Studies in Diversity Linguistics

Chief Editor: Martin Haspelmath
Consulting Editors: Fernando Zúñiga, Peter Arkadiev, Ruth Singer, Pilar Valenzuela

In this series:

1. Handschuh, Corinna. A typology of marked-S languages.

2. Rießler, Michael. Adjective attribution.

3. Klamer, Marian (ed.). The Alor-Pantar languages: History and typology.

4. Berghäll, Liisa. A grammar of Mauwake (Papua New Guinea).

5. Wilbur, Joshua. A grammar of Pite Saami.

6. Dahl, Östen. Grammaticalization in the North: Noun phrase morphosyntax in Scandinavian vernaculars.

7. Schackow, Diana. A grammar of Yakkha.

8. Liljegren, Henrik. A grammar of Palula.

9. Shimelman, Aviva. A grammar of Yauyos Quechua.

10. Rudin, Catherine & Bryan James Gordon (eds.). Advances in the study of Siouan languages and linguistics.

11. Kluge, Angela. A grammar of Papuan Malay.

12. Kieviet, Paulus. A grammar of Rapa Nui.

13. Michaud, Alexis. Tone in Yongning Na: Lexical tones and morphotonology.

ISSN: 2363-5568

The Alor-Pantar languages

History and typology
Second edition

Edited by

Marian Klamer

Marian Klamer (ed.). 2017. *The Alor-Pantar languages: History and typology.*
Second edition. (Studies in Diversity Linguistics 3). Berlin: Language Science
Press.

This title can be downloaded at:
http://langsci-press.org/catalog/book/157
© 2017, the authors
Published under the Creative Commons Attribution 4.0 Licence (CC BY 4.0):
http://creativecommons.org/licenses/by/4.0/
ISBN: 978-3-944675-94-7 (Digital)
      978-3-946234-67-8 (Hardcover)
      978-3-946234-91-3 (Softcover)
ISSN: 2363-5568
DOI:10.5281/zenodo.437098

Cover and concept of design: Ulrike Harbort
Typesetting: Sebastian Nordhoff; Timm Lichte
Proofreading: Benedikt Singpiel
Editors: Claire Bowern, Laurence Horn, and Raffaella Zanuttini, in collaboration
with Ryan Bennett, Bob Frank, Maria Piñango, Jason Shaw, and Jim Wood
Fonts: Linux Libertine, Arimo, DejaVu Sans Mono
Typesetting software: XƎLATEX

Language Science Press
Unter den Linden 6
10099 Berlin, Germany
langsci-press.org

Storage and cataloguing done by FU Berlin

Language Science Press has no responsibility for the persistence or accuracy of
URLs for external or third-party Internet websites referred to in this publication,
and does not guarantee that any content on such websites is, or will remain,
accurate or appropriate.

This volume is dedicated to the memory of Mr. Anderias Malaikosa (1964–2011), whose love for the peoples and languages of his native Alor was an inspiration to linguists both within Alor and abroad.

Contents

	Preface and acknowledgements Marian Klamer	vii
	Preface to the second edition Marian Klamer	xi
1	The Alor-Pantar languages: Linguistic context, history and typology Marian Klamer	1
2	The internal history of the Alor-Pantar language family Gary Holton & Laura C. Robinson	49
3	The relatedness of Timor-Kisar and Alor-Pantar languages: A preliminary demonstration Antoinette Schapper, Juliette Huber & Aone van Engelenhoven	91
4	The linguistic position of the Timor-Alor-Pantar languages Gary Holton & Laura C. Robinson	147
5	Kinship in the Alor-Pantar languages Gary Holton	191
6	Elevation in the spatial deictic systems of Alor-Pantar languages Antoinette Schapper	239
7	Numeral systems in the Alor-Pantar languages Antoinette Schapper & Marian Klamer	277
8	Numeral words and arithmetic operations in the Alor-Pantar languages Marian Klamer, Antoinette Schapper, Greville Corbett, Gary Holton, František Kratochvíl & Laura C. Robinson	329

9 Plural number words in the Alor-Pantar languages
   Marian Klamer, Antoinette Schapper & Greville Corbett   365

10 Participant marking: Corpus study and video elicitation
   Sebastian Fedden & Dunstan Brown   405

Index   449

Preface and acknowledgements

Marian Klamer

This volume presents some of the results of the research project 'Alor-Pantar languages: Origin and theoretical impact'. This project was one of the five collaborative research projects in the EuroCORES programme entitled 'Better Analyses Based on Endangered Languages' (BABEL) which was funded by the European Science Foundation from 2009–2012. The 'Alor-Pantar' project involved researchers from the University of Surrey (Dunstan Brown, Greville Corbett, Sebastian Fedden), the University of Alaska Fairbanks (Gary Holton, Laura Robinson), and Leiden University (Marian Klamer, Antoinette Schapper). František Kratochvíl (Nanyang Technological University) was an affiliated researcher. Brown, Corbett and Fedden (Surrey) were funded by the Arts and Humanities Research Council (UK) under grant AH/H500251/1; since April 2013, Corbett, Brown and Fedden were funded by the Arts and Humanities Research Council (UK) under grant AH/K003194/1. Robinson was funded by the National Science Foundation (US), under BCS Grant No. 0936887. Schapper was funded by the Netherlands Organisation for Scientific Research (NWO) from 2009–2012.

This volume represents the "state-of-art" of linguistic research in Alor-Pantar languages. Several chapters relate to work that has been published earlier, as explained in what follows.

Chapter 2 builds on methodology described previously in Holton et al. (2012) and Robinson & Holton (2012a), but the current chapter draws on new lexical data. In particular, the number of reconstructed proto-Alor-Pantar forms has been increased by 20% over that reported in Holton et al. (2012), and many additional cognate sets have been identified. It also differs from Robinson and Holton (2012a) in that the latter work focuses on computational methodology, arguing for the superiority of using phylogenetic models with lexical characters over traditional approaches to subgrouping, whereas chapter 2 of this volume simply applies these tools to an updated data set, omitting the theoretical justification for the methodology.

Chapter 3 revises and expands previous reconstructions within the larger Timor-Alor- Pantar family as published in Holton et al. (2012) and Schapper, Huber & Engelenhoven (2012). Chapter 3 is new in considering the relatedness of Timor-Kisar languages with the Alor-Pantar languages, while Schapper et al. 2012 was limited to the study of the internal relatedness of the Timor-Kisar languages only.

Chapter 4 is an updated and significantly expanded revision of Robinson & Holton (2012b). It differs from the latter paper in that it includes a discussion of the typological profiles of the Timor-Alor-Pantar family and its putative relatives, and has also been updated to reflect new reconstructions, especially the proto-Timor-Alor-Pantar reconstructions that are given in chapter 3.

Chapter 9 contains a discussion of plural words in five Alor-Pantar languages. The Kamang and Teiwa data were published earlier as conference proceedings (Schapper & Klamer 2011), but chapter 9 is able to revise and expand that earlier comparative work by taking into account data from three additional Alor-Pantar languages.

Chapter 10 is a newly written chapter on Alor-Pantar participant encoding, and summarizes the findings of Fedden et al. (2013) and Fedden et al. (2014). In addition, it includes a discussion of specially made video clips that have been used to collect the pronominal data, and the field manual to work with the video clips is included in the Appendix.

Crucially, all the chapters in this volume rely on the latest, most complete and accurate data sets currently available. In this respect, they all differ significantly from any of the earlier publications, as these earlier works were written either before the EuroBABEL project had even begun (e.g. Holton et al. (2012), which is essentially a revised version of a conference paper presented in 2009), or while data collection and analysis in the project was still ongoing. Where there are any discrepancies between chapters in this volume and data that was published earlier, the content of the present volume prevails.

All the chapters in this volume have been reviewed single-blind, by both external and internal reviewers. I am grateful to the following colleagues for providing reviews and helpful comments on the various chapters (in alphabetical order): Dunstan Brown, Niclas Burenhult, Mary Dalrymple, Bethwyn Evans, Sebastian Fedden, Bill Foley, Jim Fox, Martin Haspelmath, Gary Holton, Andy Pawley, Laura C. Robinson, Hein Steinhauer, and Peter de Swart.

References

Fedden, Sebastian, Dunstan Brown, Greville G. Corbett, Marian Klamer, Gary Holton, Laura C. Robinson & Antoinette Schapper. 2013. Conditions on pronominal marking in the Alor-Pantar languages. *Linguistics* 51(1). 33–74.

Fedden, Sebastian, Dunstan Brown, František Kratochvíl, Laura C. Robinson & Antoinette Schapper. 2014. Variation in pronominal indexing: lexical stipulation vs. referential properties in the Alor-Pantar languages. *Studies in Language* 38. 44–79.

Holton, Gary, Marian Klamer, František Kratochvíl, Laura C. Robinson & Antoinette Schapper. 2012. The historical relations of the Papuan languages of Alor and Pantar. *Oceanic Linguistics* 51(1). 86–122.

Robinson, Laura C. & Gary Holton. 2012a. Internal classification of the Alor-Pantar language family using computational methods applied to the lexicon. *Language Dynamics and Change* 2(2). 123–149.

Robinson, Laura C. & Gary Holton. 2012b. Reassessing the wider genetic affiliations of the Timor-Alor-Pantar languages. In Harald Hammarström & Wilco van der Heuvel (eds.), *History, contact and classification of Papuan languages* (Language and Linguistics in Melanesia Special Issue 2012, Part I), 59–87. Port Moresby: Linguistic Society of New Guinea.

Schapper, Antoinette, Juliette Huber & Aone van Engelenhoven. 2012. The historical relation of the Papuan languages of Timor and Kisar. In Harald Hammarström & Wilco van den Heuvel (eds.), *History, contact and classification of Papuan languages* (Language and Linguistics in Melanesia Special Issue 2012, Part I), 194–242. Port Moresby: Linguistic Society of Papua New Guinea.

Schapper, Antoinette & Marian Klamer. 2011. Plural words in Papuan languages of Alor-Pantar. In Peter K. Austin, Oliver Bond, David Nathan & Lutz Marten (eds.), *Proceedings of Language Documentation & Linguistic Theory (LDLT) 3*, 247–256. London: SOAS.

Preface to the second edition

Marian Klamer

This is the second edition of the volume that was originally published in 2014, as one of the first open access publications of Language Science Press. In less than three years, the first edition had more than 10,000 downloads, many of which in Indonesia, and downloads are still increasing. To us this demonstrates how important it is to use use free open access to enable both scientists and speakers of local languages in Indonesia to read this work.

In this second edition, typographical errors have been corrected, some small textual improvements have been implemented, broken URL links repaired or removed, and maps and references updated. The overall content of the chapters has not been changed.

Marian Klamer. 2017. Preface to the second edition. In Marian Klamer (ed.), *The Alor-Pantar languages*, xi–xii. Berlin: Language Science Press. DOI:10.5281/zenodo.569385

Chapter 1

The Alor-Pantar languages: Linguistic context, history and typology

Marian Klamer

> This chapter presents an introduction to the Alor-Pantar languages, and to the chapters of the volume. It discusses the current linguistic ecology of Alor and Pantar, the history of research on the languages, presents an overview of the history of research in the area and describes the state of the art of the (pre-)history of speaker groups on the islands. A typological overview of the family is presented, followed by a discussion of specific sets of lexical items. Throughout the chapter I provide pointers to individual chapters of the volume that contain more detailed information or references.

1 Introduction

The languages of the Alor-Pantar (AP) family constitute a group of twenty Papuan languages spoken on the islands of Alor and Pantar, located just north of Timor, at the end of the Lesser Sunda island chain, roughly the islands east of Bali and west of New Guinea, see Figure 1. This outlier "Papuan" group is located some 1000 kilometers west of the New Guinea mainland. The term *Papuan* is used here as a cover term for the hundreds of languages spoken in New Guinea and its vicinity that are not Austronesian (Ross 2005: 15), and it is considered synonymous with non-Austronesian. The label *Papuan* says nothing about the genealogical ties between the languages.

The Alor-Pantar languages form a family that is clearly distinct from the Austronesian languages spoken on the islands surrounding Alor and Pantar, but much is still unknown about their history: Where did they originally come from? Are they related to other languages or language groups, and if so, to which ones? Typologically, the AP languages are also very different from their Austronesian neighbours, as their syntax is head-final rather than head-initial. They

Marian Klamer. 2017. The Alor-Pantar languages: Linguistic context, history and typology. In Marian Klamer (ed.), *The Alor-Pantar languages*, 1–49. Berlin: Language Science Press. DOI:10.5281/zenodo.569386

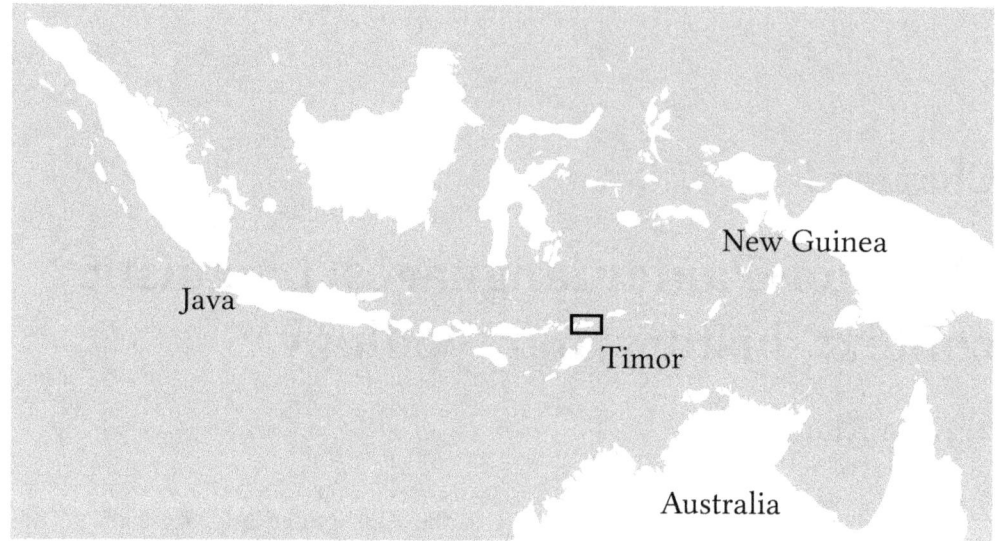

Figure 1: Alor and Pantar in Indonesia

show an interesting variety of alignment patterns, and the family has some cross-linguistically rare features.

This volume studies the history and typology of the AP languages. Each chapter compares a set of AP languages by their lexicon, syntax or morphology, with the aim to uncover linguistic history and discover typological patterns that inform linguistic theory.

As an introduction to the volume, this chapter places the AP languages in their current linguistic context (§ 2), followed by an overview of the history of research in the area (§ 3). Then I describe the state of the art of the (pre-)history of speaker groups on Alor and Pantar (§ 4). A typological overview of the family is presented in § 5, followed by information on the lexicon in § 6. In § 7, I summarize the chapter and outline challenges for future research in the area. The chapter ends with a description of the empirical basis for the research that is reported in this volume (§ 8). Throughout this introduction, cross-references to the chapters will be given, to enable the reader to focus on those chapters that s/he is most interested in.

1 The Alor-Pantar languages: Linguistic context, history and typology

2 Current linguistic situation on Alor and Pantar

There are approximately 20 indigenous Papuan languages spoken in the Alor-Pantar archipelago (§ 2.1) alongside one large indigenous Austronesian language commonly referred to as Alorese (§ 2.2). Virtually all speakers of these indigenous languages also speak the local Malay variety and/or the national language Indonesian on a regular basis for trade, education and governmental business (§ 2.3).

2.1 The Papuan languages of Alor and Pantar

The Papuan languages of Alor and Pantar as they are currently known are listed alphabetically in Table 1, and presented geographically on Figure 2. Together they form the Alor-Pantar family. The Alor-Pantar family forms a higher-order family grouping with the five Papuan languages spoken on Timor and Kisar, listed in Table 2 and presented geographically on Figure 3; together these languages constitute the Timor-Alor-Pantar family.

The language list in Table 1 is a preliminary one. In particular, it is likely that the central-eastern part of Alor, where Abui and Kamang are spoken, is linguistically richer than suggested by Table 1 and Figure 2. However, until a more principled survey of the area has been done, we stick with the labels Abui and Kamang, while acknowledging that there may be multiple languages within each of these regions.

Some of the language names of earlier works (e.g. Stokhof 1975, Grimes et al. 1997, Lewis, Simons & Fennig 2013) do not agree with what is presented here

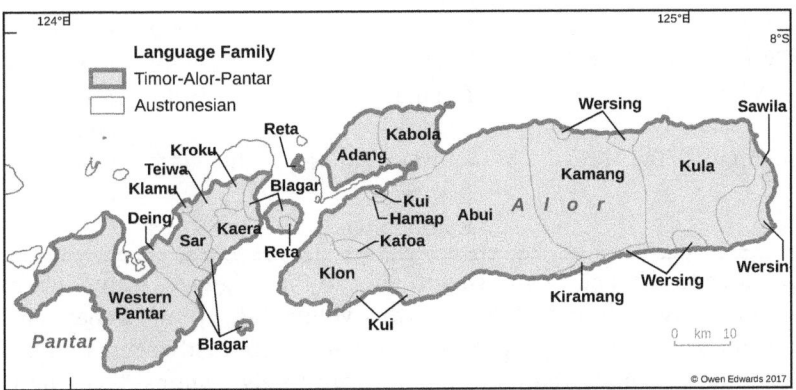

Figure 2: The languages of the Alor Pantar family. (Areas where the Austronesian language Alorese is spoken are left white.)

3

Table 1: The languages of the Alor-Pantar family.

Language†	ISO639-3	Alternate Name(s)	Pop.‡	References (selected)
Abui (AB)	abz	Papuna	17000	Kratochvíl (2007)
Adang (AD)	adn		7000	Haan (2001); Robinson & Haan (2014)
Blagar (BL)	beu	Pura	10000	Steinhauer (2014)
Deing (DE)	–	Diang, Tewa	--	
Hamap (HM)	hmu		1300*	
Kabola (KB)	klz		3900*	Stokhof (1987)
Kaera (KE)	–		5500	Klamer (2014a)
Kafoa (KF)	kpu		1000*	Baird (to appear)
Kamang (KM)	woi	Woisika	6000	Stokhof (1977); Schapper (2014a)
Kiramang (KR)	kvd		4240*	
Klon (KL)	kyo	Kelon	5000	Baird (2008)
Kui (KI)	kvd		4240*	
Kula (KU)	tpg	Tanglapui	5000*	Williams & Donohue (to appear); Donohue (1996)
Klamu	nec	Nedebang (ND)	1380*	
Reta (RT)	ret	Retta	800	
Sar (SR)	--	Teiwa?	--	
Sawila (SW)	swt		3000	Kratochvíl (2014)
Teiwa (TW)	twe	Tewa	4000	Klamer (2010a)
Wersing (WE)	kvw	Kolana	3700*	Schapper & Hendery (2014)
WesternPantar (WP)	lev	Lamma, Tubbe, Mauta, Kalondama	10300††	Holton (2010b; 2014a)

†The abbreviations in brackets are used to refer to the languages in the historical comparative chapters by Holton & Robinson (this volume[a],[b]) and Schapper, Huber & Engelenhoven (this volume). ‡Population estimates from fieldworker and/or from the published source given; starred (*) estimates from Lewis, Simons & Fennig (2013); an empty cell indicates that no number has been reported. ††This figure is from census data (Badan Pusat Statistik 2005).

1 The Alor-Pantar languages: Linguistic context, history and typology

Table 2: The Papuan languages of Timor and Kisar.

Language	ISO639-3	AlternateName(s)	Pop.†	References (selected)
Bunaq	bfn	Buna('), Bunak(e)	80.000*	Schapper (2010)
Fataluku	ddg		30000*	Engelenhoven (2009; 2010)
Makalero	mkz	Maklere	6500*	Huber (2011)
Makasai	mkz	Makasae	70000*	Huber (2008)
Oirata	oia		1220*	de Josselin de Jong (1937)

†Population estimates from fieldworker and/or from the published source given; starred (*) estimates from Lewis, Simons & Fennig (2013).

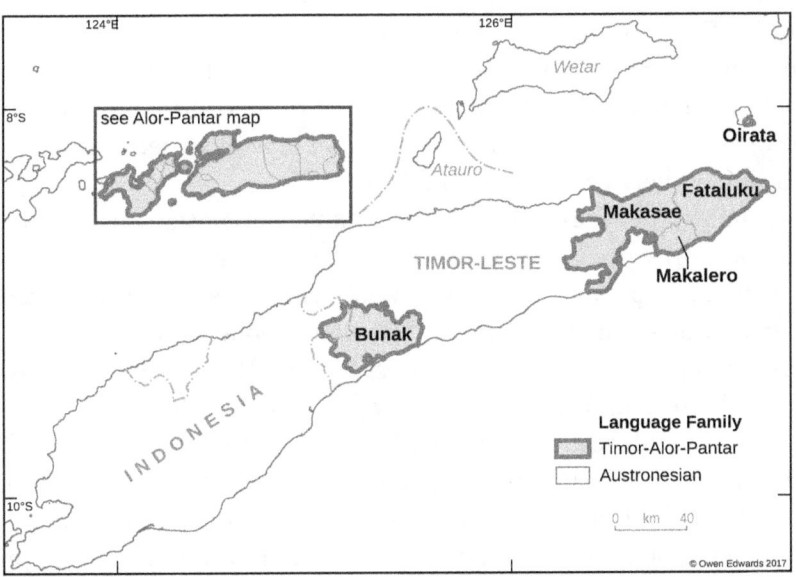

Figure 3: The Papuan languages of Timor-Alor-Pantar. (Areas where Austronesian languages are spoken are left white.)

(see also § 3). One reason may be that a language variety may either be referred to by the name of the village where it is spoken, or by the name of the ancestor village of the major clan that speaks the language, or by the clan name. The list in Table 1 aims toward more "lumping" than "splitting". The traditional criterion of mutual intelligibility is extremely difficult to apply, as speakers of the languages have been in contact for extended periods of time, and being multi-lingual is the norm in this region.

For those languages which have been the subject of recent investigation a reference is included in the table to a grammar or grammatical sketch that is published, or is about to be published. Further references to published work on the languages are presented in § 3.

2.2 Indigenous Austronesian languages on Alor and Pantar

The major indigenous Austronesian language spoken on Alor and Pantar is Alorese, also referred to as *Bahasa Alor*, "Alor", or "Coastal Alorese". Klamer (2011) is a sketch of the language. Alorese has 25,000 speakers, who live in pockets along the coasts of western Pantar and the Kabola peninsula of Alor island, as well as on the islets Ternate and Buaya (Stokhof 1975: 8-9, Grimes et al. 1997; Lewis 2009). There are reports that Alorese was used as the language of wider communication in the Alor-Pantar region until at least the mid 1970s (see Stokhof 1975: 8), but as such it did not make inroads into the central mountainous areas of Pantar or Alor, and its lingua franca function may have been limited to Pantar and the Straits in between Pantar and Alor.

The vocabulary of Alorese is clearly (Malayo-Polynesian) Austronesian. On the basis of a short word list, Stokhof (1975: 9) and Steinhauer (1993: 645) suggest that the language spoken on the Alor and Pantar coasts is a dialect of Lamaholot. Lamaholot is an Austronesian language spoken on the islands west of Pantar: Lembata, Solor, Adonara, and East Flores.[1] Recent research however indicates that Alorese and Lamaholot show significant differences in lexicon as well as grammar: Alorese and Lamaholot share only 50-60% of their basic vocabulary, severely hindering mutual intelligibility; the languages have different sets of pronouns and different possessive constructions; and, most strikingly, Alorese lacks all the inflectional and derivational morphology that is present in Lamaholot (Klamer 2011; 2012). The evidence clearly suggests that Alorese should be considered a language in its own right.

---

[1] Note that both Barnes (2001: 275) and Blust (2009: 82), Blust (2013: 87) indicate that Lamaholot is spoken on the Alor and Pantar coasts; in actual fact this is Alorese (cf. Klamer 2011).

Oral history and ethnographic observations (Anonymous 1914; Lemoine 1969; Rodemeier 2006) report local traditions about non-indigenous, Austronesian groups arriving in the northern coastal parts of Pantar around 1,300 AD whose descendants colonized the coasts of north-western Pantar and west Alor. Some of the locations mentioned are home to speakers of Alorese.[2]

Apart from Alorese, there are also languages spoken by more recent Austronesian immigrants. For instance, Bajau (or Bajo) is the language of the nomadic communities located throughout most of Indonesia which are also referred to as "sea gypsies" (cf. Verheijen 1986). There are reports that there has been a community of Bajau on Pantar since the early 1800s (Laura C. Robinson p.c.). One or more groups of Bajau came from Sulawesi, through Flores, and settled on the coast near Kabir, on Pantar island, in the 1950s. A second wave of Bajau speakers arrived from East Timor in 1999. Bajau communities are also found on Alor.

2.3 Indonesian and Alor Malay

Indonesian has been introduced relatively recently in the Alor-Pantar region, roughly correlating with the increasing number of Indonesian primary schools established in rural areas since the 1960s. Today, speakers of the Alor Pantar languages employ Indonesian and/or the local variety of Malay as language of trade, education, and governmental business.

The Alor Malay variety was already in use in the Alor-Pantar archipelago before standard Indonesian was introduced. Alor Malay is based on the Malay variety spoken in Kupang, the capital of the Indonesian province Nusa Tenggara Timor (NTT) which is located on Timor island (Jacob & Grimes 2003; Baird, Klamer & Kratochvíl Ms), though there are significant differences between the two, particularly in the pronouns.

Alor and Pantar were under (remote) Portuguese control till 1860, and Dutch colonial influence only became apparent in the first decades of the 20th century (see § 4). In 1945, van Gaalen reports that "[on the Kabola peninsula] the majority of the people can speak Malay" (1945: 30). It was probably there, and in the main town Kalabahi that most of the (few) Dutch government schools were located. But the influence of the Dutch schools must have been fairly limited, because in 1937 (after being a Dutch colony for over 60 years), only 7.5% of the children on Alor were going to school (2,089 out of a total population of 28,063 boys and

---

[2] Pandai, Baranusa and Alor are locations where Alorese is spoken today. Hägerdal (2012: 38) cites evidence that Kui and Blagar were part of the league of princedoms with Pandai, Baranusa, and Alor.

girls) (Gaalen 1945: 24, 41a). Du Bois (1960: 17) comments on the situation of Malay in schools in central Alor as being desolate, and notes in passing that in her research location Atimelang there were only about 20 boys who understood Malay (possibly implying that girls were not attending the school). The picture emerges that many areas in central and east Alor remained mostly unexposed to Malay. On the other hand, certain areas that were converted to Christianity before World War II may have been exposed to Malay earlier through the churches; this may have been the case in the Teiwa, Kaera and Western Pantar speaking areas in Pantar, and the Apui area in central Alor.

One result of the increasing use of Alor Malay and Indonesian by speakers of local Papuan languages is a rapidly on-going language shift from vernacular to languages of wider communication. None of the Alor-Pantar languages is "safe," and most are definitely endangered, in that many children are not learning the language in the home. Local languages are not used or taught in schools, as primary school teachers often have a different language background, and orthographies and dictionaries have only recently been produced for some of the languages. Language shift to Indonesian/Malay is often accelerated by urbanization and the practice of schooling children in urban centers away from their home vernacular language areas. For instance, until recently children from Pantar or east Alor went to senior high school (SMA) in Kalabahi or Kupang; only recently did Pantar get its own SMA schools, in Kabir and Baranusa. Language attitudes play an additional role in the shift to Indonesian, as the local languages lack prestige value.

3 History of research on the Alor and Pantar languages

Initial anthropological and linguistic work on Alor was carried out by Du Bois (1960 [1944]) and Nicolspeyer (1940), both working in the Abui area in central Alor. Between 1970 and 2000, research based at Leiden University resulted in a number of publications on Alor and Pantar languages. Stokhof (1975) is a 100-item word list of 17 Alor-Pantar varieties. Stokhof published language materials on Kamang, which he referred to as *Woisika* (Stokhof 1977; 1978; 1979; 1982; 1983), on Abui (Stokhof 1984) and on Kabola (Stokhof 1987). Publications on Blagar are by Steinhauer (1977; 1991; 1993; 1995; 1999; 2010; 2012; 2014). Outside of Leiden, Donohue published an article on Kula (Donohue 1996), and the *Badan* (or *Pusat*) *Pengembangan dan Pembinaan Bahasa* ('Centre for Language Development and Construction') based in Jakarta, produced some survey work on the languages of Alor (Martis et al. 2000). A grammar of Adang was completed by a native speaker of the language (Haan 2001). Between 2003 and 2007, research took place in Pantar and the western part of Alor, through a project at Leiden University that was funded with a grant from the Netherlands Organisation of Scientific Research.[3] Results of this project include work on Klon (Baird 2005; 2008; 2010), Kafoa (Baird to appear), Abui (Kratochvíl 2007; Kratochvíl & Delpada 2008a,b; Klamer & Kratochvíl 2006; Klamer & Ewing 2010; Kratochvíl 2011a,b), Teiwa (Klamer 2010a,b,c; Klamer & Kratochvíl 2006; Klamer 2011; 2012), Kaera (Klamer 2010b; 2014b), Sawila (Kratochvíl 2014) and Alorese (Klamer 2011; 2012). At the same time, Gary Holton from the University of Alaska Fairbanks, documented Western Pantar (Holton 2008; 2010b; 2011; Holton & Lamma Koly 2008; Holton 2014a,b), with funding from the US National Science Foundation, the US National Endowment for the Humanities, and the Endangered Language Documentation Programme.

In 2009, a fund from the European Science Foundation enabled a further research project on Alor-Pantar languages, now involving a group of seven researchers from the University of Alaska Fairbanks, the University of Surrey, and Leiden University. The chapters in the present volume all report on research carried out between 2009-2013 as part of this latest project.

4 History of Alor and Pantar languages and their speakers

4.1 Prehistory

The Papuan languages of Alor and Pantar all belong to a single genaealogical grouping or family (Holton et al. 2012; Holton & Robinson this volume[a]), which spread over the two islands several millennia ago. Together with the Papuan languages of Timor (cf. Table 2 above) the Alor Pantar (AP) languages (cf. Table 1 above) form the Timor Alor Pantar (TAP) family (Schapper, Huber & Engelenhoven this volume). Whenever this volume refers to the Alor-Pantar family, it must be kept in mind that this family is a subgroup of the TAP family.

One hypothesis holds that the Timor-Alor-Pantar family is a sub-branch of the Trans-New Guinea family. That is, it ultimately descends from immigrants from the New Guinea highlands who arrived in the Lesser Sundas 4,500-4,000 Before Present (BP) (Bellwood 1997: 123, Ross 2005: 42, Pawley 2005). However, recent historical comparative research (Robinson & Holton 2012; Holton & Robinson this volume[b]) shows little lexical evidence to support an affiliation with the

---

[3] Innovative research ("Vernieuwingsimpuls") project *Linguistic variation in Eastern Indonesia: The Alor-Pantar project*, led by Marian Klamer at Leiden University.

Trans New-Guinea languages (cf. Wurm, Voorhoeve & McElhanon 1975; Ross 2005).

Another hypothesis holds that the Papuans in the Lesser Sundas descend from arrivals 20,000 BP (Summerhayes 2007). While this possibility cannot be excluded, the level of lexical and grammatical similarity in the AP family does not support an age of more than several millennia, and the reconstructed vocabulary of proto-AP appears to contain Austronesian loan words such as 'betel nut' (Holton et al. 2012; Robinson 2015). Ancient Austronesian loans found across the Alor-Pantar family following regular sound changes suggest that the AP family split up after being in contact with the Austronesian languages in the area. As the Austronesians are commonly assumed to have arrived in the area ~3,000 BP (Pawley 2005: 100, Spriggs 2011), this would give the Alor-Pantar family a maximum age of ~3,000 years.

As yet, no archeological data on the Alor-Pantar archipelago is available. Archaeological research in Indonesia has been largely determined by the aim to trace the Austronesian dispersal through the archipelago, with a focus on the western islands Borneo, Sulawesi and Java (Mahirta 2006).[4] What archeological evidence we have on the Lesser Sunda islands relates to large islands such as Flores and Timor, and it suggests that the large islands were settled by Austronesians prior to smaller and more isolated islands such as Pantar and Alor.

Archaeological and anthropological studies in East Timor (O'Connor 2003; 2007; McWilliam 2007) show that the chronology of Papuan and Austronesian influence can differ by location, and that populations that now speak a Papuan language may have been Austronesian originally. Similarly, Austronesian languages may have been adopted by originally Papuan speakers.

Human genetic studies support a connection between populations of the Lesser Sundas with Papuan populations of New Guinea and Austronesians from Asia (Lansing et al. 2011; Xu et al. 2012). The Papuan (or "Melanesian"-)Asian admixture is estimated to have begun about 5,000 years BP in the western part of eastern Indonesia, decreasing to 3,000 years BP in the eastern part. This associates the Papuan-Asian admixture with Austronesian expansion (Xu et al. 2012). Debate is ongoing on the importance and details of the Austronesian expansion in Island Southeast Asia, but consensus exists that eastern Indonesia shows a "complex migration history" (Lansing et al. 2011: 263).

---

[4] The most important site in eastern Indonesia is Liang Bua in central Flores (Morwood et al. 2004), located several hundreds of kilometers west of Pantar. In mid-2012 a site was opened in Pain Haka, east Flores (investigators Simanjuntak, Galipaud, Buckley). Results are expected towards the end of 2015.

4.2 Historical records on Alor and Pantar

To date, few if any records exist on the history of the Papuan groups of Alor and Pantar.[5] Most of the written historical records refer to the large neighboring islands of Flores and Timor, and to contacts between groups on Flores and Timor on the one hand, and the coastal populations of Pantar and Alor on the other (Barnes 1996; de Roever 2002; Steenbrink 2003; Hägerdal 2010a,b; 2011; 2012 and references). It is very likely that these coastal populations were the Austronesian Alorese (§ 2.2).

One of the earliest written records is a Portuguese missionary text written after 1642, where Pantar (referred to as "Galiyao"[6]) is mentioned as a place inhabited by pagans and Muslims, together with Lewotolok and Kedang on Lembata island, located west of Pantar. Alor (referred to as "Malua") is described as an unattractive place, with few opportunities for trade and a pagan cannibal population (Hägerdal 2012: 179). It is certain that in ancient times there was traffic back and forth between Alor, Pantar, Timor, and the islands west of Pantar: traders in Kalikur, a port in north Lembata, heard from Alor traders about famous Timorese warriors who were brought to Kedang, also in north Lembata, to suppress villages of the island's interior (Barnes 1974: 10.12, Le Roux 1929: 14).

Ships of the Dutch East India Company (VOC) rarely ventured to Pantar and Alor. It was traders from Portugal who bought local products in exchange for iron, cutlasses, and axes (van Galen; see Hägerdal 2010b: 17). In the early 18th century, Portugal attempted to establish a base on Alor. Some fifty black Portuguese soldiers (originally from Africa) travelled from Larantuka in East Flores, landed in Pandai (north Pantar) in 1717 and built a church and a settlement there (Coolhaas 1979: 297, Rodemeier 2006: 78). The Portuguese made some "treaties" with local rulers, but their influence remained limited to some coastal regions in north Pantar and west Alor.[7]

---

[5] Wellfelt 2016 is a study on Alor history which appeared after this volume was written.

[6] Linguistic research on Pantar by Holton (2010a) has shown that Galiyao is used in various local Papuan languages as the indigenous name for the island of Pantar. The name originates from Western Pantar *Gale Awa*, literally 'living body'. "The appropriateness of this name is evidenced by the presence of an active volcano which dominates southern Pantar. This volcano regularly erupts, often raining ash and pyroclastic flows onto villages of the region. Even when it is not erupting, the volcano ominously vents sulfur gas and smoke from its crater. In a very real sense, the volcano is a living body." (Holton 2010a). For discussions of how the term Galiyao refers to (parts of) Pantar, see Le Roux (1929: 47); Barnes (1982: 407); Dietrich (1984); Rodemeier (1995); Barnes (2001: 277); Rodemeier (2006).

[7] The Portuguese "[handed] out Portuguese flags to some coastal rulers, among others those of Koei, Mataroe, Batoelolong, Kolana" (Gaalen 1945: 2).

The Alor archipelago was part of an areal trade network. For example, in 1851, every year more than 100 vessels came to the island, with traders from Buton and Kupang (buying rice and corn), as well as Bugis and Makassar (buying wax) (van Lynden 1851: 333). In 1853, the Portuguese gave up their claim on the Alor archipelago in exchange for the Dutch Pulau Kambing (currently known as the island Ataúru), located just north of Dili in East Timor. However, the Kui speaking areas on the southern coast of Alor remained in close contact with the Portuguese, thus prompting a Dutch military action in 1855, when the Dutch steamship Vesuvius destroyed the Kui village with its guns (Hägerdal 2010b: 18–19). Overall, however, the Dutch involvement with Alor remained limited for decades. The Dutch stationed a *Posthouder* ('post holder') at the mouth of the Kabola bay around 1861 and basically left it at that.

Only in 1910, under Governor-General Van Heutz, did the Dutch start a military campaign to put local rulers under Dutch control. Until 1945, there were regular revolts from local rulers (see the reports in Gaalen 1945: 2-9). Today, the Dutch cultural influence is most visible in the town of Kalabahi and in the Kabola peninsula.

Chinese traders have been active in the area since the end of the 19th century (Du Bois 1960: 16). These traders have likely arrived from Kupang or more remote communities, bringing with them Kupang Malay or trade Malay. Nicolspeyer (1940: 1) reports that by the late 1930s there was a 200 member strong Chinese trader community in Kalabahi engaged in the production and trade of copra. The relationship between the Chinese community and the local population must have been friendly, judging from the oral accounts of mountain population offering Chinese people refuge during the Japanese occupation in World War II.

In contrast, Nicolspeyer (1940: 8) describes the trade relations between the highlanders and the coastal populations - likely to be Alorese - in west and central Alor as mutually distrusting and hostile. Traditionally, the Alorese clans exchanged fish and woven cloth for food crops with the inland populations (cf. Anonymous 1914: 76, 81–82). Given the small size of individual Alorese clans – Anonymous (1914: 89–90) mentions settlements of only 200–300 people – , they probably exchanged women with the exogamous Papuan populations around them, or bought them as slaves.

In the east of Alor, there was contact with populations on Ataúru and Timor. Until 1965 it was not uncommon to sail from the southern coast of Alor to Ataúru island on fishing trips, and people report that this still happens today. The oral accounts of these contacts are supported by genealogies and origin myths, as well as by a number of Portuguese loanwords such as the Sawila verb *siribisi* originating in the Portuguese *serviso* 'work' (Kratochvíl, field notes). In addition, many songs in central-east Alor mention place names such as Likusaen and Maubara, which are located in the north of Timor (Wellfelt & Schapper 2013).

In 1965-1966, hundreds and possibly thousands of highlanders in Alor and Pantar were marched to Kalabahi and killed by the Indonesian forces and associated vigilantes after the alleged communist coup. Oral accounts of the atrocities still circulate among the population and the terror is palpable whenever such accounts are shared.

4.3 Contact

All of the Alor-Pantar languages show some traces of contact with Austronesian languages, but in general, borrowing from Austronesian has not been very intense. Contact with Malay and Indonesian is a relatively recent phenomenon in most of the Alor-Pantar languages. Comparing ~160 vocabulary items in 13 AP languages, Robinson (2015) finds Austronesian loan percentages to range between 4.2% (in Western Pantar) and 9.5% (in Blagar and Adang), while the majority of AP languages have only 6-7% of Austronesian loans.[8]

Of course, lexical borrowing within the Alor-Pantar family occurs as well. An example is Western Pantar *bagis* 'to wail', borrowed from Deing *bagis* 'to cry' (Holton & Robinson this volume[a]). In situations where speakers of sister languages are also geographical neighbors and in contact with each other, it is however exceedingly difficult to distinguish loans from cognates.

5 Typological overview

This section presents a general overview of the structural features of the Alor-Pantar languages. The aim is to introduce the reader to their phonology, morphology and syntax, pointing out patterns that are cross-linguistically common and patterns that are rare. Where appropriate, I refer to chapters in this volume for further discussion or illustration.

---

[8] To put this into context, roughly 7% of English vocabulary on a comparable list is borrowed from French.

5.1 Phonology

The sizes of the vowel and consonant inventories of the AP languages are transitional between the smaller vowel systems and large consonant systems of insular Southeast Asia, and the more complex vowel systems but much more reduced consonant inventories to the east, in the wider New Guinea/Oceania region (cf. Hajek 2010).

The vowel systems in Alor-Pantar involve the five cardinal vowels, possibly adding distinctions in mid vowels (e.g. Klon, Adang) and/or in length (e.g. Teiwa, Abui, Kamang). The proto-Alor-Pantar consonant inventory (Holton et al. 2012; Holton & Robinson this volume[a]) is shown in Table 3.

Table 3: Reconstructed proto-Alor-Pantar consonant inventory

	Labial	Apical	Palatal	Velar	Uvular	Glottal
Stop	p b	t d		k g	q	
Fricative		s				h
Nasal	m	n				
Glide	w		j			
Liquid		l (r)				

If it is the case that Papuan languages usually lack a distinction between /r/ and /l/ (Foley 1986, see § 5.9), then the languages of Timor, Alor and Pantar are atypical in universally distinguishing /r/ from /l/. At least two liquids must be reconstructed to proto-Timor-Alor-Pantar, the immediate parent of pAP. Interestingly, however, *r and *l occur in complementary distribution in the reconstructed phonology of proto-AP (Holton et al. 2012).

Within the Alor-Pantar family, consonant inventories are largest in Pantar, where Teiwa has 20 consonants, and Western Pantar has 16 consonants plus 10 geminates. The inventories decrease in size towards the eastern part of Alor, where Abui has 16 (native) consonants, and Kamang has 14.

While the consonant inventories of the AP languages are rather similar to each other, some variation is found in the number of fricatives and nasals. In Pantar we find consonants unique to the family: the Western Pantar geminate stops, the Teiwa pharyngeal fricative /ħ/, the Teiwa uvular stop /q/, the Kaera velar fricative /x/, and the Blagar implosive voiced bilabial stop /ɓ/. The pharyngeal fricative in particular is cross-linguistically rather uncommon (found in 2.4% of the languages of Maddieson's (2005) sample).

1 The Alor-Pantar languages: Linguistic context, history and typology

5.2 Constituent order

Overall, the AP languages are syntactically right-headed (see also chapter 4). Basic transitive clauses are verb-final, with Agent-Patient-Verb (APV) and Subject-Verb (SV) order. A refers to the more agent-like argument of a transitive verb, P to the more patient-like argument of a transitive verb, and S to the single argument of an intransitive verb.[9] (1) shows an intransitive clause followed by a transitive one. PAV is a pragmatically motivated variant in many of the Alor-Pantar languages.

(1) Teiwa (Klamer 2010a: 25)[10]
    S   V   V V   A   P   V
    Qau a ta ewar mis. Mis-an a ta man pi'i.
    good 3SG TOP return sit sit-REAL 3SG TOP grass twine
    'So she sits down again. Sitting, she twines grass.'

In adpositional phrases, postpositions follow their complement, as illustrated in § 5.8 below. Clausal negators follow the predicate:

(2) Kaera (Klamer 2014a: 114)
    Gang masu ma bino.
    3SG maybe come NEG
    'He may not come.'

In nominal phrases, determiners such as articles and demonstratives follow the noun (see Klamer et al. this volume). All AP languages have clause-final conjunctions; often these are combined with clause-initial ones, as shown in (3), where clause final *a* 'and' combines with clause-initial *xabi* 'then':

(3) Kaera (Klamer 2014a: 140)
    Gang ge-topi gu med a, xabi mampelei utug met mi kunang
    3SG 3SG.ALIEN-hat that take and then mango three take LOC children
    masik namung gu gi-ng.
    male PL that 3PL-give
    'He takes that hat of his and then takes three mangoes to give to the boys.'

---

[9] A, P and S are used as comparative concepts here, where A is the most Agent-like argument of a transitive clause, P is the least Agent-like of transitive clause, and S is the single argument of an intransitive clause (cf. Comrie 1989; Haspelmath 2011).
[10] Teiwa orthography follows IPA symbols, except: *q*=/q/, *x*=/ħ/, '=/ʔ/, *f*=ɸ, *y*=/j/, *ng* =/ŋ/.

5.3 Pronominal indexing and morphological alignment

The term 'pronominal indexing' is used here (and in Fedden & Brown this volume) to describe a structure where there is a pronominal affix on the verb and a co-referential Noun Phrase (NP) or free pronoun occur optionally in the same clause.

The pronominal indices found on the verbs in the Alor-Pantar languages are all very similar in form, pointing to a common historical origin. They are reconstructed for pAP as in Table 4 (see Holton & Robinson this volume(a),(b); Schapper, Huber & Engelenhoven this volume). The initial consonant encodes person, and the vowels *a* and *i* encode singular and plural number.

All AP languages distinguish inclusive from exclusive forms. All the modern AP languages also have reflexes of pAP *ta-, a prefix with a common or impersonal referent (compare *one* in English *One should consider this*), and a reading that is often distributive or reflexive *(each one, each other)*. In Table 4, this prefix is grouped with the singular forms because it carries the singular theme vowel *a*

Going from west to east, we find increasingly complex systems of grammatical relations involving multiple paradigms of pronominal indexes. For example, Teiwa (Pantar) has one paradigm of object prefixes (which is almost identical to the pAP paradigm in Table 4), Klon in western Alor has three paradigms (Table 5), and Abui (central Alor) has five (Table 6). Prefixes with the theme vowel *e* reflect the pAP genitive; prefixes with the theme vowel *o* occur in several languages of Alor where they have a locative function.

In AP languages, the use of these different pronominal sets is not so much determined by the grammatical role of their referent (e.g. being an object or a subject), but is mostly triggered by semantic factors. Most Alor-Pantar languages

Table 4: Reconstructed pAP P-indexing pronominal verb prefixes

1SG	*na-
2SG	*ha-
3SG	*ga-
COMMON/DISTRIBUTIVE	*ta-
1PL.EXCL	*ni-
1PL.INCL	*pi-
2PL	*hi-
3PL	*gi-

1 The Alor-Pantar languages: Linguistic context, history and typology

Table 5: Klon prefixes (Baird 2008: 69, 39).

	I	II	III
1SG	n-	ne-	no-
2SG	V-/ Ø-	e-	o-
3	g-	ge-	go-
1PL.EX	ng-	nge-	ngo-
1PL.IN	t-	te-	to-
2PL	i-	ege-	ogo-
RECP	t-	te-	to-

Table 6: Abui prefixes (Kratochvíl 2007: 78, Kratochvíl 2011b: 591).

	I (PAT)	II (LOC)	III (REC)	IV (BEN)	V (GOAL)
1SG	na-	ne-	no-	nee-	noo-
2SG	a-	e-	o-	ee-	oo-
3	ha-	he-	ho-	hee-	hoo-
1PL.EX	ni-	ni-	nu-	nii-	nuu-
1PL.IN	pi-	pi-	pu-	pii-	puu-
2PL	ri-	ri-	ru-	rii-	ruu-
DISTR	ta-	te-	to-	tee-	too-

index P on the verb, and not A, as in (4a-b). A and S are typically expressed as free lexical NPs or pronouns. Cross-linguistically, this is an uncommon pattern; it occurs in only 7% of Siewierska's (2013) sample.

(4) Teiwa (Klamer, fieldnotes)

    a. *Na Maria g-ua'*
       1SG Maria 3SG-hit
       'I hit Maria.'

    b. *Na g-ua'*
       1sg 3sg-hit
       'I hit him/her.'

One of the factors determining the indexing of P is animacy. For instance, when the P of the Teiwa verb *mar* 'take' is inanimate, it is not indexed on the verb, (5a), but when it is animate, it is indexed (5b). That is, while a verbal prefix in an Alor-Pantar language typically indexes P, not every P is always indexed on a verb.

(5) Teiwa (Klamer 2010a: 91)

  a. *Na ga'an mar.*
    1SG 3SG   take
    'I take / get it.'

  b. *Na ga-mar.*
    1SG 3SG-take
    'I follow him/her.'

In Abui, the different prefixes roughly correspond to semantically different P's. For example, in (6)-(10) the P is a patient, location, recipient, benefactive and goal, and the shape of the prefix varies accordingly.

(6) Abui (Kratochvíl 2007: 592)
Na a-ruidi
1SG 2SG.PAT-wake.up
'I woke you up.'

(7) Abui (Kratochvíl 2007: 592)
Di palootang mi ne-l   bol.
3 rattan   take 1SG.LOC-give hit
'He hit me with a rattan (stick).'

(8) Abui (Kratochvíl 2007: 592)
Fanmalei no-k   yai.
Fanmalei 1SG.REC-throw laugh
'Fanmalei laughed at me.'

(9) Abui (Kratochvíl 2007: 592)
Ma   ne ee-bol.
be.PROX 1SG 2SG.BEN-hit
'Let me hit instead of (i.e. for) you.'

(10) Abui (Kratochvíl 2007: 592)
Simon di noo-dik.
Simon 3 1SG.GOAL-prick
'Simon is poking me.'

1 The Alor-Pantar languages: Linguistic context, history and typology

In some AP languages (for instance, Abui, Kamang, and Klon) S arguments are also indexed on the verbs. Such arguments are usually more affected and less volitional, although individual languages differ in which semantic factors apply (Fedden & Brown this volume; Fedden et al. 2014). Also, lexical verb classes often play a role in the indexing of arguments.

Apart from the multiple ways to index P (the possible evolution of which is sketched in Klamer & Kratochvíl (to appear), there is also variation in the morphological alignment type of AP languages. Alignment in the AP languages is defined here relative to pronominal indexing.

The prefixes are either used in a syntactic (accusative) alignment system, or in a semantic alignment ('Split-S') system. Accusative alignment is defined here as the alignment where S and A are treated alike as opposed to P. Teiwa, Kaera, Blagar and Adang have accusative alignment, only indexing P, while S and A are free forms. An illustration is Blagar, where the same pronoun ʔana '3SG' can encode A (11) or S (12), and P is prefixed on the verb (11).

(11) Blagar (Steinhauer 2014: 208)
ʔana uruhiŋ aru ʔ-atapa-t imina
3SG deer two 3-shoot.with.arrow-LIM die
'S/he killed two deer with bow and arrow.'

(12) Blagar (Steinhauer 2014: 173)
ʔana mi bihi
3SG in run
'He/she/it runs in it.'

In Klon, however, the P prefix can also be used to index S, depending on the class the verb belongs to: one class of verbs always aligns S with A (resulting in accusative alignment), another class always aligns S with P, and a third class of verbs encodes S either as A (free pronoun) or as P (prefix), depending on its affectedness: compare (13a) and (13b).

(13) Klon (Baird 2008: 8)
 a. *A kaak*
 2SG itchy
 'You're itchy.'
 b. *E-kaak*
 2SG.II-itchy
 'You're itchy (and affected).'

Western Pantar also allows its P-prefix to index S, compare (14) and (15). Some verbs, such as *diti* 'stab' in (16)-(17) allow an alternation in the coding of a P or S with either a prefix or a free pronoun, with a difference in the degree of affectedness resulting.

(14) Western Pantar (Holton 2010b: 105-106)
Gang na-niaka.
3SG 1SG-see
'S/he saw me.'

(15) Western Pantar (Holton 2010b: 105-106)
Nang na-lama ta.
1SG 1SG-descend IPFV
'I'm going.'

(16) Western Pantar (Holton 2010b: 105-106)
Nang ga-diti.
1SG 3SG-stab
'I stabbed him.' (superficially)

(17) Western Pantar (Holton 2010b: 105-106)
Nang gaing diti.
1SG 3SG stab
'I stabbed him.' (severely)

Abui and Kamang are often found to index S by use of a prefix. The choice of prefix is determined by a mix of factors, such as the level of affectedness or volitionality of the argument (Fedden et al. 2013; 2014; see Fedden & Brown this volume).

A pattern where two arguments are indexed on a transitive verb is found in Abui, illustrated in (18)-(19). Unlike what would be expected, these are not transitive constructions expressing actions involving an affix for A and for P, but rather experience constructions where both affixes encode a P.

(18) Abui (Kratochvíl 2011b: 615)
Sieng ma he-noo-maran-i
rice cooked 3.LOC-1SG.GOAL-come.up.COMPL-PFV
'I am satiated with the rice.'

(19) Abui (Kratochvíl 2011b: 617)
Hen hee-na-minang
that 3.BEN-1SG.PAT-remember
'I remembered that.'

In sum, free pronouns exist alongside verbal affixes that index person and number of verbal arguments. There is significant variation in the choice of participant that is indexed on the verb. The Alor-Pantar languages are typologically unusual in that they index P but not A, and some of them have rich inventories of prefixes differentiating different types of P.

5.4 Possession

Possession is marked by prefixes on nouns. There are parallels with the argument indexing on verbs, particularly because inalienable possession usually involves possessors linearly preceding the possessed noun in the same way that arguments linearly precede the verb.

In all AP languages, possessive structures with alienable nouns are distinguished from possessive constructions with inalienable nouns. For example, in Abui, distinct possessive prefixes are used to encode alienable and inalienable possession, (20). In Abui, inalienable possessive prefixes have the theme vowel *a*, and alienable possessive prefixes have the theme vowel *e*.

(20) Abui (Kratochvíl 2007)

    a. *na-min*
       1SG.INAL-nose
       'my nose'

    b. *ne-fala*
       1SG.ALIEN-house
       'my house'

Prefixes with the vowel *a* reflect the proto-AP P-indexing morpheme (Table 4) while prefixes with the vowel *e* reflect the pAP genitive prefix (cf. the prefixes with theme vowels *e* in Klon (Table 5) and Abui (Table 6)).

In Teiwa, the difference between alienable and inalienable possession is expressed in a different manner: by optional versus obligatory use of the same (*a*-vowel) prefix, (21):

(21) Teiwa (Klamer 2010a: 192)

    a. *na-yaf*
       1SG.POSS-house
       'my house'

    b. *yaf*
       house
       '(a) house, houses'

    c. *na-tan*
       1SG.POSS-hand
       'my hand'

    d. *tan*
       hand
       not good for '(a) hand, hands'

The variation in the treatment of the alienable-inalienable distinction across the AP family is summarized in Table 7. (Different subscripts indicate different paradigms in a single language.)

Table 7: Encoding of alienable and inalienable possessors in some AP languages.

Location	Language name	Alienable possessor	Inalienable possessor
Pantar	Western Pantar	free form	prefix
	Teiwa	optional prefix$_a$	obligatory prefix$_a$
	Kaera	prefix$_a$	prefix$_b$
Pantar Straits	Blagar	free form	prefix
Alor	Klon	free form	prefix$_a$, prefix$_b$
	Abui	prefix$_a$	prefix$_b$
	Kamang	prefix$_a$	prefix$_b$

5.5 Plural number words

The Alor-Pantar languages exhibit a typologically unusual pattern (Dryer 2011) whereby nominal plurality is indicated via a separate number word; 'A morpheme whose meaning and function is similar to that of plural affixes in other languages' (Dryer 1989). An illustration is Teiwa *non* in (22b).

(22) Teiwa (Klamer, Teiwa corpus)

  a. *Qavif ita'a   ma gi?*
     goat where OBL go
     'Where did the goat(s) go?'

  b. *Qavif non ita'a   ma gi?*
     goat PL where OBL Go
     'Where did the (several) goats go?'; NOT *'Where did the goat go?'

Plural number words are found across Alor-Pantar and the cognates found across the family suggest that pAP had a plural number word *non. Across the AP family, there is significant variation in form, syntax and semantics of the plural number word as described in Klamer, Schapper & Corbett (this volume).

5.6 Serial verb constructions

Serial verb constructions (SVCs) are analyzed here as two or more verbs that occur together in a single clause under a single intonation contour. They share minimally one argument, and their shared argument(s) is (are) expressed maximally once. SVCs are distinguished from bi-clausal constructions by the presence of a clause boundary marker in between the clauses in the latter (a conjunction-like element, an intonational break, or a pause). The verbs in a SVC share aspect marking.

The semantic contrast between a mono-clausal construction with an SVC and a biclausal construction is illustrated by the minimally contrasting pair of Teiwa sentences in (23). Monoclausal (23a) expresses through an SVC the intransitive event of someone who died because he fell down (e.g. from a coconut tree). The biclausal construction in (23b) describes two events in clauses that are linked by the conjunction *ba*: someone is dying (e.g. because of a heart attack) and is falling down (e.g. out of a tree) as a result of this. No such conjunction-like element would occur between the verbs constituting an SVC.

(23) Teiwa (Klamer 2010a: 305)

  a. *A   ta min-an   ba'.*
     3SG TOP die-REAL fall.down
     'He died falling down.'

b. *A   ta   min-an ba   ba'.*
   3SG TOP die-REAL CONJ fall.down
   'He died then fell down.'

SVCs are frequently attested in all AP languages, and they express a wide range of notions, including direction (23a), manner (24), and aspect (25).

(24) Western Pantar (Holton 2014b: 82)
Habbang mau aname horang   sauke-yabe.
village there person make.noise dance-lego.lego
'Over there in the village people are making noise dancing lego-lego.'

(25) Teiwa (Klamer 2010a: 358)
A   bir-an   gi awan   awan   tas-an   gula'...
3SG run-REAL go far.away far.away stand-REAL finish
'She ran far away [and] stood [still]...'

SVCs in AP languages also serve to introduce event participants, for example in clauses that express a 'give'-event. This is due to the fact that the AP languages generally lack a class of simple ditransitive root verbs. (Some of the languages have one ditransitive verb, the verb 'give'.) 'Give' events involving three participants (actor, recipient, and theme) are typically expressed by means of biclausal or serial verb constructions involving the monotransitive verbs 'take' and 'give'. 'Take' introduces the theme, 'give' the recipient, and the clausal sequence or serial verb construction in which the verbs appear is then [actor [theme 'take']] [recipient 'give']]. In some of the AP languages (e.g. Kamang) the verb 'take' has been semantically bleached and syntactically reduced to become a 'defective' verb or a postposition-like element which encodes oblique constituents.

The AP 'give' constructions are illustrated by the Abui sentences in (26)-(27). In the biclausal construction in (26), the theme *hen* '3' is expressed in the first clause as a complement of *mi* 'take', while the recipient is found in the second clause, as a complement of the verb *-l / -r* 'give' (the consonant alternation encodes an aspectual distinction). In (27), the 'give' construction is monoclausal: the NP encoding the theme *nei yo* 'mine' is fronted to a position preceding both 'give' and 'take'. This would not be possible in the biclausal structure of (26).

(26) Abui (Kratochvíl, Abui corpus; cited in Klamer & Schapper 2012: 186)
Hen mi ba   Lius la   he-l-e.
3   take CONJ Lius PART 3.LOC-give-IPFV
'Just give that one to Lius.'

(27) Abui (Kratochvíl, Abui corpus; cited in Klamer & Schapper 2012: 187)
Nei   yo   la   mi   ne-r   te   yo!
1SG.POSS DEM PART take 1SG.LOC-give first DEM

'Give me mine!'

The single argument indexed on the verb 'give' is the recipient. The AP languages thus exhibit 'secundative' alignment (Dryer 1986), see Klamer (2010b) and Klamer and Schapper (2012) for discussions of this alignment type in AP languages.

5.7 Postpositions

Adpositions in AP languages follow their complement, i.e. they are postpositions. Many AP languages have adpositions encoding locations that are similar in form to (defective) locative verbs, suggesting a historical relation between items in both these word classes (Klamer to appear). For example, the Kaera postpositions *mi* 'in, on, at, into' (glossed as 'LOC') is related to the locative verbs *ming* 'be at' (see (28a-b)), while *ta* 'on' is related to the locative verb *tang* 'be on'.

(28) a. Kaera (Klamer 2014a: 118)
   Ging [abang mi] mis-o.
   3PL village LOC sit-FIN

   'They stay in the village.'

   b. *Ging abang ming gu, mis-o.*
   3PL village be.at that sit-FIN

   'Those [that] are in the village, [will] stay [there].'

In Adang too, postpositions share properties with verbs. In (29)-(30), *mi* 'be in, at' and *ta* 'be on (top of)' function as verbs in serial verb constructions.

(29) Adang (Robinson & Haan 2014: 235)
   Na ʔarabah mi mih.
   1SG Kalabahi in sit/live

   'I live in Kalabahi.'

(30) Adang (Robinson & Haan 2014: 235)
   ɛi   matɛ   nu   tang ta lamɛ eh.
   boat be.large one sea   on walk PROG

   'A large boat is travelling on the sea.'

There are also AP languages that lack adpositions altogether, Teiwa being a case in point (Klamer 2010a).

5.8 Morphological typology

Nominal morphology in AP languages is sparse. Nominal inflection is typically limited to possessive prefixing, and the nominal word-formation most frequently attested is compounding. Morphologically, verbs are the most complex word class of the AP languages. Prefixation to index arguments on verbs is very common (§ 5.3). Broadly speaking, the languages of Pantar are less agglutinative than those of central and east Alor. For example, while Teiwa (Pantar) has only one person prefix paradigm, Kamang (central Alor) has six person prefix paradigms, compare Table 8 and Table 9 (Fedden & Brown this volume).

Table 8: Teiwa person prefixes (Klamer 2010a: 77, 78)

	Prefix
1SG	*n(a)-*
2SG	*h(a)-*
3SG	*g(a)-*
1PL.EXCL	*n(i)-*
1PL.INCL	*p(i)-*
2PL	*y(i)-*
3PL	*g(i)-, ga-*

Table 9: Kamang person prefixes (Schapper 2014a: 322)

	Prefixes					
	PAT	LOC	GEN	AST[11]	DAT	DIR
1SG	*na-*	*no-*	*ne-*	*noo-*	*nee-*	*nao-*
2SG	*a-*	*o-*	*e-*	*oo-*	*ee-*	*ao-*
3	*ga-*	*wo-*	*ge-*	*woo-*	*gee-*	*gao-*
1PL.EXCL	*ni-*	*nio-*	*ni-*	*nioo-*	*nii-*	*nioo-*
1PL.INCL	*si-*	*sio-*	*si-*	*sioo-*	*sii-*	*sioo-*
2PL	*i-*	*io-*	*i-*	*ioo-*	*ii-*	*ioo-*

1 The Alor-Pantar languages: Linguistic context, history and typology

AP languages do not commonly have much derivational morphology. Some AP languages have verbal prefixes that increase valency, including a causative and/or an applicative (e.g. Blagar, Adang, Klon); but in other languages such derivations are either unproductive (Teiwa), or absent altogether (Western Pantar). In the absence of verbal derivation, serial verb constructions are often employed to introduce beneficiary or instrumental participants, or to express analytical causatives (Abui). Indeed, there is evidence that certain verbal affixes may have developed out of verbs that were originally part of serial verb constructions: in Sawila, for instance, applicative prefixes found on verbs are grammaticalized forms of verbs (cf. Klamer to appear. An illustration is the applicative prefix *li-* in *li-ilo* shine for someone / at something' (31b), which is related to the locative verb *li* 'be.DIST' (Kratochvíl 2014).

(31) Sawila (Kratochvíl 2014: 398)

a. *Laampuru ilo.*
   lamp   be.bright
   'The lamp is bright.'

b. *Laampuru li-ilo.*
   lamp   APPL-be.bright
   'The lamp is shining for someone / at something.'

Tense inflections are often lacking on verbs in AP languages, and inflections for aspect and mood remain rather limited. The languages show very little similarity in tense-aspect-mood inflections: not only are the forms different, but the values they express, and the position the morphemes take with respect to the verbal stem also show much variation. For example, Table 10 shows that aspect in Western Pantar is prefixing, while in Kaera and Kamang it is suffixing. Also, morphemes with overlapping values have very different shapes: compare the perfective of Kaera *-i* with Kamang *-ma* and imperfective Kaera *-(i)t* with Kamang *-si*.

In sum, overall, the morphological profile of languages in the AP family is simple compared to many other Papuan languages. The only affixes that have been reconstructed for proto-AP at this stage, are a paradigm of person prefixes on verbs and a third person possessive prefix on nouns (Holton & Robinson this volume[a]: Appendix).

---

[11] The assistive (AST) refers to the participant who assists in the action.

Table 10: Prefixing und suffixing of aspect morphemes

Western Pantar:	*i-*	Progressive
	a-	Inceptive
Kaera:	*-it, -t*	Imperfective
	-i	Perfective
	-ang	Continuative
Kamang:	*-si*	Imperfective
	-ma	Perfective
	-ta	Stative

5.9 Typological features of AP languages in the Papuan context

Several proposals have been made to characterize the typological profile of Papuan languages. Table 11 presents a list of typological features that have been mentioned most commonly in the literature as typical for Papuan languages (see Foley 1986; 2000; Pawley 2005; Aikhenvald & Stebbins 2007; Klamer, Reesink & van Staden 2008; Klamer & Ewing 2010). In the right-most column, I indicate whether or not a feature applies to the AP languages.

Table 11 clearly suggests that some of the syntactic typology of AP languages is much like that of other Papuan languages: object-verb order and preposed possessors (GEN-Noun) predominate, and negators and conjunctions are clause final, or at least follow the predicate. A formal distinction between alienable and inalienable possession is made in all languages. Serial verb constructions are found across the group.

AP languages are different from other Papuan languages in that they do not exhibit clause-chaining, do not have switch reference systems, never suffix subject indexes to verbs and generally do not make a formal distinction between medial and final verbs. Gender is not marked in AP languages. Unlike many other Papuan groups, the AP languages do encode clusivity in their pronominal systems, and do have a phonemic r-l distinction.

All this goes to suggest that the typology of Papuan languages is more diverse than has previously been recognized. Indeed, apart from a broadly similar head-final syntactic profile, there is very little else that the AP languages share with Papuan languages spoken in other regions (see also Holton & Robinson this volume[b]).

Table 11: Structural features in "Papuan" and in AP languages

	Typical for Papuan languages	In AP languages?
Phonology	No distinction between r/l	no
Morphology	Marking of gender	no
	Subject marked as suffix on verb	no
	Inclusive/exclusive distinction is absent in the pronominal paradigm	no
	Morphological distinction between alienable-inalienable nouns	yes
Syntax	Object-Verb	yes
	Subject-Verb	yes
	Postpositions	yes
	GEN-Noun	yes
	Clause-final negators	yes
	Clause-final conjunctions	yes
	Clause-chaining, switch reference, medial vs. final verbs	no
	Serial verb constructions	yes

6 Lexicon

In this section I summarize some of the lexical features that are typical for the AP language group.

6.1 Cognates and reconstructed vocabulary

Well over a hundred words have been reconstructed for proto-Alor-Pantar (pAP). They are listed in Holton & Robinson (this volume[a]: Appendix). Complementing these data are the additional and revised pAP reconstructions presented in Schapper, Huber & Engelenhoven (this volume: Appendix A1), which are based on lexical data from a larger language sample. As the focus of the latter chapter is to investigate the relation between the AP languages and those of Timor and Kisar, it presents reconstructions for proto-Timor as well as 89 cognates and forms of proto-Alor-Pantar and proto-Timor, reconstructed for proto-Timor-Alor-Pantar (Schapper, Huber & Engelenhoven this volume: Appendix 2 and 3).

6.2 Numerals and numeral systems

The indigenous numerals of the AP languages, as well as the indigenous structures for arithmetic operations are currently under pressure from Indonesian, and will inevitably be replaced with Indonesian forms and structures. Future generations may thus be interested in a documentary record of the forms and patterns currently used for cardinal, ordinal and distributive numerals, and the expressions of arithmetic operations (Klamer et al. this volume).

The numeral system reconstructed for pAP mixes numeral words that have a quinary and a decimal base, as shown in Table 12. That is, numeral '5' is a monomorphemic form, the numeral '7' is expressed with (reflexes of) morphemes for [5 2], '8' as [5 3], '9' as [5 4], while '10' is [10 1] (Schapper & Klamer this volume). Systems with numeral bases other than 10 such as the one reconstructed for pAP are relatively rare in the world's languages. From a typological point of view, the reconstructed form for the numeral '6' is even more interesting, as it is not composed as [5 1], as expected in a quinary system, but is rather a monomorphemic form (see Table 12).

Reflexes of the pAP numeral system are found across Alor and Pantar. In the region of the Straits between both islands, the languages underwent a separate later development, innovating some forms, as well as introducing a subtractive pattern, representing '9' as [[10] -1] and '8' as [[10] -2] (Schapper & Klamer this volume). In contrast with the AP languages, the Papuan languages spoken in Timor all have decimal systems. They have also borrowed forms from Austrone-

Table 12: Numerals and numeral system of pAP (Schapper & Klamer this volume)

'1'	*nuk	[1]
'2'	*araqu	[2]
'3'	*(a)tiga	[3]
'4'	*buta	[4]
'5'	*yiwesin	[5]
'6'	*talam	[6]
'7'		[5 2]
'8'		[5 3]
'9'		[5 4]
'10'	*qar nuk	[10 1]

sian; examples include Makalero '4', '5', '7', '9' (Huber 2011) and Bunaq '7', '8', and '9' (Schapper 2010).

6.3 Numeral classifiers

Numeral classifiers are found in numeral NPs throughout the AP family. From a Papuan point of view, this is remarkable, as few Papuan languages have numeral classifiers. In AP languages, the classifier is usually not obligatory, and it always follows the noun and precedes the numeral: [NOUN–CLASSIFIER–NUMERAL]. An illustration with the Teiwa general classifier *bag* 'CLF' is (32):

(32) Teiwa (Klamer 2014c)
Qarbau   bag ut   ga'an u
water.buffalo CLF four DEM   DIST
'those four water buffaloes'

Some of the AP languages have parallel forms for numeral classifiers. For instance, Western Pantar *waya* and Adang *beh* both originate from a noun meaning 'leaf'. However, across the AP languages, the classifiers differ significantly in form as well in their classifying function so that no classifier can be reconstructed for proto-AP. A number of AP languages have a 'general' classifier, which functions to classify nouns outside the semantic domains of other classifiers that are semantically more specific (cf. Zubin & Shimojo 1993). Illustrations are the general classifiers Teiwa *bag* (derived from a lexeme meaning 'seed', Klamer 2014c,b), and Adang *paʔ*, derived from a lexeme meaning 'non-round fruit' (Robinson & Haan 2014). Although these 'general' classifiers share a common, general classifying function, they derive from different lexical sources.

Individual languages also differ in the number of classifiers they use. For instance, Adang has 14 classifiers, while Kamang has only 2. In addition, each of the languages uses its classifiers to carve out semantic domains of a quite different nature. By way of illustration, consider the way in which the semantic categories of fruits and animals are classified. In Teiwa, fruits are classed according to their shape, while in Adang, fruits are classified together with animals and people (Robinson & Haan 2014) and Western Pantar classifies fruits with *hissa* 'contents' (Holton 2014a). On the other hand, Klon (Baird 2008) and Kamang (Schapper 2014a) do not use a classifier with fruits at all. Animals are classed with fruits and humans in Adang, but with inanimate (!) objects in Abui.

In sum, numeral classifiers appear to have developed after pAP split up, as no classifier is reconstructable for proto-AP. This is not a surprising finding, as numeral classifier sets are often highly volatile, and typically develop out of other lexical classes, such as nouns. A "spontaneous" innovative development of sets of numeral classifiers is however unusual for a Papuan group, as Papuan languages generally lack classifiers (Aikhenvald 2000: 123, Klamer 2014c).[12] Indeed, classifiers do not occur in any areal and/or genealogical cluster of Papuan languages, *except* for three areas located in eastern Indonesia where contact between Austronesian and Papuan languages has been long term and intense: Timor-Alor-Pantar, Halmahera and the Bird's Head of Papua.[13] On the other hand, classifiers are typically found in Austronesian languages, and the Austronesian languages spoken in eastern Indonesia almost universally have them (Klamer 2014b,c). It is thus plausible that long term Austronesian-Papuan contact has resulted in the diffusion of a numeral classification system into AP languages. In addition, it is likely that recent and intensive contact with Indonesian/Malay (Austronesian) has spiraled the development of the 'general' classifier type in a good number of Alor-Pantar languages as functional copies of the Indonesian general classifier *buah*. While the Indonesian classifier *buah* is derived from a noun meaning 'fruit', it has almost lost its semantic content, and functions as a general classifier today (Hopper 1986; Chung 2010).

---

[12] Numeral classifiers are absent from the overviews of Papuan features by Foley (1986; 2000) and Aikhenvald & Stebbins (2007). Aikhenvald (2000: 123) mentions ten Papuan languages with classifiers in scattered locations of Papua New Guinea: Iwam, Abau (East Sepik province), Chambri, Wogamusin, Chenapian (Lower Sepik), Angave, Tanae (Gulf Province), Folopa (Highlands), Wantoat, Awará (Morobe province).

[13] See Holton (2014a); Klamer (2014b,c) and references cited there.

Note that the contact leading to the diffusion of numeral classification systems did not involve borrowing of lexemes: no similarity in shape or semantics exists between classifiers in any Alor-Pantar language and any known classifiers of Austronesian languages spoken in the region, nor with classifiers of Indonesian/Malay. In particular, reflexes of the reconstructed proto-Malayo-Polynesian classifier *buaq, which are attested throughout the Austronesian family, are not found as classifiers in the AP languages. Neither has the grammatical structure of Austronesian numeral NPs been copied: in Austronesian NPs, the classifier follows the numeral while the position of the noun varies, thus we find [NUMERAL-CLASSIFIER-NOUN] (as in Indonesian *dua buah rumah* ['two CLF house'], 'two houses') but also [NOUN-NUMERAL-CLASSIFIER] (as in colloquial Malay *rumah dua buah* ['house two CLF']; Blust 2009: 283-284). In contrast, in AP languages, the classifier always precedes the numeral: [NOUN-CLASSIFIER-NUMERAL] (as in (32) above).

The AP classifiers thus represent neither borrowed forms nor borrowed structures. What speakers may have adopted from Austronesian, however, is the propensity to reanalyze lexemes which they already had at their disposal (such as 'seed' or 'fruit') and to grammaticalize these as sortal classifiers in numeral expressions.

6.4 Kinship terminology

Kinship terms vary between languages according to ancestor-descendant relationships: the more closely related two languages are, the more likely they are to share cognate forms, and the more likely it is that the meanings of the terms coincide. But as a social construct, kinship practice may be influenced by contact, with concomitant changes in the shape or meaning of the kin terms. The Alor-Pantar languages show enormous variation in kinship terminology and practice, in spite of the fact that many of the communities are closely bound together through ties of marriage alliance (Holton this volume). The westernmost languages distinguish both maternal and paternal cross-cousins (children of opposite-sex siblings) as ideal marriage partners, while at the opposite extreme in the highlands of Alor are found cultures which expressly forbid cross-cousin marriage. Holton (this volume) suggests that the current distribution of kinship terminologies suggests a recent drift toward symmetric exchange systems which distinguish both maternal and paternal cross-cousins, perhaps under the influence of neighboring Austronesian languages.

7 Challenges for future research

The twenty or so languages of the Alor-Pantar (AP) family constitute the westmost outlier "Papuan" group, and together with the Papuan languages of Timor, they make up the Timor-Alor-Pantar family. While this connection has been assumed for decades, the chapter by Schapper, Huber & Engelenhoven (this volume) is in fact the first publication actually *demonstrating* the relatedness using the Comparative Method. Another popular assumption is that the Timor-Alor-Pantar family is part of the Trans-New Guinea family. However, detailed investigations by Holton and Robinson in this volume indicate that there is insufficient evidence to confirm a genealogical relationship between TAP and any other family, that is, TAP must be considered a family-level isolate. The question where the Papuan languages of Timor, Alor and Pantar originate from thus yet remains unanswered, and there is yet no integrated account of the history of the Alor-Pantar region. We need detailed studies of how the languages have been in contact with each other, and to reveal more of the culture history of the speakers, more fine-grained bottom up research of targeted parts of the region is necessary, in particular combining linguistic research with results from ethnographic, archaeological, and musicological research.

Some of the typological features of Alor-Pantar languages are cross-linguistically quite rare: their strong preference to index P but not A on transitive verbs; the extreme variety in morphological alignment patterns; the use of plural number words; the existence of quinary numeral systems; the elaborate spatial deictic systems involving an elevation component; and the great variation exhibited in their kinship systems. There are bound to be more such features to be unravelled in future studies.

All the languages discussed in this volume are extremely fragile, and to keep them alive for future generations of speakers, parents must continue to speak their language with their children. We hope that this volume will create an awareness among local speakers as well as government officials and Indonesian linguists about the unique characteristics and richness of this small non-Austronesian family.

8 Data collection and archiving

Most of the data discussed in the chapters of this volume are primary data collected through fieldwork in Alor and Pantar. To collect the comparative lexical and grammatical data, fieldworkers used a combination of direct elicitation

1 The Alor-Pantar languages: Linguistic context, history and typology

through survey word lists and a set of specially prepared video clips, as well as questionnaires on specific topics. The questionnaire used for the collection of numeral words and arithmetic expressions is included in the Appendix of Klamer et al. (this volume). The set of video clips that was designed to elicit expressions of one and two-participant events in AP languages is described in Fedden & Brown (this volume). The description of the elicitation task itself is included in the Appendix of their chapter, and the set of clips is downloadable from www.smg.surrey.ac.uk/projects/alor-pantar/pronominal-marking-video-stimuli/.

All authors contributing to this volume have endeavoured to make the empirical basis on which their investigations rest as explicit as possible. To this end, most of the chapters include a section referred to as 'Sources', which lists the various sources (both published and unpublished) that were used for the chapter, their authors/collectors and the year(s) of collection. Roughly four types of data sets have been used: word lists, corpora, field notes and responses to video clips.

The word lists used for the chapters on the history of AP languages are part of a lexical database referred to as the Alor-Pantar (AP) Lexical Database, an Excel sheet with over 400 words, containing lexical survey data from Nedebang, Western Pantar (Tubbe variety), Deing, Sar (Adiabang variety), Kaera (Padangsul variety), Blagar (Warsalelang variety), Blagar (Nule variety), Kabola, Adang (Lawahing variety), Hamap, Klon, Kafoa, Abui (Atengmelang variety), Kamang, Kula, Kui, Sawila, Wersing. These word lists were collected between 2003 and 2011 by the following researchers: Louise Baird, František Kratochvíl, Gary Holton, Laura C. Robinson, Antoinette Schapper, Nick Williams, and Marian Klamer. Parts of this (slightly modified) [14] lexical database were used in Holton & Robinson (this volume[a],[b]), and Schapper, Huber & Engelenhoven (this volume). Where a more extensive lexicon of a language is available, that lexicon was used instead of the lexical survey lists. Thus, the lexical data from Teiwa, Kaera, Western Pantar, Blagar, Adang, Klon, Abui, and Sawila are from Toolbox files mutually shared among the researchers, and a published dictionary was the source for Kamang (Schapper & Manimau 2011).

The chapters on the typology of AP languages use corpora as data sets, and build on information collected by researchers in the field ("fieldnotes"). A corpus of an AP language as it is used in this volume typically consists of a Toolbox file containing various spoken texts, which have been transcribed, glossed and

---

[14] Modifications of the original survey lists include the correction of typos, and, where phonological forms are known, these have replaced the original phonetic forms. The Blagar and Adang data were replaced with data from different dialects: Adang (Pitungbang/Kokar dialect) and Blagar (Dolabang dialect).

translated by the researcher working on the language. Corpus data are cited in the text with reference to the author and the language, and refer to the sources given in the next section.

Sources

Baird, Louise	Klon corpus	Leiden University
Holton, Gary	Western Pantar corpus	University of Alaska Fairbanks
Klamer, Marian	Teiwa corpus	Leiden University
Klamer, Marian	Kaera corpus	Leiden University
Kratochvíl, František	Abui corpus	Nanyang Technological University Singapore
Kratochvíl, František	Sawila corpus	Nanyang Technological University Singapore[15]
Schapper, Antoinette	Kamang corpus	Leiden University / University of Cologne
Schapper, Antoinette & Rachel Hendery	Wersing corpus	Australian National University

Sizes of corpora vary from over 100,000 words (Abui: 120,000 words, Sawila: 108,000 words) to less than 50,000 words (Klon: 36,000 words, Teiwa: 26,000 words) to less than 20,000 words (Kaera: 19,000 words). Contents of corpora vary, too: some include oral texts as well as elicited sentences collected during the research; in other cases, a researcher may have kept elicited information separate from the oral text corpus.

Most of the data sets mentioned in this section have been archived as part of the Laiseang corpus at The Language Archive (TLA). They are accessible online at http://hdl.handle.net/1839/00-0000-0000-0018-CB72-4@view.

The responses to the video stimuli that were collected are downloadable from www.smg.surrey.ac.uk/projects/alor-pantar/pronominal-marking-video-stimuli/. They are referred to in this volume as 'Response to video clip Cx/Px, SPy', where SPy stands for the speaker number of the individual who provided the response, and C(ore) or P(eripheral) refer to the core or peripheral status of the clip in the elicitation set.

---

[15] The Sawila corpus includes work by the SIL team members Anderias Malaikosa and Isak Bantara who translated Genesis, the Gospel of Mark, and the Acts into Sawila.

1 The Alor-Pantar languages: Linguistic context, history and typology

Acknowledgments

Parts of this overview were taken from Klamer (2010a; 2011); Baird, Klamer & Kratochvíl (Ms); Holton & Klamer (in press). I thank Sebastian Fedden, Martin Haspelmath, Gary Holton, František Kratochvíl and Laura C. Robinson for their comments on an earlier version of this chapter.

Abbreviations

1	1st person	IPFV	imperfective
2	2nd person	LIM	'limitation marking' predicative suffix
3	3rd person		
A	most agent-like argument	LOC	locative
ALIEN	alienable	NEG	negator
AP	Alor-Pantar	NP	noun phrase
APPL	applicative	OBL	oblique
AST	assistive	P	most patient-like argument
BEN	benefactive	PL	plural
CLF	classifier	pAP	proto-Alor-Pantar
COMPL	completive	PART	particle
CONJ	conjunction	PAT	patient
DAT	dative	PFV	perfective
DEM	demonstrative	POSS	possessive
DIR	directional	PROG	progressive
DIST	distal	PROX	proximate
DISTR	distributive	REAL	realis
EXCL	exclusive	REC	recipient
FIN	final	S	single agreement
GEN	genitive	SG	singular
GOAL	goal	SVC	serial verb construction
INAL	inalienanable	TAP	Timor-Alor-Pantar
INCL	inclusive	TOP	topic

References

Aikhenvald, Alexandra Y. 2000. *Classifiers: A typology of noun categorization devices* (Studies in typology and linguistic theory). Oxford: Oxford University Press.

Aikhenvald, Alexandra Y. & Tonya N. Stebbins. 2007. Languages of New Guinea. In Osahito Miyaoka, Osamu Sakiyama & Micheal E. Krauss (eds.), *The vanishing languages of the Pacific Rim*, 239–266. Oxford: Oxford University Press.

Anonymous. 1914. De eilanden Alor en Pantar, residentie Timor en Onderhoorigheden. *Tijdschrift van het Koninklijk Nederlandsch Aardrijkskundig Genootschap* 31. 70–102.

Badan Pusat Statistik. 2005. *Penduduk kabupaten Alor 2005 (Hasil Registrasi)*. Kalabahi, Indonesia: Badan Pusat Statistik Kabupaten Alor.

Baird, Louise. 2005. Doing the split-S in Klon. *Linguistics in the Netherlands* 22. Doetjes. J. & J. van der Weijer (eds.). 1–12.

Baird, Louise. 2008. *A grammar of Klon: a non-Austronesian language of Alor, Indonesia*. Canberra: Pacific Linguistics.

Baird, Louise. 2010. Grammaticalisation of asymmetrical serial verb constructions in Klon. In Michael Ewing & Marian Klamer (eds.), *Typological and areal analyses: Contributions from East Nusantara*, 189–206. Canberra: Pacific Linguistics.

Baird, Louise. to appear. Kafoa. In Antoinette Schapper (ed.), *Papuan languages of Timor, Alor and Pantar: Sketch grammars*, vol. 2. Berlin: Mouton de Gruyter.

Baird, Louise, Marian Klamer & František Kratochvíl. Ms. *Alor Malay: A grammar sketch*. Manuscript, Leiden University/NTU Singapore.

Barnes, Robert H. 1974. *Kédang: A study of the collective thought of an Eastern Indonesian people*. Oxford: Clarendon Press.

Barnes, Robert H. 1982. The Majapahit dependency Galiyao. *Bijdragen tot de Taal-, Land- en Volkenkunde* 138. 407–412.

Barnes, Robert H. 1996. *Sea hunters of Indonesia. Fishers and weavers of Lamalera*. Oxford: Claredon Press.

Barnes, Robert H. 2001. Alliance and warfare in an Eastern Indonesian principality - Kédang in the last half of the nineteenth century. *Bijdragen tot de Taal-, Land- en Volkenkunde* 157(2). 271–311.

Bellwood, Peter. 1997. *The prehistory of the Indo-Pacific archipelago*. 2nd edition. Honolulu: University of Hawaii Press.

Blust, Robert Andrew. 2009. *The Austronesian languages*. Canberra: Pacific Linguistics.

Blust, Robert Andrew. 2013. *The Austronesian languages*. Revised edition. Canberra: Pacific Linguistics.

Chung, Siaw-Fong. 2010. Numeral classifier *buah* in Malay: A corpus-based study. *Language and Linguistics* 11(3). 553–577.

Comrie, Bernard. 1989. *Language universals and linguistic typology*. Oxford: Blackwell.

Coolhaas, W. Ph. 1979. *Generale missiven van gouverneurs-generaal en raden aan Heren XVII der Verenigde Oostindische Compagnie*. Vol. VII. 's Gravenhage: Martinus Nijhoff.

de Josselin de Jong, Jan Petrus Benjamin. 1937. *Studies in Indonesian culture I: Oirata, a Timorese settlement on Kisar*. Amsterdam: Noord-Hollandsche Uitgevers-Maatschappij.

de Roever, Arend. 2002. *De jacht op sandelhout: de VOC en de tweedeling van Timor in de zeventiende eeuw*. Zutphen: Leiden U. PhD thesis.

Dietrich, Stefan. 1984. A note on Galiyao and the early history of the Solor-Alor islands. *Bijdragen tot de Taal-, Land- en Volkenkunde* 140. 317–326.

Donohue, Mark. 1996. Inverse in Tanglapui. *Language and Linguistics in Melanesia* 27(2). 101–118.

Dryer, Matthew S. 1986. Primary objects, secondary objects and antidative. *Language* 62(4). 808–845.

Dryer, Matthew S. 1989. Plural words. *Linguistics* 27. 865–895.

Dryer, Matthew S. 2011. Coding of nominal plurality. In Matthew S. Dryer & Martin Haspelmath (eds.), *The World Atlas of Language Structures online*. Munich: Max Planck Digital Library. http://wals.info/chapter/33.

Du Bois, Cora. 1960. *The people of Alor*. [1944]. New York: Harper Torchbooks.

Engelenhoven, Aone van. 2009. On derivational processes in Fataluku, a non-Austronesian language in East-Timor. In W. L. Wetzels (ed.), *The linguistics of endangered languages, contributions to morphology and morpho-syntax*, 331–362. Utrecht: Netherlands Graduate School of Linguistics.

Engelenhoven, Aone van. 2010. Verb serialisation in Fataluku. The case of take. In A. Azeb, S. Völlmin, Ch. Rapold & S. Zaug-Coretti (eds.), *Converbs, medial verbs, clause chaining and related issues*, 185–211. Köln: Rüdiger Köppe Verlag.

Fedden, Sebastian & Dunstan Brown. this volume. Participant marking: corpus study and video elicitation. In Marian Klamer (ed.), *The Alor-Pantar languages*, 413–456. Berlin: Language Science Press.

Fedden, Sebastian, Dunstan Brown, Greville G. Corbett, Marian Klamer, Gary Holton, Laura C. Robinson & Antoinette Schapper. 2013. Conditions on pronominal marking in the Alor-Pantar languages. *Linguistics* 51(1). 33–74.

Fedden, Sebastian, Dunstan Brown, František Kratochvíl, Laura C. Robinson & Antoinette Schapper. 2014. Variation in pronominal indexing: lexical stipulation vs. referential properties in the Alor-Pantar languages. *Studies in Language* 38. 44–79.

Foley, William A. 1986. *The Papuan languages of New Guinea* (Cambridge language surveys). Cambridge: Cambridge University Press.

Foley, William A. 2000. The languages of New Guinea. *Annual Review of Anthropology* 29(1). 357–404.

Gaalen, G. A. M. van. 1945. Memorie van overgave van den fundgeerend controleur van Alor G. A. M. van Galen. Manuscript.

Grimes, Charles E., Tom Therik, Barbara D. Grimes & Max Jacob. 1997. *A guide to the people and languages of Nusa Tenggara* (Paradigma: Series B). Kupang: Artha Wacana Press.

Haan, Johnson Welem. 2001. *The grammar of Adang: a Papuan language spoken on the island of Alor East Nusa Tenggara - Indonesia.* Sydney: University of Sydney PhD thesis.

Hajek, John. 2010. Towards a phonological overview of the vowel and consonant systems of East Nusantara. In Michael C. Ewing & Marian Klamer (eds.), *Typological and areal analyses: Contributions from East Nusantara*, 25–46. Canberra: Pacific Linguistics.

Haspelmath, Martin. 2011. On S, A, P, T, and R as comparative concepts for alignment typology. *Linguistic Typology* 15. 535–567.

Holton, Gary. 2008. The rise and fall of semantic alignment in North Halmahera, Indonesia. In M. Donohue & S. Wichmann (eds.), *The typology of semantic alignment*, 252–276. Oxford: Oxford University Press.

Holton, Gary. 2010a. An etymology for Galiyao. University of Fairbanks.

Holton, Gary. 2010b. Person-marking, verb classes and the notion of grammatical alignment in Western Pantar (Lamma). In Michael Ewing & Marian Klamer (eds.), *Typological and areal analyses: contributions from east Nusantara*, 97–117. Canberra: Pacific Linguistics.

Holton, Gary. 2011. Landscape in Western Pantar, a Papuan outlier of southern Indonesia. In David M. Mark, Andrew G. Turk, Niclas Burenhult & David Stea (eds.), *Landscape in language*, 143–166. Amsterdam: John Benjamins.

Holton, Gary. 2014a. Numeral classifiers and number in two Papuan outliers of East Nusantara. In Marian Klamer & František Kratochvíl (eds.), *Number and quantity in East Nusantara*, 178–102. Canberra: Pacific Linguistics.

Holton, Gary. 2014b. Western Pantar. In Antoinette Schapper (ed.), *Papuan languages of Timor, Alor and Pantar: Sketch grammars*, vol. 1, 23–96. Berlin: Mouton de Gruyter.

Holton, Gary. this volume. Kinship in the Alor-Pantar languages. In Marian Klamer (ed.), *The Alor-Pantar languages*, 199–245. Berlin: Language Science Press.

Holton, Gary & Marian Klamer. in press. The Papuan languages of East Nusantara. In Bill Palmer (ed.), *Oceania*. Berlin: Mouton de Gruyter.

Holton, Gary & Mahalalel Lamma Koly. 2008. *Kamus pengantar Bahasa Pantar Barat: Tubbe - Mauta - Lamma*. Kupang, Indonesia: UBB-GMIT.

Holton, Gary & Laura C. Robinson. this volume(a). The internal history of the Alor-Pantar language family. In Marian Klamer (ed.), *The Alor-Pantar languages*, 55–97. Berlin: Language Science Press.

Holton, Gary & Laura C. Robinson. this volume(b). The linguistic position of the Timor-Alor-Pantar languages. In Marian Klamer (ed.), *The Alor-Pantar languages*, 155–198. Berlin: Language Science Press.

Holton, Gary, Marian Klamer, František Kratochvíl, Laura C. Robinson & Antoinette Schapper. 2012. The historical relations of the Papuan languages of Alor and Pantar. *Oceanic Linguistics* 51(1). 86–122.

Hopper, Paul J. 1986. Some discourse functions of classifiers in Malay. In Colette G. Craig (ed.), *Noun classes and categorization*, 309–325. Amsterdam: John Benjamins.

Huber, Juliette. 2008. *First steps towards a grammar of Makasae: a language of East Timor*. Vol. 195 (Languages of the World/Materials). München: Lincom.

Huber, Juliette. 2011. *A grammar of Makalero: a Papuan language of East Timor*. Utrecht: LOT.

Hägerdal, Hans. 2010a. Cannibals and pedlars. *Indonesia and the Malay World* 38(111). 217–246.

Hägerdal, Hans. 2010b. Van Galens memorandum on the Alor islands in 1946. An annotated translation with an introduction. Part 1. *HumaNetten* 25. 14–44.

Hägerdal, Hans. 2011. Van Galens memorandum on the Alor islands in 1946. An annotated translation with an introduction. Part 2. *HumaNetten* 27. 53–96.

Hägerdal, Hans. 2012. *Lords of the land, lords of the sea: Conflict and adaptation in early colonial Timor, 1600-1800*. Leiden: KITLV Press.

Jacob, June & Charles E. Grimes. 2003. *Kamus pengantar Bahasa Kupang–Bahasa Indonesia (dengan daftar Indonesia–Kupang)*. Kupang: Artha Wacana Press.

Klamer, Marian. 2010a. *A grammar of Teiwa* (Mouton Grammar Library 49). Berlin: Mouton de Gruyter.

Klamer, Marian. 2010b. Ditransitives in Teiwa. In Andrej Malchukov, Martin Haspelmath & Bernard Comrie (eds.), *Studies in ditransitive constructions*, 427–455. Berlin: Mouton de Gruyter.

Klamer, Marian. 2010c. One item, many faces: 'come' in Teiwa and Kaera. In Michael Ewing & Marian Klamer (eds.), *East Nusantara: Typological and areal analyses*, 203–226. Canberra: Pacific Linguistics.

Klamer, Marian. 2011. *A short grammar of Alorese (Austronesian)* (Languages of the World/Materials 486). München: Lincom.

Klamer, Marian. 2012. Papuan-Austronesian language contact: Alorese from an areal perspective. In Nicholas Evans & Marian Klamer (eds.), *Melanesian languages on the edge of Asia: challenges for the 21st century*, vol. 5 (Language Documentation & Conservation Special Publication), 72–108. Honolulu: University of Hawaii Press.

Klamer, Marian. 2014a. Kaera. In Antoinette Schapper (ed.), *Papuan languages of Timor, Alor and Pantar: Sketch grammars*, vol. 1, 97–146. Berlin: Mouton de Gruyter.

Klamer, Marian. 2014b. Numeral classifiers in the Papuan languages of Alor Pantar: A comparative perspective. In Marian Klamer & František Kratochvíl (eds.), *Number and quantity in East Nusantara*, 103–122. Canberra: Pacific Linguistics. http://pacling.anu.edu.au/materials/SAL/APL012-SAL001.

Klamer, Marian. 2014c. The history of numeral classifiers in Teiwa (Papuan). In Gerrit J. Dimmendaal & Anne Storch (eds.), *Number: constructions and semantics. Case studies from Africa, India, Amazonia & Oceania*, 135–166. Amsterdam: Benjamins.

Klamer, Marian. to appear. Typology and grammaticalization in the Papuan languages of Timor, Alor and Pantar. In Heiko Narrog & Prashant Pardeshi (eds.), *Grammaticalization from a typological perspective*. Oxford: Oxford University Press.

Klamer, Marian & Michael C. Ewing. 2010. The languages of East Nusantara: an introduction. In Michael C. Ewing & Marian Klamer (eds.), *East Nusantara: typological and areal analyses*, 1–24. Canberra: Pacific Linguistics.

Klamer, Marian & František Kratochvíl. 2006. The role of animacy in Teiwa and Abui (Papuan). In *Proceedings of BLS 32*. Berkeley Linguistic Society. Berkeley.

Klamer, Marian & František Kratochvíl. to appear. The evolution of differential object marking in Alor-Pantar languages. In Ilja Seržant & Alena Witzlack-Makarevich (eds.), *The diachronic typology of differential argument marking*. Berlin: Language Science Press.

Klamer, Marian, Ger P. Reesink & Miriam van Staden. 2008. East Nusantara as a linguistic area. In Pieter Muysken (ed.), *From linguistic areas to areal linguistics* (Studies in Language Companion Series 90), 95–149. Amsterdam: John Benjamins.

Klamer, Marian & Antoinette Schapper. 2012. The development of give constructions in the Papuan languages of Timor-Alor-Pantar. *Linguistic Discovery* 10(3). 174–207.

Klamer, Marian, Antoinette Schapper & Greville G. Corbett. this volume. Plural number words in the Alor-Pantar languages. In Marian Klamer (ed.), *The Alor-Pantar languages*, 375–412. Berlin: Language Science Press.

Klamer, Marian, Antoinette Schapper, Greville G. Corbett, Gary Holton, František Kratochvíl & Laura C. Robinson. this volume. Numeral words and arithmetic operations in the Alor-Pantar languages. In Marian Klamer (ed.), *The Alor-Pantar languages*, 337–373. Berlin: Language Science Press.

Kratochvíl, František. 2007. *A grammar of Abui: a Papuan language of Alor*. Utrecht: LOT.

Kratochvíl, František. 2011a. Discourse-structuring functions of Abui demonstratives. In Foong Ha Yap & Janick Wronae (eds.), *Nominalization in Asian languages: Diachronic and typological perspectives. Volume 2: Korean, Japanese and Austronesian languages*, 761–792. Amsterdam: John Benjamins.

Kratochvíl, František. 2011b. Transitivity in Abui. *Studies in Language* 35(3). 589–636.

Kratochvíl, František. 2014. Sawila. In Antoinette Schapper (ed.), *Papuan languages of Timor, Alor and Pantar: Sketch grammars*, vol. 1, 351–438. Berlin: Mouton de Gruyter.

Kratochvíl, František & Benediktus Delpada. 2008a. *Kamus pengantar Bahasa Abui (Abui-Indonesian-English dictionary)*. Kupang: Unit Bahasa dan Budaya (UBB).

Kratochvíl, František & Benediktus Delpada. 2008b. *Netanga neananra dei lohu naha. Abui tanga haetteng ananra. [Cerita-cerita dalam Bahasa Abui dari Takalelang. Abui stories from Takalelang.]* Kupang: Unit Bahasa dan Budaya (UBB).

Lansing, Stephen J., Murray P. Cox, Therese A. de Vet, Sean S. Downey, Brian Hallmark & Herawati Sudoyo. 2011. An ongoing Austronesian expansion in island Southeast Asia. *Journal of Anthropological Archaeology* 30. 262–272.

Le Roux, C. C. F. M. 1929. De Elcanos tocht door den Timorarchipel met Magalhães schip Victoria. In *Feestbundel, uitgegeven door het koninklijk bataviaasch genootschap van kunsten en wetenschappen bij gelegenheid van zijn 150 jarig bestaan:1778-1928*, 1–99. Weltevreden: Kolff.

Lemoine, Annie. 1969. Histoires de Pantar. *L'Homme* 9(4). 5–32.

Lewis, Paul M. (ed.). 2009. *Ethnologue: languages of the world*. 16th edn. Dallas: SIL International. http://www.ethnologue.com/web.asp.

Lewis, Paul M., Gary F. Simons & Charles D. Fennig. 2013. *Ethnologue: Languages of the world*. 17th edn. Dallas: SIL International. http://www.ethnologue.com.

Maddieson, Ian. 2005. Consonant inventories. In Martin Haspelmath, Matthew S. Dryer, David Gil & Bernard Comrie (eds.), *The World Atlas of Language Structures*, 10–13. Oxford: Oxford University Press.

Mahirta. 2006. The prehistory of Austronesian dispersal to the southern islands of eastern Indonesia. In Truman Simanjuntak, Ingrid H. E. Pojoh & Mohammad Hisyam (eds.), *Austronesian diaspora and the ethnogeneses of people in Indonesian archipelago*, 129–145. Jakarta: LIPI Press.

Martis, Non, Wati Kurnatiawati, Buha Aritonang, Hidayatul Astar & Ferr Feirizal. 2000. *Monografi kosakata dasar Swadesh di Kabupaten Alor*. Jakarta: Pusat Bahasa, Departemen Pendidikan Nasional.

McWilliam, Andrew. 2007. Austronesians in linguistic disguise: Fataluku cultural fusion in East Timor. *Journal of Southeast Asian Studies* 38(2). 355–375.

Morwood, Mike J., R. P. Soejono, R. G. Roberts, T. Sutikna, C. S. M. Turney, K. E. Westaway, W. J. Rink, J.-X. Zhao, G. D. van den Bergh, Rokus Awe Due, Hobbs D. R., M. W. Moore, M. I. Bird & L. K. Fifield. 2004. Archaeology and age of a new hominin from Flores in eastern Indonesia. *Nature* (431). 1087–1091.

Nicolspeyer, Martha Margaretha. 1940. *De sociale structuur van een Aloreesche bevolkingsgroep*. Rijswijk: Rijksuniversiteit te Leiden PhD thesis.

O'Connor, Sue. 2003. Nine new painted rock art sites from East Timor in the context of the Western Pacific region. *Asian Perspectives* 42(1). 96–128.

O'Connor, Sue. 2007. New evidence from East Timor contributes to our understanding of earliest modern human colonisation east of the Sunda shelf. *Antiquity* 81. 523–535.

Pawley, Andrew K. 2005. The chequered career of the Trans New Guinea hypothesis: recent research and its implications. In Andrew K. Pawley, Robert Attenborough, Jack Golson & Robin Hide (eds.), *Papuan pasts: cultural, linguistic and biological history of the Papuan-speaking peoples*, 67–108. Canberra: Pacific Linguistics.

Robinson, Laura C. 2015. The Alor-Pantar (Papuan) languages and Austronesian contact in East Nusantara. In Malcom Ross & I Wayan Arka (eds.), *Language change in Austronesian languages*. Canberra: Asia-Pacific Linguistics.

Robinson, Laura C. & John Haan. 2014. Adang. In Antoinette Schapper (ed.), *Papuan languages of Timor, Alor and Pantar: Sketch grammars*, vol. 1, 221–284. Berlin: Mouton de Gruyter.

Robinson, Laura C. & Gary Holton. 2012. Internal classification of the Alor-Pantar language family using computational methods applied to the lexicon. *Language Dynamics and Change* 2(2). 123–149.

Rodemeier, Susanne. 1995. Local tradition on Alor and Pantar: an attempt at localizing Galiyao. *Bijdragen tot de Taal-, Land- en Volkenkunde* 151(3). 438–442.

Rodemeier, Susanne. 2006. *Tutu kadire in Pandai-Munaseli* (Passauer Beträge zur Südostasienkunde 12). Berlin: LIT Verlag.

Ross, Malcolm. 2005. Pronouns as preliminary diagnostic for grouping Papuan languages. In Andrew K. Pawley, Robert Attemborough, Jack Golson & Robin Hide (eds.), *Papuan pasts: cultural, linguistic and biological histories of Papuan-speaking peoples*, 15–65. Canberra: Pacific Linguistics.

Schapper, Antoinette. 2010. *Bunaq: a Papuan language of central Timor*. Canberra: Australian National University PhD thesis.

Schapper, Antoinette. 2012. *Elevation and scale in two Papuan languages*. Talk presented at EuroBabel Final Conference, Leiden, 23-26 August 2012.

Schapper, Antoinette. 2014a. Kamang. In Antoinette Schapper (ed.), *Papuan languages of Timor, Alor and Pantar: Sketch grammars*, vol. 1, 285–350. Berlin: Mouton de Gruyter.

Schapper, Antoinette (ed.). 2014b. *Papuan languages of Timor, Alor and Pantar: Sketch grammars*. Vol. 1. Berlin: Mouton de Gruyter.

Schapper, Antoinette (ed.). Forthcoming. *Papuan languages of Timor, Alor and Pantar: Sketch grammars*. Vol. 2. Berlin: Mouton de Gruyter.

Schapper, Antoinette & Rachel Hendery. 2014. Wersing. In Antoinette Schapper (ed.), *Papuan languages of Timor, Alor and Pantar: Sketch grammars*, vol. 1, 439–504. Berlin: Mouton de Gruyter.

Schapper, Antoinette, Juliette Huber & Aone van Engelenhoven. this volume. The relatedness of Timor-Kisar and Alor-Pantar languages: A preliminary demonstration. In Marian Klamer (ed.), *The Alor-Pantar languages*, 99–154. Berlin: Language Science Press.

Schapper, Antoinette & Marian Klamer. this volume. Numeral systems in the Alor-Pantar languages. In Marian Klamer (ed.), *The Alor-Pantar languages*, 285–336. Berlin: Language Science Press.

Schapper, Antoinette & Marten Manimau. 2011. *Kamus pengantar Bahasa Kamang-Indonesia-Inggris (Introductory Kamang-Indonesian-English dictionary)* (UBB Language & Culture Series: A 7). Kupang: Unit Bahasa dan Budaya (BDD).

Siewierska, Anna. 2013. Verbal person marking. In Matthew S. Dryer & Martin Haspelmath (eds.), *The world atlas of language structures online*, chapter 102. Munich: Max Planck Digital Library. http://wals.info/chapter/102, accessed 2014-03-29.

Spriggs, Matthew. 2011. Archaeology and the Austronesian expansion: where are we now? *Antiquity* 85. 510–528.

Steenbrink, Karel. 2003. *Catholics in Indonesia 1808-1942. A documented history.* Leiden: KITVL Press.

Steinhauer, Hein. 1977. 'Going' and 'coming' in the Blagar of Dolap (Pura, Alor, Indonesia). *NUSA: Miscellaneous Studies in Indonesian and Languages in Indonesia* 3. 38–48.

Steinhauer, Hein. 1991. Demonstratives in the Blagar language of Dolap (Pura, Alor, Indonesia). In Tom Dutton (ed.), *Papers in Papuan linguistics*, 177–221. Canberra: Pacific Linguistics.

Steinhauer, Hein. 1993. Sisters and potential wives: where linguists and anthropologists meet: notes on kinship in Blagar (Alor). In P. Haenen (ed.), *Vrienden en verwanten, liber amicorum Alex van der Leeden*, 147–168. Leiden & Jakarta: DSALCUL/IRIS.

Steinhauer, Hein. 1995. Two varieties of the Blagar language (Alor, Indonesia). In Connie Baak, Mary Bakker & Dick van der Meij (eds.), *Tales from a concave world: Liber amicorum Bert Voorhoeve*, 269–296. Leiden: Projects Division, Department of Languages, Cultures of South-East Asia & Oceania.

Steinhauer, Hein. 1999. Bahasa Blagar Selayang Pandang. In Bambang Kaswanti Purwo (ed.), *Panorama bahasa Nusantara*, 71–102. Jakarta: Universitas Cenderawasih & Summer Institute of Linguistics.

Steinhauer, Hein. 2010. Pura when we were younger than today. In Artem Fedorchuk & Svetlana Chlenova (eds.), *Studia antropologica. A Festschrift in honour of Michael Chlenov*, 261–283. Jerusalim: Mosty Kul'tury Gesharim.

Steinhauer, Hein. 2012. Deictic categories in three languages of Eastern Indonesia. In Bahren Umar Siregar, P. Ari Subagyo & Yassir Nasanius (eds.), *Dari menapak jejak kata sampai menyigi tata bahasa. Persembahan untuk Prof. Dr. Bambang Kaswanti Purwo dalam rangka ulang tahunnya yang ke-60*, 115–147. Jakarta: Pusat Kajian Bahasa dan Budaya Universitas Katolik Indonesia Atma Jaya.

Steinhauer, Hein. 2014. Blagar. In Antoinette Schapper (ed.), *Papuan languages of Timor, Alor and Pantar: Sketch grammars*, vol. 1, 147–220. Berlin: Mouton de Gruyter.

Stokhof, W. A. L. 1975. *Preliminary notes on the Alor and Pantar languages (East Indonesia)* (Pacific Linguistics: Series B 43). Canberra: Australian National University.

Stokhof, W. A. L. 1977. *Woisika I: An ethnographic introduction* (Pacific Linguistics: Series D 19). Canberra: Australian National University.

Stokhof, W. A. L. 1978. Woisika text. *Miscellaneous Studies in Indonesian and Languages in Indonesia* 5. 34–57.
Stokhof, W. A. L. 1979. *Woisika II: Phonemics*. Canberra: Pacific Linguistics.
Stokhof, W. A. L. 1982. *Woisika riddles* (Pacific linguistics : Series D, Special publications 41). Canberra: ANU.
Stokhof, W. A. L. 1983. Names and naming in Ateita and environments (Woisika, Alor). *Lingua* 61(2/3). 179–207.
Stokhof, W. A. L. 1984. Annotations to a text in the Abui language (Alor). *Bijdragen tot de Taal-, Land- en Volkenkunde* 140(1). 106–162.
Stokhof, W. A. L. 1987. A short Kabola text (Alor, East Indonesia). In Donald C. Laycock & Werner Winter (eds.), *A world of language: Papers presented to Professor Stephen A. Wurm on his 65th birthday* (Pacific Linguistics: Series C 100), 631–648. Canberra: Research School of Pacific & Asian Studies, Australian National University.
Summerhayes, Glenn R. 2007. Island Melanesian pasts: A view from archeology. In Jonathan S. Friedlaender (ed.), *Genes, language and culture history in the Southwest Pacific*, 10–35. Oxford: Oxford University Press.
Verheijen, Jilis A. J. 1986. *The Sama/Bajau language in the Lesser Sunda Islands* (Pacific Linguistics: Series D 70). Canberra: Research School of Pacific & Asian Studies, Australian National University.
Wellfelt, Emilie. 2016. *Historyscapes in Alor. Approaching indigenous histories in Eastern Indonesia*. Linnaeus University, Sweden PhD thesis.
Wellfelt, Emilie & Antoinette Schapper. 2013. *Memories of migration and contact: East Timor origins in Alor*. Paper read at the Eighth International Convention of Asia Scholars, June 24–27, Macao.
Williams, Nick & Mark Donohue. to appear. Kula. In Antoinette Schapper (ed.), *Papuan languages of Timor, Alor and Pantar: Sketch grammars*, vol. 2. Berlin: Mouton de Gruyter.
Wurm, Stephen A., C. L. Voorhoeve & Kenneth A. McElhanon. 1975. The trans-New Guinea phylum in general. In Stephen A. Wurm (ed.), *New Guinea area languages and language study vol 1: Papuan languages and the New Guinea linguistic scene* (Pacific Linguistics: Series C 38), 299–322. Canberra: Research School of Pacific & Asian Studies, Australian National University.
Xu, Shuhua, Irina Pugach, Mark Stoneking, Manfred Kayser, Li Jin & The HUGO Pan-Asian Consortium. 2012. Genetic dating indicates that the Asian-Papuan admixture through Eastern Indonesia corresponds to the Austronesian expansion. *PNAS* 109(12). 4574–4579.

Zubin, David A. & Mitsuaki Shimojo. 1993. How general are general classifiers? With special reference to *ko* and *tsu* in Japanese. In *Proceedings of the BLS 19: general session and parasession on semantic typology and semantic universals*, 490–502.

Chapter 2

The internal history of the Alor-Pantar language family

Gary Holton

Laura C. Robinson

> This chapter demonstrates that the languages of Alor and Pantar share a common origin by applying the comparative method to primary lexical data from twelve languages sampled across the islands of the Alor-Pantar archipelago. More than one hundred proto-Alor-Pantar lexical items are reconstructed. An internal subgrouping based on shared phonological innovations is proposed and is compared to that derived using computational phylogenetic methods. It is argued that the Alor-Pantar group originally came from the region of the Pantar Strait.

1 Introduction

In this chapter we review the reconstruction of proto-Alor-Pantar (pAP) based on the comparative method. We then examine the internal relationships of the Alor-Pantar family and discuss several approaches to subgrouping. In the literature, the Alor-Pantar languages are usually considered to belong to the larger Timor-Alor-Pantar (TAP) group, which includes the Papuan languages of neighboring Timor and Kisar. The Alor-Pantar languages form a well-defined subgroup within TAP and share a common history independent of the Timor languages. The relationship between Alor-Pantar and the Timor languages is discussed in the following chapter; the wider historical relationships with languages beyond Timor-Alor-Pantar are discussed in Chapter 4.

The AP languages form one of only two large pockets of non-Austronesian languages in East Nusantara outside New Guinea (the other being North Halmahera, to which AP languages are not related – see Chapter 4). In contrast to neighboring Timor, all but one of the two dozen or so indigenous languages of the Alor-Pantar archipelago are non-Austronesian.[1] The single Austronesian language, Alorese, clearly has a more recent origin and today occupies only a few coastal outposts in the archipelago (Klamer 2011; 2012). Early reports noted a clear cultural distinction between the "non-indigenous" coastal Alorese speakers and the "indigenous" mountain populations of Alor and Pantar (Anonymous 1914: 75-8). The non-Austronesian character of the languages (as opposed to the cultures) was first recognized for Oirata, a language spoken on Kisar Island, just east of Timor de Josselin de Jong (1937), and shortly thereafter a connection was made to Abui, a language of Alor (Nicolspeyer 1940). The first evidence for the genealogical unity of the AP languages is found in Stokhof (1975), who compiled 117-item comparative wordlists for 34 language varieties. Stokhof proposed a preliminary lexicostatistical classification based on similarity judgments applied to these lexical data, emphasizing that this classification should be considered "very preliminary" (1975: 13). Holton et al. (2012) employed a much larger lexical dataset to identify regular sound correspondences and establish a reconstruction of pAP using the comparative method.

While the results of the comparative method definitively show that the AP languages form a genealogical unit, the identified phonological innovations are typologically common and do not delineate neat subgroups. After reviewing the subgrouping implications of the phonological innovations, we apply computational methods to the same data and are on this basis able to identify internal groupings. Crucially, the lexical data are coded for cognacy based on identified phonological innovations. The resulting tree of AP languages is consistent with an historical scenario whereby AP languages originate in the Pantar Strait. We begin in the following section by reviewing the recent reconstruction of pAP.[2]

---

[1] We exclude here the Austronesian language Sama-Bajo, which is spoken by recent migrants in a single community on the coast of northern Pantar.

[2] The data and reconstructions in § 2 and in the Appendix largely follow Holton et al. (2012), except in the following ways. First, we have followed Robinson & Holton (2012) in correcting some minor typos. Some of these corrections result in changes to our analyses as well. For example, retranscription of Teiwa *ki?in* 'mosquito' leads us to reconstruct *kin rather than *qin. Second, while the data in Holton et al. (2012) are primarily phonetic, here we have tried to use phonological forms where they are known. Third, we have used different dialects of Adang and Blagar (Pitungbang and Dolabang dialects, respectively) to more closely match existing publications for those languages (e.g., the sketch grammars in Schapper 2014). Fourth, we have consulted new evidence from Timor languages (see Chapter 3) to add new reconstructions or to update the pAP reconstructions based on external evidence. That new evidence has caused us to question the reconstructability of *b and *d in final position, as discussed below. Finally, we have removed pAP reconstructions for 'axe' and 'comb' because we now have evidence that these may be Austronesian loanwords that postdate the breakup of pAP.

2 Sound correspondences and reconstruction

The surge in documentary field work over the past decade (see Chapter 1) has provided a robust lexical dataset on which to base the reconstruction of pAP. The primary data source used in this chapter is a set of 400-item vocabulary lists collected for twelve different language varieties with broad geographic representation across the archipelago: Teiwa (Tw), Nedebang (Nd), Kaera (Ke), Western Pantar (WP), Blagar (Bl), Adang (Ad), Klon (Kl), Kui (Ki), Abui (Ab), Kamang (Km), Sawila (Sw), and Wersing (We). (See Figure 2 in Chapter 1.) The vocabulary list was tailored specifically to this task, taking into account three specific goals. First, the list contains basic vocabulary such as that found on a Swadesh list, tailored to include items relevant to the East Nusantara cultural and ecological region. Second, the list includes some non-basic vocabulary which may be diagnostic of shared cultural traits. For example, it includes a number of terms relating to agriculture. Our ability or inability to reconstruct these terms provides insight into the culture history of the pAP speakers and thus sheds light on AP prehistory and migration. Third, the list includes items motivated by a need to find further examples of specific sound correspondences, such as 'village' and 'crocodile', which both contain pharyngeal fricatives in Teiwa. These lists were supplemented by data from published sources and from ongoing field work by members of the EuroBABEL project. In some cases, the data present uncertainties regarding the phonemic status of particular segments, orthographic conventions, and morpheme boundaries. For example, in elicited word lists, verbs can occur with yet unanalyzed aspectual and/or modal suffixes. In this paper we only compare root forms, with affixes being identified on the basis of grammatical descriptions and recurrent endings within the lexical data. In the cognate sets presented here, material identified as fused or fossilized morphology is bracketed with '( )', while roots that obligatorily occur with affixes are marked with a hyphen, '-'.

Identification of regular consonant correspondences supports the reconstruction of a pAP inventory containing 14 consonants, as shown in Table 1. Each of these consonant reconstructions is supported by correspondence sets for each position (initial, medial, and final) in which that consonant occurs.

While we can identify regular correspondence sets supporting *r, this phoneme occurs in complementary distribution with *j. In fact, *r is the only consonant which does not occur in initial position (see Table 3 below). In contrast, glides *j and *w occur only in initial position; final glides in the modern languages derive from original vowels. The complementary distribution of *r and *j raises the possibility that *r is actually an allophone of *j in pAP. However, the /r/ ~

Table 1: Reconstructed pAP consonant inventory

	Labial	Apical	Palatal	Velar	Uvular	Glottal
Stop	p b	t d		k g	q	
Fricative		s				h
Nasal	m	n				
Glide	w		j			
Liquid		l (r)				

/l/ distinction is found in all of the modern AP languages (see Table 2 below), and at least two liquids must be reconstructed to proto-Timor-Alor-Pantar, the immediate parent of pAP (see Chapter 3).

Although a uvular stop is found in only two of the modern AP languages, the reconstruction of pAP *q is well-supported by a number of correspondence sets. In addition to Teiwa and Nedebang, which maintain *q as /q/, in Kaera the reflex of *q is /x/, which is distinct from the reflex of *k as /k/. Western Pantar collapses *q and *k as /k/ in initial position but maintains the distinction in medial position, as only the reflex of *k is geminate. Outside these four Pantar languages, the *q/*k distinction is lost. From a typological perspective the presence of the uvular stop is highly unusual. Only 2.4% of the languages in Maddieson's (2005) survey of consonant inventories contain uvular stops, though two of those languages are Trans-New Guinea (Kunimaipa and Hamtai). This figure is consistent with Hajek's (2010) survey of the phonological systems of 71 languages of East Nusantara. Hajek identifies only one language other than Teiwa which contrasts velar and uvular stops; this is the West Papuan language Tehit.

The inventory of pAP consonants is very similar to that found in many of the modern Alor-Pantar languages, and its size is typical for the East Nusantara region (Hajek 2010). Most modern AP languages differ in having a velar nasal, which is not reconstructed for pAP. As noted above most AP languages also distinguish /r/ and /l/. The consonant inventory for pAP can be compared with that for the modern language Western Pantar in Table 2.

The Western Pantar inventory exhibits several features typical of phonological developments in the modern languages. First, the uvular stop has merged with the velar stop. Second, Western Pantar has developed a velar nasal in final position. Third, Western Pantar has developed a phonemic glottal stop. The distributional restrictions on pAP consonants are summarized in Table 3. It should be noted that while *g does occur in initial position, it occurs there only in pronominal forms.

2 The internal history of the Alor-Pantar language family

Table 2: Western Pantar consonant inventory

	Labial	Alveolar	Palatal	Velar	Glottal
Stop	p b	t d		k g	ʔ
Fricative		s			h
Nasal	m	n		ŋ	
Glide	w		j		
Liquid		l r			

Table 3: Distributional restrictions on pAP consonants

	Initial	Medial	Final
b	+	+	(+)
d	+	+	(+)
g	+	+	-
p	+	+	-
t	+	+	+
k	+	+	+
q	+	+	-
s	+	+	+
h	+	-	-
m	+	+	+
n	+	+	+
l	+	+	+
(r)	-	+	+
j	+	-	-
w	+	-	-

In Holton et al. (2012), we reconstruct the voiced stops *b and *d for all positions, but after revising the reconstructions based on external data from Timor (see Chapter 3), many reconstructions which formerly ended in a voiced stop have now been revised to include further segments (i.e., 'fire', 'fish', 'sugarcane', 'sun', 'throw'). The voiced stops *b and *d are now only weakly attested in final position in our data, and it is possible that with further evidence, those few reconstructions with final *b and *d may need to be revised as well. Note that we also do not reconstruct *g in final position, so pAP may have had a restriction on final voiced stops, though these do occur in modern AP languages (e.g., Teiwa *lia:g* and Kaera *le:g* 'rattan').

The lack of final *p is robustly evidenced in our data. All instances of final *p* in the modern languages can be traced to either an original medial *p or to *b, as in Teiwa *tap* < *tapai 'pierce', or Western Pantar *hap* < *habi 'fish'.

Drawing from a comparative lexical database consisting of approximately 400 items we identify 129 cognate sets reflecting regular sound correspondences (see Appendix). There are only 127 distinct meanings, as two of the meanings, 'dog' and 'walk', are found in more than one cognate set. These forms show predominantly regular sound correspondences, as described below. However, it is important to note that several of the cognate sets cannot be reconstructed to pAP, since they are found only in a geographically restricted area. That is, in some cases lexemes appear to have been innovated. This is particularly obvious for those meanings for which we have two correspondence sets (distinguished below with subscript numerals). The supporting data for each of these sets is provided in the course of demonstrating the correspondences in the following subsections. The complete set of correspondences can be found in the Appendix.

In this section we describe the 35 consonant correspondences which we have identified in our sample of AP languages. In most cases the correspondences are conditioned by environment; we thus provide examples of the correspondences in word-initial, word-medial, and word-final position. The tables below set out the consonant correspondences, as well as the reconstructed pAP phoneme for each correspondence set. The environment (Env) column indicates whether the correspondence applies in initial (#__), medial (V__V), or final (__#) position. A zero (Ø) in a column indicates that the pAP sound in question is lost in that language. A dash (-) in a column indicates that we lack sufficient data to posit a reflex for that language. A slash (/) indicates that more than one reflex is found in that language.

2 The internal history of the Alor-Pantar language family

Transcription follows IPA conventions.[3] Geminate consonants and long vowels are indicated with a length mark (:). Word stress is transcribed here only where relevant to the correspondence in question (e.g., 'dog$_1$'). In most of the modern languages stress is on the penultimate syllable; however, stress may also be attracted to heavy syllables, as in Teiwa *ji'var* 'dog'. In addition, stress may be phonemically contrastive in some languages, as in Western Pantar *ba'wa* 'conch shell' vs. *'bawa* 'drum'.

In the tables the languages are arranged in order roughly from west to east with the western-most languages on the left and the eastern-most languages on the right. This arrangement is maintained throughout all the tables in the paper.

In the following subsections we discuss the correspondences in word-initial, word-medial, and word-final position separately for each consonant. By examining the correspondences in each position separately we are able to tease out apparent or false cognates which show the expected form in initial position but an unexpected reflex in medial or final position. Nevertheless, such irregular forms are included in correspondence sets for the sake of completeness. In these cases, the irregular forms are denoted with a preceding double dagger (‡) in the Appendix. For some of these forms, we can identify the form as borrowed from a particular source language, but for many, the reason for the irregularity has not yet been identified. Finally, we reconstruct pAP forms only when we have broad geographic evidence. That is, reflexes must be found in minimally one language of Pantar (Teiwa, Nedebang, Kaera, Western Pantar), one language of West Alor and the Pantar Strait (Blagar, Adang, Klon, Kui), and one language of East Alor (Abui, Kamang, Sawila, Wersing). Where reflexes are found only in a restricted region such as Pantar or Eastern Alor, we do not reconstruct a pAP lexeme.

2.1 Voiced stops

We reconstruct three voiced stops in labial, apical, and velar positions. Labial and apical voiced stops are well attested in initial and medial positions, and only weakly attested in final position. The evidence for a voiced velar stop in initial position is based entirely on third person pronominal forms, and there is no support for a velar stop in final position.

Initial pAP *b is retained everywhere except Abui, where it weakens to /f/, and the Eastern Alor languages Kamang, Sawila, and Wersing, where it is devoiced as /p/. This correspondence is found in 'pig', 'betel nut', 'axe', 'maize', and

---

[3] The IPA transcriptions used in this paper differ from the Indonesian-based orthographies of Alor-Pantar languages we use in other publications. Important differences include IPA /j/ = orthographic *y*, /tʃ/ = *c*, /dʒ/ = *j*.

Table 4: Alor-Pantar voiced stop correspondences

pAP	Env	Tw	Nd	Ke	WP	Bl	Ad	Kl	Ki	Ab	Km	Sw	We
*b	#_	b	b	b	b	b	b	b	b	f	p	p	p
*b	V_V	ɸ/v	f/v	b	b:	b	b	b	b	f	f	p	p
*b	_#	ɸ/v	f/v	b	p	b	b	b	b	Ø	p	p	p
*d	#_	d	d	d	d	d	d	d	d	r	t	d	d
*d	V_V	d	d	d	d:	d	d	d	d	r	t	d	d
*d	_#	r	r	d	r	d	d	d	r	r	t	d	d
*g	#_	g	g	g	g	ʔ	ʔ	g	g	h	g	g	g
*g	V_V	ħ	x	g	g:	Ø/ʔ	ʔ	g	g	h	Ø	j	l

Table 5: Alor-Pantar voiceless stop correspondences

pAP	Env	Tw	Nd	Ke	WP	Bl	Ad	Kl	Ki	Ab	Km	Sw	We
*p	#_	p	p	p	p	p	p	p	p	p	f	p	p
*p	V_V	p	p/f	p	p:	p	p	-	p	p	f	-	Ø
*t	#_	t	t	t	t	t	t	t	t	t	t	t	t
*t	V_V	t	t	t	t:	t	t	t	t	t	t	t	t
*t	_#	t	t	t	t	t	Ø	t	t	t	t	t	t
*k	#_	k	k	k	k	k	ʔ	k	k	k	k	k	k
*k	V_V	-	k	k	k:	k	ʔ	k	k	k	k	k	k
*k	_#	k	k	k	k	Ø	Ø	k	k	k	k	-	Ø
*q	#_	q	q	x	k	k/ʔ	ʔ	k	k	k	k	k	k
*q	V_V	q	q	x	k	k	Ø	k	k	k	k	k	k

Table 6: Alor-Pantar fricative correspondences

pAP	Env	Tw	Nd	Ke	WP	Bl	Ad	Kl	Ki	Ab	Km	Sw	We
*s	#_	s	s	s	s	h	h	h	s	t	s	t	t
*s	V_V	s	s/tʃ	s	s	s	h	h	s	t	s	t	t
*s	_#	s	s	s	s	h	h	h	s	t	h	t	t
*h	#_	h/ħ	Ø	Ø	h	Ø	Ø	Ø	Ø	Ø	Ø	Ø	Ø

2 The internal history of the Alor-Pantar language family

'crocodile'. Thus, Abui *fe*, Kamang *pe*, Sawila *pi*, Wersing *pei* < pAP *baj 'pig'. While the correspondence sets for initial *b are extremely regular, they are not without problems, since they may reflect borrowings. The clearest instance of this problem occurs with 'maize', which was first introduced into the region by the Dutch in the 15-16th century. AP lexemes for 'maize' represent indirect borrowings of Old Malay *batari* 'sorghum' which diffused across the languages as the crop spread. Since the historical record indicates that maize was first introduced into agriculture into western Timor, it is most likely that Austronesian languages of Timor were the proximate source for 'maize' lexemes in AP (e.g., Tetun *batar* 'maize'). We do not reconstruct a word for 'maize' to pAP, but the cognate set is included here because its consonant correspondences follow the established patterns. That is, the phonological innovations affecting pAP initial *b and final *r must postdate the introduction of the lexical item to Alor-Pantar.

Similar issues of borrowing surround the reconstruction of 'betel nut' in pAP. The betel or areca palm (*Areca catechu*) is known to have been domesticated in mainland Southeast Asia (Yen 1977). However, there is no archaeological evidence as to when the domesticated palm would have reached the Alor archipelago. There is linguistic and archaeological evidence that Proto-Austronesians in Taiwan had betel (i.e., 'betel' is reconstructable to proto-Austronesian) and that Austronesians transported betel at some points in their dispersal (Lichtenberk 1998). The similarity of the AP lexemes for 'betel' and those in surrounding Austronesian languages (e.g., Tetun *bua* 'betel', Tokodede *buo* 'betel') suggests that AP 'betel' lexemes may in fact be borrowings from Austronesian. Given this lexical likeness and the uncertainty of the timing of the arrival of betel in the region, we tentatively reconstruct a pAP (loan) lexeme for 'betel nut'.

Medial reflexes of *b are found in 'village', 'dog$_1$', 'spear', 'star', 'fish', 'tongue', 'sugarcane', 'shark', 'leg', and 'new'. These follow the same pattern as initial *b except in Teiwa, Nedebang, Western Pantar, and Abui. In Teiwa and Nedebang *b weakens to a fricative; thus, Teiwa *haɸan*, Nedebang *afaŋ* < pAP *haban 'village'. In Western Pantar *b geminates in medial position, thus, Western Pantar *hab:aŋ* 'village'. If the final vowel is lost, *b is reflected as /p/ is Western Pantar and is lost in Abui (e.g., Western Pantar *hap* < pAP *habi 'fish').

Medial gemination is a characteristic feature of Western Pantar; most pAP stops (including nasal stops) are geminated in medial position in Western Pantar (transcribed here as long consonants *b:*, *d:*, etc.). We infer that modern non-geminate medial stops in Western Pantar reflect either borrowing or innovation that took place after the gemination process. In modern Western Pantar there is a robust phonemic contrast between geminate and non-geminate consonants, as between *duba* 'slippery' and *dub:a* 'push.' Phonetic geminates do occur in some other AP languages, notably Nedebang and Sawila; however, there is little evidence that geminates have phonemic status in those languages. Furthermore, only in Western Pantar do we find geminates as a regular reflex of pAP medial stops; elsewhere they occur only sporadically.

Evidence for *b in final position is based only on a single reconstruction for 'wave'. In Holton et al. (2012), 'fish', 'tongue', 'sugarcane', and 'wave' were all reconstructed with a final *b, but with many of the cognates containing final vowels which we assumed were epenthetic. External evidence from Timor languages (see Chapter 3 and Schapper, Huber & Engelenhoven 2012) has forced us to reconstruct those final vowels for 'fish', 'tongue', and 'sugarcane'. It is possible that 'wave' also had a final vowel in pAP, though we have insufficient evidence to reconstruct that at this time.

The variation in Teiwa and Nedebang between voiced and voiceless reflexes of non-initial *b appears to be unconditioned. Nedebang *bova* 'wave' has a voiced fricative, while *a:fi* 'fish' has a voiceless fricative. Klamer (2010: 38) notes that while /ɸ/ and /v/ are distinct phonemes in Teiwa, the voiced variant is quite rare. The sporadic voicing seen in these correspondence sets may reflect a recent phonemicization of /v/.

In initial and medial positions *d is reflected as /r/ in Abui and as /t/ in Kamang. The other languages retain /d/, with the exception of Western Pantar which has a geminate in medial position, as expected. When the final vowel is lost, Teiwa, Nedebang, Western Pantar, and Kui reflect *d > r.

Initial *d correspondences are found in 'rat', 'sing', 'bird', and 'slippery'. Thus, Teiwa *dur*, Western Pantar *di*, Abui *rui*, Kamang *tui* < pAP *dur 'rat'. Medial *d correspondences are found in 'to plant', 'bat', 'right (side)', 'throw', 'fire', 'sun', and 'body hair'. Thus, Teiwa *mədi*, Western Pantar *mad:e*, Abui *marel*, Kamang *matei* < pAP *madel 'bat'. The unexpected Kaera form *wer* 'sun' is likely a borrowing from neighboring Teiwa or Nedebang, as *d is more regularly reflected as /d/ in final position, as in *od* 'throw' and *ad* 'fire'. On the other hand, Nedebang *mara* and Kaera *merei* 'bat' unexpectedly have /r/ in medial position. These forms may reflect a borrowing (from Abui); alternatively, these forms may have a more complex history in which final syllables were originally lost, leading these forms to be treated as final.

Evidence for *d in final position is based on a single correspondence set for 'garden', which is not even reconstructed to pAP. As with *b, evidence for final *d was considerably weakened in light of external evidence from Timor. The forms 'throw', 'fire', and 'sun' have all been revised to contain final vowels.

Initial *g is reflected as a glottal stop in Blagar and Adang, and as a glottal fricative in Abui. However, the reconstruction of initial *g hinges entirely on the correspondence of third person prefixal forms in pAP. These forms exhibit vowel grading which distinguishes singular, plural, genitive, and locative. In particular, all instances of initial /g/ in modern AP languages can be traced to third person pronouns. Only the third-singular bound pronoun *ga has reflexes in all languages. The third plural is attested in a few languages and can be tentatively reconstructed as *gi-. It is absent in the modern AP languages Adang, Klon, Kamang, and Abui, which have generalized their reflexes of the pAP third person singular prefix to both singular and plural contexts. A third reflex of initial *g is found in the third person genitive marker *ge(-) which indexes alienable possessors (in contrast to *ga-, which indexes inalienable possessors). The reconstruction of genitive *ge(-) is supported by the presence of reflexes in a robust geographical spread of AP languages. A final correspondence set supporting *g is found in the third person locative prefix in several languages of Alor. There is no evidence for this prefix in the languages of Pantar (Teiwa, Nedebang, Kaera, Western Pantar, Blagar), and we do not reconstruct it to pAP. Note that Kamang has a regular change of initial *g to /w/ before back vowels, hence the form wo-.

With some possible exceptions, these forms are bound, occurring as prefixes with either nominal or verbal roots. Exceptions include Adang *?e* and Klon *ge* 3GEN.[4] At this stage, we remain agnostic as to whether the pAP genitive was a free or bound form. Other free pronouns vary in their form across the modern AP languages and cannot be reconstructed to pAP (Kratochvíl et al. 2011).

The reflexes of medial *g are much more varied, but they are robustly attested in 'yellow', 'yawn', 'banana', 'garden', 'crocodile', and 'hear'. Only in Kaera, Klon, and Kui is *g retained unchanged in medial position. In Western Pantar we find the expected geminate in all forms except *bagai* 'crocodile', which may be a borrowing from Kaera. In Teiwa medial *g is reflected as a pharyngeal fricative, while in Abui it is reflected as a glottal fricative. Other languages reflect either a glottal stop, a liquid, a fricative, or zero. However, medial reflexes in Sawila and Wersing are supported by only one lexical item each.

The evidence for *g in final position is extremely weak. In the modern languages final g occurs only in the Pantar languages Teiwa and Kaera (as well as Sar, not in our sample). In our 400-item wordlist, final g is found in only eleven distinct Teiwa word forms. None of these has cognates in a central or eastern

---

[4] The Klon form is analyzed by Baird (2008) as a free form based on its ability to occur following an NP. Yet it is equally possible that Klon has homophonous bound and free genitive forms differing in distributional restrictions, analogous to WP *gai-* (bound) and *ga'ai* (free).

Alor language. Cognates with Pantar and western Alor languages do exist; however, in many cases the correspondence is between medial *g* and final *g*. For example, Teiwa *miːg*, Nedebang *miːgi*, Kaera *miag* 'yesterday'; and Teiwa *bog*, Nedebang *boga*, Western Pantar *bogːa* 'young'. Hence, it seems plausible to conclude that Teiwa and Kaera final *g* actually derive from medial *g and that pAP *g was not found in final position.

2.2 Voiceless stops

We reconstruct three voiceless stops in labial, apical, and velar positions. While all the modern languages have glottal stops, as in Adang *ʔahaɲ* 'to cry' versus *ahaɲ* 'jungle', we do not find sufficient evidence at this time to reconstruct glottal stop to pAP. In initial and medial positions pAP *p remains unchanged in all the languages except Kamang, where it weakens to /f/; Western Pantar, where it predictably geminates in medial position; and Wersing, where evidence from a single correspondence ('pierce') suggests that *p was lost in medial position. Correspondence sets reflecting *p include 'hold', 1PL.INCL, 'scorpion', 'pierce', and 'search'. Thus, pAP *p{i,u}nV > Teiwa *pin*, Blagar *pina*, Adang *puin*, Abui *pun*, Kamang *fun*, Sawila *puni* 'hold'. The devoicing of *b in Sawila and Wersing results in merger of *b and *p. Note that Western Pantar *par* 'scorpion' must be a loan from a language which preserves final *r. We find no evidence to support reconstruction of *p in final position. Rather, final /p/ in modern languages results from loss of final vowels (e.g., *tapai > Teiwa *tap* 'pierce', *habi > Western Pantar *hap* 'fish').

In initial and medial positions *t remains unchanged in all languages, with the exception of Western Pantar, which has a geminate medially as expected. The reconstruction of initial *t is supported by correspondence sets for 'recline', 'saltwater', 'short', 'stand', 'ripe', 'far' and 'tree'. Reconstruction of medial *t is supported by correspondence sets for 'dry', 'maize', 'hearth', and 'hand/arm'. Reflexes of 'dry' and 'hearth' are not sufficiently widely distributed to justify reconstruction at the level of pAP. The set for 'dry' is found only in the Pantar Strait and Central Alor languages, while the form for 'hearth' is found only in the Pantar languages. As stated earlier, we don't reconstruct pAP 'maize' since it is known to be a late borrowing from Austronesian. The resemblance between pAP *-tan 'hand/arm' and Malay *taŋan* 'hand' is superficial only and cannot be taken to indicate that the AP lexemes are Austronesian borrowings. The form *taŋan* for 'hand' is a lexical innovation of Malayic and cannot be reconstructed to higher levels of the Austronesian family: proto-Malayo-Polynesian (and proto-Austronesian) reconstructions are *lima for 'hand' and *baRa for 'arm', and it is

2 The internal history of the Alor-Pantar language family

reflexes of these proto-lexemes for 'hand' and 'arm' which are found in the Austronesian languages surrounding the AP languages. Malay has only been present in the region since the historical period, and Malay influence on the AP languages might have started as late as the beginning of the twentieth century.[5] As such, we unproblematically reconstruct pAP *tan 'hand/arm'.

Final *t is preserved in all languages except Adang, where it is lost. The reconstruction of final *t is supported by cognate sets for 'leg', 'flea', 'betel vine', and 'wound'. However, only in Teiwa, Kaera, Blagar, and Kui does the reflex of *t still occur finally. This leads to some uncertainty as to whether these forms may have been originally medial. The correspondence set for 'betel vine', for example, as it is reflected as medial *t* in more than half of the modern languages. We tentatively reconstruct this form with final *t based on two pieces of evidence. First, the Western Pantar form *meta* does not reflect gemination, which would be expected as a reflex of medial *t. Second, several of the languages have a long vowel or diphthong. We thus reconstruct *mait and presume a process of palatalization following a high front vowel. Thus, *t > tʃ/Vi_ in Adang, *t > h /Vi_ in Klon (presumably via s), and *t > s/ Vi_ in Kui, Kamang, Sawila, and Wersing.[6] In the Appendix we list only the original reflex, not the secondary development reflected in 'betel vine'. However, we note that betel vine may be introduced; see also the case of 'betel nut' in section 2.1 above.

Initially and medially, *k remains unchanged in all languages except Adang, where it is reflected as a glottal stop, and Western Pantar, where it is predictably geminated in medial position. Correspondence sets supporting initial *k include 'bone', 'dog$_2$', 'fingernail', and 'mosquito'. Note that the medial correspondence for Abui *kusɪŋ* 'fingernail' is irregular.

Medial *k is supported by correspondence sets for 'crouch', 'short', 'good', and 'lizard'. Thus, Nedebang *tuku*, Western Pantar *tuk:a*, Adang *toʔaŋ*, Klon, Kui, Wersing, Teiwa *tuk* < pAP *tukV 'short'. The lexeme 'lizard' is likely an

---

[5] It is likely that Malay was only introduced to the Papuan speakers on Alor and Pantar through the Dutch schools that were opened in early 20th century. For example, Du Bois (1944: 223) notes that among the Abui people with whom she lived in the 1930s, Malay was only known by school children. The first Dutch schools were opened on Alor in 1906; on Pantar in the 1920s (Klamer 2010: 14). In the Dutch schools, the language of education was Malay, as elsewhere in the Dutch East Indies.

[6] The alternation between alveolars and palatals in Adang reflects a phonemic split by which *d, *t, and *n have been palatalized following a vowel sequence ending in a high front vowel, as in 'betel vine' (Robinson & Haan 2014). Klon has non-phonemic palatalization in the same environment, while the closely related language Kabola (not in our sample) does not undergo palatalization.

Austronesian borrowing (cf. Alorese *take*), perhaps explaining the anomalous reflexes Adang *tɛkɔ* and Kamang *tak:eː*, the latter of which has an unexpected geminate. However, this form is geminated as expected in Western Pantar *tak:e*.

Final *k is retained in all languages except Blagar, Adang, Sawila, and Wersing, where it is lost entirely. Only two correspondence sets, 'one' and 'horn', support this reconstruction. Neither set has cognates in Sawila; however, final *k* is rare in our Sawila data set, occurring in only two forms: *werpa:k* 'frog' and *kispa:k* 'earthworm' (both lexical innovations shared with Wersing). The correspondences for final *k can be difficult to tease apart from those for medial *k, since many languages reflect later vowel epenthesis or apocope. We take the presence of a geminate in Western Pantar to be diagnostic in this regard, since Western Pantar geminates do not occur word-finally. This criterion is admittedly problematic, since it is entirely possible that vowel epenthesis preceded gemination in Western Pantar. Furthermore, Western Pantar sometimes lacks cognates for relevant lexical items, as with 'horn'.

The reconstruction of *q is supported by the presence of a post-coronal voiceless obstruent phoneme distinct from the velar stop in three Pantar languages. In Teiwa and Nedebang this is a uvular stop; in Kaera a velar fricative. Elsewhere, initial *q is reflected as /k/, with the exception of Adang, which has glottal stop, and Blagar, which shows both glottal stop and velar stop reflexes. Initial *q is found in correspondence sets for 'spear', 'itchy', and 'tens'. Blagar shows alternation between a velar and glottal reflex of *q. Note that the *r* in 'tens' behaves as a medial consonant since this numeral formative only occurs in compounds with following numeral, e.g., Teiwa *qar nuk* 'ten'.

The medial reflexes of *q are similar to those in initial position, except that Adang shows loss of medial *q. Correspondence sets supporting medial *q include 'two', 'itchy', 'white', and 'black'. Adang *kak* 'itchy' is anomalous, as it retains the medial consonant. Blagar *madʒaka* 'white' is in fact cognate due to a regular process of glide insertion between the vowels /i/ and /a/, followed by glide fortition: *miaqa > *miaka* > *mijaka* > *madʒaka*. The most interesting reflex of medial *q is found in Western Pantar. Unlike the other voiceless stops, the uvular stop is not reflected as a geminate in Western Pantar but instead as a non-geminate velar stop. In this regard Western Pantar patterns with the other Pantar languages in distinguishing reflexes of *q and *k.

In particular, *q provides an additional source for non-geminate intervocalic voiceless velar stops in Western Pantar. This in turn may inform reconstruction of final vowels in pAP. Since *q does not geminate in Western Pantar, Western Pantar *alaku* 'two' can readily be derived from *raqu, supporting reconstruction

2 The internal history of the Alor-Pantar language family

of the final vowel. On the other hand, Western Pantar *anuku* 'one' corresponds to Tw and Nd forms with velar stops, hence the reconstruction of pAP 'one' must contain a velar, not a uvular. The fact that Western Pantar *anuku* does not contain a geminate means that either it has been borrowed or that the vowel has been added following the gemination process. In the absence of any evidence for borrowing we reconstruct *nuk 'one' without a final vowel.

The evidence for *q in final position is extremely limited. One possible example is 'smoke', whose correspondences are similar to those for medial *q (Kaera *banax* and Wersing *punak*). However, the Teiwa, Nedebang, and Western Pantar reflexes are zero. Another candidate correspondence is 'rice': Western Pantar *ala* and Klon, Kui, Wersing *arak*, which compares to Teiwa *qar*, Nedebang *qara*, and Kaera *(na)xar*. If the Teiwa, Nedebang, and Kaera forms are interpreted as a result of metathesis of *r and *q, then this correspondence could also support *q in final position, namely, *araq. However, we find insufficient evidence to support reconstruction of *q in final position.

2.3 Fricatives

We reconstruct two fricatives to pAP, *s and *h. While *s occurs freely in all positions, the glottal fricative *h is restricted to initial position. Correspondence sets for *s are relatively straightforward. In initial position *s weakens to *h* in Adang, and Klon, and strengthens to *t* in Abui, Sawila, and Wersing. In the remaining languages, which include all four Pantar languages in addition to Kui and Kamang, *s is retained as *s*. Only in Blagar does the reflex of *s exhibit significant variation by position. In initial and final position Blagar has h < *s, as in Adang and Klon, while in medial position Blagar retains s < *s. Thus, pAP *siba > Blagar *hiba* 'new'; *jasi > Blagar *dʒasi* 'bad'; *bis > Blagar *bihi* 'mat', with an epenthetic final vowel which was added after the weakening of *s. In medial position Nedebang sometimes has as affricate. Thus, *jiwesin > Nedebang *jisin* 'five', but *jasi > Nedebang *jetʃi* 'bad'.

Initial correspondence sets for *s are found in 'new', 'wind', and 'shark'. Thus, Western Pantar *sab:a*, Blagar *hiba*, Adang *habar*, Klon *həba*, Kui *saba*, Abui *tifa*, Kamang *supa(ka)*, Sawila *tipea*, Wersing *təpa* < *siba 'new'. Medial correspondence sets are found in 'bad', 'fingernail', 'tooth', and 'five'. Final correspondence sets are found in 'sit', 'stand', and 'mat'.

The reconstruction of *h is supported by its presence in Western Pantar and Teiwa. The remaining languages lose original *h, though Blagar, Adang, and Klon have h < *s, and Abui has h < *g. Proto-Alor-Pantar *h did not occur in non-initial position. While *h is consistently retained in Western Pantar, Teiwa actually has two reflexes of *h, the glottal fricative *h* and the pharyngeal fricative *ħ*. This is due to a phonemic split in Teiwa, resulting from an original conditioned distribution where *ħ* occurred only before back vowels, and *h* occurred elsewhere. Modern Teiwa still tends this way, with the pharyngeal fricative generally occurring before back vowels and the glottal fricative preceding front vowels. Klamer (2010) lists only one example of a pharyngeal fricative preceding a front vowel, namely *ħer* 'yell, shout, chant, cry aloud'. This form is cognate with Western Pantar *horaŋ*, suggesting that the original form may have contained a back vowel, thus conditioning the Teiwa pharyngeal. This distinction breaks down, however, before low vowels, where a clear synchronic phonemic distinction has developed in Teiwa, as in *haɸan* 'village' (< *haban) vs. *ħaɸ* 'fish' (< *habi).

2.4 Nasals

There is a regular and unchanging correspondence of initial and medial /m/ across all the AP languages. As with the stops, *m is reflected as a geminate in medial position in Western Pantar. Correspondence sets reflecting initial and medial *m include 'come', 'betel vine', 'sit', '(be) in/on', 'fat', 'bedbug', 'horn', 'thatch', 'thick', 'walk$_1$', and 'breast'. The reconstruction of pAP initial *m is thus secure and supported by multiple cognate sets. In medial position subsequent developments may result in nasal-final forms which obey language-specific constraints. For example, Western Pantar does not admit final nasals other than velars, hence Western Pantar *haŋ* 'breast' results from later apocope, namely, pAP *hami > ham:i > ham: > ham > haŋ.

Final *m is retained as *m* in six of the twelve languages, but only in Teiwa and Kaera does it occur in final position. Blagar and Adang have a velar nasal reflex, while Klon and Kui have an alveolar nasal reflex (Kui *talama* 'six' is likely a borrowing from Abui). For many of the languages, forms reflecting final *m have an epenthetic final vowel, so that the reflex of original final *m is no longer in final position. Thus, Abui *tala:ma* < *talam 'six', *tama* < *tam 'saltwater'. Correspondence sets reflecting final *m include 'father', 'nose', 'six', and 'saltwater'. Evidence from 'saltwater' weakly supports positing the loss of final *m in Nedebang.

The behavior of the alveolar nasal mirrors that of the labial nasal in initial and medial position. Proto-Alor-Pantar *n is retained in all languages and is geminated in medial position in Western Pantar. Correspondence sets supporting initial and medial *n include 'one', 1SG, 'eat/drink', 'smoke', 'black' 'hold', 'give', 'die', 'ripe', and 'name'. Thus, pAP *nai 'eat/drink' > Teiwa, Kaera, Western Pantar, Blagar, Adang *na*, Nedebang *ina*, Klon *na:ʔ*, Kui, Wersing *nai*, Abui, Sawila *ne:*, Kamang *ne*.

2 The internal history of the Alor-Pantar language family

Final *n is reflected as a velar nasal in all languages except Teiwa, Klon, and Kui, where it is retained as *n*. The correspondence sets 'five', 'hand/arm', 'thatch', and 'fingernail' show irregularities in reflexes of final *n, perhaps due to borrowing. Nedebang *jisin* 'five' has a final alveolar rather than the expected velar and is likely borrowed from neighboring Teiwa *jusan*, while Kaera has *isim* 'five' with a final labial nasal, possibly due to influence from the following *tiam* 'six' when counting. The correspondence set for 'fingernail' is more problematic. Abui *kusiŋ* has the velar nasal as expected but shows an irregular reflex of medial *s. Western Pantar *kusi* and Klon *kuh* show irregular loss of the final nasal.

2.5 Liquids

We reconstruct two liquids *l and *r in pAP, though *r and *j may have been allophones of a single phoneme in pAP (see Section 2 above). For expository purposes we treat *r as if it were a phoneme in the present section. There is a relatively regular and unchanging correspondence of initial and medial *l* in the modern languages from which the existence of pAP *l can be posited. However, few forms are distributed widely across the languages, making it difficult to reconstruct words with initial *l. Correspondences supporting initial *l include 'rattan', 'crouch', 'bark', 'walk', and 'far'.

Medial *l is supported by correspondence sets 'axe', 'bathe', 'tongue', and 'sky'. A few languages show evidence of sporadic *l > i, for example, Wersing *jebur* 'tongue' < *–lebur. The Pantar languages Teiwa, Nedebang, and Kaera, show irregular loss of medial *l in 'six'. Kamang regularly loses *l between non-front vowels (see Chapter 3), and thus *talam > Kamang *ta:ma* is expected.

In final position, however, Teiwa, Kaera, and Kamang reflect *l > i. This final vowel may be realized phonetically as a glide in the modern languages; however, we analyze these phonemically as vowels and assume the same analysis for pAP. Adang reflects both *l* and *i* in final position. Synchronically, Adang is losing final *l* among younger speakers and certain dialects, though this only occurs following a sequence of two vowels in final position *Vil > Vi/__# (Robinson & Haan 2014). Further, Nedebang and Western Pantar lose final *l altogether. Thus, Teiwa *muħui*, Kaera *mogoi*, Western Pantar *mag:i*, Adang *mɔʔɔi*, Klon *məgol*, Kamang *mo:i*, Wersing *mulul* < pAP *mogol 'banana'. Other correspondence sets supporting final *l include 'child', 'bird', and 'bat'.

We find insufficient evidence to reconstruct *r in initial position. In non-initial position pAP clearly distinguished two liquids, and this distinction is preserved in most of the languages. In medial position Nedebang, Western Pantar, and Adang collapse *l and *r as *l* (the reflexes in Kamang are less consistent). Abui reflects *r > *j*, represented synchronically as a vowel in final position. The other languages preserve *r as such. This leaves no direct historical source for *r* in Nedebang, Western Pantar, and Adang, and we assume that *r* in these languages has been innovated or diffused from neighboring languages. In modern Western Pantar forms with *r* are infrequent and do not correspond regularly to other languages. In most cases they reflect lexical innovation, as in Western Pantar *re* 'bird' (compare pAP *(a)dVl). Correspondence sets supporting medial *r include 'two', 'water', 'sing', 'bone', 'ear', 'tail', and 'laugh'.

The correspondences for final *r are similar to those in medial position, except *r > *j* (represented here synchronically as a vowel) in Kamang and *r > Ø in Nedebang and Western Pantar.[7] Adang reflexes of final *r reflect both *l* and *i*, as do its reflexes for final *l. Correspondence sets supporting final *r include 'stone', 'scorpion', 'lime', 'maize', 'tongue', and 'moon'.

2.6 Glides

We reconstruct the two glides *w and *j to pAP. In most languages *w is preserved as *w* in all positions. In initial position only Blagar *v* and Adang *f* < *w reflect a change; other languages preserve *w. Correspondence sets supporting initial *w include 'sun', 'blood', 'stone', and 'bathe'. The form 'blood' is illustrative, as it has a reflex in every language: Teiwa *wai*, Nedebang *we*, Kaera *we*, Western Pantar *wai*, Blagar *vɛ*, Adang *foi*, Klon *weʔ*, Kui *we*, Abui *wea*, Kamang *weː*, Sawila *wiː*, Wersing *wei*.

We find insufficient evidence to reconstruct *w in non-initial position. Potential correspondences representing non-initial *w are likely either to be underlying vowels or to reflect original initial *w. For example, the root-initial consonant in the word for 'ear' is usually analyzed as a glide: Klon -*wer*, Kui *wel*, Abui *wei*, Kamang *wai*, Sawila -*wari*, and Wersing *weri*. However, regardless of the synchronic analyses these forms are likely to reflect an original vocalic form and we reconstruct pAP *uari. Apparent medial *w is also found in the word for 'lime', Kaera *awar*, Western Pantar *hauwe*, Blagar *avar*, Adang *ʔafai*, Abui *awai*, Kamang *awoi*. This correspondence matches that for initial *w and even supports reconstruction of pAP *hawar 'lime'. However, this form is likely to be an original compound; compare *war 'stone'. Another example of a potential compound containing medial *w is found in the word for 'five', reconstructed as *jiwesin.

---

[7] Some dialects of Western Pantar have *r > *l* in both medial and final position, e.g., Lamma dialect *batːal* 'maize'. However, in no dialect of Western Pantar is *r preserved as *r*, so forms such as *par* 'scorpion' must be borrowings.

Similarly, apparent reflexes of final *w are better analyzed as reflecting original vowels. For example, Western Pantar *lau*, Adang *loi/lohu*, Abui *lou*, Sawila *lu*, and Wersing *aloi* 'bark' (v.). Without additional supporting evidence we do not reconstruct *w in final position.

The initial reflexes of the palatal glide *j are relatively straightforward once a few simple rules are taken into account. In Kaera, Blagar, Adang, Kui, Kamang, Sawila, and Wersing the reflex of *j is lost before a high front vowel [i]. In Western Pantar, it becomes *h* in the same environment. Thus, Teiwa *jas*, Kaera *jas-*, Western Pantar *jasa* < pAP *jasi 'bad, broken'; but before a high front vowel Teiwa *jir*, Kaera *ir*, Kamang *ili* < *jira 'water'. Correspondence sets supporting initial *j include 'water', 'bad', 'dog$_1$', 'five', 'star', and 'laugh'.

In Kui *e:r* 'water' subsequent vowel quality changes have obliterated the environment which triggered loss of *j. Nedebang and Adang lose the initial syllable of 'dog$_1$' because the form had final stress and in those languages the initial unstressed syllable was lost. Wersing *wetiŋ* 'five' irregularly begins with *w* instead of *j*.

We do not reconstruct *j in non-initial position. Where non-initial *j* is found in modern languages we assume this is a reflex of a vowel. Examples include Nedebang *buja* 'betel nut' < *bui.

2.7 Reconstructed proto-Alor-Pantar vocabulary

Since the focus of our reconstruction is on the consonants, the vowels in the reconstructed vocabulary should be interpreted with caution. We do not make any strong claim regarding the nature of the pAP vowel system.

Having reconstructed the consonant system we can proceed with a reconstruction of pAP vocabulary. Although we identify 129 distinct lexical correspondences in our data set, not all correspondences are widely attested across the full range of languages. We reconstruct vocabulary items only when reflexes can

---

[8] A capital V stands for a vowel, where it is unclear which vowel should be reconstructed.

[9] Several AP languages show medial /g/ or reflexes of medial *g in 'laugh', leading Schapper, Huber & Engelenhoven (this volume) to reconstruct pAP *jagir. We find that the correspondences for this medial consonant are highly irregular, and therefore appear to indicate borrowing rather than inheritance. On the other hand, a number of languages unproblematically reflect *jari, so we reconstruct pAP *jari as opposed to *jagir. See the Appendix for a full list of words.

[10] Schapper, Huber & Engelenhoven (this volume) reconstruct 'new' as *siba(r) with an optional final *r. In the Timor languages, the final /r/ is found in Makalero. In the modern AP languages, only Adang has a final /r/, but the Adang reflex of pAP *r is either /l/ or /i/, so we find insufficient evidence to reconstruct 'new' with a final *r at this time.

be found in at least one language of Pantar (Teiwa, Nedebang, Kaera, Western Pantar), one language of West Alor and the Pantar Strait (Blagar, Adang, Klon, Kui), and one language of East Alor (Abui, Kamang, Sawila, Wersing). We exclude from reconstruction very obvious recent borrowings, such as 'maize', but we include some forms which are older Austronesian borrowings, such as 'pig', 'betel nut', and 'betel vine'. We know that these items/animals were introductions that roughly coincide with the arrival of the Austronesian (AN) languages in the area.[11]

Table 10 lists 117 vocabulary items which can be reconstructed at the level of pAP on the basis of the correspondence sets above. A full list of the correspondence sets with modern reflexes can be found in the Appendix.

Based on what we know of the phonotactics of the daughter languages, and on the reconstructed pAP vocabulary, we posit a (C)V(C) syllable structure for pAP, with (C)VC or CV(C) as the minimal structure for a single word. In particular, while many of the daughter languages permit words consisting of a single vowel (e.g., Western Pantar *a* 'tuber'), the reconstructed pAP vocabulary does not contain such forms, although syllables consisting of a single vowel may occur in polysyllabic words. Similarly, while some of the modern languages admit consonant clusters in word-initial onsets, which involve a second liquid second consonant (e.g., Teiwa *bluking* 'arrow', Western Pantar *bro* 'dust'), no consonant clusters are reconstructed for pAP. Underived words in pAP are typically no more than three syllables in length.

3 Internal subgrouping

In this section we consider two approaches to explaining the internal relationships of the Alor-Pantar languages. The first is based on the traditional concept of shared phonological innovations. This method robustly identifies shared history, but because the innovations cross-cut one another this method requires subjective weighting of the various innovations. We thus consider also a second less traditional approach based on computational phylogenetics applied to the lexical dataset. Here we apply two methods: split decomposition and Bayesian

---

[11] The fact that these loans can be reconstructed and show regular sound correspondences can be taken as evidence for the claim that the breakup of pAP followed the arrival of AN in the region (perhaps as recently as 3,800-3,000 BP; Spriggs (2011: 511); Pawley (2005: 100)). However, it is equally likely for later diffusions to exhibit patterns very much like regular sound correspondences. Settling this matter requires independent evidence dating pAP relative to AN.

statistical techniques. Both methods have been applied successfully to questions of wider family relationships but have only recently been used to explore internal relationships of small language families (e.g. Dunn et al. 2011). In both the traditional and computational approaches we rely on the prior application of the comparative method to establish cognate classes based on regular sound correspondences. That is, we apply these methods to true cognates rather than lexical look-alikes identified based on subjective similarity judgments.

3.1 Subgrouping based on shared phonological innovations

The sound correspondences which support reconstruction of the pAP consonant inventory allow us to identify sound changes which have occurred in the daughter languages. While there are many changes which are unique to particular languages, we can identify seventeen sound changes which are each shared by at least two languages (Table 11). Many of these changes are cross-linguistically common, and hence may be of marginal value for subgrouping, for they may have occurred independently in the languages concerned.

Additionally, many of the changes cross-cut each other, further complicating internal subgrouping. For example, the change *s > h groups Adang with Blagar and Klon, while the change *r > l groups Adang with Nedebang, Western Pantar, and Abui. This forces a somewhat subjective choice as to which sound change should be given greater weight for the purposes of subgrouping.

The most widespread of these changes is *h > Ø, which occurs in all languages except Teiwa and Western Pantar. However, this change is typologically common and may have occurred independently in several languages. We choose not to base subgrouping on this change. The second most widespread of these changes is *q > k, which occurs in all languages except the Pantar languages Teiwa, Nedebang, and Kaera. This change results in a merger of *k and *q in most daughter languages, while Teiwa, Nedebang, and Kaera keep these phonemes distinct. However, closer examination reveals that Western Pantar also distinguishes reflexes of *k and *q, though not in all positions. Western Pantar, as noted previously, geminates original stops in medial position, with the exception of *q. Thus, in medial position the Western Pantar reflexes of *k and *q are distinguished as k: and k, respectively. Using this evidence to support Western Pantar as maintaining the distinction between *k and *q we can then identify a large group of languages which merge these phonemes. The eight languages so identified are precisely the languages of Alor and the Pantar Strait, namely, Blagar, Adang, Klon, Kui, Abui, Kamang, Sawila, and Wersing. We take this change to define a subgroup labeled "Alor."

Within the Alor group we can distinguish two lower level subgroups. In the east the languages Sawila and Wersing share the innovations *b > p and *s > t. The former change is also shared with Kamang; the latter with Abui. So while it is tempting to expand this group, only Sawila and Wersing share both of these innovations, defining a subgroup we refer to as East Alor. In the west the languages Blagar and Adang share innovations *k > Ø, *g > ʔ, and *s > h, defining the Pantar Strait group (labeled "Straits" in the tree). The latter change is also shared with Klon, providing weak support for an intermediate grouping which we label West Alor. The remaining changes cross-cut these and do not provide additional subgrouping information.

The tree based on shared phonological innovations (Figure 1) differs in several ways from previous classifications based on lexicostatistics. In particular, while the eastern languages Sawila and Wersing form a subgroup, they do not constitute primary branches of pAP, as has been suggested in several previous classifications (cf. Wurm 1982; Lewis 2009). This tree has obvious geographic correlates, as shown in Figure 2 below.

The Alor subgroup defined by the merger of pAP velar and uvular stops includes all of the languages of Alor island and the intervening Pantar Straits. The languages of Pantar, with the exception of Blagar which is spoken on both Pantar and in the Straits, do not subgroup together. Within the Alor group are found two primary subgroups: East Alor at the eastern tip of the island, and West Alor comprising the western tip, the Bird's Head in the Northwest, and the Straits.

3.2 Subgrouping based on lexical characters

A second approach to subgrouping delineates subgroups according to shared cognates. For each lexical correspondence set in our data we partitioned the languages into discrete cognate classes. As with the phonological innovations discussed above, the lexical correspondence sets in our data do not all pick out the same subgroups. That is, the cognate sets delineated by some lexical items overlap with those delineated by other lexical items. These overlapping groupings can be visualized in a split graph which represents the distance between the characters in terms of numbers of splits (Figure 3). Details specific to our application of the method are laid out in Robinson & Holton (2012).

Three primary regions can be identified in the graph, each separated by significant reticulation at the center of the graph. An East Alor region groups Kamang, Wersing, and Sawila; a Central Alor region groups Kui, Klon, and Adang; and a Pantar region groups Kaera, Nedebang, Teiwa, and to a lesser extent Western Pantar. The high degree of reticulation within this latter group indicates a strong

2 The internal history of the Alor-Pantar language family

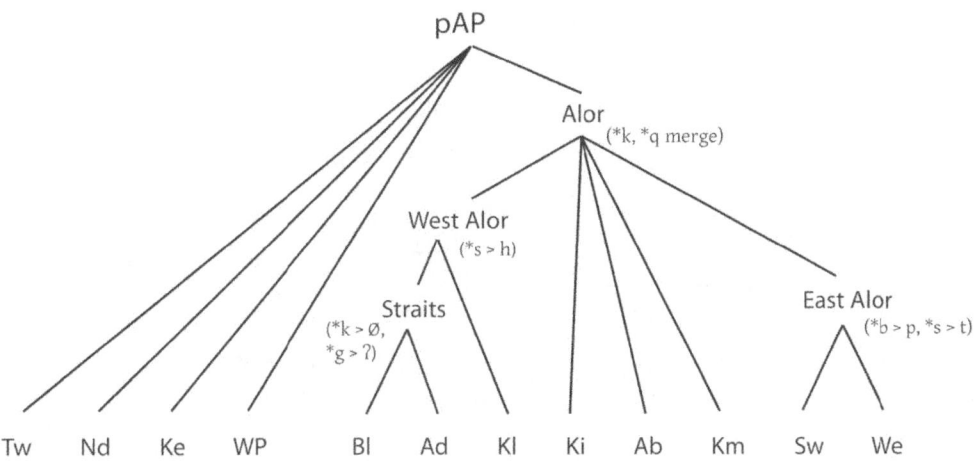

Figure 1: Subgrouping of Alor-Pantar based on shared phonological innovations

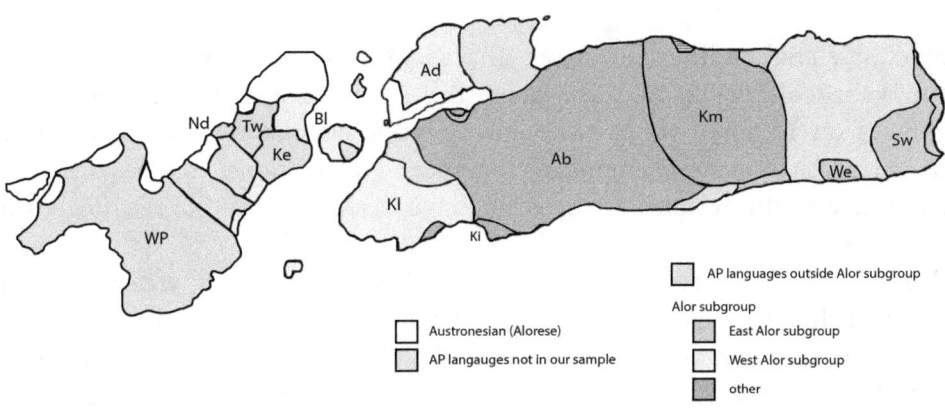

Figure 2: Distribution of subgroups defined based on shared phonological innovations

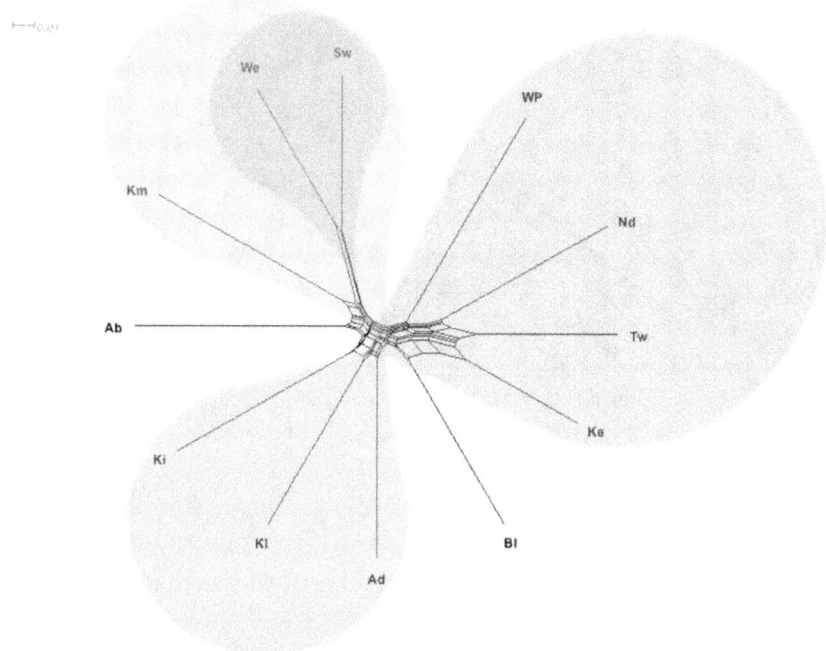

Figure 3: Split graph of lexical character coded into cognate classes, generated using NeighborNet algorithm (Huson & Bryant 2006). pAP node omitted for clarity.

conflicting signal within this region. That is, of these three regions, the Pantar group is particularly non-tree-like, suggesting a pattern of wave-like innovations in this region. In other words, although we found no shared phonological innovations to subgroup these languages together in a traditional tree based on the comparative method (Figure 1), these languages have borrowed a great deal from one another.

A greater degree of reticulation in the graph represents a less tree-like signal in the data. The degree of tree-like signal can be quantified using the delta score metric (Wichmann et al. 2011; Holland et al. 2002). The average delta score for our dataset is a moderately high $\delta = 0.29$, reflecting the fact that while some groupings do emerge in Figure 3, there is significant reticulation between those groups. The most tree-like values are found in the East Alor grouping of Kamang, Wersing, and Sawila. The Pantar group of Teiwa, Kaera, and Nedebang has delta scores similar to the mean for the entire dataset; however, the value for Western Pantar is significantly higher, suggesting that similarities between Western Pantar and the remainder of the Pantar languages may be due more to borrowing than to shared descent. An unexpected result in the graph in Figure 3 is the position of Blagar as a relative isolate within the family. In contrast to the subgrouping based on the comparative method, Blagar groups not with Adang and Klon but rather with the Pantar languages – and then only weakly so.

A second method of subgrouping based on lexical characters uses Bayesian statistical techniques to search for trees which are most compatible with the cognate classes coded in our data.[12] The results are summarized in Figure 4 as a maximum clade credibility tree. The clade credibility values listed below each node indicate the percentage of sampled trees which are compatible with that node. These values are for the most part either at or near one hundred percent (1.00), indicating that this consensus tree is compatible with almost all of the trees sampled in the analysis. Lower figures appear at exactly those nodes already shown to be problematic via the other subgrouping methods, namely Western Pantar, Abui, and Kamang.

To a large extent the groupings in the Bayesian tree are compatible with those in the split graph. First, Sawila (Sw) and Wersing (We) are shown to be closely related, a grouping which was also present in the classification based on the comparative method (Figure 1). Second, there is a Pantar grouping of Kaera (Ke), Teiwa (Tw), Nedebang (Nd), and Western Pantar (WP). Third, the position of Blagar (Bl) at the highest node coordinate to the Alor languages is consistent with its position in the split graph, though, as noted above, this differs significantly from its position in the tree based on the traditional application of the comparative method (Figure 1). On the other hand, there are also some incompatibilities between the Bayesian tree and the split graph. For example, in the tree based on lexical characters Adang (Ad) and Klon (Kl) are shown forming a group without Kui (Ki), contra both the splits graph and the tree calculated using the comparative method.

---

[12] We employ a Markov Chain Monte Carlo (MCMC) method to search through the probability space of all possible trees, using a relaxed Dollo model. Details of this implementation can be found in Robinson & Holton (2012), which compares the results of several different models, using both MrBayes 3.2.1 (Ronquist & Huelsenbeck 2003) and BEAST 1.7.2 (Drummond et al. 2012), running each model for at least 10 million iterations with a sample rate of 1000 and a burn-in of 25 percent. Each model converged after approximately 1.5 million iterations, and the best performing model (i.e., that with the highest likelihood) was found to be the relaxed Dollo model implemented in BEAST. This model has been argued to be particularly appropriate to linguistic data, since it assumes that innovations may arise only once but may be lost multiple times independently (Pagel 2009).

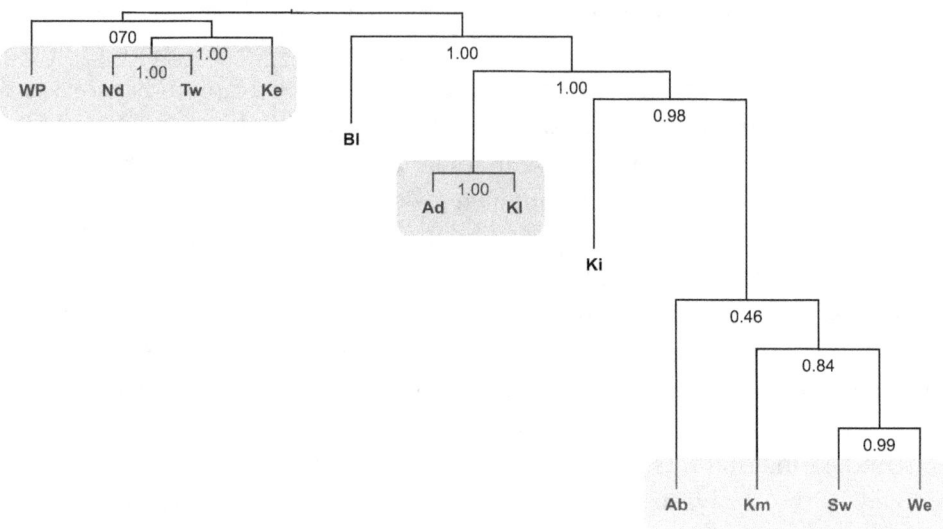

Figure 4: Bayesian MCMC maximum clade credibility tree for lexical data (relaxed Dollo model), with clade credibility values indicated. pAP node omitted

Though not immediately apparent based on visual inspection of the maximum clade credibility tree in Figure 4, the subgrouping based on lexical characters is also largely compatible with that based on phonological innovations. To demonstrate this we repeated the Bayesian analysis with the constraint that all sampled trees be compatible with the subgroups identified by the comparative method, keeping all other parameters constant.[13] We then applied a marginal likelihood analysis to the results of each model, which yielded a Bayes factor of 1.1726, only slightly favoring the constrained model over the unconstrained one.[14] The model based on lexical characters independently identifies the same subgroups found using a completely different methodology based on phonological characters, providing additional support for the robustness of the model. This lends support for those subgroups identified in the model based on lexical characters which are not found in the subgrouping based on phonological innovations. In particular, we have some evidence for the existence of an East Alor subgroup comprised of Abui (Ab), Kamang (Km), Sawila (Sw) and Wersing (We), even though this subgroup is not identified in the tree based on phonological characters.

---

[13] The authors thank Michael Dunn for suggesting this innovative approach.
[14] Marginal likelihood was estimated using Tracer 1.5 (Rambaut & Drummond 2007).

4 Discussion

The examination of sound correspondences across the Papuan languages of Alor and Pantar robustly supports the identification and reconstruction of an Alor-Pantar family. Our comparative work also allows us to propose internal subgroups within Alor-Pantar, but the overall linguistic picture is extremely complex, defying a model based solely on inheritance. Widespread multilingualism is the norm in the region, and borrowings from neighboring languages – such as Western Pantar *bagis* 'whine' from Deing *bagis* 'cry' – are extremely common.[15] Additionally, genetic studies indicate that East Nusantara, and the Alor-Pantar region in particular, is a melting pot with a long history of admixture (Mona et al. 2009), and it may well be that an analogous situation holds for languages, reflecting extensive borrowing and metatypy. Thus it is not surprising that different methods reveal different trees for the family.

The family tree based on phonological innovations identified by the comparative method (Figure 1) shows the highest level of diversity on Pantar, suggesting the languages originated in Pantar, spreading east. The tree based on the lexical characters (Figure 3) suggests that the languages of Alor originated in the Pantar Strait (around the area where Blagar is spoken today) with subsequent migration eastward. These two trees reveal different aspects of the prehistory of the AP languages. Phonological innovations show the greatest degree of diversity on Pantar, suggesting a long history of settlement there. Lexical innovations are compatible with an original settlement in the Pantar Strait. We propose that the original settlement was indeed in the area of the Pantar Strait with a very early split towards Pantar. That early settlement of Pantar led to the diversity we see there in terms of phonological innovations. The lexical innovations show less diversity on Pantar due to subsequent diffusion (as indicated by the significant reticulation for the languages of Pantar in Figure 3). As languages spread eastward from the Pantar Strait into Alor, new lexical innovations were restricted to smaller and smaller subgroups in the east, leading to the embedded structure in the tree based on lexical characters (Figure 4). However, the Pantar Strait languages (particularly Blagar and Adang) constitute a more recent linguistic area across which phonological innovations have been shared, leading to their close subgrouping in the tree based on phonological innovations (Figure 1).

While this picture is fairly complex in terms of layers of history, it is not unexpected in a region of significant warfare and shifting alliances overlaid by sev-

---

[15] Geographically, Deing lies between Western Pantar and Teiwa. It appears to be closely related to Teiwa.

eral periods of contact from different outside groups (first the ancestors of today's Muslim speakers of Alorese, then the Dutch, and now Indonesian). A more complete picture of the prehistory of the region must await evidence from other disciplines, particularly archaeology and genetics.

Appendix

Cognate sets

Here we list 129 cognate sets reflecting regular sound correspondences. There are only 127 distinct meanings, as two of the meanings, 'dog' and 'walk', are found in more than one cognate set; these are indicated with subscripts following the gloss. In the table the correspondence sets are listed alphabetically by English gloss. Languages are arranged in order roughly from west to east with the western-most languages on the left and the eastern-most languages on the right. Correspondence sets may include irregular forms when they serve to demonstrate the correspondence under discussion. In these cases the irregular forms are denoted with a preceding double dagger (‡). We reconstruct pAP forms only when we have broad geographic support in minimally one language of Pantar (Teiwa, Nedebang, Kaera, Western Pantar), one language of West Alor and the Pantar Strait (Blagar, Adang, Klon, Kui), and one language of East Alor (Abui, Kamang, Sawila, Wersing). Of these 129 correspondences, 117 reconstruct to the level of pAP.

2 The internal history of the Alor-Pantar language family

Table 7: Alor-Pantar nasal correspondences

pAP	Env	Tw	Nd	Ke	WP	Bl	Ad	Kl	Ki	Ab	Km	Sw	We
*m	#_	m	m	m	m	m	m	m	m	m	m	m	m
*m	V_V	m	m	m	m:	m	m	m	m	m	m	m	m
*m	_#	m	Ø	m	Ø	ŋ	ŋ	n	n	m	m	m	m
*n	#_	n	n	n	n	n	n	n	n	n	n	n	n
*n	V_V	-	n	n	n:	n	n	n	n	n	n	n	n
*n	_#	n	ŋ	ŋ	ŋ	ŋ	ŋ	n	n	ŋ	ŋ	ŋ	ŋ

Table 8: Alor-Pantar liquid correspondences

pAP	Env	Tw	Nd	Ke	WP	Bl	Ad	Kl	Ki	Ab	Km	Sw	We
*l	#_	l	l	l	l	l	l	l	l	l	l	l	l
*l	V_V	l	l	l	l	l	l	l	l	l	l/Ø	l	l
*l	_#	i	Ø	i	Ø	l	l/i	l	l	l	i	l	l
*r	V_V	r	l	r	l	r	l	r	r	j	l	r	r
*r	_#	r	Ø	r	Ø	r	l/i	r	r	i	i	r	r

Table 9: Alor-Pantar glide correspondences

pAP	Env	Tw	Nd	Ke	WP	Bl	Ad	Kl	Ki	Ab	Km	Sw	We
*w	#_	w	w	w	w	v	f	w	w	w	w	w	w
*j	#_	j	j	j	j	dʒ	s	Ø	j	j	j	j	j

Table 10: Reconstructed pAP vocabulary

*(a)dVl[8] 'bird'	*jari[9] 'laugh'	*por 'dry in sun'
*en(i,u) 'name'	*jasi 'bad, broken'	*p{i,u}nV 'hold'
*aman 'thatch'	*jibV 'star'	*pi- '1PL.INCL'
*aqana 'black'	*jibar 'dog'	*purVn 'spit'
*-ar 'vagina'	*jira 'water'	*pVr 'scorpion'
*araqu 'two'	*jira(n) 'fly' (v.)	*rVsi 'goanna'
*-asi 'bite'	*jiwesin 'five'	*qaba(k) 'spear'
*bagai 'crocodile'	*kin 'mosquito'	*qar- 'tens'
*bagori 'yellow'	*kusin 'fingernail'	*siba[10] 'new'
*baj 'pig'	*kVt 'flea'	*sib(a,i)r 'shark'
*-bat 'leg'	*lam(ar) 'walk'	*talam 'six'
*bis 'mat'	*-lebur 'tongue'	*tam 'saltwater'
*bob 'wave'	*lete 'far'	*tama 'fat'
*bui 'betel nut'	*luk(V) 'crouch'	*-tan 'hand/arm'
*bukan 'guard'	*lVu 'bark' (v.)	*tapai 'pierce'
*bunaq 'smoke'	*madel 'bat'	*tas 'stand'
*dar(a) 'sing'	*magi 'hear'	*tei 'tree'
*dul(a) 'slippery'	*mai 'come'	*temek 'bedbug'
*dumV 'thick'	*mait 'betel vine'	*tena 'ripe'
*dur 'rat'	*-mam 'father'	*-ten 'wake s.o.'
*ede 'burn'	*mari 'bamboo'	*tia 'recline'
*-ena 'give'	*mi '(be) in/on'	*tiara 'expel'
*ga- '3SG'	*mid 'climb'	*-tiari(n) 'close' (v.)
*ge- '3GEN'	*-mim 'nose'	*-tok 'stomach'
*gi- '3PL'	*min(a) 'die'	*tukV 'short'
*ha- '2SG'	*mis 'sit'	*-uaqal 'child'
*habi 'fish'	*mogol 'banana'	*-uari 'ear'
*haban 'village'	*mudi 'body hair'	*uasin 'tooth'
*hada 'fire, firewood'	*mudin 'plant' (v.)	*uku 'knee'
*hagur 'yawn'	*-muk 'horn'	*-wa 'mouth'
*hami 'breast'	*mVn 'rotten'	*wadi 'sun'
*has 'excrement'	*na- '1SG'	*wai 'blood'
*hasak 'empty'	*nai 'eat/drink'	*wai 'roof'
*hawar 'lime'	*nan(a) 'sibling (older)'	*war 'stone'
*hipar 'dream'	*nuk 'one'	*wata 'coconut'
*hu:ba 'sugarcane'	*oda 'throw'	*weli 'bathe'
*is(i) 'fruit'	*-ora 'tail'	*wur 'moon'

Table 11: Sound changes found in at least two languages

Change	Languages
*b>f	Teiwa, Nedebang, Abui (in Teiwa and Nedebang only non-initially)
*b>p	Kamang, Sawila, Wersing
*d>r	Abui, Kui (in Kui only finally)
*g>ʔ	Blagar, Adang
*k>Ø/_#	Blagar, Adang
*q>k	Western Pantar, Blagar, Adang (ʔ < k < *q), Klon, Kui, Abui, Kamang, Sawila, Wersing
*s>h	Blagar, Adang, Klon
*s>t	Abui, Sawila, Wersing
*h>Ø	everywhere but Teiwa and Western Pantar
*m>ŋ/_#	Western Pantar, Blagar, Adang
*n>ŋ/_#	Nedebang, Kaera, Western Pantar, Blagar, Adang, Abui, Kamang, Sawila, Wersing
*l>i/_#	Teiwa, Kaera, Adang, Kamang
*l>Ø/_#	Nedebang, Western Pantar, Abui
*r>l/V_V	Nedebang, Western Pantar, Adang, Kamang
*r>Ø/_#	Teiwa, Kaera, Western Pantar
*r>i/_#	Blagar, Kui, Abui

Gloss	pAP	Tw	Nd	Ke	WP	Bl	Ad	Kl	Ki	Ab	Km	Sw	We
'axe'[1]					baliŋ		baliŋ			faliŋ	paliŋ		
'bad, broken'	*jasi	jas	jetʃi	jas-	jasa	dʒasi	sah	jaːh				jaːti	
'bamboo'	*mari				mali	mari	mai	(du)mar		maːi	maːi		
'banana'	*mogol	muħui	‡maj	mogoi	magːi	‡mɔl	mɔʔɔi	magol			moːi		mulul
'bark' (v.)	*lVu				lau	‡orow	lou			loi		lu	aloi
'bat'	*madel	mədi	‡mara	‡merei	madːe	demεl[2]	‡madiruŋ	mədεl	madel	marel	matei ‡madiː(ku)	‡mudi:(ku)	‡mudu(k)
'bathe'	*weli	wei		wei		vela	foil	weːl	weli	-wel	-wei	wile	-weli
'bedbug'	*temek			temek		temε	‡tameʔ	tamek		tameki			mekit[3]
'betel nut'	*bui	bui	buja	bui	bu	bu	bu	bui	bui	fu		pu	pui
'betel vine'	*mait	met	mata	mat	meta	mat	metʃ	meh				maːsi	mas
'bird'	*(a)dVl	dai	‡daja		‡duŋ				mesin meːtiŋ maisi				
'bite'	*asi	si	tʃia	siː	sia		-eh	εh	adol ruwol[4] atoi			adala	adol
'black'	*aqana	qaʔan	qana	xan	‡ana	kaʔana	(l)aʔan	akan	-es	-eh			
'blood'	*wai	wai	we	wei	wai	vε	foi	weʔ	akana akan	wea	weː	akana	akeŋ
'body hair'	*mudi	mud	mudi	-mudu	-mudi			amudi	we	amur		wiː	wei
'bone'	*(a)dVl	kir	kili	kiri	kira							madi	mudi
'breast'	*hami	-ħam	ami							‡diei	ami	-aːmi	ami
'burn'	*ede	deʔ		de	-haŋ	ʔede	-eh						
'child'	*uaqal	-oqai	uaqa	-uax	wakːe	-oal	ʔai	‡ul	‡ol	‡ol		mada	‡ol
'climb'	*mid	mir			midːaŋ		mid	mid				-tiːra	
'close' (v.)	*-tiari(n)			teriŋ	‡tiariŋ	teriŋ	tel	(u)ter	(u)teri				(le)ter
'coconut'	*wata	wat	wata	wat	wata	vet	fa	‡ata	‡bat	wata	wate	wata	wata
'come'	*mai[5]	ma	ma	ma	ma	ma	ma	ma	mai	mε	meː	me	amai
'crocodile'	*bagai	baħaːi		bagai	‡bagai		baʔai	bagai	‡buai	fahai	pieː		
'crouch'	*luk(V)				lukːiŋ				luk	lukˤ[6]	lukˤ[7]		luku(k)
'die'	*min(a)	min	mina	nimin	‡hinːa	mina	min		min	moŋ		me	
'dog'	*jibar[8]	jivar	‡bar	ibar	jaˀbːe	dʒaˀbar	bel						

2 The internal history of the Alor-Pantar language family

Gloss	pAP	Tw	Nd	Ke	WP	Bl	Ad	Kl	Ki	Ab	Km	Sw	We
'dog$_2$'								ku:r	kur	ka:i	kui		
'dream'	*hipar			ipar	hip:e	ipar	apai	eper		piei	-foi		
'dry in sun'	*por			poriŋ	‡puariŋ	poriŋ	poil	upur				po:por⁹	
'dry'						‡ta?ata	ta?at	tɔkat	takata	takat			
'ear'	*uari	uar	ow	uar	uwe	veri	-fel	wer	‡wel	wei	wai	-wari	weri
'eat/drink'¹⁰	*nai	na	ina	na	na	na	na	na:?	nai	ne:	ne	ne:	nai
'empty'	*hasak	hasak		isik	hak:as¹¹					taka	saka		
'excrement'	*has	has		has		‡a:s	ah	ihi	es	‡asi	asi		atu
'expel'	*tiara	-tiar	-tiala	ter		-teri	(ate)tel					ti:ra	-(pan)ter
'far'	*lete¹²						let	let			letei		
'fat'	*tama tama?	tama?		tama		tama	tama(r) tama(d)		tama	tama(da)			
'father'	*-mam			-mam		-maŋ	-maŋ	-man	‡-ma	ma:ma			
'fingernail'	*kusin		kutʃiŋ	kusiŋ	‡kusi	‡kusil	?uhuin	‡kuh	kusin	‡kusŋ	kuisiŋ		
'fire'	*hada	har	ar	ad	had:i¹³	?ad	‡a	ada?	ar	ara	ati	ada	ada
'fish'	*habi	haɸ	afi	ab	hap	a:b	ab	ibi?	eb	afu	api	api	api
'five'	*jiwesin	jusan	‡jisin	isim	jasiŋ	‡isiŋ	iʃhiŋ	ɛweh	jesan	jetiŋ	iwesiŋ	jo:tiŋ	wetiŋ
'flea'	*kVt	‡hat			kati		‡?ut		kot				toko?¹⁴
'fly' (v.)	*jira(n)	jir-an	jila	ir	hil:aŋ	(?)ihi		ih				iriŋ	ire
'fruit'	*is(i)¹⁵	jis	itʃi	isi	‡hisa						ih	‡-si	‡-is¹⁶
'garden'		maħar	maxara		magːar		ma?ad						
'give'	*-enV	-an	-ena	-eŋ	-nia	-ɛnaŋ	-ɛn	-en	-ana		-n		-eni(r)
'good'							nɔ?	nok	noka				
'guard'	*bukan ‡boħon			bukaŋ	baukaŋ						-pukan		
'hand/arm'	*-tan	-tan	-taŋ	t:aŋ	taŋ	taŋ	taŋ	tan	tan	taŋ	taŋ	taŋ	teŋ

81

Gloss	pAP	Tw	Nd	Ke	WP	Bl	Ad	Kl	Ki	Ab	Km	Sw	We
'hear'	*magi[17]					mɛʔɛ	maʔeh	mɔgih	magi	mahi	mai	maji:ŋ	
'hearth'		tuta(h)	tutu-	tutu(k)	tutːu	tutu							
'hold'[18]	*p{i,u}nV	pin	pini	pin	pinːi	pina	puin	puin	puna	pun	fun	puni[19]	poiŋ[20]
'horn'	*muk			muk		mu	mu	mɔgih muk	muk	muk	ǂmu:		
'(be) in/on'	*mi	meʔ		mi	me	mi	mi	mi	mi	mi	mi	ma	
'itchy'		qaːq	qaqa	xaxaw	kaka	kaka	ǂkak	kaːk					
'knee'	*uku	kuʔ	uku	uku	ukːa(ŋ)	(k)uku		-uk	-uk			(taːsur)uku (seseb)uk	
'laugh'	*jari	ǂjahar	ǂgela	ǂagar	jali		asal	ǂʔagar	jeri		ǂjeːi	jara	jer
'leg'	*-bat[21]	-ɸat		-bat	-uta		-(ɛʔ)fa						
'lime'	*hawar	hor	wa	awar	hauwe	avar	ʔafai	ewer	oːr	awai	awoi		or
'lizard'		takok	taka(raːb)	tek	takːe	teke	ǂtekɔ	takek	takok	tekok	ǂtakːe:	tako	
'maize'		batar	baːta	batar	batːe	batar	batɛ	bat	batar	fat	patei	patara	peter
'mat'	*bis	bis	ǂbi:	bis	bis	bihi	buh	bus	ur	fut		ǂbuːsi	ǂbitiʔ
'moon'	*wur	wur	hula	ur		uru	ul	ur	ur		wui		ura(k)
'mosquito'	*kin	kiʔin	kim(balu)	kiŋ	kiʔ[22]	kini	ʔin	ikin	kin		kiŋ(ba)	ka(weːŋ)	ku(buŋ)
'mouth'[23]	*-wa	-aw	-wa	-ua	-wa(r)	-va	-(ar)fah			-wa	-waː	-wa	-wa
'name'	*-en(i,u)		-einu	-en	-inːu	-ɛnɛ	-ni	-nɛʔ	-enei	-ne	-nei	-ni	
'new'	*siba	ǂsib	savaʔ(ʔa)[24]	sib	sabːaːʔ[24]	hiba	haba(r)	haba	saba	tifa	supa(ka)	tipea	tapa
'nose'	*-mim			-mim	ǂ-mi	-miŋ	-miŋ	-muin	-min			-miŋi	-muiŋ
'one'	*nuk	nuk	nuku	nuk	anuku	nu	nu	nuk	nuku	nuku	nok		no
'pierce'[25]	*tapai	tap	tapa	tap	tapːa(ŋ)	tapa	tapa(ŋ)	tapa(n)	tapai	tapei	tafe	ka(weːŋ)	ta
'pig'	*baj	bai	bei	bei	bai	bɛ	boi	beʔ	bei	fe	pe	pi	pei
'plant' (v.)	*mudin	midan	mudi	muduŋ	midːiŋ	mudiŋ	mdin	mdin	medi	murui	mit	madiŋ	mədi
'rat'	*dur	dur	dur	dur	di	duru	ǂdur	dur	dur	rui	tui	daru	dur(ki)
'rattan'		liag		leːg		ʔilia	lɛ		le				
'recline'	*tia	tiʔ	taʔa	te	tiʔaŋ	tia		taː	ta	taː	taː[26]	-te	taj
'right'		jidan	jediŋ		jadːiŋ								

2 The internal history of the Alor-Pantar language family

Gloss	pAP	Tw	Nd	Ke	WP	Bl	Ad	Kl	Ki	Ab	Km	Sw	We
'ripe'	*tena			ten		tena	ten	eten	tain		iten	iti:na	
'roof'	*wai	wai	waja		wai	vai	fa	wei	wai	wa:i	iwa:h[27]		
'rotten'	*mVn	mu:n	-mini	mino		min(isa)	‡mul	muin		-mun			tama?
'saltwater'	*tam	‡ta?	ta	tam	tawa	taŋ	taŋ	tan	tan	tama	tama	tama	tama?
'scorpion'	*pVr	par		par	‡par	‡pɛl	pail	par	per	pei	‡fal	‡fal	per(buk)
'search'			lafi	rap		rapiŋ	lap		-rap					
'shark'	*sib(a,i)r[28]	siɸar	sifi	sibar	sib:u	hibir	‡tabei		sobor				
'short'	*tukV	tuk	tuku	tuk	tuk:a	tuka(ŋ)	toʔa(ŋ)	tuk	tuk	tuku[29]	tuk[30]	tuku(da)	tuk
'sibling (older)'	*nan(a)		-naŋ							na:na	puna	-na:na	-naŋ
'sing'	*dar(a)	da:r	da:la[31]	da:ro[32]	dali	dar	dal	dar	dar	jai[33]		dara	dara
'sit'	*mis	mis	misi	mis-	mis(iŋ)	mihi	mih	mih	misa	mit	‡nih	miti	amit
'six'	*talam	‡tia:m bulan	‡tiama	‡tiam buluŋ		taliŋ ‡buraŋ	talaŋ	tolan	talama	tala:ma	ta:ma		
'sky'														
'slippery'	*dul(a)			duj-banax	‡duba bun:a	dula benaka	dal bano?	du:l -bon	dula bonok	rula	tula(ka) puna	dalo:(ka) punaka	dol(ok) punak
'smoke'	*bunaq	bu:n	bun										
'spear'	*qaba(k)	‡qab	‡qaba (mali)plum	xabi	kab:i	ʔaba	ʔaba	kɔbak	kabak	kafak	kapa		
'spit'	*purVn	puran	puran	puraŋ		puruŋ	pui	paruin	puriŋ	puina	(su)pui		
'stand'	*tas	tas	tasi	tas-		tahi	toh	(ma)tɛh		(na)tet			-tati
'star'	*jibV	jiɸ	ifa(xoja)	‡ip(alaq)	hib:i	‡id	ib(iŋ)	ʔib	ib(ra)				
'stomach'	*-tok	‡-toʔ	‡-toʔo	-toki		-tow	-toʔ				-tok	-tok	-toko
'stone'	*war	war	wala	war		var	fɔi	wɔr	wor	wi	woi	wara	wor
'sugarcane'	*hu:ba	‡hub[34]	ufa	u:b	habua	ub	‡sob	aba	u:b				upa
'sun'	*wadi	war (get)	weri	‡wer	war[35]	ved	fed	‡ber	‡ber	war	wati	wadi	widi
'tail'	*ora	-or	ola	-or		-ora	ol	-ɔr	-or	-wai	(w)ui	(w)ɔ:ra	(w)ɔri
'tooth'	*uasin	usan	usiŋ	uasiŋ	wasiŋ	‡-veiŋ	fihiŋ	-weh	-wes	-weti	-weh	‡-wa	‡wesi
'tens'[36]	*qar-	qa:r-	qa-	xar-	ke-	ʔar-	‡ʔer-	kar-	kar-	‡kar-			

Gloss	pAP	Tw	Nd	Ke	WP	Bl	Ad	Kl	Ki	Ab	Km	Sw	We
'thatch'	*amen	man	maŋ	maŋ		mɛniŋ	men	ɛnɛːm[37]	amen	amen		amaŋ	ameŋ
'thick'	*dumV	‡tuʔum			dumːa							dumu	dum
'throw'	*oda			od		oda	od	oːd	or				
'tongue'	*-lebur	-livi	lefu	-leb	-lebu	‡lebul	-libu(ŋ)	-lɛb	liber	lifi	‡wot wota[38]		‡jebur
'tree'	*tei	tei	tei	tei		tɛ	ti	(ɛ)tɛʔ	(a)tei	(ba)taa	‡opui-li(m)puru		
'two'	*araqu	raq	‡raqu	rax	alaku	‡aru	alɔ	orok	oruku	ajoku	‡ok	‡jaku	‡joku
'vagina'	*-ar	-aːr				-ar	-al	-aːr	-ar	-oi	-ai	‡-la	
'village'	*haban	haɸan	aɸaŋ	abaŋ	habːaŋ	abaŋ	baŋ	ɛbɛn	aban	afɛŋ			
'wake s.o.'	*-ten		-tani	-ten				-teŋ			-tan		-teiŋ
'walk$_1$'	*lam(ar)[39]	lam(an)[40]		‡amar lama	lama	‡lamal	lamɛ	lam					lailol
'walk$_2$'											loː	loːla	
'water'	*jira	jir	jila	ir	hila	dʒar	sɛi	araː	ɛr	ja	ili	iria	ira
'wave'	*bob	boɸ	bova	boːb	‡bo		bob	boːb		fɔi			
'white'		miaq	miaqa	miex	miaka	madʒaka							
'wind'[41]							hamoi			timoi	sumui	tamuro	
'wound'	*hagur	bat	bata	ibat		bata	‡bah	‡abad	bata				
'yawn'	*bagori[42]	haħar	‡baxori	agur		boʔori	‡baʔoil	‡tagu	‡agu	ahau			
'yellow'		bahari		bagari	bugːu			bɔgor	bagura				
1PL.INCL	*pi-	pi-	pi-	pi-	pi-	pi-	pi-	pi-	pi-	pi-		pi-	
1SG	*na-	na-	na-	na-	na-	na-	na-	na-	na-	na-	na-	na-	ne-
2SG	*ha-	ha-		a-	a-	a-	a-	a-	a-	a-	a-	a-	a-
3GEN	*ge-			ga-	gai-	ʔe-	ʔe[43]	gɛ-		he-	ge-	ge-	
3LOC						ʔi-	ʔo-	go-		ho-	wo-		
3PL	*gi-	gi-		gi-	gi-	ʔi-						gi-	gi-
3SG	*ga-	ga-	ga-	ga-	ga-	ʔa-	ʔa-	g-	ga-	ha-	ga-	ga-	gV-

Notes to tables

[1] A form *balin 'axe' was reconstructed to pAP in Holton et al. (2012), but we now recognize that this is an Austronesian loan, probably from Alorese *baling*.

[2] This form has metathesized.

[3] This form has metathesized.

[4] Denotes 'chicken'.

[5] This reconstruction is strikingly similar to the Austronesian (proto-Malayo-Polynesian) form *maRi 'come', which is irregularly reflected as *ma* or *mai* in many Austronesian languages in the region (cf. Mambai (Timor) *ma*, Kambera (Sumba) *mai*). However, similar reflexes are not found in Lamaholot or Alorese, the immediate Austronesian neighbors of the Alor-Pantar languages.

[6] Denotes 'traditional dance'.

[7] Denotes 'bow, bend'.

[8] This form was not reconstructed to pAP in Holton et al. (2012) because it is not attested in Alor languages. However, based on its presence in Timor languages (see Chapter 3), we now reconstruct it to pAP.

[9] Denotes 'not quite dry'.

[10] Denotes 'eat' in Tw, Nd, WP, Ab, Km, 'eat/drink' in Ke, Bl, Sw, and 'drink' in Ad, Kl, Ki, We.

[11] This form exhibits metathesis.

[12] This form was not reconstructed to pAP in Holton et al. (2012) because of its limited distribution. However, based on its presence in Timor languages (see Chapter 3), we now reconstruct it to pAP.

[13] Denotes 'burn, of land'.

[14] Denotes 'clothing louse', with metathesis.

[15] Note similarity with proto-Austronesian *isi? 'contents', indicating that this may be a loan.

[16] Denotes 'meat'.

[17] This form was not reconstructed to pAP in Holton et al. (2012) because it is not attested in any Pantar language. However, based on its presence in Timor languages (see Chapter 3), we now reconstruct it to pAP.

[18] Reflexes of *p{i,u}nV typically encompass the meanings 'hold' and 'grab' with the difference depending on the prefixation of the verb.

[19] Sw has *wuni* 'hold' and *puni* 'hit'.

[20] We has *woiŋ* 'hold' and *poiŋ* 'hit'.

[21] This form was not reconstructed to pAP in Holton et al. (2012) due to its limited distribution. However, based on its presence in Timor languages (see Chapter 3), we now reconstruct it to pAP.

[22] Denotes 'maggot'.
[23] This form is generally part of a compound when meaning 'chin'. It seems to have historically meant 'mouth'. It is retained with that meaning in Ke, Ki, Ab, and Km. In Tw, Nd, WP, Bl, Ad, Sw, and We, the form is only retained as part of a compound meaning 'chin'.
[24] Denotes 'new sprout'.
[25] Reflexes of *tapai encompass the meanings 'pierce', 'stab' 'sew', 'plant in the ground', and 'pound rice'.
[26] Denotes 'on top'.
[27] Denotes 'thatch'.
[28] This form was not reconstructed to pAP in Holton et al. (2012) because it is not attested in the eastern languages. However, based on its presence in Timor languages (see Chapter 3), we now reconstruct it to pAP.
[29] Denotes 'piece, chunk'.
[30] Denotes 'short piece, cutting'.
[31] Denotes 'dance'.
[32] Denotes 'dance'.
[33] This form has lost the initial syllable.
[34] Denotes 'sweet'.
[35] Denotes 'shine, burn' (cf. *was* 'sun').
[36] Given that the Abui reflex is irregular, strictly speaking this set does not meet the distributional criteria for reconstruction, since there is no regular reflex in Eastern Alor.
[37] This form has metathesized.
[38] Denotes 'beat, strike (drum)'.
[39] This form was not reconstructed to pAP in Holton et al. (2012) because it is not attested in the eastern languages. However, based on its presence in Timor languages (see Chapter 3), we now reconstruct it to pAP.
[40] Tw *laman* 'follow, walk along (e.g. a path)'. WP *lama* shares this sense and is likely a borrowing from Tw, which explains the lack of gemination in the WP form.
[41] This may be an Austronesian loan. Note proto-Malayo-Polynesian *timuR 'southeast monsoon' (Blust & Trussel 2010).
[42] This form was not reconstructed to pAP in Holton et al. (2012) because it is not attested in any eastern language. However, based on its presence in Timor languages (see Chapter 3), we now reconstruct it to pAP.
[43] In Adang ʔe has been restricted to marking possessors in contrastive focus.
[44] Prefix vowel harmonizes with stem vowel.

Acknowledgements

This paper draws on the work of Holton et al. (2012) and Robinson & Holton (2012). We are particularly grateful to our co-authors of the former paper for sharing data and insights regarding the reconstruction of Proto-Alor-Pantar. Those authors are not to be blamed for errors of fact or interpretation resulting from the revisions found in the current chapter.

Abbreviations

1	1st person
2	2nd person
3	3rd person
AB	Abui
AD	Adang
AN	Austronesian languages
AP	Alor-Pantar
BL	Blagar
ENV	environment
GEN	Genitive
INCL	Inclusive
KE	Kaera
KI	Kui
KL	Klon
KM	Kamang
LOC	Locative
ND	Nedebang
pAP	proto-Alor-Pantar
PL	Plural
SG	Singular
Sw	Sawila
TAP	Timor-Alor-Pantar
Tw	Teiwa
v	verb
V	vowel
WE	Wersing
WP	Western Pantar

References

Anonymous. 1914. De eilanden Alor en Pantar, residentie Timor en Onderhoorigheden. *Tijdschrift van het Koninklijk Nederlandsch Aardrijkskundig Genootschap* 31. 70–102.

Baird, Louise. 2008. *A grammar of Klon: a non-Austronesian language of Alor, Indonesia.* Canberra: Pacific Linguistics.

Blust, Robert Andrew & Stephen Trussel. 2010. *Austronesian Comparative Dictionary, web edition.* http://www.trussel2.com/acd/.

de Josselin de Jong, Jan Petrus Benjamin. 1937. *Studies in Indonesian culture I: Oirata, a Timorese settlement on Kisar.* Amsterdam: Noord-Hollandsche Uitgevers-Maatschappij.

Drummond, Alexei J., M. A. Suchard, D. Xie & A. Rambaut. 2012. Bayesian phylogenetics with BEAUti and the BEAST 1.7. *Molecular Biology and Evolution* 29(8). 1969–1973.

Du Bois, Cora. 1944. *The people of Alor: a social-psychological study of an East Indian island.* Minneapolis: University of Minnesota Press.

Dunn, Michael, Niclas Burenhult, Nicole Kruspe, Sylvia Tufvesson & Neele Becker. 2011. Aslian linguistic prehistory: a case study in computational phylogenetics. *Diachronica* 28(3). 291–323.

Hajek, John. 2010. Towards a phonological overview of the vowel and consonant systems of East Nusantara. In Michael C. Ewing & Marian Klamer (eds.), *Typological and areal analyses: Contributions from East Nusantara*, 25–46. Canberra: Pacific Linguistics.

Holland, B. R., K. T. Huber, A. Dress & V. Moulton. 2002. Δ Plots: a tool for analyzing phylogenetic distance data. *Molecular Biology and Evolution* 19(12). 2051–2059.

Holton, Gary, Marian Klamer, František Kratochvíl, Laura C. Robinson & Antoinette Schapper. 2012. The historical relations of the Papuan languages of Alor and Pantar. *Oceanic Linguistics* 51(1). 86–122.

Huson, D. H. & D. Bryant. 2006. Application of phylogenetic networks in evolutionary studies. *Molecular Biology and Evolution* 23(2). 254–267.

Klamer, Marian. 2010. *A grammar of Teiwa* (Mouton Grammar Library 49). Berlin: Mouton de Gruyter.

Klamer, Marian. 2011. *A short grammar of Alorese (Austronesian)* (Languages of the World/Materials 486). München: Lincom.

Klamer, Marian. 2012. Papuan-Austronesian language contact: Alorese from an areal perspective. In Nicholas Evans & Marian Klamer (eds.), *Melanesian lan-*

guages on the edge of Asia: challenges for the 21st century, vol. 5 (Language Documentation & Conservation Special Publication), 72–108. Honolulu: University of Hawaii Press.

Kratochvíl, František, Sebastian Fedden, Gary Holton, Marian Klamer, Laura C. Robinson & Antoinette Schapper. 2011. *Pronominal systems in Alor-Pantar languages: Development and diachronic stability.* Paper presented at the International Conference on Historical Linguistics. Osaka, July 28.

Lewis, Paul M. (ed.). 2009. *Ethnologue: languages of the world.* 16th edn. Dallas: SIL International. http://www.ethnologue.com/web.asp.

Lichtenberk, František. 1998. Did speakers of Proto Oceanic chew betel? *Journal of the Polynesian Society* 107. 335–363.

Maddieson, Ian. 2005. Consonant inventories. In Martin Haspelmath, Matthew S. Dryer, David Gil & Bernard Comrie (eds.), *The World Atlas of Language Structures*, 10–13. Oxford: Oxford University Press.

Mona, Stefano, Katharina E. Grunz, Silke Brauer, Brigitte Pakendorf, Loredana Castri, Herawati Sudoyo, Sangkot Marzuki, Robert H. Barnes, Jörg Schmidtke, Mark Stoneking & Manfred Kayser. 2009. Genetic admixture history of Eastern Indonesia as revealed by y-chromosome and mitochondrial DNA analysis. *Molecular Biology and Evolution* 26(8). 1865–1877.

Nicolspeyer, Martha Margaretha. 1940. *De sociale structuur van een Aloreesche bevolkingsgroep.* Rijswijk: Rijksuniversiteit te Leiden PhD thesis.

Pagel, Mark. 2009. Human language as a culturally transmitted replicator. *Nature Reviews Genetics* 10(6). 405–415.

Pawley, Andrew K. 2005. The chequered career of the Trans New Guinea hypothesis: recent research and its implications. In Andrew K. Pawley, Robert Attenborough, Jack Golson & Robin Hide (eds.), *Papuan pasts: cultural, linguistic and biological history of the Papuan-speaking peoples*, 67–108. Canberra: Pacific Linguistics.

Rambaut, Andrew & Alexei J. Drummond. 2007. *Tracer, vers. 1.5.* http://beast.bio.ed.ac.uk/Tracer.

Robinson, Laura C. & John Haan. 2014. Adang. In Antoinette Schapper (ed.), *Papuan languages of Timor, Alor and Pantar: Sketch grammars*, vol. 1, 221–284. Berlin: Mouton de Gruyter.

Robinson, Laura C. & Gary Holton. 2012. Internal classification of the Alor-Pantar language family using computational methods applied to the lexicon. *Language Dynamics and Change* 2(2). 123–149.

Ronquist, F. & J. P. Huelsenbeck. 2003. MRBAYES 3: Bayesian phylogenetic inference under mixed models. *Bioinformatics* 19(1572-1574).

Schapper, Antoinette (ed.). 2014. *Papuan languages of Timor, Alor and Pantar: Sketch grammars*. Vol. 1. Berlin: Mouton de Gruyter.

Schapper, Antoinette, Juliette Huber & Aone van Engelenhoven. 2012. The historical relation of the Papuan languages of Timor and Kisar. In Harald Hammarström & Wilco van den Heuvel (eds.), *History, contact and classification of Papuan languages* (Language and Linguistics in Melanesia Special Issue 2012, Part I), 194–242. Port Moresby: Linguistic Society of Papua New Guinea.

Schapper, Antoinette, Juliette Huber & Aone van Engelenhoven. this volume. The relatedness of Timor-Kisar and Alor-Pantar languages: A preliminary demonstration. In Marian Klamer (ed.), *The Alor-Pantar languages*, 99–154. Berlin: Language Science Press.

Spriggs, Matthew. 2011. Archaeology and the Austronesian expansion: where are we now? *Antiquity* 85. 510–528.

Stokhof, W. A. L. 1975. *Preliminary notes on the Alor and Pantar languages (East Indonesia)* (Pacific Linguistics: Series B 43). Canberra: Australian National University.

Wichmann, Søren, Eric W. Holman, Taraka Rama & Robert S. Walker. 2011. Correlates of reticulation in linguistic phylogenies. *Language Dynamics and Change* (1). 205–40.

Wurm, Stephen A. 1982. *The Papuan languages of Oceania* (Ars Linguistica 7). Tübingen: Gunter Narr.

Yen, Douglas E. 1977. Hoabinhian horticulture? The evidence and the questions from northwest Thailand. In Jim Allen, Jack Golson & Rhys Jones (eds.), *Sunda and Sahul: Prehistoric studies in Southeast Asia, Melanesia and Australia*, 567–599. London: Academic Press.

Chapter 3

The relatedness of Timor-Kisar and Alor-Pantar languages: A preliminary demonstration

Antoinette Schapper

Juliette Huber

Aone van Engelenhoven

> The Papuan languages of Timor, Alor, Pantar and Kisar have long been thought to be members of a single family. However, their relatedness has not yet been established through the rigorous application of the comparative method. Recent historical work has shown the relatedness of the languages of Alor and Pantar on the one hand (Holton et al. 2012), and those of Timor and Kisar on the other (Schapper, Huber & Engelenhoven 2012). In this chapter, we present a preliminary demonstration of the relatedness of the Timor-Alor-Pantar family based on a comparison of these two reconstructions. We identify a number of regular consonant correspondences across cognate vocabulary between the two groups and reconstruct a list of 89 proto-TAP roots.

1 Introduction

This chapter looks at the historical relationship between the Papuan languages of Alor-Pantar (AP) and those of Timor-Kisar (TK). The TK group of Papuan languages consists of Bunaq, spoken in central Timor; Makasae, Makalero and Fataluku, three languages spoken in a contiguous region of far eastern Timor; and Oirata, spoken on the southern side of Kisar Island to the north of Timor. Due to their geographical proximity, AP and TK languages have typically been assumed to be related to one another (e.g., Stokhof 1975; Capell 1975). Together they have

Antoinette Schapper, Juliette Huber & Aone van Engelenhoven. 2017. The relatedness of Timor-Kisar and Alor-Pantar languages: A preliminary demonstration. In Marian Klamer (ed.), *The Alor-Pantar languages*, 91–147. Berlin: Language Science Press. DOI:10.5281/zenodo.569389

been referred to as the Timor-Alor-Pantar (TAP) family. However, there has been no substantive data-driven investigation of the claim of relatedness.

In this chapter, we test the hypothesis that AP and TK languages are related to one another through the application of the comparative method. Specifically, we compare the results of two recent reconstructions, the one of AP (Holton et al. 2012) and the other of TK (Schapper, Huber & Engelenhoven 2012). We establish that the AP and TK languages are indeed related by demonstrating that there are regular sound correspondences across cognate vocabulary between the two groups.

In comparing Holton et al. (2012) and Schapper, Huber & Engelenhoven (2012) in this chapter, we assume the existence of two nodes in the TAP tree, namely Proto-Alor-Pantar (pAP) and Proto-Timor (pTIM). Whilst pAP appears to be a robust node, the existence of pTIM is less secure. As Schapper, Huber & Engelenhoven (2012: 227-228) point out, it is possible that Bunaq and the Eastern Timor languages (reconstructed as Proto-ET in Schapper, Huber & Engelenhoven 2012) both form their own separate primary subgroups within TAP. Our aim here is not to make claims about the high-level subgrouping of the AP and TK languages, and we do not presume to definitively determine the constituency of the TK-AP tree at this stage, but merely seek to show that TK and AP languages are related. Conclusive evidence of innovations shared by Bunaq and ET languages to the exclusion of AP languages is the subject of ongoing research.

§ 2 presents the sound correspondences we find in cognate vocabulary between pAP and pTIM. § 3 summarizes our preliminary findings and discusses issues arising out of them. Appendices are included with supporting language data for any reconstructions that do not appear in Holton et al. (2012) or Schapper, Huber & Engelenhoven (2012), as well as a list of pTAP forms that can be reconstructed on the basis of the sound correspondences identified in this chapter. New, additional reconstructions have in some cases been necessary since the two articles each reconstruct only a small number of lexemes with only partial overlap between them. The sources of the lexical data used are listed in the Appendices. We also throw out several cognate sets from the AP reconstruction as they reflect borrowing from Austronesian languages.

2 Sound correspondences

In this section, we describe the consonant correspondences that we have identified between AP and TK languages. We do draw on vowel correspondences where they condition particular sound changes in consonants, but otherwise do not deal with vowels in this preliminary demonstration of relatedness. We chiefly draw attention to the correspondences in cognate vocabulary between pAP and pTIM. However, we provide the reader also with the forms of the lexemes in the TK languages as they are not available elsewhere in this volume. The argumentation and underpinning data for pAP is given in Holton & Robinson (this volume) and is based on Holton et al. (2012).

In the subsections that follow, transcription of language data adheres to IPA conventions. Long vowels are indicated with a length mark ':'. Bracketed segments '( )' are those deemed to be non-etymological, that is, typically reflecting some morpheme which has fossilized on a root. In the correspondence tables, square brackets '[]' are used where an item is cognate but doesn't reflect the segment in question. The inverted question mark '¿' is used where a cognate shows an unexpected reflex of the segment in question. Grammatical items are glossed in small caps. Reconstructions marked with '!!' are new reconstructions not found in or revised from Holton et al. (2012) or Schapper, Huber & Engelenhoven (2012). The symbol '!!' signals that the full data set on which the reconstruction in question is based is given in the Appendices. AP data supporting the additional pAP reconstructions is given in Appendix A.1 and TK data in Appendix A.2. In the text of the chapter itself, for reasons of compactness, we only give simple one-word glosses which reflect the presumed meaning of the proto-lexeme. Should the reader need more information on semantics, he can refer to the Appendices. We also do not provide information on irregular changes, such as metathesis or apocope, in the correspondence tables, except where directly relevant to the reconstruction of the segment in question. The Appendix provides the reader with fuller information on any irregularities in form or meaning in individual languages.

2.1 Reconstruction of bilabial stops

We identify two robust correspondent sets for bilabial plosives, reconstructing to pTAP *p and *b. Note that in Schapper, Huber & Engelenhoven (2012), we reconstruct a three-way distinction (*p, *b, and *f) for bilabial obstruents in pTIM, despite the fact that it is not maintained in any of the modern TK languages: Bunaq, Makasae and Makalero have merged reflexes of pTIM *p and *f, whereas in Fataluku and Oirata, *p and *b are merged. We find no evidence to support a three-way split in pTAP; instead, it looks like pTIM underwent a conditioned phoneme split, with distinct reflexes of pTAP *b in initial and non-initial positions, respectively.

Table 1 and Table 2 present the forms for these two correspondence sets respectively. In the first, pAP *p corresponds to pTIM *f in all positions. In the second, pTAP *b was retained as *b in pAP, but split to pTIM *b initially and pTIM *p non-initially. In these sets, there are two notable irregularities: (i) pAP *tiara 'expel' lost the medial bilabial that is retained in pTIM *tifar 'run'; and (ii) pAP *karab 'scratch' and pTIM *gabar 'scratch', which show an irregular correspondence of pAP *b with pTIM *b in medial position.

2.2 Reconstruction of coronal stops

There are two coronal stops, *t and *d, reconstructed to pAP, and four, *t, *d, *T and *D to pTIM. Schapper, Huber & Engelenhoven (2012) note the uncertainty of pTIM *d, which is supported by three cognate sets only, all of which are in initial position. This is played out also when comparing coronals between AP and TK languages. We can reconstruct the pTAP coronal stops *t with relative certainty, and *d, albeit with less security. The latter segment split in pTIM to *T and *D. At present, we cannot reconstruct pTIM *d to pTAP. There are, however, a substantial number of coronal correspondences which remain unexplained.

Our most consistent correspondence is pTIM *t to pAP *t and *s (Table 3). Initially, we find a steady and unchanging correspondence of pAP *t and pTIM *t, supported by a sizeable number of cognates. Only Bunaq shows a change of *t to /tʃ/ before a high front vowel. Non-initially, we find fewer cognates, but nevertheless a steady and unchanging correspondence. In two cognate sets ('sit' and 'mat'), pAP final *s preceded by *i corresponds to pTIM *t.

The reconstruction of pTAP *d is supported by only a small number of cognate sets (Table 4) and therefore still needs confirmation. In these sets, initial pAP *d corresponds to pTIM *D, while non-initial pAP *d corresponds with pTIM *T. This is consistent with what we observed with the bilabial stops, where a medial voiced stop in pAP corresponds to a voiceless stop in pTIM. Note that the cognate set for 'bird' is listed under the heading of initial *d, even though its pTIM and (arguably) pAP reflexes are in medial position. We place it there due to the fact that the sound correspondence is parallel to that for 'rat'. However, more sets supporting this reconstruction are clearly needed before we can be certain of it.

Furthermore, there are a range of cognate sets which show as yet unexplained correspondences (Table 5). In these, we find coronal correspondences between pAP and pTIM and between TK languages (especially in Bunaq and Fataluku) that don't fit well in the above given sets. More work is needed to clarify the history of the coronals in TAP.

Table 1: Correspondence sets for pTAP *p

	pAP	pTIM	Bunaq	Makasae	Makalero	Fataluku	Oirata
initial *p	*p	*f	*p, w	f	f	f	p
spit	*purVn !!	*fulu(k, n) !!	puluk	–	fulun	fulu	–
taboo	*palol !!	*falu(n)	por	falun	falun	falu	–
1PL	*pi-	*fi	–	fi	fi	afa	ap-
LOW[1]	*po !!	*ufe !!	–	he- ¿	ufe-	[ua]	[ua]
girl	*pon !!	*fana[2]	pana	fana(rae)	fana(r)	fana(r)	pana(rai)
scorpion	*pVr	*fe(r, R)e !!	wele	–	–	–	–
medial *p	*p	*f	w, Ø	f	f	f	p
face	*-pona !!	*-fanu !!	-ewen	fanu	fanu	fanu	panu
dream	*hipar	*ufar(ana) !!	waen	ufarena	ofarana	ufarana	upar(a)
run	[*tiara]	*tifar	tfiwal	[ditar]	[titar]	tifar(e)	tipar(e)
pound	*tapai	*tafa	tao[3]	–	tafa	tafa	tapa

[1] This item is a deictic marker indicating lower elevation than the deictic center. See Schapper (this volume) for more information on this deictic distinction.

[2] The bracketed *rae/r/rai* element appears to be an innovation in the Eastern Timor languages, presumably a lexical doublet or a derivational morpheme related to the nominalizing -*r* formative found in Makalero. We have no evidence for reconstructing this element higher than Proto-Eastern Timor.

[3] This would have originally been *tawo in pre-Bunaq, but in the modern language medial /w/ is not preserved before back vowels.

Table 2: Correspondence sets for pTAP *b

	pAP	pTIM	Bunaq	Makasae	Makalero	Fataluku	Oirata
inital *b	*b	*b	b	b	p	p	h
pig	*baj	*baj	–	baj	paj	paj	haj
price	*bol ‼	*bura	bol	bura	pura	pura	hura
mat	*bis	*biti ‼	–	–	piti	pet(u)	het(e)
leg	*-bat ‼	*-buta ‼	-but	buʔu	–	–	–
mountain	*buku ‼	*bugu ‼	–	buʔu	puʔu	–	–
non-initial *b	*b	*p	p, w	f	f	p	h
fish	*habi ‼	*hapi ‼	–	afi	afi	api	ahi
star	*jibV[1]	*ipi(-bere)	[bi][2]	ifi-bere	ifi	ipi(naka)	ihi
shark	*sib(a, i)r ‼[3]	*supor ‼	–	–	[su][4]	hopor(u)	–
sugarcane	*hu:ba ‼	*upa	up	ufa	ufa	upa	uha
tongue	*-lebur ‼	*-ipul	-up	ifi	ifl	epul(u)	uhul(u)
dog	*jibar ‼[5]	*Depar	zap	defa	sefar	ipar(u)	ihar(a)
other	*aben(VC) ‼	*epi ‼	ewi	–	–	–	–
scratch	*karab ‼	*gabar ¿ ‼[6]	–	–	kapar	kafur(e)	–
new	*siba(r) ‼	*(t, s)ipa(r) ¿ ‼	tip	sufa	hofar	–	–

[1] Several AP languages have a compound for 'star', although the second element does not appear to be cognate to that reconstructed for pTIM. Note also that Holton et al. (2012) gave this item as *jibC.
[2] The Bunaq form reflects the second half of the pTIM doublet that is not found in AP languages.
[3] The cognate set for this item is given in Holton et al. (2012), but no pAP reconstruction is given.
[4] The reflex of the relevant bilabial has been lost in Makalero due to apocope.
[5] The cognate set for this item is given in Holton et al. (2012), but no pAP reconstruction is given.
[6] This form shows liquid-stop metathesis. There is no evidence of *b occurring word-finally in pTIM.

3 The relatedness of Timor-Kisar and Alor-Pantar languages

Table 3: Correspondence sets for pTAP *t

	pAP	pTIM	Bunaq	Makasae	Makalero	Fataluku	Oirata
initial *t	*t	*t	t, tʃ	t	t	t	t
hand	*-tan	*-tana	-ton	tana	tana	tana	tana
sea	*tam	*mata	[mo]	–	–	mata	mata
six	*talam	*tamal ‼[1]	tomol	–	–	–	–
pound	*tapai	*tafa	tao	–	tafa	tafa	tapa
run	*tiara	*tifar	tʃiwal	ditar ¿	titar	tifar(e)	tipar(e)
sleep	*tia	*tia(r)	tʃier	taʔe	tia	taia	taja
non-initial *t	*t, *s	*t	t	t	t	t	t
tree	*tei	*hate ‼	hotel	ate	ate	ete	ete
stand	*nate(r) ¡ ‼	*nat	net	[na] ¿	nat	(a)nat(e)	nat(e)
clew	*maita ‼	*matar	mot	–	–	matar(u)	matar(a)
flat	*tatok ‼	*tetok ‼	toiʔ	–	tetuʔ	–	–
leg	*-bat ‼	*-buta ‼	but	–	–	–	–
sit	*mis	*mit	mit	mit~[mi]	mit	[(i)mir(e)] ¿	[mir(e)] ¿
mat	*bis	*biti ‼	–	–	piti	pet(u)	het(e)

[1] Bunaq /o/ is a regular reflex of pTIM *a, as seen, for instance, from the 'hand', 'sea', 'tree' and 'clew' sets.

Table 4: Correspondence sets for pTAP *d

	pAP	pTIM	Bunaq	Makasae	Makalero	Fataluku	Oirata
initial *d	*d	*D	z, s	d, s	s	c	t, s
rat	*dur	*Dura	zul	dura	sura	cura	tura
dog	*jibar ¿ !![1]	*Depar	zap	defa	seɸar	[ipar(u)] ¿	[ihar(a)] ¿
bird	*(a)dV1 !!	*haDa	hos	asa	asa	aca	asa
non-initial *d	*d	*T	t	t	t	c	t
bat	*madel	*maTa !![2]	–	–	–	maca	maṯa
fire	*hada !!	*haTa	hoto	ata	ata	aca	aṯa
sun	*wadi !!	*waTu	hot	watu	watu	wacu	waṯu
garden	*magad(a)	[*(u, a)mar][3]	[mar]	[ama]	[ama]	–	[uma]

[1] We note the irregularity of pAP *jibar 'dog' where we would expect pAP *dibar 'dog'. This is likely the result of a change pre-pAP *d > *j.
[2] The cognate set for this item is given in Schapper, Huber & Engelenhoven (2012), but no pTIM reconstruction is given.
[3] This form shows metathesis with associated loss of the syllable with pTAP *g, thus: pTAP *magad > *madag > *(u, a)mar.

Table 5: Problematic coronal cognate sets

	pAP	pTIM	Bunaq	Makasae	Makalero	Fataluku	Oirata
grandparent[1]	*tam(a, u) !!	*moTo	mata(s)	mata	mata	moco	moʈo
far	*lete !!	*eTar !!	ate	–	–	icar	–
wake	*-ten	*Tani	otin	tane	tane	tani~cani	–
coconut	*wata !!	*wa(t, D)a	hoza	wata	wata	βata	wata
P. indicus	*matar !!	*ma(t, D)ar	mazoʔ	mater	mater	matar(ia)	–
excrement	*has	*a(t, D)u !!	ozo	atu(-guʔu)	atu	atu	atu

[1] This is a reciprocal kinship term, denoting either 'grandparent' or 'grandchild'. PTIM *moTo means 'child'.

2.3 Reconstruction of velar stops

We reconstruct two velar stops for pTAP, *k and *g. We find insufficient evidence, however, for the uvular stop reconstructed for pAP in Holton et al. (2012) and Holton & Robinson (this volume).

PTAP *k and *g are retained as *k and *g in pAP, but merged to *g in pTIM. Note that, based on the comparative TAP evidence and the additional pTAP reconstructions in this chapter, we have to substantially revise Schapper, Huber & Engelenhoven's (2012) pTIM reconstructions with regard to velar stops. Concretely, we can trace only one pTIM velar back to pTAP. We find no pAP reflexes for any of the small sets of roots reconstructed for pTIM with initial *k and medial *g; those for pTIM medial *g, in particular, are rather tenuous, as noted in Schapper, Huber & Engelenhoven (2012: 212). The cognate sets that we can trace back to pTAP involve Schapper, Huber & Engelenhoven's initial *g and medial *k, and the comparative evidence is consistent with these being differential realizations of a single pTIM segment *g: initially, pTIM *g is reflected as /g/ in Bunaq and Makasae, and as /k/ in Makalero and Fataluku. We currently have no evidence for Oirata. In non-initial position, *g is reflected in Bunaq as /g/ medially and as /k/ finally, consistent with Bunaq phonotactic rules, which prohibit voiced stops from codas; in Makasae, Makalero and Fataluku, *g is reflected in non-initial position as /ʔ/, and variably as /ʔ/ and Ø in Oirata.

The cognate sets that support the reconstruction of pTAP *k are given in Table 6. As in both pTIM (Schapper, Huber & Engelenhoven 2012: 213-214) and pAP (Holton et al. 2012: 98), the reconstruction of initial *g in pTAP hinges on third person markers. Two forms are reconstructable (Table 7): a prefix *ga '3' occurring on verbs and inalienably possessed nouns, and a free form *gie '3.POSS' encoding 3rd person alienable possessors. Number marking was lost in TK languages, so the correspondence we observe is between pAP third person singular forms and pTIM third person forms which are unmarked for number (i.e., can be used in singular and plural contexts). The zero correspondence that we observe in Fataluku and Oirata is the result of the stripping off of the *g marking 3rd person (as set out in Schapper, Huber & Engelenhoven 2012: 214). In the case of the alienable possessive marker, this means we are left with reflexes of the pTIM possessive root *-ie 'POSS' alone.

In non-initial positions, we find numerous cognates reflecting pTAP *g, corresponding to pAP *g and pTIM *g as set out in Table 8.

Finally, there is as yet an insufficient number of reconstructions of pAP *q with cognates in TK languages to allow for a higher-level pTAP reconstruction. Currently, we have only Bunaq -ol 'child' (presumably reflecting pTIM *-al) as

Table 6: Correspondence sets for pTAP *k

	pAP	pTIM	Bunaq	Makasae	Makalero	Fataluku[1]	Oirata[1]
	*k	*g	g (k)	(g) ʔ	k, ʔ	k, ʔ	(ʔ) Ø
scratch	*karab ʔ	*gabar ʔ[2]	–	–	kapar	kafur(e)	–
bite	*(ta)ki ʔ[3]	*(ga)gel ʔ[3]	gagil	gaʔel	kaʔel	(ki)kiʔ(e)[4]	–
dirty	*karok ʔ	*gari ʔ	gar	raʔi	raʔi	raʔe(ne)	–
walk 1	*laka ʔ	*lagar ʔ	lagor	laʔa	laʔa	laʔa	[lare] ¿
itchy	*(i)ruk ʔ[5]	*ilag ʔ	–	ilaʔ	ileʔ	–	–
mountain	*buku ʔ	*bugu ʔ	–	buʔu	puʔu	–	–

[1] See Schapper, Huber & Engelenhoven (2012: 211-212) for more Fataluku and Oirata correspondences.
[2] This form shows liquid-stop metathesis.
[3] The bracketed initial segments in these forms reflect different inflectional prefixes which have fossilized on these verbs.
[4] The initial bracketed syllable is a fossilized reduplicated CV. This item also has the variant pronunciation *cikiʔe*.
[5] This form represents a different root from the 'itchy' root given in Holton & Robinson (this volume). See Appendix A.1 for supporting AP forms.

Table 7: Correspondence sets for pTAP 3rd person prefixes

	pAP	pTIM	Bunaq	Makasae	Makalero	Fataluku	Oirata
3	*g	*g	g	g	k	Ø	Ø
	*ga-	*g-	g-	g-	k-	–	–
3.POSS	*ge[1]	*gie	gie	gi	ki	i	ue

[1] We reconstruct this as a free form on account of the existence of free reflexes in at least two AP languages (Blagar and Adang); morphologization must thus post-date the break-up of pAP.

Table 8: Correspondence sets for pTAP *g

	pAP	pTIM	Bunaq	Makasae	Makalero	Fataluku	Oirata
	*g	*g	g, k	g, ʔ	(k) ʔ	(k) ʔ	ʔ, ∅
yellow	*bagori ‼[1]	*gabar ‼[2]	–	gabar	–	–	–
green	*(wa)logar ‼	*ugar	ugar	(h)uʔur	(h)uʔur	uʔur(eke)	uʔul(e)
laugh	*jagir ‼	*jiger ‼	higal	hiʔa	hiʔe	heʔe	–
path	*jega ‼	*jiga ‼	hik	hiʔa	hiʔa	iʔa	ia(ra)
banana	*mogol	*mugu ‼	mok	muʔu	muʔu	muʔu	muː
hear	*magi ‼[3]	*mage(n) ‼	mak	maʔen	maʔen	–	–
garden	*magad(a)	[*(u, a)mar] ‼[4]	[mar]	[ama]	[ama]	–	[uma]

[1] The cognate set for this item is given in Holton et al. (2012), but no pAP reconstruction is given.
[2] This form is apparently metathesized from pTAP *bagur(V) 'yellow'.
[3] The cognate set for this item is given in Holton et al. (2012), but no pAP reconstruction is given.
[4] This form shows metathesis with associated loss of the syllable with pTAP *g, thus: pTAP *magad > *madag > *amar. Loss of *g is found occasionally in AP languages (e.g. 'laugh', see Appendix A.1), suggesting a certain degree of instability for this segment.

cognate with pAP *-uaqal 'child'. We await further reconstructions with TK cognates for the determination of the pTAP form.

2.4 Reconstruction of fricatives

Two fricatives *s and *h can be reconstructed to pTAP. The number of cognates is still small for both phonemes, but the correspondences are relatively well-behaved.

Table 9 sets out the cognate sets for pTAP *s. Initial pTAP *s is supported by several cognate sets and has been maintained without change in pAP and pTIM. Non-initial cognates of pAP *s are difficult to find in TK languages, as many instances of reconstructed word-final *s in pAP correspond to pTIM *t (e.g., pAP *mis 'sit', *bis 'mat' and *has 'excrement').

PTAP *h can be reconstructed as a word-initial segment, but not in other positions. The segment corresponds to pTIM *h and pAP *h except before back vowels (Table 10). Based on the cognate sets available, pAP *h did not occur before back vowels. In this environment, pTAP *h changed either to *w (as in pAP *wur 'moon') or was lost (as in pAP *tei 'tree') in pAP (cf. Table 11 for the items and vocalic environments in which pAP *w is attested). The reconstruction of pTIM *h hinges on Bunaq, which retains it as /h/, while the eastern Timor languages have all lost pTIM *h (which, in turn, reflects pTAP *h). This means that where we have no Bunaq reflex (as in the 'fish' and 'breast' sets) we have no modern language attesting pTIM *h, and the presence of the phoneme can only be inferred from the fact that *h is reconstructed for the pAP cognate.

2.5 Reconstruction of glides

Two glides can be reconstructed to pTAP, *w and *j. Both appear to have only occurred in initial position. It is unclear whether the reconstructed glides could occur before all vowel qualities. Nevertheless, the cognate sets supporting these proto-phonemes are robust and show little irregularity.

The pTAP glide *w shows a stable and unchanging correspondence of *w in pAP and pTIM for the most part (Table 11). The major change is that pTAP *w is vocalized in pAP to *u root-initially on inalienably possessed nouns. In TK languages, Bunaq shows conditioned reflexes of pTAP *w, maintaining it as /w/ before front vowels, but changing it to /h/ before non-front vowels. Fataluku shows a change of *w to /β/, though we note that this is an allophone of /w/ in many languages.

3 The relatedness of Timor-Kisar and Alor-Pantar languages

Table 9: Correspondence sets for pTAP *s

	pAP	pTIM	Bunaq	Makasae	Makalero	Fataluku	Oirata[1]
initial *s	*s	*s	s	s	h, s[2]	h	s
bone	*ser ‼	*(se)sa(t, R) ‼	sesal	–	–	–	–
shark	*sib(a, i)r ‼	*supor ‼	–	–	su-	hopor(u)	–
spoon	*surV ‼	*sula	sulu	sulu	hulu	hula	sulu
weave	*sine(N) ‼	*sina	sien	sina	hina	hina	hina(na) ¿
new	*siba(r) ‼[3]	*(t, s)ipa(r) ‼[3]	tip ¿	sufa	hofar	–	–
medial *s	*s	*s	s	s	s	h	∅
meat	*iser ‼[4]	*seor	sael	seu	seur	[leura] ¿	[leura] ¿
tooth	*-uasin ‼	*-wasin ‼	[-(e)we] ¿	wasi	wasi	βahin(u)	wain(i)

[1] See Schapper, Huber & Engelenhoven (2012: 209) for more instances of Oirata cognates.
[2] Makalero seems to be part-way through a sound change s > h. See Schapper, Huber & Engelenhoven (2012: 209-211) for more cognates showing the variable s~h reflexes in Makalero.
[3] Cognates for these reconstructions show a relatively high degree of irregularity in both AP and TK indicating that there may have been variable realizations in not only pAP and pTIM, but also pTAP.
[4] Denotes 'meat' or 'game'.

Table 10: Correspondence sets for *h

	pAP	pTIM	Bunaq	Makasae	Makalero	Fataluku	Oirata
	*h (*w/Ø)	*h	h	Ø	Ø	Ø	Ø
fire	*hada !!	*haTa	hoto	ata	ata	aca	ata
fish	*habi !!	*hapi !!	–	afi	afi	api	ahi
breast	*hami	*hami !!	–	ami	–	ami(-tapunu)	–
moon	*wur	*huru	hul	uru	uru	uru	uru
tree	*tei[1]	*hate !!	hotel	ate	ate	ete	ete

[1] The loss of initial syllable may have to do with the fact that stress was apparently based on syllable weight. See also 'dog' in Appendix A.1 and Holton & Robinson (this volume).

Table 12 gives the four clear cognate sets that we have across TAP languages for pTAP *j. We see that pTAP *j is maintained as *j in pAP, but is variably lost or maintained as *j in pTIM. It may be that differing vocalic environments in pTAP conditioned the different reflexes in pTIM, but we don't have enough understanding of the history of vowels yet to determine this. There is no direct evidence for pTIM *j, that is, no TK language still reflects the proto-phoneme as /j/, but the sound correspondences between TK languages make it differentiable form sets reflecting pTIM *h (see Table 10).

2.6 Reconstruction of liquids

We identify three robust liquid correspondence sets between pAP and pTIM and as such reconstruct three pTAP liquids: *r, *R, and *l.

The most robust set is that for pTAP *r, which is reflected as *r in both pAP and pTIM (Table 13). PTAP *r is only found in non-initial positions, as are its reflexes in the daughter languages pAP and pTIM. Word-finally in polysyllabic words pTAP *r is particularly susceptible to sporadic loss, as is attested by the various irregular forms in Table 13. In one instance (pTAP *(t, s)iba(r) 'new'), the occurrence of a reflex of final *r is so erratic in both primary subgroups that we perhaps must consider it already partly lost in pTAP's daughter languages.

PTAP *R is reflected in pAP as *r and in pTIM as *l. Like pTAP *r, *R does not appear in word-initial positions and is sporadically lost word-finally in polysyllabic words. The sets supporting the reconstruction of *R (Table 14) are also fewer and less robust than for pTAP *r.

The three pTIM cognates listed in Table 15 are based on Bunaq only, in which pTIM *r and *R are merged. We have thus no means of determining whether these forms are to be reconstructed to pTAP with *r or with *R.

Cognate sets for pTAP *l are relatively infrequent in both pAP and pTIM (Table 16).[1] Cognates reflecting initial pTAP *l with pAP *l and pTIM *l (i.e., 'bark', 'new place' and 'crouch') have only a low degree of certainty. Based on the data available, there also appears to be a tendency to lose pTAP initial *l in pTIM, as in 'far', 'tongue' and 'green', but a clear conditioning environment for this is not yet obvious. Word-finally in polysyllabic words, pTAP *l is regularly lost in pTIM, as in 'banana', 'bat', 'bird' and 'taboo', However, it is retained in 'walk 2' and 'six',

---

[1] Holton & Robinson (this volume) remark that, even though correspondences appear relatively regular for initial and medial *l in pAP, they can identify only a few cognates that are widely distributed across the AP subgroup. Similarly, Schapper, Huber & Engelenhoven (2012: 216) caution that their reconstruction for pTIM *l cannot yet be called secure due to the small number of cognate sets identified.

Table 11: Correspondence sets for pTAP *w

	pAP	pTIM	Bunaq	Makasae	Makalero	Fataluku	Oirata
	*w, *u	*w	h, w	w	w	β	w
blood	*wai	*waj	ho	waj	wej	βehe	we
coconut	*wata !!	*wa(t, D)a	hoza	wata	wata	βaca	wata
stone	*war	*war	hol	–	war	–	war(aha)
sun	*wadi !!	*waTu	hot	watu	watu	βacu	waʈu
bathe	*weli	*weru	wer	waruʔ	waroʔ	βahu	wau
ear	*-uari !!	*-wali	–	wala(kuː)	wali	βali	wali
tooth	*-uasin !!	*-wasin !!	-(e)we	wasi	wasi	βahin(u)	wain(i)

Table 12: Correspondence sets for pTAP *j

	pAP	pTIM	Bunaq	Makasae	Makalero	Fataluku	Oirata
	*j	j, Ø	h, Ø	h, Ø	h, Ø	Ø	Ø
star	*jibV	*ipi(-bere)	[bi]	ifi(-bere)	ifi	ipi(-naka)	ihi
water	*jira	*ira	il	ira	ira	ira	ira
laugh	*jagir !!	*jiger !!	higal	hiʔa	hiʔe	heʔe ¿	–
path	*jega !!	*jiga !!	hik	hiʔa	hiʔa	iʔa	ia(ra)

Table 13: Correspondence sets for pTAP *r

	pAP	pTIM	Bunaq	Makasae	Makalero	Fataluku	Oirata
	*r	*r	l	r	r	r	r
run	*tiara	*tifar	tʃiwal	ditar	titar	tifar(e)	tipar(e)
moon	*wur	*huru	hul	uru	uru	uru	uru
rat	*dur	*Dura	zul	dura	sura	cura	ʈura
stone	*war	*war	hol	–	war	–	war(aha)
vagina	*-ar	*-aru	–	aru	aru	aru	aru
water	*jira	*ira	il	ira	ira	ira	ira
crawl	*er ‼	*er ‼	el	–	–	er(eke)	–
dream	*hipar	*ufar(ana) ‼	[waen] ¿	ufarena	ofarana	ufar(e)	upar(a)
meat	*iser ‼	*seor	sael	[seu] ¿	seur	leura	leura
dog	*jibar ‼	*Depar	[zap] ¿	[defa] ¿	sefar	ipar(u)	ihar(a)
bamboo	*mari	*mari	[ma] ¿	maeri	mar	–	–
P. indicus	*matar ‼	*ma(t, D)er	[mazoʔ] ¿	mater	mater	matar(ia)	–
shark	*sib(a, i)r ‼	*supor ‼	–	–	[su] ¿	hopor(u)	–
new	*siba(r) ‼	*(t, s)ipa(r) ‼	[tip] ¿	[sufa] ¿	hofar	–	–

Table 14: Correspondence sets for pTAP *R

	pAP	pTIM	Bunaq	Makasae	Makalero	Fataluku	Oirata
	*r	*l	l	l	l	l	l
spoon	*surV ‼	*sula	sulu	sulu	hulu	hula	–
tail	*-ora ‼	*-ula(ʔ)	-ulo(ʔ)	ula	ula	ula(fuka)	ula(pua)
tongue	*-lebur ‼	*-ipul	[-up] ¿	[ifl] ¿	ifl	epul(u)	uhul(u)
laugh	*jagir ‼	*jiger	higal	[hiʔa] ¿	[hiʔa] ¿	[heʔe] ¿	–
spit	*purVn ‼	*fulu(k, n) ‼	puluk	–	fulun	fulun	–
ear	*-uari ‼	*-wali	–	wala(kuː)	wali	βali	wali

Table 15: Cognate sets reconstructable to either pTAP *r or *R

	pAP	PTIM	Bunaq	Makasae	Makalero	Fataluku	Oirata
	*r	*(r, R)	–	–	–	–	–
bone	*ser ‼	*(se)sa(r, R) ‼	sesal	–	–	–	–
scorpion	*pVr	*fe(r, R)e ‼	wele	–	–	–	–
rain	*anur ‼	*ine(r, R) ‼	inel	–	–	–	–

3 The relatedness of Timor-Kisar and Alor-Pantar languages

Table 16: Correspondence sets for pTAP *1

	pAP	pTIM	Bunaq	Makasae	Makalero	Fataluku	Oirata
bark	*1	*1, Ø	1(Ø)	1(Ø)	1(Ø)	1(Ø)	1(Ø)
new place	*1Vu	*le(k)u(l) ‼	–	leu	leu	le?ul(e)	leul(e)
crouch	*lan ‼	*lan ‼	lon	–	–	–	–
far	*luk(V)	*luk ‼	lu?(-lu?)	–	–	–	–
tongue	*lete ‼	[*eTar] ‼	ate	–	–	icar	–
green	*-lebur ‼	[*-ipul]	[-up]	[ifI]	[ifI]	[epul(u)]	[uhul(u)]
banana	*(wa)logar ‼	[*ugar]	[ugar]	[hu?ur]	[(h)u?ur]	[u?ur(eke)]	[u?ul(e)]
bat	*mogol	[*mugu] ‼	[mok]	[mu?u]	[mu?u]	[mu?u]	[mu:]
bird	*madel	[*maTa] ‼	–	–	–	[maca]	[ma[a]
taboo	*(a)dVl ‼	[*haDa]	[hos]	[asa]	[asa]	[aca]	[asa]
walk 2	*palol ‼	[*falu(n)]	[por]	[falun]	[falun]	[falu]	–
six	*lam(ar) ‼	*male ‼	mele	–	–	–	–
	*talam	*tamal ‼	tomol	–	–	–	–
child	*-uaqal	*-al ‼	-ol	–	–	–	–

Table 17: Problematic liquid cognate sets

	pAP	pTIM	Bunaq	Makasae	Makalero	Fataluku	Oirata
price	*bol ‼	*bura	bol	bura	pura	pura	hura
bathe	*weli	*weru	wer	waruʔ	waroʔ	vahu ¿	wau ¿
garden	*magad(a)	*(u, a)mar	mar	[ama]	[ama]	–	[uma]
green	*(wa)logar ‼	*ugar	ugar	(h)uʔur	(h)uʔur	uʔur(eke)	uʔul(e) ¿
taboo	*palol ‼	*falu(n)	por	falun	falun	falu	–

apparently due to nasal-liquid metathesis, and in 'child' due to the loss of the item's medial syllable with *q prior to the application of the final polysyllabic deletion rule in pTIM.

Finally, there are several cases in which the appearance of liquids in AP and TK languages can be reconciled with none of the three sets we have identified here. Table 17 lists these problematic instances (the relevant segments are bolded). These sets pointedly express that we are still a long way away from a complete understanding of liquids in pTAP.

2.7 Reconstruction of nasals

Two nasals can be reconstructed to pTAP, *m and *n. For the most part, they are relatively stable and unchanging in both pAP and pTIM.

Table 18 presents a selection of the many cognate sets for pTAP *m. In word-initial position, pTAP *m corresponds unproblematically to pAP *m and pTIM *m. Identifying non-initial instances of pTAP *m is somewhat more difficult, with *hami 'breast' being the only straightforward case. Word-final *m in pAP has only non-final reflexes in pTIM, apparently because, as in the modern TK languages, word-final *m was not permitted. This issue is resolved in pTIM through metathesis of the nasal out of the final position, as in 'sea' and 'six'. Other instances of medial pTIM *m correspond to root-initial *m in pAP (as in 'garden' and 'die').

Table 19 presents the many cognate sets for pTAP *n. Initial and medial correspondences are abundant, but final correspondences are difficult to identify. PTIM *n did not appear to occur in final position; all instances of pAP final *n are either followed by a vowel or are lost in pTIM.

Table 18: Correspondence sets for pTAP *m

	pAP	pTIM	Bunaq	Makasae	Makalero	Fataluku	Oirata
initial *m	***m**	***m**	**m**	**m**	**m**	**m**	**m**
bamboo	*mari	*mari	ma	maeri	mar	–	–
banana	*mogol	*mugu ‼	mok	muʔu	muʔu	muʔu	mu:
sit	*mis	*mit	mit	mit~mi	mit	(i)mir(e)	mir(e)
bat	*madel	*maTa ‼	–	–	–	maca	maʈa
inside	*mi	*mi	mi(l)	mu(tu)	mu(tu-)	mu(cu)	mu(tu)
hear	*magi ‼	*mage(n) ‼	mak	maʔen	maʔen	–	–
non-initial *m	***m**	***m**	**m**	**m**	**m**	**m**	**m**
breast	*hami	*hami ‼	–	ami	–	ami(-tapunu)	–
sea	*tam	*mata	mo	–	–	mata	mata
six	*talam	*tamal ‼	tomol	–	–	–	–
garden	*magad(a)	*(u, a)mar ‼	mar	ama	ama	–	uma
die	*min(a)	*-umV	-ume	umu	(k)umu	umu	umu
nose	*-mim	*-muni ‼	[-inup] ¿	muni(kai)	mini	mini(ku)	–

Table 19: Correspondence sets for pTAP *n

	pAP	pTIM	Bunaq	Makasae	Makalero	Fataluku	Oirata
initial *n	*n	*n	n	n	n	n	n
stand	*nate(r) ‼	*nat	net	nat~na	nat	(a)nat(e)	nat(e)
1SG	*na-	*n- ‼	n-	–	–	–	–
eat	*nai	*nua ‼	[a~ia]	nawa	nua	una, naβa	una, nawa
one	*nuk	*uneki ‼	uen, en	[u]	[u]~un	ukani	a?uni
non-initial *n	*n	*n	n	n	n	n	n
face	*-pona ‼	*-fanu ‼	-(e)wen	fanu	fanu	fanu	panu
ripe	*tena ‼	*tena ‼	ten	tina	tina	–	–
name	*-en(i, u) ‼	*-nej	-ini(l)	naj	nej	ne	ne:(ne)
give	*-ena	*-inV	-ini	(g)ini	(k-)ini	ina	ina
wake	*-ten	*Tani	otin	tane	tane	tani~cani	–
girl	*pon ‼	*fana	pana	fana(rae)	fana(r)	fana(r)	pana(rai)
person	*anin ‼	*anu ‼	en	anu	anu	–	–
other	*aben(VC) ‼	*epi ‼	[ewi]	–	–	–	–

3 Summary of correspondences and reconstructed phonemes

For the first time since the start of TAP studies some sixty years ago (see Schapper & Huber 2012 for a historical perspective on TAP studies), we have rigorously shown in this chapter that the TAP languages form a family: the regularity of sound correspondences in cognate vocabulary demonstrates that the AP and TK Papuan languages are indeed genetically related to one another.

In Table 20, we provide an overview of the consonant correspondences we observed in cognate vocabulary between pAP and pTIM and their reconstruction in their ancestral language pTAP. In this table, we indicate whether the correspondence applies in initial (#_), medial (V_V), or final (_#) position. An empty slot means that there is no particular conditioning environment for the correspondence. The symbol 'Ø' in a column indicates that a pTAP sound is lost in the daughter language in question.

4 Discussion

Whilst we have been able to show clearly that AP and TK languages are related to one another, the comparative data presented here draws into question a number of aspects of the existing reconstructions of pAP and pTIM and necessitates revisions to these. In this final section, we will draw attention to the issues, provide a general discussion of them and suggest some possible solutions.

A major issue for the current pAP reconstruction is the apparent invalidity of many word-final consonant reconstructions. It is argued in Holton et al. (2012: 95) that the gemination of medial stops in modern Western Pantar can be used as a diagnostic for determining whether a given pAP root was consonant-final or vowel-final. Specifically, the authors claim that geminate medial stops in modern Western Pantar reflect pAP medial stops, whereas non-geminate medial stops in Western Pantar reflect an original consonant-final form, or perhaps a borrowing from another AP language. However, this argument cannot be sustained on closer inspection of the comparative evidence. Consider the items in Table 21 that are reconstructed as basically consonant final in pAP, because of the lack of stop gemination in Western Pantar. In each case, we have between three and nine reflexes in modern AP languages with a V(C) following the supposed historically final consonant. We must ask ourselves where so many additional final segments came from in so many of these languages. Holton et al. (2012) seek to explain these appearances with vowel epenthesis. Yet, under this scenario,

Table 20: Summary of sound correspondences from pTAP to pAP and pTIM

pTAP	environment	pAP	pTIM
*p		*p	*f
*b	#_	*b	*b
	V_V	*b	*p
*t	#_	*t	*t
	V_V, _#	*t, *s	*t
*d	#_	*d	*D
	V_V	*d	*T
*k		*k	*g
*g		*g	*g
*s		*s	*s
*h		*h (*w/Ø)	*h
*w		*w, *u	*w
*j		*j	*j, Ø
*r		*r	*r
*R		*r	*l
*l		*l	*l, Ø
*m		*m	*m
*n		*n	*n

we would expect to be able to predict the type of the epenthetic vowel from the shape of the root, but this is not the case; instead, the epenthetic vowels are of all different values from one item to the next and bear no apparent relationship to the vowel of the root (as defined by Holton et al. 2012). What is more, the final V(C) elements we observe in AP languages are not erratic, rather they in general adhere to correspondences observed elsewhere. This suggests that these final V(C) elements were not epenthetic to the items after the break-up of pAP, but have been inherited from pAP. This is further supported by the fact that we find clearly corresponding V(C) segments on cognate vocabulary in TK languages, meaning that the segments reconstruct to pTAP and that they were inherited into pAP. The alternative leaves us without explanation for the cognacy of the final segments in these (and other) items across the family.

Table 21: Dubious consonant-final reconstructions in AP and beyond

	'fish'	'sun'	'fire'	'coconut'	'tongue'	'ripe'	'tooth'
pTAP	*habi	*wad(u, i)	*hadi	*wata	*lebur	*tena	*-wasin
pTIM	*hapi	*waTu	*haTa	*wa(t, D)a	*-ipul	*tena	*-wasin
pAP original	*hab(i)	*wad(i)	*had(a)	*wat(a)	*-leb(ur)	*ten	*-uas
Teiwa	ħaɸ	war	ħar	wat	-livi	tanan	-usan
Nedebang	aːfi	(get)	ar	wata	-lefu	–	-usiŋ
Kaera	ab	wer	ad	wat	-leb	ten	-uasiŋ
WPantar	hap	wer	aːd	wata	-lebu	taŋ	-wasiŋ
Blagar	aːb	war	–	vet	-lebul	tena	-veŋ
Adang	aːb	ved	əda	faʔ	-lib(uŋ)	tene	-wɛhɛŋ
Klon	əbi	fɛd	ar	–	-lɛb	əten	-wɛh
Kui	eb	–	ar	bat	-liber	tain	-wes
Abui	afu	wari	ara	wata	-lifi	–	-weiti
Kamang	api	wati	ati	wate	-opui[1]	iten~iton	-weh
Sawila	api	wadi	ada	wata	-li(m)puru	itiːna	-wa
Wersing	api	widi	ada	wata	-jebur	–	-wesi

[1] Holton et al. (2012) state that these and other Kamang forms missing pAP *1 medially are irregular. However, pAP *1 is regularly lost in Kamang between non-front vowels, e.g., pAP *talam 'six' > Kamang taːm, pAP *palol 'taboo' > Kamang foːi etc. The vowel of the inalienable possessive prefix is /a/, thus providing the right environment for the loss in -opui 'tongue' of the root-initial /l/.

3 The relatedness of Timor-Kisar and Alor-Pantar languages

The problem then is how to explain medial geminate and non-geminate stops in Western Pantar. One answer would be to maintain that the difference in stop gemination was still due to a final versus non-final distinction. For example, it could be said that the loss of the final vowel occurred after the breakup of pAP but prior to the application of the gemination rule. This cannot, however, be fully sustained as WP has in some cases final vowels which clearly reflect pTAP and pAP (e.g., 'tongue'). A more attractive explanation is presented by stress-induced gemination. Although little is known about the historical prosody of TAP, it seems a good possibility that Western Pantar gemination may have been a result of final stress. This scenario is supported by and elaborated in Heston's (2016) analysis of pTAP stress, according to which closed final syllables attracted stress. Western Pantar geminate stops occur predictably before stressed final vowels (even if the syllable in question is no longer closed in modern Western Pantar). This analysis explains the lack of gemination in our examples in Table 21, with the exception of pTAP *lebur* 'tongue' and *wasin* 'tooth'. With respect to the latter, Heston (2016: 288) notes that his stress-based account does not hold for geminate s and l. The former case remains unexplained.

A second issue for the pAP reconstruction is the presence of many unexplained phonemes in a range of environments in different languages. Velar, post-velar and laryngeal consonants are a case in point. Most of the complexity in this domain is found in the languages of Pantar and the Pantar Straits, whose phoneme inventories generally include not only velar and glottal stops, but also uvular ones, as well as a velar or pharyngeal fricative next to the glottal fricative /h/. This contrasts with the situation as found in most of Alor and the TK languages, which tend to be rather simpler. Table 22 exemplifies the velar and post-velar plosives and fricatives in a language of Pantar (Teiwa), Alor (Kamang), and Timor (Bunaq).

The existing pAP reconstruction leaves a significant part of the complexity in the (post-)velar domain in the Pantar languages unexplained; for instance, it does not account for /g/ in Blagar and the relation between the various (post-)velar phonemes such as /q/ and /x/ found in different dialects of Blagar (Steinhauer 1995). It also does not explain the origin of /ʔ/ in languages other than Blagar and Adang, and does not give reflexes for pAP medial *k in Teiwa and pAP final *k in Sawila, leaving the field in question blank in the table summarising the correspondences (Holton & Robinson this volume). Finally, note a variety of irregularities in the reconstructions involving velars in Appendix 1, especially in the Pantar languages. In short, the frequency of irregularities and unexplained occurrences of (post-)velar phonemes shows how limited our understanding of

Table 22: Velar and post-velar phonemes in TAP languages

	Teiwa			
	velar	uvular	pharyngeal	glottal
plosive	k g	q		ʔ
fricative			ħ	h

	Kamang		Bunaq	
	velar	glottal	velar	glottal
plosive	k g	(ʔ)	k g	ʔ
fricative		(h)		h

this domain in AP still is, and serves as a reminder that much more extensive reconstruction work needs to be undertaken.

A similar issue is presented by the phonemic velar nasal /ŋ/ in many AP languages. This phoneme is not reconstructed for pAP, and is also absent in all of the TK languages. According to Holton & Robinson (this volume), pAP *n became /ŋ/ in word-final position in all AP languages except Teiwa, where it was retained as /n/. This historical scenario does work well for some languages, for instance, Wersing, where [ŋ] is synchronically a word-final allophone of /n/. However, in other languages, questions remain. For instance, Kamang has an unexplained contrast between /ŋ/ and /n/ in codas (e.g., *eeŋ* '2SG.POSS' versus *een* '2SG.FOC'). Similarly, the existence of /ŋ/ in coda and medial position in Teiwa is unexplained, as well as the occurrence of /ŋ/ in other positions than the final one in various languages (e.g. Sar *laŋja* 'digging stick' and Kula *ŋapa* 'father').

Vowels also present a major challenge to the reconstruction of the ancestral TAP language. The various vowel systems as illustrated in Table 23 are yet to be historically reconciled with one another. Most AP languages have a length distinction in their vowels: the most common system is 5 short and 5 long cardinal vowels (Kaera, Blagar, Abui and Kamang), though matching long vowels may be missing in the mid-vowel range (Teiwa and Klon). Blagar has a marginal length distinction with only a small number of items occurring with long vowels (Steinhauer 2014), while it is Klon's short mid-vowels that are marginal. A length distinction is entirely absent from Western Pantar's and Wersing's five vowel system and Adang's seven vowel system. A relationship, if any, between the mid-vowels in Adang and length distinctions in other languages remains to be established. Non-cardinal vowels are found in Sawila /y, y:/ and in Klon /ə/. TK languages all have simple five cardinal vowels and there is a marginal length distinction in only one language, Makalero. Stress in conjunction with length appears to have played an important role in vowel histories. For instance, Klon /ə/ seems to originate in a short, unstressed pAP *a (e.g., Klon *əbi* appears to go back to pAP *ha'bi 'fish'). In Wersing, historically short unstressed vowels are lost in words with long vowels, which in turn become short stressed vowels (e.g., Wersing *tlam* appears to go back to pAP *tala:m 'six', cf. Abui *tala:ma*). In short, much careful bottom-up reconstructive work needs to be done in order to reconcile these different systems to a single ancestral system (see Heston 2016 for a more complete stress-related account of Klon /ə/ and Heston forthcoming for a preliminary reconstruction of pTAP vowels).

In sum, with the positive establishment of the relatedness of the Papuan languages scattered across the islands of Timor, Kisar, Alor, Pantar and the Pantar Straits, a start has been made towards a history of the TAP languages. However, we are still a long way off a complete and nuanced understanding of the family and its development (cf. Schapper, Huber & Engelenhoven's (2012) statement of prospective research questions). It will be the task of future reconstructive historical work to definitively solve remaining issues in the comparative data.

Table 23: TAP vowel systems

Western Pantar	Teiwa
i u	i i: u u:
e o	e o
a	a a:

Kaera	Blagar
i i: u u:	i (i:) u (u:)
e e: o o:	e (e:) o (o:)
a a:	a (a:)

Adang	Klon
i u	i i: u u:
e o	e o o:
ɛ ɔ	ɛ ɛ: ə ɔ
a	a a:

Abui	Kamang
i i: u u:	i i: u u:
e e: o o:	e e: o o:
a a:	a a:

Sawila	Wersing
i i: y y: u u:	i u
e e: o o:	e o
a a:	a

Bunaq	Makalero
i u	i u
e o	e o
a	a

The data in these tables are from Holton (2014) for Western Pantar, Klamer (2010) for Teiwa, Klamer (2014) for Kaera, Steinhauer (2014) for Blagar, Haan (2001) for Adang, Baird (2008) for Klon, Kratochvíl (2007) for Abui, Schapper (nd[b]) for Kamang, Kratochvíl (2014) for Sawila, Schapper & Hendery (2014) for Wersing, Schapper (2010) for Bunaq, and Huber (2011) for Makalero.

Sources

Abui (Ab)	Kratochvíl (2007), Kratochvíl & Delpada (2008), Schapper fieldnotes 2010
Adang (Ad)	Robinson fieldnotes 2010
Blagar (Bl)	Robinson fieldnotes 2010
Bunaq (Lamaknen)	Schapper (nd[a]; 2010)
Deing (De)	Robinson fieldnotes 2010
Fataluku	Fataluku online dictionary,[2] van Engelenhoven fieldnotes
Hamap (Hm)	Robinson fieldnotes 2010
Kamang (Km)	Schapper (nd[b]); Schapper & Manimau (2011)
Kabola (Kb)	Robinson fieldnotes 2010
Kaera (Ke)	Klamer Kaera corpus 2005-2007
Kafoa (Kf)	Baird fieldnotes 2003
Klon (Kl)	Baird fieldnotes 2003
Ki (Ki)	Holton fieldnotes 2010
Kula (Ku)	Holton fieldnotes 2010, Nicholas Williams p.c. 2011
Makalero	Huber (2011), Huber fieldnotes 2007-2013
Makasae	Brotherson (2003); Carr (2004); Huber (2008), Huber fieldnotes 2005, 2012-2013, Language Documentation Training Center of the University of Hawaii[3]
Nedebang (Nd)	Robinson fieldnotes 2010
Oirata	de Josselin de Jong (1937), van Engelenhoven fieldnotes
Reta (Rt)	Robinson fieldnotes 2010
Sar (Sr)	Robinson fieldnotes 2010
Sawila (Sw)	Kratochvíl (nd)
Teiwa (Tw)	Klamer Teiwa corpus, Klamer & Sir (2011), Robinson fieldnotes 2010
Wersing (We)	Schapper & Hendery fieldnotes 2012, Holton fieldnotes 2010
Western Pantar (WP)	Holton & Lamma Koly (2008), Holton fieldnotes 2010

---

[2] The www.fataluku.com website, where this dictionary was found, is now defunct.
[3] The LDTC website http://ling.hawaii.edu/ldtc/ contained short sketches of various varieties of Makasae. Unfortunately, these are no longer active.

Abbreviations

1	1st person
2	2nd person
3	3rd person
ALN	alienable
AN	Austronesian
AP	Alor-Pantar
C	consonant
FOC	focus
INAL	inalienable
LOW	refers to any location down(ward) of the deictic centre
pAP	proto-Alor-Pantar
PL	plural
POSS	possessive
pTAP	proto-Timor-Alor-Pantar
pTIM	proto-Timor
SG	singular
TAP	Timor-Alor-Pantar
TK	Timor-Kisar
V	vowel

A Appendix

The orthographic conventions used in the Appendices are the following: '~' joins morphological variants of the same lexeme. In Appendix A.1 and Appendix A.2, material given in round brackets '( )' represents fossilized morphology or other unetymological material. In Appendix A.3, round brackets indicate that a given phoneme cannot be reconstructed with absolute certainty. Furthermore, 'N' is used to represent an unspecified nasal; 'L' an unspecified liquid, and 'Q' a putative postvelar stop for which we have only very weak evidence. An empty slot in the pTAP column means that the reconstructed pAP and pTIM forms, although clearly cognate, are too different to allow for a secure pTAP reconstruction.

A.1 Data supporting the additional pAP reconstructions

gloss	bark	bird	bite	bone	clew, stone circle[3]	coconut
pAP original	–	*dVl	–	–	–	*wat(a)
pAP new	*lVu	*(a)dVl	*(ta)ki	*ser	*maita	*wata
Sr	–	dal	–	–	–	wat
De	–	dal	–	–	–	wat
Tw	–	dai	–	–	–	wat
Nd	–	daya	–	–	–	wata
Ke	–	–	–	–	–	wat
WP	lau	–	–	–	–	hatua
Bl	olovi	–	(ga)ki	–	–	vet
Rt	lu	–	ki(-ki)	–	–	vat
Ad	lowo?	–	–	–	–	fa?
Hm	–	–	–	–	–	–
Kb	olowo	–	–	–	–	wa?
Ki	–	adol	–	–	–	bat
Kf	–	–	–	–	–	–
Kl	–	–	–	–	–	–
Ab	lou	–	(ta)kai	–	masaŋ ¿[4]	wata
Km	–	atul	ka(te)[1]	sɛl ¿[2]	maita	–
Ku	leloja	–	–	(gi)saja	–	gʷata
Sw	–	adala	–	sara	–	wata
We	aloi	adol	(mi)kik	(ge)seri	–	wata

[1] Metathesized form; denotes 'eat'.
[2] Kamang normally reflects pAP *r as /i/ in final position.
[3] See Rodemeier (1993) on clews in Alor.
[4] Abui normally reflects pAP *t as /t/.

gloss	crawl	die	dirty	dog	ear
pAP original	–	*minV	–	–	*-uar(i)
pAP new	*er	*min(a)	*karok[1]	*jibar[2]	*-uari
Sʀ	–	min	–	jifar	–
Dᴇ	–	miŋ	–	jewar	-war
Tᴡ	–	min	–	jifar	-uar
Nᴅ	–	miːa	–	bar	-ow
Kᴇ	–	min	–	ibar	-uar
WP	–	–	–	jabːe	-ue
Bʟ	–	(i)mina	–	jabar	-veli
Rᴛ	–	(a)mina	–	jobal	–
Aᴅ	–	miniʔ	karoʔo	bel	–
Hᴍ	–	min	–	bøl	–
Kʙ	–	mini	(na)karoʔo	bel	–
Kɪ	–	min	–	–	-uel
Kꜰ	–	(i)mon	–	–	–
Kʟ	–	–	–	–	-uɛr
Aʙ	–	moŋ	–	–	-uei
Kᴍ	eei~eel	–	–	–	-uai
Kᴜ	–	–	–	–	–
Sᴡ	–	–	–	–	uari
Wᴇ	er	–	–	–	-ueri

[1] This reconstruction must be viewed as tentative, since Kabola does not make part of the existing pAP reconstruction.

[2] Note the loss of the initial syllable in several of the daughter languages. According to Holton et al. (2012) and Holton & Robinson (this volume), this has to do with stress being based on syllable weight. The heavy *bar syllable attracts stress, which leads to the loss of the initial syllable. A similar case is, possibly, pAP *tei 'tree'.

3 The relatedness of Timor-Kisar and Alor-Pantar languages

gloss	face	far	fire	fish	flat
pAP original	–	–	*had(a)	*hab(i)	–
pAP new	*-pona	*lete	*hada	*habi	*tatok
Sʀ	–	–	–	–	–
Dᴇ	–	–	–	–	–
Tᴡ	–	–	ħar	ħaf	–
Nᴅ	–	–	ar	a:fi	–
Kᴇ	–	–	ad	ab	–
WP	–	–	–	hap	–
Bʟ	–	–	a:d	a:b	–
Rᴛ	–	–	–	–	–
Aᴅ	–	–	–	a:b	–
Hᴍ	–	–	–	–	–
Kʙ	–	–	–	–	–
Kɪ	–	–	ar	eb	–
Kꜰ	–	–	–	–	–
Kʟ	–	–	əda	əbi	–
Aʙ	-poŋ	–	ara	afu	–
Kᴍ	-funa:	letei	ati	api	tatok
Kᴜ	–	–	–	–	–
Sᴡ	–	–	ada	api	–
Wᴇ	–	–	ada	api	–

gloss	girl	grandparent grandchild	green	hear	itchy
pAP original	–	–	–	–	–
pAP new	*pon	*tam(a, u)¹	*(wa)logar⁵	*magi	*(i)ruk
Sʀ	–	–	logar	–	–
Dᴇ	–	–	alogur	–	–
Tᴡ	–	–	ajogar ¿	–	–
Nᴅ	–	–	aejaga ¿	–	–
Kᴇ	–	–	ojogi ¿	–	–
WP	–	–	haluaga	–	–
Bʟ	–	–	–	mɛʔɛ	–
Rᴛ	–	–	–	–	–
Aᴅ	–	–	–	maʔeh	–
Hᴍ	–	–	–	–	–
Kʙ	–	–	–	meʔehe	–
Kɪ	–	–	–	magi	rok
Kꜰ	–	–	–	–	–
Kʟ	–	–	wəwɛlɛŋ ¿	məgih	–
Aʙ	–	–	walaŋaj	mahi	jokuŋ
Kᴍ	fon	tam²	–	-mai	jokuŋ
Kᴜ	–	(a)tamu³	walaŋka	magin	joka
Sᴡ	–	(ga)ta:mu³	walaŋara ¿	maji:ŋ	–
Wᴇ	–	(ne)tamu⁴	walar	–	iruk

¹ This is a reciprocal term. The reflexes in the modern languages denote either 'grandparent' or 'grandchild'.

² Reciprocal grandparent-grandchild term.

³ Denotes 'grandchild'.

⁴ Denotes 'grandparent'.

⁵ While clearly cognate, the forms in this set show a variety of unexpected or irregular sound changes: Teiwa, Nedebang and Kaera normally reflect pAP *l as /l/ in initial and medial position, rather than /j/; Teiwa and Nedebang normally reflect pAP *g as /ħ/ and /x/, respectively, in medial position, rather than /g/; pAP *g is normally reflected as /g/ in Klon and /j/ in Sawila; and finally, initial /h/ in Western Pantar is usually a reflex of pAP *h, rather than *w. The pAP reconstruction must thus be seen as somewhat tentative.

gloss	laugh	leg	LOW	meat	mountain	name
pAP original	*jari	–	–	–	–	*-ain(i, u)
pAP new	*jagir[1]	*-bat	*po[2]	*iser[3]	*buku	*-en(i, u)
Sr	jehar	-fat	–	–	–	–
De	jaxar	-wat	–	–	–	–
Tw	jəħar	-fat	–	–	–	–
Nd	gela	–	–	–	–	-einu
Ke	agar	at	–	–	buku:	-en
WP	jali ¿	–	–	–	–	-iːnu
Bl	iriga	–	po	–	buku	-ene
Rt	agala	–	–	–	–	–
Ad	–	–	pɔ	hiri ¿	–	-aniŋ
Hm	–	–	–	(ma)hil	–	anɛ
Kb	jaːla	–	–	–	–	–
Ki	jeri ¿	–	–	is	–	-enei
Kf	–	–	–	(ma)heːl	–	-nɛi
Kl	əgar	–	–	(mə)hɛl	–	-ənɛʔ
Ab	–	–	pa	mahitiŋ	buku ¿[4]	-ane
Km	–	–	fuŋ	isei	buk ¿[4]	-nei
Ku	geja	–	–	–	–	–
Sw	jara ¿	–	–	isi ¿	–	-ani
We	jer ¿	–	–	(ge)is ¿	–	–

[1] Holton et al. (2012) reconstruct *jari for 'laugh'. We revise this form on the basis of the clear presence of a medial velar in the reflexes of many AP languages. Note, however, the irregular loss of reflexes of pAP *g in Western Pantar, Kui, Sawila and Wersing.

[2] See Schapper (this volume) for details on this reconstruction.

[3] The reflexes of this form denote 'game' or 'meat'. Note that there are several irregularities in this set: Adang normally reflects pAP *r as /l/, rather than /r/; and Sawila and Wersing normally reflect *s as /t/, rather than /s/.

[4] Abui normally reflects pAP *b as /f/, rather than /b/, and pAP *b is usually reflected in Kamang as /p/, rather than /b/.

gloss	new	new place	other	path	person
pAP original	*siba	–	–	–	–
pAP new	*siba(r)	*lan	*abenVC	*jega[2]	*anin
Sʀ	–	–	–	–	–
Dᴇ	sib	–	–	–	–
Tᴡ	sib	–	–	–	–
Nᴅ	sava(ʔa)	–	–	ji:ja ¿	–
Kᴇ	sib-	–	baniŋ	–	–
WP	sab:a	–	–	ja ¿	–
Bʟ	hiba	–	abeuŋ~ebeuŋ	iga ¿	–
Rᴛ	haba	–	–	viag	–
Aᴅ	habar	–	–	seʔ	–
Hᴍ	habar	–	–	seʔ	–
Kʙ	–	–	–	jeʔ	–
Kɪ	saba	–	abaŋan	–	anin(ou)
Kғ	hifa	–	afenaj	ʔijɛ	–
Kʟ	həba:	–	ebeŋ	ɛgɛʔ	anɪn(ok)
Aʙ	tɪfa	–	–	–	–
Kᴍ	supa(ka)	laŋ	–	–	-aniŋ
Kᴜ	tupa	–	–	–	aniŋ(na)
Sᴡ	tipea	la:ŋ[1]	–	–	aniŋ(ka:)
Wᴇ	təpa	laŋ[1]	–	–	aniŋ

[1] Denotes 'coast'. The relationship between the two senses is explained by the typical settlement patterns in the region: older settlements are located in high places, often on top of knolls or ridges, whilst newer settlements are downhill towards the coast.

[2] There are a number of irregularities in this set: Nedebang normally reflects medial *g as /x/, Western Pantar as /g:/, and Blagar as either Ø or /ʔ/.

gloss	price	P. indicus[3]	rain	ripe	scratch
pAP original	–	–	–	*ten	–
pAP new	*bol[1]	*matar	*anur	*tena	*karab
Sr	–	–	–	–	kəra:b
De	–	–	–	ten:aŋ	krab
Tw	–	–	–	–	–
Nd	–	–	–	tanan	(ki)kar ¿[4]
Ke	–	–	–	ten-	krabis ¿[5]
WP	–	mat:e	–	taŋ	karasi ¿[6]
Bl	–	–	onor	tena	–
Rt	(ta)beli[2]	–	–	–	–
Ad	–	–	nui	tene	–
Hm	–	–	–	tɛn	–
Kb	(ʔo)wol[2]	–	nui	tenaŋ	–
Ki	–	–	anor	tain	ukuberi
Kf	–	–	–	–	ukafi
Kl	–	mtar	–	ətɛn	kərɔb
Ab	(he)bel[2]	mitai	anui	–	kafi
Km	bol[2]	–	–	iten~iton	–
Ku	–	–	–	–	kapi
Sw	–	mata:ri	–	iti:na	kapari
We	–	–	–	–	kəpir

[1] This root is likely an Austronesian loan: PMP *bəli 'price, bride price'.
[2] Denotes 'bride price'.
[3] New Guinea Rosewood (*Petrocapus indicus*), typically referred to in Eastern Malay as *kayu merah*.
[4] Note the irregular loss of the final syllable.
[5] Semantic shift to 'claw'. Also, note the unetymological /s/, present in both Kaera and Western Pantar.
[6] While this form is very likely related, it includes several irregularities: the expected reflex of pAP *r in medial position is /l/ in Western Pantar; there is no reflex of pAP *b, which is normally reflected as /b/; and there is an unetymological /s/.

gloss	shark	spit	spoon	stand	sugarcane
pAP original	–	*purVN	–	–	*uːb
pAP new	*sib(a, i)r	*purVn	*surV[2]	*nate(r)[3]	*huːba
Sr	sifir	–	–	–	–
De	sibːir	–	–	–	–
Tw	sifar	puran	–	–	–
Nd	–	–	–	–	uːfa
Ke	sibar	puraŋ	–	–	uːb
WP	sibːu	–	–	natar ¿[4]	–
Bl	sibir[1]	puruŋ	–	–	ub
Rt	hibil	puruŋ	–	–	juwab
Ad	–	–	hur	–	soːb
Hm	–	–	–	–	–
Kb	–	paraŋ	–	–	job
Ki	sobor	puriŋ	–	–	uːb
Kf	–	–	–	natei	–
Kl	–	pərʊin	–	–	–
Ab	–	puina	tur	nate	fa
Km	–	–	suːt	–	–
Ku	–	–	–	–	pʷa
Sw	–	–	–	–	–
We	–	–	sire	–	upa

[1] Blagar normally reflects pAP *s as /h/ in word-initial position.

[2] This set shows a variety of irregularities: Adang normally reflects pAP *r as /l/ or /i/, rather than /r/; pAP *r is normally reflected as /i/ in final position in both Abui and Kamang; and Wersing normally reflects pAP *s as /t/, rather than /s/.

[3] There is a competing and morphologically unrelated form *tas 'stand', which is more widely distributed across modern AP languages (see Holton & Robinson this volume).

[4] Western Pantar normally reflects pAP *r as Ø in word-final position.

3 The relatedness of Timor-Kisar and Alor-Pantar languages

gloss	sun	taboo	tail	tongue	tooth
pAP original	*wad(i)	–	*-or	*-leb(ur)	*-uas
pAP new	*wadi	*palol	*-ora	*-lebur	*-uasin
Sr	war	–	-or	–	–
De	–	–	-or	–	–
Tw	war (get)	–	-or	-livi	-usan
Nd	weri	–	-ola	-lefu	-usiŋ
Ke	wer	–	-or	-le:b	-uasiŋ
WP	war	–	–	-lebu	-wasiŋ
Bl	ved	–	ora	-dʒebur	-veŋ
Rt	vid	–		-lebul	–
Ad	fɛd	–	olo?	-lɛb	-wɛhɛŋ
Hm	fød	–	ol	–	-fiʔiŋ
Kb	wer	–	ʔol	-leb	–
Ki	ber	–	-or	-liber	-wes
Kf	uru	–	–	-lip	-weheŋ
Kl	–	–	-or	-lɛb	-wɛh
Ab	wari	palol	–	-lifi	-weiti
Km	wati	fo:i	-(w)ui	-opei	-weh
Ku	wad	–	–	ilıp	–
Sw	wadi	–	-(w)o:ra	–	-wa
We	widi	–	wori	-jebur	-wesi

gloss	walk 1	walk 2	weave	yellow
pAP original	–	–	–	–
pAP new	*laka[1]	*lam(ar)	*sine(N)	*bagori
Sʀ	–	–	–	bahar
Dᴇ	–	–	–	bug
Tᴡ	–	lam[3]	–	baħari
Nᴅ	–	–	–	baxori
Kᴇ	–	amar ¿[4]	–	bagari
WP	–	lama	sin:aŋ	bug:a
Bʟ	–	lamar	–	bagori ¿[5]
Rᴛ	–	lamal	–	bagori
Aᴅ	–	lami	–	baʔoi
Hᴍ	–	lamɛ	–	baʔoil
Kʙ	laʔaw	–	–	baʔoil
Kɪ	lak	–	–	bagura
Kꜰ	la:ka	–	–	fijʊi
Kʟ	–	(gɛpun)lam	hnan	bʊbʊgɔr
Aʙ	la:k	–	tinei	–
Kᴍ	lo: ¿[2]	–	sine	–
Kᴜ	–	–	–	–
Sᴡ	–	–	–	–
Wᴇ	–	–	–	–

[1] This root is possibly an Austronesian loan: PMP *lakaj 'stride, take a step'.
[2] Kamang normally reflects pAP *k as /k/.
[3] Semantic shift to 'follow'.
[4] Kaera normally reflects pAP *l as /l/ in word-initial position.
[5] Blagar normally reflects pAP *g as Ø or /ʔ/ in medial position.

3 The relatedness of Timor-Kisar and Alor-Pantar languages

A.2 Data supporting the additional pTIM reconstructions

gloss	banana	bark	bat	bite	bone
pTIM original	*muku	–	–	*gakel	–
pTIM new	*mugu	*le(k)u(l)	*maTa	*(ga)gel	*(se)sa(r, R)
BUNAQ	mok	–	–	gagil	sesal
MAKASAE	muʔu	leu[1]	–	gaʔel	–
MAKALERO	muʔu	leu[1]	–	kaʔel	–
FATALUKU	muʔu	leʔul(e)[2]	maca	(ki)kiʔ(e)	–
OIRATA	mu:	leule[2]	maṭa	–	–

gloss	breast	child	crawl	crouch	dirty
pTIM original	–	–	*er(ek)	–	–
pTIM new	*hami	*-al	*er	*luk	*gari
BUNAQ	–	-ol	el	luʔ(-luʔ)[4]	gar
MAKASAE	ami	–	–	–	raʔi[5]
MAKALERO	–	–	–	–	raʔi[5]
FATALUKU	ami(-tapunu)[3]	–	er(eke)	–	raʔe(ne)[5,6]
OIRATA	–	–	–	–	–

[1] Semantic shift to 'call'.
[2] Semantic shift to 'sing'.
[3] This lexeme is a lexical doublet, i.e. originally a compound or a lexicalized parallel expression (see Schapper, Huber & Engelenhoven 2012: 224).
[4] Semantic shift to 'bent over (as with age)'.
[5] This form shows metathesis in Proto-Eastern Timor: *kari > *raki > raʔi / raʔe(ne).
[6] Semantic shift to 'littered with stones'.

gloss	dream	eat	excrement	face	far
pTIM original	–	–	–	*fenu	–
pTIM new	*ufar(ana)	*nua	*a(t, D)u	*-fanu	*eTar
BUNAQ	waen[1]	a~-ia	ozo	-ewen	ate
MAKASAE	ufarena	nawa	atu[-gu?u][2]	fanu	–
MAKALERO	ofarana	nua	atu	fanu	–
FATALUKU	ufarana	una~naβa	atu[3]	fanu	icar
OIRATA	upar(a)	una~nawa	atu[3]	panu	–

gloss	fish	flat	garden	hear	itchy
pTIM original	*api	–	*(u)mar	*make(n)	–
pTIM new	*hapi	*tetok	*(u, a)mar	*mage(n)	*ilag
BUNAQ	–	toi?[4]	mar	mak	–
MAKASAE	afi	–	ama	ma?en	ila?
MAKALERO	afi	tetu?	ama	ma?en	ile?
FATALUKU	api	–	–	–	–
OIRATA	ahi	–	uma	–	–

[1] This item shows metathesis: *waen* < *awen following on fusion from the two halves of the reconstructed doublet.

[2] The Bunaq cognate for the second half of this lexical doublet is *g-io* '3INAL-faeces', but it doesn't appear in a doublet with *ozo* 'faeces'.

[3] Semantic shift to 'belly'.

[4] The final glottal stop in Bunaq is likely a reflex of final *k in pTIM. However, more evidence is needed to substantiate this claim of relatedness.

3 The relatedness of Timor-Kisar and Alor-Pantar languages

gloss	laugh	leg	LOW	mat	mountain
pTIM original	*hika	–	–	–	–
pTIM new	*jiger	*buta	*ufe	*biti	*bugu
BUNAQ	higal	but[1]	–	–	–
MAKASAE	hiʔa	–	he-ʔ[2]	–	buʔu
MAKALERO	hiʔe	–	ufe-	piti	puʔu[3]
FATALUKU	heʔe	–	ua-ʔ[2]	pet(u)	–
OIRATA	–	–	ua ʔ[2]	het(e)	–

gloss	new	new place	nose	one	other
pTIM original	*(t, s)ifa	–	–	–	–
pTIM new	*(t, s)ipa(r)	*lan	*-muni	*uneki	*epi
BUNAQ	tip	lon	-inup ʔ[4]	uen~en	ewi[6]
MAKASAE	sufa	–	muni(kai)[5]	u	–
MAKALERO	hofar	–	mini	u~un	–
FATALUKU	–	–	mini(ku)	ukani	–
OIRATA	–	–	–	aʔuni	–

[1] Semantic shift to mean 'knee'.

[2] The reflex of pTIM *f as /h/ in Makasae and Ø in Fataluku and Oirata is irregular; /f/ is expected for Makasae and Fataluku, and /p/ for Oirata.

[3] Semantic shift to 'gable, top of house'.

[4] This item appears to show metathesis in the following stages: pTIM *-muni > *-minu > *-imun > *-inum > Bunaq -inup 'nose'. The change of *m to Bunaq p is explainable as the result of /m/ being prohibited from codas in Bunaq.

[5] The suffix -kai is frequently found in body part terms in Makasae.

[6] It seems likely that medial *p changes to /w/ in Bunaq. However, we currently lack sufficient data to support this conclusion. There has also been a semantic shift to 'foreigner'.

gloss	path	person	rain	ripe	scorpion
pTIM original	*hika	–	–	*tina(k)	–
pTIM new	*jiga	*anu	*ine(r, R)	*tena	*fe(r, R)e
BUNAQ	hik	en	inel	ten[1]	wele[4]
MAKASAE	hiʔa	anu	–	tina[2]	–
MAKALERO	hiʔa	anu	–	tina~dina[2]	–
FATALUKU	iʔa	–	–	tina[3]	–
OIRATA	ia(ra)	–	–	–	–

gloss	scratch	shark	six	spit	tooth
pTIM ORIGINAL	–	–	–	–	*wasi
pTIM NEW	*gabar	*supor	*tamal	*fulu(k, n)	*-wasin
BUNAQ	–	–	tomol	puluk	-(e)we
MAKASAE	–	–	–	–	wasi
MAKALERO	kapar	su(-amulafu)[5]	–	fulun	wasi
FATALUKU	kafur(e)	hopor(u)[6]	–	fulu	βahin(u)
OIRATA	–	–	–	–	wain(i)

[1] Semantic shift to 'be cooked, ready'.
[2] Semantic shift to 'cook'.
[3] Semantic shift to 'set alight'.
[4] It seems likely that initially before front vowels *f changes to /w/ in Bunaq. However, we currently lack sufficient data to support this conclusion.
[5] The meaning of the compound *su-amulafu* is not quite clear. It seems to refer to a large sea creature, possibly a dolphin or a dugong. The second element, *amulafu*, translates as 'human being, person'.
[6] This form is glossed as either 'shark' or 'dugong' in the different Fataluku sources.

3 The relatedness of Timor-Kisar and Alor-Pantar languages

gloss	tree	walk 1	walk 2	yellow	1SG	1PL
pTIM original	*hote	*lakor	–	–	–	–
pTIM new	*hate	*lagar[1]	*male	*gabar	*n-	*fi
BUNAQ	hotel	lagor	mele	–	n-	–
MAKASAE	ate	la?a	–	gabar	–	fi
MAKALERO	ate	la?a	–	–	–	fi
FATALUKU	ete	la?a	–	–	–	afi
OIRATA	ete	lare	–	–	–	ap-

[1] This root is possibly an Austronesian loan: PMP *lakaj 'stride, take a step'.

A.3 List of cognates and pTAP reconstruction

gloss	pTAP	pAP	pTIM
bamboo	*mari	*mari	*mari
banana	*mugul	*mogol	*mugu
bark, call		*lVu	*le(k)u(l)
bat	*madel	*madel	*maTa
bathe	*weLi	*weli	*weru
bird	*(h)adul	*(a)dVl	*haDa
bite	*ki(l)	*(ta)ki	*(ga)gel
blood	*waj	*wai	*waj
bone	*se(r, R)	*ser	*(se)sa(r, R)
breast	*hami	*hami	*hami
child	*-uaQal	*-uaqal	*-al
clew	*ma(i)ta(r)	*maita	*matar
coconut	*wata	*wata	*wa(t, D)a
crawl	*er	*er	*er
crouch	*luk(V)	*luk(V)	*luk
die	*mV(n)	*min(a)	*-umV
dirty	*karV(k)	*karok	*gari

gloss	pTAP	pAP	pTIM
dog	*dibar	*jibar	*Depar
dream	*(h)ipar	*hipar	*ufar(ana)
ear	*-waRi	*-uari	*-wali
eat	*nVa	*nai	*nua
excrement	*(h)at(V)	*has	*a(t, D)u
face	*panu	*-pona	*-fanu
far	*le(t, d)e	*lete	*eTar
fire	*hada	*hada	*haTa
fish	*habi	*habi	*hapi
flat	*tatok	*tatok	*tetok
garden	*magad	*magad(a)	*(u, a)mar
girl	*pan(a)	*pon	*fana
give	*-(e, i)na	*-ena	*-inV
grandparent	*(t, d)ama	*tam(a, u)	*moTo
green	*lugar	*(wa)logar	*ugar
hand	*-tan(a)	*-tan	*-tana
hear	*mage(n)	*magi	*mage(n)
inside	*mi	*mi	*mi
itchy	*iRak	*(i)ruk	*ilag
laugh	*jagir	*jagir	*jiger
leg	*buta	*-bat	*buta
LOW	*po	*po	*ufe
mat	*bit	*bis	*biti
meat	*isor	*iser	*seor
moon	*hur(u)	*wur	*huru
mountain	*buku	*buku	*bugu
name		*-en(i, u)	*-nej
new	*(t, s)iba(r)	*siba(r)	*(t, s)ipa(r)
new place	*lan	*lan	*lan
nose	*-mVN	*-mim	*-muni
one	*nukV	*nuk	*uneki
other	*abe(nVC)	*aben(VC)	*epi
P. indicus	*matar	*matar	*ma(t, D)ar
path	*jega	*jega	*jiga
person	*anV(N)	*anin	*anu
pig	*baj	*baj	*baj

3 The relatedness of Timor-Kisar and Alor-Pantar languages

gloss	pTAP	pAP	pTIM
pound	*tapa(i)	*tapai	*tafa
price	*boL	*bol	*bura
rain	*anu(r, R)	*anur	*ine(r, R)
rat	*dur(a)	*dur	*Dura
ripe	*tena	*tena	*tena
run	*tipar	*tiara	*tifar
scorpion	*pV(r, R)	*pVr	*fe(r, R)e
scratch	*karab	*karab	*gabar
sea	*tam(a)	*tam	*mata
shark	*sibar	*sib(a, i)r	*supor
sit	*mit	*mis	*mit
six	*talam	*talam	*tamal
sleep	*tia(r)	*tia	*tia(r)
spit	*puRV(n)	*purVn	*fulu(k, n)
spoon	*suRa	*surV	*sula
stand	*nat(er)	*nate(r)	*nat
star	*jibV	*jibV	*ipi(-bere)
stone	*war	*war	*war
sugarcane	*ub(a)	*huːba	*upa
sun	*wad(i, u)	*wadi	*waTu
taboo	*palu(l, n)	*palol	*falu(n)
tail	*-oRa	*-ora	*-ula(?)
tongue	*-lebuR	*-lebur	*-ipul
tooth	*-wasin	*-uasin	*-wasin
tree	*hate	*tei	*hate
vagina	*-ar(u)	*-ar	*-aru
wake	*tan(i)	*-ten	*Tani
walk 1	*lak(Vr)	*laka	*lagar
walk 2	*lamV	*lam(ar)	*male
water	*jira	*jira	*ira
weave	*sine(N)	*sine(N)	*sina
yellow	*bagur(V)	*bagori	*gabar
1PI	*pi	*pi-	*fi
1SG	*na-	*na-	*n-
3	*gie	*ge	*gie
3POSS	*ga-	*ga-	*g-

References

Baird, Louise. 2008. *A grammar of Klon: a non-Austronesian language of Alor, Indonesia.* Canberra: Pacific Linguistics.

Brotherson, Anna. 2003. *A spatial odyssey: Referring to space in Makasai.* Canberra: Australian National University BA (hons) thesis.

Capell, Arthur. 1975. The West Papuan phylum: General, and Timor and areas further west. In Stephen A. Wurm (ed.), *New Guinea area languages and language study*, Papuan Languages and the New Guinea linguistic scene, vol. 1, 667–716. Canberra: Research School of Pacific & Asian Studies, Australian National University.

Carr, Felicita M. 2004. *Pupuuk, Masu Moru and Data: Three genres of Makasai.* Canberra: Australian National University MA thesis.

de Josselin de Jong, Jan Petrus Benjamin. 1937. *Studies in Indonesian culture I: Oirata, a Timorese settlement on Kisar.* Amsterdam: Noord-Hollandsche Uitgevers-Maatschappij.

Haan, Johnson Welem. 2001. *The grammar of Adang: a Papuan language spoken on the island of Alor East Nusa Tenggara - Indonesia.* Sydney: University of Sydney PhD thesis.

Heston, Tyler. 2016. Stress in Proto-Timor-Alor-Pantar. *Oceanic Linguistics* 55(1). 278–289.

Heston, Tyler. Forthcoming. A first reconstruction of vowels in Proto-Timor-Alor-Pantar. *Oceanic Linguistics.*

Holton, Gary. 2014. Western Pantar. In Antoinette Schapper (ed.), *Papuan languages of Timor, Alor and Pantar: Sketch grammars*, vol. 1, 23–96. Berlin: Mouton de Gruyter.

Holton, Gary & Mahalalel Lamma Koly. 2008. *Kamus pengantar Bahasa Pantar Barat: Tubbe - Mauta - Lamma.* Kupang, Indonesia: UBB-GMIT.

Holton, Gary & Laura C. Robinson. this volume. The internal history of the Alor-Pantar language family. In Marian Klamer (ed.), *The Alor-Pantar languages*, 55–97. Berlin: Language Science Press.

Holton, Gary, Marian Klamer, František Kratochvíl, Laura C. Robinson & Antoinette Schapper. 2012. The historical relations of the Papuan languages of Alor and Pantar. *Oceanic Linguistics* 51(1). 86–122.

Huber, Juliette. 2008. *First steps towards a grammar of Makasae: a language of East Timor.* Vol. 195 (Languages of the World/Materials). München: Lincom.

Huber, Juliette. 2011. *A grammar of Makalero: a Papuan language of East Timor.* Utrecht: LOT.

Klamer, Marian. 2010. *A grammar of Teiwa* (Mouton Grammar Library 49). Berlin: Mouton de Gruyter.

Klamer, Marian. 2014. Kaera. In Antoinette Schapper (ed.), *Papuan languages of Timor, Alor and Pantar: Sketch grammars*, vol. 1, 97–146. Berlin: Mouton de Gruyter.

Klamer, Marian & Amos Sir. 2011. *Kosakata bahasa Teiwa-Indonesia-Inggris [Teiwa-Indonesian-English word list]*. Kupang, Indonesia: Unit Bahasa dan Budaya (UBB).

Kratochvíl, František. 2007. *A grammar of Abui: a Papuan language of Alor*. Utrecht: LOT.

Kratochvíl, František. 2014. Sawila. In Antoinette Schapper (ed.), *Papuan languages of Timor, Alor and Pantar: Sketch grammars*, vol. 1, 351–438. Berlin: Mouton de Gruyter.

Kratochvíl, František. nd. *Dictionary of Sawila*. Manuscript, Nanyang Technological University.

Kratochvíl, František & Benediktus Delpada. 2008. *Kamus pengantar Bahasa Abui (Abui-Indonesian-English dictionary)*. Kupang: Unit Bahasa dan Budaya (UBB).

Rodemeier, Susanne. 1993. *Lego-lego Platz und naga-Darstellung jenseitige Kräfte im Zentrum einer Quellenstudie über die ostindonesische Insel Alor*. München: Ludwig-Maximilians-Universität MA thesis.

Schapper, Antoinette. 2010. *Bunaq: a Papuan language of central Timor*. Canberra: Australian National University PhD thesis.

Schapper, Antoinette (ed.). 2014. *Papuan languages of Timor, Alor and Pantar: Sketch grammars*. Vol. 1. Berlin: Mouton de Gruyter.

Schapper, Antoinette. nd(a). Dictionary of Bunaq. Manuscript, Australian National University.

Schapper, Antoinette. nd(b). Grammar of Kamang. Manuscript, Leiden University.

Schapper, Antoinette. this volume. Elevation in the spatial deictic systems of Alor-Pantar languages. In Marian Klamer (ed.), *The Alor-Pantar languages*, 247–284. Berlin: Language Science Press.

Schapper, Antoinette & Rachel Hendery. 2014. Wersing. In Antoinette Schapper (ed.), *Papuan languages of Timor, Alor and Pantar: Sketch grammars*, vol. 1, 439–504. Berlin: Mouton de Gruyter.

Schapper, Antoinette & Juliette Huber. 2012. State-of-the-art in the documentation of the Papuan languages of Timor, Alor, Pantar and Kisar. *Wacana, Journal of the Humanities of Indonesia* (14). 1–37.

Schapper, Antoinette, Juliette Huber & Aone van Engelenhoven. 2012. The historical relation of the Papuan languages of Timor and Kisar. In Harald Hammarström & Wilco van den Heuvel (eds.), *History, contact and classification of Papuan languages* (Language and Linguistics in Melanesia Special Issue 2012, Part I), 194–242. Port Moresby: Linguistic Society of Papua New Guinea.

Schapper, Antoinette & Marten Manimau. 2011. *Kamus pengantar Bahasa Kamang-Indonesia-Inggris (Introductory Kamang-Indonesian-English dictionary)* (UBB Language & Culture Series: A 7). Kupang: Unit Bahasa dan Budaya (BDD).

Steinhauer, Hein. 1995. Two varieties of the Blagar language (Alor, Indonesia). In Connie Baak, Mary Bakker & Dick van der Meij (eds.), *Tales from a concave world: Liber amicorum Bert Voorhoeve*, 269–296. Leiden: Projects Division, Department of Languages, Cultures of South-East Asia & Oceania.

Steinhauer, Hein. 2014. Blagar. In Antoinette Schapper (ed.), *Papuan languages of Timor, Alor and Pantar: Sketch grammars*, vol. 1, 147–220. Berlin: Mouton de Gruyter.

Stokhof, W. A. L. 1975. *Preliminary notes on the Alor and Pantar languages (East Indonesia)* (Pacific Linguistics: Series B 43). Canberra: Australian National University.

Chapter 4

The linguistic position of the Timor-Alor-Pantar languages

Gary Holton

Laura C. Robinson

> The wider genealogical affiliations of the Timor-Alor-Pantar languages have been the subject of much speculation. These languages are surrounded by unrelated Austronesian languages, and attempts to locate related languages have focused on Papuan languages 800 km or more distant. This chapter draws on typological, pronominal, and especially lexical evidence to examine three hypotheses regarding the higher-level affiliations of the Timor-Alor-Pantar languages: (1) the languages are related to the North Halmaheran (West Papuan) languages; (2) the languages are part of the Trans-New Guinea family; and (3) the languages are related to the West Bomberai family, with no link to Trans-NewGuinea more broadly. We rely in particular on recent reconstructions of proto-Timor-Alor-Pantar vocabulary (chapter 3). Of the hypotheses evaluated here, we find the most striking similarities between TAP and the West Bomberai family. However, we conclude that the evidence currently available is insufficient to confirm a genealogical relationship with West Bomberai or any other family, and hence, TAP must be considered a family-level isolate.

1 Introduction

The non-Austronesian languages of the Alor and Pantar islands in eastern Indonesia have been shown to form a genealogical unit (see Chapter 2) and these, in turn, have been shown to be part of a larger family which includes the non-Austronesian languages of Timor (see Chapter 3). Here we examine the wider genealogical affiliations of the Timor-Alor-Pantar family, following Robinson &

Holton (2012).[1] Prior to this work most authors assumed a connection to Trans-New Guinea languages, based primarily on evidence from pronominal paradigms (Ross 2005). However, several other plausible hypotheses have been proposed, which we shall examine in this chapter. The Timor-Alor-Pantar (TAP) languages are surrounded on all sides by Austronesian languages, with the nearest Papuan (non-Austronesian) language located some 800 km distant.[2] Some putative relatives of the TAP family are shown in Figure 1.

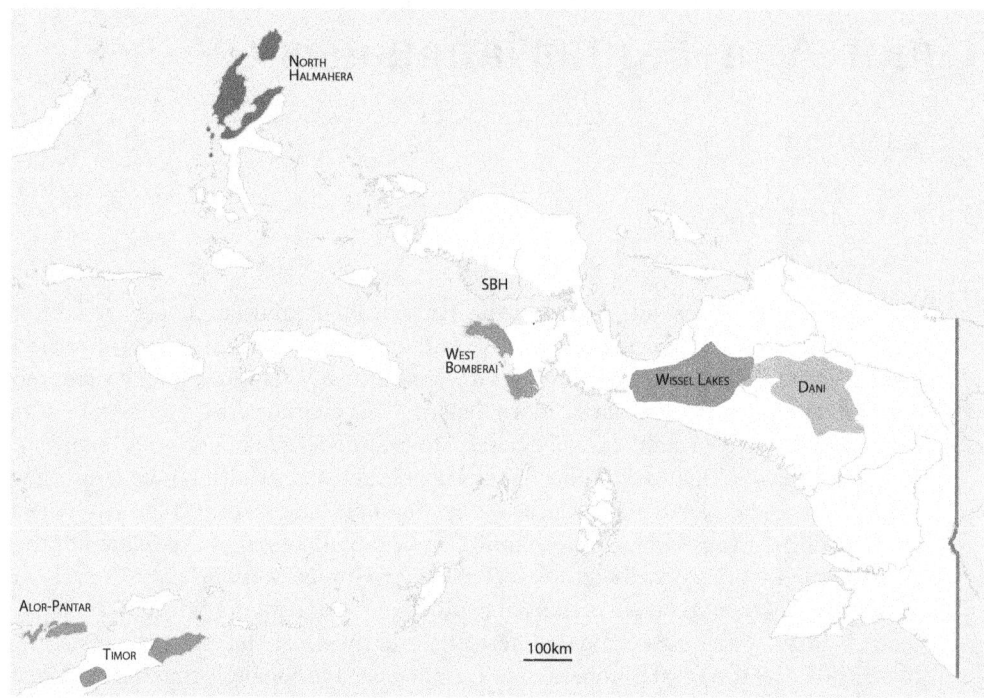

Figure 1: Location of Timor-Alor-Pantar languages (lower left) and putative related families discussed in this chapter

---

[1] This chapter differs from Robinson & Holton (2012) in that it includes a discussion of the typological profiles of the TAP family and putative relatives, and has also been updated to reflect new reconstructions, especially the proto-Timor-Alor-Pantar reconstructions in Chapter 3. In the absence of reconstructions for proto-Timor (now available in Schapper, Huber & Engelenhoven 2012) and proto-Timor-Alor-Pantar (see Chapter 3), Robinson & Holton (2012) relied exclusively on proto-Alor-Pantar reconstructions, with Timor look-alikes included where available.

[2] The extinct language of Tambora, known only from nineteenth century wordlists, was spoken some 650 km west of Pantar, and it is presumed to have been non-Austronesian (Donohue 2007a).

4 The linguistic position of the Timor-Alor-Pantar languages

In this chapter, we will consider three hypotheses about the wider relationships of the TAP family: (1) the TAP languages are related to the North Halmaheran (NH) languages; (2) the TAP languages belong to the Trans-New Guinea (TNG) family (broadly defined); and (3) the TAP languages are related to certain Papuan languages within the putative TNG family, even though the evidence linking them with TNG as a whole is indeterminate and these languages may not in fact be TNG. In order to examine the first two hypotheses we compare TAP reconstructed forms with proposed reconstructions for North Halmahera and Trans-New Guinea, respectively. In order to evaluate the third hypothesis we compare TAP reconstructions with languages from four smaller families: South Bird's Head; Wissel Lakes; Dani; and West Bomberai. Although each of these families has been claimed to be a part of some version of the larger Trans-New Guinea group, the composition of these smaller families is uncontroversial and thus allows us to evaluate potential wider affiliations while remaining agnostic as to the status of Trans-New Guinea itself. Ideally, we would compare TAP to reconstructed proto-languages for each of these four families; however, given the limited historical work done on those families, we instead choose individual languages from each family for comparison with TAP. We examine each of the three hypotheses in light of recently collected data on the TAP languages, considering pronominal, typological, and lexical evidence. Finally, we conclude with a discussion of the null hypothesis that the TAP languages form a family-level isolate.

The first hypothesis was suggested (and quickly discarded) by Capell (1944), who noted similarities between the Papuan languages of Timor and those of North Halmahera but initially refrained from asserting a genealogical relationship. By that time, the non-Austronesian character of the NH languages had long since been recognized, having been mentioned by Aa & Carel (1872) and later rigorously demonstrated by Veen (1915). Anceaux (1973), commenting on a field work report from the Pantar language Teiwa (Watuseke 1973), proposed including Teiwa and several Alor languages (Abui, Wersing, Kui) with Cowan's (1957) West Papuan group, which included NH.[3] As later formulated, Capell's (1975) West Papuan Phylum included the "Alor-Timor" languages. In fact, only one Alor language, Abui, was included in Capell's grouping, as Capell only belatedly became aware of the other extant Alor sources. Even with these additional data, Capell was quite conscious of the tenuous nature of the putative relationship between TAP (actually Alor-Timor) and North Halmahera, particularly the

---

[3] Watuseke (1973) does not identify the language as Teiwa but merely refers to it as "a language of Pantar". However, inspection of the data leaves no doubt that this is Teiwa.

lack of identifiable lexical correspondences. He thus proposed a major split between Alor-Timor (and some Bird's Head languages) on the one hand, and the rest of the West Papuan Phylum on the other. Stokhof suggested connecting TAP with several languages of the Western Bird's Head of New Guinea, concluding that "the Alor-Pantar languages form a closely related group with Cowan's West Papuan Phylum" (1975: 26). However, the putative West Papuan languages with which Stokhof compared Alor-Pantar were later reclassified as Trans-New Guinea, rendering this lexical evidence moot. More recently Donohue (2008) has revived the NH hypothesis, based largely on pronominal evidence.

With the exception of this recent work by Donohue, the second hypothesis connecting TAP with TNG has largely supplanted the NH hypothesis in the literature. Capell's (1975) paper arguing for the NH hypothesis was published with an editorial preface noting that the TAP languages should instead be included within TNG (Wurm 1975: 667). However, the accompanying paper on the TNG hypothesis in the same volume provides no data to back up this classification and instead remains skeptical as to whether TAP should be classified as Trans-New Guinea or West Papuan. In particular, the authors assert that "whichever way they [the TAP languages] are classified, they contain strong substratum elements of the other ... phyla involved" (Wurm, Voorhoeve & McElhanon 1975: 318). Only recently have additional data been provided to support the TNG hypothesis. Pawley (2001) cites lexical evidence from TAP languages in support of proto Trans-New Guinea (pTNG) reconstructions. Ross (2005) connects TAP to TNG more broadly based on pronominal evidence. Although the evidence for the TNG hypothesis is far from overwhelming, it is today the most widely received classification, appearing for example in the most recent edition of the Ethnologue (Lewis, Simons & Fennig 2013).

One of the challenges to finding support for the TNG hypothesis is the sheer size and diversity which exists within the family. Rather than only considering TNG as a whole, it is also useful to consider smaller families within TNG. Two proposals stand out. Reesink (1996) suggests connections between TAP and the South Bird's Head family (specifically the Inanwatan language). Cowan (1953) also made this connection, though he went further to group both TAP and South Bird's Head within his West Papuan Phylum. A second proposal is made by Ross (2005), who considers TAP "possibly part of a western TNG linkage" including West Bomberai, Wissel Lakes, and Dani. As Ross suggests, this more circumscribed linkage is a group of languages descended from a dialect chain and therefore characterized by overlapping innovations. In particular, Ross notes that these languages (including the Timor languages, but excluding the Alor and

4 The linguistic position of the Timor-Alor-Pantar languages

Pantar languages) all show an innovative metathesis of CV to VC in the first person singular pronoun and that the TAP languages share an innovative first person plural pronoun with the West Bomberai languages (2005: 36). We are not aware of any serious proposals connecting TAP to Papuan languages outside NH (and the West Papuan Phylum) and TNG.

The possibility that the TAP languages form a family-level isolate not demonstrably related to other Papuan languages was actually suggested by Capell, who concluded:

> Neither are the 'Papuan' languages outside New Guinea, in the Solomons, New Britain, Halmahera or Timor related to each other or to those of New Guinea. At least it cannot be assumed that any two are related.... (1944: 313)

However, this null hypothesis has not, to our knowledge, been given serious consideration in the literature. We return to this point in our conclusion (§ 6). In the meantime we evaluate the first two hypotheses in light of the typological evidence (§ 2), pronominal evidence (§ 3), and lexical evidence (§ 4). Evidence for the third hypothesis linking the TAP family with individual languages in Papua is considered in § 5.

2 Typological evidence

Given that typological features can easily cross genealogical boundaries, typological evidence for genealogical relationships should be approached with caution. Klamer, Reesink & van Staden (2008) argue that the region under consideration here—spanning from TAP to NH to New Guinea—is part of the East Nusantara linguistic area which shares a number of typological features in spite of genealogical differences among languages. Moreover, these features are not particularly unique and hence do not provide any special proof of genealogical connection in the sense of Meillet (1967). On the other hand, we feel that a volume on the Alor-Pantar languages would not be complete without a discussion of how the typological profile of the family relates to those of the surrounding Papuan languages. Nonetheless, we find little evidence for shared typological features between TAP and either the NH or TNG families. In this section we provide examples contrasting the typological profiles of these families, considering phonology (§ 2.1), morphology (§ 2.2), and syntax (§ 2.3).

2.1 Phonology

Foley (1998) suggests two typically Papuan phonological features: the presence of a single liquid phoneme and the presence of pre-nasalized stops. Neither of these putative Papuan phonological features is found in proto-Timor-Alor-Pantar (pTAP), which had at least two liquids and lacks pre-nasalized stops. The pTAP consonant inventory (based on Chapter 3), is shown in Table 1.

Table 1: pTAP consonants (based on Chapter 3)

	LABIAL	ALVEOLAR	PALATAL	VELAR	GLOTTAL
VOICELESS STOPS	p	t		k	
VOICED STOPS	b	d		g	
NASALS	m	n			
FRICATIVES		s			h
GLIDES	w		j		
LIQUIDS		l r[4]			

Nor are these features present in proto-North Halmahera (pNH), shown in Table 2.

On the other hand, both pre-nasalized stops and a single liquid phoneme are found in pTNG. Additionally, in contrast to either pTAP or pNH, pTNG contains only a single fricative (Table 3).

In many respects, these three consonant inventories are similar. Each contains two sets of stops. In pTAP and pNH, the distinction between the two sets is voicing, with one voiced set and one voiceless set. In pTNG the distinction is between oral and pre-nasalized. It is plausible that the pTNG pre-nasalized stops developed into the pTAP voiced stops. Nevertheless, considering just the four phonological features discussed above we find greater similarity between TAP and NH than between TAP and TNG, as summarized in Table 4.

---

[4] Schapper, Huber & Engelenhoven (this volume) note that there are three correspondence sets between AP on the one hand, and Timor-Kisar, on the other, and so they reconstruct a third liquid *R, but they do not speculate about the phonetic value of *R. Since none of the modern TAP languages has more than two liquids, we believe that the proto-language had just two liquids, and that the third correspondence set should be attributed to either *r or *l, with some as yet to be identified conditioning.

[5] Note that the pTNG apical stop *t may have had a flap or trill allophone (Pawley 2001: 273).

4 The linguistic position of the Timor-Alor-Pantar languages

Table 2: pNH consonants (after Wada 1980)

	LABIAL	ALVEOLAR	RETROFLEX	VELAR	GLOTTAL
VOICELESS STOPS	p	t		k	
VOICED STOPS	b	d	ɖ	g	
NASALS	m	n		ŋ	
FRICATIVES		s			h
GLIDES	w				
LIQUIDS		l	r		

Table 3: pTNG consonants (Pawley 1995; 2001)

	LABIAL	APICAL	VELAR
ORAL STOPS	p	t[5]	k
PRENASALIZED STOPS	mb	nd	ŋg
NASALS	m	n	ŋ
FRICATIVES		s	
GLIDES	w	y	
LIQUID		l	

Table 4: Summary of TAP, TNG and NH phonological features

	TAP	TNG	NH
PRE-NASALIZED STOPS	-	✓	-
SINGLE LIQUID	-	✓	-
UVULAR CONSONANT	✓	-	-
SINGLE FRICATIVE	-	✓	-

2.2 Morphology

Among the few typologically distinctive morphological features of the TAP languages is the presence of pronominal indexing of the patient-like argument of a transitive verb (P) via a pronominal prefix (see Chapter 10). Reflexes of a P prefix are widely distributed across the family and can be reconstructed to pTAP. These prefixes generally have the same form as those which index possessors on nouns, as in the Teiwa example in (1), where the third singular prefix on the verb indexes the third singular P argument, while the first singular prefix on the noun 'child' indexes the possessor.

(1) Teiwa (AP; Klamer 2010: 159)
 Name, ha?an n-oqai g-unba??
 Sir 2SG 1SG-child 3SG-meet
 'Sir, did you see (lit. meet) my child?'

However, P prefixes are in general not obligatory in TAP, and the conditions on pronominal alignment vary considerably among the individual languages of the family (Fedden et al. 2013: Chapter 10). For example, Bunaq (Timor) does not use pronominal prefixes to index inanimate P arguments. In example (2), there is no prefix on the verb because the P argument *zo* 'mango' is inanimate. In example (3), in contrast, the verb takes a third person prefix which indexes *zap* 'dog'.

(2) Bunaq (Timor; Schapper 2010: 122)
 Markus zo poi
 Markus mango choose
 'Markus chose a mango.'

(3) Bunaq (Timor; Schapper 2010: 122)
 Markus zap go-poi
 Markus dog 3-choose
 'Markus chose a dog.'

In the AP language Abui, alignment is semantic, and most non-volitional arguments are marked with pronominal prefixes, including non-volitional S arguments (Fedden et al. 2013: Chapter 10). In (4) the sole argument is volitional, so there is no marking on the verb. In (5) the first person undergoer is non-volitional and is indexed on the verb with the prefix *no-*. Likewise, in (6) the verb *wel* 'pour' takes the third person prefix *ha-* because the undergoer *Simon* is non-volitional.

4 The linguistic position of the Timor-Alor-Pantar languages

Finally, we see in (7) that even the sole argument of the verb can be indexed with a prefix if it is non-volitional.

(4) Abui (AP; Kratochvíl 2007: 80.171)
Na sei.
1SG come.down
'I come down.'

(5) Abui (AP; Kratochvíl 2007: 80.171)
Simon no-dik.
Simon 1SG-tickle
'Simon is tickling me.'

(6) Abui (AP; Kratochvíl 2007: 80.171)
Na Simon ha-wel.
1SG Simon 3-pour
'I washed Simon.'

(7) Abui (AP; Kratochvíl 2007: 80.171)
No-lila.
1SG-be.hot
'I am hot.'

A few TAP languages also permit indexing of both A and P arguments via pronominal prefixes. In such cases, the prefix paradigms for each argument are identical.

(8) Western Pantar (AP; Holton 2010)
Ke'e pi-ga-ussar.
fish 1PL-3SG-catch
'We're catching fish.'

The North Halmaheran languages also index P arguments on the verb, and as in TAP, the conditions on pronominal indexing vary considerably across different languages in the family (Holton 2008). However, pronominal indexing in NH languages differs in several respects from that found in TAP. First, not just P but also A is referenced on the verb in NH. Second, for most NH languages pronominal indexing is obligatory. Third, unlike TAP languages, the forms of A and P pronominal prefixes differ from each other in NH. That is, A and P arguments are marked by distinct paradigms, and this holds for both pronominal prefixes as well as independent pronouns. The Tobelo example in (9) illustrates these properties.

(9) Tobelo (NH; Holton 2003)
 (Ngohi) t-i-ngoriki.
 (1SG) 1SG-3SG.M-see
 'I see him.'

Moreover, in NH languages the order of verbal referents is fixed as actor-undergoer, while for TAP languages which permit two pronominal prefixes, the order may in some cases be reversed as undergoer-actor, as in (10).

(10) Western Pantar (AP; Holton fieldnotes)
 gai ya me ga-na-asang
 3POSS road LOC 3SG-1SG-say
 'I will tell him the way.' (lit., 'I will him about his road.')

Indexing of P arguments is also a prominent feature of verbs in Trans-New Guinea languages. Verbs with P arguments indexed via prefixes are found for example in the Finisterre-Huon family, and P-marking prefixes can be reconstructed at the level of pTNG (Suter 2012). Indexing of P arguments is illustrated in (11) with data from Fore, where the first person singular object is indicated with a verbal prefix.

(11) Fore (TNG; Scott 1978: 107)
 Náe na-ka-y-e.
 1SG 1SG.UND-see-3SG.ACT-DECL
 'He sees me.'

In contrast to both TAP and NH languages, pTNG indexed subjects (both A and S) via suffixes, not prefixes (Foley 2000). However, subject prefixes are not unknown in TNG languages. Foley cites Marind as an example of a Papuan language with both subject and object prefixes, noting that "Marind is the only Papuan language I know which consistently exhibits A-U-V order" (1986: 138).

(12) Marind (TNG; Drabbe 1955, cited in Foley 1986: 138)
 A-na-kipraud.
 3SG.SUBJ-1SG.OBJ-tie
 'He ties me.'

4 The linguistic position of the Timor-Alor-Pantar languages

While the Marind example in (12) may not be typical for TNG languages, it certainly shows much affinity with pronominal indexing patterns in both TAP and NH languages.

The TAP languages exhibit preposed possessor constructions, a typically Papuan feature, at least for East Nusantara (Klamer, Reesink & van Staden 2008). The possessor precedes the possessum, whether the possessor is expressed as a full noun phrase (13) or just with a pronoun (14).

(13) Western Pantar (AP; Holton fieldnotes)
yabbe si gai bla
dog that 3SG.POSS house
'the dog's house'

(14) Western Pantar (AP; Holton fieldnotes)
nai bla
1SG.POSS house
'my house'

NH languages exhibit a similar pattern of possessor-possessum order, as in the Tobelo examples below.

(15) Tobelo (NH; Holton 2003)
o-kaho ma-tau
NM-dog NM-house
'the dog's house'

(16) Tobelo (NH; Holton 2003)
ahi-tau
1SG.POSS-house
'my house'

The order possessor-possessum is also found widely among TNG languages, as illustrated by the Enga and Mian examples below.

(17) Enga (TNG; Foley 1986: 264)
namba-nyá mená
1SG-POSS pig
'my pig'

(18) Mian (TNG; Fedden 2011: 217)
 ōb   imak
 2SG.F.POSS husband
 'your husband'

The order possessum-possessor is also found in many TNG languages, particularly with inalienable nouns, as illustrated by the following examples from Fore and Barai.

(19) Fore (TNG; Scott 1978: 31)
 yaga-nene
 pig-1SG.POSS
 'my pig'

(20) Barai (TNG; Olson 1981, cited in Foley 1986)
 e   n-one
 person 1SG-POSS
 'my people'

A distinction between alienable and inalienable possession is considered a typical Papuan feature, and TAP languages share this feature. While TAP languages vary in exactly how they realize this distinction, Western Pantar is typical in realizing this distinction in the possessive pronouns. In Western Pantar the third person singular inalienable form is *ga-* rather than *gai-*, as in (21).

(21) Western Pantar (AP; Holton fieldnotes)
 ga-uta   (*gai-)
 3SG.INAL-foot (3SG.ALIEN-)
 'his/her/its foot'

Many of the TNG languages also share this distinction. In Inanwatan, alienably possessed nouns take independent pronouns, like *tigáeso* in (22), while inalienably possessed nouns take pronominal prefixes, like *na-* in (23).

(22) Inanwatan (South Bird's Head; de Vries 2004: 29, 30)[6]
 tigáe-so suqére
 3SG.F-M sago.M
 'her sago'

---

[6] The acute accent indicates lexical stress, which is distinctive in Inanwatan.

4 The linguistic position of the Timor-Alor-Pantar languages

Table 5: Summary of TAP, TNG, and NH morphological features

	TAP	TNG	NH
pronominal object prefixes (P)	✓	✓	✓
pronominal subject affixes (A/S)	(✓)	✓	✓
preposed possessors	✓	(✓)	✓
alienable/inalienable distinction	✓	✓	-

(23) Inanwatan (South Bird's Head; de Vries 2004: 29, 30)
ná-wiri
1SG-belly.M
'my belly'

While NH languages also have obligatorily possessed nouns, these languages lack a distinct inalienable possession construction. In particular, in NH languages the same possessive construction is used regardless of whether the noun is obligatorily possessed or not. In Tobelo obligatorily possessed nouns such as *lako* 'eye' (24) use the same possessive strategy as non-obligatorily possessed nouns such as *tau* 'house' (16).

(24) Tobelo (NH; Holton fieldnotes)
  a. *ma-lako*
     NM-eye
     'eye'
  b. *o-kaho ma-lako*
     NM-dog NM-eye
     'the dog's eye'
  c. *ahi-lako*
     1SG.POSS-eye
     'my eye'

The morphological features for TAP, TNG, and NH are summarized in Table 5.

2.3 Syntax

The TAP languages, like most NH and TNG (Foley 2000) languages, are right-headed and verb-final.

(25) Adang (AP; Haan 2001: 121)
 Pen ti mate sɛl alɔ ʔa-bɔʔɔi.
 John tree big CLF two 3OBV-cut
 'John cut the two big trees.'

(26) Tobelo (NH; Holton 2003)
 Ngohi o-pine t-a-ija.
 1SG NM-rice 1SG-3SG-buy
 'I bought the rice.'

(27) Mian (TNG; Fedden 2011: 344)
 Né imen-o wen-b-i=be.
 1SG taro-NC.PL eat-IPFV-1SG.SUBJ=DECL
 'I am eating taro.'

Also like the NH languages and the TNG languages, the TAP languages have postpositions, as in the Bunaq example (28), where the locative postposition *gene* follows its nominal complement *reu* 'house'.

(28) Bunaq (Timor; Schapper 2010: 104)
 neto reu gene mit
 1SG house LOC sit
 'I sit at home.'

In many TAP languages, however, the postpositions display verbal properties, as in (29), where the postposition/verb *mi* '(be) in' is modified by an aspectual marker.

(29) Adang (AP; Robinson fieldnotes)
 ʔamɔ nu meja far mi eh.
 cat one table below be.in PROG
 'A cat is beneath a table.'

Another typically Papuan feature in East Nusantara languages is the presence of clause-final negation (Klamer, Reesink & van Staden 2008). This feature is indeed found in TAP languages (30), though in NH languages the negator morpheme just follows the verb root rather than occurring in absolute final position (31).

(30) Western Pantar (AP; Holton fieldnotes)
Gang ke'e na wang yawang kauwa.
3SG.act meat eat exist agree NEG
'He doesn't like to eat meat.'

(31) Tobelo (NH; Holton 2003)
Wo-honenge-ua-ahi.
3SG.ACT-die-NEG-IPFV
'He is not yet dead.'

One notable syntactic feature absent from TAP is clause-chaining, which is one of the most distinctive features of Papuan languages in general and is particularly associated with TNG languages (Foley 1986: 175, Roberts 1997). Clause-chaining is also absent from NH languages. However, while clause-chaining may be one of the key distinguishing features of Papuan languages, it is important to note that this feature is completely absent from some TNG languages, such as Marind.

In general, syntactic features do not distinguish the TAP languages from TNG or NH (Table 6).

Table 6: Summary of TAP, TNG, and NH syntactic features

	TAP	TNG	NH
verb-final	✓	✓	✓
postpositions	✓	✓	✓
clause final negation	✓	✓	✓
clause chaining	-	(✓)	-

While the TAP languages share a number of morphological and syntactic features with TNG and NH languages, these features are typologically common, may be interrelated (such as verb-final syntax and postpositions), and they may be indicative of a linguistic area (Klamer, Reesink & van Staden 2008). We therefore do not find the typological evidence convincing of genealogical relationship.

3 Pronominal evidence

When combined with other lines of evidence, homologous pronominal paradigms can provide strong support for proposals of genealogical relatedness. However, the use of pronominal paradigms as the *sole* evidence for genealogical relatedness has been repeatedly questioned in the literature (cf. Campbell & Poser 2008). Pronominal paradigms were an important basis for the development of the Trans-New Guinea hypothesis (Wurm, Voorhoeve & McElhanon 1975), and pronouns have continued to play a starring role in attempts to subgroup the TNG languages (Ross 2005; 2006).[7] In this section we consider the strength of the pronominal evidence in evaluating the Trans-New Guinea and North Halmaheran hypotheses.

Since the full pronominal paradigm has not been reconstructed for pTAP, we consider the reconstructed pAP pronouns here. They are shown in Table 7, together with the pTNG (Ross 2005) and pNH (Wada 1980) pronouns. Note that North Halmaheran pronouns are reconstructed in two forms corresponding to actor ("subject") and undergoer ("object").

Table 7: pAP, pTNG, and pNH pronouns

	pAP	pTNG	pNH	
			ACT	UND
1SG	*na-	*na	*to-	*si-
2SG	*(h)a-	*ŋga	*no-	*ni-
3SG	*ga-	*ua, *(j)a	*mo- (FEM)	*mi- (FEM)
			*wo- (MAS)	*wi- (MAS)
			*i- (NEU)	*ja- (NEU)
1PL.INCL	*pi-	*nu, *ni	*po-	*na-
1PL.EXCL	*ni-	-	*mi-	*mi-
1DISTR	*ta-	-	-	-
2PL	*(h)i-	*nja, *ŋgi	*ni-	*ni-
3PL	*gi-	*i	*jo-	*ja-

Several structural differences are noticeable between these pronoun sets. First, AP and NH show an inclusive/exclusive distinction in first person plural which is not found in TNG. This has been argued to be an areal feature resulting from Austronesian influence (Klamer, Reesink & van Staden 2008). Second, NH but not AP or TNG distinguish gender in third person pronouns. Third, a distributive pronoun is found only in AP.

---

[7] As originally formulated, the Trans-New Guinea hypothesis linked Central and South New Guinea languages with the Finisterre-Huon languages based not on pronominal evidence but on lexical similarities (McElhanon & Voorhoeve 1970).

4 The linguistic position of the Timor-Alor-Pantar languages

We consider first the TNG pronouns. The pTNG pronominal reconstructions provide what some consider to be the strongest support for the genealogical connection between AP and TNG (Ross 2005). Both pTNG and pAP show a paradigmatic distinction between *a* in the singular and *i* in the plural. However, the correspondence is problematic due to the mismatch between the second and third person pronouns. Proto-TNG shows velar consonants in the second person forms, while pAP shows velar consonants in the third person forms. It has been suggested that the pTNG second person pronouns could have developed into the pAP second person pronouns by lenition of pTNG *ŋg > *g > *k > h. While this is possible, we find stronger evidence that the pTNG prenasalized obstruents should correspond to the pAP voiced stops (see § 4.2), if indeed the two are related at all.

Another possible scenario connecting these two paradigms is to posit a flip-flop between the second and third person pronouns, as in (32). As far as we are aware, such an inversion scenario was first proposed by Donohue & Schapper (2007).

(32) Putative flip-flop between second and third person pronouns
pTNG *ŋga '2SG' >pAP *ga- '3SG'
pTNG *ŋgi '2PL' >pAP *gi- '3PL'
pTNG *(y)a '3SG'>pAP *(h)a- '2SG'
pTNG *i '3PL'   >pAP *(h)i- '2PL'

This leaves only the fricative in the pAP second person forms unexplained, but external evidence from the Timor languages suggests that perhaps the pAP second person forms should be vowel initial (i.e., pAP *a '2SG' and *i '2PL'). While it is not impossible that the pAP pronouns descend from the pTNG pronouns in this way, connecting the two requires us to posit a flip which makes the correspondence much less striking.

The putative correspondence between the pAP and pTNG pronouns leaves at least one AP form unexplained: the AP distributive *ta- has no correspondent form in TNG. Donohue (2008) posits a connection between the AP distributive and the pNH first-singular active form *to-. According to this hypothesis the resemblance between the AP distributive and the pNH first-singular active is evidence not of a genealogical relationship but rather a borrowing relationship within a contact area encompassing the Bomberai Peninsula and South Bird's Head region. The semantic plausibility of this connection is based on an analysis of *ta- as the minimal 1/2-person pronoun in a minimal-augmented system (Donohue 2007b). However, the augmented counterpart is filled anomalously by *pi-, rather than the expected *ti-, though pAP *pi- does show striking semantic and structural similarity with pNH first person inclusive *po-. Yet in the modern Alor-Pantar languages, reflexes of *ta-, where they exist, have a clear distributive function. For example, compare the Adang first person plural inclusive (33a) with the distributive (33b).

(33) Adang (AP; Haan 2001)

    a. *Sa pi-ri bɛh.*
       3SG 1PL.INCL-ACC hit
       'She hit (all of) us.'

    b. *Sa ta-ri bɛh*
       3SG DISTR-ACC hit
       'She hit each one of us.'

The distributive function is expressed quite differently in NH languages. In Tobelo the distributive is expressed with the verb prefix *koki-* (34) rather than with a pronoun.

(34) Tobelo (NH; Holton 2003)
    ma-homoa yo-koki-honeng-oka
    NM-other 3PL-DISTR-die-PRF
    'Each of the others died.'

The AP distributive prefix is extra-paradigmatic: it does not show the vowel grading found in the other prefixes; and related independent pronouns are either absent or of limited distribution. This suggests that the pAP distributive has a distinct history from that of the other pAP pronominal forms, and that the resemblance between pNH *to '1SG' and pAP *ta '1PL.DIST' is coincidental.

The structural features of the pronominal systems are compared in Table 8. It is apparent that the AP pronominal system as a whole has relatively little in common with TNG and NH.

Given the rather speculative nature of the second-third person inversion hypothesis, the pronominal evidence does not provide very strong support for either the TNG or NH hypothesis. Nevertheless, the formal correspondence in first-person forms between AP and TNG provide tentative support for a connection between TAP and TNG.

Table 8: Summary of AP, TNG, and NH pronominal

	AP	TNG	NH
[a] singular, [i] plural	✓	✓	-
distributive pronoun	✓	-	-
inclusive/exclusive distinction	✓	-	✓
gender distinction	-	-	✓

4 Lexicon

When combined with evidence from morphological paradigms, such as pronouns, lexical evidence based on regular sound correspondences is usually considered to be compelling evidence for positing genealogical relationships between languages. Unfortunately, very little in the way of lexical evidence had been previously considered in assessing the wider genealogical relationships of the TAP languages before Robinson & Holton (2012). We consider first the lexical evidence for the NH hypothesis and then the lexical evidence for the TNG hypothesis.

4.1 Lexical evidence for the NH hypothesis

The lexical evidence for a connection between TAP and NH languages is not particularly convincing. In a list of 92 basic vocabulary terms, Capell identifies 11 which seem to show "common roots" with AP languages (1975: 685). Capell did not include data from Pantar languages and hence refers to this family as Alor-Timor. In many cases Capell's proposed Alor-Timor forms differ from the pTAP reconstructions in Chapter 3. This may be due in some cases to excessive reliance on Timor forms. In Table 9 we list Capell's Alor-Timor alongside updated pTAP forms. Where available, we use pTAP reconstructions (Chapter 3), but if no pTAP reconstruction exists, then we show lower-level reconstructions or forms from individual languages. In two cases Capell's 'Alor-Timor' form is quite different from the updated TAP form. Capell's *hele* 'stone' differs from pTAP *war but compares to Bunaq (Timor) *hol*. We have no reconstruction for 'cut' in pTAP, but Capell's form *uti* compares with Makalero (Timor) *teri*. Three of Capell's NH reconstructions are also problematic; we have noted these problems in the last column in Table 9. Capell's NH *utu 'fire' should clearly be *uku, perhaps a typographical error. Capell's *helewo 'stone' is found in Tobelo but does not reconstruct to NH. We are not able to identify Capell's *hate 'tree'; the form *gota reconstructs for the family.

Table 9: Comparison of Capell's TAP and NH, with modern TAP and NH reassessments†

	TAP (Capell)	TAP (revised)	NH (Capell)	NH (revised)
'bitter'	malara	proto-Alor (but not pAP or pTAP) *makal	*mali	
'cold'	palata	Abui, Kui palata	*malata	
'cry out'	(k)ole	Nedebang uwara, Sawila kawa, Makasae kaul 'sing'	*orehe	
'cut'	uti	Makalero teri	*tjuki	
'fall'	tapa	Western Pantar tasing, Sawila taani	*tiwa	
'fire'	ata	pTAP *hada	*utu	*uku
'flower'	buk	Blagar buma, Klon bɔːm, Kui bungan, Makasae puhu, Makalero, Bunaq buk	*hohoko	
'fly (n.)'	uhur(u)	Kaera ubar, Makalero uful, Makasae ufulae, Fataluku upuru, Oirata uhur	*guhuru	
'smell'	ʔamuhu	Teiwa min, Kaera mim-, Nedebang mini, Blagar miming, Adang muning, Klon moin, Kui mun, Wersing muing, Makasae amuh, Makalero kamuhata, also pTAP *-mVN 'nose'	*ami	
'stone'	hele	pTAP *war	*helewo	Galela teto, Tabaru madi
'tree'	ate	pTAP *hate	*hate	*gota

†Capell was not originally aware of the Pantar languages and so referred to TAP as "Alor-Timor".

4 The linguistic position of the Timor-Alor-Pantar languages

Even allowing for problematic forms in Table 9, it is difficult to infer much about regular sound correspondences from this list, since few of the correspondences repeat. A correspondence *m:*m is found in 'bitter' and 'smell'; however, the forms for 'cold' reflect a different correspondence *p:*m.

Careful inspection of Capell's proposed correspondence reveals little or no evidence for a relationship between TAP and NH languages.

Donohue (2008) lists two proposed lexical correspondences between pTAP and pNH. One of these, 'tree', is also found in Capell's list, though Donohue reconstructs pTAP *aDa. The other, pTAP *jar, pNH *aker 'water' supports a correspondence between pTAP *r and pNH *r.[8] As with Capell's similar forms, it is difficult to infer anything about sound correspondences from these two forms. Chance resemblance remains the most economical explanation, though some similarities may also be due to loans from a common source.

The lack of lexical correspondences in the data cited by Capell and by Donohue may be due in part to the unavailability of extensive lexical data for TAP. Thanks to recent work, we now have available a number of pTAP and lower-level reconstructions (see Chapters 2 and 3, and Schapper, Huber & Engelenhoven 2012). Examining the pTAP reconstructions (excluding pronouns), and drawing on pAP forms where no pTAP form is found, 63 have glosses which can also be found in Wada's (1980) pNH reconstructions or can be easily reconstructed based on existing NH data. These 63 forms are compared in Table 10.

Of these 61 forms, only 5 items (highlighted grey in Table 10) show some kind of plausible correspondence: *b:*m, *t:*t, and *k:*q. Again, with so few items it is impossible to infer anything about regular sound correspondences. And with only 8% of these basic vocabulary items showing potential cognacy, there is no clear lexical evidence for a genealogical connection between TAP and NH languages.

---

[8] Donohue actually cites the form *gala as the reconstruction for pNH 'water', rather than Wada's *aker. Moreover, the updated pTAP reconstruction for 'water' is *jira (see Chapter 3), not *jar.

Table 10: pNH forms (after Wada 1980) with TAP equivalents (after Schapper, Huber & Engelenhoven this volume), sorted alphabetically by pNH form. A double dagger ‡ indicates a pNH form which is not in Wada or a pAP form which is not reconstructed at the level of pTAP.[9]

	pNH	pTAP		pNH	pTAP
take, hold	*aho	*p(i,u)nV ‡	bird	*namo	*(h)adul
water	*aker	*jira	dream	*naner‡	*(h)ipar
blood	*aun	*waj	fish	*nawok	*habi
tail	*bikin	*-o(l,r)a[10]	ear	*ŋauk	*-wa(l,r)i
come	*bola	*mai ‡	sea	*ŋolot	*tam(a)
banana	*bole‡	*mugul	star	*ŋoma	*jib(V)
six	*butaŋa	*talam	child	*ŋopak	*-uaqal[11]
smoke	*dopo	*bunaq ‡	nose	*ŋunuŋ	*-mVN
louse/flea	*gani	*kVt ‡	eat	*odom	*nVa
salt(water)	*gasi	*tam(a)	bathe	*ohik‡	*we(l,r)i
hand	*giam	*-tan(a)	stand	*oko	*nat(er)
nail	*gitipir	*kusin ‡	they	*ona, yo	*gi- ‡
sit	*goger	*mit	belly	*pokor	*-tok ‡
bite	*goli	*ki(l)	knee	*puku	*uku ‡
tree	*gota	*hate	name	*roŋa	*-en(i,u) ‡
give	*hike	*-(e,i)na	fat/grease	*saki	*tama ‡
laugh	*hijete	*jagir	throw	*sariwi	*od ‡
village	*hoana‡	*haban ‡	two	*sinoto	*araqu ‡
spit	*hobir	*pu(l,r)V(n)	die	*soneŋ	*mV(n)
coconut	*igono‡	*wata	fruit	*sopok	*is(i) ‡
tooth	*iɲir	*-wasin	burn	*sora, soŋara	*ede ‡
spear	*kamanu	*qaba(k)‡	fly (v.)	*sosor	*jira(n) ‡
thick	*kipirin	*dumV‡	black	*tarom	*aqana ‡
tongue	*akir	*-lebu(l,r)	stone	*teto	*war
bat	*mano ‡	*madel	short	*timisi	*tukV ‡
moon	*mede	*hur(u)	pierce	*topok	*tapa(i)
ten	*mogiowok	*qar- ‡	bad	*torou	*jasi ‡
one	*moi	*nukV	drink	*udom	*nVa
betel nut	*mokoro‡	*bui ‡	fire	*uku	*hada
five	*motoha	*jiwesin ‡	he	*una, wo	*ga- ‡
			sun	*waŋe	*wad(i,u)

4 The linguistic position of the Timor-Alor-Pantar languages

4.2 Lexical evidence for the TNG hypothesis

In this section we consider the lexical evidence for the TNG hypothesis as reflected in regular sound correspondences. For this purpose we use the rather broad formulation of TNG in Pawley (2005) and Ross (2005), which includes both TAP and South Bird's Head. While no bottom-up reconstruction of proto-TNG has been completed, a set of top-down lexical reconstructions with extensive reflexes has been widely circulated as Pawley (n.d.). Some of these forms were included as support for the reconstruction of pTNG obstruents (Pawley 2001) and in other discussions of pTNG (Pawley 1998; 2012). We are not in a position here to assess the validity or quality of Pawley's reconstructions. Rather, our intent is to assess the lexical evidence for a connection between TAP and TNG based on the available data. In contrast to the NH data, the pTNG lexicon shows more striking correspondences with TAP languages. Pawley (nd) proposes 21 pTNG reconstructions with putative TAP reflexes, out of approximately 180 pTNG reconstructions. Of those, thirteen (shown in 35–47 below) appear to exhibit regular sound correspondences. Examples (35) through (40) are reconstructed to pTAP. In (35), the reconstructed pTNG form encompasses the meanings 'tree', 'wood', and 'fire', but in the TAP languages, only the latter two meanings are found. There is a separate reconstruction for 'tree' in pTAP.

(35) pTNG *inda 'tree, wood, fire', pTAP *hada 'fire, wood'

(36) pTNG *panV 'woman', pTAP *pan(a) 'girl'

(37) pTNG *amu, pTAP *hami 'breast'

(38) pTNG *na-, pTAP *nVa 'eat, drink'

(39) pTNG *kumV, pTAP *mV(n) 'die' (cf., pTim *-umV)

(40) pTNG *ata, pTAP *(h)at(V) 'excrement'

---

[9] In the pTAP / pAP reconstructions, V stands for an unidentified vowel, and N stands for an unidentified nasal. The other reconstructed consonants have their values as laid out in Table 1. The vowels, while very tentative, are assumed to have their IPA values.

[10] As mentioned in Footnote 4, Schapper, Huber & Engelenhoven (this volume), reconstruct three liquids: *l, *r, and *R based on three correspondence sets. Since none of the modern TAP languages has three liquids, we assume that *R was actually *l or *r, with some as yet to be identified conditioning, and we have therefore modified the relevant reconstructions to reflect this.

[11] Schapper, Huber & Engelenhoven (this volume) reconstruct pTAP *uaQal, where *Q is "a putative postvelar stop for which we have only very weak evidence". We prefer to render this as *uaqal, showing more transparently the value we believe this consonant would have had.

Examples (41) through (43) are found in a number of languages in both AP and Timor but have not yet been reconstructed to pTAP. Note that pTNG *L is probably a laterally released velar stop, so pharyngeal and velar fricatives would not be strange reflexes.

(41) pTNG *maL[a], Teiwa (AP) moħoʔ, Kaera (AP) *maxa*, Klon (AP) *məkɛʔ*, pTim *muka 'ground, earth'[12]

(42) pTNG *gatata, Blagar (AP) tata, Adang (AP) *taʔata*, Klon (AP) *təkat*, Kui (AP) *takata*, Abui (AP) *takata* Fataluku (Tim), Oirata (Tim) *tata* 'dry'

(43) pTNG *ini, Blagar (AP), Adang (AP) eŋ, Klon (AP), Kui (AP) -*en*, Abui (AP) -*eiŋ*, Kamang (AP) *ŋ*, Fataluku (Tim) *ina*, Makalero (Tim) *ina*, Oirata (Tim) *ina* 'eye'

Examples (44) through (47) are found in just one of the two main branches of TAP.

(44) pTNG *tukumba(C), pAP *tukV 'short'

(45) pTNG *mundu 'internal organ', Oirata (Tim) *muṭu* 'inside', Makalero *mutu* 'inside', Fataluku *mucu* 'inside', Makasae (Tim) *mutu* 'in'

(46) pTNG *sasak, Oriata (Tim) asah(a), Makasae (Tim), Fataluku (Tim) *asa*, Makalero (Tim) *hasa* 'leaf'

(47) pTNG *kitu 'leg' (possibly 'calf'), Bunaq (Tim) -*iri*, Makasae (Tim) -*iti* 'leg'

The correspondences which emerge from this set are not striking, but they are regular. Most interesting is the correspondence between the pTNG prenasalized stop and the pTAP voiced stop. Note that a correspondence between a prenasalized stop in pTNG and a voiced stop in pTAP (also a voiced stop in pAP) supports a hypothesis that pAP reflects a flip of the pTNG second person pronouns *ŋga '2SG', *ŋgi '2PL' to pAP third person pronouns *ga '3SG', *gi '3PL', respectively, although the correspondence here is velar rather than the expected alveolar, as in Table 11.

Two more forms might be included in the thirteen above, but they are somewhat problematic. The correspondence of 'neck' is based on two nasal phonemes and reflexes in just three of the nearly thirty TAP languages.

---

[12] This pTIM form is from Schapper, Huber & Engelenhoven (2012); it does not appear in Chapter 3.

4 The linguistic position of the Timor-Alor-Pantar languages

Table 11: pTNG and pTAP sound correspondences

pTNG	pTAP	examples
*t	*t	dry, short, leg, excrement
*k	*k	die, leg, short, leaf
*nd	*d	internal organ, fire
*n	*n	eat, eye, woman, 1SG, 1PL
*m	*m	die, ground, internal organ, breast
Ø	*h	fire, breast, excrement

(48) pTNG *kuma(n,ŋ)[V] (first syllable lost in some cases), Sawila (AP) -maŋ, Oirata (Tim), Fataluku (Tim) *mani* 'neck'

The form for 'lightning' likewise has a very limited distribution, with similar-looking forms occurring in just three closely related AP languages. Moreover, the vowels in the pTNG reconstruction were determined in part on the basis of the Blagar, possibly making the pTNG artificially more similar to the AP languages than otherwise warranted.

(49) pTNG *(mb, m)elak, Blagar (AP) *merax*, Retta (AP) *melak*, Kabola (AP) *mereʔ*, 'lightning'

The pTNG form for 'older sibling' shows a striking correspondence with TAP languages, but this is a nursery form, and should be excluded from determinations of genealogical similarity.

(50) pTNG *nan(a,i), pAP *nan(a), Bunaq (Tim) *nana* 'older sibling'

The pTNG form for 'to come' is also strikingly similar to the pAP, but the pAP form may have its origins in Proto-Malayo Polynesian *maRi, which is irregularly reflected as *ma* or *mai* in many Austronesian languages in the region, for example Mambai (Timor) *ma*, Manggarai (Flores) *mai*.

(51) pTNG *me-, pAP *mai 'to come'

A further four forms were excluded because their correspondences were not regular. The form for 'nose' looks promising, but pTNG *nd should correspond with pTAP *d, not a nasal.

(52) pTNG *mundu, pTAP *-mVN 'nose'

The pTNG reconstruction *wani 'who' looks similar to the Abui form *hanin* that was cited in Pawley (n.d.), but more recent research on Abui shows that 'who' is *maa*, and we know of no word *hanin* in Abui. The AP languages Adang, Hamap, and Kabola, all quite closely related, show somewhat similar forms, but the lack of correspondence in the initial consonants, combined with the limited geographic distribution, make these unlikely cognates.

(53) pTNG *wani, Adang (AP) *ano*, Hamap (AP) *hano*, Kabola (AP) *hanado* 'who'

A further two proposed cognates are simply not very similar in form to their putative TAP reflexes. The pTNG form *pululu 'fly, flutter' was originally considered cognate with Blagar (AP) *iriri, alili*, but our data show Blagar *liri*, and other cognates point to proto-Alor *liri. The competing form pAP *jira(n) has a wider distribution and is therefore reconstructed to pAP. Proto-Timor *lore suggests that Alor-Pantar *liri is older than previously assumed, but at any rate, the initial consonant from pTNG is only found in one TAP language (Fataluku (Tim) *ipile*). It seems much more likely that the resemblance between pTNG and the TAP languages is due to onomatopoeia.

(54) pTNG *pululu 'fly, flutter', Blagar (AP) *liri*, Adang (AP) *lili?*, Klon (AP) *liir*, Kui (AP) *lir*, Abui (AP) *li?*, Kamang (AP) *lila*, pTim *lore 'to fly'[13]

Likewise, further data on pTNG reconstructions for 'urine' cast doubt on the purported cognacy with TAP languages. The pTNG *[si]si, *siti, *pisi 'urine' was originally considered cognate with Oirata (Tim) *iri* 'urine, excrement'. The forms in the AP languages seem to be doublets with 'water', which is reconstructed as pTAP *jira. Although we have not established TAP correspondences for pTNG *s, there is insufficient formal similarity between the two reconstructions to retain them as cognate sets.

(55) pTNG *[si]si, *siti, *pisi 'urine', Western Pantar (AP) *jir*, Blagar (AP) *ir*, Klon (AP) *wri*, Retta (AP) *vil*, Sawila (AP) *iripiŋ* 'urine', Makalero *irih* 'urinate', Makasae *iri* 'urine', Oirata (Tim) *iri* 'urine, excrement'

In terms of lexicon, then, we are left with thirteen potential pTNG - TAP cognates and a few tentative sound correspondences (Table 11).

---

[13] Though note Makalero *uful*, Makasae *ufulae*, Fataluku *upuru*, and Oirata *uhur* 'fly (n.)'.

5 Comparison with individual languages

In the preceding section we examined evidence for a connection between TAP and TNG drawing on data from a top-down reconstruction of pTNG. Given that Pawley's putative TNG contains some five hundred languages, and that little historical reconstruction work has been done for lower level subgroups, pTNG reconstructions must be considered tentative (though some reconstructed forms are more secure than others). Hence, it is useful also to examine potential relationships of TAP directly with lower level subgroups. We focus here on four such families. The first, South Bird's Head (SBH), is not actually included in Pawley's TNG but was included in Wurm's (1982) previous formulation of TNG. This classification is detailed in Voorhoeve (1975), who along with Stokhof (1975) argues for a somewhat distant ("subphylic") connection between TAP and SBH.

The other three families considered here are all classified within Pawley's TNG. The Dani and Wissel Lakes families were part of the original core group of TNG languages proposed by Wurm, Voorhoeve & McElhanon (1975). Their membership in TNG is likely quite secure. The other TNG family considered here is West Bomberai. Like SBH, West Bomberai was originally classified by Cowan (1957) as part of the West Papuan Phylum, but it was later reclassified as TNG and included as such by Pawley. Ross (2005) also includes West Bomberai within TNG based on pronominal evidence. In fact, Ross proposes a "West Trans-New Guinea linkage" within TNG consisting of West Bomberai, Dani, Wissel Lakes, and TAP. All of these languages, including the Timor languages (but notably excluding Alor-Pantar) share an innovation whereby the pTNG first singular pronoun *na is replaced by *ani*. Ross (2005: 37) also notes that the TAP languages share with West Bomberai an innovative first-person plural form *bi (though this is an inclusive pronoun in TAP but an exclusive pronoun in West Bomberai).

In the following sub-sections we compare TAP languages to each of these four families in turn, while remaining agnostic as to the status of TAP vis-à-vis TNG. Since we lack robust reconstructions at the level of any of these families, we instead compare pTAP reconstructions (see Chapter 3) to selected individual languages from each of these families.

5.1 South Bird's Head

The South Bird's Head family is here represented by Inanwatan (ISO 639-3 szp) and Kokoda (ISO 639-3 xod). The Inanwatan pronouns are given in Table 12 (with pAP for comparison). Like the pAP and pTNG pronoun sets, these show /a/ in the singulars and /i/ in the plurals, although the Inanwatan third person singular does not follow this pattern. These are similar to the pAP pronouns in reflecting *na '1SG' instead of *an. As in the TAP languages, the pTNG first person plural pronoun *ni (if indeed Inanwatan is a TNG language) has been assigned to the exclusive, and a new form has been innovated for the inclusive. The inclusive form in Inanwatan, however, is not cognate with the inclusive in pAP. Inanwatan is also different from TAP languages in distinguishing between masculine and feminine in the third person singular.

Table 12: Inanwatan pronouns (de Vries 2004: 27-29)

	subject	possessive prefix	pAP
1SG	náiti/nári	na-	*na-
2SG	áiti/ári	a-	*(h)a-
3SG	ítigi (M)	∅	*ga-
	ítigo (F)		
1PL.INCL	dáiti	da-	*pi-
1PL.EXCL	níiti	ni-	*ni-
2PL	íiti	i(da)-	*(h)i-
3PL	ítiga	∅	*gi-

In the Inanwatan vocabulary, five forms stand out as potentially cognate with TAP.

(56) Comparison of TAP with Inanwatan (de Vries 2004)
   a. Inanwatan *mo-*, pAP *mai 'to come'
   b. Inanwatan *ni-* 'eat, drink, smoke', pTAP *nVa 'eat, drink'
   c. Inanwatan *ʔero*, pTAP *-wa(l,r)i 'ear'
   d. Inanwatan *oro*, pTAP *-ar(u) 'vagina'
   e. Inanwatan *durewo* 'wing, bird', pTAP *(h)adul 'bird'

The form for 'to come' is likely a loan from an Austronesian language (and it is not found in Timor languages). The other correspondences look promising, although we see an r:r correspondence in (d), an r:l correspondence in (e), and a correspondence between *r* and an unidentified liquid in (c).

The South Bird's Head language Kokoda also shows several promising lexical similarities with TAP, although both 'pig' and 'come' may be Austronesian loans, and the remaining items do not reconstruct to the level of pTAP. Curiously, only one of these has the same meaning as those we identified from Inanwatan even though Inanwatan and Kokoda share 20% possible lexical correspondences (de Vries 2004: 133).

(57) Comparison of TAP with Kokoda (de Vries 2004)

    a. Kokoda *ta'bai*, pTAP *baj 'pig'[14]

    b. Kokoda *kɔ'tena*, pAP *-tok 'belly, stomach'

    c. Kokoda *ɟɛria*, pAP *jira(n) 'to fly'

    d. Kokoda *mɔe*, pAP *mai 'to come'

If the suspected Austronesian loans are omitted from the list above, the number of lexical similarities between TAP and Kokoda is reduced by half to only two items.

5.2 Dani

The Dani family is here represented by Lower Grand Valley Dani (ISO 639-3 dni) for the pronouns and Western Dani (ISO 693-3 dnw) for the vocabulary. The Dani pronouns are given in Table 13 (with pAP for comparison since pTAP reconstructions are not yet available). Like the pAP and pTNG pronouns, they have the paradigmatic vowels /a/ for singulars and /i/ for plurals, plus the use of /n/ for first person, which is why Ross (2005) suggested they might be related to the TAP languages. The Dani pronouns more closely match the reconstructed pAP pronouns than either match the pTNG pronouns, in that Dani also lacks a velar consonant in the second person forms (cf. Table 7). As with pAP, the Dani pronouns could be explained by positing a flip between the second and third person pronouns. If AP were indeed TNG, then this flip could constitute evidence of shared innovation in the AP and Dani group.

Curiously, Dani shows *an* for the independent pronoun and *n(a)*- for the pronominal prefix. The pAP 1SG pronouns (both the reconstructed prefix, and the various derived independent pronouns found in individual AP languages) reflect *na-, like the pTNG *na. The Timor languages, in contrast, reflect *an in the 1SG. Donohue (p.c.) suggests that perhaps the pTNG reconstruction should instead be *an, and that many TNG languages have independently leveled the pronominal paradigm so that all the singulars are of the shape Ca. Donohue suggests that

---

[14] Robinson (2015) provides evidence that 'pig' was borrowed into pAP. It was likely also borrowed separately into pTim after the breakup of pTAP.

Table 13: Lower Grand Valley Dani pronouns (Stap 1966: 145-6), with pAP equivalents

	personal pronouns	possessive prefixes	pAP
1SG	*an*	*n(a)-*	*na-
2SG	*hat*	*h(a)-*	*(h)a-
3SG	*at*	Ø-	*ga-
1PL	*nit*	*nin-*	*pi-, *ni-
2PL	*hit*	*hin-*	*(h)i-
3PL	*it*	*in-*	*gi-

this is a simpler explanation for the pronominal distributions than claiming independent changes of *na > *an. On the other hand, the fact that the bound 1SG TNG pronoun reconstructs as *na- suggests that the CV form is older.

In the vocabulary, Western Dani shares a handful of look-alikes with the TAP languages. These are given below.

(58) Comparison of TAP with Western Dani (Purba, Warwer & Fatubun 1993)
 a. Western Dani *ji*, pTAP *jira 'water'
 b. Western Dani *mugak* 'ko banana', pTAP *mugul 'banana'
 c. Western Dani *maluk*, proto-Alor (but not pAP or pTAP) *makal 'bitter'
 d. Western Dani *nono* 'what', Adang (AP) *ano*, Hamap (AP) *hano*, Kabola (AP) *hanado* 'who'
 e. Western Dani *o* 'house', Kui (AP) *ow*, Klon (AP) *əwi*

Terms for 'water' and 'banana' are reconstructable to pTAP, but the other lookalikes occur only in the restricted geographic subset of the TAP languages, significantly increasing the probability of chance resemblance due to researcher bias. That is, with some 30 languages, there are bound to be chance resemblances with individual languages, so methodologically, we should restrict ourselves to comparing proto-language with proto-language, rather than comparing to individual daughter languages within TAP.

5.3 Wissel Lakes

The Wissel Lakes family is here represented by Ekari (ISO 639-3 ekg). The Ekari pronouns are listed in Table 14 (with pAP for comparison). As in pAP and pTNG,

4 The linguistic position of the Timor-Alor-Pantar languages

Ekari pronouns have the paradigmatic vowels /a/ for singulars and /i/ for plurals, plus the use of /n/ for first person. Like the Dani pronouns and the Timor pronouns, the Ekari pronouns show *ani* in the independent pronouns and *na-* in the prefixes. Unlike TAP and Dani, however, the Ekari pronouns show velar consonants in the second person, suggesting a straightforward inheritance from the prenasalized velars of pTNG.

We identified five potential cognates in the vocabulary; these are listed in (59) below.

(59) Comparison of TAP with Ekari (Steltenpool 1969)
 a. Ekari *nai* 'eat, drink', pTAP **nVa* 'eat, drink'
 b. Ekari *menii* 'give to him/her/them (irregular)', pTAP **-(e,i)na* 'to give'
 c. Ekari *mei* 'come', pAP **mai* 'come'
 d. Ekari *maki* 'land', Teiwa (AP) *moħoʔ*, Kaera (AP) *maxa*, Klon (AP) *məkɛʔ*, pTim **muka*
 e. Ekari *owaa* 'house', Kui (AP) *ow*, Klon (AP) *əwi*

Of these potential cognates, only 'eat' and 'give' are reconstructed to pTAP, though 'give' only matches in a subset of phonemes. As mentioned before, it is likely that both Ekari and AP borrowed 'come' from Austronesian sources (see discussion in § 4). The forms for 'house' are only found in a geographical subset of the TAP languages, leaving only 'eat, drink' and 'land' as solid-looking potential cognates.

Table 14: Ekari pronouns (Drabbe 1952), with pAP equivalents

	free	object prefix	pAP
1SG	ani	na-	*na-
2SG	aki	ka-	*(h)a-
3SG	okai̯	e-	*ga-
1DU	inai̯	-	
2DU	ikai̯		
3DU	okeai̯		
1PL	inii	ni-	*pi-, *ni-
2PL	ikii	ki-	*(h)i-
3PL	okei̯	e-	*gi-

5.4 West Bomberai

In the West Bomberai languages, stronger lexical similarities to TAP languages emerge, and we can posit tentative sound correspondences. The West Bomberai family is composed of three languages: Iha (ISO 639-3 ihp), Baham (bdw) and Karas (kgv), with the latter of these thought to be more distantly related to the other two.

The Iha pronouns are given in Table 15 (with pAP for comparison). Iha shows /o/ in the first and second person singular and /i/ in the other pronouns, paralleling the /a/ - /i/ paradigms of pTNG and pAP. Like Dani, Ekari, and the Timor languages, the Iha first person singular pronoun is VC as opposed to the CV pronouns of Inanwatan, pTNG, and pAP. Iha also shows a similar metathesis in the first person inclusive *in* from pTNG *ni. Like pTNG, Iha shows velar consonants in the second person, as opposed to the velar third person seen in pAP, suggesting that Iha did not share the proposed innovative flip of second and third person pronouns. On the other hand, one of the sound correspondences outlined below (Iha k : pAP ∅) suggests that perhaps Iha *ko* '2SG' and *ki* '2PL' correspond to pAP *(h)a- '2SG' pAP *(h)i- '2PL', respectively. The reconstruction of *h in the second person pAP pronouns is based on only two languages (Teiwa and Western Pantar), and the other AP languages have vowel-initial second person pronouns, which matches with the Iha k : pAP ∅ correspondence.

Table 15: Iha personal pronouns (Donohue, p.c.), with pAP equivalents

	Iha	pAP
1SG	on	*na-
3SG	mi	*ga-
1PL.INCL	mbi	*pi-
1PL.EXCL	in	*ni-
2PL	ki	*(h)i-
3PL	mi	*gi-

We identified thirteen potential TAP cognates in the Iha vocabulary (Donohue, p.c.), although some do not reconstruct to the level of pTAP and instead show similarities with the reconstructed pAP or forms in individual languages. The form 'eat, drink' has been reconstructed as pTNG *na- 'eat, drink'. As mentioned in § 3, the term for older sibling has been reconstructed as pTNG *nan(a,i), although this could be a nursery form.

(60) Potential cognates between Iha and TAP
   a. Iha *nwV* 'eat', pTAP *nVa 'eat, drink'
   b. Iha *tan*, pTAP *-tan(a) 'arm/hand'
   c. Iha *wor*, pAP *-o(l,r)a 'tail'[15]
   d. Iha *kar*, pTAP *-ar(u) 'vagina'
   e. Iha *wek*, pTAP *waj 'blood'
   f. Iha *ne*, pAP *-en(i,u), pTim *-nej 'name'
   g. Iha *jet*, pTAP *jagir 'laugh'
   h. Iha *mbjar*, pTAP *dibar 'dog'
   i. Iha *mħen*, pTAP *mit 'sit'
   j. Iha *iħ*, pAP *is(i) 'fruit'
   k. Iha *nen* 'older brother', Iha *nan* 'older sister', pAP *nan(a) 'elder sibling'
   l. Iha *nemehar*, Teiwa (AP) *masar* 'man, male'
   m. Iha *ja*, Blagar (AP) *dʒe* 'boat'

Based on these thirteen potential cognates in the lexicon, plus the potential cognates in the pronouns, we can suggest possible sound correspondences (Table 16).

But some of these correspondences conflict with each other. Note, for example that the h:s correspondence of 'man' and the ħ:s correspondence of 'fruit' conflict with ħ:t correspondence of 'sit'. Without more examples, it is difficult to determine whether these conflicts are due to conditioned sound change or false cognates. We posit only one conditioned correspondence, that of w:Ø before a back rounded vowel and w:w elsewhere.

The West Bomberai language Baham also shows striking similarities to TAP languages. The Baham pronouns are given in Table 17, with the pAP pronouns for comparison. In the possessives, these pronouns show a first singular *ne*, a third singular *ka*, and a first plural *ni* that appear cognate to the corresponding pAP pronouns. The third person plural may be cognate in the first segment. Other pronouns appear innovative.

The Baham vocabulary reveals thirteen potential TAP cognates. Six of these terms are also found in Iha, and three have been reconstructed for pTNG: pTNG *na- 'eat, drink', pTNG *inda 'tree', and pTNG *tukumba(C) 'short'.

(61) Potential cognates between TAP and Baham (Flassy, Ruhukael & Rumbrawer 1987)

---

[15] As mentioned above, Schapper, Huber & Engelenhoven (this volume) reconstruct a third liquid (in addition to *l and *r), but we believe that third correspondence set should be assigned to either *l or *r with an as yet to be identified conditioning.

Table 16: Possible Iha : pTAP sound correspondences

Iha	pTAP	examples
r	r	vagina, man, dog, tail
n	n	eat, name, arm, older sibling, 1SG
m	m	sit, man
w	Ø before /o/, w elsewhere	tail blood
k	Ø	vagina, blood
k	h	2SG, 2PL
h, ħ	s	man, fruit†
ħ	t	sit
mb	b	dog
mb	p	1PL.INCL
j	j	laugh, boat‡
t	t	arm
t	r	laugh
Ø	g	laugh

†Note that Teiwa [s] is the regular reflex of pAP *s, which is, in turn, the regular reflex of pTAP *s. ‡Note that Blagar [dʒ] is the regular reflex of pAP *j, which, in turn, is the regular reflex of pTAP *j.

Table 17: Baham pronouns (Flassy, Ruhukael & Rumbrawer 1987)

	personal	possessive	pAP
1SG	*anduu*	*ne*	*na-
2SG	*tow*	*te*	*(h)a-
3SG	*kpwaw*	*ka*	*ga-
1PL	*unduu*	*ni*	*pi-, *ni-
2PL	*kujuu*	*kuju*	*(h)i-
3PL	*kinewat*	*kinewaat*	*gi-

a. Baham *nowa* 'eat', pTAP *nVa 'eat, drink'
b. Iha: pTAP sound correspondences Baham *adoq* 'tree', pTAP *hada 'fire, wood'
c. Baham *toqoop*, pAP *tukV 'short'

4 The linguistic position of the Timor-Alor-Pantar languages

   d. Baham *pkwujer*, pTAP *wa(l,r)i 'ear'
   e. Baham *kaar*, pAP *-ar(u) 'vagina'
   f. Baham *wijek*, pTAP *waj 'blood'
   g. Baham *mungguo*, pTAP *mugul 'banana'
   h. Baham *wuor tare*, pTAP *o(l,r)a 'tail'
   i. Baham *waar*, pTAP *war 'stone'
   j. Baham *ɲie*, pAP *-en(i,u), pTim *-nej 'name'
   k. Baham *meheen*, pTAP *mit 'sit'
   l. Baham *jambar*, pTAP *dibar 'dog'
   m. Baham *wawa*, cf., Teiwa (AP) *wow*, Nedebang (AP) *wowa*, Kaera (AP) *wow* 'mango'

Once again, based on these thirteen potential cognates and the pronouns we can suggest potential sound correspondences (Table 18). Unsurprisingly, these correspondences are similar to the ones we propose for Iha, including a correspondence of pre-nasalized stops in Baham to voiced stops in pTAP, although the Baham form for 'tree' (cf. TAP 'fire, wood') does not fit that trend.

The West Bomberai language Karas also shows several potential cognates with TAP languages, although information on Karas is more sparse than for Iha or Baham. In the vocabulary (Donohue, p.c.), nine potential cognates were identified, six of which are also found in both Iha and Baham. Three of these are reconstructed for pTNG: *na- 'eat, drink', pTNG *me-'to come', and pTNG *amu 'breast'.

(62) Potential cognates between TAP/AP and Karas

   a. Karas *nɪn* 'eat', pTAP *nVa 'eat, drink'
   b. Karas *tan*, pTAP *-tan(a) 'arm, hand'
   c. Karas *ɔrʊn*, pTAP *o(l,r)a 'tail'
   d. Karas *bal*, pTAP *dibar 'dog'
   e. Karas *wat*, pTAP *wata 'coconut'
   f. Karas *am*, pTAP *hami 'breast'
   g. Karas *i:n*, pAP *-en(i,u), pTim *-nej 'name'
   h. Karas *mej*, pAP *mai 'to come'

Table 18: Possible Baham : pTAP sound correspondences

Baham	pTAP	examples
r	r	ear, vagina, tail, stone, dog
k	Ø	ear, vagina, blood
k	h	3SG
q	k	short
q	Ø	fire
p	Ø	short, ear
w	Ø before /o/, w elsewhere	tail blood, mango, stone, ear
n, ɲ	n	eat, name, 1SG, 1PL
m	m	banana, sit
mb	b	dog
ŋg	g/k	banana
d	d	fire
j	d	dog
t	t	short
h	t	sit
Ø	h	fire
Ø	l	banana

We can establish tentative correspondences from these forms (Table 19), although most correspondences occur only once in these data, and the final /n/ in Karas 'tail' is unexplained.

In the lexicon, then, the strongest correspondences are with West Bomberai languages, allowing us to posit some (very tentative) sound correspondences. In the pronouns, Iha shows an inclusive/exclusive distinction, with an exclusive pronoun that looks superficially similar to the reconstructed pAP inclusive pronoun *pi-. However, the sound correspondences suggest Iha mb : pTAP p, so perhaps both forms are independently innovated, with the similarity in vowels due to analogy with other pronouns in the paradigm (i.e., plurals have the vowel /i/) and the similarity in consonants due to chance. An alternative explanation would rely on borrowing, which we return to in the following section.

Table 19: Possible Karas : pAP sound correspondences

Karas	pAP	examples
m	m	come, breast
n	n	eat, arm, name
n	Ø	tail, eat
t	t	arm, coconut
r	L	tail
b	b	dog
l	r	dog
w	w	coconut
Ø	h	breast

6 Discussion

We have considered three hypotheses regarding the wider genealogical affiliations of the TAP languages. We now return to the null hypothesis proposed in § 1 (that the TAP languages are a family-level isolate) and consider the strength of the evidence with regard to each of the proposals.

The pronominal evidence points much more clearly toward a link with TNG as opposed to NH. The TAP pronouns share with TNG a vowel grading /a/ vs. /i/ in the singular vs. plural, respectively. In addition, TNG second person pronouns correspond well with TAP third person pronouns, although this correspondence requires us to posit a semantic flip between second and third person forms. This flip renders the pronominal evidence much weaker than it otherwise might be. The primary trace of similarity between the TAP and NH pronouns lies in the TAP first person distributive form, which resembles the NH first person singular. It is of course possible that the TAP pronoun system has been influenced by both TNG and NH languages, as suggested by Donohue (2008).

In the lexicon, there is no evidence supporting a genealogical connection between TAP and NH languages. The lexical evidence for a link with TNG is more promising, and a few regular sound correspondences emerge, but a critical eye limits the number to thirteen, so we cannot establish a robust connection. However, if we focus our attention just on the West Bomberai languages, the pronominal and lexical evidence looks more promising and warrants further investigation. It is possible that the TAP and Bomberai languages are related either via a deep genealogical connection or via a more casual contact relationship. If it is a genealogical relationship, it is not yet clear whether they are both part of TNG or whether they share a relationship independent of that family.

The spread of TNG is conventionally linked to the development of agriculture in the New Guinea highlands about 10,000 years ago (Bellwood 2001), with a westward spread somewhat later, perhaps around 6,000 BP (Pawley 1998). This would place any putative TAP-TNG genealogical connection at the upper limits of what is possible using the comparative method. Another possibility is that the weak signal linking TAP with Bomberai is the result not of an ancient genealogical connection, but rather of more recent contact. The West Bomberai groups, for example, have a history of slaving (Klamer, Reesink & van Staden 2008: 109). It is possible that they took Timor-Alor-Pantar peoples as slaves at some point, and that this is the source of the connection between the two groups. More investigation of the social history of pre-Austronesian contact in East Nusantara is greatly needed.

In conclusion, the existing evidence provides only weak support for a connection between TAP and Papuan languages spoken to the east. The most promising hypothesis would connect TAP with the West Bomberai languages, but even here the evidence is thin and does not support a definitive conclusion. We hope that new field research on the Bomberai languages, combined with reconstruction of proto-Bomberai, will eventually help clarify this question.

Acknowledgements

Field work on the Alor-Pantar languages was supported by grants from the Netherlands Organization for Scientific Research, the UK Arts and Humanities Council, and the US National Science Foundation (NSF-SBE 0936887), under the aegis of the European Science Foundation EuroBABEL programme. The authors are indebted to their colleagues in the EuroBABEL Alor-Pantar project for generously sharing their data and analyses, and for providing feedback on early versions of this paper. The authors also wish to thank numerous colleagues in Alor and Pantar who assisted with data collection.

Abbreviations

1	1st person	P	most patient-like argument
2	2nd person		
3	3rd person	pAP	proto-Alor-Pantor
A	most agent-like argument	pTIM	proto-Timor
ACC	accusative	PRF	perfective
ACT	actor	PL	plural
ALIEN	alienable	pNH	proto-North-Halmahera
C	consonant		
CLF	classifier	POSS	possessive
DECL	declarative	PROG	progressive
DIST	distal	pTAP	proto-Timor-Alor-Pantar
DISTR	distributive		
DU	dual	pTNG	proto-Trans-New-Guinea
EXCL	exclusive		
F	feminine	SBH	South Bird's Head
INAL	inalienable	SG	singular
INCL	inclusive	SUBJ	subject
IPFV	imperfective	TAP	Timor-Alor-Pantar
LOC	locative	TNG	Trans-New Guinea
M	masculine	UND	undergoer
N	nasal	V	verb
NC	noun class	v.	verb (given when English translation is ambiguous, e.g. 'fly (v.)'
NEG	negator		
NH	North Halmaheran		
NM	noun marker		
OBJ	object	V	vowel
OBV	obviative		

References

Aa, Robide van der & Pieter Jan Batist Carel. 1872. Een tweetal bijdragen tot de kennis van Halmahera. *Bijdragen tot de Taal-, Land- en Volkenkunde* 19. 233–239.

Anceaux, J. C. 1973. Naschrift. *Bijdragen tot de Taal-, Land- en Volkenkunde* 129(345-346).

Bellwood, Peter. 2001. Early agriculturist population diasporas? farming, language, and genes. *Annual Review of Anthropology* 30. 181–207.

Campbell, Lyle & William J. Poser. 2008. *Language classification: History and method*. Cambridge University Press.

Capell, Arthur. 1944. Peoples and languages of Timor. *Oceania* 15(3). 19–48.

Capell, Arthur. 1975. The West Papuan phylum: General, and Timor and areas further west. In Stephen A. Wurm (ed.), *New Guinea area languages and language study*, Papuan Languages and the New Guinea linguistic scene, vol. 1, 667–716. Canberra: Research School of Pacific & Asian Studies, Australian National University.

Cowan, H. K. J. 1957. A large Papuan language phylum in West New Guinea. *Oceania* 28. 159–166.

Cowan, Hendrik Karel Jan. 1953. *Voorlopige resultaten van een ambtelijk taalonderzoek in Nieuw-Guinea*. 'S-Gravenhage: Martinus Nijhoff.

de Vries, Lourens J. 2004. *A short grammar of Inanwatan: an endangered language of the Bird's head of Papua, Indonesia* (Pacific Linguistics 560). Canberra: Research School of Pacific & Asian Studies, Australian National University.

Donohue, Mark. 2007a. The Papuan language of Tambora. *Oceanic Linguistics* 46(2). 520–537.

Donohue, Mark. 2007b. *The phonological history of the languages of the non-Austronesian languages of Southern Indonesia*. Paper presented at the Fifth East Nusantara Conference, August 1-3. Kupang.

Donohue, Mark. 2008. Bound pronominals in the West Papuan languages. In Claire Bowern, Bethwyn Evans & Luisa Miceli (eds.), *Morphology and language history: In honour of Harold Koch*, 43–58. Amsterdam: John Benjamins.

Donohue, Mark & Antoinette Schapper. 2007. *Towards a morphological history of the languages of Timor, Alor, and Pantar*. Paper presented at the Fifth East Nusantara Conference. Universitas Nusa Cendana, Kupang, Nusa Tenggara Timur, Indonesia, August 1-3.

Drabbe, Peter. 1952. *Spraakkunst van het Ekagi: Wisselmeren Ned. N. Guinea*. The Hague: Martinus Nijhoff.

Drabbe, Peter. 1955. *Spraakkunst van het Marind: Zuidkust Nederlands Nieuw-Guinea*. Vol. 11 (Studia Instituti Anthropos). Wien-Mödling: Drukkerij van het Missiehuis St. Gabriël.

Fedden, Sebastian. 2011. *A grammar of Mian*. Vol. 55 (Mouton Grammar Library). Berlin: Mouton de Gruyter.

Fedden, Sebastian, Dunstan Brown, Greville G. Corbett, Marian Klamer, Gary Holton, Laura C. Robinson & Antoinette Schapper. 2013. Conditions on pronominal marking in the Alor-Pantar languages. *Linguistics* 51(1). 33–74.

Flassy, Don A. L., Constantinoepel Ruhukael & Frans Rumbrawer. 1987. *Fonologi Bahasa Bahaam*. Jakarta: Departmen Pendidikan dan Kebudayaan.

Foley, William A. 1986. *The Papuan languages of New Guinea* (Cambridge language surveys). Cambridge: Cambridge University Press.

Foley, William A. 1998. Toward understanding Papuan languages. In Jelle Miedema, Cecilia Odé & Rien A. C. Dam (eds.), *Perspectives on the Bird's Head of Irian Jaya, Indonesia*, 503–518. Amsterdam: Rodopi.

Foley, William A. 2000. The languages of New Guinea. *Annual Review of Anthropology* 29(1). 357–404.

Haan, Johnson Welem. 2001. *The grammar of Adang: a Papuan language spoken on the island of Alor East Nusa Tenggara - Indonesia*. Sydney: University of Sydney PhD thesis.

Holton, Gary. 2003. *Tobelo*. Vol. 328 (Languages of the World/Materials). München: Lincom.

Holton, Gary. 2008. The rise and fall of semantic alignment in North Halmahera, Indonesia. In M. Donohue & S. Wichmann (eds.), *The typology of semantic alignment*, 252–276. Oxford: Oxford University Press.

Holton, Gary. 2010. Person-marking, verb classes and the notion of grammatical alignment in Western Pantar (Lamma). In Michael Ewing & Marian Klamer (eds.), *Typological and areal analyses: contributions from east Nusantara*, 97–117. Canberra: Pacific Linguistics.

Klamer, Marian. 2010. *A grammar of Teiwa* (Mouton Grammar Library 49). Berlin: Mouton de Gruyter.

Klamer, Marian, Ger P. Reesink & Miriam van Staden. 2008. East Nusantara as a linguistic area. In Pieter Muysken (ed.), *From linguistic areas to areal linguistics* (Studies in Language Companion Series 90), 95–149. Amsterdam: John Benjamins.

Kratochvíl, František. 2007. *A grammar of Abui: a Papuan language of Alor*. Utrecht: LOT.

Lewis, Paul M., Gary F. Simons & Charles D. Fennig. 2013. *Ethnologue: Languages of the world*. 17th edn. Dallas: SIL International. http://www.ethnologue.com.

McElhanon, Kenneth A. & C. Voorhoeve. 1970. *The Trans-New Guinea phylum: explorations in deep-level genetic relationships* (Pacific Linguistics: Series B 16). Canberra: Research School of Pacific & Asian Studies, Australian National University.

Meillet, Antoine. 1967. *The comparative method in historical linguistics*. Paris: Champion.

Olson, Michael. 1981. *Barai clause junctures: toward a functional theory of interclausal relations.* Canberra: Australian National University PhD thesis.

Pawley, Andrew K. 1995. C. L. Voorhoeve and the Trans New Guinea phylum hypothesis. In Connie Baak, Mary Bakker & Dick van der Meij (eds.), *Tales from a concave world: liber amicorum Bert Voorhoeve*, 83–123. Department of Languages, Cultures of Southeast Asia & Oceania, Leiden University.

Pawley, Andrew K. 1998. The Trans New Guinea phylum hypothesis: a reassessment. In Cecilia Odé Jelle Miedema & Rien A. C. Dam (eds.), *Perspectives on the Bird's Head of Irian Jaya, Indonesia*, 655–690. Amsterdam: Rodopi.

Pawley, Andrew K. 2001. The Proto Trans New Guinea obstruents: arguments from top-down reconstruction. In Andrew K. Pawley, Malcolm Ross & Darrell Tryon (eds.), *The boy from Bundaberg: studies in Melanesian linguistics in honour of Tom Dutton*, 261–300. Canberra: Pacific Linguistics.

Pawley, Andrew K. 2005. The chequered career of the Trans New Guinea hypothesis: recent research and its implications. In Andrew K. Pawley, Robert Attenborough, Jack Golson & Robin Hide (eds.), *Papuan pasts: cultural, linguistic and biological history of the Papuan-speaking peoples*, 67–108. Canberra: Pacific Linguistics.

Pawley, Andrew K. 2012. How reconstructable is Proto Trans New Guinea? problems, progress, prospects. In Harald Hammarström & Wilco van den Heuvel (eds.), *History, contact and classification of Papuan languages* (LLM Special Issue), 88–164. Port Moresby: Linguistic Society of Papua New Guinea.

Pawley, Andrew K. nd. *Some Trans New Guinea phylum cognate sets.* Canberra: Department of Linguistics, Research School of Pacific & Asian Studies, Australian National University.

Purba, Theodorus T., Onesimus Warwer & Reimundus Fatubun. 1993. *Fonologi Bahasa Dani Barat.* Jakarta: Departemen Pendidikan dan Kebudayaan.

Reesink, Ger P. 1996. Morpho-syntactic features of the Bird's Head languages. In Ger P. Reesink (ed.), *Studies in Irian languages*, chap. 1.

Roberts, John R. 1997. Switch-reference in Papua New Guinea: a preliminary survey. *Papers in Papuan Linguistics* 3. Andrew K. Pawley (ed.). 101–241.

Robinson, Laura C. 2015. The Alor-Pantar (Papuan) languages and Austronesian contact in East Nusantara. In Malcom Ross & I Wayan Arka (eds.), *Language change in Austronesian languages.* Canberra: Asia-Pacific Linguistics.

Robinson, Laura C. & Gary Holton. 2012. Reassessing the wider genetic affiliations of the Timor-Alor-Pantar languages. In Harald Hammarström & Wilco van der Heuvel (eds.), *History, contact and classification of Papuan languages*

(Language and Linguistics in Melanesia Special Issue 2012, Part I), 59–87. Port Moresby: Linguistic Society of New Guinea.

Ross, Malcolm. 2005. Pronouns as preliminary diagnostic for grouping Papuan languages. In Andrew K. Pawley, Robert Attemborough, Jack Golson & Robin Hide (eds.), *Papuan pasts: cultural, linguistic and biological histories of Papuan-speaking peoples*, 15–65. Canberra: Pacific Linguistics.

Ross, Malcolm. 2006. Pronouns as markers of genetic stocks in non-Austronesian languages of New Guinea, island Melanesia and Eastern Indonesia. In Andrew K. Pawley, Malcolm Ross & Meredith Osmond (eds.), *Papuan languages and the trans New Guinea family*. Canberra: Pacific Linguistics.

Schapper, Antoinette. 2010. *Bunaq: a Papuan language of central Timor*. Canberra: Australian National University PhD thesis.

Schapper, Antoinette, Juliette Huber & Aone van Engelenhoven. 2012. The historical relations of the Papuan languages of Timor and Kisar. In Harald Hammarström & Wilco van den Heuvel (eds.), *History, contact and classification of Papuan languages*, 194–242. Language and Linguistics in Melanesia, Special Issue: On the History, Contact & Classification of Papuan languages - Part I. Port Moresby: Linguistic Society of Papua New Guinea.

Schapper, Antoinette, Juliette Huber & Aone van Engelenhoven. this volume. The relatedness of Timor-Kisar and Alor-Pantar languages: A preliminary demonstration. In Marian Klamer (ed.), *The Alor-Pantar languages*, 99–154. Berlin: Language Science Press.

Scott, Graham. 1978. *The fore language of Papua New Guinea* (Pacific Linguistics: Series B 47). Canberra: Research School of Pacific & Asian Studies, Australian National University.

Stap, Petrus A. M. van der. 1966. *Outline of Dani morphology*. 'S-Gravenhage: Rijksuniversiteit te Leiden PhD thesis. http://papuaweb.anu.edu.au/dlib/bk1/kitlv/index.html#stap-1966.

Steltenpool, J. 1969. *Ekagi-Dutch-English-Indonesian dictionary* (Verhandelingen van het KITLV 56). The Hague: Martinus Nijhoff.

Stokhof, W. A. L. 1975. *Preliminary notes on the Alor and Pantar languages (East Indonesia)* (Pacific Linguistics: Series B 43). Canberra: Australian National University.

Suter, Edgar. 2012. Verbs with pronominal object prefixes in Finisterre-Huon languages. In Harald Hammarström & Wilco van den Heuvel (eds.), *History, contact and classification of Papuan languages* (LLM Special Issue 2012-I), 23–58. Port Moresby: Linguistic Society of Papua New Guinea.

Veen, Hendrik van der. 1915. *De Noord-Halmahera'se taalgroep tegenover de austronesiese talen*. Leiden: van Nifterik.

Voorhoeve, C. L. 1975. The central and Western areas of the Trans-New Guinea phylum: Central and Western trans-New Guinea phylum languages. In Stephen A. Wurm (ed.), *New Guinea area languages and language study vol 1: Papuan languages and the New Guinea linguistic scene* (Pacific Linguistics: Series C 38), 345–460. Canberra: Research School of Pacific & Asian Studies, Australian National University.

Wada, Yuiti. 1980. Correspondence of consonants in North Halmahera languages and the conservation of archaic sounds in Galela. In *The Galela of Halmahera: A preliminary survey* (Senri Ethnological Studies 7), 497–529. Osaka: National Museum of Ethnology.

Watuseke, F. S. 1973. Gegevens over de taal van Pantar: een Irian taal. *Bijdragen tot de Koninklijk Instituut voor Taal, Land en Volkenkunde* 129. 340–346.

Wurm, Stephen A. (ed.). 1975. *New Guinea area languages and language study vol 1: Papuan languages and the New Guinea linguistic scene* (Pacific Linguistics: Series C 38). Canberra: Research School of Pacific & Asian Studies, Australian National University. http://www.papuaweb.org/dlib/bk/pl/C38/_toc.html.

Wurm, Stephen A. 1982. *The Papuan languages of Oceania* (Ars Linguistica 7). Tübingen: Gunter Narr.

Wurm, Stephen A., C. L. Voorhoeve & Kenneth A. McElhanon. 1975. The trans-New Guinea phylum in general. In Stephen A. Wurm (ed.), *New Guinea area languages and language study vol 1: Papuan languages and the New Guinea linguistic scene* (Pacific Linguistics: Series C 38), 299–322. Canberra: Research School of Pacific & Asian Studies, Australian National University.

Chapter 5

Kinship in the Alor-Pantar languages

Gary Holton

> *Although virtually all of the societies of eastern Indonesia practise some form of marital alliance between descent groups, there is an exuberant and sometimes perplexing variation in the form that such alliance systems take. (Blust 1993: 33)*

This chapter compares kinship terminologies and kinship practices in eight Alor-Pantar languages forming a broad geographic and typological sample of the family. In spite of the close genealogical relationship between the languages, there is surprisingly little evidence of shared (cognate) kinship vocabulary, and the kinship systems exhibit great variation. The westernmost languages distinguish both maternal and paternal cross-cousins (children of opposite-sex siblings) as ideal marriage partners, while at the opposite extreme in the highlands of Alor are found languages which expressly forbid cross-cousin marriage. Even among languages whose kinship systems are roughly similar, the terms themselves are often not cognate. Likewise, cognate terms often have varying semantics across the languages. The current distribution of kinship terminologies suggests a recent drift toward symmetric exchange systems which distinguish both maternal and paternal cross-cousins, perhaps under the influence of neighboring Austronesian languages.

1 Introduction

One approaches the study of kinship in Eastern Indonesia with some trepidation, for it has a chequered past. For a time Eastern Indonesia and especially East Nusantara was a nexus of kinship studies (see Fox 1980; Wouden 1968). Within linguistics a comparative approach tackled issues of the reconstruction of the proto-Austronesian kinship system and sought to understand how kinship can inform our knowledge of culture history. At the same time the study of kinship was losing its favored place in anthropological theory, as authors such as Schneider (1984) argued that the notion of kinship itself should be considered a cultural construct, not necessarily universal. While these academic trends had notably less effect on the Dutch school prevalent in Indonesian kinship studies, there has nonetheless been relatively little work on kinship in the region over the past two decades, and almost none in Alor-Pantar. More recently, a renewed interest in symbolic meaning has brought anthropological and linguistic approaches more closely in line (see Schweitzer 2000). Without revisiting the anthropological debates that have shaped the study of kinship, this chapter takes a more traditional approach to kinship, focusing first and foremost on kinship terminology. Kinship as practice may well be a cultural construct, but it is necessarily grounded in a web of linguistic terminological structure. This chapter can be read as a first step toward understanding that terminology in the Alor-Pantar languages within a comparative context.

The kinship systems in Alor-Pantar languages exhibit great variation. The westernmost languages, Blagar, Teiwa, and Western Pantar, classify siblings and parallel cousins together in distinction to cross-cousins. That is, children of same-sex siblings (parallel cousins) are classified using the same terminology as used for siblings, while children of opposite-sex siblings (cross-cousins) are classified using distinct terminology. Marriage between cross-cousins is or was until recently considered the ideal. At the opposite extreme, in the highlands of Alor, Kamang expressly forbids cross-cousin marriage. Other languages show traces of asymmetrical exchange, reflected either in their kinship terminologies, in their marriage practices, or both. These languages distinguish the relationship between a man and his female maternal cross-cousin, his mother's brother's daughter, but do not highlight the relationship between a man and his paternal female cross-cousin. Even among languages whose kinship systems are roughly similar, the terms themselves are often not cognate. Likewise, cognate terms often have varying semantics across the languages. The general picture which emerges is one of drift toward symmetric exchange. Several independent sub-patterns can be identified. These will be discussed following a description of the systems in each of the individual languages.

An important aspect of all the kinship systems considered here is the identification of cross-cousins. Children of same-sex siblings are classed as siblings, whereas children of opposite-sex siblings are cross-cousins and in some languages are considered ideal marriage partners. While this basic distinction is preserved to a greater or lesser degree across the languages, there is significant variation in kinship terminologies. Comparing these systems provides insight into the history and dispersal of the Alor-Pantar languages, as well as possible language contact scenarios.

In this chapter I compare kinship terminology in eight Alor-Pantar languages forming a broad geographic and typological sample of the family (see the Sources section at the end of this chapter for details). For all of the languages, data were obtained by eliciting genealogies for several individuals and then discussing those genealogies with both the same and other individuals in order to verify and fill in any gaps in the systems. For Western Pantar I relied also on my own fieldnotes from several years of work with the language, and for Blagar I also drew on the description in Steinhauer (1993). For those two languages the kinship terminology can be considered complete. For the remaining languages it is possible that some terms have been overlooked. Hence, the absence here of, say, a Teiwa term by which the wives of two brothers address each other should not be taken as evidence that such a term does not exist in Teiwa. It is possible that such a term does exist but has not yet been recorded.

The following section describes the kinship terminology in each of the eight languages individually. Then in § 3 these terminologies are compared across the languages. § 4 presents a brief description of marriage prescriptions. Finally, § 5 concludes with a discussion of the likely history of kinship systems in the Alor-Pantar languages.

2 Kin terminology

In the following subsections the inventory of kinship terminology is described for each of the eight languages in the sample. The descriptions begin with terminology in ego's generation and then proceeds to ascending generations, descending generations, and finally affines (kin related by marriage). A summary table of kinship terms for each language is found at the end of each subsection.[1] Since most kinship terms are obligatorily possessed in Alor-Pantar languages, the terms are cited here as bound morphemes. Full forms inflected for first-person can be derived by adding the first-person singular prefix, which is composed of an alveolar nasal plus a vowel whose quality varies by language (*n-/na-/no-/ne-*). Thus, Western Pantar *-iar* 'father'; *niar* 'my father'.

---

[1] Abbreviations used for kin type primitives are as follows: mother [M], father [F], sister [Z], brother [B], daughter [D], son [S], child [C], husband [H], wife [W], man speaking [m], woman speaking [f], elder [e], younger [y].

2.1 Western Pantar

Western Pantar has the most elaborated set of sibling/cousin terms of any language described here. A single terminology for siblings and parallel cousins includes five terms distinguished by age and relative gender (see Table 1 at the end of this section). Same-sex elder siblings are distinguished for gender, while same-sex younger siblings are not distinguished for gender. Opposite-sex siblings are not distinguished for age. The formal similarity between the form *-aipang* 'man's sister' and *-aiyang* 'woman's brother' is probably not accidental. These terms likely derive from the possessive pronoun formative *ai* (cf. *nai* 'mine', *gai* 'his/her') plus *pang* 'non-marriageable of ego's generation' and *yang* 'return from above'. So a man's sister is "that of mine which is non-marriageable"; while a woman's brother is "that of mine which descends from above", i.e., that which comes down from my descent group.

Children of same-sex siblings are classed as siblings, whereas children of opposite-sex siblings are cross-cousins. The same-sex cross-cousin terms in Western Pantar are mutually exclusive; that is, there is no general cross-cousin term which subsumes the others. Thus, *-'ar* 'man's male cross-cousin' and *-ingtamme* 'woman's female cross-cousin' refer only to same-sex, non-marriageable cross-cousins. In contrast, the term for opposite-sex cross-cousin is independent of the gender of the ego and referent. The term *baddang* 'opposite-sex cross-cousin' is often described as meaning 'marriageable' and represents the closest marriageable relationship, often said to be the ideal marriage. The terminology in ego's generation thus differs according to whether the ego is female (Figure 1) or male (Figure 2).

The term *-ai tane* is synonymous with *baddang*, though it is not used as a vocative. This term likely derives from an archaic word *ne* 'body' with a fossilized distributive possessive prefix *ta*. It is possessed using the alienable possessive paradigm, thus, *nai tane* 'my marriageable cross-cousin', or more literally, 'that of our body'. Marriageable cross-cousins may also be referred to (though not

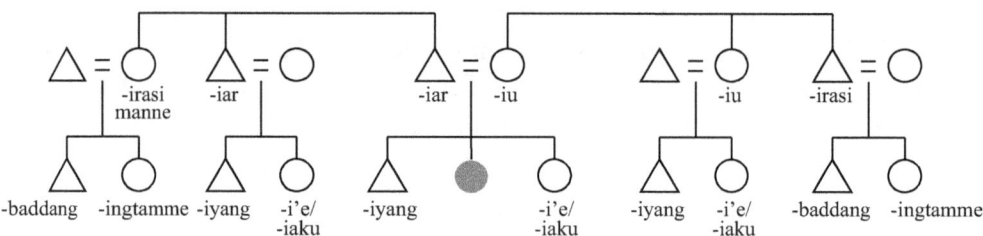

Figure 1: Western Pantar terminology in ego's and ascending generation (female ego)

5 Kinship in the Alor-Pantar languages

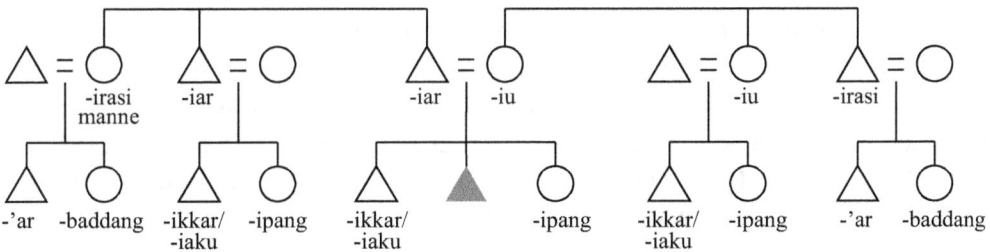

Figure 2: Western Pantar terminology in ego's and ascending generation (male ego)

addressed) by the term *wallang*, a more general term which refers to the entire mother's brother's or father's sister's descent group, including the marriageable cross-cousins. The term *wallang* contrasts with *pang*, which refers to ego's own descent group. The exchange of women from one's own descent group to one's *wallang* is highlighted in the common expression *pang wallang gar da'ai* 'one from our clan shared with the opposite clan', a figurative reference to a woman who marries outside the clan.

There is some skewing of terms in the first ascending generation. Same-sex siblings of one's parents are classed as parents, but there is no entirely separate term distinguishing father's sister from mother's brother. Mother's brother is -*irasi* (vocative *dasi*). Father's sister can also be referred to as -*irasi* but is more likely to be called by the modified term -*irasi manne* or -*irasi eu* (cf. *manne* 'wife', *eu* 'woman'). These latter terms can also denote the spouse of -*irasi*, while the spouse of -*irasi manne* is -*irasi ammu* (*ammu* 'man') or simply -*irasi*. The descending term -*airas* refers to children of one's opposite-sex siblings. Thus, -*irasi* and -*airas* are reciprocal terms. In Steinhauer's (1993) formulation -*irasi* and -*airas* denote potential parents-in-law and potential children-in-law, respectively. Indeed, these terms are used for affines as well, using the equations MB = WF and FZ = WM, characteristic of a symmetric system of marriage alliance (see § 4). That is, one's spouse's parents are denoted by the same terms used for one's parent's opposite-sex siblings, since ideally one's spouse would be the offspring of one's parent's opposite-sex sibling, i.e., a cross-cousin.

A crucial aspect of the Western Pantar kinship system is that all marriages are treated as if they were marriages between cross-cousins, even when they are not. Thus, if I marry a woman who is not my -*baddang*, I assume relationships to her kin as if she were my cross-cousin. In particular, I refer to her parents as *nirasi*, while they refer to me as *nairas*. So, affine terminology can to a large part be derived from the consanguine terminology with the assumption of cross-cousin marriage (see Figure 3).

Moreover, some rather distant relationships can appear quite close. For example, in Figure 4 the relationship between ego and C is one of cross-cousins; that is, ego calls C *na'ar*. This is true even though the biological parents of ego and C are not biological siblings. The key here is that the parents of ego and C are indeed classificatory siblings. This is because A and B, as children of same-sex siblings, are themselves classificatory siblings, hence B's sister, who is also C's mother, must also be sister to A.

The genetic distance between relationships such as those in Figure 4 does not go unnoticed, particularly with respect to the opposite-sex sibling terms -*ipang* 'man's sister' and -*iyang* 'woman's brother'. The word *haila* 'base, main, area' can be used to indicate a relationship which is perceived to be biologically closer. Thus, -*ipang haila* 'man's sister, closely related' and -*iyang haila* 'woman's brother, closely related'. The terms containing *haila* do not necessarily indicate biological siblings but are mainly contrastive in usage, indicating a closer relationship. The use of *haila* is based on the metaphor *yattu haila*, denoting the area underneath the branches of a tree (*yattu* 'tree').

Affine terminology in ego's generation is derived from sibling terminology, qualified with the gender terms *manne* 'female' and *ammu* 'male'. The choice of sibling term indicates the relationship either between ego and ego's sibling or between ego's spouse and ego's spouse's sibling. The gender qualifiers are used to indicate the gender of the referent for affine terms. Thus, -*i'e* occurs in constructions referring to 'woman's older sister', 'man's wife's elder sister' (-*i'e manne*), and 'woman's elder sister's husband' (-*i'e ammu*). Since younger siblings are not differentiated by ego's gender, the affine terms derived from -*iaku* 'younger sibling' are synonymous between spouse's sibling and sibling's spouse.

There is a paucity of Western Pantar terms referring to generations two or more removed from ego. The terms *kuba* 'old woman' and *wenang* 'old man' can be used vocatively for 'grandmother' and 'grandfather', respectively. These terms can also be used to derive polite forms of address for one's paternal grandparents, namely, *manne kuba* 'father's mother' (literally, 'female old woman') and -*ikkar wenang* 'father's father' (literally, 'man's elder brother old man'). The terms *kuba* and *wenang* can also be used referentially in conjunction with a possessive pronoun, though the reference need not be restricted to persons of the second generation above ego.

5 Kinship in the Alor-Pantar languages

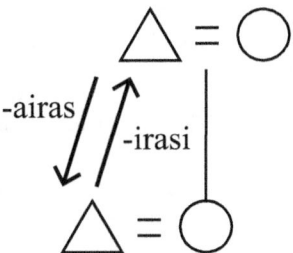

Figure 3: Western Pantar affine relations in ascending and descending generation. Terms are independent of gender of ego or referent.

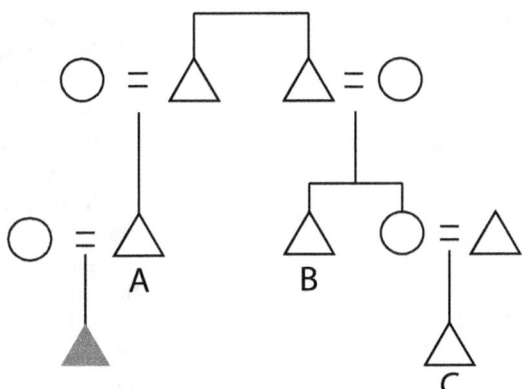

Figure 4: More distant kin relations in Western Pantar. Ego calls C *na'ar* 'man's male cross-cousin'

Table 1: Western Pantar kinship terms

-iar	F, FB	father, paternal uncle
-iu	M, MZ	mother, maternal aunt
-irasi	MB, MZH, WF, WM, HM, HF	maternal uncle
-irasi manne	FZ, MBW	paternal aunt (lit. 'female uncle')
-irasi eu		
-irasi (ammu)	FZH	paternal aunt's wife
-airas	mZC, fBC, WBC, HZC, CW, CH	child of opposite-sex sibling
-ikkar	meB	man's elder brother
-i'e	feZ	woman's elder sister
-iaku	myB, fyZ	younger same-sex sibling
-aipang	mZ	man's sister
-aiyang	fB	woman's brother
-ingtamme	fMBD, fFZD	woman's same-sex cross-cousin
-'ar	mMBS, mFZS	man's same-sex cross-cousin
-baddang /	fMBS, fFZS, mMBD, mFZD	opposite-sex cross-cousin,
wallang /		opposite clan (marriageable)
-ai tane		
pang		same clan (non-marriageable)
-imu	H	husband
-ru	W	wife
-ikkar ammu	HeB	woman's husband's elder brother
		(lit. 'male elder brother')
-ikkar manne	meBW	man's elder brother's wife
		(lit. 'female elder brother')
-i'e ammu	feZH	woman's elder sister's husband
		(lit. 'male elder sister')
-i'e manne	WeZ	man's wife's elder sister
		(lit. 'female elder sister')
-iaku ammu	HyB, fyZH	husband's younger brother,
		woman's younger sister's husband
		(lit. 'male younger sibling')
-iaku manne	WyZ, myBW	wife's younger sister, man's
		younger brother's wife
		(lit. 'female younger sibling')
wenang	FF, MF	grandfather
-ikkar wenang	FF	paternal grandfather (lit.
		'grandfather elder brother')
kuba	FM, MM	grandmother
manne kuba	FM	paternal grandmother (lit. 'female grandmother')
-wake	C, mBC, fZC	child, child of same-sex sibling
-wake ammu	S, mBS, fZS	son (lit. 'male child')
-wake eu	D, mBD, fZD	daughter (lit. 'female child')

5 Kinship in the Alor-Pantar languages

2.2 Teiwa

In Teiwa, as in many of the AP languages, there are two sets of sibling terminologies with a certain amount of overlap in usage (See Table 2 at the end of this section). The first is gender-based, distinguishing *-gasqai* 'classificatory sister' and *-ianqai* 'classificatory brother'. These terms include both siblings and parallel cousins. These terms are evidently bimorphemic, as the second contrasts with *-ian* 'cross-cousin'. The second morpheme *qai* may possibly be related to *qai* 'only' or *-oqai* 'child'. The form *-gas* on its own has no meaning. A second set of sibling terminology is age-based, distinguishing *-ka'au* 'elder sibling' and *-bif* 'younger sibling'. There is a strong preference for using the age-based terminology with same-sex siblings and using the gender-based terminology with opposite-sex siblings, but this preference does not form a strict division between the two terminologies.

Cross-cousins are not referred to by either of these terminologies but instead by the term *-ian*. Opposite-sex cross-cousins, i.e., marriageable cross-cousins, are referred to as *-dias*. In contrast to Western Pantar, cross-cousin terminology does not distinguish the gender of either the ego or the referent (see Figures 5 and 6).

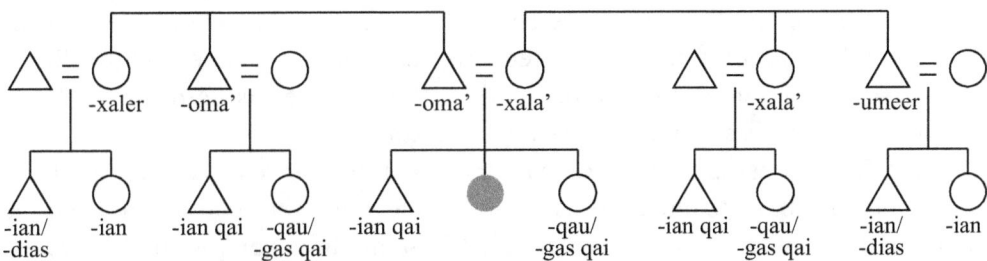

Figure 5: Teiwa terminology in ego's and ascending generation (female ego).

Marriageable cross-cousins can also be referred to as *-bruman yis,* though this term is not used as a term of address. The term *-bruman* itself indicates 'marriageable one' and may have been borrowed from neighboring Blagar *-boromung*, which is the sole term for marriageable cross-cousin in that language. The qualifier *yis* denotes 'fruit'. In Teiwa the unqualified term *-bruman* is not necessarily restricted to children of one's parent's opposite-sex sibling, but may apply more broadly. Preference for cross-cousin marriage remains strong in Teiwa, and marriages which fail to meet this criteria – that is, marriages not to one who is in the 'marriageable' category denoted by *bruman* – are not as readily integrated into the kinship system as they are in Western Pantar. As in Western Pantar marriages are treated as if they obeyed cross-cousin rules, even when they don't. Thus, one refers to the sibling of one's sibling's spouse as a cross-cousin, for had one's sibling married their cross-cousin, that person would be one's cross-cousin as well. However, in Teiwa, when a same-sex sibling marries a non cross-cousin, speakers express reluctance to call this sibling's spouse (fZH, mBW) by the term *-dias*, since in some sense this person is not really a cross-cousin. This is avoided by using the more general cross-cousin term *-ian*, or simply by addressing the sibling's spouse as *-gasqai* 'sister'.

The Teiwa kinship system contains the largest inventory of mono-morphemic terms relating to cross-cousins of any of the eight languages discussed here. Uniquely, it has distinct mono-morphemic terms referring to father's sister *-xaler* and mother's brother *-umeer*. In the other languages one or more of these terms is derived. In Western Pantar the term FZ is derived from MB (§ 2.1); in Blagar the terms MB and FZ are derived from F and M, respectively (§ 2.3). In terms of both structure and practice the Teiwa exhibits an extremely symmetrical system, with equal distinction given to the father's sister and mother's brother.

As in Western Pantar, affines in ego's generation employ the same terms as used for cross-cousins. The spouse of one's opposite-sex sibling is referred to as *-ian*, while the spouse of one's same-sex sibling is referred to as *-dias*. Affines in the descending generation are denoted *-rat*, regardless of gender, while affines in the ascending generation are denoted by the same terms used for mother's brother and father's sister, namely *-umeer* or *-xaler*.

Many Teiwa kinship terms can be further modified for relative age. All of the ascending terms can be modified with *uwaad* 'big' and *sam* 'small' to indicate relatively older or younger age, respectively (these modifiers are omitted from Figure 5 and Figure 6 above); thus, *numeer uwaad* 'my mother's elder brother'. The terms in ego's generation can be modified with *matu* 'eldest', *bak* 'middle', and

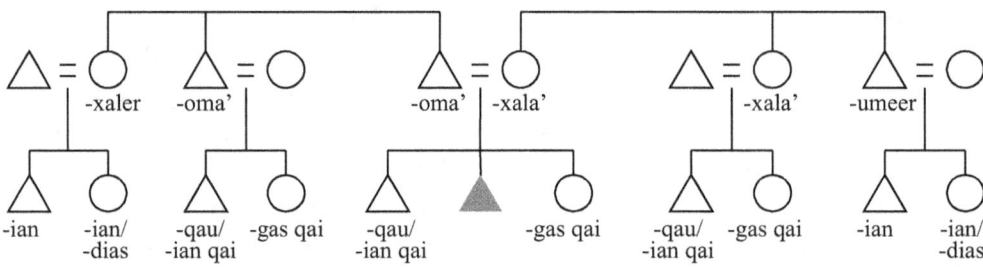

Figure 6: Teiwa terminology in ego's and ascending generation (male ego)

5 Kinship in the Alor-Pantar languages

iik 'youngest'. Terms which are not already specified for gender can be optionally specified with *eqar* 'female' or *masar* 'male'; thus, *noqai eqar* 'my daughter'.

Table 2: Teiwa kinship terms

-oma'	F, FB	father, paternal uncle
-xala'	M, MZ	mother, maternal aunt
-umeer	MB, FZH, WF, HF	maternal uncle
-xaler	FZ, MBW, HM, WM	paternal aunt
-gasqai	Z, MZD, FBD	sister, female parallel cousin
-ianqai	B, MZS, FBS	brother, male parallel cousin
-ka'au	eB, eZ, MeZC, FeBC	elder sibling, parallel cousin via parent's younger sibling
-bif	yB, yZ, MyZC, FyBC	younger sibling, parallel cousin via parent's elder sibling
-ian	MBC, FZC	cross-cousin
-dias	fMBS, fFZS, mMBD, mFZD	opposite-sex cross-cousin
-bruman yis	fMBS, fFZS, mMBD, mFZD	opposite-sex cross-cousin
-misi	H	husband
-emaq	W	wife
-rat	mZC, fBC, SW, DH	affine of descending generation
-rat masar	DH	son-in-law (lit. 'male affine')
-rat eqar	SW	daughter-in-law (lit. 'female affine')
-rat emaq	fBD, mZD, WBD, SW	daughter-in-law, daughter of opposite-sex sibling
-oqai	C	child
-rata'	FF, FM, MF, MM	grandparent
-rat qai	CC	grandchild

2.3 Blagar

Blagar (Table 3) employs a single set of gender-based terminology for classificatory siblings (siblings and parallel cousins) which distinguishes *-kaku* 'same-sex sibling' and *-edi* 'opposite-sex sibling'. Cross-cousins are distinguished by the term *-ebheang*. Additionally, cross-cousins of the opposite-sex may be optionally referred to as *-boromung*. Like its Teiwa cognate *-bruman*, the term *-boromung* distinguishes marriageable cross-cousins, or what Steinhauer refers to as "potential spouses". However, this term is avoided in the presence of the referent, in which case *-ebheang* is preferred (Steinhauer 1993: 156). The term *-ebheang* refers to all cross-cousins, regardless of the gender of ego or referent.

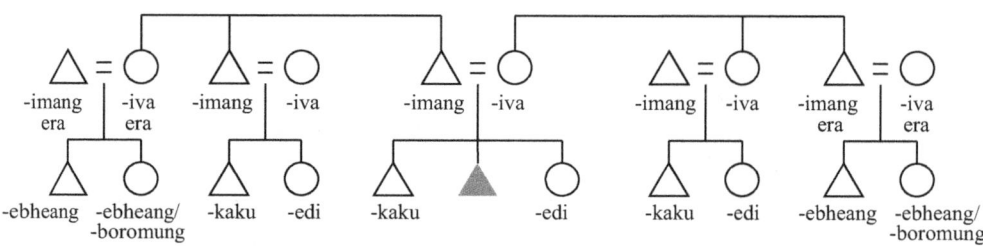

Figure 7: Blagar terminology in ego's and ascending generation (male ego)

The parents of ego's cross-cousins – i.e., ego's father's sister and her husband, and ego's mother's brother and his wife – are distinguished by compounding the classificatory mother and father terms with *era* 'base'. The reciprocal relationship is indicated by *-bhilang*. This terminology changes when cross-cousin marriages are actually realized. If ego marries his or her cross-cousin, then ego's *-imang era* and *-iva era* become simply *-idat* 'in-laws'. Similarly, these new parents-in-law now also refer to ego as *-idat* rather than *-bhilang*, so that *-idat* is its own reciprocal. Affines in ego's generation are denoted *-des*, though this term is usually restricted to same-sex referents.[2] Terms which do not inherently indicate gender may be optionally specified as *zangu* 'female' or *mehal* 'male', e.g., *nidat mehal* 'my male in-law'. Thus, *-idat zangu* 'female in-law'.

Terms which are not gender specific can be additionally marked for gender using the terms *zangu* 'female' and *mehal* 'male'; thus, *noqal zangu* 'my daugh-

---

[2] The term *-des* is not reported for the Dolap dialect described by Steinhauer (1993) but does occur in the Bama dialect as recorded in Robinson's fieldnotes. Steinhauer (pers. comm.) suggests that *-des* belongs to a different system; I include it with the other Blagar kinship terms here both because of its occurrence in Robinson's fieldnotes and because of its similarity to Teiwa *-dias* (see § 2.2).

ter'. Generations further removed from ego may be optionally specified with the modifier *zasi* (literally, 'bad'). Thus, the child of one's *-bhilang* can be referred to as *-bhilang zasi*. Further details regarding the functioning of the Blagar kinship system can be found in Steinhauer (1993).

Table 3: Blagar kinship terms

-imang	F, FB, MZH	father, paternal uncle
-iva	M, MZ, FBW	mother, maternal aunt
-imang era	MB, FZH	maternal uncle, paternal aunt's husband
-iva era	FZ, MBW	paternal aunt, maternal uncle's wife
-kaku	mB, fZ	same-sex sibling
-edi	mZ, fB	opposite-sex sibling
-ebheang	MBS, FZS, MBD, FZD	cross-cousin
-boromung	fMBS, fFZS, mMBD, mFZD	opposite-sex cross-cousin
-zangu	W	wife
-mehal	H	husband
-idat	in-law +1/-1 or +2/-2 generation	affinal kin 1 or 2 generations removed
-des	fBW, mZH, WB, HZ	affines of ego's generation
-oqal	C, fZC, mBC	classificatory child
-bhilang	mZC, fBC	child of opposite-sex sibling (potential child-in-law)

2.4 Kiraman

Kiraman employs just one primary set of terminology for ego's generation. This terminology is both age and gender based. Older and younger are distinguished for same-sex terms, while age is not distinguished for the opposite-sex terms. A second terminology is employed only for vocatives and distinguishes *baki* 'elder' from *ika* 'younger'. (Terms with strictly vocative usage are omitted from the tables.) Siblings and cousins are not distinguished via either of these terminologies. In particular, Kiraman does not obligatorily distinguish cross-cousins from siblings; however, certain cross-cousins can be optionally distinguished using the term *-eni*, which denotes both a woman's male paternal cross-cousin (fFZS) and a man's female maternal cross-cousin (mMBD). This term is its own reciprocal and denotes a marriageable relationship or a right of marriage (see § 4.2). Crucially, this term excludes a man's paternal opposite-sex cross-cousin, as well as the reciprocal relationship, a woman's maternal opposite-sex cross-cousin. The term *eni* is sometimes extended to include one's sibling's *-eni* as well – that is, a man's male paternal cross-cousin (mFZS) or a woman's female maternal cross-cousin (fMBD).

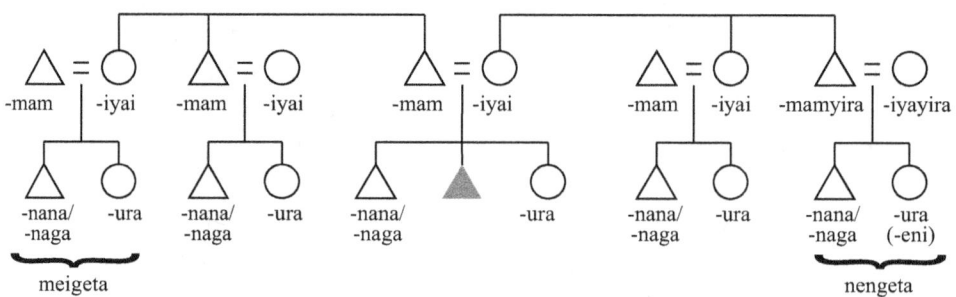

Figure 8: Kiraman terminology in ego's and ascending generation (male ego)

Kiraman ascending terminology distinguishes ego's mother's brother's side through the terms *-ma(m)yira* MB and *-iyayira* MBW, transparently derived from the terms *-mam* 'father' and *-iyai* 'mother' plus *yira* 'base'. Other ascending relationships referring to ego's parent's siblings and their spouses are denoted using the terms for mother and father modified by *baki* 'older' or *ika* 'younger', depending on the age of the referent relative to ego's mother or father, respectively. In particular, father's sister is not distinguished from mother except through the use of a relative age modifier. Descendants of one's *-mayira* and *-iyayira* can be optionally denoted *nengeta*. The reciprocal term is *meigeta*. Neither *nengeta* nor *meigeta* is used as a term of address. Descending terminology does not distinguish between biological children and children of ego's siblings but rather groups C, BC, ZC together as *-iyol* 'classificatory child'.

As in Blagar, affines in ascending and descending generations are referred to by a single term *-edat*. The term *-edat* is its own reciprocal. Affines in ego's generation are referred to as *-amo*. A man's brother-in-law may optionally be denoted *-eni*, the same term which is used to denote marriageable cross-cousins. Spouses of same-sex siblings may refer to each other as siblings, following the relative ages of their spouses. In addition, a more respectful term for the elder of two spouses of same-sex siblings is *-ina*. Thus, if A and B are brothers, and A is older than B, then B's wife calls A's wife *neina*, while A's wife calls B's wife *ika* 'younger sibling'.

5 Kinship in the Alor-Pantar languages

Table 4: Kiraman kinship terms

-mam	F, FB, FZH, MZH	father, paternal uncle
-iyai	M, MZ, FZ, FBW	mother, aunt
-ma(m)yira	MB	maternal uncle
-iyayira	MBW	maternal uncle's wife
-nana	meB, feZ, FeB elder paternal uncle	same-sex elder sibling,
-naga	myB, fyZ, FyB younger paternal uncle	same-sex younger sibling,
-ura	mZ, fB	opposite-sex sibling
baki	eB, eZ	elder sibling
ika	yB, yZ	younger sibling
nengeta	MB lineage	maternal uncle's lineage
meigeta	FZ lineage	paternal aunt's lineage
yiramei	mMBD	man's female maternal cross-cousin
yiranen	fFZS	woman's male paternal cross-cousin
-edat	WF, HF, DH, WM, HM, SW	parent-in-law, child-in-law
gei nen	H	husband
gei mei	W	wife
-eni	mMBD, fFZS, (mFZS), (fMBD), mZH, WB	marriageable cross-cousin, (sibling's marriageable cross-cousin), man's brother-in-law
-amo	fBW, HZ, mZH, WB	in-law, affine of ego's generation
-ina	HeBW, WeZH	elder same-sex in-law
-mol	HW	husband's (other) wife
-iyol	C	classificatory child
-amoku	HWC	child of husband's (other) wife

205

Terms which are not gender-specific may be optionally specified for gender using the terms *mei* 'female' and *nen* 'male'. For example, *-iyol mei* 'daughter' and *-edat nen* 'father-in-law'. Kiraman also has a distinct term *-mol* by which one wife refers to another in a polygamous marriage. These women refer to each other's children as *-amoku*.

2.5 Adang

The Adang kinship system also lacks an obligatory terminological distinction between siblings and (parallel and cross) cousins. There are two primary sets of terminologies for classificatory siblings. The first distinguishes older and younger siblings, *matu* and *di'*, respectively. The second includes the single term *-uding* 'sibling'. None of these terms is specified for gender, but each may be optionally modified with *ob* 'female' or *lote* 'male' when one wishes to specify gender. Thus, *no'uding lote* 'my female sibling', i.e., 'my sister'.

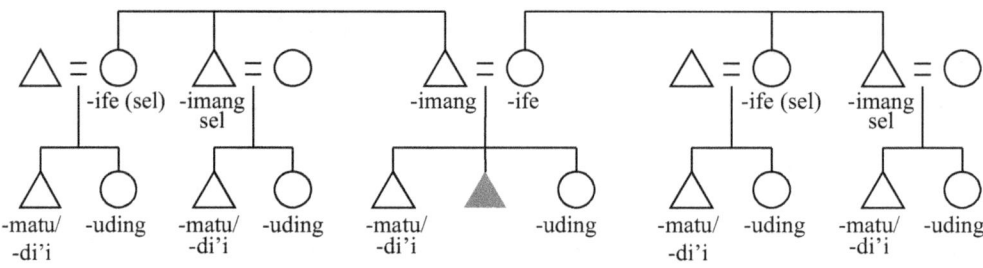

Figure 9: Adang terminology in ego's and ascending generation (male ego)

The age-based *matu/-di'* terminology has a connotation of intimacy and is preferred for biological siblings, though *-uding* can be used in this context as well. The children of one's father's brother and one's mother's sister (i.e., parallel cousins) are generally referred to as *-uding*, though the *matu/-di'* terminology is also acceptable here in certain contexts. The children of one's father's sister and one's mother's brother (i.e., cross-cousins) are almost always referred to as *-uding*; the *matu/-di'* terminology seems to be unacceptable here. This yields a kind of covert cross-cousin category, as shown in Table 5.

However, there is wide leeway in the application of this sibling terminology, and the choice between the two sibling terminologies depends greatly on pragmatics.

Co-existing with the two sibling terminologies described above is an additional layer of sibling terminology which does explicitly distinguish cross-cousins. The terms are *ob ai* 'man's female cross-cousin' (mMBD, mFZD) and *lote ai* 'woman's

5 Kinship in the Alor-Pantar languages

Table 5: Adang sibling terminologies
(✓=preferred, ?=acceptable, x=unacceptable)

	-matu/-di'	-uding
biological siblings (B, Z)	✓	?
parallel cousins (MZC, FBC)	?	✓
cross-cousins (MBC, FZC)	x	✓

male cross-cousin' (fMBS, fFZS). These terms are reciprocal, so that if A refers to B as *no'ob ai*, then B refers to A *nolote ai*. The terms derive from the gender terms *ob* 'female' and *lote* 'male' plus *ai* 'child', but when possessed the gender terms are identical to the terms for spouses, thus these cross-cousin terms translate literally as 'husband child' and 'wife child'. Though not used as terms of address, the *ob ai/lote ai* relationship is very salient to speakers, even though the referents may continue to refer to each other using the regular sibling terminology. These terms refer strictly to opposite-sex cross-cousins; Adang has no special terminology for same-sex cross-cousins.

A fourth optional distinction in ego's generation is made using the term *asel*, derived from *sel*, a term sometimes translated as 'tree' (Malay 'pohon') but which actually refers to 'area underneath, base', as in *ti sel* 'area beneath the tree' (see § 3). The term *asel* denotes one's mother's brother and descendants. Thus, maternal cross-cousins of either gender are *asel*. Like *ob ai/lote ai*, the term *asel* is not used as a term of address but rather as a description, delineating those descendants of my mother's (brother's) family. The entire mother's brother's lineage can be referred to as *asel em*, derived from *em* 'old'.

The term *sel* also occurs in ascending terminology *-imang sel* 'uncle' (MB, FB) and *-ife sel* 'aunt' (MZ, FZ). My consultants struggled with the latter term, maintaining that *sel* has no role in *nife sel* and that the modifier could equally be omitted. In contrast, *-imang sel* is clearly distinguished from *-imang* 'father'. It appears that the use of the modifier *sel* has been extended by analogy.

A woman's family may be additionally distinguished via the use of a second genitive pronominal prefix paradigm. In addition to the usual possessive paradigm with the back *o* vowel grade, Adang distinguishes a second paradigm referred to as "contrastive" (Haan 2001) which employs a front vowel grade. A male ego may use the contrastive paradigm to refer to the children of his wife's siblings, e.g., *ne'ai* 'my wife's sibling's child' (WZC, WBC). This term is only used by men; there is no corresponding term by which women can distinguish

Table 6: Adang kinship terms

-imang	F	father
-ife	M, MZ, FZ	mother, aunt
-imang sel	FB, MB	uncle
-ife sel	FZ, MZ	aunt
-matu	eB, eZ, FeBC, FeZC, MeBC, MeZC	elder classificatory sibling
-di'	yB, yZ, FyBC, FyZC, MyBC, MyZC	younger classificatory sibling
-uding	B, Z, FBC, FZC, MBC, MZC	sibling
-'ob ai	mMBD, mFZD	man's opposite-sex cross-cousin
-lote ai	fMBS, fFZS	woman's opposite-sex cross-cousin
asel	MB, MBC	mother's brother and descendants
asel em	MB lineage	mother's brother's lineage
-'ob	W	wife
-lote	H	husband
-afeng	WB, W	affine of ego's generation
bap	2nd ascending generation	grandparent
bap turtur	3rd or more ascending generation	ancestors
-'ai	C, BC, ZC	classificatory child
di'ing	CC	classificatory grandchild

their husband's sibling's children. The terms with contrastive prefix are not used as vocatives. The usual term for referring to one's biological children as well as those of one's siblings and one's spouse's siblings is *no'ai* 'my child', with optional specification for gender, *no'ai ob* 'my daughter' and *no'ai lote* 'my son'.

Affines in ego's generation are denoted by the term *-afeng*, a term which essentially means 'other' (cf. Abui *afenga*). Included in this category are the spouses of one's siblings, as well as one's spouse's siblings and their spouses. No special terms for affines in ascending and descending generations have been documented. Instead, ascending and descending affines are referred to by the same parent and child terminology used for consanguinal (biological) relations.

5 Kinship in the Alor-Pantar languages

The second ascending generation above ego is denoted *bap* 'grandparent', while more distant ascending generations are denoted *bap turtur* 'ancestors'. One's child or one's sibling is denoted *'ai*, while the second descending generation below ego is denoted by *di'ing* 'grandchild'. These terms can be further specified for gender with *ob* 'female' or *lote* 'male'.

2.6 Abui

Abui resembles Adang in having two primary terminologies for ego's generation, neither of which distinguishes between biological siblings and (parallel or cross) cousins. The first set of terminology is age-based and distinguishes *-naana* 'older sibling/cousin' from *-kokda* (or *-nahaa*) 'younger sibling/cousin'.[3] Gender is not distinguished. A second terminology is gender-based and distinguishes *-moknehi* 'same-sex sibling/cousin' from *-ura* 'opposite-sex sibling/cousin'. The choice between the two terminologies is pragmatically based and has nothing to do with the distinction between siblings and cousins. The gender-based terminology is more appropriate for older ages, whereas the age-based terminology is more appropriate for young children. The same-sex term *-moknehi* can also be used with broader semantics as a term of address even for those who are not immediate kin (Figure 10).

An additional layer of terminology for ego's generation distinguishes cross-cousins via the terms *neng fala* 'mother's brother's child' and *mayol fala* 'father's sister's child'. These terms can be used as vocatives without a possessive prefix, or they may be possessed to describe the relationship, e.g., *neneng fala* 'my mother's brother's child'. In this sense they contrast with Adang *ob ai/lote ai*, which cannot be used as vocatives. The terms *neng fala* and *mayol fala* are also reciprocals of each other, so that ego's *neng fala* calls ego *mayol fala*. These terms are derived from the words for 'man' and 'woman', plus *fala* 'house'. Descendants of one's *neng fala* are referred to as *kalieta fala*, literally 'elder house', while descendants of one's *mayol fala* are referred to as *wiil fala*, literally 'child house'.[4]

The relationship between descendants of opposite-sex siblings is diagrammed in Figure 11. The referents labeled A and B are children of opposite-sex siblings,

---

[3] Nicolspeyer (1940: 56) lists *nahaa* rather than *kokda* as the term for 'younger sibling', while both terms appear in Kratochvíl & Delpada (2008). My consultants prefer the latter term.

[4] The Takalelang variety of Abui described here differs from the Atimelang variety described by Nicolspeyer (1940). Rather than the terms *wiil fala* and *kalieta fala*, in Atimelang one finds *kokda fala* and *feng fala*, respectively. These terms are semantically similar: *wiil* 'child' vs. *kokda* 'younger'; and *kalieta* 'old' vs. *feng* 'elder'. However, Nicolspeyer indicates that the Atimelang terms *kokda fala* and *feng fala* are used to refer to the descendants of one's parents' younger and elder siblings, respectively (1940: 46).

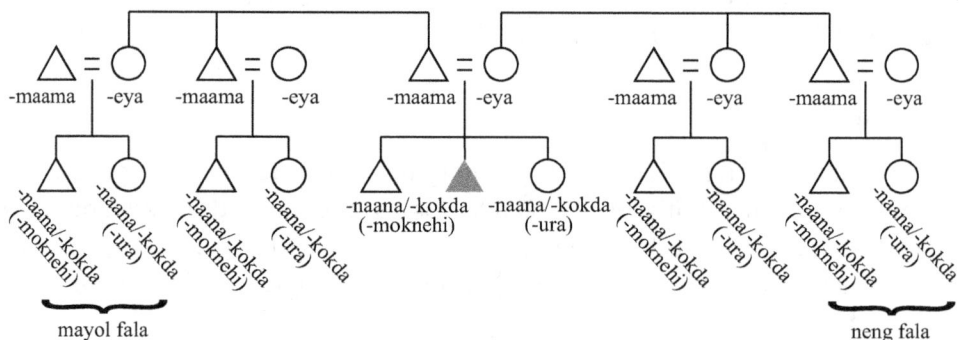

Figure 10: Abui terminology in ego's and ascending generation (male ego)

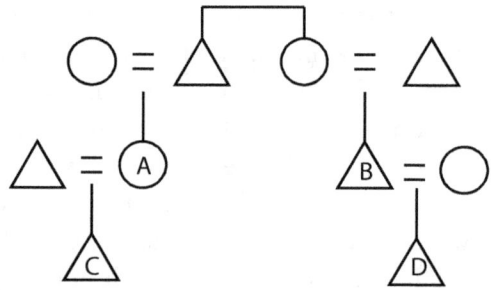

Figure 11: Abui descendants of opposite-sex siblings. C refers to D as wiil fala 'child house'; D refers to C as *kalieta fala* 'elder house'

that is, cross-cousins. A calls B *mayol fala*, literally 'female house', while B calls A *neng fala*, literally 'male house'. The children of A refer to the children of B as *wiil fala*, literally 'child house', while the children of B refer to the children of A as *kalieta fala*, literally 'elder house'.

These terms do not depend on the gender of the referent but rather on the genders of the respective siblings from which they descend. C belongs to the male side and is thus the elder house; D belongs to the female side and is thus the younger house. These terms can be used across generations as well, so that A may refer to D as either *wiil fala* or *mayol fala*; and D may refer to A as either *kalieta fala* or *neng fala*.

These descending generation terms reveal the asymmetry in the Abui system. The mother's side, through the mother's brother, is viewed as elder, while the father's side, through the father's sister, is viewed as a child. This distinction is further reflected throughout various ceremonial obligations. *Mayol fala* must always respect *neng fala*, while *neng fala* cares for *mayol fala* in an endearing way. Ascending terms in Abui distinguish siblings of one's biological parents via the modifiers *fing* 'elder, eldest' and *kokda* 'younger'. There is no distinction between opposite-sex and same-sex siblings of one's parents.

Affine terms in Abui depend on the relative gender of the referent. Opposite-sex affines are *-biena*. Male affines are *-raata*. Female affines are *-mooi*. These terms remain the same for ego's generation as well as for ascending and descending generations. Thus, *-raata* denotes a man's wife's brother and the reciprocal, a man's sister's husband; and *-raata* also denotes a man's wife's father and the reciprocal, a man's daughter's husband. The opposite-sex affine term *-biena* can also be used by spouses of opposite-sex siblings to refer to each other.

A distinct term *-mool* is used by women to refer to their husband's other wives. This term may also be used by women who are married to brothers, likely reflecting traditional levirate marriage. Further evidence of this practice can be found in the traditional Abui adage, *moknehi haba amool ri* 'sisters become *amool*', said when two sisters either marry two brothers or marry a single husband.

Abui shares with Kamang (§ 2.7) an elaborate distinction in generational levels, distinguishing three descending and four ascending generations, as shown in Table 7.

Table 7: Abui kinship terms

-maama	F, FB, MB	father, uncle
-eya	M, MZ, FZ	mother, aunt
-maama fing	MeB, FeB, MeZH, FeZH	elder uncle
-maama kokda	MyB, FyB, MyZH, FyZH	younger uncle
-eya fing	MeZ, FeZ, MeBW, FeBW	elder aunt
-eya kokda	MyZ, FyZ, MyBW, FyBW	younger aunt
-naana	eB, eZ	elder sibling
-kokda (-nahaa)	yB, yZ	younger sibling
-ura	mZ, fB	opposite-sex sibling
-moknehi	mB, fZ	same-sex sibling
-neng fala	MB, MBC	maternal uncle and descendants
-mayol fala	FZ, FZC	paternal aunt and descendants
-kalieta fala	descendants of neng fala	maternal uncle's lineage
-wiil fala	descendants of mayol fala	paternal aunt's lineage
-mayol	W	wife
-neng	H	husband
-mool	HW, HBW	husband's (other) wife
-mooi	HZ, fBW	woman's sister-in-law
-biena	HB, WZ, mBW, fZH	woman's brother-in-law, man's sister-in-law
-raata	WM, WF, WB, DH, mZH	man's brother-in-law, man's parent-in-law, man's son-in-law
-moku	C	child
-ratala	CC	grandchild
-rak beeka	CCC	great-grandchild
-kuta	2nd ascending generation	grandparent
-tungtung	3rd ascending generation	great-grandparent
-taita	4th ascending generation and above	great-great-grandparent

2.7 Kamang

Kamang kinship is described by Stokhof (1977) based on the Ateita dialect. The system described here is based on variants spoken in Apui and neighboring Silaipui districts, drawing on field work in 2010 and 2013. The two descriptions generally agree, though Stokhof is often more restrictive in delineating the semantics of certain terms. For example, Stokhof restricts the gender-based terms for ego's generation (*-namuk* 'same-sex sibling/cousin' and *-naut* 'opposite-sex sibling/cousin') to those linked through the ego's father's side. My consultants report no such restriction. This broader interpretation is also found in Schapper & Manimau (2011), where *-namuk* is defined as "same sex cousin, FBS/FZS for male or FBD/FZD for female". It may well be that the Kamang system has bleached somewhat in the four decades since Stokhof's research was conducted, so that terms which were once restricted to father's side have broadened to include both mother's and father's side.

A slightly different example type of discrepancy can be found in the terms *-namuk ela* and *-naut ela*, which both Stokhof (1977) and Schapper & Manimau (2011) define as cross-cousins on the mother's side. There is some disagreement about these terms among my consultants. Some speakers reject the terms altogether preferring instead to use the cross-cousin term *lammi*. Others accept the terms but acknowledge that the unmodified versions *-namuk* and *-naut* can also be used in this context. Most likely there are two overlapping terminological systems at work here: one distinguishing cross-cousins via the *lammi/malemi* terminology; and the other distinguishing the mother's side via *ela*. Nonetheless, Kamang today as described here still maintains significant skewing toward the maternal side in the first ascending generation.

Kamang has two primary sets of terminology for ego's generation. The first is age-based, distinguishing *-naka* 'elder sibling/cousin' and *-kak* 'younger sibling/cousin'. These terms are synonymous with *-idama* and *-idika*, respectively, and these latter terms are more commonly used in their vocative form, *dama* and *dika*, respectively. A second set of terminology is gender-based and distinguishes *-namuk* 'same-sex sibling/cousin' from *-naut* 'opposite-sex sibling/cousin'. The same-sex term *-namuk* is less likely to be used to indicate biological siblings, in which case the age-based terms are preferred. The term *-namuk* can be used more generally as a friendly way of greeting persons of the same gender as ego, even if not closely related. For both sets of terminology a biological sibling (or at least closer) relationship can be indicated by compounding the terms with *kang*. Thus, *nenaut kang* 'my (male speaking) sister' (See Figure 12).

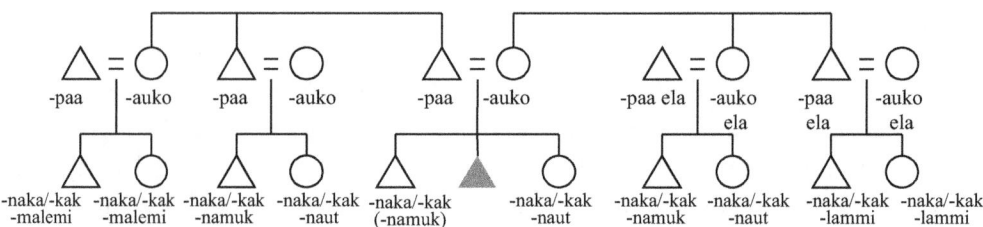

Figure 12: Kamang terminology in ego's and ascending generation (male ego)

While Stokhof reports the use of the gender-based terms for cross-cousins as well as parallel cousins, my consultants prefer to limit the use of these terms to parallel cousins (and siblings). A different set of terminology is used for cross-cousins, distinguishing *lammi* 'maternal cross-cousin' (MBC) and *malemi* 'paternal cross-cousin' (FZC). These terms are not distinguished for gender, the gender of either ego or referent, but they are reciprocal, so that if A calls B *lammi*, then B calls A *malemi*. In contrast to other Alor-Pantar languages, there is a strong taboo against marriage between cross-cousins (see § 4). The cross-cousin terms are not used as terms of address except in very specific formal contexts; instead, the usual age-based sibling terms are used. The *lammi-malemi* relationship is inherited through generations, so that the children of *lammi* and *malemi* also refer to each other as *lammi* and *malemi*. However, the restriction on marriage between *lammi* and *malemi* expires after three generations.

Kamang terminology in the first ascending generation is unique among the languages described in this chapter. Paternal terms are merged with father and mother, but maternal terms are distinguished via the modifier *ela*. This is shown in Figure 13. Some speakers merge both the maternal and paternal sides in casual reference, though they still optionally distinguish the maternal side via *ela*. In vocative address, all members of the first ascending generation are addressed as *nepaa* 'my father' or *nauko* 'my mother'.

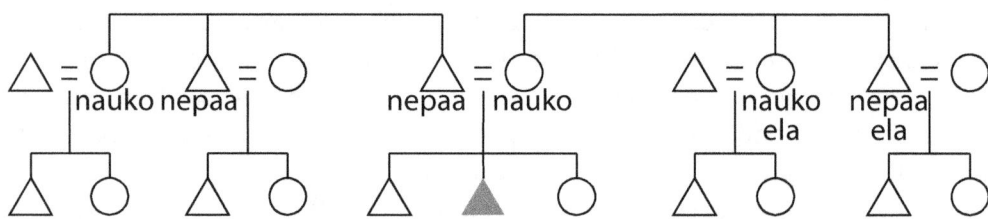

Figure 13: Kamang terms in first ascending generation

5 Kinship in the Alor-Pantar languages

Table 8: Kamang kinship terms.[5]

-paa	F, FB, FZH	father, paternal uncle
-auko	M, FZ, FBW	mother, paternal aunt
-paa idama	FeB, (MeB)	elder (paternal) uncle
-paa idika	FyB, (MyB)	younger (paternal) uncle
-auko idama	FeZ, (MeZ)	elder (paternal) aunt
-auko idika	FyZ, (MyZ)	younger (paternal) aunt
-paa ela	MB, MZH	maternal uncle
-auko ela	MZ, MBW	maternal aunt
-naka	eB, eZ, MeBC, FeBC, MeZC, FeZC	elder classificatory sibling
-kak	yB, yZ, MyBC, FyBC, MyZC, FyZC	younger classificatory sibling
-namuk	(mB), (fZ), fFBD, mFBS, fMZD, mMZS	same-sex classificatory sibling
-naut	mZ, fB, fFBS, mFBD, fMZS, mMZD	opposite-sex classificatory sibling
lammi	MBC	maternal cross-cousin
malemi	FZC	paternal cross-cousin
dum	C, MBC, MZC, FBC, FZC	classificatory child
lam	H	husband
male	W	wife
-nabeng	affine of ego's generation	
-noy	HZ, fBW	woman's sister-in-law
-mot	HBW, WZH, HW	
-nataka	WF, HF, WM, HM, DH, SW	parent-in-law, child-in-law
-ben	SWF, SWM, DHF, DHM	child-in-law's parent
tale dum	WC, HC	step-child
tale namuk	MC, FC	step-sibling

215

Affines in ego's generation are denoted by *-nabeng*. This term is its own reciprocal. Female affines may be optionally called *-noy* by a female ego. Spouses of same-sex siblings refer to each other as *-mot*. This same term is used by wives to refer to other wives sharing the same husband. In the ascending and descending generations only a single affine term is used, namely, *-nataka*. This term is independent of gender and is its own reciprocal.

2.8 Wersing

Wersing does not make an obligatory distinction between siblings and cousins, though cross-cousins are covertly distinguished, as discussed below. There are two sets of terminology for classificatory siblings (hereafter simply siblings), age-based and gender-based. The age-based terminology distinguishes *-nang* 'older sibling' from *-kaku* 'younger sibling'. The gender-based terminology consists of the single term *-arudi* 'opposite-sex sibling'. Thus, only the age-based terms may be used for same-sex siblings. The age-based terms are most commonly used also for opposite-sex siblings; the gender-based term is considered more formal or endearing.

In addition to the classificatory sibling terminologies, same-sex children of opposite-sex siblings, i.e., same-sex cross-cousins, are referred to as *-beng*. This same term is used for affines in ego's generation which are related through opposite-sex siblings. Thus, *-beng* denotes mZH, WB, fBW, HZ. These are precisely the people whose children can call ego's children *-beng*. A man's female maternal cross-cousin (mMBD) is not referred to or addressed as *-beng* but is instead tacitly considered to be a spouse, at least until the man marries someone else. Instead, a man's female maternal cross-cousin may be referred to (but not addressed) as *-mei deng*, literally 'female female-side'. A woman in turn refers to her male paternal cross-cousin by the reciprocal term *-limi deng*, literally, 'male female-side'.[6] The term *deng* itself derives from a plural marker but in this context denotes a man's mother's brother's family.

---

[5] The Kamang terms *lamta* and *maleta* have been omitted from this list. Stokhof (1977) equates *lamta* and *dum lam* but does not list *maleta*. Stokhof's definition of both *dum lam* and *dum male* is much broader, applying to a large group of kin in ego's generation. I was unable to confirm this definition with my consultants.

[6] My fieldnotes are actually inconclusive as to whether *-mei deng* and *-limi deng* can be applied also to a man's female paternal cross-cousin (mFZD) and the reciprocal woman's male maternal cross-cousin (fMBS). However, I suspect that they cannot, in which case these terms are then skewed toward the man's mother's brother's side in a way similar to that found in Kiraman (see § 4.2).

5 Kinship in the Alor-Pantar languages

Affines in ascending and descending generations are referred to by the term -*tat* 'spouse's parent, child's spouse'. In contrast to languages like Teiwa, Wersing lacks distinct terms for MB and FZ which may be employed for affines in the ascending generation. Hence, the term -*tat* is used reciprocally. The spouse of one's opposite sex sibling is -*beng* and thus treated as a same-sex cross-cousin. The same term denotes the reciprocal relationship of one's spouse's opposite-sex sibling. The spouse of one's spouse's opposite-sex sibling thus counts as an opposite-sex cross-cousin and is thus "marriageable". However, this person is generally referred to with an age-based sibling term -*nang* or -*kaku*, though never as -*arudi*, as that term is reserved for consanguine relations.

In the first ascending generation ego's parent's siblings and their spouses are all referred to by one of the terms -*paidem* 'older uncle', -*par* 'younger uncle', -*yidem* 'older aunt', -*yar* 'younger aunt' (see Figure 14). The terms -*pa* 'father' and -*ya* 'mother' are reserved for biological and adoptive parents only. No distinction is made between maternal and paternal aunts and uncles. The elder terms are clearly derived from -*pa* 'father' and -*ya* 'mother' plus *idem* 'eldest'; however, speakers do not recognize a morphological division here; nor do they view these terms as referring literally to an older or younger father or mother. The reciprocal term for -*paidem*, -*par*, -*yidem*, and -*yar*, as well as -*pa* and -*ya*, is simply -*ol* 'child'.

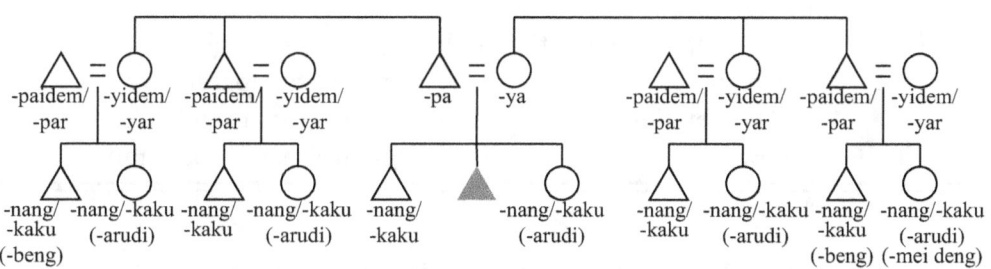

Figure 14: Wersing terminology in ego's and ascending generation (male ego)

The term -*tam* is used for kin in the second ascending and descending generations. Thus, grandchildren and grandparents address each other by the same term, *netam*. For ascending generations above this the term -*nakar*, literally 'earlier times', is used. For descending generations below this the term -*silu*, literally 'sprout, bud', is used.

Table 9: Wersing kinship terms

-pa	F	father
-ya	M	mother
-paidem	FeB, MeB	elder uncle
-par	FyB, MyB	younger uncle
-yidem	FeZ, MeZ	elder aunt
-yar	FyZ, MyZ	younger aunt
-nang	eB, eZ	elder sibling
-kaku	yB, yZ	younger sibling
-arudi	mZ, fB	opposite-sex sibling
-tat	CH, CW, WM, WF, HM, HF	parent in-law, child in-law
-beng	fMBD, fFZD, mMBS, mFZS, mZH, WB, fBW, HZ	parallel cousin
-limi deng	fFZS, (fMBS ?)	woman's male paternal (and maternal?) cross-cousin
-mei deng	mMBD, (mFZD ?)	man's female maternal (and paternal?) cross-cousin
-ol	C, BC, ZC	classificatory child
-tam	2nd ascending/descending generation	grandchild, grandparent
-nakar	3rd ascending generation and above	great-grandchild, great-grandparent
-silu	3rd descending generation and below	great-great-grandchild, great-great-grandparent

3 Summary and comparison of kinship terms

Given the close genealogical relationships between the Alor-Pantar languages, there is relatively little shared kinship vocabulary. Holton & Robinson (this volume) reconstruct just three kinship terms: 'father', 'child', and 'older sibling', though it should be noted that the methodology used to elicit vocabulary for that study may have overlooked potential cognate forms with differing semantic values. To these three we might add 'mother', for which it is difficult to propose an actual reconstruction, since it appears to be composed of a sequence of two vowels, and the vowel correspondences have yet to be worked out (see Table 10). Note that Kamang -auko 'mother' likely contains a fossilized endearment suffix

-ko. Also, while reflexes of 'older sibling' are not found in the three Pantar languages in this sample, the reconstruction is supported by Nedebang *-nang*. Two additional forms 'younger sibling' and 'opposite-sex sibling' may also be reconstructable (see Table 14), but those forms are not as widely attested as these four.

Table 10: Cognate kinship vocabulary, with reconstructed pAP forms where available (non-cognate forms in parentheses)

	'mother'	'father' *-mam	'child' -uaqal	'older sibling' -*nan(a)
Western Pantar	-au	-iba	-wakal	(-ikkar)
Teiwa	(-xala')	-oma'	-oqai	(-ka'au)
Blagar	-iva	-imang	-oqal	(-ku)
Kiraman	-iyai	-mam	-ol	-nana
Adang	-ife	-imang	-'ai	(-matu)
Abui	-eya	-maama	(-moku)	-naana
Kamang	-auko	-paa	(dum)	-naka
Wersing	-ya	-pa	-ol	-nang

Unfortunately, the reconstructions in Table 10 do not shed light on the actual structure of the kinship system, and the tag glosses given for the reconstructions should be taken as a rough indication of the relevant kin category. For example, reflexes of *mam 'father' may refer to 'F' alone, 'F, FB', or even 'F, FB, MB'. In order to understand the nature of the original Alor-Pantar kinship system we must compare the semantic structure of the kin terms, particularly as they relate to the distinction of cross-cousins and mother's brother.

The semantic distribution of the terms corresponding to the six kin type primitives in the first ascending generation are given in Table 11. The table shading indicates kin type primitives which are classed together with the same term. The table reveals that even where kinship vocabulary is cognate across languages, the terms may have differing semantic values. For example, Kamang *-paa* and Wersing *-pa* 'father' are obviously cognate, but the meaning of the Kamang form is also extended to 'father's brother' but not to 'mother's brother', which has a distinct term in Kamang. In contrast, Wersing use the same term *-paidem/-par*.

For the purposes of this comparison optional age-based modifier terms are excluded. Thus, while Abui may refer to MB as *-maama fing* or *-maama kokda*, according to whether alter is older or younger, respectively, than ego's parent, this term is here considered to be classed with *-maama* F. Wersing presents some

Table 11: Comparison of kinship categories in the first ascending generation. Shading indicates kin type primitives which are classed together with the same term.

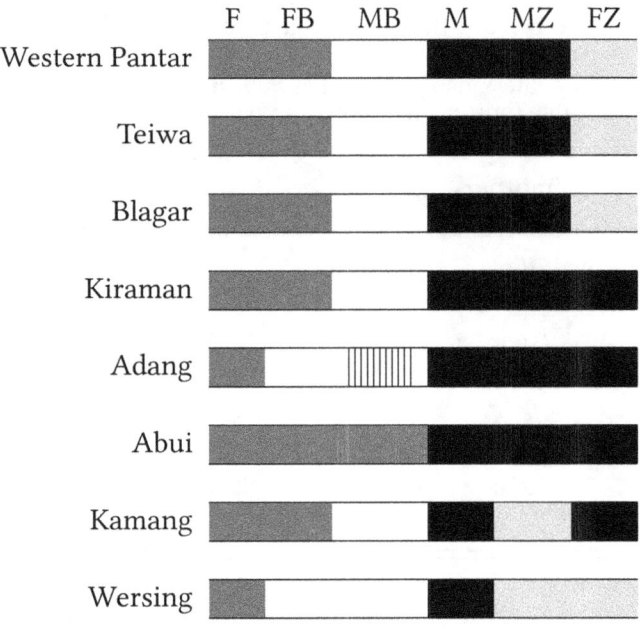

difficulties for this convention, since the Wersing terms for parents' siblings are derived from the terms for M and F together with suffixes *idem* and *-r*, depending on whether alter is older or younger, respectively, than ego's parent. However, in contrast to the Abui situation, these suffixes are not semantically transparent to Wersing speakers. While Abui *-maama kokda* is transparently 'younger father', Wersing *-par* 'FyB, MyB' is not seen by Wersing speakers as related in any way to *-pa* 'father'. Hence, for the purposes of this analysis the opaque Wersing suffixes are retained. Were the suffixes to be discarded the Wersing system would look like that found in Abui, which has only two primary terms in the ascending generation, corresponding to males and females.

Most of the languages described here have a distinct term for MB. The one marginal case is found in Adang, which classes MB and FB together as *imang sel*. However, only MB and his descendants can be denoted by the term *asel*. This suggests that the *sel* modifier has been extended from MB to FB. In any case, MB is still distinguished by a distinct term. That leaves only Abui and Wersing lacking a distinct MB term.

5 Kinship in the Alor-Pantar languages

Table 12: Comparison of F and MB terms in those languages which have a distinct MB term

	F	MB
Western Pantar (Lamma)	-iba	-irasi
Teiwa	-oma'	-umeer
Blagar	-imang	-imang era
Adang	-mang	asel
Kiraman	-mam	-mamyira
Kamang	-paa	-paa ela

For the female ascending terms, there is less consensus across the languages. The Pantar languages all distinguish FZ from M and MZ, but three languages class all female kin of the first ascending generation together. Kamang follows yet another pattern which distinguishes both male and female kin on the mother's side.

Comparing terminology across the six languages which have a distinct MB term reveals that the MB term in most cases has been derived from the term for father plus a modifier which can be translated as 'base' (Table 12). The presence of the 'base' formative is most transparent in Blagar, Kiraman, and Kamang, where the forms *era*, *yira*, and *ela*, respectively, can be identified. In Western Pantar and Teiwa the rhotic is likely a reduced form of the 'base' formative, though it does not occur synchronically as such. In the Western Pantar case a comparison with the Lamma dialect, where the word for 'father' is *-iba*, shows that the rhotic is unique to the MB term. The Adang formative *sel* also means 'base' but is used to denote MB without the *-mang* term.

The broad semantics of the 'base' forms are well articulated for Blagar in Steinhauer (1993: 156). Cognates and semantically similar terms are found across many of the Alor Pantar languages (Table 13). A prototypical usage would be Kamang *bong ela* 'base of tree'. This usage of the 'base' modifier derives from a more widespread botanic metaphor which is common throughout Eastern Indonesia (Fox 1995). Among the eight languages considered here only Wersing appears to completely lack a kinship modifier based on a botanic term (Table 13).

Turning now to ego's generation we find that these kinship terms often come in multiple overlapping sets of terminologies, and choice between terminologies may be pragmatically governed. Age-based systems for siblings are found in all of the languages except Blagar. Gender-based systems for siblings are found in all

Table 13: Use of botanic metaphors in Alor-Pantar kinship terms

language	modifier	gloss	kinship usage
Western Pantar	*haila*	'base'	close relative
Teiwa	*yis*	'fruit'	*-bruman yis* 'marriageable cross-cousin'
Blagar	*era*	'base'	*-imang era* MB, *-iva era* FZ
Kiraman	*geta*	'base'	*meigeta* FZC, *nengeta* MBC
	yira	'tree'	*-iyai yira* MBW, *-mam yira* MB
Adang	*sel*	'base'	*-imang sel* MB, FB; *asel* MBC
Abui	*iya*	'trunk'	*pi iya nuku* 'we are from one tree; related'
Kamang	*ela*	'base'	*-paa ela* MB, *-auko ela* MZ
Wersing	--	--	--

languages except Adang. Most of the gender-based systems distinguish between same-sex and opposite-sex siblings. Teiwa is unique in having gender-based sibling terms which are absolute and not dependent on relative genders of ego and alter. None of the sibling terms can be reconstructed at the level of proto-Alor-Pantar with much confidence. Only 'younger sibling' and 'opposite-sex sibling' have a very wide distribution across the languages, as shown in Table 14. But even these forms do not obey established consonant correspondences, so they are likely to have diffused.

The choice between age-based and gender-based systems is for the most part pragmatically governed, with the latter being more formal or distant. In some languages there is a strong preference for use of the age-based terms for same-sex siblings and the gender-based terms for opposite-sex siblings. In Western Pantar this preference is strictly manifested so that age-based terms are used only for same-sex siblings, while distinct terms are used for opposite-sex siblings. In addition, Western Pantar has distinct terms for male speaking and female speaking for 'elder (same-sex) sibling' and 'opposite-sex sibling'.

All of the languages have terminology for distinguishing cross-cousins. However, the languages vary as to whether: (i) cross-cousins are obligatorily distinguished; (ii) when cross-cousins are distinguished, marriageable (opposite-sex) are obligatorily distinguished from non-marriageable (same-sex) cross-cousins;

(iii) when cross-cousins are distinguished, those on MB side are distinguished from those on FZ side; and (iv) there are cross-cousin terms distinct from terms referring to the entire lineage. These distinctions are summarized in Table 15.

Table 14: Tentative reconstruction of sibling terms

	-*kak 'younger sibling'	*-ura 'opposite-sex sibling'
Western Pantar	-iaku	--
Teiwa	(-bif)	--
Blagar	--	-edi
Kiraman	-naga	-ura
Adang	(-di)	--
Abui	-kokda	-ura
Kamang	-kak	-naut
Wersing	-kaku	-arudi

Table 15: Comparison of cross-cousin distinctions

	obligatory	marriageable distinguished	maternal distinguished	distinguished from lineage
W Pantar	■	■		■
Teiwa	■			
Blagar	■			
Kiraman			■	
Adang		■	■	
Abui			■	
Kamang			■	
Wersing		■		

The languages fall into two groups along the first parameter above. Only the three Pantar languages Western Pantar, Teiwa, and Blagar obligatorily distinguish cross-cousins from siblings. In these languages cross-cousins form a distinct category and are not considered siblings. In the other languages cross-cousins can be distinguished when necessary, but they can also be referred to using the sibling terminology. Only Western Pantar obligatorily distinguishes same-sex from opposite-sex cross-cousins. In Teiwa and Blagar a single term applies to cross-cousins regardless of gender, while those of opposite gender may be optionally distinguished. As can be seen from Table 16, it is not possible to reconstruct any of the cross-cousin terminology for these languages. The Teiwa term *-ian* may be related to the term *-ianqai* 'brother'. No inferences can be drawn regarding the historical origin of the cross-cousin terms in Western Pantar and Blagar.

Table 16: Comparison of cross-cousin terms

	general	same-sex	opposite-sex
Western Pantar		*-'ar* / *-ingtamme*	*-baddang*
Teiwa	*-ian*		*-dias*
Blagar	*-ebheang*		*-boromung*

Only in Western Pantar can the opposite-sex cross-cousin term be used as a form of address. In Teiwa and Blagar this term is avoided in address by using the general form. In Wersing the opposite-sex cross-cousin term has a strong association with marriage and is thus avoided in address by using the sibling terminology instead.

The remaining five languages, all spoken on Alor, classify siblings and (parallel and cross) cousins together. However, these languages may optionally distinguish cross-cousins, and in doing so also distinguish between maternal and paternal cross-cousins. In Kiraman, Abui, Kamang, and Wersing maternal cross-cousins are referred to with a term derived from the word for 'male', while paternal cross-cousins are referred to with a term derived from the word for 'female'. In Adang only maternal cross-cousins are distinguished; there is no separate term for paternal cross-cousins. Terms for maternal and paternal cross-cousins are compared in Table 17. Kiraman also has a term *-ueni* which refers specifically to a man's maternal opposite-sex cross-cousin (mMBD) and reciprocally to a woman's paternal opposite-sex cross-cousin (fFZS). This term then extends to a man's paternal same-sex cross-cousin (mFZS), since this person is a potential spouse of one's *-eni* and is thus also referred to as *-eni*.

Here again the terms for maternal and paternal cross-cousins do not admit a reconstruction. Though Kiraman, Adang, Kamang, and Wersing derive the cross-cousin terms from the words for 'male' and 'female', they do so by the addition of different (and non-cognate) formatives.

5 Kinship in the Alor-Pantar languages

Table 17: Maternal and paternal cross-cousin terms

	MBC	FZC	derivation
Kiraman	*nengeta*	*meigeta*	*geta* 'trunk'
Adang	*asel*	--	*sel* 'base'
Abui	*neng fala*	*mayol fala*	*fala* 'house'
Kamang	*lammi*	*malemi*	*mi* 'located'
Wersing	*limideng*	*meideng*	*deng* 'side'

Affine terminology also exhibits significant variation across the languages. Where distinct terminology for cross-cousins and mother's brother exists, this same terminology is applied to affines. In ego's generation this follows logically from the observation that the spouse of ego's sibling should ideally be that sibling's cross-cousin, hence also cross-cousin to ego. Similar reasoning suggests that the parent of ego's spouse should be called by the same term as ego's mother's brother or father's sister, since those persons would be the parent of ego's cross-cousin, who would be ego's ideal marriage partner. However, only Western Pantar and Teiwa actually adopt this strategy for spouse's parent and affines of ego's generation. The terminology for affines is summarized in Table 18. The forms listed for spouse's sibling apply also to the reciprocal sibling's spouse, with appropriate adjustment for reference. Thus, Kamang *-noy* is both 'woman's brother's wife' (fBW) and also 'husband's sister' (HZ).

A single affine term **dat* can be tentatively reconstructed at the level of proto-Alor Pantar. This term probably had the general meaning of 'affine kin' but was then restricted to affines in the descending generation as affines in the ascending generation were replaced by terms denoting the parents of cross-cousins. Crucially, the reconstructed affine term is distinct from terms denoted cross-cousins, suggesting that the original kinship terminology was not based on a direct exchange system where affines would be cross-cousins.

4 Marriage prescriptions

As discussed in the previous section, special terminology for cross-cousins is found in most of the Alor-Pantar languages. However, the role of cross-cousins and that of mother's brother varies significantly across the languages. In some languages the terminology denotes a privileged marriageable relationship, based

Table 18: Comparison of affine terms

	spouse's sibling	spouse's parent	child's spouse
Western Pantar	-baddang (mBW, fZH) -ingtamme (fBW) -'ar (mZH)	-irasi	-airas
Teiwa	-ian (mZH, fBW) -dias (mBW, fZH)	-umeer/-xaler	-rat
Blagar	-des	-idat	
Kiraman	-amo -eni	-dat	
Adang	-afeng		
Abui	-biena (mBW, fZH) -amooi (fBW) -raata (mZH)	-biena	-raata
Kamang	-nabeng -noy (fBW)	-nataka	
Wersing	-beng (fBW, mZH)	-tat	

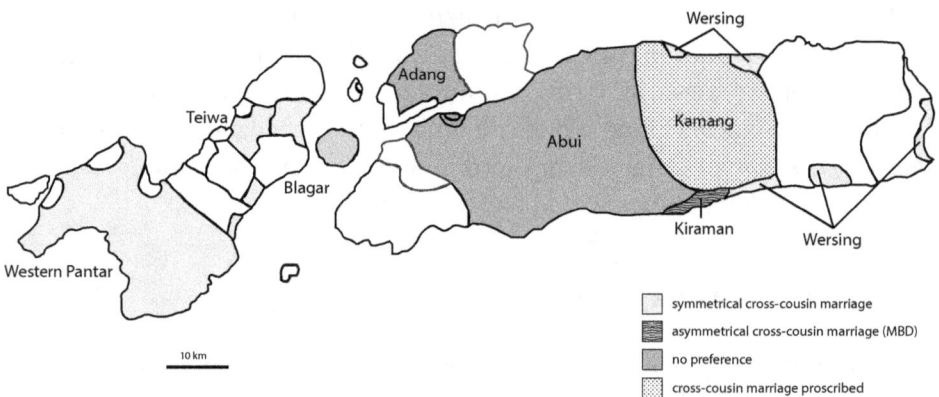

Figure 15: Geographic distribution of languages according to type of marriage prescription

5 Kinship in the Alor-Pantar languages

on symmetrical exchange. In other languages there is asymmetrical exchange with the mother's brother's side serving as the wife-givers. In yet other languages there is no marriage prescription, even though cross-cousins may be terminologically distinguished and play important roles in exchange relationships.

Some common threads in marriage practices are found in all of the Alor-Pantar languages. Descent is patrilineal and almost always patrilocal, and exchange between descent groups plays a central role in social structure, linking lineages beyond the time span of the actual marriage. The bronze kettledrum, or *moko*, plays a central symbolic role in the exchange of bride wealth, and the relative valuations of the kettledrums serves to regulate the direction of circulation of women. Distinguishing between the ideology of marriage and the actual practice of marriage is difficult without a more detailed ethnographic study of marriage and exchange, and such a study is unfortunately beyond the scope of this chapter, which is necessarily preliminary.[7] With that in mind this section focuses on a description of marriage prescriptions in the Alor-Pantar languages.

Three broad patterns of marriage prescription can be identified, as follows (see Figure 15):

(i) symmetrical systems in which the man draws a wife from either the mother's brother's or the father's sister's lineage;

(ii) asymmetrical systems in which the mother's brother's lineage serves as wife-giver;

(iii) non-prescriptive systems with no preference for marriage outside certain specific proscriptions;

In the following subsections I discuss each of these systems in turn. Within the third category we can further distinguish systems in which cross-cousin marriage is explicit ly proscribed. As shown in Figure 15 systems of marriage prescription are regionally distributed. Symmetrical systems are found throughout Pantar and on the eastern coast of Alor. Asymmetrical systems are found only in Kiraman, also located on the eastern coast of Alor. Non-prescriptive systems, including the completely proscriptive system in Kamang, are found in Central Alor

---

[7] There is as of yet still no detailed ethnographic description of marriage practices in Alor, though the reader may consult Nicolspeyer (1940) on Abui; Stokhof (1977) on Kamang; and Steinhauer (2010) on Blagar. Additional information on marriage practices can be gleaned from the ethnographic introductions to reference grammars of Teiwa (Klamer 2010), Abui (Kratochvíl 2007), and Klon (Baird 2008). Forman (1980) describes marriage customs in Makasae, a related language spoken in East Timor.

and the Bird's Head. The marriage prescriptions do not match exactly with kinship terminology, proving the point that terminology does not determine practice. Exchange has a number of dimensions in Alor-Pantar which will only be illuminated with further study.

4.1 Symmetrical exchange

In Western Pantar, Teiwa, Blagar, and Wersing cross-cousin marriage is held up as the ideal. There is symmetrical exchange with no skewing toward either the mother's or the father's side. That is, there is no preference for marriage to ego's mother's brother's child over ego's father's sister's child. Systems of symmetrical exchange are found at the two extremes of the archipelago: among the languages of Pantar in the west and in Wersing along the eastern coast of Alor (Figure 15). Here I focus on Western Pantar, since I am most familiar with the marriage customs there. I have no data on the actual extent of cross-cousin marriage, though I suspect it is quite rare. In Kedang, an Austronesian language spoken immediately to the west of Western Pantar, Barnes (1980: 88) found a conformance rate of 58% with the cross-cousin marriage prescription rule. I suspect that the rate in Western Pantar is similar, though it was likely much greater in the past.[8] Western Pantar treats all marriages as if they were between cross-cousins. However, Western Pantar recognizes a distinction between marriage established through classificatory cross-cousins, and marriage to persons outside the region who cannot be traced as cross-cousins. The former are *-baddang haila*, literally 'base cross-cousin'; while the latter are *-baddang wang gamining*, literally 'cross-cousin included'. The *-baddang wang gamining* very literally included in that, once married, they are treated as if they were in fact *-baddang* for the purposes of identifying further kinship relationships via transitivity. There is a certain circularity to this system in that *-baddang* defines the ideal marriageable relationship, yet any marriage is treated *as if* the partners were *-baddang*, effectively establishing the *-baddang* relationship by fiat.

Very rarely marriage may occur between more distantly related siblings, that is, between a man and his *-aipang wang gamining* or between a woman and her *-aiyang wang gamining*. This could happen for instance with an affine relative of one's sibling when that sibling marries into another clan. The participants in such a marriage may refer to each other as *wallang* (i.e., *-baddang*), since that is considered the ideal marriage relationship. However, this relationship is referred

---

[8] Steinhauer (2010) suggests that among the Blagar of Pura strict adherence to cross-cousin marriage had broken down by the time of the Japanese occupation in the 1940s.

to as *burang nattang*, literally 'getting together shaking hands'. At one time such a practice resulted in much stronger reprobation. In contrast, marriage between a man and his *-aipang haila* or between a woman and her *-aiyang haila* is never permitted, even today.

As in Western Pantar, in Blagar all marriages are effectively treated as if they were cross-cousin marriages. As noted in § 2.3, if marriage between ego and his or her cross-cousin is actually realized, then ego's *-imang era* and *-iva era* become simply *-idat* 'in-laws'. Similarly, these new parents-in-law now also refer to ego as *-idat* rather than *-bhilang*. The spouse of ego continues to be referred to by these parents-in-law as a classificatory child *-oqai*, since ego's cross-cousin is the child of ego's *-imang era* and *-iva era* (now *-idat*). Significantly, this remains the case even when *-bhilang* does not marry their cross-cousin. That is, whomever ego's *-bhilang* marries becomes ego's classificatory child, regardless of whether they held this status prior to the marriage. This relationship may then be propagated recursively. The result is that ego's spouse is always treated as the child of ego's potential parents-in-law (MB or FZ), hence ego's cross-cousin.

4.2 Asymmetrical exchange

Kiraman practices matrilineal cross-cousin marriage, in which the ideal marriage relationship is between a man and his matrilineal cross-cousin, i.e., his mother's brother's daughter, whom he denotes with the term *-eni*. This system is asymmetrical in that marriage between a man and his patrilineal cross-cousin is prohibited. While such potential marriage relationships are not always realized, a man is said to have the right of marriage with his *-eni*. That is, such a marriage cannot be opposed by either the man's or women's family. In contrast, marriage between a man and his paternal cross-cousin (mFZD) is prohibited. Thus, marriage exchanges, at least in the ideal, are skewed toward the man's mother's brother's side.

If one actually does marry one's *-eni* then this person is referred to as *-eni tosei* (< *tosei* 'born together'). Moreover, if one does marry one's *-eni* then the siblings of this spouse can also be referred to as *-eni*. This explains why *-eni* can sometimes be extended to denote a man's same-sex paternal cross-cousin (mFZS) or a woman's same-sex maternal cross-cousin (fMBD), since those persons are the siblings of one's ideal marriage partner. If one does not marry one's *-eni* then that person can be distinguished as *-eni yira* (< *yira* 'base', see § 3). Marriageable cross-cousins who do not actually marry each other can also be referred to as *yiramei* 'man's marriageable cross-cousin' and *yiranen* 'woman's marriageable cross-cousin', though these terms are used only referentially and not as terms of address. The reciprocal terms *yiramei* and *yiranen* refer only to relationships established through a man's maternal uncle's side, and reciprocally a woman's paternal aunt's side. There are no special terms for the man's paternal uncle's side or woman's maternal aunt's side, further reflecting the asymmetry.

4.3 Non-prescriptive systems

In the remaining languages Adang, Abui, and Kamang there is no explicit marriage prescription. Marriage with close relatives is proscribed, and in Kamang this includes also a proscription against cross-cousin marriage. In Adang marriage between cross-cousins (i.e., *ob ai* and *lote ai*) is permitted but not required or even venerated, though in the modern contexts some regard the practice as backward and are reluctant to speak openly about it. Although the cross-cousin relationship is not considered to be a potential marriage relationship in the sense of being preferential, the relationship does have additional consequences within the kinship system. For example, if two men who can both call a given woman *ob ai*, then they must call each other as brothers. The designation *asel* referring to the mother's brother's lineage does not specify a prescribed marriage relationship, but the position of *asel* carries certain rights and privileges. For example, *asel* receives additional payments during bride wealth negotiations.

In Abui marriage between cross-cousins is tolerated in present Abui society, but as in Adang the practice is not venerated or preferred. In fact, several Abui adages suggest that there may have once been a stronger taboo against cross-cousin marriage. Even today, when cross-cousins desire to marry each other they are referred to as *hiyeng akuta* 'your eyes are blind', *hiyeng awai tuk* 'you have lime in your eyes', and *hiyeng hoopa naha* 'you don't have eyes'.

In Kamang marriage between cross-cousins is strictly prohibited. This situation is unique among the Alor-Pantar languages, and Kamang speakers are keenly aware of this uniqueness. In discussing this marriage taboo, Kamang speakers describe the closeness of the *lammi-malemi* relationship as *wee makaa*, literally 'bitter blood'. In other words, the blood of *lammi* and *malemi* is too close for marriage. Relations between *lammi* and *malemi* are highly prescribed. *Lammi* loves *malemi* as one would love one's adult child, while *malemi* must respect *lammi* as an adult child would respect their parents.

5 Discussion

Having compared kinship systems across eight different Alor-Pantar languages, we are left with the question of what the original kinship system looked like in proto-Alor-Pantar. Given the preliminary nature of these data, much of the following discussion is necessarily speculative; however, it is grounded in observed facts and at least describes a plausible historical pathway which has given rise to the current diversity in kinship systems across the Alor-Pantar languages.

Given the importance of cross-cousins and mother's brother in the modern languages, our search for a common origin should naturally begin with these and related terms. As we saw in § 3, very little kinship vocabulary is reconstructable at the level of pAP, and this is especially true for cross-cousin terms. Among those languages which obligatorily distinguish cross-cousins from siblings (see Table 16), no clear correspondences emerge. Teiwa *-ian* 'cross-cousin' may well be derived from *-ianqai* 'brother', or vice-versa (cf. *qai* 'only'). Blagar *-ebheang* 'cross-cousin' shows some similarity with Alorese (Austronesian) *opung* 'cross-cousin' and hence may be a loan (note also the optional Wersing term *-beng* 'same-sex cross-cousin'). Western Pantar *-baddang* and Blagar *-boromung*, both meaning 'opposite-sex cross-cousin', may well be cognate, though the correspondence of a geminate stop with a rhotic is irregular. Note that Teiwa also has *-bruman* 'marriageable cross-cousin', though the form *-dias* is used more commonly, and *-bruman* cannot be used as a vocative.

Among those languages which do not obligatorily distinguish cross-cousins (see Table 17), we find two patterns. Kiraman, Abui, Kamang and Wersing employ terms for cross-cousins which are built from the word for 'male' or 'female' plus a modifier. The male terms indicate mother's brother's side, i.e., MBC; the female terms indicate father's sister's side, i.e., FZC. However, the choice of modifier differs in each language. Kiraman uses *geta* 'trunk'; Abui uses *fala* 'house'; Kamang uses *mi* 'located'; and Wersing uses *deng* 'side'. Thus, while no form for MBC or FZC can be reconstructed, the pattern of deriving these terms from 'male' and 'female' is shared across the three languages. The fifth language, Adang, does not use 'male' and 'female' but instead distinguishes the mother's brother's side as *asel*, based on *sel* 'trunk'. Adang has no special term for FZC. This suggests that the practice of naming cross-cousins using terms derived from 'male' and 'female' may have diffused across these languages.

The lack of a clearly reconstructable cross-cousin term in both those languages which obligatorily distinguish cross-cousins and those which do not suggests that the cross-cousin concept has diffused recently, with terminology innovated differently in the different languages – especially in those languages which now obligatorily distinguish cross-cousins (with the possible exception of Blagar -*ebheang* and Wersing *-beng*, which may be related). In those languages not only do the terms for cross-cousin differ, but the distribution of terms across gender categories differs as well. Teiwa and Blagar have both a general cross-cousin term and a special "marriageable" term for opposite-sex cross-cousins. Western Pantar and Wersing have no general term but do distinguish same-sex versus opposite-sex cross-cousins. In Western Pantar same-sex cross-cousins are distinguished for gender (man's male cross-cousin versus woman's female cross-cousin), while in Wersing it is the opposite-sex cross-cousins which are distinguished for gender. Clearly if we are to look for some point of common origin we must look to the five languages which only optionally distinguish cross-cousins.

As we have seen, the pattern of using 'male' and 'female' to derive terms for mother's brother's and father's sister's sides is shared among four of the languages which optionally distinguish cross-cousins. Upon closer examination we find a less symmetrical division between MB and FZ lines in these languages. Three of the four languages with non-obligatory cross-cousin terms have terminology which privileges the mother's lineage. Kiraman, in addition to distinguishing the MB line as *nengeta* also has a special term *-eni* which is restricted to mMBD and not mFZD. Kiraman also distinguishes MB as *-mayira* distinct from F, while FZ is classed with M. Kamang distinguishes the mother's side with the modifier *ela* 'base'. Thus, *-paa ela* 'MB' is distinct from *-paa* 'F'. In contrast, FZ is classed with M as *-auko*. Finally, Adang distinguishes the mother's brother's line as *asel*, a term which applies across generations and may denote MB as well as MBC. Only Abui lacks asymmetrical terminology distinguishing MB.

At this point it is helpful to consider the geographic distribution of the languages according to whether cross-cousins are obligatorily distinguished. Those languages with non-obligatory distinction of cross-cousins are spoken in a nearly contiguous area across the heart of Alor (see Figure 16). This region is probably even more contiguous than it appears in the figure, since Kabola, spoken in the region between Adang and Abui, has a kinship system very similar to that of Adang. Much of this region is extremely mountainous, rugged, and isolated.

In contrast, those languages which obligatorily distinguish cross-cousins from siblings are restricted to Pantar and the neighboring small island of Pura. These are primarily coastal and lowland areas (or at least places with easy access to the coast) which would have had substantially more contact with Alorese, the language spoken by Austronesian migrants who arrived in Alor during the last millennium (Klamer 2011). In this context it is notable that Alorese has a symmet-

5 Kinship in the Alor-Pantar languages

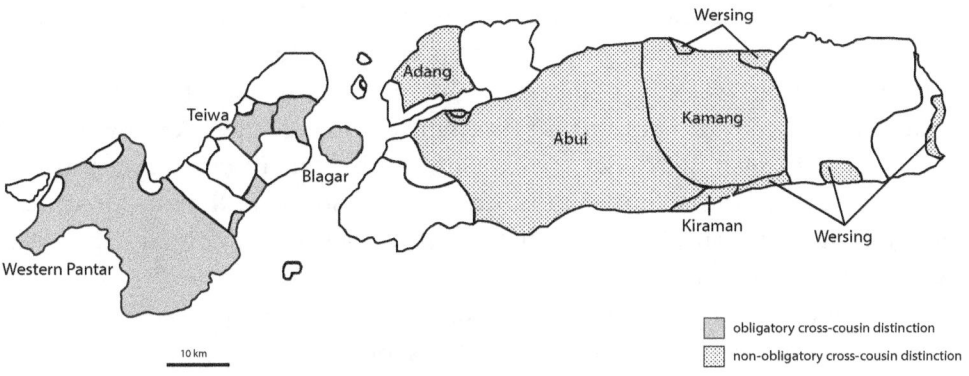

Figure 16: Geographic distribution of languages according to whether cross-cousins are obligatorily distinguished

ric alliance system which distinguishes cross-cousins from siblings (Needham 1956; Barnes 1973). In Alorese, classificatory same-sex siblings are distinguished by age: *kakang* 'elder (same-sex) sibling' versus *aring* 'younger (same-sex) sibling'; and classificatory opposite-sex siblings are distinguished for gender: *nang* 'woman's brother' versus *bineng* 'man's sister'. Both maternal and paternal cross-cousins are referred to as *opung* and may be distinguished for gender: *opung kafae* 'female cross-cousin' versus *opung kalake* 'male cross-cousin'. Moreover, these cross-cousin terms are used for affine (in-law) relations as well, yielding equations characteristic of a symmetric system. For example, *opung kalake* is both mother's brother and wife's father. The equation MB = WF implies that a man's wife must be his cross-cousin, since his mother's brother is the classificatory father of his wife. These same equations hold in Western Pantar and Teiwa, though not in the other languages, which largely retain reflexes of the original pAP affine term *dat (see Table 18). This suggests that in Western Pantar and Teiwa the original affine term has been replaced by the cross-cousin term under pressure from a shift to a symmetric alliance system.

Marriage practices may also be a result of contact with Alorese. Preference for cross-cousin marriage is strongest among the westernmost languages Western Pantar, Teiwa, and Blagar – i.e., those languages which have likely had the most contact with Alorese. The preference for cross-cousin marriage is strongest in Western Pantar, where the equation W = MBD = FZD holds, with the result that all marriages are treated as if they were between cross-cousins. At the other end of the spectrum, Kamang explicitly forbids marriage between cross-cousins.

In the more remote regions of central Alor, people view the concept of cross-cousin marriage as a coastal practice, often choosing to refer to it by its local Malay designation, *lake ruma - bini ruma*, literally 'house husband - house wife', rather than using equivalent terms from their own languages. Among Kamang speakers, where such marriages are explicitly forbidden, discussion of this relationship generated derisive laughter. Among Abui speakers there is an attitude of ambivalence. One speaker noted that "some people do that now, and the elders have seen that it is okay".

Further evidence that the preference for cross-cousin marriage is an innovation comes from the prevalence of terms for spouse's sibling which are distinct from terms for cross-cousin (see Table 18 above). In a system of direct exchange based on cross-cousin marriage we would expect cross-cousins to be equated with affines in ego's generation, for, in such a system, ego's spouse's sibling should also be a cross-cousin. Yet this equation again holds only in the westernmost languages, where obligatory cross-cousin distinctions have emerged.

Taken together this evidence, while admittedly circumstantial, suggests that the Alor-Pantar kinship system was originally non-prescriptive, with no distinctions between siblings and cousins. These systems then underwent drift toward prescriptive systems under influence of the Austronesian migrants. Some evolved asymmetric systems with preference for maternal cross-cousin marriage; while others evolved symmetric systems. Whether or not this historical scenario is correct must await further data and analysis. In the meantime it can be hoped that the data presented here go some way toward providing a fuller picture of kinship terminology in Alor-Pantar. Whatever the exact nature of proto-Alor-Pantar kinship may have been, it is clear that the family today shows enormous variation in both kinship terminology and practice, in spite of the fact that the various language communities are closely bound together through ties of marriage alliance. The Alor-Pantar languages thus provide fertile ground for the investigation of the ways kinship systems may evolve.

Sources

Data sources are as follows. Western Pantar is based on the author's own field work, primarily in 2007. Teiwa is based on Klamer (2010) and field work by Laura C. Robinson in 2010 and 2011 and by the author in 2013. Blagar is based on published data in Steinhauer (1993) as well as field work by Robinson in 2011. Kiraman is based on the author's field work in 2010 and 2013. Adang is based on field work by Robinson in 2010 and 2011 and by the author in 2013. Abui is based on Kratochvíl & Delpada (2008) and field work by the author in 2013. Kamang is based on Stokhof (1977), Schapper & Manimau (2011), and the author's field work in 2010 and 2013. Wersing is based on the author's work in 2010 and 2013. Alorese (Austronesian) is based on Needham (1956) and Barnes (1973). The author has conducted primary field work with all languages discussed in this chapter except Blagar, and in all cases the author accepts full responsibility for any errors of fact or interpretation.

Acknowledgments

I wish to acknowledge the many speakers who assisted with research on kinship terms in Alor-Pantar languages, especially: Mahalalel Lamma Koly, Nathan Lamma Koly, Amos Sir, Yarid Malaimakuni, Marlon Adang, Benny Delpada, Yulius Mantaun, Agus Mantaun and Ans Retebana, among many others. I also thank Marian Klamer, James Fox, and Hein Steinhauer for their critical comments on an earlier draft of this chapter.

Abbreviations

B	brother
C	child
D	daughter
e	elder
F	father
f	woman speaking
H	husband
M	mother
m	man speaking
S	son
W	wife
y	younger
Z	sister

References

Baird, Louise. 2008. *A grammar of Klon: a non-Austronesian language of Alor, Indonesia*. Canberra: Pacific Linguistics.

Barnes, Robert H. 1973. Two terminologies of symmetric prescriptive alliance from Pantar and Alor in Eastern Indonesia. *Sociologus* 23. 71–89.

Barnes, Robert H. 1980. Concordance, structure, and variation: Considerations of alliance in Kedang. In James J. Fox (ed.), 68–97. Cambridge: Cambridge University Press.

Blust, Robert Andrew. 1993. Austronesian sibling terms and culture history. *Bijdragen tot de Taal-, Land- en Volkenkunde* 149(1). 22–76.

Forman, Shepard. 1980. Descent, alliance, and exchange ideology among the makassae of East Timor. In James J. Fox (ed.), 152–177. Cambridge: Cambridge University Press.

Fox, James J. (ed.). 1980. *The flow of life: essays on Eastern Indonesian*. Cambridge: Cambridge University Press.

Fox, James J. 1995. *Origin structures and systems of precedence in the comparative study of Austronesian societies*. Paper read at Austronesian Studies Relating to Taiwan, Symposium Series of the Institute of History and Philology, Academia Sinica, at Taipei.

Haan, Johnson Welem. 2001. *The grammar of Adang: a Papuan language spoken on the island of Alor East Nusa Tenggara - Indonesia*. Sydney: University of Sydney PhD thesis.

Holton, Gary & Laura C. Robinson. this volume. The linguistic position of the Timor-Alor-Pantar languages. In Marian Klamer (ed.), *The Alor-Pantar languages*, 155–198. Berlin: Language Science Press.

Klamer, Marian. 2010. *A grammar of Teiwa* (Mouton Grammar Library 49). Berlin: Mouton de Gruyter.

Klamer, Marian. 2011. *A short grammar of Alorese (Austronesian)* (Languages of the World/Materials 486). München: Lincom.

Kratochvíl, František. 2007. *A grammar of Abui: a Papuan language of Alor*. Utrecht: LOT.

Kratochvíl, František & Benediktus Delpada. 2008. *Kamus pengantar Bahasa Abui (Abui-Indonesian-English dictionary)*. Kupang: Unit Bahasa dan Budaya (UBB).

Needham, Rodney. 1956. A note on kinship and marriage on Pantara. *Bijdragen tot de Taal-, Land- en Volkenkunde* 112-113. 285–290.

Nicolspeyer, Martha Margaretha. 1940. *De sociale structuur van een Aloreesche bevolkingsgroep*. Rijswijk: Rijksuniversiteit te Leiden PhD thesis.

Schapper, Antoinette & Marten Manimau. 2011. *Kamus pengantar Bahasa Kamang-Indonesia-Inggris (Introductory Kamang-Indonesian-English dictionary)* (UBB Language & Culture Series: A 7). Kupang: Unit Bahasa dan Budaya (BDD).

Schneider, David M. 1984. *A critique of the study of kinship*. Ann Arbor: University of Michigan.

Schweitzer, Peter P. 2000. Introduction. In Peter P. Schweitzer (ed.), *Dividends of kinship: Meanings and uses of social relatedness*, 1–32. New York: Routledge.

Steinhauer, Hein. 1993. Sisters and potential wives: where linguists and anthropologists meet: notes on kinship in Blagar (Alor). In P. Haenen (ed.), *Vrienden en verwanten, liber amicorum Alex van der Leeden*, 147–168. Leiden & Jakarta: DSALCUL/IRIS.

Steinhauer, Hein. 2010. Pura when we were younger than today. In Artem Fedorchuk & Svetlana Chlenova (eds.), *Studia antropologica. A Festschrift in honour of Michael Chlenov*, 261–283. Jerusalim: Mosty Kul'tury Gesharim.

Stokhof, W. A. L. 1977. *Woisika I: An ethnographic introduction* (Pacific Linguistics: Series D 19). Canberra: Australian National University.

Wouden, F. A. E. van. 1968. *Types of social structure in Eastern Indonesia*. Translated by Rodney Needham. Original edition, Sociale structuurtypen in de Groote Oost. The Hague: Marinus Nijhoff.

Chapter 6

Elevation in the spatial deictic systems of Alor-Pantar languages

Antoinette Schapper

> This chapter provides a formal and semantic typology of the highly elaborate spatial deictic systems involving an elevation component found in the Alor-Pantar languages. The systems show a high degree of variation both in the number of paradigms of elevation-marked terms as well as in the number of semantic components within the different elevational domains. The chapter further considers the history and reconstructability of an elevational system to proto-Alor-Pantar, observing that the elevation distinction itself is very stable in the deictic systems of the AP languages, but that the terms of the systems are not always stable and that the systems are often subject to elaboration.

1 Introduction

Elevation in a spatial deictic system is where a referent's location or trajectory is identified as being at a certain elevation relative to the deictic centre (abbreviated as 'DC'). Elevation is a common component of systems of spatial reference in several language areas: it is pervasive in the Tibeto-Burman (Bickel 2001; Cheung 2007; Post 2011) and New Guinea (Senft 1997; 2004; Diessel 1999; Levinson 1983) areas, and less common but recurrent in pockets of the Americas (e.g., Uto-Aztecan languages such as Guarjío, Miller 1996), Australia (e.g., Dyirbal, Dixon 1972: 48) and the Caucasus (e.g., East Caucasian languages, Schulze 2003). In the typological and descriptive literature, many terms have been used to describe elevation components in spatial deictic systems, including: "environmental space deixis" (Bickel 2001), "altitudinal case markers" (Ebert 2003), "height" (Dixon 2003), "vertical case" (Noonan 2006), "spatial coordinate systems" (Burenhult 2008), and "topographical deixis" (Post 2011).

In this chapter I further the typological study of spatial deictic systems with an elevation component by surveying the elevation-expressing terms in Alor-Pantar (AP) languages. Every AP language possesses elevation-expressing terms in at least two domains: (i) set of motion verbs (labelled here "elevational motion verbs") expressing that a trajectory is at a certain elevation relative to the deictic centre (go up, come down, go across, etc.), and (ii) set of non-verbal items (generically referred to here as "elevationals") expressing that a location is at a certain elevation relative to the deictic centre. The synchronic part of this chapter focuses on the use and function of the second of these sets and any additional elevational sets a language might have. These items show much morphosyntactic variation, in contrast to elevational verbs which have near-identical distributions across the AP languages.[1] I further consider the history and reconstructability of an elevational system to proto-Alor-Pantar, observing that the elevation distinction itself is very stable in the deictic systems of the AP languages, but that the terms of the systems are not always stable and that the systems are often subject to elaboration.

The chapter is structured as follows. In § 2, I set out the terminology and conventions that I will use in describing the elevational systems. In § 3, I describe the elevational systems of seven AP languages. For each language I discuss the number of elevation terms in the system, both within and across paradigms which contain elevation-marked terms. I highlight the variation that exists in the elaboration of the systems as well as in the morpho-syntactic behaviour of the items in the individual systems. In § 4, I turn to the history of AP elevational systems. Using data from eleven AP languages, I reconstruct the proto-AP elevational system and look at how different languages have expanded and complicated the inherited system. § 5 concludes the discussion and considers briefly the potential typological significance of AP elevational systems. All data is cited in a unified transcription in order to avoid confusion due to different orthographic practices for different languages. The sources for the data cited are given throughout the text of the chapter, but are also summarized in the 'Sources' section before the References.

2 Terminological preliminaries

The various labels that we saw in the previous section are indicative of the lack of standardized terminology to describe deictic systems with an elevational com-

---

[1] Note that I do not deal with how elevation terms are influenced by pragmatic and other contextual factors or by ultimate orientation effects (see Schapper 2012 for discussion of some of these effects in two Timor-Alor-Pantar languages).

6 Elevation in the spatial deictic systems of Alor-Pantar languages

ponent. In this section, I define the terminology for the different categories we encounter to be used throughout this chapter.

Of primary importance are the labels given to elevational heights. I distinguish three heights of elevation in basic glosses, as set out in (1). I avoid terms such as "below", "above", etc. as used by other authors, since these are typically relational terms whose locative reference does not hinge on a speech participant (speaker and/or addressee). For instance, in the sentence *The cat is below the chair*, the position of speech participants does not have any impact on the locative relation between the cat and the chair.

(1) 'HIGH': refers to any location situated *up(ward of)* the deictic centre;
'LOW': refers to any location situated *down(ward of)* the deictic centre;
'LEVEL': refers to any location situated *level with* the deictic centre.

There are very different ways in which an entity can be 'HIGH', 'LOW' or 'LEVEL' relative to the deictic centre. The most sophisticated typology of this is set out in Burenhult (2008). He identifies three kinds of systems (Burenhult 2008: 110-111) (see Table 1).

Table 1: Types of spatial coordinate system (Burenhult 2008: 110-111).

Global elevation	projects general search domains above or below the level of the deictic centre, with an axis from the deictic centre to the referent can but need not be strictly vertical (e.g., there anywhere above, below, etc.)
Verticality	projects very narrow search domains along a truly vertical axis running at a right angle through the deictic centre, invoking a sense of exactly above/overhead or below/underneath (e.g., there straight up, there directly below, etc.)
Geophysical elevation	projects search domains which restrict themselves to elevation as manifested in features of the geophysical environment and are not used to refer to the vertical dimension in general (e.g., there uphill, there downstream, etc.)

The AP languages have, for the most part, systems of global elevation. There are languages in which geophysics plays a role in mapping the elevation system onto the landscape, but this does not limit the systems from referring to locations as, for instance, only uphill or downhill. An example of this comes from Wersing: in this, elevational motion verbs *-a* 'go.LOW' and *-mid* 'go.HIGH' are often translated by speakers as 'go towards the sea' and 'go towards the mountains'. However, it does not follow that this is a geophysical system, since when we move speakers to a non-coastal environment, the verbs can still be applied despite the absence of the sea-land dichotomy in physical geography. In addition, AP languages may also incorporate elements of other elevational types into otherwise globally elevated systems. In § 3.5, we will see that, whilst Adang marks only global elevation in its elevationals, demonstratives and elevational motion verbs, it also has a special set of directional elevationals containing dedicated geophysical elevation terms as well as extra elevation terms in the HIGH domain marked for different degrees of verticality. Two languages, Western Pantar and Kamang, also incorporate the steepness of the slope into their elevational systems, which in essence is also a means of distinguishing greater or lesser degrees of verticality in elevational deixis.

In several AP languages which I will discuss, elevation-marked terms occur in paradigms with terms that are not marked for elevation. I refer to any term in a paradigm with elevation-marked terms which is not marked for elevation as 'UNELEVATED'. For those that are elevation-marked, I use the label 'ELEVATED'. Note that I avoid describing ELEVATED terms as "distal" as compared to the UNELEVATED terms with which they occur in paradigms. ELEVATED terms, in many instances, seem to form a separate system that contrasts with their UNELEVATED counterparts in terms of speech participant-anchoring. This means that, whereas UNELEVATED terms take one of their speech participants (speaker or addressee) as the deictic centre, ELEVATED terms refer to locations relative to the speech situation as a whole. However, on account of their only vague locational reference, they are not typically used in relation to items that are very close to a speaker. Labels such as "distal" (DIST) and "proximal" (PROX) as well as "addressee-anchored" (ADDR) and "speaker-anchored" (SPKR) will be used only in reference to UNELEVATED terms.[2] The terms 'NEAR' and 'FAR' are used instead for the few occasions in which we find distance-related distinctions between ELEVATED terms.

Finally, I use the term "elevational" to refer to the sets of non-verbal items denoting a location that is at a certain elevation relative to the deictic centre.

---

[2] This glossing of demonstratives is taken from Schapper & San Roque (2011). See their discussion and illustration of the meanings and uses of such demonstratives.

6 Elevation in the spatial deictic systems of Alor-Pantar languages

I use the term "locational" to refer to paradigms of ELEVATED and UNELEVATED terms referring to locations. This means, ELEVATED locationals are "elevationals", while UNELEVATED locationals are functional equivalents to such items as English "here" and "there". However, I avoid the common label given to these ("demonstrative adverbs", as, e.g., in Diessel 1999) since locationals in AP languages are not typically restricted to adverbial positions, but can often also occur as predicates and in NPs. I reserve the term "demonstrative" for an NP constituent that refers to an entity by locating it in space. By contrast, locationals, including elevationals, denote a location relative to which a referent can be identified in space. The morpho-syntax of elevationals in individual languages will be described in § 3.

3 Alor-Pantar elevational systems

The expression of elevation is considered in seven AP languages from across the archipelago. I discuss languages in order of the complexity of their elevational systems. Complexity here is calculated by looking at both the number of elevation-marked terms and the number of semantic components within the different elevational domains. The relative complexity of the different AP systems is discussed at the end of this section (§ 3.8).

3.1 Wersing

Wersing has one of the simpler elevational systems, with a total of nine elevation-marked terms. There are three elevationals for the three elevational heights, each matched with motion verbs denoting movement to and from the deictic centre (Table 2). No additional semantic distinctions are made in the elevational or verbal paradigm.[3]

Wersing elevationals can be used as one-place predicates encoding the location of a NP referent at an elevation relative to the speaker. Example (2) illustrates this predicative use.

(2) Wersing (Schapper & Hendery 2014: 457)
   *Sobo ba **tona**.*
   house ART HIGH
   'The house is up there.'

---
[3] This section is based on Schapper & Hendery (2014: 457-458).

Table 2: Wersing elevation terms

	Elevationals	Elevational motion verb From DC	To DC
LEVEL	*mona*	*-wai*	*-mai*
HIGH	*tona*	*-mid*	*-dai*
LOW	*yona*	*-a*	*-sir*

The elevationals also have non-predicative uses where they locate an action or an entity as at a particular elevation. In these contexts the elevational follows the clausal element(s) over which it has scope. In (3) the elevational *mona* follows the NP headed by *pei* 'pig' and denotes the elevation of the pig at the time of its still breathing. In (4) *yona* follows the verbal predicate *aki* 'call' and denotes the elevation at which the calling takes place.

(3) NP scope Wersing (Schapper & Hendery (2014: 457))
*Pei ba **mona** de ge-kiŋ sesai.*
pig ART DOWN IPFV 3-breathe breath
'The pig (that is) over there is still breathing.'

(4) Predicate scope Wersing (Schapper & Hendery (2014: 248))
*David aki **yona**.*
David call DOWN
'David calls (from) down there.'

3.2 Teiwa

Teiwa also has a simple 9-term elevational system (Table 3). Like Wersing, elevationals and elevation-marked motion verbs distinguish the three elevational heights and no additional semantic distinctions are made.

Teiwa elevationals occur predicatively, where they indicate the elevational height of the NP referent, as in (5).

(5) Teiwa (Klamer 2010: 142)
*Uy nuk un **maraqai**.*
3SG one CONT HIGH
'Is a person up there?'

6 Elevation in the spatial deictic systems of Alor-Pantar languages

Table 3: Teiwa elevation terms

	Elevationals	Elevational motion verb	
		From DC	To DC
LEVEL	*wunaxai*	*wa*	*ma*
HIGH	*maraqai*	*mir*	*daa*
LOW	*yaqai*	*yix*	*yaa*

Elevationals in Teiwa can also occur in positions both before and after predicates. In (6) *maraqai* precedes the postpositional predicate *uyan me?*, and locates it as at a higher elevation than the speaker. In (7) *yaqai* after the verb *yix* denotes the location resulting from the motion as at a lower elevation than the speaker.

(6) Teiwa (Klamer 2010: 141)
   A ***maraqai*** uyan me?.
   3SG HIGH mountain in
   'He's in the mountains up there.'

(7) Teiwa (Klamer, fieldnotes)
   Iman yix-in ***yaqai***.
   3PL go.LOW-REAL LOW
   'They went down there.'

3.3 Abui

In Abui elevational motion verbs maintain the simple three-way distinction already observed in Wersing and Teiwa. However, the elevationals show an extra degree of elaboration in the HIGH and LOW spheres, with a distance contrast being added between NEAR and FAR locations. The LEVEL sphere does not show this extra semantic component.

Abui elevationals can be predicates, as for instance in (8) where *oro* denotes elevation of the branch in relation to the speaker. Where they indicate the ele-

---

[3] The syntactic classification of the elevationals is that of the present author. Kratochvíl (2007) includes elevationals in a single class with the demonstratives *do, o, to, yo*, and the articles *hu* and *nu*. These two sets have different syntactic distributions from the set of elevationals I identify. See Schapper & San Roque (2011) for details on the morphosyntactic properties of Abui demonstratives. The distributional characteristics of Abui elevations are set out in the main text here.

Table 4: Abui elevation terms

		Elevationals	Elevational motion verb From DC	To DC
LEVEL		*oro*	*we*	*me*
HIGH	NEAR	*ó* †	*marei*	*maraŋ*
	FAR	*wó*		
LOW	NEAR	*ò*	*pa*	*sei*
	FAR	*wò*		

† Accents mark tone. The rising accent marks high tone, while the grave accent marks low tone. See Kratochvíl (2007: 60)

vation at which an action takes place, elevations occur directly before a verb, as with the predicative verb *burok* 'move' in (9).

(8) Abui (Kratochvíl, Abui corpus)
 *Bataa ha-taŋ   dara **oro**.*
 tree 3.POSS-arm still LEVEL
 'The tree branch is still over there.'

(9) Abui (Kratochvíl, Abui corpus)
 *Bataa ha-taŋ   dara **oro**   burok.*
 tree 3.POSS-arm still LEVEL move
 'The tree branch is still moving over there.'

Abui elevationals can also occur in NPs. In an NP headed by a noun the elevational follows the head, but to the left of any article or demonstrative marking the right periphery of the NP. For instance, in (10) the LEVEL elevational *oro* follows the NP head *fu* 'betel' but precedes the demonstrative *do*. It indicates the elevation at which the betel palm is found. An elevational can also occur in an NP without a head noun. In this case the elevational is the head of the NP and the referent of the NP is the location indicated by the elevational. In (11) the LOW elevational *ò* heads the NP marked by the article *nu* and the demonstrative *do*. This NP occurs in the postpositional phrase headed by *=ŋ* and denotes the goal location for the motion dignified by the elevational verb *pa* 'go down'.

(10) Abui (Kratochvíl, Abui corpus)
 Di yaa [fu **oro** do]_NP mia.
 3 go betel LEVEL DEM in
 'He went to this betel (palm) (which is) over here.'

(11) Abui (Kratochvíl, Abui corpus)
 ... ha-bukaŋ dikaŋ mi [ò **nu** do]_NP=ŋ pa.
 ... 3.POSS-thimble again take LOW.FAR ART DEM=LOC go.LOW
 '... (he) again goes to take his thimble to down there.'

3.4 Blagar

Blagar has a plethora of elevation terms, with a total of 32 elevation-marked forms. These occur in paradigms with speech participant-anchored terms (Table 5). Blagar has five locationals. These appear both as independent words and as constituents of multiple sets of derived items (bolded in Table 5). These particles consist of the three elevationals, *mo* 'LEVEL', *do* 'HIGH' and *po* 'LOW', plus two UNELEVATED speech participant-anchored locationals, *ʔa* 'PROX.SPKR' and *ʔu* 'PROX.ADDR'. Only the elevational motion verbs, which have different etymologies, do not include the basic elevationals in their forms.

The elevationals occur in two positions: between the subject and its predicate, as in (12), and following the predicate, as in (13). The different positions are associated with different epistemic values. The clause-medial position connotes epistemic certainty on the part of the speaker, while the clause-final position connotes epistemic accessibility to the addressee, that is, that the addressee is or could be aware of the situation described in the clause (Hein Steinhauer, p.c.).[4]

(12) Blagar (Steinhauer, p.c.)
 ʔana **po** ab na.
 3SG.SUBJ LOW fish eat
 'S/he eats fish down there (for sure).'

(13) Blagar (Steinhauer, p.c.)
 ʔana ab na **po**.
 3SG.SUBJ fish eat LOW
 'S/he eats fish down there (as you may know).'

---

[4] Schapper & San Roque (2011) describe similar epistemic uses of demonstratives in TAP languages. Blagar appears to be unique in its use of different syntactic positions of deictic particles to denote different levels of epistemic accessibility.

Table 5: Blagar elevation terms

		Locationals
LEVEL		*mo*
HIGH		*do*
LOW		*po*
UNELEVATED	PROX.SPKR	ʔa
	PROX.ADDR	ʔu

		Stative verbs				
		be as much as	be as big as	be as high as	be at	be at vis
LEVEL		*monoaŋ*	*movaŋ*	*mohukaŋ*	*moʔe*	*momo*
HIGH		*donoaŋ*	*dovaŋ*	*dohukaŋ*	*doʔe*	*dodo*
LOW		*ponoaŋ*	*povaŋ*	*pohukaŋ*	*poʔe*	*popo*
UNELEVATED	PROX.SPKR	ʔanoaŋ	ʔavaŋ	ʔahukaŋ	ʔaʔe	ʔaʔa
	PROX.ADDR	ʔunoaŋ	ʔuvaŋ	ʔuhukaŋ	ʔuʔe	ʔuʔu

		Demonstratives		Manner adverbs
		Basic	Collective	
LEVEL		*ʔamo*	*ʔanamo*	*molaŋ*
HIGH		*ʔado*	*ʔanado*	*dolaŋ*
LOW		*ʔapo*	*ʔanapo*	*polaŋ*
UNELEVATED	PROX.SPKR	*ʔaŋa*	*ʔanaŋa*	*ʔalaŋ*
	PROX.ADDR	*ʔaŋu*	*ʔanaŋu*	*ʔulaŋ*

	Elevational motion verbs	
	From DC	To DC
LEVEL	*va*	*ma*
HIGH	*mida*	*da*
LOW	*ʔipa*	*ya*
UNELEVATED	*ʔila*	*hoʔa*

6 Elevation in the spatial deictic systems of Alor-Pantar languages

The derived demonstratives (basic and collective) occur marking the right-hand periphery of the NP either with (14) or without a noun head (15).

(14) Blagar (Steinhauer 2012)
 [Hava kiki ʔa-na-**po**]ₙₚ kaʔana.
 house little DEM-COLL-LOW black
 'That group of little houses down there is black.'

(15) Blagar (Steinhauer 2012)
 ʔini [ʔa-**mo**]ₙₚ mi mihi.
 3PL.SUBJ DEM-LEVEL LOC sit
 'They live in that (place) over there.'

The derived manner adverbs occur in one of two positions: (i) preceding the subject (16), or (ii) following the predicate (17).

(16) Blagar (Steinhauer 2012)
 ʔu-laŋ ana tia.
 PROX.ADDR-like 2SG.SUBJ sleep
 'That is how you sleep.'

(17) Blagar (Steinhauer 2012)
 Ana tia-t ʔa-laŋ.
 2SG.SUBJ sleep-MNR PROX.SPKR-like
 'You sleep like this.'

Derived stative verbs refer to measurement (18), and static location (19).

(18) Blagar (Steinhauer 2012)
 Ne hava **do**-vaŋ.
 1SG.POSS house HIGH-big.as
 'My house is as big as the one up there.'

(19) Blagar (Steinhauer 2012)
 ʔana mida **do**-ʔe.
 3SG.SUBJ go.HIGH HIGH-be.at
 'S/he went up and is up there.'

Table 6: Adang elevation terms (reanalysed from Haan 2001)

		Locationals		Demonstratives
		Basic	Directional	
LEVEL		mɔŋ malɛ	falɛ	hɛmɔ
HIGH		tɔŋ madɔŋlɛ adaŋlɛ taʔlɛ talɛ	midlɛ	hɛtɔ
LOW		pɔŋ	iplɛ hɛllɛ lifaŋlɛ	hɛpɔ
UNELEVATED	PROX.SPKR PROX.ADDR	ɔŋ		hɔʔɔ ho

	Elevational motion verbs	
	From DC	To DC
LEVEL	fa	ma
HIGH	mid	madɔŋ
LOW	ip	hɛl
UNELEVATED	sam	hoʔ

3.5 Adang

Adang has 22 elevation-marked terms occurring in a paradigm with UNELEVATED terms (Table 6). Elevation terms are divided across three word classes: locationals, demonstratives and elevational motion verbs. These are described below.

Elevational motion verbs follow the simple 6-term pattern that we have seen for all AP discussed thus far. ELEVATED demonstratives have a three-way elevational contrast marked by *mɔ* 'LEVEL', *tɔ* 'HIGH' and *pɔ* 'LOW', while their UN-ELEVATED counterparts are essentially characterizable by the absence of these morphemes. The largest elevational word class is the ELEVATED locationals, or elevationals. These divide into two sets, basic and directional, that are distinguished from one another both formally and semantically. The basic set has the elevation-marking morphemes we saw in the ELEVATED demonstratives marked with -ŋ and occurs in a paradigm with an UNELEVATED term. The directional set of elevationals differs from the basic set in that they are derived from other roots with the suffix -lɛ and do not have UNELEVATED counterparts.

Semantically, the contrast between the basic and directional elevationals is in the first place the type of elevation they reference. Basic elevationals refer to global elevation. In the directional set, different terms have different elevational reference. In Table 7 I set out the elevational reference and the sources of roots of the directional elevationals. The two geophysical elevationals in Adang reference a trajectory between the inland mountains where Adang villages are traditionally located and the coastal lowlands away from Adang villages. The two vertical elevationals reference a location that is vertically HIGH in relation to the DC. The difference between *taʔlɛ* and *talɛ* appears to be one of the contact relationship between the DC and the referent location. *Taʔlɛ* references a location straight up from the DC without being in contact with the DC, while *talɛ* references a location that is directly on top of and in contact with the DC. Finally, the directional elevationals with global elevational reference are built from elevation-marked motion verbs. They differ referentially from the basic set which also refers to elevation globally with reference to location as being towards ('WARDS') or away ('AWAY') from the DC, according to what elevational motion verb is the root (see Table 7).

Despite the formal and semantic differences between basic and directional elevationals, they have the same syntactic distributional properties and cannot cooccur in the clause. This indicates that they are of one and the same word class. They occur in three positions.

First, an elevational can occur as an independent clausal predicate. This is seen in (20) with the basic elevational *tɔŋ* 'HIGH' and in (21) with the directional elevational *iplɛ* 'LOW-AWAY'.

(20) Adang (Haan 2001: 192)
 Aru nu tɔŋ.
 deer one HIGH
 'There is a deer up there.'

(21) Adang (Haan 2001: 192)
 Bel iplɛ.
 dog LOW.AWAY
 'There are dogs down there (away from the speaker).'

Table 7: Sources of Adang directional elevationals.

Geophysical:	*adaŋlɛ*	MOUNTAIN.WARDS	< *adaŋ*	'mountain'
	lifaŋlɛ	COAST.WARDS	< *lifaŋ*	'anchor'
Vertical:	*taʔlɛ*	HIGH.VERTICAL	< *ta*	'(put) on'
	talɛ	ON.VERTICAL		
Global:	*midlɛ*	HIGH.AWAY	< *mid*	'go.HIGH'
	madɔŋlɛ	HIGH.WARDS	< *madɔŋ*	'come.HIGH'
	iplɛ	LOW.AWAY	< *ip*	'go.LOW'
	hɛllɛ	LOW.WARDS	< *hɛl*	'come.LOW'
	falɛ	LEVEL.AWAY	< *fa*	'go.LEVEL'
	malɛ	LEVEL.WARDS	< *ma*	'come.LEVEL'

Second, elevationals can occur adverbially before a predicate and its (if any) adjunct. In (22) the basic elevational *mɔŋ* 'LEVEL' indicates the locational setting for the verbal predicate *tuf* 'stand' and its adjunct *bana mi* 'in the forest'. In (23) the directional elevational *iplɛ* 'LOW.DC-AWAY' modifies the simple verbal predicate *tar* 'lie down'.

(22) Adang (Robinson & Haan 2014: 237)
      Ti   taʔat ho   **mɔŋ** bana mi tuf=eh.
      tree dry   DEM LEVEL   forest IN stand=PROG
      'The dry stick is standing over there in the forest.'

(23) Adang (Haan 2001: 191)
      Bel **iplɛ**   tar=eh.
      dog LOW.AWAY   lie.down=PROG
      'There are dogs lying down down there (in a direction away from the speaker).'

Finally, elevationals can also occur with an NP. Where an elevated demonstrative also occurs in the NP, then the elevational and demonstrative must match in elevational marking. The NP headed by *bel* 'dog' is modified by the basic LEVEL elevational and the LEVEL demonstrative in (24) and by a directional LOW elevational and the LOW demonstrative in (25).

(24) Adang (Haan 2001: 188)
Bel **mɔŋ hɛmɔ** matɛ.
dog LEVEL DEM.LEVEL big
'That dog over there is large.'

(25) Adang (Haan 2001: 188)
Bel **iplɛ hɛpɔ** matɛ.
dog LOW.AWAY DEM.LOW big
'That dog over there is large.'

Table 8 summarizes the permitted combinations of demonstrative and elevationals. Note that the only exception to the matching of elevations between demonstratives and elevationals within an NP is with *talɛ* 'ON.VERTICAL'. This elevational refers to the location of *another entity on* the NP referent. Thus, the NP referent may be specified with a demonstrative as being HIGH, LOW or LEVEL in relation to the speaker as DC, and then also be located on another entity by means of *talɛ*. The possibility of these combinatorics is illustrated in (26) and (27).

(26) Adang (Haan 2001: 188)
Namɛ be **talɛ hɛmɔ** fail.
person mango ON.VERTICAL DEM.LEVEL sell
'Someone is selling those mangoes on the others mangoes (the upper group of mangoes) over there.'

(27) Adang (Haan 2001: 188)
Bel **talɛ hɛpɔ** matɛ.
person ON.VERTICAL DEM.LOW big
'That dog up here from the others down there is big.'

3.6 Western Pantar

Western Pantar has a total of 26 elevation-marked terms, occurring in paradigms with speech participant-anchored terms (Table 9). As in Blagar and Adang, elevation marking is repeated across multiple paradigms of different word classes in Western Pantar. These are: locationals, demonstratives and elevational motion verbs.

The number of elevational motion verbs is higher than in the AP languages looked at thus far. This is due to an extra distinction between steep versus non-steep appearing in the verbs denoting motion away from the deictic centre. The

Table 8: Combinations of ELEVATED demonstratives and elevationals (adapted from Haan 2001: 188)

	Demonstrative	Elevational
HIGH	hɛtɔ	mɔŋ midlɛ madɔŋlɛ adaŋlɛ taʔlɛ talɛ
LOW	hɛpɔ	pɔŋ iplɛ hɛllɛ lifaŋlɛ talɛ
LEVEL	hɛmɔ	mɔŋ falɛ malɛ talɛ

high number of elevation-marked terms found in the three elevation-marked word classes is, however, chiefly due to the existence of multiple paradigms of locationals and demonstratives in Western Pantar. Locationals and demonstratives have distinct paradigms for specific versus non-specific reference, and demonstratives further have separate paradigms for visible versus non-visible referents. Across the locational and demonstrative paradigms, marking for location has the same forms derived from the basic (i.e., non-specific) locationals. These are the three elevationals, *mau* 'LEVEL', *dau* 'HIGH' and *pau* 'LOW' (bolded in Table 9), plus the two UNELEVATED speech participant-anchored locationals, *iga* 'PROX.SPKR' and *ina* 'DIST.SPKR'. Specific-marked forms of locationals and demonstratives are derived by means of *s-* prefixed onto the basic locationals (28). Demonstratives are derived from the elevationals by *-gu* for the visible paradigm and *-m(e)* for the non-visible paradigm (29).

6 Elevation in the spatial deictic systems of Alor-Pantar languages

Table 9: Western Pantar elevation terms (adapted from Holton 2007 and Holton 2014)

		Locationals		Demonstratives			
				visible		invisible	
		NSPEC	SPEC	NSPEC	SPEC	NSPEC	SPEC
LEVEL		*mau*	*smau*	*maugu*	*smaugu*	*maume*	*smaume*
HIGH		*dau*	*srau*	*daugu*	*sraugu*	*daume*	*sraume*
LOW		*pau*	*spau*	*paugu*	*spaugu*	*paume*	*spaume*
UNELEVATED	PROX.SPKR	*iga*	*siga*	*aiga*	*saiga*	*igamme*	*sigamme*
	DIST.SPKR†	*ina*	*sina*	*aina*	*saina*	*inamme*	*sinamme*

		Elevational motion verbs	
		From DC	To DC
LEVEL		*wa*	*ma*
HIGH	STEEP	*mia*	*middaŋ*
	NSTEEP	*rauŋ*	
LOW	STEEP	*pia*	*yaŋ*
	NSTEEP	*dakaŋ*	

† The distal means away from speaker or other established deictic centre, not necessarily close to addressee.

(28) Western Pantar (Holton 2011)
[*Ging spaugu*]_{NP}   *kuaŋ*   *i-pariŋ*.
3PL   SPEC.LOW.VIS.DEM moko.drum 3PL-surrender
'Those who are the ones visible down there will hand over the moko drums.'

(29) Western Pantar (Holton 2011)
[*Aname ye daum*]_{NP}   *is*   *taŋ tiʔaŋ kor id-dia*.
person one HIGH.NVIS.DEM banyan on sleep snore PROG-go
'Someone who is up there in a banyan tree sleeping and snoring away.'

Western Pantar elevationals occur as predicates denoting the location of a NP referent at an elevation relative to the speaker. Example (30) illustrates this predicative use.

(30) Western Pantar (Holton, p.c.)
   Hinani=b **srau**?
   what=FOC SPEC.HIGH
   'What is up there?'

Within the clause, elevationals follow the element whose location they denote, and thus may appear clause-medially or -finally. For instance, in (31) the LOW elevational *pau* follows the subject *eu* 'girl' and denotes the location of her at the time of calling. In (32) *pau* denotes the location of the object *habbaŋ* 'village' which it follows, while in (33) *mau* denotes the location of the pre-subject locative adjunct *habbaŋ* 'village' which it follows.

(31) Western Pantar (Holton, Western Pantar corpus)
   Eu **pau** *asaŋ* ,...
   girl LOW say ...
   'The girl down there says, ...'

(32) Western Pantar (Holton, Western Pantar corpus)
   Sinam   bila taŋ misiŋ i   habbaŋ **pau** *ya   saukaŋ*
   SPEC.NVIS.DEM hill top sit 3PL.RFLX.POSS village LOW toward watch
   pia.
   go.LOW.STEEP
   '(They) sat on the top of the mountain there and looked down at their village.'

(33) Western Pantar (Holton & Lamma Koly 2008: 97)
   Habbaŋ **mau** *aname horaŋ   sauke-yabe.*
   village LEVEL person make.noise women.dance
   'Over in the village people are making noise dancing lego-lego.'

Elevationals in clause-final position indicate the location at which the preceding predicate takes place. For instance, final *pau* in (34) denotes that the event of *teri* 'anchoring' is at lower elevation than the deictic centre. Similarly, in (35) final *dau* signals that the motion denoted by *mia* 'go.HIGH.STEEP' is higher in elevation than the deictic centre.

(34) Western Pantar (Holton, Western Pantar corpus)
   *Asaŋ sibaŋ   tukka yallu paum   i-teri   **pau**.*
   say driftwood short one LOW.NVIS.DEM PROG-anchor LOW
   'Apparently, there's a short (piece of) driftwood caught down there.'

(35) Western Pantar (Holton, Western Pantar corpus)
Manne gaŋ a-wake siŋ usiŋ ga-r halli wa im-mia
woman 3SG 4-child this cradle 3-with cry go.LEVEL PROG-go.HIGH.STEEP
dau.
HIGH
'His wife cradled her child while crying over him going back up there.'

3.7 Kamang

Kamang elevation terms are given in Table 10. The Kamang elevational paradigms have more terms than most AP languages due to the presence of two additional semantic components in the HIGH and LOW domains, namely, direction and distance. Direction has to do with the angle of the path taken or referenced location relative to the angle of the slope. Using a DIRECT elevation term means that the path taken follows the angle of the slope directly (i.e., at its steepest), whilst an INDIRECT elevation term means that the path traverses across the angle of the slope or that the referenced location is off to the side of angle of the slope. Distance is only marked in the INDIRECT domain, and is concerned with whether the path taken is short or long or the referenced location is near or far. Thus, using a NEAR elevation term means traversing across a slope for a short distance, while using a FAR one means traversing across a slope for a long distance.

Table 10: Kamang elevation terms

| | | | Elevationals | Elevational motion verbs | |
				From DC	To DC
LEVEL			*muŋ*	*we*	*me*
HIGH	DIRECT		*tuŋ*	*te*	*taaŋ*
	INDIRECT	NEAR	*mutuŋ*	*wete*	*metaaŋ*
		FAR	*tumuŋ*	*tewe*	*taaŋme*
LOW	DIRECT		*fuŋ*	*fe*	*yaaŋ*
	INDIRECT	NEAR	*muhuŋ*	*wehe*	*yaaŋme*
		FAR	*fumuŋ*	*fewe*	

Kamang elevationals occur adverbially, directly before a predicate or a predicate and its object. For instance, in (36) *mutuŋ* denotes the location from which the calling takes place, and in (37) *tuŋ* gives the location on the slope where the stumbling takes place. An elevational may also occur following a motion verb specifying the resultant location of the motion, as in (38) where the elevational *tuŋ* follows its corresponding elevational verb *te*.

(36) Kamang (Schapper 2014a: 306)
   *Nok sue   koo **mutuŋ** wo-iti-si.*
   one come stay LEVEL 3.LOC-call-IPFV
   'Somebody was calling him from over there.'

(37) Kamang (Schapper 2014a: 306)
   *Markus **tuŋ**   wuleh sama   kawaila-ma.*
   Markus HIGH.DRCT slope middle stumble-PFV
   'Markus stumbled on the slope up (which is) up there.'

(38) Kamang (Schapper 2014a: 306)
   *Nal te   **tuŋ**.*
   1SG go.HIGH.DRCT HIGH.DRCT
   'I go up top.'

3.8 Summary

AP languages invariably have elevation marking in a set of non-verbal elevationals and in a paradigm of elevational verbs. In the preceding sections, we have seen some of the variety that elevational systems contain.

AP languages vary significantly in the number of elevation terms, the number of paradigms over which they occur and the extra semantic components that are added within the three elevational heights (summarized in Table 11).

Minimally, AP languages have 9 elevation terms, with three elevationals and six elevational motion verbs distinguishing three elevations. A much higher number of terms are found in languages such as Blagar, Adang and Western Pantar, which have elevation marking morphology reiterated over multiple paradigms of different word classes, including in particular demonstratives (one extra paradigm in Adang, two in Blagar and four in Western Pantar), verbs (six extra paradigms in Blagar) and adverbs (one extra paradigm in Blagar).

The number of elevation-marked terms has also been increased by adding semantic distinctions within the three elevational heights. Adang has the greatest number of semantic elaborations, with geophysical, vertical and directional terms being added in the elevationals to the standard global elevationals. Kamang

6 Elevation in the spatial deictic systems of Alor-Pantar languages

Table 11: Overview of elaboration of elevational systems in AP languages

	elevation marked forms	paradigms with elevationals	extra semantic features
Wersing	9	2	0
Teiwa	9	2	0
Abui	11	2	1
Blagar	32	10	0
Adang	22	4	3
Western Pantar	26	8	1
Kamang	20	2	2

adds two new semantic components to its elevation-marked terms, directionality and distance. Western Pantar and Abui add one extra semantic distinction, steepness and distance respectively.

Added semantic components are typically limited to either particular elevational domains or to particular paradigms of elevation-marked terms. Table 12 presents an overview of the distribution of these across AP languages. A cell with '1' represents a domain without semantic elaboration, whilst higher numerals (bolded) indicate the presence of semantic elaborations.

We see that it is not typical to elaborate in the LEVEL domain. Only Adang has more than one LEVEL term in its elevationals, due to the regular derivation of directional elevationals from elevation-marked verbs (*falɛ* < *fa* 'GO.LEVEL', *malɛ* < *ma* 'come.LEVEL'). All other languages restrict their elaborations to the HIGH and LOW domains. Semantic elaborations are typically also limited to one paradigm and are not elaborated over all paradigms. Abui and Adang limit their extra distinctions to elevationals, while Western Pantar limits it to elevational motion verbs denoting movement away from the DC. Kamang is unusual in that it has almost the same semantic elaborations in both its elevationals and elevational verbs. Asymmetries in the number of extra distinctions are present in Adang and Kamang, while Abui and Western Pantar apply the semantic elaboration to all parts of the paradigm.

The syntax of elevation-marked terms also shows variation between languages. Focusing on the elevationals (or "ELEVATED locationals", items referring to a loca-

Table 12: Number of elevation-marked terms by elevational domain and word class

	Elevationals			Elevational motion verbs					
				From DC			To DC		
	LEVEL	HIGH	LOW	LEVEL	HIGH	LOW	LEVEL	HIGH	LOW
Wersing	1	1	1	1	1	1	1	1	1
Teiwa	1	1	1	1	1	1	1	1	1
Abui	1	2	2	1	1	1	1	1	1
Blagar	1	1	1	1	1	1	1	1	1
Adang	3	6	4	1	1	1	1	1	1
Western Pantar	1	1	1	1	2	2	1	1	1
Kamang	1	3	3	1	3	3	1	3	2

tion at a specified elevation), we observed a range of syntactic differences from one language to the next. In Table 13, I summarize the ability of AP elevationals to occur predicatively, adverbially and within the NP.

Table 13: Overview of syntax of elevationals in AP languages

	predicative	Adverbial		(Ad-)Nominal	
		medial	final	w/ noun head	w/o noun head
Wersing	yes	yes	no	no	no
Teiwa	yes	yes	yes	no	no
Abui	yes	yes	no	yes	yes
Blagar	no	yes	yes	no	no
Adang	yes	yes	no	yes	no
Western Pantar	yes	yes	yes	no	no
Kamang	no	yes	yes	no	no

In all but two languages (Kamang and Blagar), elevationals occur as independent clausal predicates indicating the elevation at which the subject was to be located. Blagar does not allow elevationals predicatively, and instead has a derived paradigm of stative elevational verbs which fulfill the same function as predicative elevationals in other AP languages.

6 Elevation in the spatial deictic systems of Alor-Pantar languages

All languages allow their elevationals to occur clause-medially, when adverbial. However, only four languages (Teiwa, Blagar, Western Pantar and Kamang) allow elevationals to occur clause-finally. Yet, even where the clausal position was the same, there were, differences from language to language in the function and constituency of elevationals in adverbial use. The most common clause-medial function of an elevational was to mark that the situation or event denoted by the following predicate took place at a certain elevation. This was found for Wersing, Teiwa, Abui, Adang and Kamang clause-medial adverbial elevationals, but not in Blagar and Western Pantar. In Blagar the choice of clausal position of an elevational reflected not spatial but epistemic differences, with clause-medial position signalling certainty on the part of the speaker and clause-final position signalling epistemic accessibility of knowledge of the event to the addressee. In Kamang, by contrast, the clausal position of an elevational reflects a different kind of location: clause-medially an elevational denotes the location at which the following predicate take places, whereas clause-finally an elevational denotes a location resulting from the predicate. In Western Pantar, making a clause-final versus clause-medial distinction is misleading because the constituency of an elevational is the same in both positions: Western Pantar elevationals follow the element whose location they denote, medially these are NPs and finally these are verbs.

In the nominal domain, we also observed variation in how individual languages could use elevationals. All but Abui and Adang did not allow elevationals to occur in the NP. Abui allowed elevationals not only to occur within an NP alongside a head noun, but also to head the NP itself, while Adang only allowed elevationals to occur within a head noun.

In short, elevation marking in AP languages is characterized by diversity not only in the sheer number of terms that systems contain, but also in the semantic components and syntactic behaviour of those terms.

4 History of AP elevation terms

Thus far our explorations of AP elevational systems have been synchronic, describing the internal structures of the systems one language at a time. Today, even if the majority of elevational systems in AP languages are little explored, the quantity and quality of existing information is sufficient for the formulation of historical hypotheses about the elevational system of their common ancestor, proto-AP (pAP).

In Table 14, I present the reconstructable elevational forms of pAP. These reconstructions are made by comparing the terms in the systems found in modern AP languages. The one peculiarity of this reconstructed system is that the LOW elevational domain has two competing reconstructions in the elevational particles (*po versus *yo) and in the elevational verbs denoting motion towards the DC (*seri versus *ya(ŋ)). The evidence for these will be discussed in subsequent sections.

Table 14: pAP elevation terms

	Elevationals	Elevational motion verbs	
		From DC	To DC
LEVEL	*mo	*wai	*mai
HIGH	*do	*mid(a)	*medai(ŋ)
LOW	*po *yo	*ipa	*seri *ya(ŋ)

In Sections 4.1 and 4.2, I look at the evidence for the different forms in the reconstructed proto-paradigms of elevationals and elevational verbs respectively. Finally, in § 4.3, I consider the mechanisms by which the proto-system has been complicated and additional distinctions have been built up. In the following subsections, I draw on data not only from the seven languages already discussed in § 3, but also from an additional four languages, Kaera, Klon, Kui, and Sawila. In these languages, individual basic elevation terms are known but the semantics and morpho-syntax of the elevation system are not fully understood or described.[5]

4.1 Proto-elevationals

Table 15 presents pAP elevationals and their reflexes in the eleven modern AP languages for which we have data. Bolding in the table selects the cognate parts of the modern reflexes.

---

[5] The following language abbreviations are used in tables in subsequent sections: Tw Teiwa, KE Kaera, WP Western Pantar, BL Blagar, AD Adang, KL Klon, KI Kui, AB Abui, KM Kamang, Sw Sawila, and WE Wersing.

6 Elevation in the spatial deictic systems of Alor-Pantar languages

Table 15: Reflexes of pAP elevationals

	pAP	Lg	Reflexes
LEVEL	*mo	WP	mau
		Bl	mo
		Ad	mɔŋ
		Km	muŋ
		We	mona
		Sw	mana
HIGH	*do[a]	WP	dau
		Ke	de
		Bl	do
		Ad	tɔŋ
		Kl	ta
		Km	tuŋ
		We	tona
		Sw	tana
LOW	*po	WP	pau
		Ke	pe
		Bl	po
		Ad	pɔŋ
		Km	fuŋ
	*yo	Tw	yaqai
		Ki	iyo
		We	yona
		Sw	yana

[a] Languages of the Alor subgroup show an irregular sound change in this morpheme from *d > t. The phoneme *d is preferred as the earlier form on the basis of a *d being found in cognates in Timor languages.

Reflexes of all four morphemes are found in non-contiguous areas of both Alor and Pantar. The distribution also does not conform to any known subgroups of the AP languages, thus justifying the reconstruction of the four morphemes to the highest level, pAP.

We see from Table 15 that "bare", that is unaffixed, reflexes of the proto-elevationals are found in Western Pantar, Kaera and Blagar. In West Pantar, Blagar and Adang, these morphemes are found across multiple paradigms of different word classes. Notably, several modern AP languages have reflexes suffixed with a nasal segment. This, I suggest, traces back to an enclitic postposition, pAP *=ŋ 'LOC'.[6] Abui reflects the proto-morpheme as =ŋ 'LOC' (see example 11), an enclitic postposition closely resembling the probable original function of *=ŋ. In other AP languages, *=ŋ is preserved fused onto a range of location-signifying words. Many AP languages have postpositions marked with *=ŋ, for instance: on Blagar *taŋ* 'on top of', but not on Kamang *taa* and Abui *taha*, or on Wersing *miŋ* 'in', but not on Kamang *mi*, Klon *mi* and many more < *mi 'in(side)'.

The four languages for which we have reflexes of proto-elevationals marked with *=ŋ 'LOC' are Adang, Kamang, Wersing and Sawila. In the latter three the morpheme is fused on, whilst in Adang reflexes of *=ŋ only occur on one paradigm and the basic elevational forms combine with other affixes in other paradigms (e.g., *hɛ-* in the demonstratives, or *-lɛ* in directional elevationals). In the East Alor languages, Wersing and Sawila, the forms have further fossilized suffixed with *-a*, a morpheme of unknown significance at this stage.[7] It appears that *=ŋ was used originally on the elevationals to make them into locative predicates. This is seen in that, whilst Blagar and Western Pantar cannot use their "bare" elevationals as predicates, the elevationals marked with *=ŋ as in Adang, Wersing and Sawila can be predicates. From there, *=ŋ would have become fixed on the elevationals, even in adverbial function where it would not have been needed originally in pAP, as is suggested by the adverbial use of "bare" elevationals in Blagar and Western Pantar.

---

[6] I give this morpheme its phonetic rather than phonemic value for ease of explication. It seems likely that, as in many modern AP languages, in pAP the velar nasal was a word-final allophone of pAP *n.

[7] Wersing has an enclitic article =*a* 'ART' which marks NPs for specificity, and a suffix -*a* which marks realis mood on verbs. Note there is some evidence for the existence of elevationals in Wersing without -*a*. In Schapper and Hendery, Wersing corpus., there are two instances of *yoŋ* that were said by an informant to have the same meaning as *yona*.

4.2 Proto-elevational verbs

Table 16 presents pAP elevational verbs and their reflexes in the eleven modern AP languages for which we have data. Differences between the reconstructed meaning and the modern meaning of the verbs are given below the table.

The reconstruction of the paradigm with proto-forms of the verbs in the LEVEL and HIGH domains is robust and well-supported. Reflexes of these are found throughout the Alor-Pantar area with consistent form-meaning pairings. Some small irregularity is observed in the sound correspondences of reflexes, particularly amongst the reflexes of *medai(ŋ) 'come.LOW'. Teiwa *daa*, Kaera and Blagar *da* and Wersing *dai* all show loss of the initial syllable of *medai(ŋ). It is likely that the initial syllable of the verb was unstressed (i.e., *me'dai(ŋ)), as is often found in Alor-Pantar roots made up of a light-heavy syllable series. Historical loss of initial unstressed syllables has been observed repeatedly in AP languages (Holton et al. 2012: 93, 111).

The reconstruction of proto-forms of elevational verbs in the LOW domain is more complex due to the existence of two competing 'come.LOW' forms, *seri and *ya(ŋ). The majority of AP languages have a reflex of only one of these two. Typically, Pantar languages have reflexes of *ya(ŋ) for 'come.LOW', while west Alor languages have reflexes of *seri for 'come.LOW'. Only east Alor languages have reflexes of both, with a reflex of *seri for 'come.LOW' and a reflex of *ya(ŋ) for 'go.LOW', while no reflexes of *pia are found, as would be expected for 'go.LOW'.[8] At this stage, both *ya(ŋ) and *seri are reconstructed to pAP, because evidence for reconstructing one over the other is thin. The slightly wider distribution of reflexes of *ya(ŋ) might be taken to indicate that this was the earlier term, and that *seri was introduced into the elevational verb paradigm soon after the breakup of the proto-language. One potential source for this introduction would be verbs such as Kamang *silaŋ* 'descend', a verb which is not part of the elevation paradigm proper as it is not anchored to a deictic centre as elevational verbs are.

4.3 Elaborations of the proto-system

Having reconstructed the elevational system of pAP, we are now in a position to investigate changes to pAP elevational system and establish various developmental paths that have been taken by individual languages or groups of languages since the breakup of the pAP. Note that I am concerned here not with adding

---

[8] East Alor forms a well-defined low-level subgroup and it is reasonable to assume that this shared characteristic among the languages goes back to their common ancestor, proto-East Alor.

Table 16: Reflexes of pAP elevational verbs.

LEVEL	*wai					
	WP	wa	Ad	fa	Km	we
	Tw	wa	Kl	wa	We	wai
	Ke	wa	Ki	bai	Sw	we
	Bl	va	Ab	we		
	*mai					
	WP	ma	Ad	ma	We	mai
	Tw	ma	Kl	ma	Ki	mai
	Ke	ma	Ab	me		
	Bl	ma	Km	me		
HIGH	*mid(a)					
	WP	mia	Ad	mid	We	mid
	Tw	mir	Kl	mid	Sw	mide
	Ke	mid	Ki	mira		
	Bl	mida	Ab	marei		
	*medai(ŋ)					
	WP	middaŋ	Ad	madɔŋ	We	dai
	Tw	daa	Kl	mde	Sw	made
	Ke	da	Ki	maran		
	Bl	da	Ab	maraŋ		
LOW	*ipa					
	WP	pia	Ad	ip	Ab	pa
	Ke	ip	Kl	ip	Km	fe
	Bl	ʔipa	Ki	pa†		
	*seri					
	Ad	hɛl	Ki	sei	We	sir
	Kl	her	Ab	sei	Sw	sire
	*ya(ŋ)					
	WP	yaŋ	Bl	ya	Sw	yaa‡
	Tw	yaa	Km	yaaŋ		
	Ke	ya	We	a‡		

† This term in Kui has shifted meaning to 'go west', instead of 'go.LOW'. This new meaning makes sense as a conventionalization due to the local geography whereby west Alor is significantly less mountainous and overall at a much lower elevation than east Alor, as per Windschuttel (2013).
‡ Means 'go.LOW' instead of expected 'come.LOW'.

6 Elevation in the spatial deictic systems of Alor-Pantar languages

further elevation-marked terms to the set through innovative morphology (e.g., Adang directional elevationals marked with *-lɛ*), so much as with the processes by which distinctions within the elevational system are elaborated.

The first observation to be made is that the pAP elevational system has often altered where new elevation terms (i.e., not reflecting the proto-terms) have emerged. Abui elevationals are an example of this, since reflexes of pAP elevationals are entirely absent in this language (see Table 4). Abui has innovated new terms with a tonal distinction between HIGH and LOW elevations, with a further distance contrast being added between near and far locations, the latter marked by /w/, the former by its absence. Western Pantar complicates its system of elevational motion verbs towards the DC by incorporating the innovative verbs *diakaŋ* and *rauŋ* into the paradigm alongside *mia* and *pia*, reflexes of the pAP elevational motion verbs *mid(a) 'go.HIGH' and *pia 'go.LOW'. *Diakaŋ* and *rauŋ* have been incorporated into the paradigm for motion along gentle slopes, thereby causing the restriction of meaning of the inherited verbs to be for steeper slopes. Holton (p.c.) notes that for some speakers the innovative steep terms, *diakaŋ* and *rauŋ*, have even largely replaced the inherited gentle slope terms, *mia* and *pia*, in casual speech.

The second mechanism of elaboration of sets of elevation-marked terms is compounding basic terms together to create "mediated" distinctions. Consider the forms of the Sawila elevational motion verbs presented in Table 17.

In the HIGH and LOW domains we see that there are not the expected two terms each, but instead five each. The DIRECT terms denoting movement along an axis following the line of a slope straight up or straight down reflect individual pAP elevation terms. The INDIRECT terms denote a movement that traverses across the slope diagonally and are formed by compounding different proto-terms together. The compounding process is not completely regular: there is some inconsistency in the terms that are compounded together in the verbs denoting motion toward the DC.[9] Nevertheless, the etymologies for the terms are clear, as set out in Table 18.

Kamang presents a more complex example of system elaboration, involving compounding of terms across all elevational word classes not just verbs, as well as paradigm regularization. Looking at the forms of Kamang elevation-marked terms in Table 10, we see particular morphemic "atoms" are used to build up the elaborated terms in a semi-regular manner. DIRECT terms are simplest, being built thus: (i) the elevational domain is marked by a single consonant *t-* for HIGH, either *f-* or *y-* for LOW and either *m-* or *w-* for LEVEL, and (ii) the word class is

---

[9] The difference between high INDIRECT terms denoting motion towards the DC is not understood (František Kratochvíl, p.c.). As such I have not attempted to supply any more precise characterization of these. Kula has a similar system to Sawila, but the meanings of all compound elevational terms are also not yet well understood (Nicholas Williams, p.c.).

Table 17: Sawila elevational motion verbs (Kratochvíl 2014 and Kratochvíl, Sawila corpus)

		Elevationals	Elevational motion verbs	
			From DC	To DC
LEVEL		*mana*	*we*	*me*
HIGH	DIRECT	*anna*	*midde*	*made*
	INDIRECT		*waamide*	*mamade*
				madaame
LOW	DIRECT	*yana*	*yaa*	*sire*
	INDIRECT		*wayaa*	*masire*
				mayaa

Table 18: Sources of Sawila elevational motion verbs

HIGH domain		
DIRECT	*midde*	< *mid(a) 'go.high'
	made	< *medai(ŋ) 'come.high'
INDIRECT	*waamidde*	< *wai 'go.level' + *mid(a) 'go.high'
	mamade	< *mai 'come.level' + *medaiŋ 'come.high'
	madaame	< *medai(ŋ) 'come.high' + *mai 'come.level'
LOW domain		
DIRECT	*yaa*	< *ya(ŋ) 'come.low'
	sire	< *sire 'come.low'
INDIRECT	*wayaa*	< *wai 'go.level' + *ya(ŋ) 'come.low'
	masire	< *mai 'come.level' + *sire 'come.low'
	mayaa	< *mai 'come.level' + *ya(ŋ) 'come.low'

6 Elevation in the spatial deictic systems of Alor-Pantar languages

marked by *-u-ŋ* for elevationals, by *-e* for elevational motion verb from DC and by *-aaŋ* for elevational motion verb from the DC. This pattern is perfectly illustrated by Kamang's HIGH DIRECT terms: *tuŋ* 'HIGH.DRCT', *te* 'go.HIGH.DRCT' and *taaŋ* 'come.HIGH.DRCT'. Of these, only *tuŋ* is inherited from pAP, while *te* and *taaŋ* are Kamang innovations following the pattern of morphemic atoms.

Irregularities in the formation of non-compounded elevation terms in Kamang stem from cases in which the morphemic atoms have not been fully applied (as explained further below), and instead there is retention of etymological forms. Table 19 presents an overview of the non-compounded elevation terms in Kamang, followed by their expected but non-occurring form (marked with **) if they were formed on the morphemic atom pattern, and their relationship to pAP terms.

Table 19: Kamang non-compounded elevation-marked terms and their etymologies

	Elevationals	Elevational motion verbs	
		From DC	To DC
LEVEL	*muŋ*	*we*	*me*
		**me	**maaŋ
	< pAP *mo-ŋ	< pAP *wai	< pAP *mai
HIGH	*tuŋ*	*te*	*taaŋ*
	< pAP *do-ŋ	< pAP **mid(a)*	< pAP **medai(ŋ)*
LOW	*fuŋ*	*fe*	*yaaŋ*
			**faaŋ
	< pAP *po-ŋ	< pAP *ipa	< pAP **yaa(ŋ)*

In Table 19, we see that the appearance of both *m-* and *w-* in the formation of LEVEL motion verbs is a result of the retention of reflexes of pAP *wai 'go.LEVEL' alongside *mai 'come.LEVEL'. If the formation of these terms were to conform to the atomic pattern, we would find the forms **me and **maaŋ instead. In the LOW domain, *fuŋ* and *fe* are inherited terms that follow the morphemic atom pattern, while *yaaŋ* is a retention of a reflex of pAP **yaa(ŋ)* that does not conform to the pattern expected when using the morphemic atoms.

Table 20: Sources of Kamang INDIRECT elevation terms.

High domain		
NEAR INDIRECT terms		
ELEVATIONAL:	mutuŋ	< mu 'LEVEL'+ tu 'HIGH.DRT'+ŋ
Motion verb from DC	wete	< we 'GO.LEVEL'+te 'GO.HIGH.DRT'
Motion verb to DC	metaaŋ	< me 'COME.LEVEL'+taaŋ 'COME.HIGH.DRT'
FAR INDIRECT terms		
ELEVATIONAL:	tumung	< tu 'HIGH.DRT'+mu 'LEVEL'+ŋ
Motion verb from DC	tewe	< te 'GO.HIGH.DRT' we 'GO.LEVEL'
Motion verb to DC	taaŋme	< taaŋ 'COME.HIGH.DRT'+me 'COME'.LEVEL
Low domain		
NEAR INDIRECT terms		
ELEVATIONAL:	muhuŋ	< mu 'LEVEL'+fu 'HIGH.DRT'+ŋ
Motion verb from DC	wehe	< we 'GO.LEVEL'+ fe 'GO.LOW.DRT'
Motion verb to DC	yaaŋme	< yaaŋ 'COME.LOW.DRT'+me 'COME.LEVEL'
FAR INDIRECT terms		
ELEVATIONAL:	fumuŋ	< fu 'HIGH.DRT'+mu 'LEVEL'+ŋ
Motion verb from DC	fewe	< fe 'GO.LOW.DRT'+ we 'GO.LEVEL'
Motion verb to DC	yaaŋme	< yaaŋ 'COME.LOW.DRT'+me 'COME.LEVEL'

These basic forms that are established by this set in Kamang are then compounded together to create complex indirect terms in the HIGH and LOW domains. NEAR INDIRECT terms are built by prefixing the LEVEL morpheme onto the DIRECT term of the corresponding word class, while FAR INDIRECT terms are built by prefixing the DIRECT morpheme onto the LEVEL morpheme of the corresponding word class. The composition of these terms is set out in Table 20. Also, in this set of compounds, we find irregularity: the expected form **meyaaŋ for 'COME.LOW.INDRCT.NEAR' does not appear, instead yaaŋme is used for near and far indirect motion. This gap in the Kamang paradigm shows that the elaboration of such systems is not as regular as we might anticipate for a process in which morphemes are so transparent.

In sum, AP languages have elaborated the inherited elevational system by bringing innovative new terms often alongside reflexes of terms from the proto-system and/or by combining reflexes of the original system together to create complex forms with "mediated" (i.e., INDIRECT or diagonal directions) semantics.

5 Conclusion

All AP languages have rich systems of spatial deixis with elevation components. The languages show significant similarity in the basic, core system in which elevation terms occur, namely, in both a verbal and non-verbal domain consistently contrasting LEVEL, HIGH, and LOW elevations. The shared characteristics of the systems can be traced back to a paradigm of elevationals and a paradigm of elevational motion verbs in the ancestral language, pAP. Despite their common origin, modern AP elevational systems display noteworthy differences in the number of terms, paradigms and semantic features they have. Individual languages have complicated the basic system by: (i) reiterating the elevational distinction in multiple, additional domains (e.g., Blagar, Western Pantar), (ii) adding additional terms through innovative morphology (e.g., Adang lɛ- elevationals), or (iii) compounding basic terms together to create more distinctions (e.g., Kamang, Sawila). The result is that the AP languages today display the kind of diversity in the details of their morphology, syntax and semantics of their elevational systems that is typical of other domains in the group.

Typologically, the AP systems are remarkable for their complexity, which is much greater than that found in Papuan languages elsewhere for which deictic systems with elevational components have been described (see, e.g., Heeschen 1982; 1987). Other Papuan languages only ever have three terms for the three elevational heights and do not reiterate the elevational distinctions across multiple parts of the lexicon. We might conjecture that the semantic elaborations of elevational domains with features such as distance, steepness and directionality that we have observed in AP languages are rare cross-linguistically, and parallels remain to be identified in a world-wide survey of elevational systems.

The persistent occurrence of elevational distinctions across word classes in AP languages can be usefully understood in terms of the preexisting concept of "semplates" (Levinson & Burenhult 2009). A semplate is defined as "a configuration consisting of distinct sets or layers of lexemes, drawn from different semantic subdomains or different word classes, mapped onto the same abstract semantic template" (Levinson & Burenhult 2009: 154). This fits well with the basic AP pattern in which locationals and motion verbs are organized by a semantic template differentiating the three elevational domains. The interesting feature of AP elevational semplates is their overtness in many instances: Adang, Blagar, Western Pantar use the same morphemes to reiterate the elevational semplate across word classes, while, as we saw in § 4.2, Kamang has in part discarded inherited lexemes and developed a system of morphemic atoms used to form complex subnodes in the elevational semplate. Thus, the AP elevational systems studied here not only present new evidence for the existence of Levinson & Burenhult's (2009) templates, but also have the potential to illuminate the diachronic processes by which abstract semplates may become productive and increasingly overt in their marking.

Sources

Abui	Kratochvíl Abui corpus, Kratochvíl (2007)
Adang	Haan (2001); Robinson & Haan (2014)
Blagar	Steinhauer (1977; 1991; 2012; 2014), p.c.
Kaera	Klamer (2014)
Kamang	Schapper (2012; 2014a)
Klon	Baird (2008), Baird Klon corpus
Kui	Windschuttel (2013)
Sawila	Kratochvíl (2014), Sawila Toolbox dictionary, p.c.
Teiwa	Klamer (2010), fieldnotes, Teiwa corpus
Wersing	Schapper & Hendery (2014)
Western Pantar	Holton (2007; 2011; 2014), Western Pantar corpus, p.c., Holton & Lamma Koly (2008)

Acknowledgments

Thanks go to Hein Steinhauer, Gary Holton and František Kratochvíl for answering my many questions on the elevation terms in the languages of their expertise. I would also like to thank Juliette Huber for the very useful discussions on elevation terms in Makasae and Makalero, related languages spoken on Timor. Information on these languages does not appear in this chapter, but comparison with them informed some of the reconstructions made here. Any errors are, of course, my own.

Abbreviations

2	2nd person	LOC	Locative
3	3rd person	LOW	refers to any location situated down(ward of) the deictic centre
4	4th person		
AB	Abui		
AD	Adang	NP	Noun phrase
ADDR	Addressee-anchored	NSPEC	non-specific
AP	Alor-Pantar	NSTEEP	non-steep
ART	Article	NVIS	Non-visible
BL	Blagar	pAP	proto-Alor-Pantar
DC	Deictic Centre	PL	Plural
DEM	Demonstrative	POSS	Possessive
DIST	Distal	PROG	Progressive
DRCT	Direct	PROX	Proximal
HIGH	refers to any location situated up(ward of) the deictic centre	REAL	Realis
		RFLX	Reflexive
		SG	Singular
INDRCT	Indirect	SPEC	Specifier
IPFV	Imperfective	SPKR	Speaker-anchored
KE	Kaera	STEEP	steep
KI	Kui	SUBJ	Subject
KM	Kamang	Sw	Sawila
LEVEL	refers to any location situated level with the deictic centre	Tw	Teiwa
		VIS	Visible
		WE	Wersing
		WP	Western Pantar

References

Baird, Louise. 2008. *A grammar of Klon: a non-Austronesian language of Alor, Indonesia*. Canberra: Pacific Linguistics.

Bickel, Balthasar. 2001. Deictic transposition and referential practice in Belhare. *Journal of Linguistic Anthropology* 10(2). 224–247.

Burenhult, Niclas. 2008. Spatial coordinate systems in demonstrative meaning. *Linguistic Typology* 12. 99–142.

Cheung, Candice Chi-Hang. 2007. On the noun phrase structure of Jingpo. *USC Working Papers in Linguistics* 3. 32–56.

Diessel, Holger. 1999. *Demonstratives: form, function, and grammaticalization.* Vol. 42 (Typological Studies in Language). Amsterdam: John Benjamins.

Dixon, R. M. W. 1972. *The Dyirbal language of North Queensland.* Vol. 9 (Studies in Linguistics). Cambridge: Cambridge University Press.

Dixon, R. M. W. 2003. Demonstratives: a cross-linguistic typology. *Studies in Language* 27(1). 61–112.

Ebert, Karen H. 2003. Kiranti languages: an overview. In Graham Thurgood & Randy J. LaPolla (eds.), *The Sino-Tibetan languages* (Routledge Language Family Series), 505–517. London: Routledge.

Haan, Johnson Welem. 2001. *The grammar of Adang: a Papuan language spoken on the island of Alor East Nusa Tenggara - Indonesia.* Sydney: University of Sydney PhD thesis.

Heeschen, Volker. 1982. Some systems of spatial deixis in Papuan languages. In Jürgen Weissenborn & Wolfgang Klein (eds.), *Here and there. Cross-linguistic studies in deixis and demonstration.* 81–109. Amsterdam: John Benjamins.

Heeschen, Volker. 1987. Oben und Unten. In Mark Münzel (ed.), *Neuguinea. Nutzung und Deutung der Umwelt.* Vol. 2, 601–618. Frankfurt am Main: Museum für Völkerkunde.

Holton, Gary. 2007. *Directionals and spatial deixis. An Overview of Western Pantar.* http://www.uaf.edu/alor/langs/western-pantar/directionals.html..

Holton, Gary. 2011. Landscape in Western Pantar, a Papuan outlier of southern Indonesia. In David M. Mark, Andrew G. Turk, Niclas Burenhult & David Stea (eds.), *Landscape in language,* 143–166. Amsterdam: John Benjamins.

Holton, Gary. 2014. Western Pantar. In Antoinette Schapper (ed.), *Papuan languages of Timor, Alor and Pantar: Sketch grammars,* vol. 1, 23–96. Berlin: Mouton de Gruyter.

Holton, Gary & Mahalalel Lamma Koly. 2008. *Kamus pengantar Bahasa Pantar Barat: Tubbe - Mauta - Lamma.* Kupang, Indonesia: UBB-GMIT.

Holton, Gary, Marian Klamer, František Kratochvíl, Laura C. Robinson & Antoinette Schapper. 2012. The historical relations of the Papuan languages of Alor and Pantar. *Oceanic Linguistics* 51(1). 86–122.

Klamer, Marian. 2010. *A grammar of Teiwa* (Mouton Grammar Library 49). Berlin: Mouton de Gruyter.

Klamer, Marian. 2014. Kaera. In Antoinette Schapper (ed.), *Papuan languages of Timor, Alor and Pantar: Sketch grammars,* vol. 1, 97–146. Berlin: Mouton de Gruyter.

Kratochvíl, František. 2007. *A grammar of Abui: a Papuan language of Alor.* Utrecht: LOT.

Kratochvíl, František. 2014. Sawila. In Antoinette Schapper (ed.), *Papuan languages of Timor, Alor and Pantar: Sketch grammars*, vol. 1, 351–438. Berlin: Mouton de Gruyter.
Levinson, Stephen & Niclas Burenhult. 2009. Semplates: a new concept in lexical semantics? *Language* 85(1). 153–174.
Levinson, Stephen C. 1983. *Pragmatics*. Cambridge: Cambridge University Press.
Miller, Wick R. 1996. *Guarijó: gramática, textos, y vocabulario*. Mexico City: Instituto de Investigaciones Antropológicas, Universidad Nacional Autónoma de México.
Noonan, Michael. 2006. *Contact-induced change in the Himalayas: the case of the Tamangic languages*. Paper presented at the International Colloquium on Language Contact and Contact Languages, University of Hamburg, July 6-8, 2006.
Post, Mark. 2011. Topographical deixis and the Tani languages of North-East India. In G. Hyslop, S. Morey & M. Post (eds.), *North East Indian linguistics*, 137–154. New Delhi: Cambridge University Press India.
Robinson, Laura C. & John Haan. 2014. Adang. In Antoinette Schapper (ed.), *Papuan languages of Timor, Alor and Pantar: Sketch grammars*, vol. 1, 221–284. Berlin: Mouton de Gruyter.
Schapper, Antoinette. 2012. *Elevation and scale in two Papuan languages*. Talk presented at EuroBabel Final Conference, Leiden, 23-26 August 2012.
Schapper, Antoinette. 2014a. Kamang. In Antoinette Schapper (ed.), *Papuan languages of Timor, Alor and Pantar: Sketch grammars*, vol. 1, 285–350. Berlin: Mouton de Gruyter.
Schapper, Antoinette (ed.). 2014b. *Papuan languages of Timor, Alor and Pantar: Sketch grammars*. Vol. 1. Berlin: Mouton de Gruyter.
Schapper, Antoinette & Rachel Hendery. 2014. Wersing. In Antoinette Schapper (ed.), *Papuan languages of Timor, Alor and Pantar: Sketch grammars*, vol. 1, 439–504. Berlin: Mouton de Gruyter.
Schapper, Antoinette & Lila San Roque. 2011. Demonstratives and non-embedded nominalisations in the Papuan languages of south-east Indonesia. *Studies in Language* 35(2). 378–406.
Schulze, Wolfgang. 2003. The diachrony of demonstrative pronouns in East Caucasian. In Dee Ann Holisky & Kevin Tuite (eds.), *Current trends in Caucasian, East European and Inner Asian linguistics: papers in honor of Howard I. Aronson*, 291–348. Amsterdam: John Benjamins.
Senft, Gunter. 1997. *Referring to space: studies in Austronesian and Papuan languages* (Oxford Studies in Anthropological Linguistics 11). Oxford: Clarendon Press.

Senft, Gunter. 2004. *Deixis and demonstratives in Oceanic languages.* Canberra: Pacific Linguistics.

Steinhauer, Hein. 1977. 'Going' and 'coming' in the Blagar of Dolap (Pura, Alor, Indonesia). *NUSA: Miscellaneous Studies in Indonesian and Languages in Indonesia* 3. 38–48.

Steinhauer, Hein. 1991. Demonstratives in the Blagar language of Dolap (Pura, Alor, Indonesia). In Tom Dutton (ed.), *Papers in Papuan linguistics*, 177–221. Canberra: Pacific Linguistics.

Steinhauer, Hein. 2012. Deictic categories in three languages of Eastern Indonesia. In Bahren Umar Siregar, P. Ari Subagyo & Yassir Nasanius (eds.), *Dari menapak jejak kata sampai menyigi tata bahasa. Persembahan untuk Prof. Dr. Bambang Kaswanti Purwo dalam rangka ulang tahunnya yang ke-60*, 115–147. Jakarta: Pusat Kajian Bahasa dan Budaya Universitas Katolik Indonesia Atma Jaya.

Steinhauer, Hein. 2014. Blagar. In Antoinette Schapper (ed.), *Papuan languages of Timor, Alor and Pantar: Sketch grammars*, vol. 1, 147–220. Berlin: Mouton de Gruyter.

Windschuttel, Glenn. 2013. *Space and deixis in Kui.* Paper Presented at the Workshop on the Languages of Melanesia, Australian National University, 23-26 May 2013.

Chapter 7

Numeral systems in the Alor-Pantar languages

Antoinette Schapper

Marian Klamer

> This chapter presents an in-depth analysis of numeral forms and systems in the Alor-Pantar (AP) languages. The AP family reflects a typologically rare combination of mono-morphemic 'six' with quinary forms for numerals 'seven' to 'nine', a pattern which we reconstruct to go back to proto-AP. We focus on the structure of cardinal numerals, highlighting the diversity of the numeral systems involved. We reconstruct numeral forms to different levels of the AP family, and argue that AP numeral systems have been complicated at different stages by reorganisations of patterns of numeral formation and by borrowings. This has led to patchwork numeral systems in the modern languages, incorporating to different extents: (i) quaternary, quinary and decimal bases; (ii) additive, subtractive and multiplicative procedures, and; (iii) non-numeral lexemes such as 'single' and 'take away'. Complementing the historical reconstruction with an areal perspective, we compare the numerals in the AP family with those of the Austronesian languages in their immediate vicinity and show that contact-induced borrowing of forms and structures has affected numeral paradigms in both AP languages and their Austronesian neighbors.

1 Introduction

Numerals and numeral systems have long been of typological and historical interest to linguists. Papuan languages are best known in the typological literature on numerals for having body-part tally systems and, to a lesser extent, restricted numeral systems which have no cyclically recurring base (Laycock 1975; Lean 1992; Comrie 2005a). Papuan languages are also typologically interesting for the fact that they often make use of bases of other than the cross-linguistically most

 Antoinette Schapper & Marian Klamer. 2017. Numeral systems in the Alor-Pantar languages. In Marian Klamer (ed.), *The Alor-Pantar languages*, 277–329. Berlin: Language Science Press. DOI:10.5281/zenodo.569393

frequent decimal and vigesimal bases, such as quinary (Lean 1992) and senary bases (Donohue 2008; Evans 2009).

In this chapter we present an in-depth analysis of numeral forms and systems in the Alor-Pantar (AP) languages. Typologically, the family reflects a rare combination of mono-morphemic 'six' with quinary forms for numerals 'seven' to 'nine', a pattern which we reconstruct back to proto-AP. We focus on the structure of cardinal numerals, highlighting the diversity of the numeral systems involved. We reconstruct numeral forms to different levels of the AP family, and argue that AP numeral systems have been complicated at different stages by reorganizations of patterns of numeral formation and by borrowings. This has led to patchwork numeral systems in the modern languages, incorporating to different extents: (i) quaternary, quinary and decimal bases; (ii) additive, subtractive and multiplicative procedures, and; (iii) non-numeral lexemes such as 'single' and 'take away'. We complement the genealogical perspective with an areal one, comparing the numeral systems of the AP languages with those of the Austronesian languages in their immediate vicinity to study if and how contact has affected the numeral paradigms.

This chapter centres on numeral data from 19 Alor-Pantar language varieties spanning east to west across the AP archipelago, presented collectively in Appendix A.1. As a motivated phonemic orthography is yet lacking for many of the varieties in our sample, all the data is presented in a broad IPA transcription. The fieldworkers who collected the data are recognized in the 'Sources' section at the end of the chapter.

We begin with an overview of the terminology used throughout this chapter in § 2 and a brief note on sound changes in numeral compounds in § 3. We then describe how cardinal numerals are constructed across the AP languages: 'one' to 'five' are discussed in § 4, 'six' to 'nine' in § 5, and numerals 'ten' and above in § 6. § 7 looks at the AP numeral systems in typological and areal perspective, while § 8 summarizes our findings.

2 Terminological preliminaries

Numerals are 'spoken normed expressions that are used to denote the exact number of objects for an open class of objects in an open class of social situations with the whole speech community in question' (Hammarström 2010: 11). A numeral system is thus the arrangement of individual numeral expressions together in a language.

7 Numeral systems in the Alor-Pantar languages

Numeral systems typically make use of a base to construct their numeral expressions.[1] A "base" in a numeral system is a numerical value n which is used repeatedly in numeral expressions thus: $xn \pm/xy$, that is, numeral x is multiplied by the base n plus, minus or multiplied by numeral y (Comrie 2005b, Hammarström 2010: 15).[2] Many languages have multiple bases. For instance, Dutch numerals have five different bases: *tien* '10', *honderd* '100', *duizend* '1000', *miljoen* '100,000', *miljard* '1,000,000'. These bases are all powers of ten (10, 10^2, 10^3, 10^6, 10^9). However, the higher powers are not typically considered important in defining a numeral system type; the lowest base gives its name to the whole system, that is, Dutch would be characterized as a "decimal" or "base-10" numeral system.

In this chapter we deal with several "mixed numeral systems". We define a "mixed numeral system" as a numeral system in which there are multiple bases that are *not* simply powers of the lowest base. So, we do not consider Dutch to have a mixed numeral system, since all its higher bases are powers of its lowest base, *tien* '10'. By contrast, a language such as Ilongot (Table 1) would be considered to have a mixed quinary-decimal system because: (i) it uses a quinary base to form numerals 'six' to 'nine', and (ii) a decimal base to form numerals 'ten' and higher. 'Ten' is not a power of 'five' and therefore the language can be considered to "mix" numeral bases.

It is important to note that isolated cases of a particular mathematical procedure being used in the formation of a numeral do not constitute an instance of another 'base' in a numeral system. For instance, Ujir (Table 1) forms 'seven' by means of the addition of 'six' and 'one'. Yet 'six' is not a base in Ujir, since there are no other numerals in the language formed with additions involving 'six'. Similarly, 'two' and 'four' are not bases in Ujir, because neither is used recursively in forming numerals. The formation of 'eight' through the multiplication of 'two' and 'four' is a procedure limited to 'eight'.

In this chapter, we are concerned with the internal composition of cardinal numerals, that is, if and how they are made up out of other numeral expressions. We call a monomorphemic cardinal a "simplex numeral", and one that is composed of more than one numeral expressions a "complex numeral". To describe (i) the arithmetic relation between component elements in a complex numeral,

---

[1] Notable exceptions, i.e., numeral systems without bases, are the body-tally systems mentioned above, and the languages discussed in Hammarström (2010: 17-22).

[2] We do not adopt the notion of 'base' of Greenberg (1978) where 'base' is defined as a serialized multiplicand upon which the recursive structure of *all* higher complex numerals is constructed. That is, even where a language has for instance a small sequence of numerals formed on a non-decimal pattern (e.g., '5 2' for 'seven', '5 3' for 'eight', and '5 4' for 'nine'), if '10' is the higher, more productive base, then the language is classed as having a decimal system only.

Table 1: Examples illustrating the notion of "base"

	Ilongot Austronesian Philippines		Ujir Austronesian Indonesia	
	Analysis	Expression	Analysis	Expression
1	1	sit	1	set
2	2	dewa	2	rua
3	3	teyo	3	lati
4	4	opat	4	ka
5	5	tambiaŋ	5	lima
6	5 + 1	tambiaŋno sit	6	dubu
7	5 + 2	tambiaŋno dewa	6 + 1	dubusam
8	5 + 3	tambiaŋno teyo	4 x 2	karua
9	5 + 4	tambiaŋno opat	9	tera
10	10	tampo	10	uisia
11	10 + 1	tampo no sit	10 + 1	uisia ma set
15	10 + 5	tampo no tambiaŋ	10 + 5	uisia ma lima
20	2 x 10	dowampo	2 x 10	uirua
21	2 x 10 + 1	dowampo no sit	2 x 10 + 1	uirua ma set
25	2 x 10 + 5	dowampo no tambiaŋ	2 x 10 + 5	uirua ma lima
30	3 x 10	teyompo	3 x 10	uilati
BASES	5-10		10	

and (ii) the role of component elements in arithmetic operations, the following terms are used:

- "additive numeral": a numeral where the relation between components parts of a complex numeral is one of addition. The component parts are "augend" and "addend". So, for example, in the equation 5 + 2 = 7, the augend is 5 and the addend is 2.

- "subtractive numeral": a numeral where the relation between component parts of a complex numeral is one of subtraction. The component parts are "subtrahend" and "minuend". So, for example, in the equation 10 - 2 = 8, the subtrahend is 2 and the minuend is 10.

- "multiplicative numeral": a numeral where the relation between components parts of a complex numeral is one of multiplication. The component parts are "multiplier" and "multiplicand". So, for example, in the equation 3 x 2 = 6, the multiplier is 3 and the multiplicand is 2.

Throughout this chapter we rely on the definitions made in this section, and the reader is referred to this section for clarification of terminology.

3 A brief note on sound changes and numerals

In this chapter we posit reconstructions of numerals to proto-Alor-Pantar (pAP) and several lower subgroups within the AP group. Many of the sound correspondences on which these reconstructions are based are part of regular correspondence sets discussed in Holton et al. (2012) and Holton & Robinson (this volume).

However, the history of numerals also involves formal changes which cannot be couched in terms of regular sound correspondences. Many irregular changes observed in numerals arise from members of compounds fusing together over time. In the history of AP numerals, two types of change are associated with the compounding process: (i) segmental reduction in the members of a compound, (ii) dissimilation of segments across members of a compound.

Examples of segmental reduction in numeral compounds are widespread in AP languages. For instance, in the Atoitaa dialect of Kamang, numerals 'seven' to 'nine' are formed with *iwesiŋ* 'five' followed by a numeral 'one' to 'four'. This is illustrated for 'six' in (1). In forming the compound, the medial syllable of 'five', /we/, is lost due to a shift in stress to the penultimate syllable. Unreduced forms involving two distinct phonological forms are only produced by speakers when explaining numeral formation and have not been observed in naturalistic speech, indicating that the reduced form is already well incorporated into speakers' lexicons.

(1) Variation in the realization of Kamang (Atoitaa) 'six'

    a. *iwesiŋ nok* [iˈwesiŋ ˈnok] (careful speech)
       five   one
       'six'

    b. *isiŋnok* [iˈsiŋnok] (normal speech)
       five.one
       'six'

Similarly, in Sawila we find that 'six' can be realized both in unreduced form as two distinct numerals (*joːtiŋ* 'five' [plus] *suna* 'one') and in reduced form as set out in (2).

(2) Variation in the realization of Sawila 'six'

a. *jo:tiŋ suna* (careful speech)
   five one
   'six'

b. *jo:tsuna* (normal speech)
   five.one
   'six'

Dissimilation of segments across members of a compound is also found. An example is Klon *tidorok* 'eight', a form which must have involved consonant dissimilation of the protoform *turarok (see Table 5) and a hypothetical intermediate form like **tudarok (§ 5.2.2).

In short, the reconstruction of numerals must take into account regular sound changes as well as irregular changes in the members of compounds.

4 Numerals 'one' to 'five'

The numerals 'one' to 'five' are for the most part simple mono-morphemic words in Alor- Pantar. Table 2 presents an overview with the reconstructions to proto-Alor-Pantar (pAP).[3] The Proto-AP numerals 'one' to 'five' have been retained in most of its descendants. Only in eastern Alor have numerals in this range been innovated.

A non-etymological initial /a/ is present on Western Pantar 'one' and 'four' and Reta 'one'. This development is apparently due to analogy with the numerals 'two' and possibly 'three'. Such analogical adjustments in numeral forms, sometimes referred to as 'onset runs' (Matisoff 1995), are cross-linguistically relatively common.[4] The prothetic /a/ is also found on Western Pantar 'thousand' which can be realized as either *ribu* or *aribu*, an Austronesian loan.

---

[3] Not all elements of the reconstructed forms as they are given here are motivated in this chapter; see the reconstructed sound changes reported on in Holton et al. (2012) and Holton & Robinson (this volume).

[4] For example, in the Austronesian language Thao (Taiwan), initial /s/ in *susha 'two' was replaced by /t/ (*tusha*) in analogy to the onsets of *ta* 'one' and *turu* 'three' (Blust 2009: 274). The initial /d/ on 'nine' in Slavonic languages (e.g., Russian *dévjat*) is thought to have arisen due to the influence of the following numeral, Common Slavonic *desętĭ, 'ten' PIE *dekm̥(t) (Comrie 1992: 760). Winter (1969) discuses how the form for 'four' influences 'five' in Indo-European languages. These examples illustrate that '[a]nalogy is a powerful factor in counting, in both alliteration and rhyme, such that regular sound laws can be broken.' (Sidwell 1999: 256).

7 Numeral systems in the Alor-Pantar languages

Table 2: AP numerals 'one' to 'five'

		'one'	'two'	'three'	'four'	'five'
Proto-AP		*nuk	*araqu	*(a)tiga	*buta	*jiwesiŋ
Pantar	Western Pantar	anuku	alaku	atiga	atu	jasiŋ
	Deing	nuk	raq	atig	ut	asan
	Sar	nuk	raq	tig	ut	jawan
	Teiwa	nuk	haraq ~ raq	jerig	ut	jusan
	Kaera	nuk(u)	(a)rax-	(i/u)tug	ut	isim
Straits	Blagar-Bama[5]	nuku	akur	tuge	ut	isiŋ
	Blagar-Dolabang	nu	aru	tue	buta	isiŋ
	Reta	anu	alo	atoga	buta ~ wuta	avehaŋ
W Alor	Kabola	nu	olo	towo	ut	iweseŋ
	Adang	nu	alo	tuo	ut	ifɨhiŋ
	Hamap	nu	alo	tof	ut	ivehiŋ
	Klon	nuk	orok	toŋ	ut	eweh
	Kui	nuku	oruku	siwa	usa	jesan
C & E Alor	Abui	nuku	ajoku	sua	buti	jetiŋ
	Kamang	nok	ok	su	biat[6]	iwesiŋ
	Sawila	(sundana)†	jaku	tuo	(ara:siːku)	joːtiŋ
	Kula	(sona)	jakwu	tu	(arasiku)	jawatena
	Wersing	no	joku	tu	(arasoku)	wetiŋ

†Brackets indicate forms not reflecting proto-Alor-Pantar reconstructions.

283

The etymologies of the AP numerals 'two' and 'five' have been the subject of some speculation and typological interest. In his early comparative study on Alor-Pantar languages, Stokhof (1975: 21) makes two observations about these AP numerals which are not supported by our data. First, his claim that AP languages frequently use the root 'tooth' to express 'five' is not supported by more recent historical work on the family, which reconstructs 'five' as pAP *jiwesin, and 'tooth' as *-uas(in) (Holton & Robinson this volume). It should also be noted that no known cognitive link exists between 'five' and 'tooth', unlike the link between 'five' and 'hand' (Majewicz 1981; 1984; Heine 1997). Second, contra Stokhof, pAP *(a)tiga 'three' is not a loan word from Malay, despite the similarity with Malay *tiga* 'three'. Whilst there is evidence of Austronesian influence in pAP,[7] there is no evidence of influence from Malay. Malay first arrived in the Alor-Pantar region in colonial times,[8] thousands of years after the likely break-up of pAP. If there were an Austronesian numeral 'three' borrowed into the family, this would more likely be similar to proto-Austronesian *telu 'three' (Blust 2009: 268) instead of Malay *tiga*. The Austronesian languages surrounding Alor-Pantar reflect proto-Austronesian *telu. For instance, Alorese (an Austronesian language spoken on the coasts of Pantar and Alor) has *tilu*, Kedang (on Lembata) has *telu*, the language of Atauro (a small island of the north coast of Timor) has *hetelu* and Tetun Fehan (on Timor) has *tolu*.

In short, AP languages have by and large cognate forms for numerals 'one' to 'five' that reflect monomorphemic lexemes inherited from proto-AP.

5 Numerals 'six' to 'nine'

Unlike numerals 'one' to 'five' which show significant stability across the AP group, numerals 'six' to 'nine' have undergone several changes in their history.

---

[5] Liquid-stop metathesis has occurred in Blagar-Bama *akur* 'two', but not in other Blagar dialects.

[6] In Abui and Kamang, the vowels in 'four' display some irregular patterns. For Kamang, it is necessary to posit the following metathesis: Proto-Alor Pantar *buta < *bita < biat.

[7] For instance, pAP *bui 'betel nut' is probably borrowed from Austronesian (proto-West Malayo-Polynesian) *buyuq 'leaf of betel vine' (Blust nd).

[8] The function of Malay as the *lingua franca* of the Dutch East Indies appears irrelevant for Alor-Pantar, as the area was under (remote) Portuguese control till 1860, and Dutch colonial influence only became apparent in the first decades of the 20th century (Klamer 2010: 14 and references cited there). There is no evidence that Malay was used as a trade language in the Alor archipelago in pre-colonial times. On the other hand, there is anecdotal evidence that Alorese was used for interethnic communications in Pantar and coastal parts of west Alor until the mid 20th century (Klamer 2011).

7 Numeral systems in the Alor-Pantar languages

In most AP languages, 'six' is morphologically simple, but in a subset of the languages bi-morphemic 'six' [5+1] has been innovated (§ 5.1). The numerals 'seven', 'eight', and 'nine' show more complex histories, with some being historically constructed by addition to a quinary base [5+n] and others by subtraction from a decimal base [10-n] (§ 5.2).

5.1 Numeral 'six': Simplex and compound forms

In most AP languages, the form 'six' is mono-morphemic, as shown in Table 3. Four languages have a compound 'six': Western Pantar in the west, and Alor, Sawila and Kula in the east. Kamang and Wersing display both patterns across their dialects: Kamang-Takailubui and Wersing-Pureman have simplex 'six', while Kamang-Atoitaa and Wersing-Kolana have compound 'six'.

The simplex numeral 'six' reconstructs as pAP *talam 'six'. It is generally assumed that a base-five system originates from counting the fingers of one hand. In such a system, the numeral 'six' often involves crossing over from one hand to the other,[9] and may etymologically be related to words like 'cross over' (Majewicz 1981; 1984, Lynch 2009: 399-401). Synchronic evidence that pAP *talam may have been such a 'cross-over' verb comes from Sawila, which has a modern form *talamaŋ* 'step on, change legs in dance'.

AP compounds for 'six' are composed of two juxtaposed numeral morphemes. In several AP languages, compounds for 'six' have replaced etymological *talam 'six'. There appears to have been three independent innovations of this kind. One area where this has happened is eastern Alor, represented by Sawila, Kula and Wersing in Table 4. Kula, Sawila and Wersing-Kolana have replaced *talam 'six' with a base-five compound, as set out in (3). Whereas Sawila and Kula use 'one' in the compounds, the morpheme *nuŋ* used in Wersing-Kolana for the '[plus] one' part of the compound is not identical to the synchronic numeral 'one', which is *no*. Rather, *nuŋ* appears to be a reflex of a distinct pAP lexeme *nakuŋ 'single', which is reflected in, for example, Kamang *nukuŋ* 'single', and Western Pantar *nakkiŋ* 'single'.

(3) Formation of 'six' in eastern Alor languages
Sawila:
jo:tiŋsundana 'six' < *jo:tiŋ* 'five' [plus] *sundana* 'one'
Kula:

---

[9] Cross-linguistically, other strategies to express 'six' include (in bodily counting routines) touching or grabbing the wrist (Evans 2009; Donohue 2008), or using the etymon 'fist' (Plank 2009: 343). We do not find any such practices in Alor-Pantar.

jawatensona 'six' < *jawetena* 'five' [plus] *sona* 'one'
Wersing-Kolana:
wetiŋnuŋ 'six' < *wetiŋ* 'five' [plus] *nuŋ* 'single'

As these three languages are in close contact with each another, it is likely that the innovative use of a base-five compound for 'six' has diffused among them. This has probably happened relatively recently, since the members of the compounds are transparently related to existing cardinals. Older compounds show more divergence between the compound members and the individual numerals these derive from (cf. the formally less transparent base-five compounds

Table 3: AP numerals for 'six'

		simplex 'six'	compound 'six'
Proto-AP		*talam	
Pantar	Western Pantar		*hisnakkuŋ*
	Deing	*talaŋ*	
	Sar	*tejaŋ*	
	Teiwa	*tia:m*	
	Kaera	*tia:m*	
Straits	Blagar-Bama	*tajaŋ*	
	Blagar-Dolabang	*taliŋ*	
	Reta	*talaun*	
W Alor	Kabola	*talaŋ*	
	Adang	*talaŋ*	
	Hamap	*talaŋ*	
	Klon	*tlan*	
	Kui	*talama*	
C & E Alor	Abui	*tala:ma*	
	Kamang-Takailubui	*ta:ma*	
	Kamang-Atoitaa		*isiŋnok*
	Sawila		*jo:tiŋsundana*
	Kula		*jawatensona*
	Wersing-Pureman	*təlam*	
	Wersing-Kolana		*wetiŋnuŋ*

discussed in § 5.2.1). The view that the transparent base-five forms are innovations is confirmed by the fact that Wersing-Pureman, the dialect spoken in –what according to oral traditions is– the Wersing homeland, preserves etymological, simplex 'six': *tǝlam*.

In the north-central Alor language Kamang, the formation of 'six' differs between dialects, as set out in (4). The Atoitaa dialect has a base-five compound of 'five [plus] one', while the dialect of Atoitaa reflect pAP *talam 'six'.

(4) Formation of 'six' in Kamang dialects
Kamang-Atoitaa: *isiŋnok* 'six' < *iwesiŋ* 'five' [plus] *nok* 'one'
Kamang-Takailubui: *ta:ma* 'six'

Other language varieties in central Alor (Suboo, Tiee, Moo and Manetaa), also have *ta:ma* 'six'. The dominance of etymological 'six' in the area indicates that the Atoitaa Kamang pattern is a recent innovation, probably occurring by extending the base-five pattern used in forming 'seven' through 'nine' to also include 'six'.

In contrast to the transparent additive compounds found in the languages of eastern and north-central Alor, Western Pantar 'six' is structured more opaquely. There are two morphemes in Western Pantar *hisnakkuŋ* 'six': (i) *his-*, a morpheme which has no independent meaning and; (ii) *-nakkuŋ*, a morpheme originating in the Western Pantar verb *nakkiŋ* 'be single, alone' (< pAP *nakung 'single'). The two morphemes are still apparent in the distributive form of 'six', *hisnakkuŋ~nakkuŋ* 'six~REDUP' 'six by six', where the second element reduplicates, contrasting with the distributive of monomorphemic numerals, e.g., *alaku~alaku* 'two~REDUP' 'two by two' (Klamer et al. this volume). The initial *his-* morpheme of the compound appears to be a borrowing of an Austronesian numeral 'one' (< pAN *esa ~ isa). Initial [h] in the Western Pantar form *his-* is a non-phonemic consonant that appears before /i/, so that the underlying phonological form of *his-* is in fact /is-/. This matches well with the forms of the 'one' numeral in many nearby Austronesian languages on Flores (e.g. Nage *esa* 'one') and Timor (e.g. Tokodede *iso* 'one').

The distinct elements of the Western Pantar compound 'six' indicate that this numeral must have developed independently from the base-five forms for 'six' as found in central-east Alor languages. It appears that Western Pantar *hisnakkuŋ* represents a partial calque of the base-five pattern found in Austronesian languages of Timor. In Tokodede and Mambae, 'six' is formed as 'five-and-one': Mambae *lim-nain-ide*, Tokodede *lim-woun-iso*. However, the initial *lim* 'five' is typically dropped, leaving simply 'and-one' to denote 'six': Mambae *nain-ide*, Tokodede *woun-iso*. Western Pantar *hisnakkuŋ* may have borrowed Austronesian 'one' for the first half (*his*), while for the second half it uses a native element meaning 'single'. The resulting combination 'one-single' is, then, a mediation of numeral constructions from different languages.

5.2 Numerals 'seven' to 'nine'

The AP languages invariably have compound forms for 'seven', 'eight', 'nine', 'ten' and the decades. The compounds are constructed in two distinct ways. One is the additive base-five compound [5+n] (§ 5.2.1), the second a subtractive base-ten compound [10-n] (§ 5.2.2).

5.2.1 Additive base-five compounds

Numerals 'seven' to 'nine' that are historically formed as additive base-five numeral (i.e., [5 2] 'seven', [5 3] 'eight', [5 4] 'nine') are found in both Pantar and central-east Alor. Table 4 presents an overview.

Table 4: Numerals 'seven' to 'nine' in Pantar and central-east Alor

		'seven' 5 2	'eight' 5 3	'nine' 5 4
Pantar	Deing	*jewasrak*	*santig*	*sanut*
	Sar	*jisraq*	*jinatig*	*jinaut*
	Teiwa	*jesraq*	*jesnerig*	*jesnaʔut*
	Kaera	*jesrax-*	*jentug*	*jeniut*
C&E Alor	Abui	*jetiŋajoku*	*jetiŋsua*	*jetiŋbuti*
	KamangTakailubui	*wesiŋok*	*wesiŋsu*	*wesiŋbiat*
	KamangAtoitaa	*isiŋok*	*isiŋsu*	*isiŋbiat*
	Sawila	*jo:tiŋjaku*	*jo:tiŋtuo*	*jo:tiŋara:siiku*
	Kula	*jawatenjakwu*	*jawatentu*	*jawatenarasiku*
	Wersing	*wetiŋjoku*	*wetiŋtu*	*wetiŋarasoku*

The languages of central-east Alor construct 'seven' to 'nine' with an additive base-five system that is synchronically transparent. That is, speakers of these languages readily parse their numerals 'seven' to 'nine' as being composed of the synchronic numeral 'five' followed by 'two', 'three', or 'four', as set out in (5).

(5) Compound 'seven' to 'nine' in central-east Alor

7 Numeral systems in the Alor-Pantar languages

		'seven'	< 'five'	[plus] 'two'
a.				
	Abui	jetiŋajoku	< jetiŋ	ajoku
	Kamang (T)	wesiŋok	< wesiŋ	ok
	Kamang (A)	isiŋok	< iwesiŋ	ok
	Sawila	jo:tiŋjaku	< jo:tiŋ	jaku
	Kula	jawatenjakwu	< jawatena	jakwu
	Wersing	wetiŋjoku	< wetiŋ	joku
b.		'eight'	< 'five'	[plus] 'three'
	Abui	jetiŋsua	< jetiŋ	sua
	Kamang (T)	wesiŋsu	< wesiŋ	su
	Kamang (A)	isiŋsu	< iwesiŋ	su
	Sawila	jo:tiŋtuo	< jo:tiŋ	tuo
	Kula	jawatentu	< jawatena	tu
	Wersing	wetiŋtu	< wetiŋ	tu
c.		'nine'	< 'five'	[plus] 'four'
	Abui	jetiŋbuti	< jetiŋ	buti
	Kamang (A)	isiŋbiat	< iwesiŋ	biat
	Kamang (T)	wesiŋbiat	< wesiŋ	biat
	Sawila	jo:tiŋara:si:ku	< jo:tiŋ	ara:si:ku
	Kula	jawatenarasiku	< jawatena	arasiku
	Wersing	wetiŋarasoku	< wetiŋ	arasoku

By contrast, languages of the Pantar subgroup have compounds for numerals 'seven' through 'nine' that are synchronically non-transparent. The patterns found across the Pantar languages show certain regularities, indicating that the reductions were probably already present in their immediate ancestor, proto-Pantar (pP).[10] In (6) we present the reconstructed numeral compounds and their constituent numeral roots. Only the major changes leading to the forms in the modern languages are detailed here.

The final segments /in/ of pP *jiwasin 'five' were already lost in pP 'seven'. This was followed by the loss of (probably unstressed) medial /wa/ in the subgroup containing Sar, Teiwa and Kaera (proto-Central Pantar, pCP). In the pP-forms of 'eight' and 'nine', medial /we/ of *jewasin 'five' was lost, as well as the final /a/

---

[10] The sub-groups within the AP group that we name here are based purely on evidence from formal and phonological (often sporadic and/or irregular) changes shared between languages in their numerals. The reconstruction of pAP in Holton et al. (2012) is too preliminary and coarse-grained to pick up any real subgrouping evidence. We take the detailed study of numerals that we make here to be indicative of how we may go about identifying AP subgroups in the future.

of *(a)tiga 'three'. In pCP 'eight' and 'nine', a metathesis of /an/ to /na/ occured,[11] followed by a reduction of the resulting /sn/ cluster to /s/ in the group containing Sar and Kaera (proto-Central East Pantar, pCEP).

(6) Developments in proto-Pantar cardinals 'seven' to 'nine'
    a. 'seven':
        pP *jewasin 'five' [plus] *raqo 'two' > *ˌewasˈraqo > pCP *jesraqo
    b. 'eight':
        *jewasin 'five' [plus] *atiga 'three' > *jeˈsantig > pCP *jesnatig > pCEP *jenatig
    c. 'nine':
        pP *jewasin 'five' [plus] *ut 'four' > *jeˈsanut > pCP *jesnaut > pCEP *jenaut

The presence of base-five numerals for 'seven' through 'nine' in separate groups of the AP languages at opposite ends of the archipelago, coupled with the absence of any other equally widely attested forms for these numerals, is a strong indication that a base-five system was used in proto-AP 'seven' through 'nine'.

The difference between base-five numerals in Pantar and central-east Alor languages is merely in the transparency of formatives in the compound numerals. While in the Pantar group base-five compounds have been reduced to such an extent that they are no longer transparent, the central-east Alor languages have retained base-five as a transparent and productive system.

5.2.2 Subtractive base-ten compounds and extensions

The second strategy of creating numerals 'seven' through 'nine' found in the AP languages is subtraction, that is, [10-3] for 'seven', [10-2] for 'eight' and [10-1] for 'nine'. This strategy is found in the Straits and West Alor languages. Table 5 sets out the numerals under discussion in this group along with their reconstructed forms in the ancestor language proto-Straits-West-Alor (pSWA). The final two language in Table 5, Kui and Western Pantar, have innovated their own distinctive forms as indicated by the brackets. They are nevertheless included here because, as will be seen in § 5.2.3, they both include some of the formatives distinctive of pSWA numerals 'seven' to 'nine'.

The subtractive basis for the formation of Straits-West-Alor numerals 'seven' through 'nine' is evident from the remnants of reflexes of proto-AP *(a)tiga 'three',

---

[11] The medial glottal stop in the Teiwa form appears to have been inserted as a syllable boundary marker as the adjacent vowels /au/ of pCP *jesnaut began to harmonize in Teiwa.

7 Numeral systems in the Alor-Pantar languages

Table 5: Numerals 'seven' to 'nine' in the Straits and West Alor

		'seven'	'eight'	'nine'
proto-Straits-West-Alor		*ɓutitoga 7 3	*turarok [10]-2	*ˌtukaˈrinuk [10]-1
Straits	Blagar-Bama	titu	tuakur	tukurunuku
	Blagar-Dolabang	ɓititu	tuaru	turinu
	Reta	bititoga	tulalo	tukanu
West Alor	Kabola	wutito	turlo	tiʔinu
	Adang	itito	turlo	tiʔenu
	Hamap	itito	turalo	tieu
	Klon	usoŋ	tidorok	tukainuk
South-West Alor	Kui	(jesaroku)	(tadusa)	(jesanusa)
Pantar	Western Pantar	(betalaku)	(betiga)	(anukutannaŋ)

*araqu 'two' and *nuk 'one' in the final syllables of modern forms, as set out in (7). Bolding indicates the matching strings of segments.

(7) Formatives 'three', 'two', and 'one' in Straits-West-Alor 'seven' through 'nine'

    a.   'seven' Compare: 'three'
      Blagar-B: *titu*   *tuge*
      Blagar-D: *ɓititu*   *tue*
      Reta: *bititoga*   *atoga*
      Kabola: *wutito*   *towo*
      Adang: *itito*   *tuo*
      Hamap: *itito*   *tof*
      Klon: *usoŋ*   *toŋ*

    b.   'eight' Compare: 'two'
      Blagar-B: *tuakur*   *akur*
      Blagar-D: *tuaru*   *aru*
      Reta: *tulalo*   *alo*
      Kabola: *turlo*   *alo*
      Adang: *turlo*   *alo*
      Hamap: *turalo*   *alo*
      Klon: *tidorok*   *orok*

c.   'nine'   Compare: 'one'
   Blagar-B: *tukurunuku*   *nuku*
   Blagar-D: *turinu*   *nu*
   Reta: *tukanu*   *anu*
   Kabola: *tiʔinu*   *nu*
   Adang: *tiʔenu*   *nu*
   Hamap: *tieu*   *nu*
   Klon: *tukainuk*   *nuk*

Two different subtractive bases are apparent in the modern forms: (i) in 'eight' and 'nine', there is a synchronically unanalysable initial morpheme, which is followed by reflexes of 'two' and 'one', and; (ii) in 'seven', we see an augend that we argue below to be a borrowed reflex of proto-Austronesian *pitu 'seven', with reflexes of 'three' as addend. We discuss these two constructions now in turn.

The unanalysable initial elements in the compounds for 'eight' (*tur-) and 'nine' appear to go back to a single morpheme pre-proto-Straits-West-Alor *tukari, originally meaning something like '[ten] less' or '[ten] take away'. On this reconstruction, pre-pSWA *tukari was already reduced to *tur- in pSWA 'eight', but maintained in 'nine'. We suggest that *tukari meant 'less' or 'take away' rather than 'ten' for two reasons. First, the reconstructed pAP *qar 'ten' (Holton et al. 2012) has a distinct form which cannot be reconciled with pre-pSWA *tukari. Second, to assign *tukari the meaning 'ten' would imply that the numerals formed by subtraction would be composed of a simple sequence of the subtrahend and the minuend. This would be a cross-linguistically unusual pattern and is judged to be unlikely here, but by no means impossible.

We analyse these subtractive numerals as originally constructed along the lines of 'ten less one', 'ten less two', and 'ten less three'. However, over time, the numeral overtly denoting 'ten' was dropped and 'less one' was conventionalized to mean 'nine', 'less two' to mean 'eight', and 'less three' to mean 'seven'. In turn, it appears that pre-pSWA *tukari was reanalysed as a subtrahend rather than the actual morpheme expressing the subtraction. This is seen in its replacement by another base in pSWA 'seven', the other subtrahend that is apparent in the modern numerals, *ɓuti-. We propose that this is a borrowed numeral which is a reflex of proto-Austronesian *pitu 'seven'. It is followed by reflexes of pAP *(a)tiga 'three' to denote 'seven', and has replaced the pre-pSWA morpheme *tukari in the numeral 'seven', as laid out in Table 6.

In other words, Proto-Straits-West-Alor *ɓutitoga is composed of *ɓuti, a borrowed base that is a reflex of PAN *pitu 'seven', conjoined with *toga* as a reflex of pAP *(a)tiga 'three'. The Straits-West-Alor languages are located along a

7 Numeral systems in the Alor-Pantar languages

Table 6: Pre-Proto-Straits-West-Alor and Proto-Straits-West-Alor 'seven' to 'nine'

		'seven'	'eight'	'nine'
Pre-pSWA	stage I	*tukari**toga** less.**three**	*tukari**arok** less.**two**	*tukari**nuk** less.**one**
	stage II	*ɓuti**toga** seven.**three**		
pSWA		*ɓutitoga	*turarok	*tukarinuk

narrow and busy strait where language contact with Austronesian speakers is highly plausible. The motivation for borrowing an Austronesian base for 'seven' may have been Austronesian cultural influence. Among Austronesian groups in eastern Indonesia, 'seven' is a culturally significant numeral (e.g., Flores (Forth 2004: 221); Kedang on Lembata (Barnes 1982: 14-18); Tetun Fehan on Timor (Van Klinken 1999: 102) and Kambera on east Sumba (Forth 1981: 212-213)).

The resulting proto-Straits-West-Alor numeral compound 'seven' was, however, a mediation of the contact and the native numeral. By borrowing the numeral for 'seven', the Austronesian pattern was emulated, but by maintaining the original minuend 'three' along with the new Austronesian numeral functioning as subtrahend, the native Straits-West-Alor subtractive pattern was also partially preserved.

Such a rearrangement in which a numeral is formed mathematically incorrectly may appear unusual, but parallels are found in other languages of the area. For instance, in the Manufahi dialect of Bunaq (a language related to the Alor-Pantar languages spoken on Timor (Schapper 2010)), 'six' is denoted by *tomoluen*, a compound of etymological 'six' and 'one'. Bunaq-Manufahi is spoken in an area dominated by speakers of the Austronesian language Mambae and all Bunaq-Manufahi spreakers also speak Mambae. As discussed in § 5.1, Mambae has a quinary system for the formation of numerals 'six' to 'nine'. The Bunaq-Manufahi pattern of forming 'six' mediates between the native Bunaq pattern of *tomol* 'six' and Mambae *lim-nain-ide* 'five-and-one' > 'six', by combining *tomol* 'six' and *uen* 'one'.

In an alternative analysis, proto-Straits-West-Alor *ɓutitoga 'seven' would be a compound of proto-Alor-Pantar *buta 'four' and *(a)tiga 'three' [4 3]. The advantage of this etymology is that no borrowing from Austronesian is invoked. However, the analysis implies that proto-Straits-West-Alor innovated a numeral with a quaternary base as the initial member of an additive compound. This would effectively add a completely new (fourth) type to the structural inventory of numeral system types found in AP numerals.

Recall that AP numerals have (i) additive compounds with quinary bases as first element (e.g. 5[+]2), (ii) multiplicative compounds with quaternary bases as second (*not* first) element [e.g. 2[x]4], and (iii) subtractive compounds ([10]−2). While we cannot exclude the possibility that a (proto-)language invents a completely new structural type for a single numeral, we believe this scenario to be less likely than the borrowing plus reanalysis scenario outlined above.

It should be added that there is no evidence that a new [4 3] pattern could have been borrowed from neighbouring Austronesian language(s), as [4 3] 'seven' is not attested anywhere in the region (Schapper & Hammarström 2013). Numerals with a quaternary base are found in the region, but these are all multiplicative forms: [2 4] (Flores) or [4 2] (Lembata) 'eight' (see Table 13 and Appendix A.2).

5.2.3 Other mixed systems for 'seven' to 'nine'

In the previous section it was mentioned that 'seven' through 'nine' in Kui and Western Pantar include formative elements of the Straits West Alor system. However, the formatives are part of different systems, using a range of bases.

In (8) we set out the formatives found in Kui 'seven' to 'nine'. We can see that Kui has replaced the proto-Straits-West-Alor subtractive numerals for 'seven' and 'nine' with additive base-five numerals [5 2], [5 4]. The numeral *tadusa* 'eight' follows a different pattern, apparently being built from two morphemes: (i) the first element *tad-* appears to reflect the subtractive morpheme *tur- (< pre-pSWA *tukari) used in forming pSWA *turarok 'eight' (see Table 6), and (ii) the second element *usa* is the Kui numeral 'four' (< pAP *buta 'four').

(8) Formatives in Kui 'seven' to 'nine'

    a. 'seven':
       jesaroku < *jesan* 'five' [plus] *oruku* 'two'

    b. 'eight':
       tadusa < *tad- usa* 'four'

    c. 'nine':
       jesanusa < *jesan* 'five' [plus] *usa* 'four'

It appears that in Kui 'eight' has been imperfectly remodelled on a multiplication pattern 'two [times] four' [2x4]. The original proto-Straits-West-Alor *turarok 'eight', historically composed of pre-pSWA *tukari 'less' and pre-PSWA *arok 'two', appears to have been reduced and reanalysed from subtractive 'minus two' to multiplicative '[two] times'. This new base was then combined with *usa* 'four' to reach 'eight'. The /d/ in Kui *tadusa* 'eight' appears to have arisen through liquid dissimilation of the two /r/'s in the adjacent syllables. That is, as we see also in Klon *tidorok* 'eight', dissimilation applied such that *turarok took on a hypothetical form like **tudarok. In the history of Kui, the *arok element of hypothetical **tudarok was then replaced with *usa* 'four' to create **tudusa 'eight' with the vowel changes u > o > a leading to modern Kui *tadusa* 'eight'.

In (9) we set out the formatives found in Western Pantar 'seven' to 'nine'. We can see that proto-Straits-West-Alor subtractive numeral *tukarinuk 'nine' have been replaced by an innovative, but still subtractive form composed of the numeral 'one' denoting the subtrahend and the lexical verb 'take away' signalling the subtraction. The numerals 'seven' and 'eight' follow a different, innovative pattern in which *be-* ~ *bet-*, reflecting *ɓuti- as also used in the formation of proto-Straits-West-Alor *ɓutitoga 'seven', is combined with 'two' and 'three' to form 'eight' and 'nine' respectively.

(9) Formatives in Western Pantar 'seven' to 'nine'

a. 'seven':
betalaku < *bet-* '?' *alaku* 'two'
b. 'eight':
betiga < *be-* '?' *tiga* 'three'
c. 'nine':
anukutannaŋ < *anuku* 'one' *tannaŋ* 'take away'

Synchronic evidence for their poly-morphemic status includes the distributive formation of 'seven', which takes the right-most element as the base for the reduplication Klamer et al. (this volume): *betalaku~talaku* 'seven~REDUP' 'seven by seven', *betiga~tiga* 'eight~REDUP' 'eight by eight', and *anuktannaŋ~tannaŋ* 'nine~REDUP' 'nine by nine'. The segmentation in distributives appears to be a historical relic. This is suggested by the irregularities in the distributive derivation of 'seven': there has been a reanalysis of the morpheme boundary between *bet-* and *alaku* 'two' to become *be-talaku,* analogous to the segmentation of the numeral *betiga* 'three'. The reanalysis points to speakers not being able to decompose the complex numerals into their orginal forms.

Thus, in Western Pantar, *ɓuti- has been adopted not as a minuend (as in proto-Straits-West-Alor 'seven'), but as an augend. We posit that proto-Western Pantar originally had an additive base-5 system in which 'seven' and 'eight' were formed by means of compounds of 'five [plus] two' and 'five [plus] three' respectively, as set out in stage I in Table 7. In stage II, pre-Western Pantar 'five' is replaced by a reflex of proto-Austronesian *pitu 'seven' borrowed either directly from an Austronesian language under the same forces for pre-proto-Straits-West-Alor as described in § 5.2.2, or perhaps more likely from a ([pre]-proto)-Straits-West-Alor language. In stage III, the pattern of using *ɓuti- as an augend for the formation of 'seven' in stage II is extended to the formation of 'eight' (Table 7).

Table 7: Proto-W Pantar developments leading to modern W Pantar 'seven', 'eight'

		'seven'	'eight'
Proto-WP	stage I	*jasiŋalaku five.two	*jasiŋatiga five.three
	stage II	*ɓutialaku seven.two	
	stage III		*ɓutiatoga seven.three

In sum, in Kui, the proto-Straits-West-Alor subtractive numerals for 'seven' and 'nine' have been replaced by additive base-five forms [5 2] and [5 4], while 'eight' has become a base-four compound [2x4]. In Western Pantar, on the other hand, the proto-Straits-West-Alor subtractive numeral 'nine' has been replaced by an innovative, but still subtractive form composed of the numeral 'one' denoting the subtrahend and the lexical verb 'take away'. Western Pantar 'seven' and 'eight' involve a borrowed and reanalysed quinary base.

6 Numerals 'ten' and above

6.1 Numeral 'ten': multiplied base-ten compound

Table 8 presents the numerals 10, 20 and 30. A decimal base *qar 'ten' is reconstructable to proto-Alor-Pantar. This is reflected across AP languages, with the exception of central-eastern Alor, where languages eastwards of Kamang reflect innovative proto-Central-East-Alor (pCEA) *adajaku 'ten'. This form indicates that a quinary base may have at some point replaced the decimal base in these languages: the second element of the compound *adajaku 'ten' is homophonous with *jaku '2' so that it appears to be composed as [(5?) x 2].

7 Numeral systems in the Alor-Pantar languages

Table 8: Numerals 'ten' and the formation of decades

		'ten'	'twenty'	'thirty'
Pantar	Western Pantar	ke†anuku	ke alaku	ke atiga
	Deing	qar nuk	qar raq	qar atig
	Sar	qar nuk	qar raq	qar tig
	Teiwa	qa:r nuk	qa:r raq	qa:r jerig
	Kaera	xar nuko	xar raxo	xar tug
Straits	BlagarBama	qar nuku	qar akur	qar tuge
	BlagarDolabang	ʔari nu	ʔari aru	ʔari tue
	Reta	kara nu	kara alo	kara atoga
West Alor	Kabola	kar nu	kar ho(ʔ)olo	kar towo
	Adang	ʔer nu	ʔer alo	ʔer tuo
	Hamap	air nu	air alo	air tof
	Klon	kar nuk	kar orok	kar toŋ
	Kui	kar nuku	kar oruku	kar siwa
C&E Alor	Abui	kar nuku	kar ajoku	kar sua
	Kamang	ata:k nok	ata:k ok	ata:k su
	Sawila	ada:ku	ada:ku maraku	ada:ku matua
	Kula	adajakwu	mijakwu	mitua
	Wersing	adajoku	adajoku mijoku	adajoku mitu

†In Western Pantar the final consonant of *qar underwent irregular loss at the word-internal morpheme boundary.

In the modern AP languages, reflexes of *qar for the most part do not stand alone but must be combined with another numeral in order to signify. Decades (numerals denoting a set or series of ten such as '10', '20', '30' etc.) in AP languages are typically formed by combining the decimal base with a multiplicand indicating the decade. Thus, 'ten' is composed of a reflex of *qar and 'one' [10 1], 'twenty' of 'ten' and 'two' [10 2], 'thirty' of 'ten' and 'three' [10 3], and so on for higher decades.

In the east of Alor we find deviations from this majority pattern for forming decades. First, Sawila, Kula and Wersing do not denote 'ten' by 'ten [times] one' [10 1] as elsewhere, but employ the numeral 'ten' alone without 'one'. Second, in the formation of decades higher than 'ten', these languages do not simply juxtapose numerals to express multiplication of the base-ten, but mark it with a prefix (Kula/Wersing *mi-* and Sawila *m(a)-*) on the multiplicand. These are verbal prefixes which have developed from the proto-AP postposition *mi 'be in' (Holton & Robinson this volume). Attached to numerals *mi-* 'TIME' derives frequency verbs such as 'to do twice' in the Alor languages Kamang and Klon.[12]

(10) Kamang (Schapper, field notes)
 Alma uh ok an-iŋ=daŋ kai **mi-ok**.
 person CLF two thus-SET=WHEN cheer TIME-two
 'Two people('s heads) means (we) cheer twice.'

(11) Klon (Baird 2008)
 ... mid beh go-duur o **mi-orok** ...
 ... climb branch 3-cut DEM TIME-two ...
 '... (he) climbed up (and) cut the branch twice...'

In the east of Alor, prefix *mi-* occurs on multiplicands to denote decades 'twenty' and above. This appears an extension of how *mi-* derives frequency verbs and ordinals from cardinals. In other words, the construction used to express higher decades in eastern Alor languages can be paraphrased as 'ten twice' for 'twenty', 'ten thrice' for 'thirty', and so on. In Kula, the use of *mi-* in the decade construction has conventionalized to such an extent that *adajakwu* 'ten' can be left off entirely, with the prefixed multiplicand carrying the decade meaning alone. That is, *mi-jakwu* for instance, would etymologically denote 'twice' or 'second', but is now used alone to mean 'twenty'.

6.2 Numerals within decades

A 'decade' is a numeral which is a set or series of ten (e.g., '20', '30' etc.). The term 'numeral within decades' is used here to refer to any numeral expression such as 'eighteen', 'eighty-nine' etc., involving an operator word that signifies addition.[13] In AP languages, an additive operator separates the decades from the numerals 'one' to 'nine', as illustrated in Table 9.

The additive operator is not used to combine decades, hundreds or thousands with each other, as illustrated with '1999' in several languages in (12).

---

[12] By contrast, *mi* derives ordinals in the Pantar-Straits languages Kaera, Blagar and Adang (Klamer et al. this volume).

[13] Such operators are referred to variously in the typological literature as 'marker of addition', 'additive marker' or 'additive link'. See, e.g., Greenberg (1978: 264-265); Hanke (2010: 73).

7 Numeral systems in the Alor-Pantar languages

Table 9: AP language compounds for 'eighteen'

		'ten'	'one'	OPERATOR	'eight'
Pantar	West Pantar	ke	anuku	wali	betiga
	Teiwa	qa:r	nuk	rug	jesnerig
	Kaera	xar	nuk	beti	jentug
Straits	Blagar-Bama	qar	nuku	wali	tuakur
	Blagar-Dolabang	ʔari	nu	belta	tuaru
W Alor	Adang	er	nu	faliŋ	turlo
	Klon	kar	nuk	awa	tidorok
C&E Alor	Abui	kar	nuku	wal	jetiŋsua
	Kamang	ata:k	nok	wa:l	isiŋsu
	Sawila	ada:ku		garisiŋ	jo:tiŋtua
	Kula	adajakwu		arasɨŋ	jawatentu
	Wersing	adajoku		weresiŋ	wetiŋtu

(12)   1000 1   100   9   10   9   OPER 9
     Teiwa: ribu nuk ratu jesnaʔut   qa:r jesnaʔut   rug jesnaʔut
     W Pantar: ribu   ratu nuktannaŋ ke nuktannaŋ wali nuktannaŋ
     Abui: rifi nuku aisaha jetiŋbuti   kar jetiŋbuti   wal jetiŋbuti
     Kamang: ribu nuk asaka isiŋbiat   ata:k isiŋbiat   wa:l isiŋbiat

An additive operator *wali(ŋ) can be reconstructed to proto-Alor-Pantar. In modern AP languages, the operator is for the most part a semantically empty lexeme without meaning outside of the numeral formula. However, some modern languages have homophonous lexical verb roots with semantics plausibly related to the additive operator: Teiwa and Kaera *wal* are verbs meaning 'fill, full', and Abui *wal-* is a verb meaning 'gather more'. These might suggest that the proto-AP additive linker *wali(ŋ) was a lexeme meaning 'add, (do) again'.

Not all modern AP languages reflect the reconstructed operator. Kaera and Blagar-Dolabang have apparently related operators, while Teiwa has a unique form *rug*. In eastern Alor languages, the additive operators (Kula *arisɨŋ*, Sawila *garisiŋ*, Wersing *weresiŋ*) are the result of shared borrowing from an Austronesian language of Timor, most likely Tokodede. The Austronesian languages of eastern Timor invariably use 'more' with a variant of the form /geresin/ as the additive operator in numerals. Examples are provided in (13).

299

(13) Additive operators in 'eleven' in the Austronesian languages of eastern Timor

	ten	OPERATOR	one
Tokodede	sagulu	geresi	iso
Kemak	sapulu	resi	sia
Tetun	sanulu	resin	ida
Mambae	sagul	resi	kid
Atauro	seŋulu	resi	hea

6.3 Multiples of 'hundred' and 'thousand'

In most AP languages, bases for 'hundred' and 'thousand' cannot be used as numerals on their own. That is, they must be juxtaposed with a following multiplicand, so that 'one hundred' is [100x1], 'two hundred' [100x2] '200', and so on (Table 10). A handful of languages do not conform to this pattern. Western Pantar *ratu*, Kui *asaga*, Kula *gasaka* and Wersing *aska* 'hundred' can be used independently to denote '100'. Western Pantar *ribu* is also able to independently denote '1000', but may also appear with the unrelated form *je* to make *ribu je* '1000'. *Je* is also used in the ordinal 'first' (Klamer et al. this volume). Sawila *dana* and Kula *dena* are reductions of a different proto-form *sundana 'one' (compare the forms for 'one' in Table 2).

Across much of Alor we find reflexes of a form *a(j)saka 'hundred', but it is not clear to what level this form should be reconstructed. The languages of Pantar, Straits and West Alor have borrowed an Austronesian form reflecting PAN *Ratus 'hundred'.[14] There is no evidence of an indigenous AP numeral for 'thousand'; all AP languages have borrowings from Austronesian reflecting PAN *libu 'thousands'. Possible source languages include Malay (*ratus* 'hundreds', *ribu* 'thousands'), or Lamaholot (spoken on Adonara, Lomblen, Solor and Flores located west of Pantar), which employs the bases *ratu* 'hundreds' and *ribu* 'thousands'. Austronesian languages in eastern Timor are not probable sources as they reflect neither PAN *R in 'hundred' (e.g., Tetun, Kemak and Tokodede *atus* 'hundred') nor PAN *b in 'thousand' (e.g., Tetun and Tokodede *rihun*, Kemak *lihur* 'thousand').

---

[14] In proto-Austronesian *R represents an alveolar or uvular trill, contrasting with Proto-Austronesian *r which is thought to have been an alveolar flap.

Table 10: Numerals with bases '100' and '1000'

		'100'	'200'	'1000'	'2000'
Pantar	West Pantar	ratu	ratu alaku	(a)ribu (ye)	ribu (alaku)
	Deing	aratu nuk	aratu raq	aribu nuk	aribu raq
	Sar	ratu nuk	ratu raq	ribu nuk	ribu raq
	Teiwa	ratu nuk	ratu (ha)raq	ribu nuk	ribu (ha)raq
	Kaera	ratu nuk	ratu rax-	ribu nuk	ribu rax-
Straits	Blagar-Bama	ratu nuku	ratu akur	ribu nuku	ribu akur
	Blagar-Dolabang	ratu nu	ratu aru	ribu nu	ribu aru
	Reta	ratu anu	ratu alo	ribu ano	ribu alo
W Alor	Kabola	rat nu	rat ho(?)olo	rib nu	rib ho(?)olo
	Adang	rat nu	rat alo	rib nu	rib alo
	Hamap	rat nu	rat alo	—†	—
	Klon	eska nok	eska orok	—	—
	Kui	asaga	asaga oruku	rab nuku	rab oruku
C & E Alor	Abui	aisaha nu	aisaha ajoku	rifi nuku	rifi ajoku
	Kamang (L/U)	asaka nok	asaka ok	libu nok	libu ok
	Sawila	asaka dana	asaka jaku	ri:bu dana	ri:bu jaku
	Kula	gasaka	gasaka jakwana	rib dena	—
	Wersing	aska	aska joku	ribu no	—

† '—' denotes that no data is available for this numeral

Table 11: Morpheme patterns in AP cardinals 'five' through 'ten'

	'five'	'six'	'seven'	'eight'	'nine'	'ten'
Northern Pantar	5	6	5 2	5 3	5 4	10 1
Central Alor	5	6	5 2	5 3	5 4	10 (1)
East Alor	5	5 1	5 2	5 3	5 4	10
Wersing Kolana	5	5 single	5 2	5 3	5 4	10
Kui	5	6	5 2	[2] 4	5 4	10 1
Straits-West-Alor	5	6	7 3	[10] less 2	[10] less 1	10 1
Western Pantar	5	5 single	7 2	7 3	1 take away [10]	10 1

7 Alor-Pantar numerals from a typological and areal perspective

In this section, we consider how forms and systems used in the composition of AP numerals relate to those used in other languages. First, we place the AP numeral systems in a broad typological perspective (§ 7.1); next, we take an areal perspective, addressing the question to what extent the AP systems are similar to those of the surrounding Austronesian languages, and suggest where contact could have played a role in shaping the numerals (§ 7.2).

7.1 Typological rarities in AP numeral(s)

In Table 11 we summarize the various systems that AP languages use to form cardinals 'five' through 'ten'. The Arabic numerals represent the numeral morphemes used in compounds, and the English words represent the lexical items that combine with those formatives. Thus, a compound numeral like Wersing Kolana *wetiŋnuŋ* 'six' would be transcribed as '5 single' as it is made up of *wetiŋ*, the morpheme for '5', and a lexeme *nuŋ*, meaning 'single', while a compound numeral like Teiwa *jesraq* 'seven' would be transcribed as '5 2' as it is a compound of morphemes for '5' and '2'. Square brackets '[]' represent absent surface elements that are assumed to be part of the earlier numeral construction as we reconstructed it, while round brackets '( )' represent elements which may or may not be present depending on the details of the language in question.

Two major typological points are of interest in the AP numeral systems. The first is that they combine a mono-morphemic 'six' with base-five compounds for numerals 'seven' to 'nine'. We reconstruct this system for proto-AP, and it is presently reflected in languages of northern Pantar and central Alor. Crosslinguistically, this is a rather uncommon numeral system; it is much more common to have a system where the quinary base is used in forming all numerals 'six' through nine',[15] as attested in the languages of east Alor. However, because pAP *talam 'six' is a reflex of the higher pTAP *talam 'six' (Schapper, Huber & Engelenhoven this volume), this form must be considered older than the quinary numeral for 'six'. In other words, where we find [5 1] 'six', this is viewed as a later extension of the quinary system that was already in use for 'seven' through 'nine' in proto-AP.[16]

A second point of typological interest are the subtractive decimal systems used in the Straits-West-Alor languages, where numerals 'seven' through 'nine' are formed by subtraction,[17] while 'six' is monomorphemic. Systems like this, where subtraction is used in the formation of more than one numeral, and where such subtractive forms occur *alongside* a monomorphemic form for 'six', are crosslinguistically uncommon.

7.2 AP numerals in their areal context

It is useful to complement the genealogical perspective of sections 4 to 6 with an areal perspective, and compare the numeral system patterns in the AP languages with those of the Austronesian languages in their immediate vicinity, to see what this might tell us about the history of AP numerals. Where similar forms or patterns are found, we may ask whether there is evidence that these are contact-induced. In this section, we look at the evidence that may suggest influence from AP languages into nearby Austronesian languages, followed by

---

[15] Harald Hammarström, p.c. 2012, based on his extensive numeral database reported on in Hammarström (2010).

[16] This contrasts with the view expressed by Vatter, who considered monomorphemic 'six' to be a 'deviation'('Abweichung') from the base-five compounds 'six' (1932: 279-280).

[17] This is independent of the substitution of the Austronesian base into 'seven'.

the evidence suggesting influence in the opposite direction. We also point out cases where the data currently available are inconclusive.

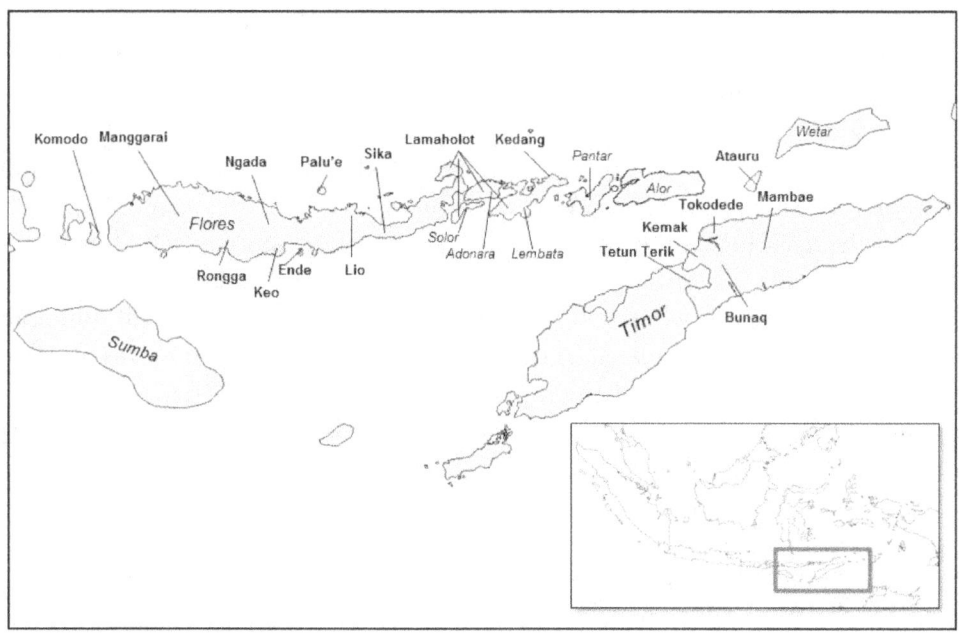

Figure 1: Austronesian languages to the west and south of Alor-Pantar. Names in bold are language names, names in italics are names of islands.

It is a well-established fact that proto-Austronesian (pAN) had a decimal system, with numerals 'one' through 'nine' all being simple mono-morphemic words. Blust (2009: 268) claims that outside of Melanesia few Austronesian languages have innovated complex - additive, subtractive or multiplicative - numerals for 'one' to 'ten'. The Austronesian languages around AP, however, show a notable clustering of just such innovations. We compiled numeral data for 32 Austronesian languages spoken west and south-east of Alor and Pantar (see Appendix A.2 and A.3). In these, we observe three distinct patterns of innovations in the formation of numerals 'six' through 'nine', reflected in nine modern Austronesian languages (Table 13). These are: the Timor pattern (1-5, 5+1, 5+2, 5+3, 5+4, 10), the Lembata pattern (1-7, 4x2, 5+4, 10), and the Flores pattern (1-5, 5+1, 5+2, 2x4, 10-1, 10). Proto-Austronesian numerals are provided for comparative purposes in the top row.

7 Numeral systems in the Alor-Pantar languages

Table 12: Mixed numeral systems in proto-Austronesian and the Austronesian languages of Flores, Lembata and Timor (1-5)

		'one'	'two'	'three'	'four'	'five'
	pAN	*esa ~ *isa	*duSa	*telu	*Sepat	*lima
Flores	Rongga	(e)sa	ɹua	telu	wutu	lima
	Ende	sa	zua	tela	wutu	lima
	Ngadha	esa	zua	telu	vutu	lima
	Nage	esa	d'ua	telu	wutu	lima
	Kéo †	haʔesa	ʔesa rua	ʔesa tedu	ʔesa wutu	ʔesa dima
	Lio	əsa	rua	təlu	sutu	lima
Lembata	Kedang*	>udeʔ	sue	tælu	>apaʔ	leme
Timor	Mambae	id	ru	teul	fat	lim
	Tokodede	iso	ru	telo	pat	lim

† Kéo numerals appear with the default classifier ʔesa and/or the prefix ha 'one'.
* In Kedang orthography />/ preceding a vowel encodes that vowel as breathy (Samely 1991).

Innovative quinary numerals are found in the Austronesian languages across the three innovative types. In the north-central Timor languages, Tokodede and Mambae, we have quinary numerals for numerals from 'six' through 'nine', a pattern that stands out against the typically conservative numerals systems of the Austronesian languages elsewhere on Timor (Naueti being an exception, see Schapper & Hammarström (2013) on the possible reasons for the quinary numerals in Naueti). It is notable that the close inland relative of Tokodede and Mambae, Kemak, has no base-5 numerals (see Appendix A.3). The appearance of this pattern in these languages may be a result of contact with speakers of AP languages spoken on the south and east coast of Alor, such as Kula, Sawila and Wersing, located just a short sea crossing from the north of Timor. There is some linguistic evidence that contacts between these Alor groups and those of north-central Timor existed: the additive operators in the central-east Alor languages Sawila, Kula and Wersing (see Table 9) seem to be borrowed from Tokodede (§ 6.2). In addition, oral traditions record contacts between groups in south-east Alor and north Timor. For instance, eastern Alor groups almost invariably trace their origins to pre-historic migrations from Timor (Wellfelt & Schapper 2013, Wellfelt pers. comm. 2013). Similarly, many songs in central-east Alor are sung in the Tokodede language and mention place names such as Likusaen and Maubara,

Table 13: Mixed numeral systems in proto-Austronesian and the Austronesian languages of Flores, Lembata and Timor (6-10)

		'six'	'seven'	'eight'
	pAN	*enem	*pitu	*walu
Flores	Rongga	lima esa 5 1	limaɹua 5 2	ɹuambutu 2 4
	Ende	limasa 5 1	limazua 5 2	ruabutu 2 4
	Ngadha	lima esa 5 1	limarua 5 2	ruabutu 2 4
	Nage	lima esa 5 1	lima zua 5 2	zua butu 2 4
	Kéo †	ʔesa dima ʔesa 5 1	ʔesa dima rua 5 2	ʔesa rua mbutu 2 4
	Lio	lima əsa 5 1	lima rua 5 2	rua mbutu 2 4
Lembata	Kedang*	>ænæng	pitu	butu rai 4 2?
Timor	Mambae	limnai nide 5 1	limnai rua 5 2	limnai telu 5 3
	Tokodede	wouniso [5] 1	wouru [5] 2	woutelo [5] 3

		'nine'	'ten'	
	pAN	*siwa	*puluq	
Flores	Rongga	taraesa [10] 1	sambulu 1 10	
	Ende	trasa [10] 1	sabulu 1 10	
	Ngadha	teresa [10] 1	habulu 1 10	
	Nage	tea esa [10] 1	sa bulu 1 10	
	Kéo †	ʔesa tera ʔesa [1 10] 1	hambudu 1 10	
	Lio	təra əsa [10] 1	sambulu 1 10	
Lembata	Kedang*	leme >apaʔ 5 4	pulu 1 10	
Timor	Mambae	limnai pata 5 4	sikul	
	Tokodede	woupat [5] 4	sagulu 1 10	

† Kéo numerals appear with the default classifier ʔesa and/or the prefix ha 'one'.
* In Kedang orthography />/ preceding a vowel encodes that vowel as breathy (Samely 1991).

which are located in the north of Timor in the area where Tokodede is spoken (Wellfelt & Schapper 2013). However, as Wellfelt & Schapper (2013) argue, the directionality of the influence in the contact relations retrievable from such oral traditions and linguistic evidence is firmly flowing from Timor to Alor. The borrowing of quinary numerals from AP into Timor languages thus would appear to go against the other borrowing patterns, including that seen thus far in numerals. As such, whilst Alorese quinary numerals are the only such systems that are in contact with the Tokodede and Mambae and seem the best candidate for the innovative numeral formation, it remains to be explained why this pattern was able to spread to the Timor languages, when in oral traditions and language it is the Timor groups that are the source of influence on Alor and not a recipient of it.

The origin of the base-five numerals in the central-eastern Flores languages Rongga, Ende, Ngadha, Nage, Kéo, and Lio is yet more obscure. There is mounting evidence of a non-Austronesian substrate in the Austronesian languages of the Flores region (see, e.g., Capell 1976; Klamer 2012). Accordingly, we may hypothesize that the quinary forms of the Flores languages reflect a prehistoric Papuan (or non-Austronesian) substrate that had a quinary system for the lower cardinals. However, we currently lack any evidence to link the languages forming the substrate in the central-eastern Flores region to the AP languages as we know it today – the Flores substrate could just as well be part of a different non-Austronesian group.

For Kedang on north Lembata, however, we are on a firmer ground to say that it formed its numeral 'nine' on the basis of the quinary patterns used for 'six' through 'nine' in the AP languages of northern Pantar, which is located just east of the Kedang speaking area on Lembata (see Figure 1). Note that the Lamaholot dialects spoken around Kedang in south and west Lembata all lack quinary numerals (see Appendix A.2) so that Kedang 'nine' stands out as being different from its immediate Austronesian neighbours. In his ethnographic study of the Kedang, Barnes (1974) noted that the Kedang speakers are culturally very different from the Lamaholot groups on Lembata, instead showing cultural similarities with the AP groups of Alor and Pantar. For instance, unlike the Lamaholot, the Kedang are known for 'the number of gongs [they] own and especially in the fact that [these] are used as bridewealth' (Barnes 1974: 15), which is also a common practice in AP groups. The unique quinary form of Kedang 'nine' may well be a trace of cultural contact between Kedang and AP speakers on Pantar, for instance in bridewealth negotiations involving gongs.

In turn, we now investigate to what extent the numeral systems in AP languages have been influenced by nearby Austronesian languages. In sections 4-6, we saw that some AP languages employ numerals containing morphemes that have been borrowed from Austronesian languages, in the following five contexts:

1. A reflex of pAN *pitu was borrowed into the Straits-West Alor languages as a base in the numeral 'seven'.

2. The Western Pantar numeral 'six' *hisnakkung* has an initial element *his*- that is a likely Austronesian borrowing (< PAN esa~*isa 'one'), and *hisnakkung* represents a partial calque of the [5 1] pattern found in Austronesian languages of Flores.

3. An additive operator with the approximate form /geresin/ was borrowed into east Alor languages from Tokodede (north Timor).

4. Reflex(es) of pAN *Ratus 'hundred' were borrowed from the Flores-Lembata Austronesian languages into the languages of Pantar, and to a lesser extent Alor.

5. Reflex(es) of pAN *libu 'thousand' were borrowed from Flores-Lembata Austronesian languages into AP languages across the board.

The pattern for Kui *tadusa* 'eight' seems to be formed a multiplicative pattern 2x4 due to the second element appearing to be derived from *usa* 'four'. This multiplicative pattern is otherwise unknown in AP languages, but is found in the Austronesian languages of central-eastern Flores (Ende, Lio, Ngadha, Rongga, Keo). Whilst the Kui are today not directly adjacent to any of the Austronesian languages of Flores with multiplicative 'eight', there are indications that they may have had fairly intensive contact with Austronesian speakers from the west. Kui oral tradition holds that the royal family of the group migrated to Alor from Flores (Emilie Wellfelt pers. comm.). Hägerdal (2012: 38, fn. 36) cites evidence that the Kui were part of a league consisting of the five princedoms Pandai, Baranusa, Blagar, Alorese and Kui. Today, Pandai, Baranusa and Alor are locations where Alorese is spoken, an Austronesian language closely related to Lamaholot in the Flores region (Klamer 2011; 2012). In the historical period, the Kui king is also widely recorded to have owned boats running trade routes between Alor and Kupang in West Timor and islands of the Solor archipeligo (Emilie Wellfelt pers. comm., Hägerdal 2012). It is therefore possible that the Kui were once in close contact with speakers of (an) Austronesian language(s) from the Flores region, and that this contact might be the ultimate source of their base-4 numeral 'eight'.

Finally, recall that forming 'nine' by subtraction ([10]-1) is found in the AP languages of Straits-West-Alor, while in the Austronesian languages of central-east Flores, monomorphemic 'nine' (proto-Austronesian *siwa) has been replaced with a subtractive compound containing two formatives: a reflex of proto-Austronesian *esa 'one', and an unanalysable initial element (*tar). There is no obvious explanation how the subtractive 'nine' entered this group of Flores languages. Neither can we explain the origin of the subtractive pattern in proto-Straits-West-Alor. We have argued that in this proto-language, subtractive 'nine' replaced the original pAP base-five form of 'nine' [5 4], and involved reflexes of pAP *nuk 'one', subsequently extending the subtractive system to 'eight' and 'seven'. So it is the subtractive pattern that is similar across the Flores and Straits-West Alor groups, not the lexemes themselves. The geographical closeness of the groups, combined with the relative rarity of subtractive systems in both Austronesian and Alor-Pantar languages, may be suggestive of a (possibly ancient) structural diffusion. On the other hand, we cannot exclude the possibility that the forms were innovated independently in both groups: as Schapper & Hammarström (2013) point out, innovation of subtractive numerals has occured independently in proto-Malay, central Maluku and south-east Sulawesi.

In short, contact-induced borrowings of both forms and structures ('matter' and 'patterns') have played a role in shaping some of the numerals in the Alor-Pantar and nearby Austronesian languages. Some contacts took place in historical times, and are supported by historical and ethnographic data, others are likely to be of more ancient date and must remain hypothetical. There are also similarities that cannot be traced back to contact.

8 Conclusions and discussion

From this comparative study of the numeral paradigms in 19 AP language varieties we draw three types of conclusions: (i) about the morphological make up of the numeral compounds; (ii) about typological rarities in the AP numeral systems, and (iii) about the subgrouping and history of the AP language group.

Morphologically, AP cardinals above 'six' consist of minimally two formatives. Additive base-five forms involve two (reflexes of) numerals and no marker for addition. Subtractive base-ten forms involve a numeral and an unanalysable initial element that appears to go back to a morpheme originally meaning something like 'less' or 'take away'. With one exception, the numerals 'ten' are compounds of 'ten' and 'one', and the decades are formed accordingly. Numerals 'one hundred' and 'one thousand' are structured in the same way, expressing multiplication of the base with juxtaposed numerals in which the highest numeral precedes the lowest. Numerals in between decades are expressed as phrases, involving an additive operator (proto-AP *wali(ŋ) 'add, (do) again').

Typologically, the constellations of numerals 'six' through 'nine' in AP represent two rare patterns. The first rarity is the combination of a mono-morphemic 'six' with quinary forms 'seven' through 'nine' found in many languages across the two islands, and reconsructed to proto-AP. The second rarity is the occurrence of subtractive base-ten systems alongside a monomorphemic 'six' as found in the Straits-West-Alor languages. Typologically interesting are the mathematically 'incorrect' numerals found in some of the languages: a 'seven' that mathematically should be 'four' (Straits-West Alor), a 'seven' and 'eight' that mathematically should be 'nine' and 'ten' (Western Pantar), and an 'eight' that would literally translate as 'minus four' in Kui. These forms all arose through reanalysis of the numeral value of the base as different from its etymological source. Finally, it is of typological interest to consider the non-numeral lexemes that are incorporated into AP numerals: the (ad)verbs 'less' and 'take away' as part of subtractive numerals; *mi-*, an originally locative morpheme deriving decades; and the word 'single' standing in for the numeral 'one' in compound numerals for 'six'.

Historically, this study has provided information on the numeral system of proto-AP, and additional details on affiliations and distinctions between members of the AP group that may be used as evidence to construct particular subgroups within the family. The proto-AP numeral system was a mixed quinary and decimal system, with a monomorphemic 'six' (i.e. 1, 2, 3, 4, 5, 6, [5 2], [5 3], [5 4], [10 1]). The arithmetic operations involved were addition and multiplication. Over time, the system was complicated by reorganizations of patterns as well as borrowings of numeral bases, or patterns, or both. As a result, some modern languages have introduced subtractive procedures instead of, or along with, addition and multiplication. Some languages incorporated non-numeral formatives into their numerals.

Numeral forms were reconstructed to different nodes in the AP family, as summarized in Table 14. The table is to be read from left to right. The left-most column represents the oldest numeral forms, that is, those that can be reconstructed to proto-AP. Numerals 'one' through 'six' in this proto-language were monomorphemic forms, while 'seven' through 'nine' were regular quinary forms. The right-hand columns represent numeral innovations which can be reconstructed to different subgroups of the AP family.[18]

---

[18] The ordering of right-hand columns is by number of languages; it should not be interpreted as representing a chronology of the age of subgroups in the case of proto-Straits-West-Alor (pSWA) and proto-Pantar (pP). Naturally, proto-Central-East-Alor (pCEA), proto-East Alor

Table 14: Numeral (pattern) reconstructions for 'one' through 'ten' in AP subgroups

	Proto-Alor-Pantar	Proto-Straits-West-Alor	Proto-Pantar	Proto-Central-East-Alor	Proto-East Alor	Proto-East Alor Montane
'one'	*nuk					*sundana
'two'	*araqu					
'three'	*(a)tiga					
'four'	*buta					
'five'	*yiwesin					
'six'	*talam				*arasiku	
'seven'	5 2	*butitoga	*yewasraqo			
'eight'	5 3	*turarok	*yesantig			
'nine'	5 4	*tukarinuk	*yesamut			
'ten'	*qar			*adayaku		

7 Numeral systems in the Alor-Pantar languages

Translated into a tree, the reconstruction of numerals in AP languages yields the structure in Figure 2.

We see that that there are patterns and forms found in the Pantar languages (except Western Pantar) are clearly separate from those in the languages of Alor; the Straits West Alor languages (Blagar, Reta, Kabola, Adang, Hamap, Klon) share patterns and forms amongst themselves that are not shared with other AP languages; and we argued the same to be the case for the languages of central and east Alor. The subgrouping membership of the Kui and Western Pantar is problematic; their grouping within pSWA is tentative and rests on their possessing some innovative morphemes (i.e., reflexes of *ɓuti- and *tukari) in common with the main Straits-West Alor languages proper, though with different functions in Kui and Western Pantar.

The preliminary reconstruction of Proto-AP based on sound changes as reported in Holton et al. (2012) and (Holton & Robinson this volume) focuses on showing the relatedness of all AP languages. Little work has been done on the sound changes defining lower-level subgroups of AP languages. Nevertheless, there are some correspondences that can be observed. For instance, the pSWA subgroup we define (without the problematic inclusion of Kui and Western Pantar) is also supported by the sound change *s > h. Further study of lower level sound changes is needed to test whether all the subgroups we posit here on the basis of the morphological evidence of numerals are valid.

In sum, cardinal numerals in the Alor-Pantar languages are fertile ground for understanding how diverse numeral systems can evolve in related languages. In particular, Alor-Pantar languages provide us with unique, typological insights into the historical changes and influences that can complicate and prompt reorganizations of patterns of numeral formation and borrowings into the numeral paradigm.

(pEA) and proto-East Alor Montane (pEAM) can be taken to represent a chronological sequence, since pEA forms a subgroup of pCEA, and pEAM a subgroup of pEA.

7 Numeral systems in the Alor-Pantar languages

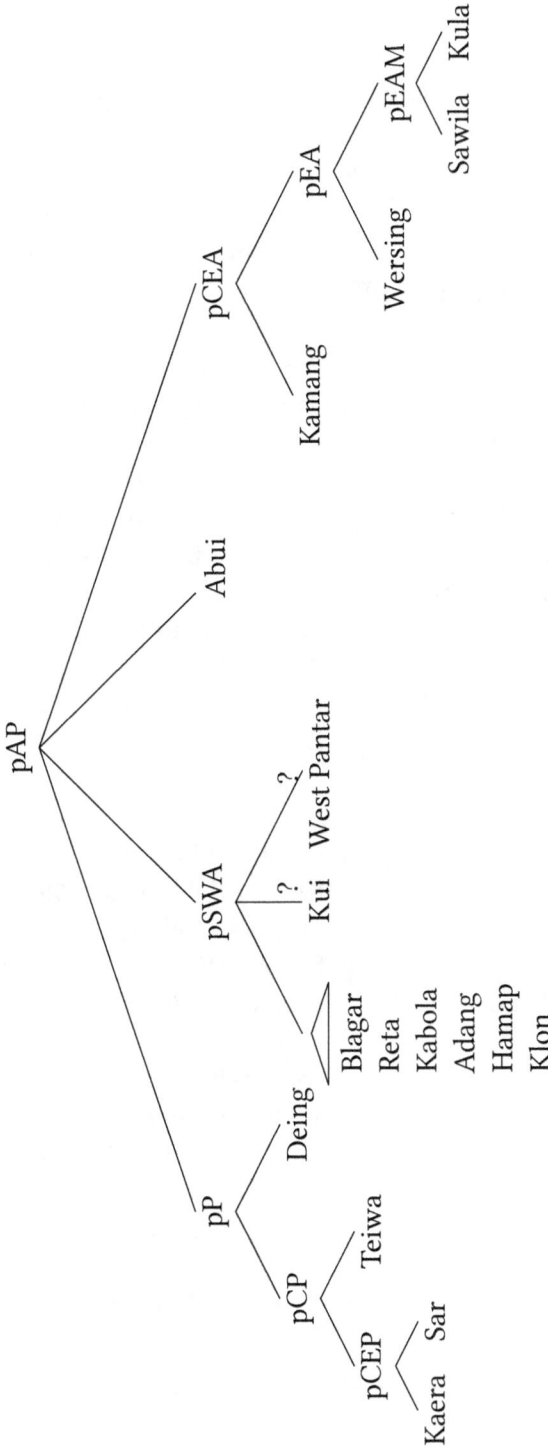

Figure 2: Tree of the AP languages based on numeral innovations

9 Sources

Sources of the language data cited in the text and the Appendices are given in the table below. We provide information about the dialect in cases where unpublished sources are used, or where multiple dialects are cited.

Abui (AP)	Kratochvíl (2007), Schapper fieldnotes 2010
Adang (AP, Pitungbang dialect)	Robinson fieldnotes 2010
Alorese (AN)	Klamer (2011)
Amarasi (AN)	Bani & Grimes (2011)
Atauro (AN)	Schapper fieldnotes 2007
Blagar (AP, Bama dialect)	Robinson fieldnotes 2010
Blagar (AP, Dolabang dialect)	Hein Steinhauer p.c. 2011
Bunaq (TAP, Lamaknen)	Schapper (2010)
Bunaq (TAP, Manufahi)	Schapper fieldnotes 2007
Dadu'a (a.k.a. Galoli) (AN)	Penn (2006)
Dhao	Grimes, Ranoh & Aplugi (2008)
Deing (AP)	B. Volk fieldnotes 2008
Ende (AN)	Aoki & Nakagawa (1993)
Hamap (AP)	Baird fieldnotes 2003
Idate (AN)	Klamer fieldnotes 2002
Ilongot (AN)	ABVD
Kabola (AP)	Robinson fieldnotes 2010
Kaera (AP)	Klamer fieldnotes 2005
Kamang (AP)	Schapper fieldnotes 2010, 2011
Kedang (AN)	Samely (1991)
Kemak (AN, Atabai dialect)	Klamer fieldnotes 2002
Kéo (AN)	Baird (2002)
Klon (AP)	Baird (2008)
Komodo (AN)	Verheijen (1982)
Kui (AP)	Baird fieldnotes 2003, Holton fieldnotes 2010
Kula (AP)	Holton fieldnotes 2010, Nicholas Williams p.c. 2011
Lakalei (AN)	Klamer fieldnotes 2002

7 Numeral systems in the Alor-Pantar languages

Lamaholot (AN, Lewoingu dialect)	Nishiyama & Kelen (2007)
Lamaholot (AN, Lewotobi dialect)	Naonori Nagaya p.c. 2011
Lamaholot (AN, Lewolema dialect)	Pampus (2001)
Lamaholot (AN, Solor dialect)	Klamer fieldnotes 2002
Lamaholot (AN, Adonara)	Philippe Grangé p.c. 2011
Lamaholot (AN, Lamalera dialect)	Keraf (1978)
Lio (AN)	Sawardo, Tarno & Kusharyanto (1987: 127-137, 44, 57, 60, 75, 110), Arndt (1933)
Mambae (AN, Ainaro dialect)	Schapper fieldnotes 2007
Manggarai (AN)	Verheijen (1967: 518); Verheijen (1970: 173)
Nage (AN)	Gregory Forth p.c. 2011
Ngadha (AN)	Arndt (1961)
Palu'e (AN)	ABVD
Reta (AP)	Robinson fieldnotes 2010
Rembong (AN)	Verheijen (1978)
Rongga (AN)	Arka et al. (2007)
Sar (AP)	Baird fieldnotes 2003; Robinson fieldnotes 2010
Sika (AN)	Pareira & Lewis (1998); Calon (1890)
Teiwa (AP)	Klamer (2010)
Tetun Fehan (AN)	Van Klinken (1999: 100)
Tokodede (AN, Licissa dialect)	Schapper fieldnotes 2007
Uab Meto (AN)	Middelkoop (1950: 421-424)
Ujir (AN)	Schapper fieldnotes
Waima'a (AN)	Hull (2002)
Western Pantar (AP)	Holton (nd)
Wersing (AP)	Holton fieldnotes 2010, Schapper & Hendery (2014)

A Appendix

A.1 Cardinal numerals in the Alor-Pantar languages

Varieties within a language are indicated by the name of one of the places where the dialect is spoken, though often dialects cover more than one place.

Table 15: Numerals 'one' through 'four'

Location	Language	'one'	'two'	'three'	'four'
Pantar	Western Pantar	*anuku*	*alaku*	*atiga*	*atu*
	Deing	*nuk*	*raq*	*atig*	*ut*
	Sar	*nuk*	*raq*	*tig*	*ut*
	Teiwa	*nuk*	*(ha)raq*	*jerig*	*ut*
	Kaera	*nuk(u)*	*(a)rax-*	*(i/u)tug*	*ut*
Straits	Blagar-Bama	*nuku*	*akur*	*tuge*	*ut*
	Blagar-Dolabang	*nu*	*aru*	*tue*	*ɓuta*
	Reta	*anu*	*alo*	*atoga*	*w/ɓuta*
W Alor	Kabola	*nu*	*olo*	*towo*	*ut*
	Adang	*nu*	*alo*	*tuo*	*ut*
	Hamap	*nu*	*alo*	*tof*	*ut*
	Klon	*nuk*	*orok*	*toŋ*	*ut*
	Kui	*nuku*	*oruku*	*siwa*	*usa*
C&E Alor	Abui	*nuku*	*ajoku*	*sua*	*buti*
	Kamang (Atoitaa)	*nok*	*ok*	*su*	*biat*
	Kamang (Takailubui)	*nok*	*ok*	*su*	*biat*
	Sawila	*sundana*	*jaku*	*tuo*	*ara:si:ku*
	Kula	*sona*	*jakwu*	*tu*	*arasiku*
	Wersing	*no*	*joku*	*tu*	*arasoku*

7 Numeral systems in the Alor-Pantar languages

Table 16: Numerals 'five' through 'nine'

Location	Language	'five'	'six'	'seven'	'eight'	'nine'
Pantar	Western Pantar	jasiŋ	hisnakkuŋ	betalaku	betiga	anukutannaŋ
	Deing	asan	talaŋ	jewasrak	santig	sanut
	Sar	jawan	tejaŋ	jisraq	jinatig	jinaut
	Teiwa	jusan	tia:m	jesraq	jesnerig	jesnaʔut
	Kaera	isim	tia:m	jesrax-	jentug	jeniut
Straits	Blagar-Bama	isiŋ	tajaŋ	titu	tuakur	tukurunuku
	Blagar-Dolabang	isiŋ	taliŋ	bititu	tuaru	turinu
	Reta	avehaŋ	talaun	bititoga	tulalo	tukanu
W Alor	Kabola	iweseŋ	talaŋ	wutito	turlo	tiʔinu
	Adang	ifihiŋ	talaŋ	ititɔ	turlo	tiʔenu
	Hamap	ivehiŋ	talaŋ	itito	turalo	tieu
	Klon	eweh	tlan	usoŋ	tidorok	tukainuk
	Kui	jesan	talama	jesaroku	tadusa	jesanusa
C & E Alor	Abui	jetiŋ	tala:ma	jetiŋajoku	jetiŋsua	jetiŋbuti
	Kamang (Takailubui)	wesiŋ	ta:ma	wesiŋok	wesiŋsu	wesiŋbiat
	Kamang (Atoitaa)	iwesiŋ	isiŋnok	isiŋok	isiŋsu	isiŋbiat
	Sawila	jo:tiŋ	jo:tiŋsundana	jo:tiŋjaku	jo:tiŋtuo	jo:tiŋara:si:ku
	Kula	jawatena	jawatensona	jawatenjakwu	jawatentu	jawatenarasiku
	Wersing	wetiŋ	wetiŋnuŋ	wetiŋjoku	wetiŋtu	wetiŋarasoku

Table 17: Numerals 'ten' and the formation of decades

		'ten'	'twenty'	'thirty'
Pantar	Western Pantar	ke anuku	ke alaku	ke atiga
	Deing	qar nuk	qar raq	qar atig
	Sar	qar nuk	qar raq	qar tig
	Teiwa	qa:r nuk	qa:r raq	qa:r jerig
	Kaera	xar nuko	xar raxo	xar tug
Straits	Blagar-Bama	qar nuku	qar akur	qar tuge
	Blagar-Dolabang	ʔari nu	ʔari aru	ʔari tue
	Reta	kara nu	kara alo	kara atoga
West Alor	Kabola	kar nu	kar ho(ʔ)olo	kar towo
	Adang	ʔer nu	ʔer alo	ʔer tuo
	Hamap	air nu	air alo	air tof
	Klon	kar nuk	kar orok	kar toŋ
	Kui	kar nuku	kar oruku	kar siwa
C & E Alor	Abui	kar nuku	kar ajoku	kar sua
	Kamang	ata:k nok	ata:k ok	ata:k su
	Sawila	ada:ku	ada:ku maraku	ada:ku matua
	Kula	adajakwu	mijakwu	mitua
	Wersing	adajoku	adajoku mijoku	adajoku mitu

Table 18: Numerals with bases '100' and '1000'

		'100'	'200'	'1000'	'2000'
Pantar	West Pantar	ratu	ratu alaku	(a)ribu (ye)	ribu (alaku)
	Deing	aratu nuk	aratu raq	aribu nuk	aribu raq
	Sar	ratu nuk	ratu raq	ribu nuk	ribu raq
	Teiwa	ratu nuk	ratu (ha)raq	ribu nuk	ribu (ha)raq
	Kaera	ratu nuk	ratu rax-	ribu nuk	ribu rax-
Straits	Blagar-Bama	ratu nuku	ratu akur	ribu nuku	ribu akur
	Blagar-Dolabang	ratu nu	ratu aru	ribu nu	ribu aru
	Reta	ratu anu	ratu alo	ribu ano	ribu alo
W Alor	Kabola	rat nu	rat ho(?)olo	rib nu	rib ho(?)olo
	Adang	rat nu	rat alo	rib nu	rib alo
	Hamap	rat nu	rat alo	–†	–
	Klon	eska nok	eska orok	–	–
	Kui	asaga	asaga oruku	rab nuku	rab oruku
C & E Alor	Abui	aisaha nu	aisaha ajoku	rifi nuku	rifi ajoku
	Kamang (A/T)	asaka nok	asaka ok	libu nok	libu ok
	Sawila	asaka dana	asaka jaku	ribu dana	ribu jaku
	Kula	gasaka	gasaka jakwana	rib dena	–
	Wersing	aska	aska joku	ribu no	–

† '–' denotes that no data is available for this numeral

A.2 Numerals 'one' to 'ten' in Austronesian languages W of Alor-Pantar

Table 19: Numerals 'one' to 'five' in Austronesian languages W of Alor-Pantar.

Location	Language	'one'	'two'	'three'	'four'	'five'
	PAN	*esa~*isa	*duSa	*telu	*Sepat	*lima
Komodo	Komodo	sa, se-	rua	telu	paʔ	lima
Flores	Manggarai	esa	sua	telu	pat	lima
	Rongga	(e)sa	ɹua	telu	wutu	lima
	Rembong	sa, saʔ	zta	telu	pat	lima
	Ende	sa	zua	tela	wutu	lima
	Ngadha	esa	zua	telu	vutu	lima
	Nage	esa	ɗua	telu	wutu	lima
	Kéo†	haʔesa	ʔesa rua	ʔesa tedu	ʔesa wutu	ʔesa dima
	Lio	əsa	rua	təlu	sutu	lima
	Sika	ha	rua	tɛlu	hutu	lima
	Palu'e	a	rua	təlu	ɓa	lima
	Lamaholot-Lewoingu	toʔu	rua	təlo	pak	lema
	Lamaholot-Lewotobi	toʔu	rua	təlo	pa	lema
	Lamaholot-Lewolema	toʔu	rua	təlo	pat	lema
Solor	Lamaholot-Solor	toʔu	rua	təlo	pa	lema
Adonara	Lamaholot-Adonara	toʔu	rua	təlo	pat	lema
Lembata (Lomblen)	Lamaholot-Lamalera	tou	rua	telo	pa	lema
	Kedang†	>udeʔ	sue	tælu	>apaʔ	leme
	Alorese-Baranusa	to	rua	talau	pa	lema
Pantar	Alorese-Alor Kecil	tou	rua	telo	pa	lema

† Kéo numerals appear with the default classifier ʔesa and/or the prefix ha 'one'. In Kedang orthography />/ preceding a vowel encodes that vowel as breathy (Samely 1991)

7 Numeral systems in the Alor-Pantar languages

Table 20: Numerals 'six' to 'ten' in Austronesian languages W of Alor-Pantar

Location	Language	'six'	'seven'	'eight'	'nine'	'ten'
	PAN	*enem	*pitu	*walu	*siwa	*puluq
Komodo	Komodo	nemu	pitu	walu	siwa	pulu, sampulu
Flores	Manggarai	enem	pitu	alo	ciok	pulu cempulu cepulu campulu
	Rongga	limaesa	limaɹua	ɹuambutu	taraesa	sambulu
	Rembong	non	pitu?	walu?	siwa?	(se)puluh / pulu?
	Ende	limasa	limazua	ruabutu	trasa	sabulu
	Ngadha	limaesa	limarua	ruabutu	teresa	habulu
	Nage	lima esa	lima zua	zua butu	tea esa	sa bulu
	Kéo†	ʔesa dima ʔesa	ʔesa dima rua	ʔesa rua mbutu	ʔesa tera ʔesa	ha mbudu
	Lio	lima əsa	lima rua	rua mbutu	təra əsa	sambulu
	Sika	ɛna	pitu	walu	hiwa	pulu pulu ha
	Palu'e	əne	ɓitu	valu	iva	apulu
	Lamaholot-Lewoingu	nəmən	pito	buto	hiwa	pulo
	Lamaholot-Lewotobi	namu	pito	buto	hiwa	pulo
	Lamaholot-Lewolema	nəm(ə)	pito	buto	hiwa	pulok
Solor	Lamaholot-Solor	nəmũ	pito	wutu	hiwa	pulo? pulok
Adonara	Lamaholot-Adonara	nəm(ə)	pito	buto	hiwa	pulo
Lembata (Lomblen)	Lamaholot-Lamalera	nemu	pito	buto	hifa	pulo
	Kedang†	>ænæŋ	pitu	buturai	leme>apaʔ	pulu
	Alorese-Baranusa	namu	pito	buto	hifa	karto
Pantar	Alorese-Alor Kecil	nemu	pito	buto	hifa	kartou

† Kéo numerals appear with the default classifier ʔesa and/or the prefix ha 'one'. In Kedang orthography />/ preceding a vowel encodes that vowel as breathy (Samely 1991)

321

A.3 Numerals 'one' to 'ten' in Austronesian languages S & E of Alor-Pantar

Table 21: Numerals 'one' to 'five' in Austronesian languages S & E of Alor- Pantar

Location	Language	'one'	'two'	'three'	'four'	'five'
	PAN	*esa~*isa	*duSa	*telu	*Sepat	*lima
Rote	Dhao	ətʃi	dua	təke	əpa	ləmi
Atauro	Atauro	hea	herua	hetelu	heat	helima
Western Timor	Uab Meto	mɛse	nua	tenu	ha	nim
	Amarasi	es	nua	teun~tenu	ha:	ni:m~nima
North-Central Timor	Mambae	id	ru	teul	fat	lim
	Tokodede	iso	ru	telo	pat	lim
Central Timor	Kemak	sia	hurua	telu	pa:t	həlima
	Lakalei	isa	rua	telu	at	lima
	Idate	wisa	rua	telu	at	lima
South-Central Timor	Tetun Fehan	ida	rua	tolu	ha:t	lima
North-Eastern Timor	Waima'a	se	kairuo	kaitelu	kaiha:	kailime
	Dadu'a	isa	warua	watelu	wa:k	walima

7 Numeral systems in the Alor-Pantar languages

Table 22: Numerals 'six' to 'ten' in Austronesian languages S & E of Alor-Pantar

Location	Language	'six'	'seven'	'eight'	'nine'	'ten'
	PAN	*enem	*pitu	*walu	*siwa	*puluq
Rote	Dhao	əna	piɖa	aru	tʃeo	tʃaŋuru
Atauro	Atauro	henen	heitu	heau	hese	seŋulu
Western Timor	Uab Meto	nɛ	hitu	fanu‡	seo / sio	boʔɛs†
	Amarasi	nee	hiut~hitu	faun~fanu	seo / sea	boʔes
North-Central Timor	Mambae	limnainide	limnairua	limnaitelu	limnaipata	sikul
	Tokodede	wouniso	wouru	woutelo	woupat	sagulu
Central Timor	Kemak	hənem	hitu	balu	sibe	sapulu
	Lakalei	nen	hitu	walu	sia	sakulu
	Idate	nen	hitu	walu	sia	sanulu
South-Central Timor	Tetun Fehan	neen	hitu	walu	siwi	sanulu
North-Eastern Timor	Waima'a	kainena	kaihitu	kaikaha	kaisiwe	base
	Dadu'a	wanee	waʔitu	waʔao	wasia	sanulu

† *Boʔɛs* probably derives from *bua ès* 'one collection' according to Middelkoop (1950: 421).

‡ *Fanu* 'eight' is used in the sense of 'many' "by reversing the last syllable" (i.e. as *faun*) (Middelkoop 1950: 422).

Abbreviations

—	no data available	D	Blagar-D > Blagar-Dolabang
~REDUP	reduplication	E	Eastern
A	refers to the most agent-like argument of a canonical transitive verb	PAN	proto-Austronesian
		PAP	proto-Alor Pantar
		PCEA	proto-Central East Alor
		PCEP	proto-Central East Pantar
ABVD	Austronesian Basic Vocabulary Database (Greenhill, Blust & Gray 2005-2007)	PCP	proto-Central Pantar
		PEA	proto-East Alor
		PEAM	proto-East Alor Montane
		PP	proto-Pantar
AN	Austronesian	PSWA	proto-Straits-West-Alor
AP	Alor-Pantar	PTAP	proto-Timor-Alor-Pantar
B	Blagar B > Blagar-Bama	TAP	Timor-Alor-Pantar
		W	West
C	Central	WP	Western Pantar

References

Aoki, Eriko & Satoshi Nakagawa. 1993. *Endenese-English dictionary.* Unpublished manuscript.

Arka, I Wayan, Fransiscus Seda, Antonius Gelang, Yohanes Nani & Ivan Ture. 2007. *A Rongga-English dictionary with an English-Rongga finderlist.* https://openresearch-repository.anu.edu.au/handle/1885/29891.

Arndt, Paul. 1933. *Li'onesisch-Deutsches Wörterbuch.* Ende-Flores: Arnoldus-Druckerei.

Arndt, Paul. 1961. *Wörterbuch der Ngadhasprache* (Studia Instituti Anthropos 15). Posieux (Fribourg, Suisse): Anthropos-Institut.

Baird, Louise. 2002. *A grammar of Kéo: An Austronesian language of East Nusantara.* Australian National University PhD thesis.

Baird, Louise. 2008. *A grammar of Klon: a non-Austronesian language of Alor, Indonesia.* Canberra: Pacific Linguistics.

Bani, Heronimus & Charles E. Grimes. 2011. *Ethno-mathematics in Amarasi: how to count 400 ears of corn in 60 seconds.* Handout from talk given at the International Conference on Language Documentation and Conservation. University of Hawaii, February 11–13 2011.

Barnes, Robert H. 1974. *Kédang: A study of the collective thought of an Eastern Indonesian people.* Oxford: Clarendon Press.

Barnes, Robert H. 1982. Number and number use in Kédang, Indonesia. *Man* 17(1).
Blust, Robert Andrew. 2009. *The Austronesian languages*. Canberra: Pacific Linguistics.
Blust, Robert Andrew. nd. *Blust's Austronesian Comparative Dictionary*. http://www.trussel2.com/acd/.
Calon, L. F. 1890. Woordenlijstje van het dialect van Sikka. *Tijdschrift voor Indische Taal-, Land- en Volkenkunde* 33. 501–530.
Capell, Arthur. 1976. Austronesian and Papuan 'mixed' languages: general remarks. In Stephen A. Wurm (ed.), *New Guinea area languages and language study*, 527–579. Canberra: Pacific Linguistics.
Comrie, Bernard. 1992. Balto-Slavonic. In Jadranka Gvozdanović (ed.), *Indo-Eropean numerals* (Trends in Linguistics 57), 717–833. Berlin: Mouton de Gruyter.
Comrie, Bernard. 2005a. Endangered numeral systems. In Jan Wohlgemuth & Tyko Dirksmeyer (eds.), *Bedrohte Vielfalt: Aspekte des Sprach(en)tods [Endangered diversity: aspects of language death]*, 203–230. Berlin: Weißensee Verlag.
Comrie, Bernard. 2005b. Numeral bases. In Martin Haspelmath, Matthew S. Dryer, Bernard Comrie & David Gil (eds.), *World atlas of language structures*, 530–533. Oxford: Oxford University Press.
Donohue, Mark. 2008. Complexities with restricted numeral systems. *Linguistic Typology* 12. 423–429.
Evans, Nicholas. 2009. Two *pus* one makes thirteen: Senary numerals in the Morehead-Maro region. *Linguistic Typology* 13. 321–335.
Forth, Gregory. 1981. *Rindi: An ethnographic study of a traditional domain in Eastern Sumba*. The Hague: Martinus Nijhoff.
Forth, Gregory. 2004. *Nage birds: classification and symbolism among an Eastern Indonesian people*. London: Routledge.
Greenberg, Joseph H. 1978. Generalizations about numeral systems. In Joseph H. Greenberg (ed.), *Universals of human language*, vol. 3, 250–295. Stanford: Stanford University Press.
Greenhill, Simon J., Robert Andrew Blust & Russell D. Gray. 2005-2007. *The Austronesian Basic Vocabulary Database (ABVD)*. http://language.psy.auckland.ac.nz/austronesian/.
Grimes, Charles E., Ayub Ranoh & Helena Aplugi. 2008. *Lil Dhao (Ndao) online dictionary*. Kupang. http://e-kamus2.org/index.html.
Hammarström, Harald. 2010. Rarities in numeral systems. In Jan Wohlgemuth & Michael Cysouw (eds.), *Rethinking universals: How rarities affect linguistic theory*, 11–60. Berlin: Mouton de Gruyter.

Hanke, Thomas. 2010. Additional rarities in numeral systems. In Jan Wohlgemuth & Michael Cysouw (eds.), *Rethinking universals: How rarities affect linguistic theory*, 61–90. Berlin: Mouton de Gruyter.

Heine, Bernd. 1997. *Cognitive foundations of grammar*. Oxford: Oxford University Press.

Holton, Gary. nd. *Western Pantar lexicon*. Accessed 06 December, 2011. http://www.uaf.edu/alor/langs/western-pantar/lexicon/.

Holton, Gary & Laura C. Robinson. this volume. The internal history of the Alor-Pantar language family. In Marian Klamer (ed.), *The Alor-Pantar languages*, 55–97. Berlin: Language Science Press.

Holton, Gary, Marian Klamer, František Kratochvíl, Laura C. Robinson & Antoinette Schapper. 2012. The historical relations of the Papuan languages of Alor and Pantar. *Oceanic Linguistics* 51(1). 86–122.

Hull, Geoffrey. 2002. *Waimaha (Waima'a)* (East Timor Language Profiles 2). Dili: Instituto Nacional de Linguística/Universidade Nacional de Timor-Leste.

Hägerdal, Hans. 2012. *Lords of the land, lords of the sea: Conflict and adaptation in early colonial Timor, 1600-1800*. Leiden: KITLV Press.

Keraf, Gregorius. 1978. *Morfologi dialek Lamalera*. Jakarta: Universitas Indonesia PhD thesis.

Klamer, Marian. 2010. *A grammar of Teiwa* (Mouton Grammar Library 49). Berlin: Mouton de Gruyter.

Klamer, Marian. 2011. *A short grammar of Alorese (Austronesian)* (Languages of the World/Materials 486). München: Lincom.

Klamer, Marian. 2012. Papuan-Austronesian language contact: Alorese from an areal perspective. In Nicholas Evans & Marian Klamer (eds.), *Melanesian languages on the edge of Asia: challenges for the 21st century*, vol. 5 (Language Documentation & Conservation Special Publication), 72–108. Honolulu: University of Hawaii Press.

Klamer, Marian, Antoinette Schapper, Greville G. Corbett, Gary Holton, František Kratochvíl & Laura C. Robinson. this volume. Numeral words and arithmetic operations in the Alor-Pantar languages. In Marian Klamer (ed.), *The Alor-Pantar languages*, 337–373. Berlin: Language Science Press.

Kratochvíl, František. 2007. *A grammar of Abui: a Papuan language of Alor*. Utrecht: LOT.

Laycock, D. C. 1975. Observations on number systems and semantics. In Stephen A. Wurm (ed.), *Papuan languages and the New Guinea linguistic scene*, 219–233. Canberra: Pacific Linguistics.

Lean, Glendon. 1992. *Counting systems of Papua New Guinea and Oceania*. Papua New Guinea University of Technology PhD thesis.

Lynch, John. 2009. At sixes and sevens: the development of numeral systems in Vanuatu and New Caledonia. In Bethwyn Evans (ed.), *Discovering history through language: Papers in honour of Malcolm Ross*, 391–411. Canberra: Pacific Linguistics.

Majewicz, Alfred F. 1981. Le rôle du doigt et de la main et leurs désignations dans la formation des systèmes particuliers de numération et de noms de nombres dans certaines langues. In Fanny de Sivers (ed.) (ed.), *La main et les doigts dans l'expression linguistique* (LACITO – Documents Eurasie 6), 193–212. Paris: SELAF.

Majewicz, Alfred F. 1984. Le rôle du doigt et de la main et leurs désignations en certaines langues dans la formation des systèmes particuliers de numération et des noms de nombre. *Lingua Posnaniensis* 28. 69–84.

Matisoff, James A. 1995. Sino-Tibetan numerals and the play of prefixes. *Bulletin of the National Museum of Ethnology (Osaka) [Kokuritsu Minzokugaku Hakubutsukan Kenkyuu Hookoku]* 20(1). 105–252.

Middelkoop, P. 1950. Proeve van een Timorese grammatica. *Bijdragen tot Taal-, Land- en Volkenkunde* (106). 375–517.

Nishiyama, Kunio & Herman Kelen. 2007. *A grammar of Lamaholot, Eastern Indonesia: the morphology and syntax of the Lewoingu dialect* (Languages of the World/Materials 467). München: Lincom.

Pampus, Karl-Heinz. 2001. *Mue Moten Koda Kiwan: Kamus Bahasa Lamaholot, Dialek Lewolema, Flores Timur*. Frankfurt: Frobenius-Institut Frankfurt am Main.

Pareira, M. Mandalangi & E. Douglas Lewis. 1998. *Kamus Sara Sikka - Bahasa Indonesia*. Ende, Flores, Indonesia: Penerbit Nusa Indah.

Penn, David. 2006. *Introducing Dadu'a*. University of New England PhD thesis.

Plank, Frans. 2009. Senary summary so far. *Linguistic Typology* 13. 337–345.

Samely, Ursula. 1991. *Kedang (Eastern Indonesia): Some aspects of its grammar* (Forum phoneticum 46). Hamburg: Helmut Buske.

Sawardo, P. Wakidi, Y. Lita Tarno & S. Kusharyanto. 1987. *Struktur Bahasa Lio*. Jakarta: Pusat Pembinaan dan Pengembangan Bahasa.

Schapper, Antoinette. 2010. *Bunaq: a Papuan language of central Timor*. Canberra: Australian National University PhD thesis.

Schapper, Antoinette & Harald Hammarström. 2013. Innovative numerals in Austronesian languages outside of Oceania. *Oceanic Linguistics* 52(2). 425–456.

Schapper, Antoinette & Rachel Hendery. 2014. Wersing. In Antoinette Schapper (ed.), *Papuan languages of Timor, Alor and Pantar: Sketch grammars*, vol. 1, 439–504. Berlin: Mouton de Gruyter.

Schapper, Antoinette, Juliette Huber & Aone van Engelenhoven. this volume. The relatedness of Timor-Kisar and Alor-Pantar languages: A preliminary demonstration. In Marian Klamer (ed.), *The Alor-Pantar languages*, 99–154. Berlin: Language Science Press.

Sidwell, Paul. 1999. The Austroasiatic numerals from 'one' to 'ten' from a historical and typological perspective. In Jadranka Gvozdanović (ed.), *Numeral types and changes worldwide*, 253–271. Berlin: Mouton de Gruyter.

Stokhof, W. A. L. 1975. *Preliminary notes on the Alor and Pantar languages (East Indonesia)* (Pacific Linguistics: Series B 43). Canberra: Australian National University.

Van Klinken, Catharina. 1999. *A grammar of the Fehan dialect of Tetun, an Austronesian language of west Timor*. (C-155). Canberra: Pacific Linguistics.

Vatter, E. 1932. *Ata Kiwan. Unbekannte Bergvölker im tropischen Holland*. Leipzig: Bibliographisches Institut.

Verheijen, Jilis A. J. 1967. *Kamus Manggarai: Manggarai-Indonesia & Indonesia-Manggarai*. Vol. 1. 's-Gravenhage: Nijhoff.

Verheijen, Jilis A. J. 1970. *Kamus Manggarai: Manggarai-Indonesia & Indonesia-Manggarai*. Vol. 2. 's-Gravenhage: Nijhoff.

Verheijen, Jilis A. J. 1978. *Bahasa Rembong di Flores Barat*. Vol. 3. Ruteng: S.V.D.

Verheijen, Jilis A. J. 1982. *Komodo: Het eiland, het volk en de taal* (Verhandelingen van het Koninklijk Instituut voor Taal-, Land- en Volkenkunde 96). The Hague: Martinus Nijhoff.

Wellfelt, Emilie & Antoinette Schapper. 2013. *Memories of migration and contact: East Timor origins in Alor*. Paper read at the Eighth International Convention of Asia Scholars, June 24–27, Macao.

Winter, Werner. 1969. Analogischer Sprachwandel und semantische Struktur. *Folia Linguistica* 3. 29–45.

Chapter 8

Numeral words and arithmetic operations in the Alor-Pantar languages

Marian Klamer

Antoinette Schapper

Greville Corbett

Gary Holton

František Kratochvíl

Laura C. Robinson

> The indigenous numerals of the AP languages, as well as the indigenous structures for arithmetic operations are currently under pressure from Indonesian, and will inevitably be replaced with Indonesian forms and structures. This chapter presents a documentary record of the forms and patterns currently in use to express numerals and arithmetic operations in the Alor-Pantar languages. We describe the structure of cardinal, ordinal and distributive numerals, and how operations of addition, subtraction, multiplication, division, and fractions are expressed.

1 Introduction

Numeral systems are more endangered than languages. Cultural or commercial superiority of one group over another often results in borrowing of numerals, or replacements of parts or all of a numeral system, even in a language that itself is not endangered (Comrie 2005). In the Alor-Pantar (AP) context, the national language, Indonesian, plays a dominant role in education and commerce, and

Marian Klamer, Antoinette Schapper, Greville Corbett, Gary Holton, František Kratochvíl & Laura C. Robinson. 2017. Numeral words and arithmetic operations in the Alor-Pantar languages. In Marian Klamer (ed.), *The Alor-Pantar languages*, 329–365. Berlin: Language Science Press. DOI:10.5281/zenodo.569396

this will inevitably lead to the replacement of the numerals and the arithmetic expressions with Indonesian equivalents. It is therefore crucial to keep a record of the forms and patterns as they are currently used for future reference, and this chapter aims to be such a documentary record.

The patterns described in this chapter fall into two broad classes, pertaining to two distinct linguistic levels: the word (§ 2) and the clause or sentence (§ 3). At the word level we describe how numeral words are created, discussing the structure of cardinals (§ 2.1), ordinals (§ 2.2) and distributives (§ 2.3). At the clause and sentence level, we describe the constructions that contain numerals and function to express the arithmetic of addition (3.1), subtraction (§ 3.2), multiplication (§ 3.3), division (§ 3.4), and fractions (§ 3.5). § 4 presents a summary and conclusions.

Details on the data on which this chapter is based are given in the Sources section at the end of this chapter. Adang, Blagar, Kamang and Abui are each very diverse internally. The data presented in this chapter are from the Dolap dialect of Blagar, the Takailubui dialect of Kamang, the Lawahing dialect of Adang, and the Takalelang dialect of Abui. These dialect names refer to the place where the variety is spoken.

2 Operations to create numeral words

Most of the cardinals in AP languages are historically morphologically complex forms. Within and across the languages we find variation in choice of numeral base, the type of operations invoked for the interpretation of the composite elements, and the ways in which these operations are expressed (§ 2.1). Ordinals in AP languages are possessive constructions that are derived from cardinals, where the ordered entity is the grammatical possessor of the cardinal (§ 2.2). Distributive numerals in AP languages are also derived from the cardinal, by reduplicating it partially or fully. When the cardinal contains more than one morpheme, generally only the right-most formative is reduplicated (section 2.3.3). In all cases, the numeral words follow the noun they quantify. Cardinals may be preceded by a classifier, if the language has them.

2.1 Cardinal numerals

By cardinal numerals, we understand the set of numerals used in attributive quantification of nouns (e.g., 'three dogs'). In enumeration, the numeral follows the noun in all AP languages (N NUM), as in Teiwa *yaf haraq* 'house two' > 'two

8 Numeral words and arithmetic operations in the Alor-Pantar languages

houses'. If a language uses a sortal or mensural classifier, the classifier occurs between the noun and the numeral (N CLF NUM). The same cardinals that are used in enumeration are also used for non-referential counting (*one, two, three, four, five, etc.*), and all the AP languages use the same numeral forms to count small animates (ants, flies, bees, or house lizards), large animates (children, dogs, or pigs), and inanimates (houses, rocks, stars, or coconut trees).

In all the AP languages we surveyed, the cardinal numbers 'one' to 'five' are morphologically simple forms, as illustrated in Table 1. The composition of 'six' varies. Most of the AP languages have a monomorphemic 'six', an example is Teiwa *tiaam*. Bi-morphemic forms for 'six' are composed of (reflexes) of 'five' and 'one', e.g., Kula *yawaten sona*. The cardinals 'seven' and higher consist of minimally two formatives in all AP languages. Often, these forms involve reflexes of 'five', 'one', 'two', 'three' and 'four', as illustrated in Table 1, though other patterns are also attested (Schapper & Klamer this volume).

Table 1: 'One' through 'nine' in Teiwa (Pantar) and Kula (East Alor)

Cardinal	Analysis	Teiwa	Kula
1	1	*nuk*	*sona*
2	2	*(ha)raq*	*yakwu*
3	3	*yerig*	*tu*
4	4	*ut*	*arasiku*
5	5	*yusan*	*yawatena*
6	5 1		*yawaten sona*
6	6	*tiaam*	
7	5 2	*yes raq*	*yawaten yakwu*
8	5 3	*yes nerig*	*yawaten tu*
9	5 4	*yes na'ut*	*yawaten arasiku*

From the above it can be inferred that the AP languages have at most six mono-morphemic numerals. This number is significantly fewer than the number we find in many European languages. Present-day English, for example, has twelve mono-morphemic cardinal numerals (Von Mengden 2010: 26).

Both within and across the AP languages we find variation in the way cardinals are composed (cf. Stump 2010). First, in choice of numeral base: in all systems both quinary ('base-five') and decimal ('base-ten') bases are used. Table 1 includes examples of numerals with a quinary base (*yes* in Teiwa, *yawaten* in Kula). A decimal base is used in numerals 'ten' and above; an illustration is Teiwa *qaar* in *qaar nuk* 'ten' and *qaar raq* 'twenty'.

Second, the type of operations invoked for the interpretation of the morphemes that make up the compound numerals vary between addition (Abui *yeting buti* 'nine'< *yeting* 'five' + *buti* 'four'), subtraction (Adang *tiʔi nu* 'nine' < *tiʔi* (semantically opaque), *nu* 'one' < 'minus one') and multiplication (Western Pantar *ke atiga* 'thirty' < *ke* 'ten' x *atiga* 'three'). Of these, subtraction is the least frequent.

Third, different types of operations are involved in the derivation of cardinals: typically they involve simple juxtaposition of bases (e.g., Abui *kar nuku* 'ten' < *kar* 'ten', *nuku* 'one'), but in some cases, a lexeme is added that expresses the operation (e.g., the operator *wal* signifying addition in numerals 11-19, e.g., Abui *kar nuku **wal** nuku* 'eleven'.

The number compounds in AP languages are all exocentric, that is, they lack a morphological head. In this respect they contrast with nominal compounds, which are typically endocentric (e.g., Teiwa *xam yir* 'milk' < *xam* 'breast', *yir* 'water', where the rightmost element is the head). As both nominal and numeral compounds have stress on their final member, we can analyse both types of compounds as prosodically right-headed across the board in Alor-Pantar.

In the Pantar languages in particular, the synchronic morphological make-up of numeral compounds can be rather obscure. For instance, Teiwa *yesnerig* 'eight' is not a transparent compound of synchronic *yusan* 'five' + *yerig* 'three'. In contrast, the languages of Central and East Alor have more transparent numeral compounds, for instance Abui *yetingsua* 'eight' < *yeting* 'five' + *sua* 'three'. Phonologically, however, in all the languages of the sample discussed here, we can still recognize compound forms because they consist of two stressed phonological words, the second of which has primary stress. (We return to this issue in § 2.3.2 below.)

We have not attested an AP language with a number word for 'null' or 'zero'. The absence of entities is rather expressed predicatively, using a word meaning '(be) empty', such as Teiwa *hasak* in (1). [1] In the Teiwa idioms in (1), a subject precedes a nominal predicate that is headed by the place pronoun *i* 'it.(place)', so that absent entities are expressed as "X is (an) empty place(s)", compare ((1) (a-b).

(1) Teiwa

    a. *Guru*   [*i*   *hasak*]$_{PRED}$
        teacher(IND) it.(place) empty'
        'No / zero teachers'

---

[1] Compare proto-Alor-Pantar *hasak (Holton & Robinson this volume), reflected in Western Pantar *hakkas*, Kaera *isik*, Abui *taka*, Kamang *saka*.

b. *Yaf* [*i* *hasak*]ₚᵣₑ𝒹
 house it.(place) empty
 'No / zero people'

In sum, AP languages have up to six morphologically simple cardinals; in all AP languages, the non-borrowed cardinals 'seven' and up are morphologically complex. Most cardinals are compounds, consisting of two or more morphemes in apposition, the second of which gets word stress. The definition of the morphological structure of these compounds varies along three dimensions: the choice of base, the arithmetic operations invoked for the interpretation of the cardinals that make up the numeral, and the ways in which these arithmetic operations are expressed.

2.2 Ordinal numerals

Ordinal numerals are words that identify the position that a given member of a set occupies relative to other members of the same set (e.g., 'the third dog'). The main function of ordinal numerals is thus to indicate the position of an entity in an ordered sequence.

All AP languages have distinct forms for cardinal and ordinal numerals, and all of them have ordinal numbers associated with any cardinal from 'two' and above. Ordinals in AP languages are derived from cardinals, which is a cross-linguistically common pattern (Stolz & Veselinova 2013). Variation exists only in the expression of 'first', which in some of the languages is unrelated to the numeral 'one', as discussed below.

The derivation of ordinals involves a third person possessive pronoun or prefix at the left periphery of the cardinal numeral. The ordered entity functions grammatically as the possessor of the cardinal number. For example, Kamang *dum yeok* 'child 3.POSS-two', lit. 'child its-two' > 'second child'.

Within the ordinal possessive constructions, three areal patterns are discernible. The first pattern is that of the languages of Pantar and the Straits, where the possessive ordinal construction includes an additional element specific for ordinals. The second pattern is found in Central-East Alor, where ordinals are also expressed like possessive constructions, but without including an additional ordinal element. The third pattern is found in Kula and Sawila in East Alor, where the ordinals involve an applicative verb. We discuss the three patterns in turn.

In the languages of Pantar and the Straits, possessive constructions like those in (2) are the base for ordinal constructions such as those in (3), where the elements *maing*, *ma* or *mi* occur between the possessor prefix and the numeral.

(Full paradigms of ordinal constructions are presented in the Appendix A.1.)

(2) W Pantar *aname gai*   *bla*
    Teiwa   *masar ga-*   *yaf*
    Kaera   *masik ge-*   *ma*
    Blagar   *mehal ʔe-*   *hava*
    Adang   *nami ʔo-*   *bang*
             man   3.POSS house

'the man's house'

(3) W Pantar *aname gai*   *maing atiga*
    Teiwa   *masar ga-*   *ma- yerig*
    Kaera   *masik ge-*   *mi- tug*
    Blagar   *mehal ʔe-*   *mi- tue*
    Adang   *nami ʔo-*   *mi- towo -mi*
             man   3.POSS ORD- three -ORD

'the third man'

In Western Pantar, the ordinal element is a free form *maing*; in Teiwa, Kaera, Blagar, and Adang it is a bound morpheme (*ma-* or *mi-*). The ordinal elements are formally similar to existing words in the respective languages: Western Pantar *mayang* 'to place', Teiwa *ma* 'come, OBL', and Kaera/Blagar/Adang *mi* 'OBL' (<pAP *mai 'come' and *mi 'be in/on' Holton & Robinson this volume). Synchronically, the semantic and syntactic link between these free forms and the ordinal markers is obscure. It may be that the ordinal morphemes express notions that are (historically) related to notions of placement or location at a particular numeral rank. However, their position preceding the numeral does not parallel the position of verbs and oblique markers, which in AP languages always *follow* their nominal complement. Note however, that the ordinals in Adang involve two identical morphemes: one preceding and one following the numeral. This might reflect an earlier structure where the ordinal marker followed the numeral, paralleling the position of case markers and verbs.

The second areal pattern of ordinal constructions is found in Central-East Alor, where ordinal constructions are also possessive constructions but now without an ordinal element included. Compare the constructions in (4) and (5). The basic possessive construction in (4) includes a possessor, an alienable possessive prefix and a possessum. In the ordinal constructions in (5), the ranked entity is the possessor of the numeral indicating the rank.

(4) Nominal possessive construction in Central-East Alor
Kamang *lami ge- kadii*
Abui *neng he- fala*
man 3.POSS- house
'the man's house'

(5) Ordinal construction in Central-East Alor
Kamang *lami ge- su*
Abui *neng he- sua*
man 3.POSS- three
'the third man'

In East Alor, ordinal structures that diverge from both these areal patterns are found in Kula and Sawila. Kula (Nick Williams, p.c. 2013) and Sawila ordinals employ applicative verbs involving the cognate prefixes *we-/wii-*, illustrated in (6) and (8). In Kula ordinals this verb combines with a possessive structure, (7). In Sawila, possessive constructions are not used in ordinals, (9).

(6) Kula
wanta gi-we-araasiku
day 3.POSS-APPL-four
'the fourth day'

(7) Kula
Maria gi-skola
Maria 3.POSS-school
'Maria's school'

(8) Sawila
imyalara wii-tua
man APPL-three
'the third man'

(9) Sawila
imyalara gi-araasing
man 3.POSS-house
'the man's house'

In all AP languages, the ordinals for 'second' and higher are regularly derived. There is no limit in the creation of ordinals on the basis of higher, morphologically more complex, cardinals.

Some variation exists, however, in the expression of 'first'. Adang and Kamang form 'first' by the regular process used for 'second' and above. Teiwa and Abui use forms for 'first' that are unrelated to the numeral 'one', compare (10) (a-b) and (11) (a-b). In Teiwa, the regular derivation from *nuk* does not exist, (10)(b); in Abui, it does exist, but has a different meaning ('the only/single/particular'), (11)(b). Western Pantar has two options to express 'first'. One is to use the regular construction derived from *(a)nuku* 'one', as in (12)(a) while the other option is to use a different root *ye* (12)(b) with an unclear etymology. There is a functional difference between Western Pantar ordinal based on *anuku* which is often used in predicative contexts ('you are the first'), and *ye*, which is preferred in attributive contexts ('my first child').

(10) Teiwa

    a. *uy   ga-xol*
       person 3.POSS-first
       'first person'

    b. **uy   ga-ma   nuk*
       person 3.POSS-ORD one

(11) Abui

    a. *ama   he-teitu*
       person 3.POSS-first
       'first person'

    b. *ama   he-nuku*
       person 3.POSS-one
       '(the) only/single person, particular person'

(12) Western Pantar

    a. *aname gai   maing anuku*
       person 3.POSS ORD   one

    b. *aname gai   maing ye*
       person 3.POSS ORD   one
       'first person'

In sum, the AP languages regularly derive ordinals from numerals with a possessor morpheme, so that syntactically the ordinal construction is a possessed nominal phrase. Apart from the third person possessor morpheme, which is used across the board, ordinals vary in structure when we go from west to east. In the western languages (Pantar-Straits-West Alor) special morphemes are employed which may be etymologically related to free forms encoding locations, though synchronically, this relation is not transparent. In the eastern languages, ordinals involve an applicative morpheme. At least three of the AP languages have an ordinal 'first' involving a root that is different from the cardinal 'one'. This is in line with the cross-linguistic tendency for languages with ordinals unrelated to cardinals to confine them to the lowest numerals (Stolz & Veselinova 2013).

2.3 Distributive numerals

2.3.1 Forms and distribution of distributives

Distributive numerals function to express notions such as 'one by one' or 'in groups of three'. AP languages create distributive numerals by reduplication of the cardinal numeral, or a part of it. Cross-linguistically, reduplication is the most common strategy to form distributives: in about 33% of the 251 languages in Gil's (2013) sample, distributives are created in this way. As Gil points out, the reduplicative strategy is iconically motivated: repeated copies of the cardinal correspond to multiple sets of objects.

Distributive numerals follow the noun or pronoun they modify, as illustrated in (13–16). Distributives can modify different clausal arguments; for example, an actor subject in (13) and (14) or a patient object in (15).

(13) Teiwa
Iman nuk~nuk aria-n.
3PL RDP~one arrive-REAL
'They arrived one by one.'

(14) Abui
Ama rifi~rifi sei hel buku nu
person RDP~thousand come.down.CONT TOP land SPEC
he-waalri.
3.LOC-gather.in.COMPL
'People came in thousands to that place.'

(15) Teiwa
   Yi   ma   gula   yerig~yerig   mat.
   2PL come sweet RDP~three   take
   'You take three sweets each.'

In some AP languages distributives may float outside the NP to a position adjacent to the verb; an example is Adang, (16). The exact restrictions and possibilities of such constructions across the AP languages remain a topic for future research; here we focus on the morphological shape of the distributives.

(16) Adang
   Sunuiɲ papan du   teweng al~alu   [allo].
   3PL   board DEF carry   RDP~two
   'They carry the board two by two (i.e., two at a time).'

The following sections describe how distributives are derived: the regular patterns are discussed in § 2.3.2, and the irregularities in § 2.3.3. Full paradigms of distributives in five languages of our sample are given in the Appendix.

2.3.2 Regular distributive formation

Regular distributive formation in Alor-Pantar involves reduplication of (a part of) the cardinal number. In complex numerals it is usually the right-most element, the prosodic head (§ 2.1), that is the base for the reduplication. The result is a distributive form that contains word-internal reduplication.

Even in languages where the morphological make-up of compound cardinals is synchronically opaque, such as Teiwa, distributive reduplication splits the cardinal in two parts, and only the rightmost element, the prosodic head, is reduplicated; see the numerals 'seven' to 'nine' in Table 2. Also in numerals that contain an operator expressing addition, it is the right-most morpheme that is reduplicated, see (17–19) below.

In Adang, distributives are formed by partial reduplication, as shown in Table 3. In the mono-morphemic forms 'one' through 'six', reduplication copies the first two segments (CV or VC) of the cardinal. Note that this analysis assumes that distributive 'two' *allo* and 'five' *iwwihing* are (historical) contractions of *al-alu* and *iw-iwing*. Numerals 'seven' to 'nine' are subtractive compound forms, in which the right-most element is the base for the reduplication (cf. *to* < *towo* 'three', *lo* < *alu* 'two', *nu* < *nu* 'one').

8 Numeral words and arithmetic operations in the Alor-Pantar languages

Table 2: Teiwa cardinals and distributives

	Cardinal	Distributive
1	*nuk*	*nuk~nuk*
2	*raq*	*raq~raq*
3	*yerig*	*yerig~yerig*
4	*ʔut*	*ʔut~ʔut*
5	*yusan*	*yusan~yusan*
6	*tiaam*	*tiaam~tiaam*
7	*yes**raq***	*yesraq~raq*
8	*yesn**erig***	*yesnerig~rig*
9	*yesna**ʔut***	*yesnaʔut~ʔut*

Table 3: Adang cardinals and distributives

	Cardinal	Distributive
1	*nu*	*nu~nu*
2	*alu* [alu]	*al~lo* [alːo] †
3	*towo*	*to~towo*
4	*ʔut*	*ʔu~ʔut*
5	*iwihing*	*iw~wihing*
6	*talang*	*ta~talang*
7	*wit**to***	*witto~to*
8	*tur**lo***	*turlo~lo*
9	*tiʔi**nu***	*tiʔinu~nu*

† Synchronically, the vowel in the distributive *allo* has a distinct quality from the vowel in the cardinal.

Across the AP family, the formation of distributives by reduplicating (parts of) cardinals is a productive process. It applies not only to frequent or morphologically simple numerals such as 'one' or 'two', but also to less frequent and morphologically complex numerals like '27' in (17), '201' in (18), and '1054' in (19). It must be noted that, while it is difficult to imagine a distributive context for numerals like these, speakers are able to mechanically derive their distributive form.

(17) Abui
Kar ayoku wal yeting ayok~ayok-da
ten two ADD five RDP~two-get.CONT
'in groups of 27'

(18) Distributive for '201'
            100   2   ADD RDP~1
W Pantar: *ratu   alaku wali   ye~ye*
Teiwa: *ratu   raq   rug   nuk~nuk*
Abui: *aisaha ayoku wal   nuk~nukda*
Kamang: *ataak ok   waal no~nok*

(19) Distributive for '1054'
            1000 1   10   5   ADD RDP~4
W Pantar: *(a)ribu nuk ke   yasing wali atu~atu*
Teiwa: *ribu   nuk qaar   yusan rug   ut~ut*
Abui: *rifi   nuku kar   yeting wal   buk~bukna*
Kamang: *ribu   nok ataak wesing waal bye~biat*

In sum, distributives are productively derived from cardinals by reduplicating part of or the whole cardinal base. In morphologically complex forms, the rightmost element is the prosodic head and the reduplicative base.

2.3.3 Irregularities in distributive formation

Exceptions to the regular derivations are mainly found in the formation of the morphologically complex low numerals 'six' to 'nine'. The irregularities include: (i) irregular segmental changes in reduplicated forms; (ii) irregular patterns of partial vs. full reduplication; and (iii) irregular choice of reduplicative base.

Abui shows the greatest amount of formal difference between its cardinal and distributive numerals, as shown in Table 4. The distributives are reduplicated verbal constructions: their verbal status is clear from the suffixes *-da/-na/-ra* which

8 Numeral words and arithmetic operations in the Alor-Pantar languages

encode light verbs and (continuative) aspect (Kratochvíl 2007). In Table 4, the parts printed in bold show the irregular relation between Abui cardinals and the numeral morphemes used in distributives.

Table 4: Abui cardinals and distributives

	Cardinal	Distributive
1	nuk**u**	nuk~nuk-da
2	ayok**u**	ayok~ayok-da
3	s**u**a	s**ui**~s**ui**-da
4	bu**ti**	bu**k**~bu**k**-na
5	ye**ting**	ye**k**~ye**k**-na
6	tala**ama**	tala**n**~tala**n**-ra

In Kamang distributives, the reduplicant varies in shape. In the numerals 'one' to 'four' and 'six', a morpheme with the shape (C)VV is reduplicated, while in the numeral 'five' and the complex numerals built on it—'seven' through 'nine'—the reduplicant has the shape CVCV. This is shown in Table 5.

Table 5: Kamang distributive numeral formation

	Cardinal	Reduplicant shape	Distributive
nok	'1'	CV	no~nok
ok	'2'	V	o?~ok[2]
su	'3'	CV	su~su
biat	'4'	CVV	bie~biat
wesing	'5'	CVCV	wesi~wesing
taama	'6'	CVV	taa~taama

Kamang has an irregular choice of reduplicative base. Compare the reduplicants (in bold-face) in the numerals 'seven' to 'nine' in Table 6. We see that Abui reduplicates only the right-most numeral, resulting in word-internal reduplication, which is consistent with the regular distributive pattern in AP languages

---

[2] The glottal stop in this form is phonetic. It is required to break up the sequence of like vowels in separate syllables. Speakers insist on including it in writing in order to distinguish /o/ from /o:/, orthographically {oo}.

(§ 2.3.2). By contrast, Kamang reduplicates the initial element *wesing*. As main stress is on the final syllable of the numerals in Kamang just as it is in Abui, we analyse this as a choice of reduplicative base in Kamang distributives which diverges from the overall pattern of AP languages.

Table 6: Reduplication of base-5 numerals in Abui and Kamang

	Abui	Kamang
'7'	*yeting**ayok**~ayokda*	***wesi**~wesingok*
'8'	*yeting**sui**~suida*	***wesi**~wesingsu*
'9'	*yeting**buk**~bukna*	***wesi**~wesingbiat*

In sum, AP languages derive distributive numerals by partial or full reduplication of the cardinal. In complex numerals, the right-most element is the prosodic head and as a rule this item is the base for the reduplication. Exceptions to the regular derivations of distributives are mainly found in the formation of the morphologically complex low numerals 'six' through 'nine' in Central-East Alor, and include segmental changes in reduplicated forms (Abui); irregular patterns of reduplication (Abui, Kamang), and an irregular choice of reduplicative base (Kamang).

3 Structures expressing arithmetic operations

To complete the catalogue of numeral expressions in AP languages, this section presents the basic arithmetic operations in which numbers are combined. We describe addition (section 3.1), subtraction (section 3.2), multiplication (section 3.3), division (section 3.4), and fractions (section 3.5). To elicit math constructions from speakers was generally easy and not forced at all. This is remarkable in light of the fact that for none of the languages is it the case that children acquire or use these arithmetic expressions in school: the language of education in Alor-Pantar is Indonesian.

3.1 Addition

Across Alor-Pantar, addition takes the shape of imperative sentences involving more than one verb. In such constructions, the agent or actor is not expressed and the added numerals are the arguments of verbs in a serial construction. The number that represents the sum amount is a predicate that follows a clause-coordinating element. Languages may abbreviate the expression by omitting a verb or the clause-coordinator. Examples (20) through (24) illustrate 'three plus three is six':

(20) Western Pantar
Atiga ma³ atiga tang tiggung (allang) hisnakkung
three come three on add (then) six
'Bring three, add on three, (then) [get] six.'

(21) Teiwa
Yerig ma yerig taxa' si a tiaam
three come three add SIM 3SG six
'Add three with three so (it's) six.'

(22) Adang
Towo med towo ta talang.
three take three add six
'Take three add three (it's) six.'

(23) Abui
Sua mi sua-ng h-ai maiye talaama
three take three-SEE 3.PAT-add.to if six
'If you add three to three, (it's) six.'

(24) Kamang
Su me su wo-tte an-ing=bo taama
three take three 3.LOC-add thus-SET=CONJ six
'Add three to three makes six.'

3.2 Subtraction

Just like addition, subtraction is also expressed in imperative sentences. Syntactically, the subtrahend (i.e., the numeral subtracted) is expressed as the complement of transitive verbs such as 'throw away X', 'split off X', 'move X', or 'take X'. The grammatical role of the minuend (i.e., the numeral subtracted from) is less clear. As is the case with the sum of addition, the result of the subtraction typically occurs as the predicate of a separate clause, following a clause coordinating element. Examples (25) through (30) illustrate 'five minus two is three':

---

[3] *Ma* may be omitted; in that case there must be a pause between both occurrences of *atiga*.

(25) Western Pantar
Yasing alaku sussung   allang (gang) atiga.
five   two   throw.away then   (3SG) three
'Discard two from five then there are three.'

(26) Teiwa
Muxui kam yusan, haraq ma   ga-fa'   mai ha   si,
banana CLF five   two   come 3SG-split.off save then SIM
kam yerig qai.
CLF three only
'Five bananas, split off two [to] save then only three [are left].'

(27) Adang
Iwihing a-no'   kurung alu towo
five   CAUS-affect less   two three
'Five minus two is three.'

(28) Abui
Yeting nu   ayoku=ng ha-bel   maiye he-pot   sua
five   SPEC two=LOC 3.PAT-subtract if   3.ALIEN-remainder three
'If two is subtracted from five, the remainder is three.'

(29) Abui
Yeting nu   ayoku mi-a   maiye sua
five   SPEC two   take-DUR if   three
'If two is taken from five, it is three.'

(30) Kamang
Wesing ok wo-met   an-ing=bo   su.
five   two 3.LOC-take thus-SET=CONJ three
'Take two from five thus there are three.'

3.3 Multiplication

The strategy used in multiplication is variable. All languages start with the multiplicant, but its shape differs. In Western Pantar and Teiwa it is an underived cardinal followed by a demonstrative, while in Abui it is a morphologically derived distributive (§ 2.3). Examples (31) through (34) illustrate 'five times four is twenty':

8 Numeral words and arithmetic operations in the Alor-Pantar languages

(31) Western Pantar
Attu si gaunung me yasing allang (gang) ke alaku.
four that just on five then 3SG ten two
'Five on just that four then (it's) twenty.'

(32) Teiwa
Ut ga'an tag-an ma-yusan si, a qaar raq.
four that count-REAL come-five SIM 3SG ten two
'Count these four five times and it's twenty.'

(33) Abui
Buk~bukna ha-lakda nu ming yekna maiye kar
RDP~group.of.four 3.PAT-count.CONT SPEC about five.times if ten
ayoku.
two
'If a group of four is counted five times, it is twenty.'

Kamang expresses multiplication with an applicative verb derived from a cardinal base by prefixing *mi-*. (Compare Teiwa, where the applicative derivation is used for fractions, see § 3.5).

(34) Kamang
Biat=a mi-wesing an-ing=bo ataak ok.
four=SPEC APPL-five thus-SET=CONJ ten two
'Five times these four makes twenty.'

3.4 Division

Expressions for division involve the transitive verbs 'split' and 'divide' in Western Pantar, Teiwa, and Adang. The following examples illustrate 'ten divided by two is five':

(35) Western Pantar
Ke anuku daai alaku allang yasing
ten one split two then five
'Ten split (by) two then (it's) five.'

(36) Teiwa
Qaar nuk paxai g-et haraq si yusan.
ten one divide 3sg-eye two SIM five
'Ten divided in two parts (lit. eyes), then (it's) five.'

(37) Adang
 'Air nu 'aba'ang ʔo-alu   iwihing
 ten one divide   POSS-two five
 'Ten divided (by) two (is) five.'

Note that the order of the verb relative to its complement 'two' in (35)-(40) is unexpected, as it goes against the canonical AP object-verb order, found in subtraction (§ 3.2). Note that the equivalent expression in Indonesian/Malay is *sepuluh bagi dua (adalah) lima* lit. 'ten divide two (is) five', with verb complement order. It may be the case that the constructions in (35)-(40) are calques from Indonesian/Malay.

Abui divisions are expressed as imperative sentences with regular serial verb constructions, where the result follows a coordinating element, see (38). Kamang expresses a fraction by marking the dividing numeral with *wo-*, the same prefix that is used to express, for instance, fractions resulting from an action, e.g., *bo'ne wo-ok* 'hit into two pieces', (39).

(38) Abui
 Kar nuku nu   mi   ayoku he-yeng   maiye yek~yekna
 ten one SPEC take two   3.LOC-divide if   RDP~group.of.five
 'If a ten is divided into two (you get) a group of five.'

(39) Kamang
 Ataak nok=a   wo-ok   an-ing=bo   wesing
 ten   one=SPEC 3.LOC-two thus-set=CONJ   five
 'Ten divided into two makes five.'

3.5 Fractions

Expressions for fractions show much variety across the AP languages. Western Pantar, Teiwa and Adang express fractions using a verb, while Kamang uses fraction adverbs, and no fractions appear to exist in Abui.

Western Pantar derives fractions productively with the verb 'divide', (40). In Teiwa, expressions for fractions contain an applicative verb derived from a cardinal base by prefixing *g-un-*, a fossilized combination of a 3SG object prefix and an applicative prefix *un-*. The fraction verb occurs as second verb in a serial verb construction, (41):

8 Numeral words and arithmetic operations in the Alor-Pantar languages

(40) Western Pantar
Ye daai atiga, ye daai attu
one divide three one divide four
'one third, one fourth'

(41) Teiwa
Taxaran g-un-yerig, g-un-ut, g-un-qaar nuk
divide 3SG-APPL-three 3SG-APPL-four 3SG-APPL-ten one
'a third, a fourth, a tenth' (lit. 'Divide into three, four, ten')

(42) Adang
Nu 'aba'ang ʔo-ut
one divide POSS-four
'one fourth'

In Kamang, fractions are verbs derived by prefixing *wo-* '3.LOC' to the numeral base, as in (43). In (44), the derived verb is part of a resultative serial verb construction.

(43) Kamang
wo-ok, wo-su, wo-biat, wo-ataak
3.LOC-two 3.LOC-three 3.LOC-four 3.LOC-ten
'half, a third, a fourth/quarter, a tenth'

(44) Kamang
Nala le nok katee wo-biat.
1SG mango one eat 3.LOC-four
'I eat a fourth of the mango.', 'I eat the mango in fourths.'

Abui does not seem to have a construction dedicated to derive fractions. It does have a word for 'half' that is unrelated to 'two':

(45) Abui
Nalama pingai nuku ahama
cooked.rice plate one half
'One and a half plates of rice'

Words for 'half' that are unrelated to 'two' are also found in Western Pantar, Teiwa, and Adang, as shown below. In Western Pantar, 'half' can be a nominal *gamme* 'half, portion', but also a fraction involving the verb 'divide', compare

(46–47). In Teiwa, 'half' may be a nominal (*qaas* 'side, half', *abaq* 'half' in 48–49), but may also be expressed by an applicative verb derived from 'two', as in (50).

(46) Western Pantar
Gang maggi gamme na
3SG banana half eat
'He ate half a banana.'

(47) Western Pantar
ye daai alaku
one divide two
'half'

(48) Teiwa
Ha wou ga'an tu'un qaas na-mian
2SG mango that peel side 1SG-give
'Peel that mango (and) give me half.'

(49) Teiwa
Yir sluan abaq
water glass half
'half a glass of water'

(50) Teiwa
Taxaran g-un-raq
divide 3SG-APPL-two
'half'

(51) Adang
na be bo'oden solo 'adi no'o me-nani?
1SG mango half only eat can or-not
'Can I only eat half a mango?'

4 Summary and conclusions

The majority of cardinal numerals in AP languages are morphologically complex expressions—most are compounds. These forms have quinary or decimal bases, though mathematical operations always employ a decimal base. No AP language has a numeral 'null' or a word for 'zero'—the absence of entities is expressed predicatively instead.

8 Numeral words and arithmetic operations in the Alor-Pantar languages

Ordinals are derived from cardinals by means of a third person possessor morpheme. Syntactically, ordinals are possessive phrases where the ranked numeral is possessed by the ranked item. In the languages of Pantar, the Straits and West Alor, ordinal constructions also contain a dedicated ordinal morpheme; an applicative morpheme is used in the ordinals of languages of Central and East Alor.

Most languages derive distributives from cardinals by reduplicating part or whole of the cardinal. In complex forms, the right-most lexeme, which is the prosodic head of the compound, is taken as the base for the reduplication. This applies even to those forms that are synchronically morphologically opaque. Kamang is exceptional in that it reduplicates the left-most element of the compound rather than the prosodic head, and in Abui, distributives and cardinals are only indirectly related.

Across the languages, there is more homogeneity in the expressions of addition and subtraction than there is in the expression of multiplication and division. Addition and subtraction typically take the shape of imperative sentences. In additive expressions, the added numerals each have their own predicate. The second numeral is often the grammatical object of a transitive verb ('add X') that has an implied subject, the imperative addressee. In subtraction, the subtrahend is also the object of a transitive verb ('throw away X') but the grammatical role of the 'minuend' is less clear. In both addition and subtraction, the result follows a clause coordinating element.

The strategies used in multiplication, division, and fractions vary significantly across the languages. While all the languages express multiplication by a multiplicant followed by a verb, the morpho-syntactic shape of the multiplicant and the choice of verb differ. In expressions for division, the number of verbs involved range from zero to two, and word orders in the western languages go against the head-final order that is typical for AP and follow the order of Indonesian/Malay, suggesting they may be calques. Across the AP languages, the expression of fractions shows the largest variety. The lack of homogeneity in the expressions for multiplication, division and fractions suggests that these expressions are more labile than those for addition and subtraction, which is probably due to their lower frequency in everyday language.

The indigenous numeral forms of the AP languages, as well as the indigenous structures for arithmetic operations are currently under pressure from Indonesian as the language of interethnic trade and national education. This will inevitably lead to their replacement with Indonesian forms and constructions. This chapter keeps a snapshot of them for future generations.

M. Klamer, A. Schapper, G. Corbett, G. Holton, F. Kratochvíl & L. C. Robinson

4.1 Sources

The data sets on which this paper is based were collected from 2010-2012 by the authors. We used a questionnaire on numerals designed in 2010 by Marian Klamer and Antoinette Schapper for the purpose of documenting the numerals and numeral systems in AP languages (see Appendix B). The core dataset discussed in this chapter thus comes from questionnaires filled in for Teiwa (by Klamer and Robinson), Western Pantar (by Holton), Adang (by Robinson), Abui (by Kratochvíl and Schapper), and Kamang (by Schapper). Comparative information on additional languages was provided through personal communication with Hein Steinhauer (Blagar), Nick Williams (Kula), František Kratochvíl (Sawila) and Marian Klamer (Kaera).

8 Numeral words and arithmetic operations in the Alor-Pantar languages

A Appendix

A.1 Ordinal and Distributive Numerals

Table 7: Western Pantar ordinals in a construction with *bla* 'house' and *aname* 'person'

1st	bla/aname	gai	maing	ye
	bla/aname	gai	maing	anuku
2nd	bla/aname	gai	maing	alaku
3rd	bla/aname	gai	maing	atiga
4th	bla/aname	gai	maing	atú
5th	bla/aname	gai	maing	yasing
6th	bla/aname	gai	maing	hisnakkung
7th	bla/aname	gai	maing	betalaku
8th	bla/aname	gai	maing	betiga
9th	bla/aname	gai	maing	anuku tannang
10th	bla/aname	gai	maing	ke anuku
100th	bla/aname	gai	maing	ratu

Table 8: Teiwa ordinals with *yaf* 'house' and *uy* 'person'

1st	yaf/uy	ga-		xol†
2nd	yaf/uy	ga-	ma-	ga-mar [gama'gamar] '3s-ORD-3s-take'
	yaf/uy	ga-	ma-	raq
3rd	yaf/uy	ga-	ma-	yerig
4th	yaf/uy	ga-	ma-	ut
5th	yaf/uy	ga-	ma-	yusan
6th	yaf/uy	ga-	ma-	tiaam
7th	yaf/uy	ga-	ma-	yes raq
8th	yaf/uy	ga-	ma-	yes nerig
9th	yaf/uy	ga-	ma-	yes na?ut
10th	yaf/uy	ga-	ma-	qaar nuk
100th	yaf/uy	ga-	ma-	ratu nuk

†Teiwa *ga-nuk* means 'one from a group', *ga-ma-nuk* is not a Teiwa word.

Table 9: Kaera ordinals with *ma* 'house' and *ui* 'person'

1st	ma/ui	(ge-)		tuning (*tuni* 'gate', *tuning* 'placenta')
2nd	ma/ui	ge-	mi	(a)raxo
3rd	ma/ui	ge-	mi	(u)tug
4th	ma/ui	ge-	mi	ut
5th	ma/ui	ge-	mi	isim
6th	ma/ui	ge-	mi	tiam
7th	ma/ui	ge-	mi	yesraxo
8th	ma/ui	ge-	mi	yentug
9th	ma/ui	ge-	mi	yeniut
10th	ma/ui	ge-	mi	xar nuko
100th	ma/ui	ge-	mi	ratu nuko

Table 10: Adang ordinals with *bang* 'house' and *nami* 'person'

1st	bang/nami	ʔo-	mi-	nu	mi
2nd	bang/nami	ʔo-	mi-	alu	mi
3rd	bang/nami	ʔo-	mi-	towo	mi
4th	bang/nami	ʔo-	mi-	ut	mi
5th	bang/nami	ʔo-	mi-	(i)wihing	mi
6th	bang/nami	ʔo-	mi-	talang	mi
7th	bang/nami	ʔo-	mi-	witto	mi
8th	bang/nami	ʔo-	mi-	turlo	mi
9th	bang/nami	ʔo-	mi-	tiʔinu	mi
10th	bang/nami	ʔo-	mi-	ʔ,air nu	mi
100th	bang/nami	ʔo-	mi-	rat nu	mi

8 Numeral words and arithmetic operations in the Alor-Pantar languages

Table 11: Abui ordinals with *fala* 'house' and *ama* 'person'

1st	fala/ama	he-	teitu
	fala/ama	he-	nuku
2nd	fala/ama	he-	ayoku
3rd	fala/ama	he-	sua
4th	fala/ama	he-	buti
5th	fala/ama	he-	yeting
6th	fala/ama	he-	talaama
7th	fala/ama	he-	yeting ayoku
8th	fala/ama	he-	yeting sua
9th	fala/ama	he-	yeting buti
10th	fala/ama	he-	kar nuku
100th	fala/ama	he-	aisaha nuku

Table 12: Kamang ordinals for *kadii* 'house' and *alma* 'person'

1st	kadii / alma	ye-	nok
2nd	kadii / alma	ye-	ok
3rd	kadii / alma	ye-	su
4th	kadii / alma	ye-	biat
5th	kadii / alma	ye-	wesing
6th	kadii / alma	ye-	taama
7th	kadii / alma	ye-	wesing ok
8th	kadii / alma	ye-	wesing su
9th	kadii / alma	ye-	wesing biat
10th	kadii / alma	ye-	ataak nok
100th	kadii / alma	ye-	asaka nok

Table 13: Sawila ordinals with *araasing* 'house' and *imyalara* 'man'

1st	araasing/imyalara	wii-	suna
2nd	araasing/imyalara	wii-	yaku
3rd	araasing/imyalara	wii-	tuo
4th	araasing/imyalara	wii-	araasiiku
5th	araasing/imyalara	wii-	yooting
6th	araasing/imyalara	wii-	yootsuna
7th	araasing/imyalara	wii-	yootingyaku
8th	araasing/imyalara	wii-	yootingtuo
9th	araasing/imyalara	wii-	yootingaraasiiku
10th	araasing/imyalara	wii-	adaaku
100th	araasing/imyalara	wii-	asaka

Table 14: Distributive numerals in Pantar-West Alor languages

	Western Pantar	Teiwa	Adang-Lawahing
1	ye~ye	nuk~nuk	nu-nu
2	alaku~alaku	raq~raq	al-lo
3	atiga~atiga	yerig~yerig	to-towo
4	atu~atu	ʔut~ʔut	u-ut
5	yasing~yasing	yusan~yusan	iw-wihing
6	hisnakkung~nakkung	tiaam~tiaam	ta-talang
7	betalaku~talaku	yesraq~raq	witto-to
8	betiga~tiga	yesnerig~rig	turlo-lo
9	anuktannang~tannang	yesnaʔut~ʔut	ti'inu-nu
10	ke anuku~nuku	qaar nuk~nuk	ʔair nu-nu
11	ke anuku wali ye~ye	qaar nuk rug nuk~nuk	ʔair nu waling nu-nu
100	ratu~ratu	ratu nuk~nuk	rat nu-nu
1000	aribu~aribu	ribu nuk~nuk	rib nu-nu

8 Numeral words and arithmetic operations in the Alor-Pantar languages

Table 15: Distributive numerals in Central-East Alor languages

	Abui	Kamang
1	nuk~nukda	no~nok, nokda~nokda
2	ayok~ayokda	o~ok
3	sui~suida	su~su
4	buk~bukna	bye~biat
5	yek~yekna	wesi~wesing
6	talan~talanra	taa~taama
7	yeting ayok~ayokda	wesi~wesingok
8	yeting sui~suida	wesi~wesingsu
9	yeting buk~bukna	wesi~wesingbiat
10	kar nuk~nukda	ataak no~nok
11	kar nuku wal nuk~nukda	ataak nok waal no~nok
100	aisaha nuk~nukda	asaka no~nok
1000	rifi nuk~nukda	ribu no~nok

M. Klamer, A. Schapper, G. Corbett, G. Holton, F. Kratochvíl & L. C. Robinson

A.2 Numeral Questionnaire used in the field

A.2.1 Numerals

It is preferred to elicit the data for this questionnaire using words and constructions in the language of investigation as much as possible. The Malay examples below are not given as prompts to be translated, but rather as additional background for you to help you steer a discussion in Malay. Expressions containing numerals and ordinals, and morphological derivations relating to numerals and ordinals in the AP languages are expected to be quite different from what they are in Malay.

A.2.2 Tasks

1. Ask a person to count in sequence from 1-20 and record this.

2. Elicit 1-100 on paper. Appendix 1: answer sheet.

3. Elicit higher cardinals 2000, 3000,..., 10.000. Appendix 2: answer sheet.

4. Elicit 100-1000 on paper. Suggestion: You could give (a) speaker(s) an empty notebook to work on this at their leisure at home. After they have written up all the numbers, please go over it, to check

   - if the writing is legible
   - if you know which letter is used for which sound
   - if this letter-sound correspondence in their orthography is consistent (or consistent enough to be used by us)
   - if there are any (possible) morphemes or morpheme boundaries that need additional elicitation or discussion –these notes can go with the manuscript.

5. Elicit expressions for basic calculations if any exist:

   - 3 + 3 = 6: *3 tambah 3 sama dengan enam*
   - 5 − 2 = 3: *lima kurang dua sama dengan tiga*
   - 4 x 5 = 20: *empat kali lima sama dengan dua puluh*
   - 10 : 2 = 5: *sepuluh bagi 2 sama dengan lima*

6. If expressions for basic calculations don't exist, or if they are borrowed or calqued from Malay, can consultants think of any other strategies how such basic calculations can be done? Situations to suggest could include:

8 Numeral words and arithmetic operations in the Alor-Pantar languages

- talking about the number of children alive in a family (e.g. 8 children born, 3 died as babies, 5 are still alive),
- counting / adding / subtracting pupils in a class setting
- cigarettes in a packet
- members of the church who have newly arrived / have left / died
- multiplying/dividing rupiahs earned by a group of people
- measuring land to buy or sell e.g. to build a house on
- etc.

7. Elicit the years 1978, 1999, 2010. If there is no consensus or consistency across speakers, please note down any differences you notice.

8. Elicit fractions, if they exist
    - half
    - one third
    - quarter
    - try smaller fractions?
    - a tenth

   Please ask for examples in context, e.g. *Saya bisa makan setengah buah manggo saja* 'I can only eat half a mango', *Tolong berikan sepertiga/seperempat (bagian) saja* 'Please give me a third/quarter only'.

9. If expressions for fractions don't exist, can consultants think of other ways to talk about parts of fruits, subgroups of people, parts of piece of land?

10. Ordinals: Elicit 1st-10th e.g., *Saya lihat barisan anak di muka rumah. Yang pertama bernama... yang kedua... yang ketiga...* etc.

    Please try also for higher ones: contrast *Anggota gereja yang ketiga* 'the third member of the church' with *anggota yang kesepuluh, yang keratus, yang keseribu ...* It is best to use a local language prompt here, as the higher ones are ungrammatical in Malay!

A.2.3 Points for further elicitation

1. Is there a word for zero?

2. Is there an indigenous word for million/*jutah*?

3. Are there indigenous numbers higher than million?

4. Distinguish non-referential counting (1, 2, 3, ... 10) and enumeration (*satu ekor ayam, dua orang, tiga buku, sepuluh rumah*): are different numerals used?

5. Check if there is a contrast in counting small animates versus large animates and animate vs. inanimate entities:
    - Small animates
        - ant/*semut*
        - fly/*lalat*
        - bee/*lebah*
        - house lizzard/*cecak*
    - Large animates
        - child/*anak*
        - dog/*anjing*
        - pig/*babi*
    - Inanimates
        - house/*rumah*
        - rock/*batu karang*
        - star/*bintang*
        - coconut tree/*pohon kelapa*

6. Note down the distribution of cardinals as part of NP (in 'attributive' function), for example in a context like:

    Ada tiga orang di rumah. Dua orang pergi ke kota, satu orang tinggal di rumah. 'There are three people at home. Two went to town, one stayed at home.'

    - Is the position of numeral w.r.t. noun fixed or is there variability? E.g. *Orang tiga* vs *tiga orang* in the above example.

8 Numeral words and arithmetic operations in the Alor-Pantar languages

- If there is variability, check if it is related to higher vs. lower cardinals. E.g. Malay
    - *Ada dua orang di rumah* **vs.** *ada orang dua di rumah*
    - *Ada sebelas orang di rumah* **vs** *ada orang sebelas di rumah*
    - *Ada lima puluh orang di rumah* **vs.** *ada orang lima puluh di rumah*
- What is the position of the numeral in the NP if it contains a demonstrative? E.g. *Those five girls...*
    - *Dua orang itu ada di rumah, Orang dua itu ada di rumah, Sebelas orang itu ada di rumah, Orang sebelas itu ada di rumah,* etc.

7. Is there any agreement morphology between numeral and noun?

8. Note down the distribution of cardinals as predicate (in 'predicative' function), if they are used as such, e.g.:
    - *Waktu itu kami masih bertiga* 'At that time we were still three';
    - *Mereka datang berlima, berdua mereka pergi* 'They came with five and left with two'

9. If cardinals may be used in predicative function, can a higher numeral also be used as such? Note that this not generally possible in Malay, where the predicative *ber-* construction is not productively used with higher numerals: **Waktu itu kami berdua puluh*. Instead one would say *Waktu itu kami duapuluh orang* 'We were twenty at the time'.
    - Check e.g. 12, 15, 20, 35, 50, 76, 95.

10. In Malay, certain particular high cardinals do appear in the *ber-* construction: *Kami akan datang berseribu* 'we will come (as) a (group of) thousand'. So perhaps a language does not treat all higher cardinals in the same way.
    - Check e.g. 1000, 2000, 100, 500, 1 000 000, 2 000 000

11. Can cardinals be used as elliptical for a fuller NP (subject or object): *Mau berapa buah pisang? Saya mau dua (dua buah/dua pisang)*

12. Can cardinals be used as abstract entities, e.g. in contexts like:
    - *Nomor HP saya mulai dengan angka/nomor tiga* 'My mobile phone number starts with digit/number three'

- *Waktu mengajar anak menulis guru bilang:* "*Coba menulis angka/nomor dua dan angka dua belas sekarang*" 'When the teacher taught the children to write, he said: " Please write digit/number two and number/digit 12 now'.

Try the same with some higher numerals:

- *Guru bilang kepada anak: Angka dua puluh itu masih terlalu kecil* 'that number 20 is still too small'

Try the same for *angka lima belas, tiga puluh, seratus, seribu, dua ribu, (se)jutah.*

13. **Reduplication of cardinals**: Can numerals be reduplicated? If so, give some examples in sentential context.
    - Try 1, 2, 3, 4, 5, 10, 12, 17, 15, 20, 50, 100, 500, 1000.

14. What does the reduplication mean? E.g. Malay *beribu-ribu orang datang ke kota itu* 'People came in thousands to that town' (vs. *ribuan orang* 'thousands of people')

15. Does reduplicated 'one' have any special meaning? E.g. Bunaq *uen~uen* means 'same, equal'; Kamang *no-nok* 'one by one'.

16. Where do numeral reduplications occur: before or after the noun? Before or after the verb? Please provide some example sentences.

17. Do reduplicated numerals occur as part of NPs in 'attributive' function (as in Malay *beribu-ribu orang*)? Or do they occur in 'predicative' function?

18. Check reduplication of NPs encoding subject/actor vs NPs encoding object/undergoer:
    - *Dua orang laki-laki membawa papan. Satu demi satu mereka membawa papan* = one carrier at the time vs.
    - *Dua orang laki-laki membawa papan. Mereka membawa papan satu demi satu* = one plank at the time

19. Note down the **distribution of Ordinals**:
    - as part of NP:
        - *Orang pertama yang membeli tv adalah Markus* 'The first person to buy a radio was Markus'

8 Numeral words and arithmetic operations in the Alor-Pantar languages

- as sth. similar to a non-verbal predicate:
    - *Lidia adalah orang pertama yang pergi ke Kupang* 'Lidia was the first person who went to Kupang'
- with an inanimate noun:
    - *Mereka masuk jalan kedua*
    - *Kepala desa membangunkan rumahnya kedua*(or *rumah keduanya*) *pada tahun yang lalu*
- modifying the predicate, in adverbial-like function:
    - *Mereka pergi ke Kupang pada kali yang kedua.*

20. Are the ordinals etymologically clearly related to cardinals? e.g. Indonesian ordinal *pertama* is not derived from cardinal *satu*.

21. Are there any words that are used like ordinals but have no numeral or ordinal root?

22. **Plural marking**: Is plural marked with an affix?

23. Does the language have a plural word? E.g. *non* 'PLURAL' in Teiwa.

    A plural word is a morpheme whose meaning and function is similar to that of plural affixes in other languages, but which is a separate word that functions as a modifier of the noun. Plural words are overrepresented in isolating or analytic languages, in languages with classifiers, and in head-marking languages (cf. M. Dryer, Plural words, *Linguistics* 27 (1989), 865-895.)

    Questions 24-29 only apply when the language has a plural word:

24. If the language has a plural word, do you observe any animacy or size effects in the use of the plural word? Check:
    - *orang perempuan*
    - *kakak perempuan*
    - *anak laki-laki*
    - *babi, anjing*
    - *tikus, burung*
    - *nyamuk, semut, lebah, lalat*

- *batu kecil, jarum, kancing*
- *kendi, panci, mok*
- *batu karang, pohon kelapa*
- *bintang*
- *rumah*

25. Plural words as 'numerals': Can plural word and numeral co-occur? (If so, this could be evidence that they belong to different categories.)

26. Can plural word and non-numeral quantifiers (*beberapa, semua, sedikit, banyak*) co-occur?

27. Can plural word and possessor noun co-occur?

28. Can plural word and possessive prefix co-occur?

29. Plural words are reported to derive from e.g. third person plural pronoun, plural article, words meaning *all* or *many*, nouns meaning *group* or *set*, classifier,... etc. Do you have ideas about the possible diachronic origin of the plural word in the language of study?

30. **Quantifiers (non-numeral)** *semua, banyak, sedikit, beberapa* What does the quantifier inventory look like for

    - Countable objects
        - *orang, babi, anjing, rumah, kursi, gelas*
    - Uncountable objects or masses
        - *garam, gula, air, nasi, jagung (?), semut, lebah, lalat,*
        - *gunung-gunung (?), awan-awan (?)*
    - Liquids
        - *air, air susu, anggur, arak, teh*
    - Edibles
        - *buah pinang, daun papaya, daging babi, ikan*

31. Do particular semantics play a role in the interpretation of the value of the quantifiers? (e.g. (un)expected/(un)wanted value, e.g. many people come to church, more than expected, or when only a little bit of gas is sold less than expected (*misalnya kalau banyak orang datang ke g<ereja, lebih dari harapan (atau hanya sedikit minyak dijual, kurang dari harapan*).

32. **Classifiers**: We will make a separate questionnaire & stimuli for this at a later stage. If you have made some observations about the classifiers, please include them here.

A.2.4 Numerals 1–100

No	Language:	Notes
1		
2		
...		
99		
100		

A.2.5 Higher cardinals

No	Language:	Notes
1000		
2000		
...		
9000		
10 000		

Abbreviations

=	clitic boundary	CONJ	conjunction	PL	plural
~	reduplication	CONT	continuous	POSS	possessive
1	1st person	DEF	definite	PRED	predicate
2	2nd person	DUR	durative	RDP	reduplication
3	3rd person	IND	Indonesian	SG	singular
ALIEN	alienable	LOC	locative	SIM	simultaneous
AP	Alor-Pantar	N	noun	SPEC	specific
APPL	applicative	NP	noun phrase	TOP	topic
CAUS	causative	NUM	numeral	V	verb
CLF	classifier	ORD	ordinal		
COMPL	completive	PAT	patient		

M. Klamer, A. Schapper, G. Corbett, G. Holton, F. Kratochvíl & L. C. Robinson

References

Comrie, Bernard. 2005. Endangered numeral systems. In Jan Wohlgemuth & Tyko Dirksmeyer (eds.), *Bedrohte Vielfalt: Aspekte des Sprach(en)tods [Endangered diversity: aspects of language death]*, 203–230. Berlin: Weißensee Verlag.

Dryer, Matthew S. 1989. Plural words. *Linguistics* 27. 865–895.

Gil, David. 2013. Distributive numerals. In Matthew Dryer & Martin Haspelmath (eds.), *The World Atlas of Language Structures online*, chap. 54. Munich: Max Planck Digital Library. http://wals.info/chapter/54.

Holton, Gary & Laura C. Robinson. this volume. The internal history of the Alor-Pantar language family. In Marian Klamer (ed.), *The Alor-Pantar languages*, 55–97. Berlin: Language Science Press.

Kratochvíl, František. 2007. *A grammar of Abui: a Papuan language of Alor*. Utrecht: LOT.

Schapper, Antoinette & Marian Klamer. this volume. Numeral systems in the Alor-Pantar languages. In Marian Klamer (ed.), *The Alor-Pantar languages*, 285–336. Berlin: Language Science Press.

Stolz, Thomas & Ljuba Veselinova. 2013. Ordinal numerals. In Matthew Dryer & Martin Haspelmath (eds.), *The World Atlas of Language Structures online*, chap. 53. Munich: Max Planck Digital Library. http://wals.info/chapter/53.

Stump, Gregory. 2010. The derivation of compound ordinal numerals: Implications for morphological theory. *Word Structure* 3(2). 205–233.

Von Mengden, Ferdinand. 2010. *Cardinal numerals: Old English from a cross-linguistic perspective*. Berlin: Mouton de Gruyter.

Chapter 9

Plural number words in the Alor-Pantar languages

Marian Klamer

Antoinette Schapper

Greville Corbett

> In this chapter, we investigate the variation in form, syntax and semantics of the plural words found across the Alor-Pantar languages. We study five AP languages: Western Pantar, Teiwa, Abui, Kamang and Wersing. We show that plural words in Alor-Pantar family are diachronically instable: although proto-Alor-Pantar had a plural number word *non, many AP languages have innovated new plural words. Plural words in these languages exhibit not only a wide variety of different syntactic properties but also variable semantics, thus likening them more to the range exhibited by affixal plural number than previously recognized.

1 Introduction

The majority of the world's languages express nominal plurality by affixation. After affixation, the use of independent plural words is the most widespread strategy: it is used in 16% of Dryer's (2011) sample of 1066 languages. Yet, 'plural words' have received remarkably little attention since their preliminary treatment in Dryer (1989). In this chapter, we build on Schapper & Klamer (2011) in furthering the investigation of plural words using data from the Alor-Pantar (AP) languages, which are of great typological interest.

A plural word is "a morpheme whose meaning and function is similar to that of plural affixes in other languages, but which is a separate word" (Dryer 1989: 865; Dryer 2007: 166). Plural words are the most common example of a more general category, that of grammatical number words – a number of languages

Marian Klamer, Antoinette Schapper & Greville Corbett. 2017. Plural number words in the Alor-Pantar languages. In Marian Klamer (ed.), *The Alor-Pantar languages*, 365–403. Berlin: Language Science Press. DOI:10.5281/zenodo.569397

employ singular or dual words as well as plural words. For Dryer, to be a plural word a lexeme must be the prime indicator of plurality: "I do not treat a word as a plural word if it co-occurs with an inflectional indication of plural on the noun" (1989: 867). Dryer further makes a distinction between 'pure' number words and other kinds of number expressions: "We can [...] distinguish 'pure' plural words, which only code plurality, from articles that code number in addition to other semantic or grammatical features of the noun phrase, in which these articles are the sole indicator of number in noun phrases". Thus the bar is set quite high: plural words are the prime indicator of plurality, and in the pure case they have this as their unique function.

Plural words in Alor-Pantar languages carry also a range of additional semantic connotations beyond simple plurality, including completeness, abundance, individuation, and partitivity. These are interrelated to the other options the individual languages have for marking plurality. This means that our discussion of plural words in Alor-Pantar languages necessarily also touches on other plurality expressing strategies available in the languages. We will see that the form, syntax and semantics of plural words across the Alor-Pantar languages display a high degree of diversity.

This paper is structured as follows. § 2 introduces the lexical forms of the plural words of the languages and the sources of the data discussed in this paper. § 3 discusses their syntax, while § 4 looks in detail at the semantics of the plural words. § 5 places AP plural words in a wider typological context, and § 6 presents our conclusions.

2 Plural number words across Alor-Pantar

Plural words are found across the Alor-Pantar languages, as shown in Table 1. Cognate forms attested in Teiwa (West Pantar), Klon (West Alor) and Kamang (Central-East Alor) indicate that a plural word *non can be reconstructed for proto-Alor-Pantar (pAP). Western Pantar, Abui, Wersing, Kula and Sawila do not reflect this item, and instead appear to have innovated new lexemes for plural words. Several AP languages in our sample (Klon, Abui, Wersing, Kula and Sawila) have two plural words encoding different kinds of plurality, though the other languages do have a range of plural-marking strategies in addition to their plural word. There are also Alor-Pantar languages for which no plural word has been attested; an example is Kaera (North-East Pantar; Klamer 2014a).

In all Alor-Pantar languages, nouns are uninflected for number, and a noun phrase without a plural word can refer to any number of individuals. For in-

9 Plural number words in the Alor-Pantar languages

Table 1: Cognate and non-cognate plural words in Alor-Pantar languages

Language	Reflecting *non	Not reflecting *non	Source
Western Pantar		*maru(ng)*	Holton & Lamma Koly (2008); Holton (2012; 2014), p.c.
Teiwa	*non*		Klamer (2010), Teiwa corpus; Schapper and Klamer (2011)
Adang	*nun*		Robinson & Haan (2014)
Klon	*(o)non*	*maang*	Baird (2008), Klon corpus, p.c.
Abui		*loku, we*	Schapper fieldnotes; Kratochvíl (2007), Abui corpus
Kamang	*nung*		Schapper Kamang corpus, 2014, fieldnotes; Schapper & Manimau (2011); Stokhof (1978; 1982)
Wersing		*deing, naing*	Schapper & Hendery (2014), fieldnotes, Wersing corpus; Malikosa (nd)
Kula		*du(a), araman*	Nicholas Williams p.c.
Sawila		*do, maarang*	František Kratochvíl p.c.

stance, Teiwa *qavif* 'goat' in (1a) can be interpreted as either singular or plural, depending on the context. Those Alor-Pantar languages that have a plural word use it to express plurality: 'more than one'. Illustrations are Teiwa *non* in (1b), and Klon *onon* in (2b-c). The plural word pluralizes the preceding nominal expression. In none of the AP languages we investigated is the plural word obligatory when plural reference is intended.

(1) Teiwa (Klamer, Teiwa corpus)

    a. *Qavif itaʔa ma gi?*
       goat where OBL go
       'Where did the goat(s) go?'

b. *Qavif non itaʔa ma gi?*
   goat PL where OBL go
   'Where did the (several) goats go?'; *'Where did the goat go?'

(2) Klon (Baird, Klon corpus, p.c.)

   a. *Ge-ebeng   go-thook.*
      3.GEN-friend 3-meet
      '(He) met his friend(s).'[1]

   b. *Ge-ebeng   onon go-thook.*
      3.GEN-friend PL   3-meet
      'His friends met him'/'(He) met his friends.'
      (*'(He) met his friend.'; *'(They) met their friend.')

   c. *Ininok onon ge-ebeng   go-thook.*
      person PL   3.GEN-friend 3-meet
      'The people met their friend.'

While plural words only occur with third person referents, none of the languages seems to have semantic restrictions on which referents can be marked plural. For instance, in all the languages we examined, both animate and inanimate entities can be pluralized. There does not seem to be a preference to use a plural word more often with animate than with inanimate nouns, or vice versa. In Wersing, for example, the plural word can be used to signal the plurality of a human (3), animal (4) or inanimate referent (5). There is similarly no difference in the plural marking of large versus small referents, as illustrated for Western Pantar *raya* 'chief' (6) and *bal* 'ball' (7). *Bal marung* 'ball PL' in (7) refers to an unspecified number of balls. This can be a small number of balls, say two or three; it does not have to be a large number of balls.

(3) Wersing (Schapper & Hendery 2014: 469)
    ..., *saku deing bias ol   tamu   poko dein=a ge-pai ge-tai...*
    ... adult PL   usually child grandchild small PL=ART 3-make 3-sleep
    '..., the adults would usually [do it] to make the children and grandchildren sleep...'

---

[1] Compare *Iniq ge-ebeng go-thook* 'They met his friend(s)', where the non-singular pronoun *iniq* encodes the subject (Baird, p.c.).

(4) Wersing (Schapper & Hendery 2014: 469)
*Ne-karbau wari ne-wai deing=na yeta le-gadar.*²
1SG-buffalo and 1SG-goat PL=FOC 2PL.AGT APPL-guard
'You watch out for my buffaloes and my goats.'

(5) Wersing (Schapper & Hendery 2014: 469)
Kiki deing aso ge-mira susa.
flower PL also 3-inside suffer
'The flowers were also suffering.'

(6) Western Pantar (Holton 2012)
Raya marung wang hundar.
chief PL exist amazed
'The chiefs were amazed.' (*'The chief is amazed.')

(7) Western Pantar (Holton 2012)
Bal marung mea tang pering.
ball PL table on pour
'A bunch of balls are spread out on the table.'

Where the plural words do differ from plural affixes in other languages is in their shape and distribution: they are for the most part free word forms, and they need not occur next to the noun they pluralize. This is illustrated in (8), where Teiwa *non* occurs next to the adjective *sib* 'clean' while pluralising *gakon* 'his shirt'. Similarly in (9) we see Adang *nun* follows the verb *matɛ* 'large' modifying the head noun *ti* 'tree'.

(8) Teiwa (Klamer, Teiwa corpus)
Uy masar ga-kon sib non gaʔan, ma tonaʔ.
person male 3SG.POSS-shirt clean PL DEM come collect
'Those clean shirts of that man, collect them.'

(9) Adang (Robinson & Haan 2014: 252)
Pen ti matɛ nun ʔa-bɔʔɔi.
Pen tree large PL 3INCL.OBJ-cut
'Pen cut some large trees.'

---

² Here the plural word must have scope over both nouns, such that this example cannot be read to mean "my buffalo and my goats".

Plural words in AP languages cannot co-occur with a numeral in a single NP. For instance, in Teiwa, a noun can be pluralized with either a plural word or with a numeral (plus optional classifier) (10a-b), but not with both at the same time (10c). Adang shows the same restriction; the plural word *nun* cannot co-occur with a numeral, compare (11a-b).[3]

(10) Teiwa (Klamer, Teiwa corpus)

    a. *war non*
       rock PL

       '(several/many) rocks'

    b. *war (bag) haraq*
       rock CLF two

       'two rocks'

    c. **war (bag) haraq non*
       rock CLF two PL

       Intended: 'two rocks'

(11) Adang (Robinson & Haan 2014: 253)

    a. *sɛi   nun ho ʔuhuɲ ɛ bɛŋ   tanib*
       water PL DEF pour and other draw.water.from.well

       'Pour out that little bit of water and get some more from the well.'

    b. **sɛi   nun alɔ ho ʔuhuɲ ɛ bɛŋ   tanib*
       water PL two DEF pour and other draw.water.from.well

       Intended: 'Pour out the two bits of water and get some more from the well.'

In sum, proto-Alor-Pantar had a plural word of the shape **non*. Some Alor-Pantar languages inherited both form and function, others innovated a plural word. The languages under investigation do not show restrictions on which referents can be marked plural, and in none of the languages does the plural word co-occur with a numeral in an NP.

---

[3] A combination of a mass noun and a numeral is also ungrammatical: **sɛi ut* 'water four' (Haan 2001: 296).

3 Syntax of plural words in Alor-Pantar

The plural words investigated in Dryer (1989) are very heterogeneous in their categorial properties. They belong to one of the following classes: (i) articles; (ii) numerals; (iii) grammatical number words like singular, dual, trial; (iv) a closed class of noun modifiers; and (v) a class of their own. Dryer concludes that "there is little basis for using the term [plural word] as a syntactic category" (1989: 879).

In this section, we investigate the syntax of plural words in Western Pantar (§ 3.1), Teiwa (§ 3.2), Kamang (§ 3.3), Abui (§ 3.4) and Wersing (3.5). For each language, we describe the template of the NP as well as the position and combinatorial properties of the plural word. We confirm Dryer's observation that there is little syntactic unity in plural words across languages. Our description focuses on the following issues:

1. Does the plural word occur in the NP?
2. How does the plural word behave in respect to quantifiers in the NP?
3. Can the plural word alone form an NP?

The languages under discussion differentiate the plural word from other syntactic classes. We will see that significant variation exists in terms of which syntactic class the plural word class resembles most. In Wersing, the plural word shares many properties with nouns, while in Kamang the plural word is most similar to pronouns. In Western Pantar and Teiwa, the plural words are comparable with numerals and quantifiers.

3.1 Western Pantar

The template of the Western Pantar NP is presented in (12) (Holton 2014). The NP is maximally composed of a head noun (N) followed by an adjective in the attribute slot (ATTR), followed by numeral phrases with an optional classifier ((CLF) NUM) or a plural word (PL), a demonstrative (DEM) and an article (ART).

(12) Template of the Western Pantar NP[4]
 [N ATTR{(CLF) NUM / PL}DEM ART]$_{NP}$

Western Pantar has no dedicated slot for (non-numeral) quantifiers, as these behave like adjectives or like nouns: adjectival quantifiers go in the ATTR slot

---

[4] Western Pantar does not have relative clauses.

(13), while nominal quantifiers occur in apposition to the NP, to the right of the article (14).

(13) Western Pantar (Holton 2014)
   Wakke-wakke haweri wang Tubbe birang kalalang.
   child~RDP many exist T. speak know
   'Most/many children can speak the Tubbe language.'

(14) Western Pantar (Holton 2014)
   [[*Hai bloppa sing*]~NP~ *der*]~NP~ *ga-r diakang.*
   2SG.POSS weapon ART some 3SG-with descend
   'Bring down some of your weapons.' [publia152]

Nominal plurality is expressed by the plural word *maru(ng)*, (15).[5] The use of numerals is illustrated in (16), and (17)-(18) show that numeral and plural word do not co-occur in a single NP.

(15) Western Pantar (Holton 2012)
   Bal marung mea tang pering.
   ball PL table on pour
   'A bunch of balls are spread out on the table.'

(16) Western Pantar (Holton 2012)
   Bal ara atiga, kalla yasing, mea tang ti?ang.
   ball large three small five table on set
   'Three large balls and five small balls are sitting on the table.'

(17) Western Pantar (Holton 2012)
   a. **ke?e kealaku maru*
      fish twenty PL
      Intended: 'twenty fish'
   b. **ke?e bina maru*
      fish CLF PL
      Intended: 'twenty fish'

---

[5] *Marung* has cognate forms in three AP languages: Klon *maang*, Kula *araman* (with liquid nasal metathesis) and Sawila *maarang* (Schapper & Huber Ms.)

(18) Western Pantar (Holton 2012)

    a. *keʔe maru kealaku
       fish PL   twenty
       Intended: 'twenty fish'

    b. *keʔe maru bina
       fish PL   CLF
       Intended: 'twenty fish'

Maru(ng) cannot substitute for a whole NP and function independently as a verbal argument, compare (19a) and (19b).

(19) Western Pantar (Holton 2012)

    a. *Raya marung lama ta.*
       chief PL   walk IPFV
       'The chiefs walk.'

    b. **Marung lama ta.*
       PL   walk IPFV
       Intended: 'They walk.'

In sum, Western Pantar *marung* can only be used as a nominal attribute within an NP. It is in complementary distribution with adjectival quantifiers and numerical expressions and lacks nominal properties.

3.2 Teiwa

The template of the Teiwa NP is presented in (20). The NP is maximally composed of a head noun (N) followed by an attributive (ATTR) noun, derived nominal or adjective, followed by a numeral phrase (indicated by {})consisting of either a numeral with an optional classifier ((CLF) NUM) or a plural word with an optional quantifier (PL (Q)), a demonstrative (DEM) and a demonstrative particle in the article (ART) slot.

(20) Template of the Teiwa NP[6]
    [N ATTR{(CLF) NUM / PL (Q)} DEM ART]_NP

In the DEM slot, we often find *gaʔan* (glossed as 'that.KNWN'), a 3SG object pronoun that also functions as a demonstrative modifier of nouns. In the ART slot are the demonstrative particles *u* 'DISTAL' and *a* 'PROXIMATE'. These particles occupy the NP-final position, marking definiteness and/or the location of NP referent with respect to the speaker.

The plural word has its own slot within the NP. It cannot combine with numeral constituents as those in (21a); compare (21b) with (22a-c). However, *non* can be combined with a quantifier in an NP, as shown in (23) and (24). Note that *dum* 'many/much' is used contrastively here.

(21) Teiwa (Klamer, Teiwa corpus)

    a. *war (bag) haraq*
       rock CLF two

       'two rocks'

    b. *war non*
       rock PL

       'rocks'

(22) Teiwa (Klamer, Teiwa corpus)

    a. **war haraq non*
       rock two PL

       Intended: 'two rocks'

    b. **war bag haraq non*
       rock CLF two PL

       Intended: 'two rocks'

    c. **war bag non*
       rock CLF PL

       Intended: 'two rocks'

(23) Teiwa (Klamer, Teiwa corpus)
Hala [qavif non dum]$_{NP}$ *pin aria?*?
someone goat PL many hold arrive

'Were many [rather than few] goats brought here?'

(24) Teiwa (Klamer, Teiwa corpus)
[Wat non dum]$_{NP}$ *usan ma!*
coconut PL many pick.up come

'Pick up the many coconuts.' [situation: there are many coconuts in a pile of various kinds of fruits, and the order is to pick up these, not the rest]

Non does not substitute for an NP and cannot function independently as a verbal argument, either with or without the distal demonstrative particle *u* that functions as an (grammatically optional) article in (25b-c). It must always remain part of the NP, as shown by the ungrammaticality of (25d).

(25) Teiwa (Klamer, Teiwa corpus)

    a. [*G-oqai non u*]_{NP} *min-an tau.*
       3SG-child PL DIST die-REAL PFV
       'Her children (lit. those her children) have died.'

    b. *[*Non u*]_{NP} *min-an tau.*
       PL DIST die-REAL PFV
       Intended: 'They have died.'

    c. *[*Non*]_{NP} *min-an tau.*
       PL die-REAL PFV
       Intended: 'They have died.'

    d. *[*G-oqai u*]_{NP} *non min-an tau.*
       3SG-child DIST PL die-REAL PFV
       Intended: 'Her children (they) have died.'

Just as Western Pantar *maru(ng)*, Teiwa *non* can occur in an NP that stands in apposition with a pronoun (26):

(26) Teiwa (Klamer, Teiwa corpus)
    [*Kemi non*]_{NP} *iman xap gu-uyan mat...*
    ancestor PL they bride 3.OBJ-search take
    '(Our) ancestors (they) searched for brides...'

It is possible for an NP with *non* to be part of the subject of numeral predication if the numeral predicate also contains a classifier, as illustrated in (27), where *bag* is the generic numeral classifier (Klamer 2014b) and combines with *tiaam* 'six'. The plural word *non* is part of the subject NP, and is grammatically optional. Subjects pluralized with *non* can thus occur with a numeral predicate.

However, an NP with *non* cannot be the subject of a quantifier predication with *dum* 'many/much', compare (28a-b). This is because the Teiwa plural word *non* often has the connotation of 'many' and 'plenty' (see § 4.2). A subject NP like the one in (28) already implies that there are 'many/plenty goats', so that combining it with a predicate 'be many' in (28b) is semantically redundant.

375

(27) Teiwa (Klamer, Teiwa corpus)
 [Ga-qavif (non)]_{NP} [un bag tiaam]_{Pred}
 3SG-goat PL CONT CLF six
 'His goats are six.'

(28) Teiwa (Klamer, Teiwa corpus)

  a. [Ga-qavif]_{NP} [un dum]_{Pred}
   3SG-goat CONT many
   'His goats are many.'

  b. *[Ga-qavif non]_{NP} [un dum]_{Pred}
   3SG-goat PL CONT many
   Intended: 'His many/plenty goats are many.'

The fact that *non* does not combine with a numeral in a single NP suggests that it patterns with the numeral word class. However, unlike numerals, *non* cannot combine with a classifier. On the other hand, *non* can combine with the quantifier *dum* 'much/many' in a single NP, which a numeral cannot do. However, at the same time, *non* does not pattern with the class of quantifiers for two reasons. First, such quantifiers can occur as predicates, while *non* cannot, (29a-b); and second, non-numeral quantifiers can occur both inside the NP (30a) as well as outside of it, adjacent to the verb (30b), while *non* must remain within the NP. In (30c) the NP contains *non*, and the ungrammaticality of (30d) shows that *non* cannot occur in the position adjacent to the verb.

(29) Teiwa (Klamer, Teiwa corpus)

  a. *Masar* [un dum]_{Pred}
   male CONT many
   'There are many men.' (Lit. 'Males are [being] many.')

  b. **Masar* [un non].
   male CONT PL
   Intended: 'There are many/several males.'

(30) Teiwa (Klamer, Teiwa corpus)

  a. [Qavif dum ga?an]_{NP} hala tatax.
   goat many that.KNWN someone chop
   'Many (known) goats were chopped up.'

b. [*Qavif ga?an*]~NP~ hala   dum tatax.
   goat that.KNWN someone many chop

   'Many of these (known) goats were chopped up.'

c. [*Qavif non ga?an*]~NP~ hala   tatax.
   goat PL that.KNWN someone chop

   'These (known) goats were chopped up by someone.'

d. *[*Qavif ga?an*]~NP~ hala   non tatax
   goat that.KNWN someone PL chop

   Intended: 'These (known) goats were chopped up.'

In sum, Teiwa *non* does not have any nominal properties, shares some of the distributional properties of numerals and quantifiers, and constitutes its own syntactic class.[7]

3.3 Kamang

The template of the Kamang noun phrase (NP) is presented in (31). The NP is maximally composed of a head noun (N) followed by its attribute (ATTR), a numeral phrase (NUM), a relative clause (RC), a demonstrative (DEM) and an article (ART). The article marks the right edge of an NP and is used to nominalize (i.e., create NPs from) clauses and other non-nominal phrases in the language. In addition, a Kamang NP can occur with a range of items co-referential with it in a slot outside the NP, called here the NP-appositional (APPOS) slot (discussed further below). The apposition between an NP and an item in the NP-appositional slot is syntactically tight: there is no intonational break or pause between NP and appositional item, and no item may intervene between them. For more details on the status of the APPOS slot or for discussion of the other NP slots, see Schapper (2014a).

(31) Template of the Kamang NP (Schapper 2014a)
     [N~HEAD~ ATTR NUMP RC DEM ART]~NP~ Appos

---

[7] In addition to the plural word, Teiwa has four dedicated pronoun series for referents of different quantificational types: (i) the dual paradigm (*we two*, etc.), (ii) the "X and they" paradigm (*you (sg/pl) and they, s/he/they and they; I/we (incl/excl) and they*), (iii) the "X alone" paradigm (*I alone, you alone*, etc.) and (iv) the "X as a group of …" paradigm (*we/you/they as a group of x numbers*) (Klamer 2010: 82-85). The plural word cannot co-occur with these pronouns. Teiwa has no associative plural word. To express associative plural notions, a form from the special pronoun series "X and they" is used, e.g., *Rini i-qap a-kawan aria' wad* 'Rini 3-and.they 3-friend arrive today', '*Today Rini arrived with her friends*'.

The Kamang plural word *nung* is conspicuously absent from the template in (31). In Kamang *nung* does not occur within the NP, but directly follows it. That is, it occurs to the right of the NP article, where one is expressed. For example, in (32) and (33) *nung* follows the specific ('SPEC') and definite ('DEF') articles respectively. The alternative order with the article following *nung* is not grammatical: **nung=a* 'PL=SPEC' and **nung=ak* 'PL=DEF'. In short, *nung* only occurs in the NP-appositional slot.

(32) Kamang (Schapper, fieldnotes)
Almakang laising-laung=a nung yeʔ-baa   sue.
people   youthful=SPEC PL   3.SBEN-say arrive
'Go tell the young people to come.'

(33) Kamang (Schapper, fieldnotes)
Muut=ak   nung iduka.
citrus=DEF PL   sweet
'The citrus fruits are sweet.'

By contrast, other Kamang quantifiers can occur within the NP, i.e., to the left of the NP-defining article. Non-numeral quantifiers such as *adu* 'many/much' occupy the ATTR slot within the NP and cannot float out of it, as seen in (34).

(34) Kamang (Schapper, fieldnotes)

　a. *sibe   adu=a*
　　 chicken many=SPEC
　　 'the many chickens'

　b. **sibe=a   adu*
　　 chicken=SPEC many
　　 Intended: 'the many chickens'

Kamang does not have a syntactic class of non-numeral quantifiers; items denoting *many, few, a little*, etc. are adjectives and occur in the ATTR slot of the NP. Numeral quantifiers occur with a classifier in the NUMP. The unmarked position for the NUMP is within the NP to the left of the article (35a), and the marked position is post-posed into the NP-appositional slot outside the NP (35b). The latter position is less frequent and pragmatically marked, functioning to topicalize the enumeration of the NP referent.

(35) Kamang (Schapper, fieldnotes)

    a. *sibe*   [*uh su*]$_{\text{NumP}}$=*a*
        chicken CLF three=SPEC
        'the three chickens'

    b. *sibe*=*a*   [*uh su*]$_{\text{NumP}}$
        chicken=SPEC CLF three
        'the chickens, the three ones'

The plural word shares distributional properties in common not only with a NumP but also with a pronoun, since the NP-appositional position can also host a pronoun. In (36) we see that a pronoun (36a) and a plural word (36b) respectively can both occur in the slot following an NP. In these examples, the parts of the free translations in curly brackets are the semantics contributed by the items in the appositional slot.

(36) Kamang (Schapper, fieldnotes)

    a. *almakang*=*ak gera*
        people=DEF 3.CONTR
        'the {specific group of} people {not some other group}'

    b. *almakang*=*ak nung*
        people=DEF PL
        'the {multiple} people'

The Kamang plural word has a distribution similar to that of an NP in two respects. Firstly, *nung* can substitute for a whole NP, where reference is sufficiently clear. For instance, in (37) *nung* is the sole element representing the S of the verb *sue* 'come'. Secondly, like an NP, a plural word can itself occur with a pronoun in the NP appositional slot where no NP is expressed, as in (38).

(37) Kamang (Schapper, fieldnotes)
     [*Nung*]$_{\text{NP}}$ *sue*.
     PL   arrive
     '{Multiple} (people) arrived.'

(38) Kamang (Schapper, fieldnotes)
     [*Nung*]$_{\text{NP}}$ *gera*$_{\text{APPOS}}$ *sue*.
     PL   3.CONTR arrive
     '{Multiple other} (people) arrived.'

Nung is not compatible with any other quantificational items. That is, despite its occurring outside the NP, marking an NP with *nung* means that other quantificational items cannot occur in the NP. This is seen in the examples in (39) where *nung* cannot grammatically co-occur with the numeral quantifier *su* 'three' (39a) and with the non-numeral quantifier *adu* 'many' (39b).

(39) Kamang (Schapper, fieldnotes)

    a. **sibe   uh su   nung*
       chicken CLF three PL
       Intended: 'three chickens'

    b. **sibe   adu   nung*
       chicken many PL
       Intended: 'many chickens'

In addition to the plural word, Kamang has multiple dedicated quantificational pronoun series to signal different quantificational types.[8] For instance, we see the third person pronouns forms for group plurality and universal quantification in (40) and (41) respectively. The plural word cannot co-occur with these pronouns.

(40) Kamang (Schapper, fieldnotes)
Geifu   loo   maa.
3.GROUP walk go
'They go together (as a group).'

(41) Kamang (Schapper, fieldnotes)
Gaima bisa wo-ra=bo   pilan.
3.ALL can 3.LOC-wear=LNK lego-lego
'They all can wear (them) and dance in a lego-lego.'

The use of quantificational pronouns with NPs is illustrated in (42) and (43). We see in these examples that the quantificational pronouns fill the appositional slot in the same manner as the plural word *nung* and signal the plurality of the referents of the preceding NP.

---

[8] There are four "quantifying" pronominal paradigms in Kamang: (i) the "alone" paradigm (*I alone/on my own, we alone/on our own*, etc.), (ii) the dual paradigm (*we two*, etc.- only in non-singular numbers), (iii) the "all" paradigm (*we all*, etc.- only in non-singular numbers), and (iv) the "group" paradigm (*we together in a group*, etc.- only in non-singular numbers). See Schapper (2014a) for full set of Kamang pronominal paradigms.

(42) Kamang (Schapper, fieldnotes)
[*Mane ang*]~NP~ *geifu*~APPOS~ *mauu.*
village DEM 3.GROUP war

'Those villages make war together (against another village).'

(43) Kamang (Schapper, fieldnotes)
[*Arita pang*]~NP~ *gaima*~APPOS~ *luaa-ra   lai-ma.*
leaf DEM 3.ALL whither-AUX finished-PFV

'All the leaves have withered completely.'

Finally, Kamang has a suffix marking associative plurality, *-lee* 'ASSOC'. This suffix can occur on kin terms or proper names, as in (44) and (45) respectively. Nouns marked by *-lee* cannot be modified by any other NP elements. The plural word *nung* does not occur in such contexts.

(44) Kamang (Schapper, fieldnotes)
..., *ge-dum-lee   see   silanta malii*
... 3.GEN-child-ASSOC arrive mourn mourn

'..., her children and their associates come to mourn.'

(45) Kamang (Schapper, fieldnotes)
Marten-lee   n-at   tak.
Marten-ASSOC 1SG-from run

'Marten and his associates run away from me.'

So, the Kamang plural word occurs outside the NP and shares distributional properties of pronouns. The semantics of the plural word also intersects with pronouns, in particular, the quantificational pronouns whose functions are to denote different number features.

3.4 Abui

The template of the Abui NP is presented in (46).[9] The NP is composed of a head noun (N) followed by its attribute (ATTR). The Abui plural word *loku* is not etymologically related to the plural word that is reconstructable for pAP. It has a variable position with respect to the relative clause (RC), being able to either precede or follow the plural word. The plural word occurs inside the NP and thus always occurs to left to the determiner (DET).

---

[9] The morphosyntactic analysis and glossing of Abui presented here is that of Schapper, and differs from that presented in Kratochvíl (2007). Examples are individually marked as to source.

(46) Template of the Abui NP
[N ATTR {PL RC / RC PL } DET]_NP

The variable position of *loku* in relation to the relative clause is illustrated in (47) and (48). In (47) *loku* appears after the relative clause but before the demonstrative *yo*. In (48) *loku* precedes both the relative clause and the article *nu*. The two plural word positions are mere variants of one another; extensive elicitation and the examination of corpus data have revealed no difference in the scope or semantics correlating with the plural word's position, although corpus frequency and speaker judgments point to the position preceding the relative clause as being preferred.

(47) Abui (Kratochvíl, Abui corpus)
[...*oto he-amakaang* [*ba h-omi mia*]_RC *loku yo*]_NP *mi pak*
car 3.GEN-person REL 3.GEN-inside in PL DEM take cliff
mahoi-ni
gather-PFV
'...those people who were inside the car were taken over the [edge of the] cliff.'

(48) Abui (Kratochvíl, Abui corpus)
[*Sieng loku* [*ba uti mia*]_RC *nu*]_NP *sik bakon-i mi melang*
rice PL REL garden in ART pluck rip.off.PFV-PFV take village
sei.
come.down
'Pluck off [all] the rice that is in the garden [and] take it down to the village.'

Loku cannot co-occur in an NP together with any quantifiers; numeral (49a) or non-numeral (49b). However, it is possible for an NP with *loku* to be the subject of both numeral and non-numeral quantifier predications (50a-b). This indicates that, whilst double marking of quantification/plurality is not permitted within the NP, there is no semantic redundancy in the quantificational values of the Abui plural word and other quantifiers. In this respect, Abui *loku* differs from Teiwa *non* (§ 3.2).

(49) Abui (Schapper, fieldnotes)

a. **He-wiil taama loku nu mon-i.*
3.GEN-child six PL ART die.PFV-PFV
Intended: 'His six children died.'

b. *He-wiil   faring loku nu   mon-i.
   3.GEN-child many PL   ART die.PFV-PFV
   Intended: 'His many children died.'

(50) Abui (Schapper, fieldnotes)

a. He-wiil   loku nu taama.
   3.GEN-child PL   ART six
   'His children were six.' i.e., 'He had six children.'

b. He-wiil   loku nu faring.
   3.GEN-child PL   ART many
   'His children were many.' i.e., 'He had many children.'

Loku can be used to modify a third person pronoun, as in (51) and (52). Abui has no number distinction in the third person of its pronominal series. By using *loku* the plural reference can be made explicit.

(51) Abui (Kratochvíl, Abui corpus)
    Hel loku abui   yaa ut   teak.
    3   PL   mountain go garden watch
    'They went to the mountains to check the garden.'

(52) Abui (Kratochvíl, Abui corpus)
    Hel loku he-sepatu   he-tawida.
    3   PL   3.GEN-shoe 3.GEN-be.alike
    'They have the same shoes.'

Loku must co-occur with a noun or with the third person pronoun *hel*. It cannot stand alone in an NP.

In addition to the general plural word *loku*, Abui has an associative plural word, *we* 'ASSOC'. This item only appears marking proper names for humans and has the meaning '[name] and people associated with [name]' and occurs directly after the noun it modifies, as in (53a). When *loku* is used in the same context (53b), the reading is not one of associative plurality, but of individualized plurality. *Loku* and *we* can co-occur, and either can precede the other, as shown in (53c).

(53) a. Abui (Schapper, fieldnotes)
       Benny we   ut   yaa.
       Benny ASSOC garden go.to
       'Benny and his associates go to the garden.'

383

b. *Benny loku ut yaa.*
Benny PL garden go.to
'Different individuals called Benny go to the garden.'

c. *Benny loku we / Benny we loku ut yaa.*
Benny PL ASSOC / Benny ASSOC PL garden go.to
'Two or more people called Benny go to the garden.'

Connected to its individualising semantics, *loku* may be used with verbs to make expressions for collections of people. Examples are given in (54).

(54) a. Abui (Kratochvíl 2007: 155)
pe loku
near PL
lit. 'the near ones'; i.e. 'neighbours'

b. *firai loku*
run PL
lit. 'the running ones'; i.e. 'runners'

c. *walangra loku*
fresh PL
lit. 'the new ones'; i.e. 'the newcomers, the Malays'

Abui differs from the more western languages (such as Western Pantar and Teiwa) in that it has two plural words marking different kinds of plurality.

3.5 Wersing

The template for the Wersing noun phrase (NP) is given in (55). Modifiers follow the head noun of the NP (N_{HEAD}). They are an attribute (ATTR), a numeral (NUM) or the plural word(PL), and a relative clause (RC). Right-most in the NP is a determiner (DET). See Schapper & Hendery (2014) for details and full illustration of the Wersing NP.

(55) Template of the Wersing NP
$[N_{HEAD}$ ATTR NUM/PL RC DET$]_{NP}$

The Wersing plural word is *deing*. As is clear from template (55), it occurs in the NP in the same slot as a numeral. It cannot be used in combination with a numeral or any non-numeral quantifier (which are typically simple intransitive verbs that appear in the ATTR slot), as illustrated in (56).

9 Plural number words in the Alor-Pantar languages

(56) Wersing (Schapper and Hendery, Wersing corpus)

    a. **aning weting deing*
       person five   PL
       Intended: 'five people'

    b. **aning bal deing*
       person many PL
       Intended: 'many people'

Deing need not occur with an overt noun in the NP, but can stand alone so long as the referent can be retrieved from the discourse context. So, for instance, the head noun *gis* in (57a) can be elided, as in the following examples (57b-d). What is more, the NP can be reduced to the plural word (57d) where there is neither noun head nor article.

(57) Wersing (Schapper and Hendery, Wersing corpus)

    a. *g-is   kebai dein=a*
       3-content young PL=ART
       'their (coconut) young flesh'

    b. *kebai dein=a*
       young PL=ART
       'the young (flesh)'

    c. *dein=a*
       PL=ART
       'the (young flesh)'

    d. *deing*
       PL
       'the (young flesh)'

Like Kamang and the other eastern Alor languages, and Teiwa on Pantar, Wersing has multiple pronominal paradigms dedicated to denoting particular quantities of referents, for instance, universal quantification ('ALL') (58) and group plurality ('GROUP') (59).[10] Such quantificational pronouns also play an important

---

[10] There are five "quantifying" pronominal paradigms in Wersing: (i) the "alone" paradigm (*I alone (no one else)*, etc.), (ii) the "independent" paradigm (*I on my own without help*, etc.), (iii) the dual paradigm (*we two*, etc.- only in non-singular numbers), (iv) the "all" paradigm (*we all*, etc.- only in non-singular numbers), and (v) the "group" paradigm (*we together in a group*, etc.- only in non-singular numbers) (Schapper & Hendery 2014).

role in marking plurality of NP referents in Wersing. In (60) we see, for instance, the 3rd person pronoun *genaing* being used to signal the plurality of the referents of the preceding NP.[11]

(58) Wersing (Schapper & Hendery 2014: 463)
 Tanaing dra bo!
 1PL.INCL.ALL sing EMPH
 'Let's sing.'

(59) Wersing (Schapper & Hendery 2014: 479)
 Nyawi nyi-mit o!
 1PL.EXCL.GROUP 1PL.EXCL-sit EXCLAM
 'Let's sit together!'

(60) Wersing (Schapper & Hendery 2014: 495)
 Ge-siriping genaing beteng ge-dai.
 3-root 3.ALL pull 3-come.up
 'All its roots were pulled right up.'

Wersing *deing* can nevertheless mark plurality for non-singular numbers of topic pronouns, as in (61) and (62). In this respect, then, the Wersing plural word is not like a pronoun as in Kamang, but a distinct item which can modify any NP head, nominal or pronominal.

(61) Wersing (Schapper and Hendery, Wersing corpus)
 Gai dein=a mona min-a.
 3.TOP PL=ART ACROSS be.at-REAL
 'They are all over there.'

(62) Wersing (Schapper and Hendery, Wersing corpus)
 Nyai deing o-min-a.
 1PL.EXCL.TOP PL HERE-be.at-REAL
 'We are all here.'

Wersing has a further plural word, *naing*, which marks associative plurality. This form has been observed only marking personal names, as in (63) and (64).

---

[11] A pronoun of this paradigm can also be marked with *-le*, as in: *Aning ge-naingle kamar ming=te nanal te-mekeng* (3.ALL-PL room be.in=CONJ thing RECP-exchange) 'All of those who are in the room exchange things'. The *-le* suffix does not appear on nouns or any other pronominal series in Wersing; it is likely cognate with the Kamang associative plural marker *-lee* (see § 3.3).

As an associative plural word, it doesn't have the ability to stand in for a NP. Like *deing*, *naing* cannot occur with other quantifiers, numeral and non-numeral.

(63) Wersing (Malikosa nd)
Petrus naing g-aumeng ga-pang ge-pai.
Peter ASSOC 3-fear 3-dead 3-make
'Peter and the others were afraid to die.'

(64) Wersing (Malikosa nd)
Yesus naing lailol gewai Kapernaum taing.
Jesus ASSOC walk 3-go Kapernaum reach
'Jesus and the others walked onto Kapernaum.'

3.6 Summary

Most Alor-Pantar languages have inherited a plural word, but they show much variation in the syntactic properties of this word. Table 2 presents a summary of the variable syntax discussed in the previous sections.

Table 2: Variable syntax of five Alor-Pantar plural words

	Teiwa	W Pantar	Kamang	Abui	Wersing
Is plural word part of NP?	yes	yes	no	yes	yes
Can plural word stand alone in NP?	no	no	–	no	yes
Can the plural word and non-numeral quantifier co-occur?	yes	no	no	no	no
Can plural word and numeral co-occur?	no	no	no	no	no

The table reveals the gradient differences between plural words in Alor-Pantar languages. Kamang stands out from the other four languages for the fact that the plural word is not part of the NP. Of the languages that do have their plural word in the NP, the plural word cannot typically stand alone in the NP, but requires another, nominal, element be present. In Wersing, however, this is only the case for the associative plural word *deing*; its plural number word can form independent NPs. Alor-Pantar plural words are prohibited from co-occurring with quantifiers.

No language allows co-occurrence with a numeral quantifier and only Teiwa permits co-occurrence with a non-numeral quantifier.

These different properties mean that in all five languages, plural word(s) constitutes a word class of its own, with only partial overlap with other morpho-syntactic classes of words. In Western Pantar, the plural word shares much with adjectival quantifiers and numerical expressions. In Teiwa, the plural word patterns mostly with non-numeral quantifiers. In Kamang and Wersing, plural words pattern similarly to quantificational pronouns in denoting the number of a preceding noun. However, Wersing *deing* behaves much more like a nominal element. Nominal properties are also visible in the Abui word *loku*, particularly in its frequent use with verbs to form expressions for collections of people.

In short, Alor-Pantar plural words are a morpho-syntactically diverse group of items that are seemingly united only by their semantic commonalities. Yet, as we will see in the following sections, even the semantics of plurality reveal more variability than might have been expected.

4 Semantics of plural words in Alor-Pantar

In all five languages, the plural words code plurality alongside other notions. In this section, we review three additional connotations of the plural word.

4.1 Completeness

The Western Pantar plural word *maru(ng)* typically imparts a sense of entirety, completeness, and comprehensiveness, as in (65):

(65) Western Pantar (Holton, Western Pantar corpus)
Ping   pi   mappu   maiyang, lokke   maiyang saiga si,
1PL.INCL 1PL.INCL.POSS fishpond place   fishtrap place   DEM ART
gai   ke?e maru si   aname ging   haggi kanna.
3.POSS fish PL   ART person 3PL.ACT take already
'We placed our fishponds, placed our fish traps, and then people took all the fish.'

Its sense of comprehensiveness and entirety explains why NPs pluralized with *maru(ng)* can be the subject of the nominal predicate *gaterannang* 'all' expressing universal quantity, as in (66), while combinations of *marung* and mid-range quantifiers such as *haweri* 'many' are absent in the Western Pantar corpus. It also explains why *marung* is not compatible with a numeral predicate, as in (67), as these indicate a quantity of a certain number rather than universal quantity.

(66) Western Pantar (Holton 2012)
[*Aname marung*] *ging gaterannang dia wang pidding.*
people PL they all go exist spread
'All the people spread out [to look for them]' (Holton 2012) (Lit. 'All people they were all going spreading ...')

(67) Western Pantar (Holton 2012)
*[*Aname marung*] *ging kealaku dia wang pidding.*
people PL they twenty go exist spread
Intended: 'All people they were twenty going spreading...'

Finally, *marung* is used with count nouns, and cannot combine with mass nouns such as *halia* 'water', (68). In this respect, *marung* contrasts with the plural words in Abui, Wersing, Kamang and Teiwa, which can combine with mass nouns (sections 4.2, 4.3.1).

(68) Western Pantar (Holton, p.c.)
**halia marung*
water PL
Intended: 'several containers of water'; 'multiple waters'

The connotation of comprehensiveness is also found in Abui *loku*. That is, the inclusion of *loku* signals that the whole mass of saliva was subject to the swarming of the birds in (69) and that all the available corn had to be stowed away (70) in an orderly fashion, so as to use the maximum capacity of the basket.

(69) Abui (Kratochvíl, Abui corpus)
... *kuya do sila nahang oro he-ya he-puyung loku*
... bird DEM much everywhere LEVEL 3.GEN-mother 3.GEN-saliva PL
do he-afai.
DEM 3.GEN-swarm
'Those birds were everywhere there, swarming over the saliva of his mother.'

(70) Abui (Kratochvíl, fieldnotes)
Fat loku mi ba buot he-rei
corn PL take CONJ back.basket 3.GEN-stow
'Stow all the corn in the basket.'

The sense of comprehensive quantity expressed by *loku* ('all') is relative to the situation at hand ('all that is there'). As a result, *loku* can occur with the universal quantifier *tafuda* 'all', as in (71).

(71) Abui (Kratochvíl, Abui corpus)
Ama [ne-mea   loku] tafuda takaf-i   do   n-omi
person 1SG.GEN-mango PL   all   steal-PFV DEM 1SG.GEN-inside
he-ukda
3.GEN-shock
'All my mangos got stolen, it really shocked me.'

In Wersing, the sense of comprehensiveness is found when the plural word is used together with an already plural topic pronoun. For instance, in (72) the use of *deing* implies that the whole set of those who were expected are present.

(72) Wersing (Schapper, fieldnotes)
Tai   deing o-min-a.
1PL.INCL.TOP PL   HERE-be.at-REAL
'We are all here.'

4.2 Abundance

In Teiwa and Wersing, using the plural word can add the sense that the referent occurs in particular abundance.

While the core semantics of Teiwa *non* is plural 'more than one' or 'several', it often has the connotation of 'many, plenty', as in (73). This is not true for all plural words in AP languages.

(73) Teiwa (Klamer, Teiwa corpus)
   a. *in   non*
      it.thing PL
      'plenty of things'
   b. *in   bun   non*
      it.thing bamboo PL
      'plenty of pieces of bamboo'
   c. *wou non*
      PL mango
      'plenty of mangos'

9 Plural number words in the Alor-Pantar languages

Especially when combining with nouns referring to utensils or consumables, the plurality of *non* often has the connotation 'plenty'. A similar reading is imposed when *non* combines with small objects such as flowers or insects. As these come in sets of conventionally large numbers, the use of *non* implies that their set is larger than expected. For instance, *haliwai non* in (74) refers to black ants as crawling into the sarong in unexpected numbers.

(74) Teiwa (Klamer, Teiwa corpus)
…*a mis-an haliwai non daa nuan gom ma yiri u si,…*
3SG sit-REAL black.ant PL ascend cloth inside come crawl DIST SIM

'…(while) he sat (unexpectedly many) black ants came crawling into his sarong,…'

There are other specific readings that *non* may get, varying according to the type of nominal referent and the pragmatics of the situation. For example, when *non* combines with objects such as seeds, chairs, or rocks, it may imply that they occur in a set that has an unusual configuration which is more disorderly than the conventional one, such as when seeds are spilled across the floor rather than in a bag or a pile, or when chairs are scattered around the room instead of organized around a table. Finally, *non* may also code that the set is non-homogeneous, e.g., *war non* may refer to 'several rocks', but also to 'rocks of various kinds and sizes'.

Wersing also reflects this sense, when referring to inanimates, especially where they have little individuation. In (75) the use of *deing* to modify *wor* 'rock' and *inipak* 'sand' suggests that an abundance of these items are swept up by the wind. Without the plural word, there would be no indication of the amount of rock and sand moved by the wind.

(75) Wersing (Schapper, fieldnotes)
Tumur lapong gai ge-tati=sa, wor anta inipak lang=mi dein=a
east.wind wind 3.A 3-stand=CONJ rock or sand beach=LOC PL=ART
ge-poing ge-dai medi aruku le-ge-ti.
3-hit 3-go.up take dry.land APPL-3-lie

'When the east wind blows, a mass of rocks and sand from the beach is lifted up and deposited on dry land (beyond the beach).'

Such senses of abundance have not been observed with the plural word in Western Pantar or Kamang.

4.3 Individuation

The use of a plural word often imposes an individuated reading of a referent, that is, that the referent is not an undifferentiated mass but rather is composed of an internally cohesive set of individuals of the same type. For instance, consider the contrast between the *we* and the *loku* plural in Abui in (76a-b), repeated from example (53) in § 3.4. The associative plural *we* gives a reading of a closely-knit group of individuals centred on one prominent individual, Benny. By contrast, the *loku* plural, when it is used in the same context, imposes a referentially heterogeneous or individualized reading whereby multiple distinct people of the same name are being referred to. This difference is also characteristic of the Wersing plural words *deing* 'PL' and *naing* 'ASSOC'.

(76) Abui (Schapper, fieldnotes)

    a. *Benny we ut yaa.*
       Benny ASSOC garden go.to
       'Benny and his associates go to the garden.'

    b. *Benny loku ut yaa.*
       Benny PL garden go.to
       'Different individuals called Benny go to the garden.'

There are two contexts in which we find a particular tendency of plural words in AP to impose individualized readings on the nouns they modify. These are discussed in the following subsections.

4.4 Individuation of mass to count

While they are typically used with count nouns, plural words may combine with mass nouns, provided these are recategorized. Combining a plural word with a mass noun indicates that it is interpreted as a count noun. For instance, Teiwa *yir* 'water' is interpreted as a mass in (77a), but gets an individuated reading in (77b) when it combines with *non*. In Kamang (78a) the noun *ili* 'water' combined with *nung* is individuated just like when it combines with the numeral *nok* 'one' (78b).[12]

---

[12] As we saw in § 4.1, Western Pantar *maru(ng)* does not have this individuating function due to the sense of comprehensiveness and completeness of the word.

(77) Teiwa (Klamer, Teiwa corpus)

    a. *Na yir ma gelas mia?.*
       1SG water OBL glass fill
       'I fill the glass with water.'

    b. *Na yir non ma drom mia?.*
       1SG water PL OBL drum fill
       'I fill the drum with several containers of water.'

(78) Kamang (Schapper & Klamer 2011)

    a. *ili nung*
       water PL
       '{multiple individual} waters'

    b. *ili nok*
       water one
       'a water'

The plural words in Abui and Wersing also occur together with mass nouns with readings of abundance, as discussed already in § 4.2. Western Pantar *marung* cannot combine with mass nouns.

4.5 Clan or place name to members

When Abui *loku* is combined with the name of a clan or a place name, the expression refers to the members belonging to that clan (79) or issuing from that place (80), a use that can be extended to the question word *te* 'where' (81).

(79) Abui (Kratochvíl 2007: 165)
    Afui Ata loku
    clan.name PL
    'people of the Afui Ata clan'

(80) Abui (Kratochvíl 2007: 166)
    Kafola loku
    Kabola PL
    'people from Kabola'

(81) Abui (Kratochvil, fieldnotes)
Edo te loku, naana?
2SG.FOC where PL older.sibling
'Where are you from, bro?'

A similar use is attested for Teiwa *non* when it is used to make an ethnonym from a clan name (82). However, Teiwa *non* cannot combine with place names.

(82) Teiwa (Klamer, Teiwa corpus)
Teiwa non gaʔan itaʔa ma gi?
clan.name PL that.KNWN where OBL go
'Where did that group of Teiwa [people] go to?'

This function of the plural word is not known to occur in Western Pantar, Kamang or Wersing. In Kamang this kind of plurality is encoded by the combination of a place name with a group plural pronoun, as in (83).

(83) Kamang (Schapper, fieldnotes)
Ga wo-suk-si=bo gafaa Takailubui geifu mauu-h=a,...
3.AGT 3.LOC-think-IPFV=LNK 3.ALONE Takailubui 3.GRP war-PURP=SPEC
'They think that if they alone make war against the people of Takailubui,...'

4.6 Partitive

Plural words also occur in contexts of partitive plural reference. This means that the plural can be used to pick out a part or group of referents from a larger set.

The Kamang plural word *nung* can be used for partitive plural reference, often with contrast between different subsets of referents. For instance, in (84) *nung* is used twice to divide the set of citruses into the multitude that are sweet and the multitude that are sour. Similarly, in (86) *nung* is used twice to contrast the sub-set of people who went to Molpui with the sub-set that went to the nearby village.

(84) Kamang (Stokhof 1982: 40)
Muut=ak nung iduka, ah=a nung alesei.
citrus=PL PL sweet CNCT=SPEC PL sour
'Some of these citrus fruits, others are sour.'

(85) Kamang (Stokhof 1978: 57)
Nung gera ye-iyaa ai Molpui wo-oi ye-te, nung
PL 3.CONTR 3.GEN-return take M. 3.LOC-to 3.GEN-go.up PL
gera yeeisol ye-iyaa ai mane wo-oi
3.CONTR straight 3.GEN-return take village 3.LOC-towards
ye-wete.
3.GEN-go.up.across
'Some of them went home going up to Molpui, others went straight home going up across to the village.'

The Wersing plural word can be used also in partitive plural reference, but does not typically make explicit contrasts between subsets using the plural word over multiple NPs. For instance, in (87) *deing* refers to a subset of candle nuts that have not yet been crushed, the other set is not explicitly mentioned but must simply be inferred from the discourse context. In (88), the other member of the whole (namely the speaker himself) is singular and so is not marked with the plural word, but he is contrasted with the set of others who are teaching other languages. This second plural set is accordingly marked with *deing*.

(86) Wersing (Schapper, fieldnotes)
Deing de naung.
PL IPFV NEG
'Some are still not done.'

(87) Wersing (Schapper, fieldnotes)
Naida Abui ge-lomu ong ge-tenara, pang=sa te-nong
1PL.EXCL.TOP Abui 3-language use 3-teach DEM=CONJ 1PL.INCL-friend
aumang dein=a Pantara ge-lomu ong ge-tenara war Sawila ge-lomu.
other PL=ART Pantar 3-language use 3-teach and Sawila 3-language
'I will teach them Abui and other friends of ours will teach them Pantar and Sawila.'

Such a contrastive use of the plural word has not been attested in Western Pantar and Abui, but may be a sense present in Teiwa *non*, see (22) and (23) (§ 3.2).

4.7 Vocative

A term of address, relation or kin can be also marked with a plural to express a plural vocative. Western Pantar *marung* has a vocative use in (89). Teiwa *non* can be used in vocatives with kin terms, for instance, when starting a speech (90) or in a hortative (91).

(88) Western Pantar (Holton, Western Pantar corpus)
Wenang marung hing yadda mising, nang na-ti?ang.
Mr PL PL NOT.YET sit I 1SG-sleep
'You all keep sitting, I'm going to sleep.'

(89) Teiwa (Klamer, Teiwa corpus)
Na-rat qai non oh!
1SG.POSS-grandchild PL EXCL
'Oh my grandchildren!'

(90) Teiwa (Klamer, Teiwa corpus)
Na-gas qai non, tup pi gi ina.
1SG-female.younger.sibling PL get.up 1PL.INCL go eat
'My (female) friends, let's get up to eat.'

Abui *loku* also can be present in vocative contexts with relational nouns (91) or kin terms (92).

(91) Abui (Schapper, fieldnotes)
Ne-feela loku, yaa fat ho-aneek.
1SG.GEN-friend PL go corn 3.LOC-weed
'My friends, go weed the corn.'

(92) Abui (Schapper, fieldnotes)
Ne-fing loku, me!
1SG.GEN-elder.sibling PL come
'My siblings, come on already.'

There is no reason to expect that plural words should not be usable in vocatives. Yet, the plural word is not found in Kamang or Wersing vocatives. In Kamang, there are a range of special vocatives for calling (a) child(ren) or (b) friend(s). A Kamang vocative suffix, when used, means that a noun cannot be further modified, for instance, with the plural word.

4.8 Summary

Plural words code more than plurality; they have additional connotations and usages which vary across the languages as summarized in Table 3.

Table 3: Semantics of Alor-Pantar plural words

	Teiwa	Abui	Wersing	W Pantar	Kamang
Completeness	no	yes	yes †	yes	no
Vocative	yes	yes	no	yes	no
Individuation: mass>count	yes	yes	no	no	yes
Individuation: name>members	yes	yes	no	no	no
Abundance	yes	no	yes ‡	no	no
Partitive	no	no	yes	no	yes

† On topic pronouns only. ‡With inanimates only.

5 Typological perspectives on plural words in AP languages

We saw in § 1 that a good deal of what was known of the typology of plural words is due to Matthew Dryer's work, in particular Dryer (1989; 2011) and to a lesser extent Dryer (2007). Dryer (2011) documents the use of plural words in the coding of nominal plurality. In doing so, Dryer wanted to prove the existence of a phenomenon that was not generally recognized, and his definitions reflect that. As mentioned in § 1, for Dryer, to be a plural word an item must be the prime indicator of plurality, and in the pure case they have this as their unique function. Based on this constrained characterization, Dryer shows that plural words nevertheless show considerable diversity.

First, while being by definition non-affixal, they vary according to their degree of phonological independence. Second, they show great variety in the word class to which they belong; they may be integrated (to a greater or lesser degree) into another class, or form a unique class. The examples from the Alor-Pantar languages show vividly the variety of plural words in this regard: in all of them, plural words form a unique class on their own, which is however integrated into another class - but which class is variable across the languages. For instance, in Teiwa, the plural word is part of the noun phrase and behaves largely like a nominal quantifier, while in Kamang, rather than actually being part of the noun phrase, the plural word distributes as a noun phrase itself.

Third, plural words may have different values. In this respect they are perhaps poorly named. Dryer (1989: 869) suggests that "grammatical number words" would be a better term, since he gives instances of singular words and dual words. This is an area where Alor-Pantar languages indicate how the typology can be taken forward. When we look at the full range of "ordinary" number values, those associated with affixal morphology, we distinguish 'determinate' and 'indeterminate' number values (Corbett 2000: 39-41). Determinate number values are those where only one form is appropriate, given the speaker's knowledge of the real world. If a language has an obligatory dual, for instance, this would be a determinate number value since to refer to two distinct entities this would be the required choice. However, values such as paucal or greater plural are not like this; there is an additional element to the choice. We find this same distinction in the Alor-Pantar number words: for instance, Teiwa *non* signals not just plurality but has the connotation of abundance (like the greater plural).

Fourth, a key part of the typology of number systems is the items to which the values can apply. Two systems may be alike in their values (say both have singular and plural) but may differ dramatically in that in one language almost all nominals have singular and plural available, while in the other plurality may be restricted to a small (top) segment of the Animacy Hierarchy. The data from Alor-Pantar languages are important in showing how this type of differentiation applies also with number words. With affixal number, we find instances of recategorization; these are found particularly where a mass noun is recategorized as a count noun, and then has singular and plural available. We see this equally in Alor-Pantar languages such as Kamang where *nung* is used with *ili* 'water', when recategorized as a count noun.

Furthermore, number words are not restricted to appearing with nouns. In Abui, plural *loku* can occur with a third person pronoun; *hel* is the third singular pronoun, which can be pluralized by *loku*. While this is of great interest, other languages go further. A fine example is Miskitu, a Misumalpan language of Nicaragua and Honduras. Number is marked by number words (Green ms. Andrew Koontz-Garboden, p.c.), singular (*kum*) and plural (*nani*). Pronouns take the plural word, rather like nouns:

(93) Miskitu (Green ms. Andrew Koontz-Garboden, p.c.)
 Yang nani kauhw-ri.
 1   PL   fall-1.PST.INDF
 'We (exclusive) fell.'

This example, like all those cited above from Alor-Pantar languages, helps to extend the typology of number words; as we gather a fuller picture, the typology of number words becomes increasingly like that of affixal number.

6 Conclusions

Proto-Alor-Pantar had a plural word of the shape *non. Some daughter languages inherited this form, others innovated one or more plural words. In none of the five AP languages investigated here do restrictions apply on the type of referents that can be pluralized with the plural word, and all of them prohibit a combination of the plural word and a numeral in a single constituent.

The syntax of the plural word varies. In each language investigated here the word constitutes a class of its own. In Western Pantar, the plural word shares much with adjectival quantifiers and numerical expressions, in Teiwa it patterns mostly with non-numeral quantifiers, and in Kamang, Abui and Wersing plural words function very much like nouns. The plural words in the five languages behave differently, so that it is not possible to establish a category of plural word that is cross-linguistically uniform.

The plural words all code plurality, but in all five languages they have additional connotations, such as expressing a sense of completeness or abundance. A plural word may also function to impose an individuated reading of a referent, or to pick out a part or group of referents from a larger set. Plural words are used to express plural vocatives. None of the additional senses and functions of the plural words is shared across all of the five languages.

What our study shows is that, even amongst five typologically similar and genetically closely related languages whose ancestor had a plural word, the original plural word has drifted in different syntactic directions and developed additional semantic dimensions, showing a degree of variation that is higher than any other inherited word.

Acknowledgments

We are grateful to the following colleagues for answering our questions and gracefully sharing their data: Gary Holton for Western Pantar, František Kratochvíl and Benny Delpada for Abui, and Louise Baird for Klon. We are also very grateful to Mary Darlymple and Martin Haspelmath for their comments on an earlier version of this paper.

Abbreviations

=	clitic boundary	FOC	focus
~	reduplication	GEN	genitive
1	1st person	INCL	inclusive
2	2nd person	INDF	indefinite
3	3rd person	IPFV	imperfective
ACT	actor	KNWN	known
AGT	agent	LNK	linker
ALL	all	LOC	locative
AP	Alor-Pantar	N	noun
APPL	applicative	NP	noun phrase
APPOS	apposition	NUM(P)	numeral (phrase)
ART	article	OBJ	object
ASSOC	associative	OBL	oblique
ATTR	attribute slot	pAP	proto-Alor-Pantar
AUX	auxiliary	PFV	perfective
CLF	classifier	PL	plural
CNCT	connector	POSS	possessive
CONJ	conjunction	PST	past
CONT	continuous	PURP	purposive
CONTR	contrastive focus	RC	relative clause
DEF	definite	RDP	reduplication
DEM	demonstrative	REAL	realis
DET	determiner	SBEN	self-benefactive
DIST	distal	SG	singular
EMPH	emphasis	SPEC	specific
EXCL	exclusive	TOP	topic
EXCLAM	exclamation	W (Pantar)	Western Pantar

References

Baird, Louise. 2008. *A grammar of Klon: a non-Austronesian language of Alor, Indonesia.* Canberra: Pacific Linguistics.

Corbett, Greville G. 2000. *Number* (Cambridge Textbooks in Linguistics). Cambridge: Cambridge University Press.

Dryer, Matthew S. 1989. Plural words. *Linguistics* 27. 865–895.

Dryer, Matthew S. 2007. Noun phrase structure. In Timothy Shopen (ed.), *Language typology and syntactic description. Complex constructions*, vol. 2, 151–205. Cambridge: Cambridge University Press.

Dryer, Matthew S. 2011. Coding of nominal plurality. In Matthew S. Dryer & Martin Haspelmath (eds.), *The World Atlas of Language Structures online*. Munich: Max Planck Digital Library. http://wals.info/chapter/33.

Green, Tom. ms. Covert clause structure in the Miskitu noun phrase. Unpublished paper. Cambridge, MA.

Haan, Johnson Welem. 2001. *The grammar of Adang: a Papuan language spoken on the island of Alor East Nusa Tenggara - Indonesia*. Sydney: University of Sydney PhD thesis.

Holton, Gary. 2012. *Number in the Papuan outliers of East Nusantara*. Paper presented at the International Conference on Austronesian Linguistics, Bali, 5 July 2012. Bali: International Conference on Austronesian Linguistics.

Holton, Gary. 2014. Western Pantar. In Antoinette Schapper (ed.), *Papuan languages of Timor, Alor and Pantar: Sketch grammars*, vol. 1, 23–96. Berlin: Mouton de Gruyter.

Holton, Gary & Mahalalel Lamma Koly. 2008. *Kamus pengantar Bahasa Pantar Barat: Tubbe - Mauta - Lamma*. Kupang, Indonesia: UBB-GMIT.

Klamer, Marian. 2010. *A grammar of Teiwa* (Mouton Grammar Library 49). Berlin: Mouton de Gruyter.

Klamer, Marian. 2011. *A short grammar of Alorese (Austronesian)* (Languages of the World/Materials 486). München: Lincom.

Klamer, Marian. 2014a. Kaera. In Antoinette Schapper (ed.), *Papuan languages of Timor, Alor and Pantar: Sketch grammars*, vol. 1, 97–146. Berlin: Mouton de Gruyter.

Klamer, Marian. 2014b. The history of numeral classifiers in Teiwa (Papuan). In Gerrit J. Dimmendaal & Anne Storch (eds.), *Number: constructions and semantics. Case studies from Africa, India, Amazonia & Oceania*, 135–166. Amsterdam: Benjamins.

Kratochvíl, František. 2007. *A grammar of Abui: a Papuan language of Alor*. Utrecht: LOT.

Malikosa, Anderias. nd. *Yesus Sakku Geleworo Kana*. Unpublished manuscript. Kupang, Indonesia.

Robinson, Laura C. & John Haan. 2014. Adang. In Antoinette Schapper (ed.), *Papuan languages of Timor, Alor and Pantar: Sketch grammars*, vol. 1, 221–284. Berlin: Mouton de Gruyter.

Schapper, Antoinette. 2014a. Kamang. In Antoinette Schapper (ed.), *Papuan languages of Timor, Alor and Pantar: Sketch grammars*, vol. 1, 285–350. Berlin: Mouton de Gruyter.

Schapper, Antoinette (ed.). 2014b. *Papuan languages of Timor, Alor and Pantar: Sketch grammars*. Vol. 1. Berlin: Mouton de Gruyter.

Schapper, Antoinette & Rachel Hendery. 2014. Wersing. In Antoinette Schapper (ed.), *Papuan languages of Timor, Alor and Pantar: Sketch grammars*, vol. 1, 439–504. Berlin: Mouton de Gruyter.

Schapper, Antoinette & Juliette Huber. Ms. A reconstruction of the Timor-Alor-Pantar family: phonology and morphology. Manuscript, Leiden University and Lund University.

Schapper, Antoinette & Marian Klamer. 2011. Plural words in Papuan languages of Alor-Pantar. In Peter K. Austin, Oliver Bond, David Nathan & Lutz Marten (eds.), *Proceedings of Language Documentation & Linguistic Theory (LDLT) 3*, 247–256. London: SOAS.

Schapper, Antoinette & Marten Manimau. 2011. *Kamus pengantar Bahasa Kamang-Indonesia-Inggris (Introductory Kamang-Indonesian-English dictionary)* (UBB Language & Culture Series: A 7). Kupang: Unit Bahasa dan Budaya (BDD).

Stokhof, W. A. L. 1978. Woisika text. *Miscellaneous Studies in Indonesian and Languages in Indonesia* 5. 34–57.

Stokhof, W. A. L. 1982. *Woisika riddles* (Pacific linguistics : Series D, Special publications 41). Canberra: ANU.

Chapter 10

Participant marking: Corpus study and video elicitation

Sebastian Fedden

Dunstan Brown

> The Alor-Pantar languages are particularly interesting for examining the relative importance of referential properties as opposed to lexical stipulation in determining pronominal marking on the verb. In this chapter we take a detailed look at the patterns of pronominal marking on verbs in the existing corpora of three languages, Abui, Kamang and Teiwa. These differ in relation to the importance of these factors. There is a continuum with event properties, such as volitionality and affectedness at one end, and stipulation or arbitrary association of prefixes with verbs at the other end. Abui is located at one end of this continuum, because event semantics play a major role. Teiwa is located at the other end, with the lexical property of object animacy as the major determinant of prefixal marking. Between these two extremes we find Kamang. We also argue that lexical properties such as animacy, as opposed to event properties, create the means for arbitrary classes to develop. We complement the corpus study with data from video experimentation using 42 specially prepared video stimuli, in which we systematically varied animacy and volitionality values for participants in one and two-participant events.

1 Introduction

The Alor-Pantar languages sometimes index event participants using pronominal indexing on the verb. The factors that determine when this happens vary significantly across the languages. For some, referential properties dependent on the semantics of the event (e.g., volitionality and affectedness) play a major role, while for others it appears that the indexing is lexically determined by the verb.

 Sebastian Fedden & Dunstan Brown. 2017. Participant marking: Corpus study and video elicitation. In Marian Klamer (ed.), *The Alor-Pantar languages*, 403–447. Berlin: Language Science Press. DOI:10.5281/zenodo.569399

In order to illustrate the range of possibilities, we concentrate on three languages: Teiwa, Kamang and Abui. For a map, see the introduction to this volume. These three languages have been chosen as they constitute three representative types in the micro-typology of the Alor-Pantar languages.

Our main source of data are the respective corpora of Teiwa (Klamer, Teiwa corpus), Kamang (Schapper, Kamang corpus) and Abui (Kratochvíl, Abui corpus). In additon we use the following sources: Teiwa (Pantar; Klamer (2010a); Klamer, fieldnotes; Robinson, fieldnotes), Kamang (Eastern Alor, Schapper & Manimau (2011); Schapper, fieldnotes) and Abui (Central-Western Alor; Kratochvíl (2007; 2011); Kratochvíl, fieldnotes; Schapper, fieldnotes).

An important source of data are 42 specially designed videos created to represent events varying with respect to specific semantic variables (participant number, animacy, volitionality) (see Fedden et al. 2013). For Abui and Teiwa we present the data for the associated video elicitation experiments. For Kamang our video data show that prefixation occurs very often, although less so than for Abui. In order to understand Kamang's place in the typology, with its set of obligatorily prefixed verbs that must be conventionally associated with a particular prefix type, rather than this being determined by semantic values, we present data from the sources listed above.

We focus especially on the difference between properties expressing a relationship between participants and events, namely affectedness in Abui and Kamang and volitionality in Abui, on the one hand, and the lexical properties of words (animacy, verb classes) in Teiwa, on the other hand. We find that Abui, Kamang and Teiwa are located at different points on a continuum of lexical stipulation: Abui is at one end, where event semantics play the greatest role, and Teiwa is at the other end, where lexical properties play the greatest role, with Kamang located somewhere between these two extremes.

The languages under investigation can be contrasted along further dimensions: *alignment type* and *number of prefix series*. Abui and Kamang have semantic alignment, Abui being more fluid in its alignment than Kamang, as we will see in the course of this chapter. Teiwa, on the other hand, has accusative syntactic alignment. Finally, the Alor languages Abui and Kamang have multiple prefix series, five and six, respectively, while the Pantar language Teiwa has only one.

It is important to bear in mind that we are not dealing with morphological case in the Alor-Pantar languages but with indexing on the verb. In this chapter we use the term 'pronominal indexing' to describe a structure where there is a pronominal affix on the verb[1] and a co-referent noun phrase or free pronoun

---

[1] In the Alor-Pantar languages pronominal indices are exclusively prefixal.

optionally (indicated by brackets) in the same clause, as in (1). Co-reference is indicated by the index *k*. There is no pronominal indexing in (2). As the Alor-Pantar languages have APV and SV word order any overt A or S precedes the verb.[2]

(1)   (noun phrase$_k$/free pronoun$_k$) prefix$_k$-verb[3]

(2)   (noun phrase/free pronoun) verb

We concentrate in this chapter on animacy and volitionality since these were varied systematically in the video stimuli. We also discuss affectedness and its impact on indexation in Kamang and Abui. As affectedness is a complex issue (Tsunoda 1985; Beavers 2011) we decided to exclude it as a factor from the video elicitation task when we were designing the video stimuli.

Similar factors to those found in constructions involving pronominal prefixes in the Alor-Pantar languages have been reported for differential object marking, including animacy (Bossong 1991; Croft 1988; Aissen 2003), specificity (Heusinger & Kaiser 2005), and affectedness (Hopper & Thompson 1980; Tsunoda 1981; 1985; Heusinger & Kaiser 2011). Volitionality is, among other things, argued to play a role in differential subject marking in Hindi (Mohanan 1990).

In § 2 and § 3 we briefly sketch the systems of syntactic and semantic alignment in Abui, Kamang and Teiwa, and discuss the number of prefix series that one finds in these languages, respectively. In § 4 we discuss our video elicitation method. We discuss the effects of animacy and volitionality in § 5. Teiwa does not use indexing to directly represent information about events and participants but relies strongly on verb classes, conventionally associated with animacy, but also with a high degree of arbitrary stipulation. Although verb classes also play a role in Abui and Kamang, indexing in these languages is used to directly encode information about events and participants, such as volitionality and affectedness in Abui, and affectedness in Kamang. Finally in § 6, we summarize and give a conclusion of our findings.

---

[2] We use the following primitives for core participants: S for the single argument of an intransitive verb, A for the more agent-like argument of a transitive verb, and P for the more patient-like argument of a transitive verb.

[3] The co-occurrence of a pronominal prefix and a co-referent free pronoun is generally restricted in the Alor-Pantar languages but the constraints for this differ between the languages. In some languages the co-occurrence of the free pronoun and pronominal prefix is possible under certain circumstances, but we do not address the issue here.

2 Alignment

The person prefixes found on the verbs in the Alor-Pantar languages are all very similar in form, pointing to a common historical origin.[4] However, pronominal indexing is conditioned by a variety of constraints which differ between the languages. Teiwa, a language of Pantar, has syntactic alignment (accusative), whereas both Kamang, from eastern Alor, and Abui, from central western Alor, have semantic alignment. Although there is no case marking on noun phrases, alignment can be defined relative to pronominal indexing.

For almost all Teiwa verbs the following holds: only P's are indexed whereas S's and A's are never indexed. There is a small subset of three reflexive-like verbs which index the S (see below). Generally, therefore, Teiwa treats S like A and unlike P and can be said to have syntactic alignment of the accusative type. In Abui and Kamang P's are also indexed, as are more patient-like S's (S_P), while more agent-like S's (S_A) are not indexed. As in Teiwa, A's are not indexed. Such systems in which S's behave differently depending on semantic factors are generally called semantic alignment systems (Donohue & Wichmann 2008) or active/agentive systems (Mithun 1991).

The Alor-Pantar languages are of interest at the macro-typological level for a number of reasons. First, the nominative-accusative alignment system in Teiwa's prefixal marking is typologically the most common (Siewierska 2004: 53), yet in Teiwa it is associated with the rare property of marking only the person of the P on the verb (Siewierska 2013). Second, the Alor-Pantar languages which have semantic alignment are subject to differing semantic factors in determining their pronominal indexing, including animacy, volitionality and affectedness. These are, of course, implicated in many phenomena of a wider macrotypological interest.

For almost all Teiwa verbs, S's are encoded with a free pronoun, as illustrated in (3) and (4).

(3) Teiwa (Klamer 2010a: 169)
    A   her.
    3SG climb
    'He climbs up.'

---

[4] Similar prefixes occur on nouns to mark possession. There are parallels, particularly because inalienable possession usually involves possessors linearly preceding the possessed in the same way that arguments linearly precede the verb.

(4) Teiwa (Response to video clip P04_wake.up_07, SP3)
 A   uri.
 3SG wake.up
 'He wakes up.'

An example of an indexed S is provided in (5). Teiwa has only three verbs which follow this pattern. These are *-o'on* 'hide', *-ewar* 'return' and *-ufan* 'forget'.

(5) Teiwa (Klamer 2010a: 98)
 Ha h-o'on.
 2SG 2SG-hide
 'You hide.'

Indexation of P on the Teiwa verb is associated with animacy of P. In the Teiwa corpus (Klamer, Teiwa corpus) indexing is restricted to 49 out of 224 transitive verbs (types), i.e., ~22%, comprising 44 verbs which always index P and five verbs in which the presence of the index depends on the animacy value of P. The rest of the transitive verbs never index their object. This is illustrated in (6) below for the prefixing transitive verb *-unba'* 'meet', where the object is animate and in the third person singular, while the subject is in the second person singular. In (7), we see the non-prefixing transitive verb *ari'* 'break', which typically takes an inanimate object.

(6) Teiwa (Klamer 2010a: 159)
 Name, ha'an n-oqai   g-unba'?
 sir   2SG 1SG.POSS-child 3-meet
 'Sir, did you see (lit. meet) my child?'

(7) Teiwa (Klamer 2010a: 101)
 Ha'an meja ga-fat   ari'.
 2SG   table 3.POSS-leg break
 'You broke that table leg!'

Kamang, on the other hand, has semantic alignment, where the S is coded like the A, in (8), or like the P, if the S is affected in (9).

(8) Kamang (Response to video clip C03_dance_05, SP13)
 Almakang=a pilan.
 people=SPEC dance.lego-lego
 'The people are dancing a *lego-lego* (traditional dance).'

(9) Kamang (Schapper 2014a: 324)
Na-maitan-si.
1SG.PAT-hunger-IPFV
'I'm hungry.'

Some verbs allow alternation between having a prefix and an affected S and having no prefix and a non-affected S. This is illustrated in (10), where the dog runs off because it was chased away, whereas (11) does not have this affected meaning.

(10) Kamang (Schapper 2014a: 236)
Kui ge-tak.
dog 3.GEN-run
'The dog ran off (was forced to run).'

(11) Kamang (Schapper 2014a: 326)
Kui tak.
dog run
'The dog runs.'

Kamang indexes P's, for instance on the verbs *-tan* 'wake someone up' and *-tak* 'see' in examples (12) and (13), respectively.

(12) Kamang (Response to video clip P07_wake.up.person_19, SP15)
[...] *ge-pa-l   sue   ga-tan.*
[...] 3.GEN-father-CONTR_FOC arrive 3.PAT-wake_up
'[...] his father comes and wakes him.'

(13) Kamang (Response to video clip C19_be.afraid.of.axe_40, SP15)
Ga sue   paling ga-tak.
3SG arrive axe   3.PAT-see
'He comes and sees the axe.'

Abui also has semantic alignment. An important semantic factor in the indexing of S's is volitionality. Volitional S's are expressed with a free pronoun and no prefix, as in (14). Non-volitional S's are indexed with a prefix, as in (15), where a free pronoun can optionally be used. The free translations try to capture the difference in volitionality involved here.

(14) Abui (Kratochvíl 2007: 15)
Na laak.
1SG leave
'I go away.'

(15) Abui (Kratochvíl 2007: 15)
(Na) no-laak.
(1SG) 1SG.REC-leave
'I (am forced to) retreat.'

These Abui examples do not involve transitive verbs, but there is a natural connection with the situation in Teiwa. Prefixation in Teiwa is typical of animate objects, and objects are, among other things, expected to be non-volitional (Givón 1985: 90, Malchukov 2005: 79, Heusinger & Kaiser 2011: 4). It is semantic factors, such as volitionality, which leads Kratochvíl (2007: 177-178, 257) to treat the Abui system as based on actor and undergoer roles (Foley & Van Valin 1984), rather than notions of subject and object, which can more easily be applied to Teiwa.

Abui indexes P's. There are no verbs in the corpus which are never prefixed. An example of a prefixed transitive verb indexing a P is (16). Animacy is much less important in Abui; both *fik* 'pull' and *-bel* 'pull' in (16) would be prefixed, even if their P's were inanimate. Another example, with the verb *-kol* 'tie', is given in (17).

(16) Abui (Response to video clip C01_pull_person_25, SP8)
Wiil neng nuku di de-feela   ha-fik   ha-bel-e.
child male one   3ACT 3.AL.POSS-friend 3.PAT-pull 3.PAT-pull-IPFV
'A boy is pulling his friend.'

(17) Abui (Kratochvíl 2007: 91)
Maama di   bataa ha-kol.
father 3ACT wood 3.PAT-tie
'Father ties up the wood.'

For some Abui verbs a difference of affectedness in the P can be encoded by the choice of prefix, namely a prefix from the LOC series for a lower degree of affectedness and a prefix from the PAT series for a higher degree of affectedness. We take this up in § 5.1.2 below.

To sum up the role of conditions, Abui and Kamang index P's and some S's. This is in part determined by affectedness (in Abui and Kamang) and volitionality (in Abui). In both languages lexical verb classes also play a role to some degree, in Kamang more than in Abui. Teiwa indexes P's in part determined by animacy. The role of animacy in Teiwa in the formation of verb classes will be taken up in § 5.3.

3 Number of person prefix series

All Alor-Pantar languages have at least one series of person prefixes. In the languages which have only one series, like Teiwa and Western Pantar (Holton 2010), this is always the series which is identified by *a*-vowels in the singular and *i*-vowels in the plural.[5] The Teiwa prefixes are given in Table 1.

Table 1: Teiwa person prefixes (Klamer 2010a: 77, 78)

	Prefix
1SG	*n(a)-*
2SG	*h(a)-*
3SG	*g(a)-*
1PL.EXCL	*n(i)-*
1PL.INCL	*p(i)-*
2PL	*y(i)-*
3PL	*g(i)-, ga-*

Abui and Kamang are innovative in that they developed multiple prefix series. The Abui prefixes are given in Table 2.

For each series of prefixes Abui has two contrasting types for the third person. The α-type starts with /d/ and indexes an actor.[7] The β-type starts with /h/ and indexes an undergoer. The difference between the α-type and the β-type is illustrated by the following two examples (18) and (19), respectively.

---

[5] Teiwa actually has four verbs for which a difference between an animate and an inanimate object can be encoded by the choice of two different prefixes in the third person only. We discuss this alternation in detail in § 5.3.

[6] Ø- before vowel.

[7] Kratochvíl (2007: 78-79) calls these "3ı" (our α-type) and "3ıı" (our β-type).

Table 2: Abui person prefixes

	Prefixes				
	PAT	REC	LOC	GOAL	BEN
SG	n(a)-	no-	ne-	noo-	nee-
2SG	a-[6]	o-	e-	oo-	ee-
3 (α-TYPE)	d(a)-	do-	de-	doo-	dee-
3 (β-TYPE)	h(a)-	ho-	he-	hoo-	hee-
1PL.EXCL	ni-	nu-	ni-	nuu-	nii-
1PL.INCL	pi-	po-/pu-	pi-	puu-/poo-	pii-
2PL	ri-	ro-/ru-	ri-	ruu-/roo-	rii-

(18) Abui (Kratochvíl 2007: 185)
   Fani el   da-wel-i.
   PN before 3.PAT-pour-PFV
   'Fani washed himself.' [α-type prefix: *da-*]

(19) Abui (Kratochvíl 2007: 185)
   Fani el   ha-wel-i.
   PN before 3.PAT-pour-PFV
   'Fani washed him.' [β-type prefix: *ha-*]

Kamang has six prefix series. The Kamang prefixes are given in Table 3.

Having multiple person prefix series is not restricted to Alor-Pantar languages with semantic alignment. For example, Adang (Haan 2001; Robinson & Haan 2014) has syntactic alignment like Teiwa (i.e., only P's are indexed with a prefix) but, having three series, more readily fits with the semantically aligned languages Abui and Kamang along this dimension of the micro-typology.

4 Video elicitation

As our goal is to compare across related languages we are faced with the problem of how to obtain comparable data. Translation-based elicitation brings with it the danger that the responses are heavily biased towards the constructions of the meta-language, and prompted elicitation using the target language brings with

Table 3: Kamang person prefixes. In the third person prefixes, /g/ can be realized as [j] before front vowels, i.e., in the GEN and DAT series.
†The assistive (AST) indexes the participant who assists in the action.

	PAT	LOC	Prefixes GEN	AST†	DAT	DIR
1SG	na-	no-	ne-	noo-	nee-	nao-
2SG	a-	o-	e-	oo-	ee-	ao-
3	ga-	wo-	ge-	woo-	gee-	gao-
1PL.EXCL	ni-	nio-	ni-	nioo-	nii-	nio-
1PL.INCL	si-	sio-	si-	sioo-	sii-	sio-
2PL	i-	io-	i-	ioo-	ii-	io-

it, among other things, well known difficulties of determining exactly what the consultant is making a judgment about and the extent to which they are trying to accommodate the researcher. We therefore decided to choose video elicitation, as this obviates many of the problems associated with other techniques. While this method entails substantial preparatory work, we can have more confidence in the results.

4.1 Video stimuli

We used 42 short video elicitation stimuli specifically designed to investigate the impact that various semantic factors have on the patterns of pronominal marking in the Alor-Pantar languages. The full set of video clips can be downloaded from www.smg.surrey.ac.uk/projects/alor-pantar/pronominal-marking-video-stimuli. A list of the clips and instructions on how to use them are provided in the appendix.

Given that we are dealing with some systems where there is semantic alignment and others where there is a syntactic alignment system conditioned partly by semantic factors, it made sense to test the role of conditions which have been identified either for semantic alignment or for their salience in marking grammatical relations such as objects. Animacy is important in Teiwa (Klamer 2010a: 171; Klamer & Kratochvíl 2006) and volitionality, telicity, and the stative/active distinction were identified as major factors in the typological work on semantic alignment systems (Arkadiev 2008; Klamer 2008 on semantic alignment in eastern Indonesia). We therefore chose the following five factors, each with two possible values:

10 Participant marking: Corpus study and video elicitation

1. Number of participants: 1 vs. 2

2. Animacy: Animate vs. Inanimate

3. Volitionality: Volitional vs. Non-volitional

4. Telicity: Telic vs. Atelic[8]

5. Dynamicity: Stative vs. Dynamic[9]

From this, we constructed a possibility space in which we systematically varied the values. The value for *animacy* only varies for S and P. The factor *volitionality* varies only with respect to S and A.

There are therefore 32 (2^5) possibilities or cells in the possibility space. Two of these value combinations are logically incompatible, namely the combination of [−Animate] and [+Volitional] and the combination of [+Telic] and [−Dynamic]. As there generally are no volitional inanimates or telic states, we eliminated these value combinations. This eliminated 7 cases from the one-participant predicates. (There are 4 telic states and 3 additional volitional inanimates. The fourth case with the combination "volitional inanimate" is also a telic state.) For two-participant verbs, only 4 cases had to be eliminated, namely the four telic states. As volitionality and animacy are coded for different participants, a combination of these does not cause a problem.

Telicity and dynamicity have not been identified for the Alor-Pantar languages but we designed the experiment to include these factors because they have been repeatedly recognized as factors which impact on the realization of participant-related information in semantically aligned languages (see Arkadiev (2008) and references therein). On the potential effect of telicity, see Fedden et al. (2013). Dynamicity did not have an effect on the indexation patterns in our video elicitation task. We will say no more about these two factors here.

The factors definiteness and specificity which are also well-known to have an effect on participant marking (Aissen 2003) were not tested because video elicitation is not the right technique to investigate those. The values of discourse-related factors like definiteness and specificity cannot be systematically varied in any straightforward way in video elicitation.

---

[8] We define *telic* loosely as "denoting a change of state" and *atelic* as an "unbounded process or activity".

[9] We use the definition given by Comrie (1976: 49): "With a state, unless something happens to change that state, then the state will continue [...]. With a dynamic situation, on the other hand, the situation will only continue if it is continually subject to a new input of energy [...]".

We tested 21 factor combinations (32-7-4=21). For practical fieldwork purposes, we created a core set of video stimuli for each of the combinations and a peripheral set. Fieldworkers would use the core set as the first task and then the peripheral set where possible. For the languages discussed here both sets were completed. Because there are two sets for each of the 21 combinations, there are 42 clips. For each set the order of the clips was randomized. The order in which the clips were to be shown was fixed after randomization.

4.2 Speakers and procedure

The video stimuli were administered to a total of 11 male native speakers (four for Abui, four for Kamang and three for Teiwa).[10] The video clips were shown to individual participants or groups of participants, one of whom was the primary speaker whose responses were recorded. Elicitation was conducted in Indonesian. Descriptions of the scenes in the clips were elicited using neutral cues, such as *Apa yang lihat?* 'What did you see?' or *Apa yang terjadi?* 'What happened?'. If the initial description did not include a verb which roughly corresponded to the English verb in the clip label, the field experimenters probed for the intended verb in a minimal way. All sessions were audio-recorded and the responses transcribed.

Responses that we counted as valid had to conform to the specific factor combination for which they were given as a description. For example, the description of the clip "hear person" had to involve an animate entity as the object, e.g., "hear the man". So responses involving a non-person referent, such as "he hears the man's voice" were not counted for the relevant feature combination. Tables giving the proportion of prefixed verbs measured against the total of valid responses for a certain factor or combination of factors are used to show the effect of animacy or volitionality on prefixation. Figures are given for individual speakers as well as aggregated data for all speakers of each language. All percentages are conventionally rounded to yield whole numbers.

5 Participant properties

In this section we focus on the difference between properties expressing a relationship between participants and events (affectedness, volitionality) on the one hand and lexical properties (animacy, verb classes) on the other.

---

[10] For the purpose of citing examples anonymously we assigned each speaker a code (SP1 to SP15). This range also includes one speaker of Western Pantar and three speakers of Adang. We say nothing about these two languages here.

While volitionality as a term suggests that it is exclusively a property of a human (or at least an animate) participant it is typically not a property of the lexical semantics of nouns that they are volitional or non-volitional agents. Nouns such as *person, child,* or *man* can be used in contexts in which they may be subject to non-volitional acts (e.g., fall) or volitional ones (e.g., walk), while they remain constant in their values for animacy. This means that a distinction on the basis of volitionality would not yield an exhaustive partition of the lexicon in the way that the animate-inanimate opposition would. Typically, volitionality is a property of a participant which is observed in the context of an event. In this sense we can attribute it to the event as a whole. Volitionality as we use it here (or the absence thereof) is more likely a part of the lexical semantics of verbs, as can be seen in examples like 'stumble', 'trip', 'fall', and 'vomit'. But, as with the noun examples mentioned, it is possible to find verbs where there is no requirement that their lexical semantics are committed to a value for volitionality. This entails that, while volitionality may be relevant for some verbs such as the ones we mention, it does not partition the verb lexicon in the way that animacy partitions the noun lexicon. Animacy, on the other hand, is a lexical property. As Hurford (2007: 43) notes in his discussion of the pre-linguistic basis for semantics, animacy is a more permanent property and is 'less perception dependent'.

5.1 Abui

Of the three languages in our sample Abui shows the greatest flexibility of combining verbs with prefixes from different series. However, the PAT prefix series is much more lexically limited than the other inflections in Abui. Verbs that take this prefix are the only verbs showing lexical classing, i.e., the absence of alternation.

5.1.1 Inflection classes in Abui

The discussion here is based on a detailed examination of the prefixal behaviour of 210 verbs. The numbers reflect the state of the documentation and analysis of the language at present (see Kratochvíl, Abui corpus).

For 33 Abui verbs inflection with a PAT prefix is either obligatory or optional. Table 4 presents the distribution of the PAT prefix across the whole sample (all percentages rounded to whole numbers). Obligatory inflection with a PAT prefix means that a verb has to have a prefix and that the prefix has to be from the PAT prefix series. In other words, these verbs exclusively appear with the PAT prefix. This is the case for 14% of the verbs in the sample (29 out of 210 verbs). Within optional PAT verbs we distinguish two cases. First, there are the verbs that always require a prefix, and this may be from any series, including the PAT series. These are a minority (4 out of 210 verbs, or 2% in Table 4). Second, there are the verbs that may occur without a prefix or with a prefix, from any series, including the PAT series. These form a substantial subset (68 out of 210 verb or 32% in Table 4).

Table 4: Distribution of the Abui PAT prefixes

	PAT obligatory	PAT optional	
	Prefix required	A prefix is required	A prefix is not required
Total (of 210 verbs)	29 verbs 14% (29/210)	4 verbs 2% (4/210)	68 verbs 32% (68/210)

There are 29 verbs in our sample which obligatorily occur with the PAT prefix. Examples are *-ieng* 'see s.o./sth.', *-kai* 'drop s.o./sth.', *-lal* 'laugh', *-rik* 'hurt s.o.' and *-tamadia* 'repair sth.'.[11] An example with *-ful* 'swallow s.o./sth.' is provided in (20) As the verbs which obligatorily take a PAT prefix do not form a semantic class we treat them as an inflection class, defined by the fact that these verbs can only occur with a PAT prefix.

(20) Abui (Kratochvíl 2007: 463)
Kaai afu ha-ful.
dog fish 3.PAT-swallow
'The dog swallowed the fish.'

For 72 verbs the PAT prefix is optional. Four of these always require a prefix, i.e., the verb cannot occur without a prefix. These are *-dak* 'grab firmly s.o./sth.', *-luol* 'follow, collect s.o./sth.', *-k* 'throw at s.o./sth.; feed s.o./sth.' and *-maha* 'want'. An example is given in (21).

(21) Abui (Kratochvíl 2007: 364)
Kokda di ha-luol we hu ama fen-i.
younger 3ACT 3.PAT-follow leave SPEC person injure.COMPL-PFV
'When the younger one followed him, people killed (him).'

---

[11] The addition of *someone* (s.o.) and/or *something* (sth.) in the glosses indicates whether a verb can appear with an animate or an inanimate P in the corpus. If there is no such addition, e.g., *maha* 'want' the prefix indexes the S.

68 verbs optionally take PAT but occurrence without a prefix is also possible. Examples of these are *(-)aahi* 'take away sth.', *(-)dik* 'stab s.o./sth.', *(-)wik* 'carry s.o./sth.' and *(-)yok* 'cover s.o./sth.'. An example is given in (22), where the verb *(-)wik* 'carry s.o./sth.' occurs without a prefix.

(22) Abui (Kratochvíl 2007: 502)
Na ne-sura wik-e.
1SG 1SG.AL.POSS-book carry-IPFV
'I carry my book.'

The verbs which optionally occur with a PAT prefix can take a prefix from at least one other series instead of PAT. The majority of these verbs can alternate between the REC, LOC, GOAL, and BEN prefixes, whereby semantic differences in the indexed participant are observable when alternating one prefix with another.

To sum up, apart from lexical classing found in verbs which only occur with the PAT prefix, the Abui prefix system is highly fluid and verbs can occur with most, perhaps all of the prefixes, or be unprefixed. In the following sections we deal in turn with affectedness and volitionality as factors which impact on the prefixation patterns.

5.1.2 Affectedness in Abui

Affectedness is one of the factors that has an impact on pronominal indexing in Abui. Affected participants undergo a persistent change. On affectedness as a criterion for high transitivity, see Hopper & Thompson (1980) and Tsunoda (1981; 1985). On affectedness as a parameter of semantic distinctness between the two participants of a transitive clause, see Næss (2004; 2006; 2007).

Affectedness is clearly a relation between a participant and an event because, while the participant is the affected entity, the predicate contains the information whether the change of state is entailed (Beavers 2011: 337).

Abui allows the expression of different degrees of affectedness by choosing between the PAT and the LOC prefix series for P, as illustrated in Table 5.

The LOC series is chosen if the change of state in P is either not entailed, e.g., *he-pung* 'hold sth.' vs. *ha-pung* 'catch sth.', or if it is that P is less strongly affected *he-dik* 'stab s.o./sth.' vs. *ha-dik* 'pierce s.o./sth. through' or *he-lak* 'take sth. apart' vs. *ha-lak* 'demolish sth.'. The PAT series on the other hand is chosen if P is highly affected and a change of state in P is entailed. Full examples for *-dik* are provided in (23) and (24).

Table 5: Degrees of affectedness in Abui (Abui Kratochvíl 2011: 596; p.c.)

Lower degree of affectedness: LOC prefix	Higher degree of affectedness: PAT prefix
he-dik 'stab s.o./sth.'	*ha-dik* 'pierce s.o./sth. through'
he-akung 'cover sth.'	*h-akung* 'extinguish sth.'
he-pung 'hold sth.'	*ha-pung* 'catch sth.'
he-komangdi 'make sth. less sharp'	*ha-komangdi* 'make sth. completely blunt'
he-lilri 'warm sth. up (water)'	*ha-lilri* 'boil sth. (water)'
he-lak 'take sth. apart'	*ha-lak* 'demolish sth.'

(23) Abui (Kratochvíl 2007: 194)
Rui ba tukola mi-a ma-i yo wan e
rat LNK hole be.in-DUR be.PROX-PFV DEM already before
he-dik-i?
3.LOC-prick-PFV
'Has that rat that was in a hole already been stabbed?'

(24) Abui (Kratochvíl 2007: 194)
Rui tukola mi-a hare bataa mi ha-dik-e!
rat hole be.in-DUR so wood take 3.PAT-stab-IPFV
'There are rats in the hole, so take a stick and run them through!'

These Abui examples show the impact of different degrees of affectedness depending on which prefix series is chosen for the indexing of P.

5.1.3 Volitionality in Abui

Next we deal with the factor of volitionality. Volitionality in a linguistic context has been defined in various ways in the literature which make sense intuitively, but to our knowledge there has been no serious attempt to formalize volitionality in a way that Beavers (2011) did for affectedness. Hopper & Thompson (1980: 286) define volitionality as the "degree of planned involvement of an A[gent] in the activity of the verb". DeLancey (1985: 52) equates volitionality with conscious control over the activity of the verb. Furthermore, it has been observed in the literature that control and volition often coincide (Tsunoda 1985: 392; DeLancey

1985: 56) and that instigation is sometimes used interchangeably with control (Næss 2007: 45). On volition as an entailment which identifies (Proto-)Agents, see Dowty (1991).

As we noted, volitionality may be a property associated with nouns denoting human (or some animate) participants, but many nouns of this type are non-committal as to the volition of what they denote. This contrasts with animacy, where a noun either denotes an animate or an inanimate entity. For verbs there is also no requirement that their lexical semantics be committed to a value for volitionality, but this information can be encoded by the choice of indexing they take. Animacy, on the other hand, is a lexical property. Hence, where volitionality is involved, this is a semantic factor associated with the event as a whole.

In Abui, a language with semantic alignment, volitionality is an important factor. It determines whether an S is indexed. The absence of a prefix signals volitional S's, whereas free pronouns are outside the system of volitionality and non-volitionality. This is illustrated with the following pair: *na laak* [1SG leave] 'I go away' vs. *(na) no-laak* [(1SG) 1SG.REC-leave] 'I (am forced to) retreat'. These examples illustrate this with the first person, which has the potential to differ in terms of volitionality. We can therefore identify a relative scale with respect to the factors, where affectedness is about the event and volitionality can be about the event, but where the lexical semantics of certain items restricts the possibilities for its application.

In the video elicitation task Abui had the most instances of prefixation of the S in one-place predicates (Table 6).

Table 6: Indexation of S's in one-place predicates in Abui (responses to the video stimuli)

	SP8	SP9	SP10	SP11	All
One-place predicates	17	12	10	12	51
Prefixed	8	6	4	5	23
Proportion	47%	50%	40%	42%	45%

A proportion of 45% is very high in comparison to Teiwa, where S's were not indexed at all in the video elicitation tasks, and to Kamang, where an average of 19% of S's were indexed.

As we shall see, non-volitionality, when combined with animacy, appears to play a bigger role in prefixation in Abui intransitives than in any of the other languages. This is consistent with Kratochvíl's analysis of Abui as a semantically aligned language. Free pronouns on their own, that is without a co-referent prefix, are reserved for typical agents, i.e., participants who have volition with respect to the event and are not affected by it. The set of free pronouns includes the third person pronoun *di*,[12] which can appear on its own or be adnominal following a noun phrase. In our experiment, there were no instances where an S was encoded with *di* in any of the responses. In all cases noun phrases without *di* were used, for example in (25).

(25) Abui (Response to video clip P20_run_06, SP8)
Ama nuku furai ba weei.
man one run and go
'A man is running along.'

Other examples from the experiment are: *mit* 'sit', *natet* 'stand' and *it* 'lie'. Further examples from the Abui corpus are: *ayong* 'swim', *kalol* 'foretell (fortune or the future)', *kawai* 'argue', *luuk* 'dance', *miei* 'come', *taa* 'lie', *yaa(r)* 'go'. Semantically, these are mainly motion verbs, posture verbs, and social activities. Typically these express their S with a free pronoun and not a prefix because they typically denote events with volitional participants.

Free pronouns can be combined with a co-referent prefix (in the third person this needs to be an α-type prefix) to express reflexive situations, in which the agent is volitional but also affected by his (own) action. As there are no examples of this construction in the responses to the video elicitation task, a textual example is given in (26).

(26) Abui (Kratochvíl 2007: 203)
Ata di do-kafi-a.
PN 3ACT 3.REC-scrape-DUR
'A. scratches himself (intentionally).' [α-type prefix: *do-*]

In the video elicitation tasks, non-volitional S's are expressed only with a prefix. An example of this is given in (27).

(27) Abui (Response to video clip P09_person.fall_14, SP 9)
Neng nuku laak-laak-i ba me la da-kaai yo eya!
man one walk-walk-PFV and come just 3.PAT-stumble DEM EXCLAM
'A man walks along and stumbles there, whoops!' [α-type prefix: *do-*]

---

[12] The free pronoun *di* is probably of verbal origin and has grammaticalized from the auxiliary *d* 'hold' (Kratochvíl 2011). Participants marked with *di* are mainly humans, but nonhuman participants of considerable agentive force, e.g., a storm, are also possible.

10 Participant marking: Corpus study and video elicitation

In the responses to the video elicitation task, α-type prefixes were exclusively used in the descriptions of one-participant events. In each case the prefix cross-references the sole participant in the event denoted by the verb. Prefixes of the α-type are used with non-volitional S's, namely the S of *minang* 'wake up', *liel* 'tall', *lal* 'laugh', *kaai* 'stumble', and *yongf* 'forget' (which was employed in descriptions of the sleep event [i.e., video clip C05_sleep_11]). Speakers also very consistently used α-type prefixes with volitional S's with the two positional verbs *ruid* 'rise, stand up' and *reek* 'lie'.

(28) Abui (Response to video clip P21_stand.up_02, SP11)
 Wil neng da-ruid-i ba laak-i.
 child male 3.PAT-stand.up-PFV and leave-PFV
 'The guy stands up and leaves.' [α-type prefix: *da-*]

However, just looking at the effect of volitionality alone on the coding in the experiment does not give us a clear picture. The proportions for non-volitional and volitional S's are about equal (see Table 7).

Table 7: Indexation of non-volitional and volitional S's in Abui (responses to the video stimuli)

	SP8	SP9	SP10	SP11	All
Non-volitional S	11	6	4	6	27
Prefixed	5	3	2	2	12
Proportion	45%	50%	50%	33%	44%
Volitional S	6	6	6	6	24
Prefixed	3	3	2	3	11
Proportion	50%	50%	33%	50%	46%

The impact of non-volitionality becomes more obvious when one looks at non-volitional animate S's. Of all S's in one-place predicates, non-volitional animate S's are most likely to be indexed (Table 8).

In Abui animate S's that are non-volitional are indexed with a prefix for an average of 69% of the cases, whereas animate S's (55%), volitional animate S's (46%), and inanimate (and thus by definition non-volitional) S's (9%) show much lower proportions. This pattern may have a functional explanation, in that use of prefixation encodes information that the default expectation is not met that an animate participant is volitional.

Table 8: Indexation of non-volitional animate S's in Abui (responses to the video stimuli)

	SP8	SP9	SP10	SP11	All
Non-volitional AND animate S	6	4	3	3	16
Prefixed	4	3	2	2	11
Proportion	66%	75%	66%	66%	69%

In sum, Abui has a high degree of semantic fluidity, and prefixation patterns depend on the factors affectedness and volitionality. We now turn to the neighbouring language Kamang, in which arbitrary inflection classes (at least synchronically) play a larger role than in Abui.

5.2 Kamang

Kamang, like Abui, has semantic alignment and several prefix series. However, in Kamang the actual use of prefixes differs radically from Abui. Kamang is more restricted in terms of the possible combinations of verbs with prefixes than Abui. More than in Abui, lexical classes in Kamang play an important role in determining prefixation patterns of the S in intransitive clauses and the P in transitive clauses. We have based our analysis of Kamang on a corpus of 510 verbs (Schapper, Kamang corpus; Schapper & Manimau (2011)). In Kamang the primary verb class divide is between:

(i) *Obligatorily prefixed verbs*: These require a prefix on the verb in order to be well-formed. The prefix comes from one of the six series, is lexically fixed for each verb and does not alternate. For verbs in this group the different prefixal inflections have no obvious semantic functions, but rather define arbitrary inflection classes. Of the 510 verbs in the corpus, 166 are obligatorily prefixed (approx. 33%).

(ii) *Non-obligatorily prefixed verbs*: These do not require a prefix. Where prefixes are added to these verbs they have semantically transparent functions. Prefixation can either be argument-preserving, whereby prefixation of the verb does not add another argument or alter the valency of the verb, or argument-adding, whereby the prefix indexes an additional argument. 344 verbs belong into this class (approx. 67%).

We see in Table 9 that there is a substantial difference in the prefixal requirements of transitive and intransitive verbs (all percentages rounded to whole numbers). In the classification of verbs as either intransitive or transitive we follow Schapper & Manimau (2011).

Table 9: Kamang verbs (obligatorily prefixed and non-obligatorily prefixed)

	Obligatorily prefixed	Non-obligatorily prefixed
Transitive	45% (113/250 verbs)	55% (137/250 verbs)
Intransitive	20% (53/260 verbs)	80% (207/260 verbs)
Total (of 510 verbs)	33% (166/510 verbs)	67% (344/510 verbs)

Almost half of the transitive verbs that we sampled from the corpus are obligatorily prefixed, whereas substantially fewer of the intransitive verbs (only 20%) are.

5.2.1 Inflection classes in Kamang

As noted, one third of the verbs in Kamang are obligatorily prefixed and fall into arbitrary inflection classes. All of these verbs require a prefix and the prefix series is lexically fixed and independent of verb semantics.

Table 10 presents the percentages of obligatorily prefixed intransitive verbs across inflection classes. The prefix indexes S. Well over half occur in the PAT inflection, whereas less than one fifth goes in each of the LOC and GEN inflection classes. The remainder is made up of the AST class. There are no instances of obligatorily prefixed intransitive verbs outside these four inflection classes.

Table 10: Proportion of obligatorily prefixed intransitive verbs by prefix class

PAT	LOC	GEN	AST
65% (33 verbs)	15% (8 verbs)	18% (11 verbs)	<2% (1 verb)

Table 11 presents the percentages of obligatorily prefixed transitive verbs across inflection classes (rounded to whole numbers). The prefix indexes P. Over half of these verbs belong to the LOC inflection, while roughly 35% are in the PAT inflection. The remainder is made up by a handful of transitive verbs from the other four inflections.

Table 11: Proportion of obligatorily prefixed transitive verbs by prefix class

PAT	LOC	Other
35% (46 verbs)	60% (82 verbs)	<5% (9 verbs)

The distribution of verbs over these classes is independent of verb semantics. Within the obligatorily prefixed intransitive verbs -*waawang* 'remember', -*mitan* 'understand' and -*pan* 'forget' have similar semantics, yet they belong to the inflection classes PAT, GEN, and AST, respectively. Similarly, -*iwei* 'vomit', -*tasusin* 'be sweaty' and -*wilii* 'defecate' belong to the classes PAT, LOC, and GEN. Within the obligatorily prefixed transitive verbs -*set* 'shake up and down' belongs to PAT, while -*gaook* 'shake back and forth' belongs to LOC. Similarly, -*kut* 'stab s.o./sth.' belongs to PAT and -*fanee* 'strike, shoot s.o./sth.' to GEN. The inflection classes DAT and DIR contain one verb each and are therefore too small for any common semantics to be discernible.

In the following examples we illustrate the inflection classes in Kamang. For each class we give an intransitive and a transitive example and provide a list of verbs so the reader can further appreciate that classing is independent of verb semantics.

Examples (29) and (30) show an intransitive verb encoding S with a PAT prefix and a transitive verb encoding P with a PAT prefix, respectively.

(29) Kamang (Response to video clip P21_stand.up_02, SP12)
      Lami   saak nok ga-serang   maa we.
      husband old   one 3.PAT-get.up walk go
      'A guy gets up and goes.'

(30) Kamang (Schapper & Manimau 2011: 73)
      Gal na-kut.
      3   1SG.PAT-stab
      'He stabbed me.'

Examples of intransitive verbs in the PAT inflection class are: -*iloi* 'feel nauseous', -*ook* 'shiver, tremble', and -*tan* 'collapse, fall over'. Examples of transitive verbs in the PAT inflection class are: -*asui* 'disturb s.o./sth.', -*beh* 'order s.o./sth.', and -*kut* 'stab s.o./sth.'.

10 Participant marking: Corpus study and video elicitation

Examples (31) and (32) below show an intransitive verb encoding S with a LOC prefix and a transitive verb encoding P with a LOC prefix, respectively.

(31) Kamang (Schapper & Manimau 2011: 286)
No-tasusing.
1SG.LOC-sweat
'I'm sweaty.'

(32) Kamang (Schapper & Manimau 2011: 50)
Ga bong=a wo-gaook.
3AGT tree=SPEC 3.LOC-shake.back.and.forth
'He shook the tree.'

Examples of intransitive verbs in the LOC inflection class are: *-biee* 'angry' and *-tasusin* 'sweaty'. Examples of transitive verbs in the LOC inflection class are: *-aakai* 'trap, trick s.o./sth.', *-eh* 'measure sth.' and *-ra* 'carry (s.o./sth.)'.

Examples (33) and (34) below show an intransitive verb encoding S with a GEN prefix and a transitive verb encoding P with a GEN prefix, respectively.

(33) Kamang (Schapper, fieldnotes)
Ne-soona-ma.
1SG.GEN-slip-PFV
'I slipped over.'

(34) Kamang (Schapper, fieldnotes)
Leon ne-fanee-si.
Leon 1SG.GEN-shoot-IPFV
'Leon shoots at me.'

Examples of intransitive verbs in the GEN inflection class are: *-foi* 'dream', *-iyaa* 'go home', *-laita* 'shy', *-taiyai* 'cooperate, work together', and *-wilii* 'defecate'.

There are only two transitive verbs in the GEN inflection class, namely *-fanee* 'strike, shoot s.o./sth.' and *-towan* 'carry sth. on a pole between two people'.

Examples (35) and (36) below show an intransitive verb encoding S with an AST prefix and a transitive verb encoding P with an AST prefix, respectively.

(35) Kamang (Schapper & Manimau 2011: 103)
Oo-pan-si naa.
2SG.AST-forget-IPFV NEG
'Don't you forget.'

(36) Kamang (Schapper & Manimau 2011: 131)
Dum kiding=a ga-filing woo-tee.
child small=SPEC 3.POSS-head 3.AST-protect

'The child protected his head.'

The number of verbs in the AST inflection class is very small. Transitive verbs are *-sui* 'dry sth. off', *-tee* 'protect sth.', and *-waai* 'be facing s.o./sth.'. There is only one intransitive verb *-pan* 'forget'. Like other cognition verbs and sensory perception verbs in Kamang (e.g., *-mitan* 'understand', *-mai* 'hear') this verb is intransitive. This is seen by the fact that it is unable to occur with an NP encoding the stimulus in its basic form, such as that in example (35) above, as shown in (37). The stimulus – or better said that which is to be remembered – must be retrieved simply from the discourse context. To explicitly include an extra participant with such a verb is possible in two ways: (i) by using an applicative morpheme, such as *wo-* in (38), or (ii) by having a complement clause following the clause with the cognition verb, as in (39).

(37) Kamang (Schapper 2014a: 324)
*Mooi oo-pan-si naa.
banana 2SG.AST-forget-IPFV NEG

'Don't you forget the bananas.'

(38) Kamang (Schapper, fieldnotes)
Mooi wo-oo-pan-si naa.
banana APPL-2SG.AST-forget-IPFV NEG

'Don't you forget the bananas.'

(39) Kamang (Schapper, fieldnotes)
Oo-pan-si naa mooi met.
2SG.AST-forget-IPFV NEG banana take

'Don't you forget to bring the bananas.'

Class size decreases even further in the inflection classes DAT with *-sah* 'block s.o./sth.' and DIR with *-surut* 'chase s.o.'. They each include a single transitive verb only. There are no intransitive verbs in either DAT or DIR.

To sum up, obligatorily prefixed verbs in Kamang fall into inflection classes. Synchronically, there is no semantically transparent reason why one prefixal inflection is used with one verb and another inflection with another one. The relation between prefix and verb is simply lexically fixed. None of these verbs can ever occur without a prefix. We now turn to prefixation in non-obligatorily prefixed verbs and the semantic factor of affectedness which influences the prefixation patterns.

5.2.2 Affectedness in Kamang

Affectedness can be identified as a semantic factor which plays a role in indexing in non-obligatorily prefixed verbs in Kamang. It is a property expressing a relationship between participants and events. Stative verbs like *saara* 'burn' or *suusa* 'be in difficulty' take a LOC prefix to express that the S is affected. In (40), the S is affected in its entirety. Kamang expresses this by indexing the S with a LOC prefix on the verb. On the other hand, in (41), where the S is less affected, the prefix is absent.

(40) Kamang (Schapper 2014a: 325)
Kik   nok wo-saara.
palm.rib one 3.LOC-burn
'A palm rib burns down/on (i.e., is consumed over time).'

(41) Kamang (Schapper 2014a: 325)
Kik   nok saara.
palm.rib one burn
'A palm rib burns.'

The possibility of indexing affected participants with a prefix is not restricted to inanimates. Compare (42), with an inanimate, and (43), with an animate participant.

(42) Kamang (Schapper, fieldnotes)
Buk   taa kamal.
mountain top cold
'The mountains are cold.' (i.e., 'In the mountains, it is cold.')

(43) Kamang (Schapper, fieldnotes)
No-kamal-da-ma.
1SG.LOC-cold-AUX-PFV
'I have cooled.' (i.e., 'My fever has come down.')

In (42) *kamal* 'cold' describes a constant property, whereas in (43) it denotes a change of state in an (animate) participant affected by the process of the dropping of their body temperature.

In sum, affectedness plays an important role in the indexing patterns in Kamang. In contrast to Abui the degree of lexical stipulation is much higher. While Abui coerces only one sixth of its verbs into one fixed inflection, namely the PAT inflection, Kamang (unevenly) assigns one third of its verbal vocabulary to six inflection classes. Because of practical constraints we have sampled a larger number of Kamang verbs than is the case for Abui or Teiwa. It is a reasonable expectation that a larger sample size would give us the opportunity to see the verbs more evenly distributed across the classes, and yet Kamang does not show this. This suggests that this contrast between Abui and Kamang is a real and important factor.

In the remainder of this chapter we look at the importance of animacy as a factor in Teiwa.

5.3 Animacy and verb classes in Teiwa

Teiwa has syntactic alignment, whereby only P's are indexed on the verb. This is a rare type cross-linguistically, occurring in only 7% of the languages from Siewierska's (2013) WALS sample. Animacy is the core semantic factor which plays a role in whether an object is indexed on the verb. It has often been observed in the literature that objects are typically not animate, definite, or specific and that it is marked, if they are animate, definite, or specific in a given context (see for example Givón (1976); Aissen (2003); also see Bickel (2008: 205-205). There is a cross-linguistically robust association between marked objects and topicality. This association may have been obscured by grammaticalization, but what we still find in some languages is that marked objects are associated with semantic features typical of topics, such as animacy (Dalrymple & Nikolaeva 2011: 2).

In the video elicitation task, all three Teiwa participants used prefixes exclusively with animate objects of transitive verbs. The number of prefixes used is too small to say anything reliable about the possible impact of (non-)volitionality on prefixation. Participants consistently used prefixes for the same three verbs, all of which are transitive and have animate objects. These are *-tan (tup)* [lit. call get.up] 'wake someone up', *-u'an* 'hold someone in one's arms', and *-arar* 'be afraid of someone'. An example is given in (44).

(44) Teiwa (Response to video clip P07_wake.up.person_19, SP4)
 Kri   nuk ma   bif goqai ga-tan-an   tup.
 old.man one come child   3-call-REAL get.up
 'An old man comes and wakes up a small child.'

Having an animate object is not a sufficient condition for the object to be indexed by a prefix. In our experiment, many animate objects were not indexed with a prefix. In fact, indexation of an animate object in Teiwa accounts for 50% of the instances, as in Table 12.

Table 12: Prefixation with animate P's in Teiwa

	SP2	SP3	SP4	All
Animate P's	5	6	7	18
Prefix	3	3	3	9
Proportion	60%	50%	43%	50%

The results suggest that the animacy of the object cannot be the whole story. It is therefore worth considering whether (a) the rule of object indexation is at all productive in Teiwa and if so, whether (b) the effects we have observed in relation to a property of the object might more readily be associated with the verb itself.

To address the first question we did a corpus search for Teiwa inspired by the quantitative method in Baayen (1992) and subsequent work based on that. The Teiwa corpus we used for this consists of about 16,900 words of which roughly one third is elicited material. The assumption is that, if a morphological process is productive in a language, hapax legomena in the corpus will exhibit it. The basic intuition behind this is that lower frequency items will need to rely on the creativity associated with rules, whereas memory will have a greater role in relation to high frequency items. Therefore, if in Teiwa most instances of transitive verbs with animate objects which occur only once have a prefix, then the rule can be considered productive. If, on the other hand, there is no difference in the behaviour of the hapax legomena, i.e., if there is a more or less even split, then it is impossible to conclude anything.

The results for transitive verb hapaxes are summarized in Table 13. The number before the slash includes hapaxes in elicited material, the number after the slash excluded elicited items.

Bear in mind that we did not search for all verb hapaxes, only transitive ones. The number of intransitive verb hapaxes is not relevant to the question whether morphological rules in transitive verbs are productive, as intransitive verbs are not prefixed in Teiwa at all.

These results strongly indicate that prefixation of animate objects is indeed productive in Teiwa and not an artefact associated with high frequency. 88.8%

Table 13: Hapax legomena of transitive verbs in Teiwa

	Total number of hapaxes	With prefix	Proportion
With animate object	9 / 7	8 / 6	88.8%/85.7%
With inanimate object	13 / 12	1 / 1	7.7%/8.3%

of transitive verb hapaxes with an animate object actually also have a prefix. If the elicited hapaxes (2 in total) are eliminated, the proportion is still 85.7%. Conversely, if we look at transitive verbs with an inanimate object, only about 8% of the hapaxes have prefixes. Of course, the Teiwa corpus is nowhere near as large in its coverage as the ones Baayen used, but they give us the best evidence we can obtain at the moment.

Having established that object indexation seems to be a productive rule in Teiwa we turn to the second question, namely whether the observed animacy effects might be associated with the verb itself.

If prefixation in Teiwa were purely a matter of sensitivity to the animacy property of the object, rather than a manifestation of the class to which a verb belongs, we would expect one and the same verb to alternate between prefixation and non-prefixation, depending on the animacy of the object it happened to be taking. This, however, is typically not the case. There are instances where the very same verb has a prefix regardless of the animacy value of the object. This is illustrated for the verb *-uyan*, which is prefixing in (45), where it appears with an animate P, and also prefixing in (46), where it appears with an inanimate P:

(45) Teiwa (Klamer 2010a: 88)
 A   qavif ga-uyan gi si   ...
 3SG goat 3-search go SIM
 'He went searching for a goat, [...]'

(46) Teiwa (Klamer 2010a: 340)
 ... ha gi ya'   siis   nuk ga-uyan pin aria'.
   2SG go bamboo_sp. dry one 3-search hold arrive
 '[...] You go look for dry bamboo to bring here.'

The converse case is more frequent. There are many transitive verbs that never index their P, regardless of its animacy value. This is illustrated in (47) and (48) where the verb *tumah* occurs with an animate and an inanimate P, respectively.

10 Participant marking: Corpus study and video elicitation

The examples (49) and (50) illustrate this for the serial verb construction *ta tas* [on stand] 'stand on'. The verb does not have a pronominal index regardless of the animacy value of the object.

(47) Teiwa (Response to video clip C13_bump_into_person_38, SP4)
Uy   masar nuk wa kri   tumah.
person male   one go old_man bump
'A man is going and bumps into an old man.'

(48) Teiwa (Response to video clip C16_bump_into_tree_42, SP4)
Kri   nuk tewar wa tei   tumah.
old_man one walk go tree bump
'An old man walks and bumps into a tree.'

(49) Teiwa (Response to video clip C04_step.on.person_32, SP4)
Bif goqai ma   oma' ta tas
child   come father on stand
'A child comes and steps on his father.'

(50) Teiwa (Response to video clip C20_step.on.banana_33, SP4)
kri   nuk ma   moxoi muban ta tas   [...]
old.man one come banana ripe   on stand [...]
'An old man comes and steps on a ripe banana ...'

In Teiwa we find the formation of a class of prefixed vs. a class of not prefixed verbs based on the animacy value of the objects a verb typically occurs with. There are four classes of verbs.

The first class of transitive verbs consists of prefixed verbs. These always index their P with a prefix and they typically occur with animate objects. A separate noun phrase constituent may optionally be present. In addition to the transitive verbs used in the video elicitation task *-arar* 'be afraid of s.o.', *-tan (tup)* [lit. call get.up] 'wake s.o. up', and *-u'an* 'carry s.o.', further examples from the corpus are: *-ayas* 'throw at s.o.', *-bun* 'answer s.o.', *-fin* 'catch s.o.', *-lal* 'show to s.o.', *-liin* 'invite s.o.', *-pak* 'call s.o.', *-panaat* 'send to s.o.', *-regan* 'ask s.o.', *-rian* 'look after s.o.', *-sas* 'feed s.o.', *-soi* 'order s.o.', *-tiar* 'chase s.o.', *-ua'* 'hit s.o.', *-'uam* 'teach s.o.', and *-wei* 'bathe s.o.'.

The second class of transitive verbs consists of unprefixed verbs. These never index their P and typically occur with inanimate objects. A separate noun phrase constituent may optionally be present. Examples from the video elicitation task are: *si'* 'wash sth.', *miman* 'smell sth.', and *wuraq* 'hear sth.'. Further examples from the corpus are: *bali* 'see s.o./sth.', *bangan* 'ask for sth.', *boqai* 'cut sth. up', *dumar* 'push sth. away', *hela* 'pull sth.', *mat* 'take sth.', *me'* 'be in sth.', *moxod* 'drop s.o./sth.', *ol* 'buy sth.', *pin* 'hold s.o./sth.', *qas* 'split sth.', *taxar* 'cut sth. in two', *tian* 'carry sth. on head or shoulder'.

An explanation of the behaviour of the verb (i.e., whether it has a prefix) based on verb semantics is likely to fail. Verbs with similar semantics can vary, such as the verb 'to cradle' in (51), in contrast to the verb 'to hold' in (52):

(51) Teiwa (Response to video clip P15_hold.person_24, SP3)
Kri   nuk g-oqai   g-u'an-an   tas-an.
old_man one 3-child 3-cradle-REAL stand-REAL
'An old man is standing cradling his child.'

(52) Teiwa (Klamer 2010a: 436)
Qau ba   iman ta   mauqubar g-oqai pin bir-an   gi [...]
good SEQ 3PL TOP frog   3-child hold run-REAL go
'So they hold the baby frog and go, [...].'

Some verbs which typically occur with inanimates, e.g., *pin* 'hold', could well occur with animates, as in (52). It is very difficult to identify certain verb semantics which would be associated with the verb taking a prefix. Generally, when looking at verbs of similar semantics, some verbs will have a prefix while others do not.

As mentioned above, it is not the case that prefixation in Teiwa is purely a matter of sensitivity to the animacy property of the object, but rather a manifestation of the class to which a verb belongs. We do, however, find a few cases where one and the same verb alternates between prefixation and non-prefixation or between two different sets of prefixes, depending on the animacy of the object the verb happened to be taking. Such verbs make up the classes 3 and 4, respectively.

Transitive verbs of class 3 either have a prefix and an animate object or no prefix and an inanimate object. This class is small and consists of five verbs, given in Table 14.

For these verbs the animate-inanimate distinction constitutes an agreement feature realized by the presence or the absence of the prefix.

Transitive verbs of class 4 select one prefix set with animate objects and another prefix set with inanimate objects. This class comprises only four items, listed in Table 15.

10 Participant marking: Corpus study and video elicitation

Table 14: Transitive verbs with or without prefix (class 3)

-dee	'burn s.o.'	dee	'burn sth.'
-mai	'keep for s.o.'	mai	'save sth.'
-mar	'follow s.o.'	mar	'take/get sth.'
-mian	'give to s.o.'	mian	'put at sth.'
-sii	'bite s.o.'	sii	'bite (into) sth.'

Table 15: Transitive verbs taking different prefixes (class 4)

-kiid	'cry for s.o.'	'cry about sth.'
-tad	'strike s.o.'	'strike at sth.'
-wultag	'talk to s.o.'	'talk about sth.'
-wulul	'tell s.o.'	'tell sth.'

Class 4 shows alternation between two different prefixes in the 3rd person. Inanimate objects are indexed with the normal *ga-* prefix whereas animate objects take an augmented form (with a glottal stop). Compare examples (53) and (54).

(53) Teiwa (Klamer 2010a: 92)
Ha gi ga'-wulul.
2SG go 3.AN-talk
'You go tell him.'

(54) Teiwa (Klamer 2010a: 92)
Ha gi ga-wulul.
2SG go 3-talk
'You go tell it (i.e., some proposition)!'

This contrast exists in the third person only. Although the first and second persons are always animate they nonetheless take the unaugmented prefix forms with the class 4 verbs, e.g., *ha gi na-wulul/*na'-wulul* 'You go tell me'.

There is a potential issue in these examples because the semantic roles of the non-subject arguments in (53), a human recipient, and (54), a proposition or message expressed as the object, are different but this need not concern us because Teiwa (as indeed all Alor-Pantar languages) has secundative alignment (Klamer

2010b: 449, 454).[13] This means that the language generally treats recipients (and goals, including those of ballistic motion and comitatives) like patients, both of which are indexed with a prefix, e.g., *-an* 'give to s.o.', *-honan* 'come to s.o.', *-ayas* 'throw at s.o.', and *-yix* 'descend with s.o.'. Therefore it is fully expected that the non-subject arguments in (53) and (54) – despite their difference in semantic role – are both indexed with a prefix. For the verbs in class 4, we can see the development of a small inflectional paradigm in which the animate-inanimate distinction constitutes an agreement feature realized by different prefix types. Importantly, it also contrasts with class 3, which in essence realizes the same animate-inanimate distinction, but uses prefixation vs. lack of prefixation to do it rather than different prefix forms. These are therefore examples of arbitrary inflection classes, as the same animate-inanimate distinction (in classes 3 and 4) has different reflexes depending on the verb. So there is strong evidence for Teiwa contrasting with Abui and Kamang, and this appears to be associated with a move from semantic related factors to a greater role for animacy and verb classes.

6 Discussion and conclusion

The Alor-Pantar languages are of significant macrotypological interest for pronominal indexing, because they show contrasting behaviours in terms of the degree to which purely lexical information is involved. For Abui, prefixation is determined to a greater extent by the semantics of the event, rather than the semantics associated directly with the lexical item. Volitionality and affectedness are interpreted at the level of the event itself, rather than a constant and indefeasible part of a verb's semantics. For Kamang, which has what would still be broadly defined as a semantic alignment system, affectedness also plays a role, but there appears to be greater scope for arbitrary association between a prefix-class and a particular verb, so that verbs are more restricted in terms of the choice of prefix with which they may occur. It is reasonable to infer that the restriction of a given verb to one prefix series, as happens in Kamang, results from the strengthening of associations between particular verbs and the prefix series on the basis of those verbs' frequent occurrences in constructions related to the original event-related semantics. These prefixes then become conventionally associated with subsets of verbs, as is the case in Kamang, and are restricted to those verbs. In contrast with Kamang, for Teiwa animacy plays an important role in effecting this conventional association. While we cannot be entirely sure about the diachronic scenario, the

---

[13] On the notion of secundative alignment, see Dryer (1986).

10 Participant marking: Corpus study and video elicitation

most entrenched conventionalization is associated with the prefix series which is the oldest, namely the PAT series.

The video elicitation task confirms the importance of animacy in Teiwa. There is interesting interaction of animacy and volitionality in Abui, where volitionality and animacy work together to increase the likelihood of the intransitive subject (S) being indexed on the verb. Our experimental method confirmed the fascination of the Alor-Pantar languages for understanding the role of the usual suspects in realizing grammatical relations. While it is possible to identify roles for the different factors, their influence is manifested in different ways and to different degrees. This is further evidence that it is impossible to assume a direct relationship between the semantics and the formal realization of indexation. The experiment shows that none of these systems of indexation is semantically fully transparent. Being an animate P is not a sufficient condition to be indexed in Teiwa. Many animate P's are, in fact, not indexed and the number of verbs which alternate between having an animate object, which is indexed with a prefix, or having an inanimate object, which is not indexed or indexed with a different prefix, is quite small.

The three Alor-Pantar languages considered in this chapter provide important typological insights into the relationship between referential properties and lexical stipulation as evinced in a language's patterns of pronominal indexing. In all of the languages we have discussed here, properties of the verb play some role. In the semantically aligned languages, this emerges from the lexical semantics of verbs with regard to affectedness or volitionality. But we can observe a change in orientation from properties expressing a relationship between participants and events, as in Abui and Kamang, to properties involving lexical features of the verb itself. Semantic factors in events are reinterpreted as constraints on individual verbs. The role of animacy is increasingly important in Teiwa. The language has a very small set of verbs (classes 3 and 4) in which animacy figures as an agreement feature. Thus, in Teiwa a conventionalization has taken place where verb classes become associated with the animacy value of the objects with which the verbs in a given class typically occur.

Across the three languages, the nature of the semantic restrictions on pronominal indexing differs, and animacy is a property which actually allows for arbitrary classes to emerge, much more so than affectedness and volitionality. This is because it classifies the argument of the verb according to animacy but also involves an expectation based on the verb's own semantics (about the properties of the objects it selects for), while at the same time not directly classifying the relationship between the participant and the event. Given this dual nature of animacy, there is therefore a strong potential for properties based on what is expected to clash with what actually occurs, and there is greater potential for arbitrary classes to emerge. A reasonable hypothesis is that the Teiwa system represents one possible trajectory within Alor-Pantar from a system which is highly dependent on the event semantics to one where the restrictions on prefixes lead to a much smaller number of verbs being prefixed.

A Appendix

A.1 The Video Elicitation Task

A.1.1 Background

These short video elicitation stimuli are a means to systematically study the variation in the patterns of pronominal marking in the Papuan languages of Alor and Pantar. The design of an elicitation task consisting of video clips, which systematically vary the parameters under investigation, is inspired and influenced by the video elicitation tools developed by the Max Planck Institute for Psycholinguistics in Nijmegen. See Bohnemeyer, Bowerman & Brown (2001); Bowerman et al. (2004) and Evans et al. (2004).

All Alor-Pantar languages share the typologically rare trait that they mark objects or undergoers on the verbs, rather than subjects or actors (Siewierska 2013). However, there is considerable within-group variation as to how this is done and also what the relevant semantic parameters are which govern the indexation patterns. For instance, Teiwa (Klamer 2010a) aligns its arguments on a nominative-accusative basis indexing the object of some (but not all) transitive verbs. The prime factor which determines whether a verb indexes its object is animacy (Klamer & Kratochvíl 2006; Klamer 2010a). Abui (Kratochvíl 2007; 2011), on the other hand, has a semantic alignment system, in which the undergoer is marked on the verb. In intransitive clauses, more undergoer-like arguments are indexed, e.g., 'He is ill', whereas more actor-like ones are not, e.g., 'He runs'.

Although the video clips were designed with the argument-indexing typology of the Alor-Pantar languages in mind they can readily be used to elicit patterns of participant marking in languages which employ case and/or adpositions or a combination of argument indexing and case/adpositional marking.

A.1.2 Task

A.1.2.1 Materials The task consists of 42 video clips to be described by the consultants. The clips have been divided into two sets, a core set and a peripheral set, each consisting of 21 clips. From the pair of clips for each combination of factors, one clip is in the core set, one is in the peripheral set. The clips have been randomly ordered within their sets and afterwards been numbered from C01 to C21 (core set) and P01 to P21 (peripheral set).

The clips are named in the following way, e.g., C14_sit.down_01.mp4.

The initial letter identifies a clip as belonging either to the core (C) or the peripheral (P) set. The letter is followed by a number, which indicates the order in which the clips are to be tested. Then comes a short characterization of the event shown in the clip. The final number before the file extension refers to the number of the clip before randomization.

For example: C14_sit.down_01.mp4 – This clip belongs to the core set, it is number 14 in the randomized clip order, it depicts a man sitting down, before randomization it was clip number 01, and it is a MP4-file.

Do test the clips on your laptop before you go to the field!

A.1.2.2 Requirements Laptop with Windows Media Player (or indeed any player which handles MPEG-4 video files) or Quicktime (for Mac). The videos have a sound track which is not essential for understanding what is going on but which provides ambient sounds, so make sure you turn up the volume on your laptop. Without sound the clips will probably feel less natural. Record responses on audio- and/or video-tape with an external microphone.

A.1.2.3 Number of speakers Run the stimuli with four different couples of speakers. If feasible, it might be a good idea to have one speaker describe the clips to the other, who is sitting behind the computer screen and is not able to see the clips. That way the speaker doing the experiment has someone to address when describing the clips. If this is not feasible or undesirable for any reason, having both speakers looking at the clips will also be fine. For each speaker, you should record full meta-data, such as age, sex, education, language used in the task, other languages known by the speaker, etc. Of course, it is fine to run the experiment with individual speakers rather than pairs of speakers.

A.1.2.4 Procedure

1. Make sure you audio- and/or video-tape each elicitation session.

2. You and your speaker(s) sit in front of the laptop. Explain to each speaker that they will see scenes in which someone does something or something happens, and that they should afterwards describe what happened. You then prompt them after each clip, saying "Can you describe the scene?". You can stop prompting speakers in this way once it's no longer necessary.

3. You can repeat a clip as often as you need to, if the speaker wants to see it again. You can also go back to a previous clip, if necessary. If the speaker does not recognize an object in a clip you can explain what it is.

10 Participant marking: Corpus study and video elicitation

4. It is crucial that you get a description of the event depicted in the clip that includes a verb which roughly corresponds to the English verb in the clip label. If that does not happen you might have to probe for the intended verb.

For example, it is conceivable that a speaker describes a scene in which a man is "lying" on the ground as "There is a man on the ground". Similarly, if a speaker gives a description of possible intentions the agent might have, like "He's cleaning up' (for *wash plate*), or "He wants the man to come to him" (for *pull person*), or a very general description of the scene, you should immediately probe for the intended verb. If a speaker uses a serial verb construction make sure this is the most basic way of encoding the event.

A.1.2.5 Further probing and elicitation While carrying out the procedure outlined above opportunities for further probing might come up. This does not have to be done with every single speaker.

In some cases, you might want to probe further whether the indexing patterns of a verb change when the animacy value of the object/undergoer changes. It might for example be possible to use some of the verbs of spatial configuration, such as 'stand' and 'lie', with inanimates (as in English). Or you might want to find out what happens to the indexing patterns, if a child falls instead of a coconut?

Another point for further probing is following up on any alternative verbs which a speaker might have used in the description of a particular event. What is the exact meaning of the verb? What are its indexing patterns?

It might be worth enquiring further into what happens to indexation when the volitionality of the Agent (e.g., Agent does something inadvertently) or the telicity of the event (e.g., 'eating bananas' vs. 'eat a banana up') change. It'll probably turn out quite quickly whether something is going on there.

Some events might be described with a serial verb construction. When this happens, make sure that this is the most basic way of encoding the event.

Finally, for the clips where it makes sense, you could ask the speakers to imagine that they themselves *did* what was shown in the clip or that it *happened to them*. Ask them to imagine that they went home to their family and told them about it. This would yield a 1st person singular participant (in the agent or patient role) and will be helpful in finding out about or excluding person effects. Again, it will not be necessary to do this with all speakers and it might well turn out that it only works with some.

A.1.2.6 List of video clips Below is a list of all video clips for the task. Each row provides information on the combination of factors which define a given cell in the possibility space. For each cell, there are two clips. The verb describing the main event in each clip is given numbered from 01-42 (which is the original numbering). There is a short description of the event depicted in each clip. Finally, the name of the clip file is given. Core set video clips appear in boldface. The full set of video clips can be downloaded from http://www.smg.surrey.ac.uk/projects/alor-pantar/pronominal-marking-video-stimuli/.

participants	volitional	telic	animate	stative	event	Description	Clip file name
1	+	+	+	−	**1 sit down**	Person sitting down.	C14_sit.down_01
1	+	+	+	−	2 stand up	Person standing up.	P21_stand.up_02
1	+	−	+	+	3 stand	Person standing.	P17_stand_03
1	+	−	+	+	**4 lie**	Person lying on the ground.	C10_lie_04
1	+	−	+	−	**5 dance**	People dancing.	C03_dance_05
1	+	−	+	−	6 run	Person running across the frame.	P20_run_06
1	−	+	+	−	7 wake up	Person waking up suddenly.	P04_wake.up_07
1	−	+	+	−	**8 fall asleep**	Person sitting, falling asleep.	C06_fall.asleep_08
1	−	+	−	−	**9 fill up**	Glass being filled from bottle.	C09_fill.up_09
1	−	+	−	−	10 go out	Flame goes out.	P03_go.out_10
1	−	−	+	+	**11 sleep**	Person sleeping.	C05_sleep_11
1	−	−	+	+	12 be tall	Two people, one tall and one short.	P05_be.tall_12
1	−	−	+	−	**13 laugh**	Person laughing.	C07_laugh_13
1	−	−	+	−	14 fall	Person slipping and falling.	P09_person_fall_14
1	−	−	−	+	15 be big	One big and two small stones.	P18_be.big_15
1	−	−	−	+	16 be long	One long and three short logs.	C17_be.long_16
1	−	−	−	−	17 fall	Coconut falling.	C15_fall_17
1	−	−	−	−	18 burn	Burning house.	P10_burn_18
2	+	+	+	−	19 wake s.o. up	Person waking another person up.	P07_wake.up.person_19
2	+	+	+	−	**20 run to s.o.**	Child running to parent.	C12_run.to.person_20
2	+	+	−	−	21 eat sth.	Person eating a banana.	C11_eat.banana_21
2	+	+	−	−	22 wash sth.	Person washing plate.	P16_wash.plate_22
2	+	−	+	+	**23 lean on s.o.**	Child leaning on parent.	C02_lean.on.person_23

10 Participant marking: Corpus study and video elicitation

participants	volitional	telic	animate	stative	event	Description	Clip file name
2	+	−	+	+	24 *hold* s.o.	Person holding child.	P15_hold.person_24
2	+	−	+	−	25 *pull* s.o.	A pulling B.	C01_pull.person_25
2	+	−	+	−	26 *smell* s.o.	A sniffing at B, disgusted face.	P01_smell.person_26
2	+	−	−	+	27 *lean* on sth.	Person leaning on house.	C21_lean.on.house_27
2	+	−	−	+	28 *hold* sth.	Person hugging a tree.	P13_hold.tree_28
2	+	−	−	−	29 *pull* sth.	Child pulling a log.	C18_pull.log_29
2	+	−	−	−	30 *smell* sth.	Person sniffing at food, disgusted face.	P02_smell.food_30
2	−	+	+	−	31 *fall onto* s.o.	Banana drops on person's stomach.	P19_fall.onto.person_31
2	−	+	+	−	32 *step* on s.o.	Child stepping on lying person.	C04_step.on.person_32
2	−	+	−	−	33 *step* on sth.	Person stepping on a banana.	C20_step.on.banana_33
2	−	+	−	−	34 *fall onto* sth.	Banana falling onto log.	P11_fall.onto.log_34
2	−	−	+	+	35 *be* afraid of s.o.	Child afraid of snake.	C08_be.afraid.of.snake_35
2	−	−	+	+	36 *bend* person	Rock bending someone's back.	P08_bend.person_36
2	−	−	+	−	37 *hear* s.o.	A hears B calling out and turns head.	P12_hear.person_37
2	−	−	+	−	38 *bump* into s.o.	A bumping into B.	C13_bump.into.person_38
2	−	−	−	+	39 *bend* sth.	Log lying on a plank bending it.	P14_bend.plank_39
2	−	−	−	+	40 *be* afraid of sth.	Person afraid of axe.	C19_be.afraid.of.axe_40
2	−	−	−	−	41 *hear* sth.	A hears noise and turns head.	P06_hear.noise_41
2	−	−	−	−	42 *bump* into sth.	Person walking into a tree.	C16_bump.into_tree_42

Acknowledgments

This chapter presents an overview of the results reported in two earlier papers, "Conditions on pronominal marking in the Alor-Pantar languages" by Sebastian Fedden, Dunstan Brown, Greville G. Corbett, Marian Klamer, Gary Holton, Laura C. Robinson and Antoinette Schapper, published in *Linguistics* 51(1): 33-74 in March 2013, and "Variation in pronominal indexing: lexical stipulation vs. referential properties in the Alor-Pantar languages" by Sebastian Fedden, Dunstan Brown, František Kratochvíl, Laura C. Robinson and Antoinette Schapper published in *Studies in Language* 38(1): 44-79 in May 2014. This chapter also has an additional section on the video elicitation to be used by others for further comparative work. We would like to thank the editor and two anonymous reviewers. The work reported here was supported under the European Science Foundation's EuroBABEL program (project "Alor-Pantar languages: origin and theoretical impact"). At the time of this write-up, Fedden and Brown were funded by the Arts and Humanities Research Council (UK) under grant AH/K003194/1. We thank this funding body for its support. *Correspondence address:* Sebastian Fedden, Surrey Morphology Group, School of English and Languages, University of Surrey, Guildford GU2 7XH, United Kingdom. E-mail: s.fedden@surrey.ac.uk.

Abbreviations

1	1st person	GOAL	goal
2	2nd person	INCL	inclusive
3	3rd person	IPFV	imperfective
ACT	actor	LOC	locative
AGT	agent	PAT	patient
AL	alienable	PFV	perfective
AN	animate	PL	plural
AST	assistive	PN	personal name
AUX	auxiliary	POSS	possessive
BEN	benefactive	REAL	realis
COMPL	completive	REC	recipient
CONTR_FOC	contrastive focus	SEQ	sequential
DIR	directional	SG	singular
DUR	durative	SIM	simultaneous
EXCL	exclusive	SPEC	specific
EXCLAM	exclamative	TOP	topic
GEN	genitive	V	verb

References

Aissen, Judith. 2003. Differential object marking: Iconicity and economy. *Natural Language and Linguistic Theory* 21(3). 435–483.

Arkadiev, Peter. 2008. Thematic roles, event structure, and argument encoding in semantically aligned languages. In Mark Donohue & Søren Wichmann (eds.), *The typology of semantic alignment*, 101–117. Oxford: Oxford University Press.

Baayen, R. Harald. 1992. Quantitative aspects of morphological productivity. In Geert Booij & Jaap van Marle (eds.), *Yearbook of morphology*, 109–149. Dordrecht: Kluwer Academic Publishers.

Beavers, John. 2011. On affectedness. *Natural Language and Linguistic Theory* 29(2). 335–370.

Bickel, Balthasar. 2008. On the scope of the referential hierarchy in the typology of grammatical relations. In Greville G. Corbett & Michael Noonan (eds.), *Case and grammatical relations. Papers in honour of Bernard Comrie*, 191–210. Amsterdam: John Benjamins.

Bohnemeyer, Jürgen, Melissa Bowerman & Penelope Brown. 2001. Cut and break clips. In Stephen C. Levinson & Nick J. Enfield (eds.), *Manual for the field season 2001*, 90–96. Nijmegen: Max Planck Institute for Psycholinguistics.

Bossong, Georg. 1991. Differential object marking in Romance and beyond. In Dieter Wanner & Douglas A. Kibbee (eds.), *New analyses in Romance linguistics, selected papers from the XVIII linguistic symposium on Romance languages 1988*, 143–170. Amsterdam: Benjamins.

Bowerman, Melissa, Marianne Gullberg, Asifa Majid & Bhuvana Narasimhan. 2004. Put project: the cross-linguistic encoding of placement events. In Asifa Majid (ed.), *Field manual volume 9*, 10–24. Nijmegen: Max Planck Institute for Psycholinguistics.

Comrie, Bernard. 1976. *Aspect*. Cambridge: Cambridge University Press.

Croft, William. 1988. Agreement vs. case marking in direct objects. In Michael Barlow & Charles A. Ferguson (eds.), *Agreement in natural languages. Approaches, theories, descriptions*, 159–180. Stanford: Center for the Study of Language & Information.

Dalrymple, Mary & Irina Nikolaeva. 2011. *Objects and information structure*. Cambridge: Cambridge University Press.

DeLancey, Scott. 1985. On active typology and the nature of agentivity. In Frans Plank (ed.), *Relational typology*, vol. 2, 47–60. Berlin: Mouton.

Donohue, Mark & Søren Wichmann. 2008. *The typology of semantic alignment*. Oxford: Oxford University Press.

Dowty, David. 1991. Thematic proto-roles and argument selection. *Language* 67(3). 547–619.
Dryer, Matthew S. 1986. Primary objects, secondary objects and antidative. *Language* 62(4). 808–845.
Evans, Nicholas, Stephen C. Levinson, Nick J. Enfield, Alice Gaby & Asifa Majid. 2004. Reciprocal constructions and situation type. In Asifa Majid (ed.), *Field manual volume 9*, 25–30. Nijmegen: Max Planck Institute for Psycholinguistics.
Fedden, Sebastian, Dunstan Brown, Greville G. Corbett, Marian Klamer, Gary Holton, Laura C. Robinson & Antoinette Schapper. 2013. Conditions on pronominal marking in the Alor-Pantar languages. *Linguistics* 51(1). 33–74.
Foley, William A. & Robert Van Valin. 1984. *Functional syntax and universal grammar*. Cambridge: Cambridge University Press.
Givón, Talmy. 1976. Subject, topic, and grammatical agreement. In Charles Li (ed.), *Subject and topic*, 57–98. New York: Academic Press.
Givón, Talmy. 1985. Ergative morphology and transitivity gradients in Newari. In Frans Plank (ed.), *Relational typology*, 89–107. Berlin: Mouton de Gruyter.
Haan, Johnson Welem. 2001. *The grammar of Adang: a Papuan language spoken on the island of Alor East Nusa Tenggara - Indonesia*. Sydney: University of Sydney PhD thesis.
Heusinger, Klaus von & Georg Kaiser. 2005. The evolution of differential object marking in Spanish. In Klaus von Heusinger & Georg Kaiser (eds.), *Proceedings of the workshop "specificity and the evolution/emergence of nominal determination systems in Romance"*, 33–70. Konstanz: Universität Konstanz.
Heusinger, Klaus von & Georg Kaiser. 2011. Affectedness and differential object marking in Spanish. *Morphology* 21(1). 1–25.
Holton, Gary. 2010. Person-marking, verb classes and the notion of grammatical alignment in Western Pantar (Lamma). In Michael Ewing & Marian Klamer (eds.), *Typological and areal analyses: contributions from east Nusantara*, 97–117. Canberra: Pacific Linguistics.
Hopper, Paul J. & Sandra A. Thompson. 1980. Transitivity in grammar and discourse. *Language* 56(1). 251–299.
Hurford, James R. 2007. *The origins of meaning: language in the light of evolution* (Studies in the Evolution of Language 8). Oxford: Oxford University Press.
Klamer, Marian. 2008. The semantics of semantic alignment in Eastern Indonesia. In Mark Donohue & Søren Wichmann (eds.), *The typology of semantic alignment*, 221–251. Oxford: Oxford University Press.
Klamer, Marian. 2010a. *A grammar of Teiwa* (Mouton Grammar Library 49). Berlin: Mouton de Gruyter.

Klamer, Marian. 2010b. Ditransitives in Teiwa. In Andrej Malchukov, Martin Haspelmath & Bernard Comrie (eds.), *Studies in ditransitive constructions*, 427–455. Berlin: Mouton de Gruyter.

Klamer, Marian & František Kratochvíl. 2006. The role of animacy in Teiwa and Abui (Papuan). In *Proceedings of BLS 32*. Berkeley Linguistic Society. Berkeley.

Kratochvíl, František. 2007. *A grammar of Abui: a Papuan language of Alor*. Utrecht: LOT.

Kratochvíl, František. 2011. Transitivity in Abui. *Studies in Language* 35(3). 589–636.

Malchukov, Andrej. 2005. Case pattern splits, verb types and construction competition. In Mengistu Amberber & Helen de Hoop (eds.), *Competition and variation in natural languages: The case for case*, 73–117. Amsterdam: Elsevier.

Mithun, Marianne. 1991. Active/agentive case marking and its motivations. *Language* 67(3). 510–546.

Mohanan, Tara. 1990. *Arguments in Hindi*. Stanford: Stanford University PhD thesis.

Næss, Åshild. 2004. What markedness marks: The markedness problem with direct objects. *Lingua* 114(9-10). 1186–1212.

Næss, Åshild. 2006. Case semantics and the agent-patient opposition. In Leonid Kulikov, Andrej Malchukov & Peter de Swart (eds.), *Case, valency and transitivity*, 309–327. Amsterdam: John Benjamins.

Næss, Åshild. 2007. *Prototypical transitivity*. Amsterdam: John Benjamins.

Robinson, Laura C. & John Haan. 2014. Adang. In Antoinette Schapper (ed.), *Papuan languages of Timor, Alor and Pantar: Sketch grammars*, vol. 1, 221–284. Berlin: Mouton de Gruyter.

Schapper, Antoinette. 2014a. Kamang. In Antoinette Schapper (ed.), *Papuan languages of Timor, Alor and Pantar: Sketch grammars*, vol. 1, 285–350. Berlin: Mouton de Gruyter.

Schapper, Antoinette (ed.). 2014b. *Papuan languages of Timor, Alor and Pantar: Sketch grammars*. Vol. 1. Berlin: Mouton de Gruyter.

Schapper, Antoinette & Marten Manimau. 2011. *Kamus pengantar Bahasa Kamang-Indonesia-Inggris (Introductory Kamang-Indonesian-English dictionary)* (UBB Language & Culture Series: A 7). Kupang: Unit Bahasa dan Budaya (BDD).

Siewierska, Anna. 2004. *Person*. Cambridge: Cambridge University Press.

Siewierska, Anna. 2013. Verbal person marking. In Matthew S. Dryer & Martin Haspelmath (eds.), *The world atlas of language structures online*, chapter 102.

Munich: Max Planck Digital Library. http://wals.info/chapter/102, accessed 2014-03-29.

Tsunoda, Tasaku. 1981. Split case-marking in verb-types and tense/aspect/mood. *Linguistics* 19(5-6). 389–438.

Tsunoda, Tasaku. 1985. Remarks on transitivity. *Journal of Linguistics* 21. 385–396.

Name index

Aa, Robide van der, 149
Aikhenvald, Alexandra Y., 28, 32
Aissen, Judith, 405, 413, 428
Anceaux, J. C., 149
Anonymous, 7, 12, 50
Aoki, Eriko, 314
Aplugi, Helena, 314
Arka, I Wayan, 315
Arkadiev, Peter, 412, 413
Arndt, Paul, 315

Baayen, R. Harald, 429
Badan Pusat Statistik, 4
Baird, Louise, 4, 7, 9, 17, 19, 32, 37, 59, 124, 227, 272, 298, 314, 367
Bani, Heronimus, 314
Barnes, Robert H., 6, 11, 228, 233, 235, 293, 307
Beavers, John, 405, 417, 418
Bellwood, Peter, 9, 184
Bickel, Balthasar, 239, 428
Blust, Robert Andrew, 6, 33, 86, 191, 282, 284, 304, 324
Bohnemeyer, Jürgen, 437
Bossong, Georg, 405
Bowerman, Melissa, 437
Brotherson, Anna, 125
Brown, Dunstan, 16, 19, 20, 26, 35
Brown, Penelope, 437
Bryant, D., 72
Burenhult, Niclas, 239, 241, 271, 272

Calon, L. F., 315
Campbell, Lyle, 162
Capell, Arthur, 91, 149, 307
Carel, Pieter Jan Batist, 149
Carr, Felicita M., 125
Cheung, Candice Chi-Hang, 239
Chung, Siaw-Fong, 32
Comrie, Bernard, 15, 277, 279, 282, 329, 413
Coolhaas, W. Ph., 11
Corbett, Greville G., 23, 398
Cowan, H. K. J., 173
Cowan, Hendrik Karel Jan, 150
Croft, William, 405

Dalrymple, Mary, 428
de Josselin de Jong, Jan Petrus Benjamin, 5, 50, 125
de Roever, Arend, 11
de Vries, Lourens J., 158, 159, 174, 175
DeLancey, Scott, 418
Delpada, Benediktus, 9, 125, 209, 235
Diessel, Holger, 239, 243
Dietrich, Stefan, 11
Dixon, R. M. W., 239
Donohue, Mark, 4, 8, 148, 150, 163, 167, 183, 278, 285, 406
Dowty, David, 419
Drabbe, Peter, 156, 177
Drummond, Alexei J., 73, 74
Dryer, Matthew S., 22, 23, 25, 365, 371, 397, 434

Name index

Du Bois, Cora, 8, 12, 61
Dunn, Michael, 69

Ebert, Karen H., 239
Engelenhoven, Aone van, viii, 4, 5, 9, 16, 30, 34, 35, 58, 67, 91–94, 98, 100, 101, 105, 107, 123, 137, 148, 152, 167–170, 179, 303
Evans, Nicholas, 278, 285, 437
Ewing, Michael C., 9, 28

Fatubun, Reimundus, 176
Fedden, Sebastian, viii, 16, 19, 20, 26, 35, 154, 158, 160, 404, 413
Fennig, Charles D., 3–5, 150
Flassy, Don A. L., 179, 180
Foley, William A., 14, 28, 32, 152, 156–159, 161, 409
Forman, Shepard, 227
Forth, Gregory, 293
Fox, James J., 191, 221

Gaalen, G. A. M. van, 8, 11, 12
Givón, Talmy, 409, 428
Gray, Russell D., 324
Green, Tom, 398
Greenberg, Joseph H., 279, 298
Greenhill, Simon J., 324
Grimes, Charles E., 3, 6, 7, 314

Haan, John, 4, 25, 32, 61, 65, 252, 272, 367, 369, 370, 411
Haan, Johnson Welem, 4, 9, 124, 160, 164, 207, 250–254, 272, 370, 411
Hägerdal, Hans, 7, 11, 12, 308
Hajek, John, 14, 52
Hammarström, Harald, 278, 279, 294, 303, 305, 309

Hanke, Thomas, 298
Haspelmath, Martin, 15
Heeschen, Volker, 271
Heine, Bernd, 284
Hendery, Rachel, 4, 124, 243, 244, 272, 315, 367–369, 384–386
Heston, Tyler, 121, 123
Heusinger, Klaus von, 405, 409
Holland, B. R., 72
Holton, Gary, vii, viii, 4, 9–11, 13, 14, 16, 20, 24, 27, 28, 30, 32, 33, 35, 37, 50, 54, 58, 70, 73, 85–87, 91–93, 96, 100, 101, 103, 106, 107, 118–122, 124, 125, 128, 131, 134, 147, 148, 155–157, 160, 161, 164, 165, 218, 255, 256, 265, 272, 281, 282, 284, 289, 292, 298, 312, 315, 332, 334, 367, 369, 371–373, 389, 410
Hopper, Paul J., 32, 405, 417, 418
Huber, Juliette, viii, 4, 5, 9, 16, 30, 31, 34, 35, 58, 67, 91–94, 98, 100, 101, 105, 107, 118, 123–125, 137, 148, 152, 167–170, 179, 303, 372
Huelsenbeck, J. P., 73
Hull, Geoffrey, 315
Hurford, James R., 415
Huson, D. H., 72

Jacob, June, 7

Kaiser, Georg, 405, 409
Kelen, Herman, 315
Keraf, Gregorius, 315
Klamer, Marian, viii, 4, 6, 7, 9, 15, 18, 19, 22–28, 30–32, 35, 37, 50, 58, 61, 64, 124, 125, 151, 154,

157, 160–162, 184, 227, 232, 234, 244, 245, 272, 284, 287, 295, 298, 300, 307, 308, 314, 315, 331, 365–367, 375, 377, 393, 404, 406, 407, 410, 412, 430, 432, 433, 437
Kratochvíl, František, 4, 7, 9, 17–21, 27, 37, 59, 124, 125, 155, 209, 227, 235, 245, 246, 268, 272, 314, 341, 367, 381, 384, 393, 404, 409–412, 416–418, 420, 437
Kusharyanto, S., 315

Lamma Koly, Mahalalel, 9, 125, 256, 272, 367
Lansing, Stephen J., 10
Laycock, D. C., 277
Le Roux, C. C. F. M., 11
Lean, Glendon, 277, 278
Lemoine, Annie, 7
Levinson, Stephen, 271, 272
Levinson, Stephen C., 239
Lewis, E. Douglas, 315
Lewis, Paul M., 3–6, 70, 150
Lichtenberk, František, 57
Lynch, John, 285

Mahirta, 10
Majewicz, Alfred F., 284, 285
Malchukov, Andrej, 409
Malikosa, Anderias, 367, 387
Manimau, Marten, 35, 125, 213, 235, 367, 404, 422–426
Martis, Non, 8
Matisoff, James A., 282
McElhanon, Kenneth A., 10, 150, 162, 173
McWilliam, Andrew, 10

Meillet, Antoine, 151
Middelkoop, P., 315, 323
Miller, Wick R., 239
Mithun, Marianne, 406
Mohanan, Tara, 405
Mona, Stefano, 75
Morwood, Mike J., 10

Nakagawa, Satoshi, 314
Næss, Åshild, 417, 419
Needham, Rodney., 233, 235
Nicolspeyer, Martha Margaretha, 8, 12, 50, 209, 227
Nikolaeva, Irina, 428
Nishiyama, Kunio, 315
Noonan, Michael, 239

O'Connor, Sue, 10
Olson, Michael, 158

Pagel, Mark, 73
Pampus, Karl-Heinz, 315
Pareira, M. Mandalangi, 315
Pawley, Andrew K., 9, 10, 28, 68, 150, 152, 153, 169, 184
Penn, David, 314
Plank, Frans, 285
Poser, William J., 162
Post, Mark, 239
Purba, Theodorus T., 176

Rambaut, Andrew, 74
Ranoh, Ayub, 314
Reesink, Ger P., 28, 150, 151, 157, 160–162, 184
Roberts, John R., 161
Robinson, Laura C., vii, viii, 4, 9, 10, 13, 14, 16, 25, 27, 28, 30, 32, 35, 50, 61, 65, 70, 73, 87, 93, 100, 101, 106, 107, 121, 122,

Name index

128, 134, 147, 148, 165, 175, 218, 252, 272, 281, 282, 284, 298, 312, 332, 334, 367, 369, 370, 411
Rodemeier, Susanne, 7, 11, 127
Ronquist, F., 73
Ross, Malcolm, 1, 9, 10, 148, 150, 162, 163, 169, 173, 175
Ruhukael, Constantinoepel, 179, 180
Rumbrawer, Frans, 179, 180

Samely, Ursula, 305, 306, 314, 320, 321
San Roque, Lila, 242, 245, 247
Sawardo, P. Wakidi, 315
Schapper, Antoinette, viii, 4, 5, 9, 13, 16, 23–26, 30–32, 34, 35, 50, 58, 67, 91–95, 98, 100, 101, 105, 107, 118, 123–125, 131, 137, 148, 152, 154, 160, 163, 167–170, 179, 213, 235, 240, 242–245, 247, 258, 272, 293, 294, 303, 305, 307, 309, 314, 315, 331, 365, 367–369, 372, 377, 380, 384–386, 393, 404, 408, 422–427
Schneider, David M., 192
Schulze, Wolfgang, 239
Schweitzer, Peter P., 192
Scott, Graham, 156, 158
Senft, Gunter, 239
Shimojo, Mitsuaki, 31
Sidwell, Paul, 282
Siewierska, Anna, 406, 428, 437
Simons, Gary F., 3–5, 150
Sir, Amos, 125
Spriggs, Matthew, 10, 68
Stap, Petrus A. M. van der, 176
Stebbins, Tonya N., 28, 32
Steenbrink, Karel, 11

Steinhauer, Hein, 4, 6, 8, 19, 121, 122, 124, 193, 202, 203, 221, 227, 228, 234, 249, 272
Steltenpool, J., 177
Stokhof, W. A. L., 3, 4, 6, 8, 50, 91, 173, 213, 216, 227, 235, 284, 367, 394, 395
Stolz, Thomas, 333, 337
Stump, Gregory, 331
Summerhayes, Glenn R., 10
Suter, Edgar, 156

Tarno, Y. Lita, 315
Thompson, Sandra A., 405, 417, 418
Trussel, Stephen, 86
Tsunoda, Tasaku, 405, 417, 418

Van Klinken, Catharina, 293, 315
van Staden, Miriam, 28, 151, 157, 160–162, 184
Van Valin, Robert, 409
Veen, Hendrik van der, 149
Verheijen, Jilis A. J., 7, 314, 315
Veselinova, Ljuba, 333, 337
Von Mengden, Ferdinand, 331
Voorhoeve, C., 162
Voorhoeve, C. L., 10, 150, 162, 173

Wada, Yuiti, 153, 162, 168
Warwer, Onesimus, 176
Watuseke, F. S., 149
Wellfelt, Emilie, 11, 13, 305, 307
Wichmann, Søren, 72, 406
Williams, Nick, 4
Windschuttel, Glenn, 266, 272
Winter, Werner, 282
Wouden, F. A. E. van, 191
Wurm, Stephen A., 10, 70, 150, 162, 173

Name index

Xu, Shuhua, 10

Yen, Douglas E., 57

Zubin, David A., 31

Language index

Abau, 32
Abui, 3, 4, 8, 9, 14, 16–22, 24, 25, 27, 35, 36, 50, 51, 55–61, 63–66, 68, 69, 73, 74, 76, 77, 79–86, 120, 122–125, 127–136, 149, 155, 166, 170, 172, 209–212, 219, 220, 222–224, 226, 227, 230–232, 234, 245–247, 259–262, 264, 266, 267, 272, 273, 283, 284, 286, 288, 289, 297, 299, 301, 313, 314, 316–318, 330, 332, 335, 336, 340–342, 344, 346, 347, 349, 350, 353, 355, 366, 367, 371, 381–384, 387–390, 392–399, 404–406, 408–411, 415–422, 428, 434, 435
Adang, 4, 8, 13, 14, 19, 25, 27, 31, 35, 50, 51, 55, 56, 59–66, 68–70, 73, 75–77, 79–86, 102, 120–122, 124, 125, 127–136, 160, 164, 166, 170, 172, 176, 206–209, 219–226, 230–232, 234, 242, 250–253, 258–264, 266, 267, 271–273, 283, 286, 291, 297, 299, 301, 312–314, 316–319, 330, 332, 334, 336, 338, 339, 345–347, 350, 352, 354, 367, 369, 370
Alorese, 3, 6, 9, 11, 50, 62, 76, 85, 231–233, 235, 284, 285, 307, 308, 314, 320, 321
Amarasi, 314, 322, 323
Angave, 32
Apui, 8
Atauro, 300, 314, 322, 323
Austronesian language(s), 1, 3, 5, 6, 10, 13, 31–33, 50, 57, 60–62, 68, 85, 86, 92, 133, 136, 141, 148, 162, 171, 174, 175, 177, 228, 231, 232, 234, 235, 278, 280, 282, 284, 287, 288, 293, 294, 296, 299, 300, 302–309, 314, 320, 322
Awará, 32

Baham, 178–182
Bajau, 7
Barai, 158
Bird's Head language(s), 149, 150
Blagar, 4, 8, 13, 14, 19, 22, 27, 35, 51, 55, 56, 59–64, 66, 68–70, 73, 75–77, 79–86, 102, 120–122, 124, 125, 127–136, 166, 170–172, 179, 192, 193, 199, 200, 202–204, 219–224, 226–228, 231, 233–235, 247–249, 253, 258–266, 271–273, 283, 284, 286, 291, 297, 299, 301, 312–314, 316–319, 324, 330, 334, 350
Bomberai language(s), 149, 150, 173, 178, 179, 181–184

Language index

Bunaq, 5, 31, 91–114, 116, 117, 121, 122, 124, 125, 137–141, 154, 160, 165, 166, 170, 171, 293, 314

Chambri, 32
Chenapian, 32

Dadu'a, 314, 322, 323
Dani language(s), 149, 150, 173, 175, 177, 178
Deing, 4, 13, 35, 75, 125, 127–136, 283, 286, 288, 297, 301, 313, 314, 316–319, 385
Dhao, 314, 322, 323
Dutch, 279
Dyirbal, 239

East Caucasian language(s), 239
Ekari, 176–178
Ende, 305, 307, 308, 314, 320, 321
Enga, 157

Fataluku, 5, 91, 93–106, 108–114, 116, 117, 125, 137–141, 166, 170–172
Finisterre-Huon language(s), 156
Folopa, 32
Fore, 156, 158

Galela, 166
Guarjío, 239

Hamap, 4, 35, 125, 127–136, 172, 176, 283, 286, 291, 297, 301, 312–314, 316–319
Hamtai, 52
Hindi, 405

Idate, 314
Iha, 178, 179, 181

Ilongot, 279, 280, 314
Inanwatan, 158, 159, 173, 174, 178
Indonesian, 3, 7, 8, 13, 30, 32, 55, 76, 329, 330, 342, 346, 349, 361
Iwam, 32

Kabola, 4, 8, 35, 61, 125, 127–136, 171, 172, 176, 232, 283, 286, 291, 297, 301, 312–314, 316–319
Kaera, 4, 8, 9, 14, 15, 19, 22, 25, 27, 28, 35, 36, 51, 52, 54–56, 58–66, 68–70, 72, 73, 76, 77, 79–86, 120, 122, 124, 125, 127–136, 166, 170, 177, 181, 262–266, 272, 273, 283, 286, 288, 289, 297, 299, 301, 313, 314, 316–319, 332, 334, 350, 352, 366
Kafoa, 4, 9, 35, 125, 127–136
Kamang, 3, 4, 8, 14, 19, 20, 22, 24, 26–28, 32, 35, 36, 51, 55–66, 68–70, 72–74, 76, 77, 79–86, 120–122, 124, 125, 127–136, 170, 172, 192, 211, 213–216, 218–227, 230–233, 235, 242, 257–267, 269–273, 281, 283–289, 296–299, 301, 313, 314, 316–319, 330, 332, 333, 335, 336, 340–342, 345–347, 349, 350, 353, 355, 360, 366, 367, 371, 377–381, 385–389, 391–399, 404–408, 410, 411, 414, 419, 422–428, 434, 435
Kambera, 85, 293
Karas, 178, 181, 183
Kedang, 228, 284, 293, 305, 307, 314, 320, 321
Kemak, 300, 305, 314, 322, 323
Keo, 308

Language index

Kiraman, 4, 203, 205, 206, 219–227, 229, 231, 232, 234
Klon, 4, 9, 14, 16, 19, 21, 22, 27, 32, 35, 36, 51, 55, 56, 59, 61, 63–66, 68–70, 73, 76, 77, 79–85, 120, 122–125, 127–136, 166, 170, 172, 176, 177, 227, 262–264, 266, 272, 282, 283, 286, 291, 295, 297–299, 301, 312–314, 316–319, 366–368, 372, 399
Kokoda, 173–175
Komodo, 314, 320, 321
Kui, 4, 12, 35, 51, 55, 56, 58, 59, 61, 63, 64, 66, 68–70, 73, 76, 77, 79–86, 120, 125, 127–136, 149, 166, 170, 172, 176, 177, 262, 263, 266, 272, 273, 283, 286, 290, 291, 294, 296, 297, 300, 301, 308, 310, 312–314, 316–319
Kula, 4, 8, 35, 122, 125, 127–136, 267, 283, 285, 286, 288, 289, 297–301, 305, 313, 314, 316–319, 331, 333, 335, 350, 366, 367, 372
Kunimaipa, 52
Kéo, 305, 307, 314, 320, 321

Lakalei, 314, 322, 323
Lamaholot, 6, 85, 300, 307, 308, 315, 320, 321
Lio, 305, 307, 308, 315, 320, 321
Lower Grand Valley Dani, 175

Makalero, 5, 31, 91, 93, 95–103, 105, 106, 108–114, 116, 117, 123–125, 137–141, 165, 166, 170, 172, 272
Makasae, 5, 91, 93, 95–103, 105, 106, 108–114, 116, 117, 125, 137–141, 166, 170, 172, 227, 272
Malay, 3, 7, 8, 12, 13, 32, 60, 61, 133, 234, 284, 300, 346, 349, 356, 357, 359, 360
Mambai, 85, 171, 287, 293, 300, 305, 307, 315, 322, 323
Manggarai, 171, 315, 320, 321
Marind, 156, 161
Mian, 158, 160
Miskitu, 398

Nage, 287, 305, 307, 315, 320, 321
Naueti, 305
Nedebang, 4, 35, 51, 52, 55–70, 72, 73, 76, 77, 79–86, 120, 125, 127–136, 166, 181, 219
New Guinea language(s), 239
Ngadha, 305, 307, 308, 315, 320, 321
North Halmaheran language(s), 149, 151–153, 155, 156, 159–162, 164–167, 169, 183

Oirata, 5, 50, 91, 93, 95–103, 105, 106, 108–114, 116, 117, 125, 137–141, 166, 170–172
Old Malay, 57

Palu'e, 315, 320, 321
Portuguese, 12, 13
proto-Alor, 166, 172, 176
proto-Alor-Pantar, 14, 16, 21, 23, 27, 30, 31, 50–60, 63–70, 74, 76–78, 80–87, 92–123, 126–136, 141–143, 162–164, 166, 167, 169–172, 174–183, 219, 222, 225, 231, 233, 234, 240, 261–267, 269, 271, 273, 278, 281–286, 289, 290, 292–294, 296, 298,

299, 303, 309–313, 332, 334, 366, 370, 381, 399, 400
proto-Austronesian, 57, 60, 85, 191, 284, 292, 296, 300, 304–306, 308, 309, 320–323
proto-Bomberai, 184
proto-Central East Alor, 296, 310–313
proto-Central East Pantar, 290
proto-Central Pantar, 289, 290, 313
proto-East Alor, 265, 311–313
proto-East Alor Montane, 311–313
proto-Eastern Timor, 92, 95, 137
proto-Malay, 309
proto-Malayo-Polynesian, 33, 60, 85, 86, 133, 136, 141, 171
proto-North-Halmahera, 152, 153, 162–164, 167, 168
proto-Pantar, 289, 290, 310, 311, 313
proto-Straits-West-Alor, 290–296, 309–312
proto-Straits-West-Pantar, 313
proto-Timor, 30, 92–120, 126, 127, 137–143, 170, 172, 177, 181
proto-Timor Alor Pantar, 30, 52, 91–98, 100–105, 107–113, 115, 116, 118–121, 126, 127, 141–143, 148, 152, 165–169, 171, 174–182, 303
proto-Trans-New-Guinea, 150, 152, 156, 162, 163, 169–173, 176–179, 181
proto-West Malayo-Polynesian, 284
proto-Western Pantar, 295, 296

Rembong, 315, 320, 321
Reta, 4, 125, 127–136
Retta, 171, 172, 282, 283, 286, 291, 297, 301, 312, 313, 315–319
Rongga, 305, 307, 308, 315, 320, 321
Russian, 282

Sama-Bajo, 50
Sar, 4, 35, 59, 122, 125, 127–136, 283, 286, 288, 289, 297, 301, 313, 315–319
Sawila, 4, 9, 12, 27, 35, 36, 51, 55–64, 66, 68–70, 72–74, 76, 77, 79–86, 120, 121, 123–125, 127–136, 166, 171, 172, 262–264, 266–268, 271–273, 281–283, 285, 286, 288, 289, 297, 299–301, 305, 313, 316–319, 333, 335, 350, 354, 366, 367, 372, 395
Sika, 315, 320, 321
South Bird's Head language(s), 150, 173, 174

Tabaru, 166
Tambora, 148
Tanae, 32
Tehit, 52
Teiwa, 4, 8, 9, 14–19, 21–24, 26, 31, 36, 50–52, 54–66, 68–70, 72, 73, 75–77, 79–86, 120–122, 124, 125, 127–136, 149, 154, 166, 170, 178, 179, 181, 192, 193, 199–202, 217, 219–224, 226–228, 231, 233, 234, 244, 245, 259–263, 265, 266, 272, 273, 283, 286, 288–290, 297, 299, 301, 303, 313, 315–319, 330–332, 334, 336, 338–340, 344–348, 350, 351, 354, 366, 367, 369–371, 373–377, 382, 384, 385, 387–399, 404–407, 409–411, 419, 428–436, 456
Teiwa, 391
Tetun, 57, 300
Tetun Fehan, 284, 293, 315, 322, 323

Language index

Thao, 282
Tibeto-Burman language(s), 239
Tobelo, 156, 157, 159–161, 164
Tokodede, 57, 287, 299, 300, 305, 307, 308, 315, 322, 323
Trans-New Guinea language(s), 9, 10, 34, 52, 148–153, 156–159, 161–165, 169, 183

Uab Meto, 315, 322, 323
Ujir, 279
Uto-Aztecan language(s), 239

Waima'a, 315, 322, 323
Wantoat, 32
Wersing, 4, 35, 36, 51, 55–57, 59–66, 68–70, 72–74, 76, 77, 79–86, 120, 122–125, 127–136, 149, 166, 216–226, 228, 231, 232, 235, 242–245, 259–266, 272, 273, 283, 285–289, 297, 299–302, 305, 313, 315–319, 366–369, 371, 384–397, 399
West Papuan language(s), 150, 151, 173
Western Dani, 175, 176
Western Pantar, 4, 8, 9, 11, 13, 14, 20, 22, 24, 27, 28, 31, 35, 36, 51–53, 55–66, 68–70, 73, 75–77, 79–86, 118, 120–122, 124, 125, 127–136, 155–158, 161, 166, 172, 178, 192–200, 219–224, 226, 228, 231–234, 242–244, 253–264, 266, 267, 271–273, 282, 283, 285, 287, 290, 291, 294–297, 299–301, 308, 310, 312, 313, 315–318, 332, 334, 336, 340, 344–347, 350, 351, 354, 366–369, 371–373, 375, 384, 387–389, 391–397, 399, 400, 410
Wissel Lakes language(s), 149, 150, 173, 176
Wogamusin, 32

Subject index

actor, 409, 410
additive numeral, 278, 280, 287, 288, 294–296, 298–300, 304, 308–310
adposition, 15, 25, 29, 160, 161, 245, 246, 298
affectedness, 403–406, 408, 409, 414, 417–419, 427, 434, 435
agreement, 434
alienability, 21, 22, 28, 29, 59, 100, 104, 120, 126, 158, 159, 194, 334, 344
alignment, 19, 25, 34, 154, 406
animacy, 17, 331, 368, 391, 397, 398, 404–407, 409, 412, 414, 419, 421, 427–432, 434, 435
apocope, 62, 64, 93, 96
aspect, 24, 27, 160

borrowing, 12, 13, 30, 33, 50, 57–60, 62–68, 73, 75, 85, 86, 92, 118, 133, 136, 141, 163, 167, 174, 175, 177, 182, 231, 278, 282, 284, 287, 292–294, 296, 299, 300, 305, 307–310, 312, 329, 333, 356

cardinal numeral(s), 278, 279, 286, 290, 298, 302, 307, 309, 312, 316, 330–333, 335, 337–342, 344–346, 348, 349, 356, 358–361, 363

clause-chaining, 28, 29, 161
conjunction, 15, 23, 28, 29, 400
conventionalization, 434, 435

definiteness, 413
deixis, 34, 95, 126, 239–243, 247, 253, 255, 256, 265, 271, 273
demonstrative, 242, 243, 245–255, 258, 264, 273, 371, 373, 375, 377, 382, 400
derivation, 6
determiner, 15
dialect chain, 150
differential object marking, 405
differential subject marking, 405
direction, 24, 242, 250–252, 257–259, 264, 267, 271
distributive, 162
distributive numerals, 330, 337–342, 344, 349, 351, 354, 355

elevation, 95, 239–248, 250–272
epenthesis, 58, 62–64, 118, 119

free pronoun, 404, 406, 408, 419, 420

gender, 28

inflection, 6
inflection classes, 415, 423, 426
innovation, 30, 32, 50, 57, 60, 62, 66, 68–75, 92, 95, 150, 151, 234, 269, 271, 285, 287, 290, 295,

Subject index

304, 305, 307, 310, 312, 313, 366, 370, 399
isolate language(s), 149, 151, 183

kinship, 33, 34, 99, 191, 193, 195, 198, 200–203, 205, 206, 208, 212, 213, 215, 218–222, 225, 228, 231, 232, 234, 235, 396

lexical stipulation, 404, 415, 428, 435

manner, 24
metathesis, 63, 85, 86, 93, 96, 98, 101, 103, 115, 127, 137–139, 151, 178
metatypy, 75
mood, 27
motion, 240, 242–248, 250, 251, 253, 255–260, 262, 267–271
multiplicative numeral, 278, 280, 294, 295, 304, 308

negation, 15, 29, 160
nominalization, 95, 377
numeral classifier, 31–33, 305, 306, 320, 321, 330, 331, 361–363, 370, 371, 373, 375, 376, 378, 400
Nusa Tenggara Timor, 7

object, 407, 409, 428–432
ordinal numeral(s), 298, 300, 330, 333–337, 349, 351–354, 356, 357, 360, 361

palatalization, 61
person, 406, 410, 433
plural (number) word, 365–375, 377–400
plurality, 22, 34, 59, 100, 126, 162, 163, 173, 175, 182, 183, 362

possession, 6, 21, 22, 26–29, 59, 100, 104, 120, 126, 154, 157–159, 180, 194, 196, 207, 209, 273, 330, 333–336, 349, 362, 369, 372, 388, 396, 400
prefix alternation, 416, 417, 423, 430, 432, 433
productivity, 429
pronominal indexing, 403–406, 417, 435
pronoun, 6, 7, 16, 28, 29, 148–150, 154, 155, 158, 159, 161–165, 173, 175–177, 179, 180, 182, 183, 194, 196, 207, 332, 333, 337, 362, 368, 371, 373, 375, 377, 379–381, 383, 385, 386, 388, 390, 394, 397, 398
pronouns, 178

reduplication, 101, 287, 295, 330, 337, 338, 340–342, 349, 360, 400
referential properties, 403, 435
right-headed, 15, 159

secundative alignment, 434
semantic alignment, 404, 406–408, 412, 419, 420, 422, 435
serial verb construction(s), 23, 24, 27, 29, 342
simplex numeral, 279, 285, 287, 303, 309, 310
sound change, 278, 281, 282, 312
specificity, 405, 413
subject, 409, 435
subtractive numeral, 278, 280, 288, 290, 292–296, 303, 304, 309, 310
switch reference, 28, 29
syntactic alignment, 404, 406, 428

Subject index

telicity, 412
tense, 27

undergoer, 409, 410

valency, 27
verb classes, 404, 414, 422, 428, 430, 431, 435
verb-final, 15, 159
video stimuli, 412
volitionality, 155, 403–406, 408, 409, 412, 414, 418, 420, 421, 434, 435
vowel harmony, 86

www.ingramcontent.com/pod-product-compliance
Lightning Source LLC
Chambersburg PA
CBHW080753300426

44114CB00020B/2716